THE
PUBLIC GENERAL ACTS
1973

with
Lists of the Public General Acts
and Local Acts
and a Table of the Effect of Legislation
and an Index

[IN THREE PARTS]

PART I

LONDON
HER MAJESTY'S STATIONERY OFFICE
1974
£18·25 net.
(for three parts)

ISBN 0 11 840124 6

c

The Public General Acts
which received the Royal Assent in 1973
in which year ended the TWENTY-FIRST
and began the TWENTY-SECOND YEAR
of the Reign of HER MAJESTY
QUEEN ELIZABETH THE SECOND
and
ended the Third Session
and began the Fourth Session
of the Forty-Fifth Parliament of the
United Kingdom of Great Britain
and Northern Ireland

d

Printed by C. H. BAYLIS, C.B.
Controller of Her Majesty's Stationery Office and
Queen's Printer of Acts of Parliament

CONTENTS

[There were no General Synod Measures in 1973]

f

TABLE I

Alphabetical List of

the Public General Acts of 1973

TABLE II

Chronological List of

the Public General Acts of 1973

* Consolidation Act.

* Consolidation Act.

TABLE III

Alphabetical List of

the Local and Personal Acts of 1973

THE PUBLIC GENERAL ACTS OF 1973

Consolidated Fund Act 1973

1973 CHAPTER 1

An Act to apply a sum out of the Consolidated Fund to the service of the year ending on 31st March 1973.

[13th February 1973]

Most Gracious Sovereign,

WE, Your Majesty's most dutiful and loyal subjects, the Commons of the United Kingdom in Parliament assembled, towards making good the supply which we have cheerfully granted to Your Majesty in this session of Parliament, have resolved to grant unto Your Majesty the sum hereinafter mentioned; and do therefore most humbly beseech Your Majesty that it may be enacted, and be it enacted by the Queen's most Excellent Majesty, by and with the advice and consent of the Lords Spiritual and Temporal, and Commons, in this present Parliament assembled, and by the authority of the same, as follows:—

1. The Treasury may issue out of the Consolidated Fund of the United Kingdom and apply towards making good the supply granted to Her Majesty for the service of the year ending on 31st March 1973 the sum of £590,988,000.

Issue out of the Consolidated Fund for the year ending 31st March 1973.

2. This Act may be cited as the Consolidated Fund Act 1973.

Short title.

A

National Theatre and Museum of London Act 1973

1973 CHAPTER 2

An Act to raise the limits imposed by section 1 of the National Theatre Act 1949 and section 13 of the Museum of London Act 1965 on the grants which may be made under those sections.   [13th February 1973]

B E IT ENACTED by the Queen's most Excellent Majesty, by and with the advice and consent of the Lords Spiritual and Temporal, and Commons, in this present Parliament assembled, and by the authority of the same, as follows:—

Revised limits.
1949 c. 16.
1946 c. 31.
1969 c. 11.

1.—(1) In section 1 of the National Theatre Act 1949 (which, as modified by Order in Council under the Ministers of the Crown (Transfer of Functions) Act 1946 and by the National Theatre Act 1969, authorises the Secretary of State to make contributions not exceeding £3,750,000 in respect of the cost of erecting and equipping a national theatre) for the words " (not exceeding £3,750,000) " there shall be substituted the words " (not exceeding £5,700,000) ".

1965 c. 17.

(2) In section 13 of the Museum of London Act 1965 (which authorises the Secretary of State to make grants not exceeding in the aggregate £150,000 in respect of the cost of furnishing and equipping any premises in which the collections vested in the Governors of the Museum of London are, or are to be, housed) for the words " not exceeding in the aggregate £150,000 " there shall be substituted the words " not exceeding in the aggregate £300,000 ".

Short title, citation and repeal.

2.—(1) This Act may be cited as the National Theatre and Museum of London Act 1973; and the National Theatre Act

1949 and subsection (1) of section 1 above may be cited together as the National Theatre Acts 1949 and 1973; and the Museum of London Act 1965 and subsection (2) of section 1 above may be cited together as the Museum of London Acts 1965 and 1973.

(2) **The** National **Theatre** Act 1969 is hereby repealed.   1969 c. 11.

Sea Fish Industry Act 1973

1973 CHAPTER 3

An Act to relax certain time limits under the Sea Fish Industry Act 1970 with respect to grants and loans under the Act and with respect to the White Fish Marketing Fund and the Herring Marketing Fund.

[13th February 1973]

B E IT ENACTED by the Queen's most Excellent Majesty, by and with the advice and consent of the Lords Spiritual and Temporal, and Commons, in this present Parliament assembled, and by the authority of the same, as follows:—

Extension of time limits.
1970 c. 11.

1.—(1) In section 49 of the Sea Fish Industry Act 1970 (which enables grants to be made in accordance with schemes under the section to owners or charterers of fishing vessels or vessels handling the catch, but by subsection (4) requires an application for a grant to have been made before 1st January 1974), subsection (4) is hereby repealed; and the operation of section 51 of that Act (reimbursement of Isle of Man herring subsidies) shall be extended accordingly.

(2) The following provisions of the Sea Fish Industry Act 1970, that is to say,—

(a) sections 22(1) and 35(1) (Exchequer loans to White Fish Authority or Herring Industry Board), and sections 24(2) and 37(2) (payment into White Fish Marketing Fund or Herring Marketing Fund of principal repaid on certain Exchequer loans); and

(b) sections 23(1) and 36(1) (Exchequer grants to Authority or Board);

shall have effect as if in each of those provisions any reference to the end of the year 1972 were a reference to the end of the year

1973 or any later date that may be prescribed for that provision by order of the Ministers.

(3) An order made under subsection (2) above shall be contained in a statutory instrument made before the end of the year 1973 or, as the case may be, before the date or last date prescribed by a previous order so made for the provision in question; but an order made under that subsection shall be of no effect unless it is approved by a resolution of the Commons House of Parliament.

(4) In section 24(6) and in section 37(6) of the Sea Fish Industry 1970 c. 11. Act 1970 (which require the White Fish Marketing Fund and the Herring Marketing Fund to be wound up as soon as may be after the end of the year 1972) for the reference to the end of the year 1972 there shall be substituted a reference to the date up to which payments may under the section continue to be made into the Fund there mentioned.

(5) Sections 28, 43 and 58(2) of the Sea Fish Industry Act 1970 (which make provision as to the operation of that Act in relation to Northern Ireland) shall have effect as if any reference therein to Part I or to Part II of the Act included subsections (2), (3) and (4) above in so far as they affect that Part; and, subject to section 58(2) of that Act, " the Ministers " in subsection (2) above means the Minister of Agriculture, Fisheries and Food, the Secretary of State concerned with the sea fishing industry in Scotland and the Secretary of State concerned with the sea fishing industry in Northern Ireland.

2.—(1) This Act may be cited as the Sea Fish Industry Act Citation and 1973, and the Sea Fish Industry Act 1970 and this Act may be extent. cited together as the Sea Fish Industry Acts 1970 and 1973.

(2) It is hereby declared that this Act, except as it affects section 51 of the Sea Fish Industry Act 1970, extends to Northern Ireland, but subject to the provision made by section 1(5) above.

Atomic Energy Authority (Weapons Group) Act 1973

1973 CHAPTER 4

An Act to transfer to the Secretary of State the Weapons Group of the United Kingdom Atomic Energy Authority, and for connected purposes; and to modify section 2 of the Atomic Energy Authority Act 1954 in respect of the Authority's power to do work on explosive nuclear devices.   [6th March 1973]

B E IT ENACTED by the Queen's most Excellent Majesty, by and with the advice and consent of the Lords Spiritual and Temporal, and Commons, in this present Parliament assembled, and by the authority of the same, as follows:—

Transfer of Atomic Energy Authority Weapons Group to Secretary of State.

1.—(1) On a day appointed by the Secretary of State by order made by statutory instrument the undertaking of the United Kingdom Atomic Energy Authority (" the Authority ") shall cease to comprise so much of it as is known as the Weapons Group ; and it shall on and after that date, be for the Secretary of State (and not the Authority, except under contract to the Secretary of State, or by his direction or with his approval) to carry on any activities which before that day were activities of the Group and involved the doing of work on explosive nuclear devices.

(2) On the appointed day there shall be transferred to the Secretary of State for Defence by virtue of this Act and without further assurance—

(a) all such lands and premises as immediately before the appointed day are the property of the Authority and were on 1st November 1972 the property of the

Authority and recorded in the Authority's books as held by the Weapons Group ;

(*b*) without prejudice to the foregoing but subject to the following subsection, all such property, rights, liabilities and obligations as immediately before the appointed day belonged to or were incumbent upon the Authority and appertained to the Weapons Group.

(3) There are excepted from the transfer effected by subsection (2) above any rights, liabilities or obligations of the Authority under—

(*a*) any contract of employment ;

(*b*) any agreement for the rendering by a person of services to the Authority in his capacity as a member of the Authority ; or

(*c*) any pension scheme or agreement relating to a pension scheme ;

and there are also excepted from that transfer the interests, property, rights, liabilities and obligations specified in the Schedule to this Act (patents and other industrial property).

2.—(1) Every person who, immediately before the appointed Weapons day, is an employee of the Authority engaged in the Weapons Group Group shall on that day cease to be employed by the Authority employees. but may, in pursuance of arrangements made by the Secretary of State in connection with the transfer to him of the Weapons Group, be taken into employment in the civil service of the State ; and notwithstanding anything in section 22 of the Redundancy Payments Act 1965 (implied or constructive termination of 1965 c. 62. contract) the operation of this subsection in relation to any person shall not be treated for the purposes of that Act as a termination by the Authority of that person's contract of employment.

(2) Nothing in subsection (1) above affects the office of special constable held by any person who, immediately before the appointed day, is a special constable by virtue of section 3 of the Special Constables Act 1923 as applied by Schedule 3 to the 1923 c. 11. Atomic Energy Authority Act 1954, and who as from that day 1954 c. 32. becomes employed in the civil service of the State in pursuance of the arrangements referred to in that subsection ; nor shall the subsection affect any duty, power or privilege of such a person in his capacity as a special constable in relation to any premises transferred by virtue of section 1 of this Act ; but in relation to such a special constable section 3(2) of the said Act of 1923 (control of constables and power to suspend or terminate their appointments) shall, as from the appointed day, have effect as if any reference to the department on whose nomination he was appointed was a reference to the Secretary of State.

(3) A person who—

    (*a*) on or after the appointed day ceases to be employed by the Authority (whether under subsection (1) above or otherwise) and as from ceasing to be so employed becomes employed in the civil service of the State in pursuance of the arrangements referred to in subsection (1) ; and

    (*b*) was, immediately before ceasing to be so employed, included in a pension scheme maintained by the Authority or would (had he remained in that employment) have become eligible for inclusion in such a pension scheme on attaining an age or fulfilling a condition specified in the scheme,

may continue to be included in the scheme or, as the case may be, retain his eligibility to be included in it, until such time as he becomes subject to a scheme made by the Minister for the Civil Service under section 1 of the Superannuation Act 1972 ; and the Authority's pension scheme may continue to apply to any such person notwithstanding that he is no longer an employee of the Authority.

1972 c. 11.

Powers of Secretary of State in relation to transfer under s. 1.

    3.—(1) The Secretary of State may give such directions extending or restricting the operation of section 1 of this Act as he may consider expedient for the purpose of making minor adjustments of the property, rights, liabilities and obligations transferred by subsection (2) of that section, in order to facilitate the carrying on by him of activities which before the appointed day were activities of the Weapons Group, or to facilitate the carrying on by the Authority of any other activities ; and any directions under this subsection may in particular provide for dividing and apportioning any property, rights, liabilities or obligations between the Secretary of State and the Authority, and for the variation or cancellation of any lease, licence or agreement for a lease to which he and they were parties immediately before the appointed day.

    (2) The Secretary of State may give directions excepting from the operation of section 1 of this Act any books or other documents which in his opinion are not required for use in connection with the carrying on by him of activities which before the appointed day were activities of the Weapons Group, or extending the operation of that section to any books or other documents which in his opinion are required for such use.

    (3) No directions shall be given under subsection (1) or (2) above after the end of the period of two years beginning with the appointed day.

(4) Subject to the next following subsection, a certificate issued by the Secretary of State to the effect that any property of the Authority was, or was not, transferred by virtue of section 1, or that any rights, liabilities or obligations of the Authority specified in the certificate were, or were not, so transferred shall be conclusive evidence of the matters stated in the certificate; but the issue of a certificate under this subsection shall not prevent a subsequent direction being given under subsection (1) or (2) above in relation to any property, rights, liabilities or obligations to which the certificate relates.

(5) Before giving any direction or issuing any certificate under this section in relation to any matter the Secretary of State shall consult the Authority; and on giving any direction or issuing any certificate thereunder the Secretary of State shall send a copy of it to the Authority.

4.—(1) Where immediately before the appointed day there is in force an agreement which— General transitional provisions.

    (*a*) confers or imposes on the Authority any rights, liabilities or obligations which are transferred to the Secretary of State by virtue of section 1 of this Act; and

    (*b*) refers (in whatever terms, and whether expressly or by implication) to the Authority or to a member or officer of the Authority,

the agreement shall have effect, in relation to anything falling to be done on or after that day, as if for that reference there were substituted a reference either to the Secretary of State or to such person as he may appoint for the purposes of the agreement.

(2) Where any right, liability or obligation is transferred to the Secretary of State by virtue of this Act, he and all other persons shall, on and after the appointed day, have the same rights, powers and remedies (and in particular, the same rights as to the taking or resisting of legal proceedings) for ascertaining, perfecting or enforcing that right, liability or obligation as they would have had if it had at all times been a right, liability or obligation of the Secretary of State; and any legal proceedings by or against the Authority which relate to any property, right, liability or obligation transferred to the Secretary of State by virtue of this Act, and are pending immediately before the appointed day, may be continued on and after that day by or against the Secretary of State.

(3) In subsection (2) above, any reference to legal proceedings shall be construed as including a reference to any application to an authority, and any reference to the taking or resisting of legal proceedings shall be construed accordingly.

(4) Any instrument shall, so far as may be necessary for or in consequence of any transfer effected by this Act, have effect as if references to, or which are to be construed as references to, the Authority, or any member or officer of the Authority, were or, as the case may require, included references to the Secretary of State.

Additional provision as to technical information, etc.

5.—(1) Where the Secretary of State thinks it necessary or expedient for the purposes of any activities carried on or to be carried on by him, he may by directions given to the Authority, after consultation with them, require them to make available to him, on such terms as to payment or otherwise as he thinks appropriate—

(*a*) facilities for, and information relating to, the use of any invention, design or trade mark excepted from transfer by section 1(3) of this Act; and

(*b*) any technical information in the possession of, or available to, the Authority, other than information which the Authority are precluded by contract from disclosing.

1958 c. 38.
1949 c. 87.
1949 c. 88.

(2) Nothing in subsection (1) above is to be taken as prejudicing any provision of the Defence Contracts Act 1958, nor any provision of the Patents Act 1949 or the Registered Designs Act 1949 relating to the use for services of the Crown of patents and registered designs; but in relation to the use of any such invention or design as is referred to in subsection (1)(*a*) above, being property of the Authority, section 46(3) of the Patents Act 1949 and paragraph 1(3) of Schedule 1 to the Registered Designs Act 1949 (Crown use on terms to be agreed with the patentee, or registered proprietor, or in default of agreement to be settled by the court) shall each have effect with the substitution for the words " as may be agreed " onwards of the words " as the Secretary of State may determine to be appropriate ".

(3) The Secretary of State shall at the request of the Authority enter into arrangements with them for securing that they have access—

(*a*) to any property of theirs which in consequence of this Act is for the time being in the custody or control of the Secretary of State; and

(*b*) to any technical information which was available to them before the appointed day and is required by them for the purposes of any part of their undertaking which is not transferred by this Act;

including (but without prejudice to the generality of the foregoing) arrangements for enabling servants of the Authority to inspect and take copies of documents which before the appointed day were the property of the Authority and are for the time being in the custody or control of the Secretary of State.

6.—(1) The Authority shall not by virtue of anything in section 2 of the Atomic Energy Authority Act 1954 (general powers in relation to production, use and disposal of atomic energy and to carrying out research, etc.) have power to engage in any work, whether by way of research, experiment, development, production or otherwise, on any explosive nuclear device, whether for war-like applications or otherwise, except in accordance with arrangements made with the Secretary of State. Powers of Authority in relation to atomic weapons development, etc.
1954 c. 32.

(2) In section 2(2) of the said Act of 1954, in paragraph (i) of the proviso (which precludes the Authority from developing or producing weapons otherwise than in accordance with such arrangements, but makes an exception for certain work on explosive nuclear assemblies) the words from " except that " to the end of the paragraph are hereby repealed.

7. Property vested in the Secretary of State for Defence by virtue of section 1 of this Act shall not be treated as so vested by way of sale for the purposes of section 12 of the Finance Act 1895 (which requires Acts to be stamped as conveyances on sale in certain cases). Stamp duty.
1895 c. 16.

8. There shall be paid out of money provided by Parliament— Financial provisions.

    (a) any expenses incurred by the Secretary of State in carrying on any such activities as are referred to in section 1(1) of this Act, or otherwise carrying this Act into effect ;

    (b) any increase attributable to this Act in the sums payable out of such money under any other enactment.

9.—(1) In this Act "the appointed day" means the day appointed by the Secretary of State for the purposes of section 1(1). Interpretation and supplementary provisions.

(2) For the purposes of this Act—

    (a) property, rights, liabilities and obligations of the Authority shall be taken at any time to be property, rights, liabilities and obligations appertaining to the Weapons Group ; and

    (b) persons shall be taken at any time to be employees of the Authority engaged in that Group,

if at that time they are property held, rights acquired, liabilities or obligations incurred or persons employed by the Authority (as the case may be) wholly or mainly for the purposes of, or in the course of carrying on, that part of the Authority's undertaking known as the Weapons Group (as distinct from the Authority's undertaking in general or any other part of that undertaking in particular) ; and the question whether at a particular time property of the Authority was held for the purposes of the Weapons Group, or in the course of carrying on any activities of the Group, shall be determined (in case of doubt) by reference to the Authority's books, and entries in those books with respect to any property shall be conclusive as to how it was held at the time in question, regardless of who at that time had custody of it.

(3) For the avoidance of doubt it is hereby declared that—

(*a*) any reference in this Act to property of the Authority is a reference to property whether situated in the United Kingdom or elsewhere, and

(*b*) any reference in this Act to rights, liabilities or obligations of the Authority is a reference to rights to which the Authority is entitled or (as the case may be) liabilities or obligations to which the Authority is subject, whether under the laws of the United Kingdom or of a part of the United Kingdom or under the laws of any country or territory outside the United Kingdom ;

and it shall be the duty of the Authority and of the Secretary of State, in the case of any property situated in any country or territory outside the United Kingdom which is transferred by virtue of this Act, or in the case of any rights, liabilities or obligations of the Authority under the laws of any such country or territory which are so transferred, to take all such steps as may be requisite for perfecting the transfer.

(4) Except as provided by sections 1 and 6 of this Act, nothing in this Act is to be construed as taking away from the Authority any power, right, liability or obligation expressly conferred on them by name by any enactment.

Citation.   **10.** This Act may be cited as the Atomic Energy Authority (Weapons Group) Act 1973.

SCHEDULE

<small>PATENT AND OTHER RIGHTS RESERVED TO ATOMIC ENERGY AUTHORITY</small>

Scope of reservation

1. Any interest of the Authority in a patent, registered design, registered trade mark or copyright.

2. Any rights, liabilities or obligations of the Authority so far as arising—

   (*a*) from an application for the grant of a patent or for the registration of a design or a trade mark, where the application was pending immediately before the appointed day ;

   (*b*) from any invention (whether patented or not) made before that day ;

   (*c*) from the use by the Authority before that day of an unregistered trade mark.

3. Any property of the Authority consisting of drawings, models, specifications or designs, or of documents relating thereto (including documents relating to the application or operation of any process or technique), other than those relating to any explosive nuclear device.

4. Any rights, liabilities or obligations of the Authority so far as arising—

   (*a*) from any licence or assignment (whether to or by the Authority) of an invention, design, copyright or trade mark, or from an agreement for such a licence or assignment ; or

   (*b*) from any agreement with respect to the making of an application for a patent or for the registration of a design or trade mark ; or

   (*c*) from any agreement requiring the Authority to provide, or enabling them to receive, technical information or assistance of any description.

Interpretation

5. In the above paragraphs any reference to a patent, or to a registered design, or to copyright, shall include a patent granted or design registered or copyright subsisting under the laws of a country or territory outside the United Kingdom ; and any reference to a trade mark shall include a trade mark subsisting or registered under the laws of any such country or territory.

Housing (Amendment) Act 1973

1973 CHAPTER 5

An Act to extend the operation of the Housing Act 1971 and to make further provision as to the imposition of conditions on the sale of houses by local authorities under the Housing Act 1957.   [6th March 1973]

B E IT ENACTED by the Queen's most Excellent Majesty, by and with the advice and consent of the Lords Spiritual and Temporal, and Commons, in this present Parliament assembled, and by the authority of the same, as follows:—

Extension of powers to give financial assistance for housing in certain areas.

1971 c. 76.

1.—(1) The Housing Act 1971 (under section 1 of which the increased financial assistance for housing improvement in development areas and intermediate areas for which sections 2 and 3 provide is available only in respect of works completed before the expiration of a period of two years beginning with 23rd June 1971) shall have effect in relation to any local government area as defined in subsection (4) of the said section 1 for a further period of one year; and the word "three" shall accordingly be substituted for the word "two" in paragraph (b) of subsection (1) and in both places where it occurs in subsection (2) of that section.

(2) For the paragraph which follows the Table in section 2(1) of the said Act of 1971 (increased financial assistance in England and Wales) there shall be substituted the following paragraphs:—

"The substitution by this Table in section 16(2) of the Housing Act 1969 for three quarters of 90 per cent. shall not apply where the local authority grant is an improvement grant which—

(a) if the application for it was approved before 4th August 1972, is less than three quarters of the approved expense;

(*b*) if the application was approved on or after that date, is less than whichever of the following amounts is the smaller, namely—

(i) three quarters of the approved expense ;

(ii) the maximum permissible amount of grant.

For the purposes of the application to any case of the foregoing paragraph the maximum permissible amount of grant is the maximum amount payable in that case by virtue of subsections (2) and (3) of section 5 of the Housing Act 1969."

(3) For the paragraph which follows the Table in section 3(1) of the said Act of 1971 (increased financial assistance in Scotland) there shall be substituted the following paragraphs : —

" The substitutions by this Table in section 35 of the Housing (Financial Provisions) (Scotland) Act 1968 shall not apply where the local authority grant is an improvement grant which—

(*a*) if the application for it was approved before 4th August 1972, is less than three quarters of the approved expense ;

(*b*) if the application was approved on or after that date, is less than whichever of the following amounts is the smaller, namely—

(i) three quarters of the approved expense ;

(ii) the maximum permissible amount of grant.

For the purposes of the application to any case of the foregoing paragraph the maximum permissible amount of grant is the maximum amount payable in that case by virtue of section 29(1) of the Housing (Financial Provisions) (Scotland) Act 1968."

(4) Where a single grant or contribution under the Housing 1969 c. 33. Act 1969 or the Housing (Financial Provisions) (Scotland) Act 1968 c. 31. 1968 is payable in respect of a number of dwellings, and the works required for the provision or improvement of one or more of those dwellings have been completed before the expiration of the period of three years mentioned in section 1 of the Housing Act 1971 (as amended by subsection (1) above) but 1971 c. 76. the remaining works have not been so completed, section 2 or as the case may be, section 3 of the said Act of 1971 shall have effect in relation to such portion of the grant or contribution as is attributable, in the opinion of the local authority or, as the case may be, the Secretary of State, to the completed works.

(5) Any expenses of the Secretary of State which are attributable to the provisions of this section shall be defrayed out of money provided by Parliament.

(6) There shall be paid into the Consolidated Fund any sums which, in consequence of the provisions of this section, are to be so paid under any other Act.

Conditions on sale of houses by local authorities.
1957 c. 56.

2. Section 104 of the Housing Act 1957 (which empowers local authorities to dispose of houses provided under Part V of that Act) shall have effect, in relation to a disposition by way of sale where the consent of the Secretary of State to the sale was given on or after 16th August 1972—

(*a*) with the substitution in paragraph (*a*) of subsection (3) (which provides for the imposition of conditions on sales of such houses) of the words " relevant period " for the words from " period " to " sale " ;

(*b*) with the addition after subsection (3) of the following subsection : —

"(3A) In subsection (3) above " relevant period " means—

(*a*) if no greater period is authorised or required by the Secretary of State, any period not exceeding five years from the completion of the sale ;

(*b*) if a greater period is authorised or required by him, that period."

Citation, etc.

3.—(1) This Act may be cited as the Housing (Amendment) Act 1973.

(2) The Housing Acts 1957 to 1972 and this Act may be cited together as the Housing Acts 1957 to 1973.

(3) The Housing (Scotland) Acts 1966 to 1972 and this Act (except section 2 above) may be cited together as the Housing (Scotland) Acts 1966 to 1973.

(4) This Act does not extend to Northern Ireland.

Furnished Lettings (Rent Allowances) Act 1973

1973 CHAPTER 6

An Act to amend the provisions of the Housing Finance Act 1972 and the Housing (Financial Provisions) (Scotland) Act 1972 to provide rent allowances for certain persons occupying dwellings under contracts to which Part VI of the Rent Act 1968 applies or would apply but for section 70(3)(*a*) or (*b*) thereof, or contracts to which Part VII of the Rent (Scotland) Act 1971 applies or would apply but for section 85(3)(*a*) or (*b*) thereof, and for certain tenants under furnished lettings of housing authority dwellings; and for connected purposes.   [22nd March 1973]

BE IT ENACTED by the Queen's most Excellent Majesty, by and with the advice and consent of the Lords Spiritual and Temporal, and Commons, in this present Parliament assembled, and by the authority of the same, as follows:—

1.—(1) The Housing Finance Act 1972 shall have effect subject to the amendments set out in Schedule 1 to this Act.

(2) Until 29th April 1973 (on which date local authorities are required by paragraph 2 of Schedule 1 to this Act to bring into operation schemes varying or replacing their existing rent allowance schemes so as to take account of the amendments set out in that Schedule)—

    (*a*) nothing in this Act shall invalidate the existing allowance scheme of a local authority or cause the authority to be

Rent allowances for tenants of furnished dwellings in England and Wales.
1972 c. 47.

regarded as being in breach of section 20(1) of the Housing Finance Act 1972 (which requires allowance schemes to conform with Schedules 3 and 4 thereto), and

(*b*) that Act shall continue to apply in relation to the existing scheme as if this Act had not passed.

Rent allowances for tenants of furnished lettings in Scotland.
1972 c. 46.

2.—(1) The Housing (Financial Provisions) (Scotland) Act 1972 shall have effect subject to the amendments set out in Schedule 2 to this Act.

(2) Until such time as a local authority bring into or are required to bring into operation under section 16 of the Housing (Financial Provisions) (Scotland) Act 1972 a scheme varying or replacing their existing allowance scheme so as to take account of the said amendments—

(*a*) nothing in this Act shall invalidate that existing scheme or cause the authority to be regarded as being in breach of section 17(1) of that Act (which requires allowance schemes to conform with Schedules 2 and 3 thereto), and

(*b*) that Act shall continue to apply in relation to the existing scheme as if this Act had not passed.

Financial provisions.

3.—(1) There shall be paid out of money provided by Parliament any increase in the sums payable out of money so provided under any Act other than this Act which is attributable to any provision of this Act.

(2) There shall be paid into the Consolidated Fund any increase in the payments to be made to, or to be recoverable by, the Secretary of State under any Act other than this Act which is attributable to any provision of this Act.

Citation, etc.

4.—(1) This Act may be cited as the Furnished Lettings (Rent Allowances) Act 1973.

(2) The Housing Acts 1957 to 1973 and this Act (except section 2, subsection (3) below and Schedule 2) may be cited together as the Housing Acts 1957 to 1973.

(3) The Housing (Scotland) Acts 1966 to 1972 and this Act (except section 1, subsection (2) above and Schedule 1) may be cited together as the Housing (Scotland) Acts 1966 to 1973.

(4) This Act does not extend to Northern Ireland.

SCHEDULES

SCHEDULE 1

AMENDMENTS TO HOUSING FINANCE ACT 1972

1. In section 18(3)(*b*), the words " or without payment of rent " are hereby repealed.

2. In section 19(1), for " not later than 1st January 1973 " there shall be substituted " on 29th April 1973 ".

3. In section 19(3), the words " or without payment of rent " are hereby repealed.

4. In section 19(4), there shall be inserted at the end the words " or who, being a qualified person within the meaning of subsection (12) below, occupies a dwelling under a contract to which Part VI of the Rent Act 1968 (furnished lettings) applies or would apply but for section 70(3)(*b*) thereof.

5. In section 19(6), there shall be inserted at the end the words " or if, being a qualified person within the meaning of subsection (12) below, he occupies a dwelling under a contract with the Crown Estate Commissioners to which Part VI of the Rent Act 1968 would apply but for section 70(3)(*a*) thereof ".

6. In section 19(7), there shall be inserted after " case " the words " or he occupies a dwelling under a Part VI letting " and after " tenants) " the words " applies, or ".

7. In section 19(8), after " rebate ", where first occurring, there shall be inserted " or allowance ".

8. In section 19, after subsection (8), there shall be inserted the following new subsection:—

> " (8A) A local authority, and the Greater London Council, shall treat as if he were a private tenant under a Part VI letting any person who occupies a Housing Revenue Account dwelling let by them if—
>
> > (*a*) there is attributable to the use of furniture a proportion of the rent which is substantial, having regard to the value of that use to him, and
> >
> > (*b*) he is a qualified person within the meaning of subsection (12) below,
>
> and accordingly shall provide in their allowance scheme for (or, in the case of the Greater London Council, shall bring into operation on 29th April 1973 an allowance scheme providing for) the grant to any such person of an allowance equal in amount to the allowance to which he would have been entitled if he had been such a private tenant."

9. In section 19(10), there shall be inserted after " rebates " in the first and third places where it occurs the words " or allowances " and

SCH. 1   there shall be inserted after " section 18 " the words " or subsection (8A) ".

10. In section 19, after subsection (11), there shall be inserted the following new subsections:—

" (12) The occupier of a dwelling is a qualified person for the purposes of this section if—

(*a*) the authority to whom he applies for an allowance or rebate are of the opinion (arrived at in accordance with such guidance as may be given by the Secretary of State) that he would suffer hardship if the allowance or rebate were not granted, or

(*b*) he is a person falling within a description specified in that behalf in regulations made by the Secretary of State.

(13) Where the Secretary of State proposes to make regulations under subsection (12) above he shall refer the proposals to the Advisory Committee on Rent Rebates and Rent Allowances constituted under section 23 below in order that that Committee may consider them and advise on them.

(14) Regulations under subsection (12) above shall be made by statutory instrument and shall be subject to annulment in pursuance of a resolution of either House of Parliament ".

11. In section 20(7), in the proviso, there shall be inserted after " section 19(8) " the words " (8A) or (10) ".

12. In section 23(1) there shall be inserted at the end the words " or making orders under section 25(3A) of this Act, or to the descriptions of persons to be specified in regulations under section 19(12) of this Act ".

13. In section 24(5), after " their rebate scheme " there shall be inserted " or their allowance scheme, as may be appropriate," and after " their tenants " there shall be inserted " of Housing Revenue Account dwellings ".

14. In section 24(6), after " their rebate scheme " there shall be inserted " or their allowance scheme, as may be appropriate,".

15. In section 24(10), after " private tenant " there shall be inserted " or to a person who, if he were a qualified person within the meaning of section 19(12) of this Act, would be a private tenant " and for " currently operated " there shall be substituted " which, at the time of the granting of the tenancy, is being operated ".

16. In section 24(11), after " a dwelling " there shall be inserted " or for a person who, if he were a qualified person within the meaning of section 19(12) of this Act, would be a private tenant of a dwelling "; for " currently operated " there shall be substituted " which, at the time of the insertion, is being operated "; for " 1st January 1973 " in each place where it occurs, there shall be substituted " 29th April 1973 "; and for " 30th June 1973 " there shall be substituted " 30th September 1973 ".

17. In section 25(1), after " of the rent " there shall be inserted " (or, in the case of an allowance, the occupational element of the residue of the rent remaining after deducting any amounts falling to be deducted by virtue of paragraph 14 of Schedule 4 to this Act) ", and there shall be inserted at the end " Provided that in the case of a Part VI letting where the rent includes payment for the use of furniture, the ' rent which is eligible to be met by a rebate or an allowance ' shall be the smallest of the following amounts, namely—

   (*a*) the sum arrived at under the foregoing provisions of this subsection increased by one quarter;

   (*b*) the rent, exclusive of any part thereof attributable to rates;

   (*c*) rent for the dwelling registered under section 74 of the Rent Act 1968." 1968 c. 23.

18. For section 25(2) there shall be substituted the following subsection:—

   " (2) For the purposes of subsection (1) above ' the occupational element ' of any rent, or of the residue of any rent, means the amount thereof—

      (*a*) less a sum equal to any part of the rent attributable to rates, and

      (*b*) subject to any regulations made under this section, exclusive of any part of the rent or residue which is fairly attributable to the use of furniture or the provision of services."

19. In section 25, after subsection (3), there shall be inserted the following new subsection:—

   " (3A) The Secretary of State may by order amend paragraph (*a*) of the proviso to subsection (1) above so as to alter the increase thereunder either generally or in relation to authorities of a specified description ".

20. In section 25(4) there shall be inserted after " Regulations " the words " and orders ".

21. After section 25 there shall be inserted the following new section:—

"Power to vary or revoke scheme.   25A. A scheme under any provision of this Part of this Act may vary or revoke a previous scheme thereunder."

22. In section 26(1), there shall be inserted, in such positions as retain the alphabetical order, the following new definitions:—

   " ' dwelling ' has the same meaning as in Part VI of the Rent Act 1968;

   " ' Part VI letting ' means a contract to which Part VI of the Rent Act 1968 applies, or would apply but for section 70(3)(*a*) or (*b*) thereof; "

23. In section 26(1)—

   (*a*) in the definition of " allowance scheme " there shall be inserted after " made under " the words " subsection (8A) or "; and (*b*) in the definition of " landlord ", the words " Part II of " are hereby repealed.

24. In section 104(1), in the definition of " dwelling ", there shall be inserted before " means " the words " except in Part II of this Act ".

25. In Schedule 3, in paragraph 1(1)(*c*), there shall be inserted at the end " (as defined in section 25 of this Act) ".

26. In Schedule 4, in paragraph 14(1), there shall be inserted at the end the following:—

1968 c. 23.

" (*h*) where the rent is payable in respect of a Part VI letting, any rent paid in excess of rent for the dwelling registered under section 74 of the Rent Act 1968 and (after making the deduction (if any) required for disregarding that excess), any remaining rent paid in excess of the fair rent for the dwelling, as estimated by the authority on the basis that any furniture, services or board provided under the letting are disregarded except, as respects furniture or services, to the extent that they would fall to be taken into account (in pursuance of regulations made under section 25(3) of this Act) in calculating the occupational element of the rent ".

27. In Schedule 4, in paragraph 14, the following new sub-paragraph shall be inserted after sub-paragraph (3):—

" (3A) For the purpose of estimating a fair rent under this paragraph an authority may consult any rent officer appointed by virtue of section 40 of the Rent Act 1968 for the registration area in which the dwelling is situated."

28. In Schedule 10, in the heading to paragraph 9, the words " *before the coming into force of this Act* " are hereby repealed.

29. In Schedule 10, in paragraph 9, for " the coming into force of this Act " there shall be substituted " the coming into operation of that provision ".

Section 2.

1972 c. 46.

SCHEDULE 2

AMENDMENTS TO HOUSING (FINANCIAL PROVISIONS) (SCOTLAND) ACT 1972

1. In section 16(1), for " 1st January 1973 " there shall be substituted " 1st October 1973 or such earlier date as the Secretary of State may by order made by statutory instrument appoint ".

2. In section 16(3), there shall be added at the end the words " or who, being a qualified person within the meaning of subsection (8) of this section, is a lessee under a contract to which Part VII of the Act of 1971 (furnished lettings) applies or would apply but for section 85(3)(*b*) thereof, other than a contract under which the interest of the lessor belongs to a housing authority ".

3. In section 16(5), there shall be added at the end the words " or if, being a qualified person within the meaning of subsection (8) of this section, he occupies a house under a contract with the Crown Estate Commissioners to which Part VII of the Act of 1971 would apply but for section 85(3)(*a*) thereof ".

4. In section 16, after subsection (6), there shall be added the following new subsections:—

" (7) A local authority shall treat as if he were a private tenant any person who, being a qualified person within the meaning of subsection (8) of this section—

(*a*) occupies a house let to him by a housing authority and who is not, by reason of section 15(3) of this Act, entitled to a rent rebate; or

(*b*) occupies a house (other than a house to which the housing revenue account relates) let to him by a local authority, and who is not treated as a private tenant by virtue of subsection (6) of this section, because, if he occupied a house to which the housing revenue account relates, he would not be entitled to a rent rebate by reason of the said section 15(3).

(8) A person is a qualified person for the purposes of subsection (3), (5) or (7) of this section if—

(*a*) the local authority are of the opinion (arrived at in accordance with such guidance as may be given by the Secretary of State) that he would suffer hardship if an allowance were not granted, or

(*b*) he is a person falling within a description specified in that behalf in regulations made by the Secretary of State.

(9) Before making regulations under subsection (8) above the Secretary of State shall consult with such associations of local authorities as appear to him to be concerned and with any local authority with whom consultation appears to him to be desirable, unless the Secretary of State is satisfied that there was such consultation before the coming into operation of the Furnished Lettings (Rent Allowances) Act 1973, which in his opinion was sufficient for the purpose.

(10) Regulations under subsection (8) above shall be made by statutory instrument and shall be subject to annulment in pursuance of a resolution of either House of Parliament."

5. After section 18 there shall be inserted the following section:—

" Power to vary or revoke scheme.   18A. A scheme under any provision of this Part of this Act may vary or revoke a previous scheme thereunder."

6. In section 20(1), after " private tenant " there shall be inserted " or to a person under a furnished letting ".

7. In section 22(1), there shall be inserted, in such positions as retain the alphabetical order, the following new definitions:—

" ' furnished letting ' means a contract to which Part VII of the Act of 1971 applies or would apply but for section 85(3)(*a*) and (*b*) thereof, other than a contract under which the interest of the lessor belongs to a housing authority, and includes a tenancy under which a person is treated as a private tenant by virtue of section 16(7) of this Act;

' lessee ' and ' lessor ' have the meanings respectively assigned to them by section 100(1) (interpretation of Part VII) of the Act of 1971; ".

8. In section 22(1)—

(*a*) in the definition of " landlord ", the words " Part II of " are hereby repealed; and

(*b*) in the definition of " rent ", after " authority " there shall be inserted " other than a tenant who is treated as a private tenant by virtue of section 16(7) above ".

9. In Schedule 3, in paragraph 15(1)(*f*), there shall be inserted after " apply " the words " or in respect of a furnished letting ".

10. In Schedule 3, in paragraph 15(1), there shall be inserted at the end the following—

" (*g*) where the rent is payable in respect of a furnished letting—

(i) any rent paid in excess of rent for the dwelling-house registered under section 89 of the Act of 1971 where the letting is a contract to which Part VII of that Act applies, and

(ii) (after making the deduction (if any) required for disregarding that excess), any remaining rent paid in excess of 125 per cent. of the rent, as estimated by the authority, which would be determined to be a fair rent for the dwelling-house if the letting were a regulated tenancy, on the basis that furniture and services provided under the letting are disregarded except so far as any amount of the rent payable in respect of their use falls to be treated as rent by virtue of section 21 of this Act."

11. In Schedule 3, in paragraph 15, the following new sub-paragraph shall be inserted after sub-paragraph (3)—

" (3A) For the purpose of estimating a fair rent under this paragraph an authority may consult any rent officer appointed by virtue of section 37 of the Act of 1971 for the registration area in which the dwelling-house is situated."

Concorde Aircraft Act 1973

1973 CHAPTER 7

An Act to make further provision for financial support in connection with the production in the United Kingdom of the supersonic aircraft known as the Concorde. [22nd March 1973]

BE IT ENACTED by the Queen's most Excellent Majesty, by and with the advice and consent of the Lords Spiritual and Temporal, and Commons, in this present Parliament assembled, and by the authority of the same, as follows:—

1.—(1) Section 8 of the Industrial Expansion Act 1968 (Government finance for Concorde project) shall be amended as follows.

(2) For subsection (3) (limit on Government finance and date by which Government loans to be repayable and guarantees to expire) there shall be substituted the following subsection:—

> " (3) Subject to subsection (4) below, the aggregate of—
>
> > (a) the principal outstanding in respect of loans made by the Secretary of State under such arrangements as aforesaid;
> >
> > (b) the amount for which the Secretary of State is liable under guarantees of the repayment of principal given by him under such arrangements; and
> >
> > (c) any sums which have been paid by the Secretary of State pursuant to such guarantees of the repayment of principal and have not been repaid to him,
>
> shall not at any time exceed £250 million."

Finance for Concorde project.

1968 c. 32.

(3) In subsection (4) (amount to which the limit imposed by subsection (3) may be raised by order) for the words " £100 million " and " £125 million " there shall be substituted, respectively, the words " £250 million " and " £350 million ".

Short title.

2. This Act may be cited as the Concorde Aircraft Act 1973.

Coal Industry Act 1973

1973 CHAPTER 8

An Act to provide for the capital reconstruction of the National Coal Board; to make provision with respect to borrowing by the Board or its subsidiaries, and with respect to their powers to give guarantees in connection with loans; to confer on the Secretary of State new or extended powers to make grants or other payments to the Board or to other producers of coking coal, or to or in respect of workers in the coal industry made redundant; to authorise the appointment of additional members of the Board ; and for purposes connected with those matters.   [22nd March 1973]

B E IT ENACTED by the Queen's most Excellent Majesty, by and with the advice and consent of the Lords Spiritual and Temporal, and Commons, in this present Parliament assembled, and by the authority of the same, as follows:—

1.—(1) All outstanding liabilities of the National Coal Board (in this Act referred to as " the Board ") to the Secretary of State in respect of the principal of or interest on sums borrowed from him by the Board before the end of the current financial year (including any sums deemed to have been so borrowed by virtue of section 2(1) of the Act of 1965) shall be extinguished at the end of the current financial year. *Capital reconstruction of National Coal Board.*

(2) In the accounts of the Board for the current financial year the total net book value of the Board's fixed assets, as shown in their accounts for the financial year of the Board ending in March 1972, and after making due allowance for depreciation, acquisitions, disposals and other matters occurring during the current financial year, shall be reduced by £275 million (being an amount calculated by reference to the over-valuation of certain of those assets).

(3) The accumulated deficit of the Board on their revenue account at the end of the current financial year, as reported by the auditors of the Board, shall be deemed to be extinguished at the end of the current financial year.

(4) The Board shall be deemed to have borrowed from the Secretary of State at the end of the current financial year a sum equal to the amount of the liabilities referred to in subsection (1) of this section, less the aggregate of the following amounts, that is to say—

    (a) the amount of £275 million referred to in subsection (2) of this section, and

    (b) the amount of the accumulated deficit referred to in subsection (3) of this section ;

and the assets of the National Loans Fund shall accordingly be reduced by an amount corresponding to the aggregate of those amounts.

(5) The sum deemed to have been borrowed by the Board as mentioned in subsection (4) of this section shall be deemed to have been borrowed under subsection (2) of section 1 of the Act of 1965 (which relates to borrowing otherwise than by way of temporary loan) and shall be deemed to have been lent to the Board at the end of the current financial year by the Secretary of State under subsection (6) of that section.

(6) It shall not be necessary for the Treasury, in approving for the purposes of section 28(1) of the Act of 1946 the rate of interest on the sum deemed by virtue of subsection (5) of this section to have been lent to the Board, to approve that rate in accordance with subsection (2) of section 5 of the National Loans Act 1968 (criteria for fixing or approving rates of interest), and accordingly that subsection shall not apply to the approval of the rate of interest on that sum.

1968 c. 13.

(7) In this section " the current financial year " means the financial year of the Board ending with 31st March 1973.

Borrowing powers of the Board and its subsidiaries and powers to guarantee loans.

2.—(1) The following provisions shall be substituted for subsections (3) and (4) of section 1 of the Act of 1965 (borrowing powers of the Board) in relation to any time on or after 1st April 1973, that is to say—

    " (3) Without prejudice to subsection (4) of this section, the aggregate amount outstanding in respect of the principal of—

        (a) sums borrowed by the Board otherwise than from any of their wholly owned subsidiaries (including the sum which under section 1(4) of the Coal Industry Act 1973 is deemed to have been so borrowed), and

    (*b*) sums borrowed by any wholly owned subsidiary of
the Board otherwise than from the Board or from
another such subsidiary,

shall not exceed £550 million or such greater sum, not
exceeding £700 million, as the Secretary of State may specify
by order made by statutory instrument.

    (4) The aggregate of the amounts outstanding in respect
of sums borrowed temporarily by the Board under subsection (1) and subsection (2A) of this section—

    (*a*) shall not at any time exceed such limit as the
Secretary of State may from time to time direct,
and

    (*b*) at the end of any financial year of the Board shall
not be such as to permit any accumulated deficit
on the Board's revenue account to exceed £50
million or such lesser or greater sum, but not
exceeding £100 million, as the Secretary of State
with the approval of the Treasury may specify
by order made by statutory instrument."

    (2) In accordance with any general authority given by the
Secretary of State with the approval of the Treasury, the Board
may under subsection (1) or subsection (2A) of section 1 of
the Act of 1965 borrow temporarily from any person other
than the Secretary of State any sum which they have power
to borrow under either of those subsections with the consent of
the Secretary of State.

    (3) With the consent of the Secretary of State and the approval
of the Treasury the Board may borrow (otherwise than by way
of temporary loan) from the Commission of the European
Communities or from the European Investment Bank (established by Article 129 of the E.E.C. Treaty) any sum in sterling
which the Board have power to borrow from the Secretary of
State under section 1(2) of the Act of 1965.

    (4) It is hereby declared for the avoidance of doubt that
references in section 1 of the Act of 1965 to borrowing by the
Board do not include borrowing by subsidiaries of the Board.

    (5) The Board shall not make any loan to any of their sub-
sidiaries except with the consent of the Secretary of State and
the approval of the Treasury or in accordance with any general
authority given by the Secretary of State with the approval of
the Treasury.

    (6) The Board shall not exercise their power to guarantee the
repayment by any person of money lent to him, or the payment
of interest on money lent to any person, unless the Secretary of
State gives his consent or it is exercised in accordance with a
general authority given by the Secretary of State.

(7) It shall be the duty of the Board to exercise their control over their wholly owned subsidiaries so as to secure that no such subsidiary guarantees the repayment by any person of money lent to him, or the payment of interest on money lent to any person, except with the consent of the Secretary of State or in accordance with a general authority given by him.

S.I. 1972
Nos. 468, 469.

(8) The Coal Industry (Borrowing Powers) Order 1972 (which increased to £950 million the limit imposed by subsection (3) of section 1 of the Act of 1965) and the Coal Industry (Accumulated Deficit) Order 1972 (which increased to £100 million the limit on the accumulated deficit of the Board) are hereby revoked as from the end of March 1973.

Extension of power to make grants to Board in connection with pit closures.

3.—(1) The financial years of the Board in respect of which grants may be made by the Secretary of State to the Board under section 1 of the Act of 1971 shall include the financial years ending in March 1975 and in March 1976 respectively.

(2) Grants made under that section in respect of any financial year of the Board shall not in the aggregate exceed one-half of the relevant expenditure of the Board for that financial year; and, in the case of the financial year ending in March 1974, that limit shall have effect in substitution for the limit (namely, one-third of the relevant expenditure) specified in section 1(3)(c) of the Act of 1971.

(3) The limit of £24 million imposed by subsection (3) of section 1 of the Act of 1971 on the aggregate amount of the grants under that section shall have effect as a limit on the aggregate amount of the grants made under that section in respect of expenditure for the period consisting of the financial years of the Board ending in March 1972 and in March 1973 respectively.

(4) The grants made under that section in respect of expenditure for the period consisting of the financial years 1974-1976 shall not in the aggregate exceed £60 million.

(5) The Secretary of State may by order direct that the financial years of the Board in respect of which grants may be made under that section shall also include the financial years ending in March 1977 and in March 1978 respectively; and, if such an order is made, the grants so made in respect of expenditure for the period consisting of the financial years 1974-1976 and those two further financial years shall not in the aggregate exceed £100 million.

(6) In this section " relevant expenditure " has the meaning assigned to it by section 3(3)(b) of the Act of 1965, and any reference to expenditure for any financial year of the Board shall be construed as mentioned in section 1(4) of the Act of 1971.

4. In section 3 of the Act of 1967 (which as amended by the Act of 1971 enables the Secretary of State to make schemes providing for payments to persons becoming redundant before 31st March 1974) there shall be made the following amend- ments:—

(*a*) in subsection (1), after the words "making of pay- ments to" there shall be inserted the words "or in respect of" and for the words "31st March 1974" there shall be substituted the words "28th March 1976 or, if the Secretary of State by order so directs, 26th March 1978";

(*b*) after subsection (1) there shall be inserted the following subsections—

"(1A) The payments to be made under a scheme under this section shall be either—

(*a*) payments by the Secretary of State to per- sons to whom the scheme applies in accord- ance with subsection (1) of this section, or

(*b*) payments by the Secretary of State to the Board in respect of the carrying out by the Board of arrangements relating to conces- sionary coal.

(1B) If such an order as is mentioned in sub- section (1) of this section is made by the Secretary of State, the aggregate amount of the payments made by him under this section during the period consist- ing of the financial years 1974-1976 and of the financial years of the Board ending in March 1977 and in March 1978 respectively shall not exceed £100 million; and, if no such order is made, the aggregate amount of the payments so made during the financial years 1974-1976 shall not exceed £60 million.";

(*c*) after subsection (4) there shall be inserted the following subsection—

"(4A) The power to make such an order as is mentioned in subsection (1) of this section shall be exercisable by statutory instrument, but shall not be exercisable unless a draft of the order has been laid before the Commons House of Parliament and approved by a resolution of that House.";

(*d*) in subsection (5), at the end, there shall be added the words "'concessionary coal' means coal supplied free of charge or at reduced prices and 'the financial years 1974-1976' means the financial years of the Board ending in March 1974, March 1975 and March 1976 respectively".

Reimburse-
ment of
Board's
contributions
towards
increased
pensions.

5.—(1) Subject to the following provisions of this section, the Secretary of State may, out of moneys provided by Parliament, make payments to the Board reimbursing to the Board the whole or part of the amount of the Board's contributions towards benefits payable under the mineworkers' pension scheme, in so far as those contributions—

(*a*) are attributable to any approved increase in those benefits, and

(*b*) are contributions towards benefits payable in respect of any part of the period beginning on 1st April 1973 and ending with the financial year of the Board which comes to an end in March 1976 or, if the Secretary of State by order so directs, ending with the financial year of the Board which comes to an end in March 1978.

(2) The aggregate amount of the payments made by the Secretary of State under this section—

(*a*) if an order is made under subsection (1)(*b*) of this section, shall not exceed £40 million, or

(*b*) if no such order is made, shall not exceed £25 million.

(3) For the purpose of exercising his powers under subsection (1) of this section, the Secretary of State shall consult the Board before determining whether to reimburse to the Board the whole of the amount referred to in that subsection or to reimburse to the Board part and, if so, what part of that amount ; and no such determination shall be made except with the approval of the Treasury.

(4) For the purposes of this section the amount of the Board's contributions towards benefits payable under the mineworkers' pension scheme shall be taken to be such amount as is certified in that behalf by the auditors of the Board ; and the proportion of that amount which is attributable to an approved increase in those benefits shall for those purposes be taken to be such proportion as is certified by those auditors to be so attributable.

(5) So much of the contributions made by the Board as is reimbursed under this section shall not be treated as relevant expenditure for the purposes of section 3 of the Act of 1965.

(6) In this section—

(*a*) " the mineworkers' pension scheme " means any scheme established under that name by the Board in pursuance of regulations made under section 37 of the Act of 1946, in the form in which any such scheme (whether as originally established or as subsequently amended) is for the time being in force ; and

(*b*) any reference to an approved increase in the benefits payable under the mineworkers' pension scheme is a reference to any amount by which, in consequence of any amendment made with the approval of the Secretary of State before, on or after 1st April 1973 and coming into force on or after that date, the amount of the benefits of any description so payable is greater than it would have been in accordance with the mineworkers' pension scheme as in force immediately before that date.

6.—(1) For the purpose of promoting the sale of coal by the National Coal Board to the Central Electricity Generating Board or the South of Scotland Electricity Board during the period consisting of the financial years 1974-1976, the Secretary of State with the approval of the Treasury may out of moneys provided by Parliament make payments to the National Coal Board. *Payments for promoting sale of coal to Electricity Boards.*

(2) The aggregate amount of the payments made by the Secretary of State under this section shall not exceed £50 million or such greater sum, not exceeding £100 million, as the Secretary of State may by order specify.

(3) Payments made by the Secretary of State under this section may be made subject to such conditions as the Secretary of State with the approval of the Treasury may determine.

7.—(1) Subject to the following provisions of this section, the Secretary of State with the approval of the Treasury may, out of moneys provided by Parliament, make grants to the Board towards any cost incurred by the Board in any of the financial years 1974-1976 in building up and maintaining stocks of coal or coke. *Grants in connection with stocks of coal or coke.*

(2) For the purposes of this section no account shall be taken—

(a) of any stocks of coal or coke for the time being owned by the Board except in so far as they exceed such quantity as the Secretary of State may determine, or

(b) of any stocks of coal or coke for the time being owned by the Board in excess of 30 million tonnes.

(3) The Secretary of State may by order direct that subsection (1) of this section shall have effect as if, after the words " financial years 1974-1976 ", there were inserted the words " or of the financial years of the Board ending in March 1977 and in March 1978 respectively ".

(4) The aggregate amount of the grants made by the Secretary of State under this section—

(a) if an order is made under subsection (3) of this section, shall not exceed £70 million, or

(b) if no such order is made, shall not exceed £40 million.

B

(5) Grants under this section may be made subject to such conditions as the Secretary of State with the approval of the Treasury may determine.

Grants in respect of coking coal.

8.—(1) For the purpose of contributing towards measures for securing supplies of coke for use in blast furnaces by the iron and steel industry in the United Kingdom and in other countries comprised in the European Coal and Steel Community, the Secretary of State with the approval of the Treasury may, out of moneys provided by Parliament, make grants to the Board or to any other person to whom this section applies.

(2) This section applies to any person carrying on in Great Britain a business which consists of or includes the production of coking coal.

(3) Grants made by the Secretary of State under this section shall be made in respect of coking coal supplied for use in the manufacture of coke, where the coke is to be manufactured for such use as is mentioned in subsection (1) of this section ; and any such grants may be made subject to such conditions as the Secretary of State with the approval of the Treasury may determine.

(4) The power to make grants under this section shall be exercisable at any time during the financial years 1974-1976 or, if the Secretary of State by order so directs, shall be exercisable during those financial years and during the financial years of the Board ending in March 1977 and in March 1978 respectively.

(5) The aggregate amount of the grants made by the Secretary of State under this section—

   (*a*) if an order is made under subsection (4) of this section, shall not exceed £75 million, or

   (*b*) if no such order is made, shall not exceed £45 million.

Regional grants.

9.—(1) For the purpose of assisting the Board in moderating contraction of the coal mining industry in Great Britain, the Secretary of State, having regard to the fact that the industry is heavily concentrated in assisted areas, may with the approval of the Treasury make, out of moneys provided by Parliament, grants to the Board during any of the financial years 1974-1976 of such amount as, subject to the next following subsection, he may consider requisite for that purpose.

(2) The aggregate amount of the grants made by the Secretary of State under this section shall not exceed £210 million.

(3) Grants under this section may be made subject to such conditions as the Secretary of State with the approval of the Treasury may determine.

(4) In this section " the coal mining industry " means the aggregate of the activities falling within the heading numbered 101 (coal mining) in Order II in the Standard Industrial Classification as defined by section 6(2) of the Industry Act 1972, and " assisted area " means an assisted area as so defined. 1972 c. 63.

10. The limit imposed by section 2(2) of the Act of 1946 on Increase in the number of members of the Board other than the chairman membership shall be raised from eleven to fourteen. of Board.

11. There shall be paid out of moneys provided by Parliament Administrative any increase attributable to this Act in the sums so payable in expenses. respect of administrative expenses of the Secretary of State.

12.—(1) In this Act— Interpretation,

and provisions
" the Act of 1946 " means the Coal Industry Nationalisation as to orders.
Act 1946 ; 1946 c. 59.

" the Act of 1965 " means the Coal Industry Act 1965 ; 1965 c. 82.

" the Act of 1967 " means the Coal Industry Act 1967 ; 1967 c. 91.

" the Act of 1971 " means the Coal Industry Act 1971 ; 1971 c. 16.

" the Board " means the National Coal Board ;

" the financial years 1974-1976 " means the financial years of the Board ending in March 1974, March 1975 and March 1976 respectively ;

" subsidiary " shall be construed in accordance with section 154 of the Companies Act 1948, and " wholly owned 1948 c. 38. subsidiary " shall be construed in accordance with subsection (4) of section 150 of that Act.

(2) Except in so far as the context otherwise requires, any reference in this Act to an enactment shall be construed as a reference to that enactment as amended or extended by or under any other enactment.

(3) Any power to make orders under this Act shall be exercisable by statutory instrument.

(4) No power to make an order under this Act shall be exercisable unless a draft of the order has been laid before the Commons House of Parliament and approved by a resolution of that House.

(5) Any power conferred by any provision of this Act to make an order shall include power to vary or revoke the order by a subsequent order made under that provision.

Amendments
and repeals.

13.—(1) The enactments specified in Schedule 1 to this Act shall have effect subject to the amendments set out in that Schedule (being amendments consequential upon the preceding provisions of this Act).

(2) The enactments specified in Schedule 2 to this Act are hereby repealed to the extent specified in the third column of that Schedule.

Short title,
citation, com-
mencement
and extent.

14.—(1) This Act may be cited as the Coal Industry Act 1973.

(2) The Coal Industry Acts 1946 to 1971 and this Act may be cited together as the Coal Industry Acts 1946 to 1973.

(3) The following provisions of this Act, that is to say, section 2(1) and so much of Schedule 2 as repeals section 2(1) of the Act of 1965 or as relates to the Act of 1967 or the Act of 1971, shall come into operation on 1st April 1973.

(4) This Act does not extend to Northern Ireland.

SCHEDULES

SCHEDULE 1

CONSEQUENTIAL AMENDMENTS

1. In section 2(2) of the Act of 1946, for the words "not less than eight nor more than eleven other members" (substituted by section 1(1) of the Coal Industry Act 1949) there shall be substituted the words "not less than eight nor more than fourteen other members".

2. In section 27(4) of the Act of 1946, after the words "section 1 of the Coal Industry Act 1965" (substituted by the Act of 1971) there shall be added the words "or under section 2(3) of the Coal Industry Act 1973".

3. In section 1 of the Act of 1965—

(*a*) in subsection (5), at the end, there shall be added the words "or with section 2(3) of the Coal Industry Act 1973";

(*b*) after subsection (7) there shall be added the following subsection—

"(8) Any power conferred by a provision of this section to make an order shall include power to vary or revoke the order by a subsequent order made under that provision ; but no such power shall be exercisable unless a draft of the order has been laid before the Commons House of Parliament and approved by a resolution of that House."

4. In section 1 of the Act of 1971—

(*a*) in subsection (2), after the words "30th March 1974" there shall be inserted the words "or for such subsequent years as are provided for by or under subsection (1) or subsection (5) of section 3 of the Coal Industry Act 1973";

(*b*) in subsection (3), for the words "shall not exceed in the aggregate £24 million" there shall be substituted the words "in respect of the two years ending with 31st March 1973 shall not exceed in the aggregate £24 million, and grants so made in respect of any subsequent years shall not exceed in the aggregate the limits imposed by subsections (4) and (5) of section 3 of the Coal Industry Act 1973"; and for paragraph (*c*) there shall be substituted the following—

"(*c*) in the case of the year 1973-74 and subsequent years, one half".

SCHEDULE 2

ENACTMENTS REPEALED

Chapter	Short Title	Extent of Repeal
1949 c. 53.	The Coal Industry Act 1949.	In section 1, subsection (1).
1965 c. 82.	The Coal Industry Act 1965.	In section 2, subsections (1) and (2).
1967 c. 91.	The Coal Industry Act 1967.	Section 1.
1971 c. 16.	The Coal Industry Act 1971.	Section 3. In section 4, in subsection (1), paragraph (*c*).

Counter - Inflation Act 1973

1973 CHAPTER 9

An Act to establish a Price Commission and a Pay Board;
to authorise the formulation of the principles to be
applied by those bodies; to afford powers of control
over prices, pay, dividends and rents; to provide for
the furnishing of information about rates ; and for
connected purposes.   [22nd March, 1973]

BE IT ENACTED by the Queen's most Excellent Majesty, by and
with the advice and consent of the Lords Spiritual and
Temporal, and Commons, in this present Parliament
assembled, and by the authority of the same, as follows:—

PART I

THE AGENCIES

1.—(1) There shall be established two Agencies to be called
respectively the Price Commission and the Pay Board.

(2) Each Agency shall, subject to subsection (5) below, consist
of not less than five and not more than twelve members
appointed by the Secretary of State and the Minister of Agriculture, Fisheries and Food (acting jointly), in the case of the Price
Commission and by the Secretary of State, in the case of the Pay
Board.

(3) Her Majesty may, by Order in Council, provide for the
amalgamation of the Price Commission and the Pay Board into
a single Agency, to be known by such name as may be specified
in the Order.

(4) An Order in Council under subsection (3) above—

> (*a*) shall be subject to annulment in pursuance of a resolu-
> tion of either House of Parliament ;
>
> (*b*) may contain supplemental and incidental provisions ;
> and

*Establishment
of two
Agencies:
the Price
Commission
and the Pay
Board.*

(c) may make consequential amendments in any enactment, including this Act.

(5) The Secretary of State may, by an order contained in a statutory instrument subject to annulment in pursuance of a resolution of either House of Parliament—

   (a) direct that the minimum or maximum number of members of each Agency shall be a number greater or less than that specified in subsection (2) above ;

   (b) vary or revoke any previous order made by virtue of this subsection ;

and an order made by virtue of this subsection may provide for the composition of the two Agencies to differ.

(6) The provisions of Schedule 1 to this Act shall have effect in relation to the advisory role of the Agencies and incidental matters relating to each of the Agencies, their members, officers, servants and proceedings.

Code for
guidance
of Agencies.
   2.—(1) The Treasury shall prepare a code for the purposes of this Act, and it shall be the duty of the Agencies to have regard to that code in performing their functions under this Act.

The Treasury shall from time to time make such changes in the code as appear to them to be required.

(2) The code may include practical guidance for those concerned in decisions on levels of prices and pay.

(3) The code, and any change in the code, shall be contained in an order made by statutory instrument, and may be varied or revoked by a subsequent order so made.

(4) Before making an order under this section the Treasury shall consult—

   (a) such representatives of consumers, persons experienced in the supply of goods or services, employers and employees and other persons as they think appropriate, and

   (b) except in the case of the first order made under this section, the Agencies.

(5) An order made under this section shall cease to have effect at the expiration of a period of one month beginning with the date on which it was made unless, before the expiration of that period of one month, the order has been approved by a resolution of each House of Parliament.

In reckoning the said period of one month no account shall be taken of any time during which Parliament is dissolved or prorogued or during which both Houses are adjourned for more than four days.

(6) An order under this section may provide for different parts of the code to come into force on different dates.

PART II

PRICES, PAY, DIVIDENDS AND RENTS

3.—(1) This Part of this Act shall come into force on the date on which the first order under section 2 of this Act is made.

(2) Subject to the following provisions of this section, the period for which section 2 of the Counter-Inflation (Temporary Provisions) Act 1972 has effect in accordance with section 1 of that Act shall terminate on the date when this Part of this Act first comes into force.

(3) No order or notice under section 6 of this Act shall apply where the relevant transaction (as defined by the order or notice) is effected before 29th April 1973, and for the purposes of subsection (1) of the said section 2 (prices and charges) and of the other provisions of the said section 2 as they relate to subsection (1), the period for which section 2 has effect shall terminate on 29th April 1973.

(4) No order under section 11 of this Act shall apply to increases of rent (as defined in the order) taking place before 29th April 1973, or to new lettings (as so defined) taking place before that date, and for the purposes of subsection (4) of the said section 2 (rents) the period for which the said section 2 has effect shall terminate on 29th April 1973.

(5) Nothing in this section shall be taken as extending the period for which the said section 2 would have effect apart from this section.

4.—(1) Subject to the provisions of this section, this Part of this Act shall cease to have effect at the expiration of a period of three years beginning with the date on which it first comes into force.

(2) The period for which this Part of this Act is in force may at any time be terminated by Her Majesty by Order in Council.

(3) If an Order is made under subsection (2) above, Her Majesty may by Order in Council again bring this Part of this

PART I

Commence-
ment of
Part II.

1972 c. 74.

Duration and
reactivation
of Part II.

Act into force for a period ending not later than 31st March 1976.

(4) An Order under subsection (3) above shall not be made unless a draft of the Order has been approved by resolution of each House of Parliament.

Prices and pay

Notification of price and pay increases, and approvals and consents.

5.—(1) The Minister may, in such cases as appear to him appropriate, by order make provision to ensure that the Agencies receive notice of increases in any prices, charges or remuneration in time to consider whether the increases conform with the relevant provisions of the code, and whether the Agencies should exercise the powers conferred by the following provisions of this Act in order to prevent those increases.

(2) The order may provide that, until the end of the period given for consideration of the proposed increase by the Agency, any implementation of the increase constitutes a contravention of the order.

(3) The length of notice required by an order under this section shall not exceed eight weeks.

(4) Schedule 2 to this Act shall have effect as respects—

(*a*) procedures for obtaining the Agencies' approval for increases, and

(*b*) procedures for giving consents overriding the Agencies' orders and notices about prices, charges and remuneration.

(5) An order under this section or under the said Schedule 2 may be made to come into force before the time when this Part of this Act is in force, and may require notices to be given before that time.

(6) An order under this section shall be subject to annulment in pursuance of a resolution of either House of Parliament.

Powers of Price Commission.

6.—(1) The Price Commission shall exercise the powers conferred by this section in such ways as appear to them appropriate for the purpose of ensuring that the provisions of the code which concern prices and charges are implemented.

(2) For the said purpose the Price Commission may restrict any prices or charges for the sale of goods or the performance of services in the course of business, where the relevant transaction is effected at a time when this Part of this Act is in force.

(3) The powers conferred by subsection (2) above shall be exercisable by order, or by notice given to the person, or each of the persons, selling the goods or performing the services subject to the restriction.

(4) Before making or giving an order or notice under this section (other than one which only removes or lessens a restriction), the Price Commission shall give 14 days notice to the persons selling the goods or performing the services which would be subject to the restriction, and shall afford to those persons an opportunity of making written representations to the Price Commission.

(5) If, in the case of an order under this section, it appears to the Price Commission to be impracticable to give notice under subsection (4) above to all the persons selling the goods or performing the services, they may instead publish 14 days notice of their intention to make the order in the Gazette and in such other ways as may be prescribed, and shall afford to all those persons an opportunity of making written representations to the Price Commission.

(6) Where an order or notice under this section is contravened, the liability for the contravention attaches to the person selling the goods or performing the services.

(7) This section has effect subject to section 3(3) of this Act.

7.—(1) The Pay Board shall exercise the powers conferred by this section in such ways as appear to them appropriate for the purpose of ensuring that the provisions of the code which concern remuneration are implemented.

Powers of Pay Board.

(2) For the said purpose the Pay Board may restrict any kind of remuneration for a period when this Part of this Act is in force.

(3) The powers conferred by subsection (2) above shall be exercisable by order, or by notice given to the person, or each of the persons, paying the remuneration subject to the restriction.

(4) Before making or giving an order or notice under this section (other than one which only removes or lessens a restriction), the Pay Board shall give 14 days notice—

(*a*) to the person or persons paying the remuneration which would be subject to the restriction, and

(*b*) to any organisation or organisations of workers which appear to the Pay Board to be concerned,

and shall afford to those persons an opportunity of making written representations to the Pay Board.

(5) If it appears to the Pay Board—

(*a*) in the case of an order, that it is impracticable to give notice under subsection (4) above to all the persons paying the remuneration, or

(*b*) in any case, that a substantial number of those receiving the remuneration are not represented by any organisation of workers,

PART II

the Pay Board shall publish 14 days notice of their intention to make the order, or to give the notice, in the Gazette and in such other ways as may be prescribed.

(6) Where an order or notice under this section makes it illegal to pay remuneration of any amount, it shall also be illegal to enter into any agreement or arrangement whereby the employer makes to, or for the benefit of, the employee some payment, whether called remuneration or not, to compensate for the remuneration which it is illegal to pay ; and an employer who enters into any such agreement or arrangement, or makes any payment pursuant to any such agreement or arrangement, contravenes the provisions of the order or notice.

Power to modify Acts about prices and pay.

8.—(1) The Minister may by order direct that—

(*a*) any provision of any Act, whether passed before this Act or later, which relates to prices, charges or to remuneration or other terms or conditions of employment, or

(*b*) any provision having effect under any Act within paragraph (*a*) above,

shall, while this Part of this Act is in force, have effect subject to such exceptions, modifications or adaptations as may be specified in the order.

(2) An order under this section shall be subject to annulment in pursuance of a resolution of either House of Parliament.

Restrictions on insurance premiums.

9.—(1) The Secretary of State shall have power to restrict insurance premiums, where the relevant transaction is effected at a time when this Part of this Act is in force.

(2) The powers conferred by subsection (1) above shall be exercisable by order, or by notice given to the insurer, or each of the insurers, affected by the notice.

(3) An order or notice under this section may make provision for the giving of consents by the Secretary of State to the doing of anything otherwise prohibited by the order or notice.

(4) Before making or giving an order or notice under this section (other than one which only removes or lessens a restriction), the Secretary of State shall give 14 days notice to the insurers who would be affected by the order or notice, and shall afford to them an opportunity of making written representations to the Secretary of State.

(5) If, in the case of an order under this section, it appears to the Secretary of State to be impracticable to give notice under subsection (4) above to all the said persons, the Secretary of State may instead publish 14 days notice of his intention to make

the order in the Gazette and in such other ways as may be
prescribed, and shall afford to all those persons an opportunity
of making written representations to the Secretary of State.

(6) Where an order or notice under this section is contravened,
the liability for the contravention attaches to the insurer who
charges the insurance premium.

(7) An order under this section shall be subject to annulment
in pursuance of a resolution of either House of Parliament.

Dividends and rent

10.—(1) The Treasury shall have power to restrict the declara- Restrictions
tion or payment of ordinary dividends by companies at any on dividends.
time when this Part of this Act is in force.

(2) The powers conferred by subsection (1) above shall be
exercisable by order, or by notice given to the company, or
each of the companies, affected by the notice.

(3) Without prejudice to the generality of subsection (1)
above, an order or notice under this section may—

(a) provide for the basis on which any comparison is to
be made with the declaration or payment of any earlier
dividends by the companies concerned;

(b) prohibit any company to which it applies from making
any such distribution as may be specified in the order
or notice;

(c) prohibit any such company from assuming any obligation, whether conditional or otherwise, to make any
such distribution as may be so specified; and

(d) make provision for the giving of consents, whether by
the Treasury or by one of the Agencies, to the doing
of anything otherwise prohibited by the order or notice.

(4) This section shall apply to every company incorporated
under the law of any part of the United Kingdom; but nothing
in this section shall apply to companies not so incorporated.

(5) An order under this section shall be subject to annulment
in pursuance of a resolution of either House of Parliament.

11.—(1) The Minister may by order provide for restricting Orders about
or preventing increases of rent which take place, or would take rent.
place, while this Part of this Act is in force, or for restricting
rent payable on new lettings which take place while this Part
of this Act is in force.

(2) The supplemental and incidental provisions that may be
made by an order under this section may include provisions
excluding, adapting or modifying any provision contained in, or

PART II having effect under, any Act (whether passed before this Act or later) which relates to rent, and in the exercise of any power to make regulations or other instruments under any such Act regard may be had to matters connected with the operation of this section.

(3) An order under this section shall be subject to annulment in pursuance of a resolution of either House of Parliament.

(4) This section has effect subject to section 3(4) of this Act.

PART III

PRICE CONTROL RELATED TO VALUE ADDED TAX

Introduction of value added tax: temporary power to control prices and charges.

1972 c. 41.

1968 c. 2.

12.—(1) Subject to subsection (2) below, the powers conferred on the Minister by this section shall be exercisable, as respects relevant transactions effected on or after 1st April 1973, where he considers it expedient for the purpose of ensuring that prices and charges correctly reflect—

(a) the introduction of value added tax and car tax, and the abolition of purchase tax and selective employment tax, by the Finance Act 1972 ;

(b) alterations in the rates of customs and excise duties payable in respect of spirits, beer, wine, British wine, tobacco, matches and mechanical lighters, being alterations first having statutory effect by virtue of Resolutions of the House of Commons made in March 1973 under the Provisional Collection of Taxes Act 1968.

(2) The Minister shall not exercise the powers conferred on him under this section except so far as appears to him to be necessary to prevent or offset excess prices or charges in relevant transactions effected on or before 30th June 1973.

(3) For the said purpose the Minister may, as respects relevant transactions, restrict any prices or charges for the sale of goods or the performance of services in the course of business.

(4) The powers conferred by subsection (3) above shall be exercisable by order contained in a statutory instrument, or by notice given to the person, or each of the persons, selling the goods or performing the services subject to the restriction.

(5) No order or notice shall be made or given under this section to take effect after 30th June 1973 ; but any such order or notice may be expressed to have effect for any period not exceeding three months, notwithstanding that the period ends after that date.

(6) An order or notice made or given under this section—

(a) may be framed in any way whatsoever ;

(b) may define " relevant transaction " both for the purposes of the order or notice and for the purposes of any provision of this section in relation to the order or notice ;

(c) may be varied or revoked by a subsequent order or notice so made or given ;

but the variation or revocation of an order or notice under this section shall not affect liability for any offence committed before the variation or revocation takes effect.

(7) Any person who is designated in accordance with paragraph 2 of Schedule 4 to this Act may perform the Minister's functions of restricting prices and charges by means of the giving of notices under this section.

(8) A transaction shall not be invalid because it involves a price or charge which exceeds the limit imposed in relation to that transaction by an order or notice under this section ; but the person paying the price or charge shall be entitled to recover the amount representing the excess unless he is a person who is himself liable to punishment by reason of his having aided, abetted, counselled or procured the offence committed under this Act by the other party to the transaction.

(9) Where an order or notice under this section is contravened, the liability for the contravention attaches to the person selling the goods or performing the services.

(10) There is no contravention of an order or notice under this section if what has been done is authorised by the consent in writing of the Minister ; and, in the case of a notice given by a person designated as mentioned in subsection (7) above, the consent in writing of any such person shall have the same effect for the purposes of this subsection as if it had been given by the Minister.

PART IV

MISCELLANEOUS

13.—(1) The Minister may, not later than 30th April 1973, by order direct that any order, regulation, byelaw or other instrument—

Power to modify subordinate legislation about prices and charges.

(a) which has effect under any Act passed before this Act, and

(b) which relates to prices or charges,

shall have effect subject to such exceptions, modifications or adaptations as appear to the Minister to be expedient for the purpose of ensuring that prices and charges correctly or sufficiently reflect the introduction of value added tax and car tax, and the abolition of purchase tax and selective employment tax, by the Finance Act 1972.

1972 c. 41.

PART IV   (2) An order under this section relating to a byelaw made by a local authority may authorise the local authority having power to amend the byelaw, or a committee of the authority, to amend it by resolution.

(3) Any amendment of an instrument made in pursuance of this section shall have effect as if made under the same power as that under which the instrument was made, and accordingly may be amended by a subsequent instrument made in exercise of that power.

(4) An order under this section shall be contained in a statutory instrument subject to annulment in pursuance of a resolution of either House of Parliament.

Protected tenancies.

1968 c. 23

14.—(1) For paragraph (*a*) of section 1(1) of the Rent Act 1968 (protected tenancies) there shall be substituted the following paragraphs:—

" (*a*) where the appropriate day in relation to the dwelling-house fell before the date of the passing of the Counter-Inflation Act 1973—

(i) the dwelling-house on the said appropriate day had a rateable value exceeding, if it is in Greater London, £400 or, if it is elsewhere, £200, and

(ii) the dwelling-house on the date of the passing of the said Act of 1973 had a rateable value exceeding if it is in Greater London, £600, or, if it is elsewhere, £300, and

(iii) the dwelling-house on 1st April 1973 has a rateable value exceeding, if it is in Greater London, £1,500 or, if it is elsewhere, £750, or

(*aa*) where the appropriate day in relation to the dwelling-house falls on or after the date of the passing of the said Act of 1973, but before 1st April 1973—

(i) the dwelling-house on the said appropriate day had a rateable value exceeding, if it is in Greater London, £600, or, if it is elsewhere, £300, and

(ii) the dwelling-house on 1st April 1973 has a rateable value exceeding, if it is in Greater London, £1,500, or, if it is elsewhere, £750, or

(*aaa*) where the appropriate day in relation to the dwelling-house falls on or after 1st April 1973, the dwelling-house on the said appropriate day has or had a rateable value exceeding, if it is in Greater London, £1,500 or, if it is elsewhere, £750, or. "

(2) In section 1(3) of the Rent Act 1968 (questions on limits of rateable value) for the words " subsection (1)(*a*) " there shall be substituted the words " subsection (1) ".

(3) So much of section 89 of the Housing Finance Act 1972 as relates to the said section 1 of the Rent Act 1968 (being provisions superseded by subsection (1) above) shall cease to have effect.

(4) Schedule 5 to this Act shall have effect for supplementing this section, and in that Schedule this section is referred to as " the principal section ".

(5) References to this Act in sections 15 to 21 of this Act, and in Schedules 1 to 4 to this Act, shall not include references to this section.

PART V

SUPPLEMENTAL

15.—(1) The Minister, or either Agency, may for the purposes of this Act by notice require any person—

  (a) to furnish, whether by periodical returns or by other means, such estimates or other information as may be specified or described in the notice, or

  (b) to produce to an officer of the Minister, or of either Agency, being an officer duly authorised for the purpose, any documents so specified or described.

(2) The Minister may for the purposes of this Act by order—

  (a) require any class or description of persons specified in the order to furnish to the Minister, or to either Agency, such periodical or other returns containing estimates or other information as may be so specified or described, or

  (b) require any person carrying on a business, or any class or description of persons who carry on a business, to keep such records as may be so specified or described.

(3) A notice or order under this section may specify the way in which, and the time within which, it is to be complied with and, in the case of a notice requiring the production of documents, the facilities to be afforded for making extracts from, or taking copies of, the documents.

(4) Nothing in this section shall be taken to require a person who has acted as counsel or solicitor for any person to disclose any privileged communication made to him in that capacity.

(5) A notice or order given or made under this section may be varied or revoked by a subsequent notice or order so given or made, and an order under this section shall be contained in a statutory instrument.

(6) This section shall have effect only during any period in which Part II of this Act is in force ; but the power conferred by subsection (1) above shall continue to be exercisable, at any

PART V

time when Part II has ceased to be in force, for the purpose of acquiring information or documents in relation to the bringing of proceedings for an offence under Part II or the doing of anything preparatory, or with a view, to the bringing of such proceedings.

Power
to obtain
information
about rates
from rating
and other
authorities.

16.—(1) The Secretary of State may by order made before 1st April 1974 require any rating or other authority to which this section applies to furnish to him such information as the order may specify in relation to—

(a) any rate made, or precept or requisition issued, by the authority for the financial year 1973-74 or any part of that year, or

(b) any rate, precept or requisition which they propose to make or issue for the financial year 1973-74 or 1974-75 or any part of either of those years.

(2) Without prejudice to the generality of subsection (1) above, any such order may require an authority to which it applies to furnish information as to—

(a) the authority's estimated future expenditure and income,

(b) the amount of their proposed rate, precept or requisition,

(c) the estimated product of a penny rate in their area,

(d) the amount of, and the estimates made in relation to, the authority's expenditure and income in any previous year, and

(e) the assumptions about inflation, population changes, rate support grant, and other relevant matters on which the authority's proposals are based,

and may require the authority to furnish any information called for by the order before such time as may be specified in the order.

(3) The authorities to which this section applies are—

(a) in England and Wales, rating authorities within the meaning of section 1 of the General Rate Act 1967 and authorities having power to issue a precept to a rating authority,

1967 c. 9.

(b) in Scotland, local authorities, joint boards and joint committees within the meaning of the Local Government (Scotland) Act 1947 and regional water boards and water development boards within the meaning of the Water (Scotland) Act 1967, and

1947 c. 43.

1967 c. 78.

(c) in Northern Ireland, district councils established under the Local Government Act (Northern Ireland) 1972.

1972 c. 9 (N.I.).

(4) Where an authority to which subsection (6) of section 12 of the General Rate Act 1967 applies (precept to be issued, or information to be given, not less than twenty-one days before the

beginning of the year or half year in which the rate concerned is to be levied) propose to issue a precept, the Secretary of State may, if he considers that the requirement in the said subsection (6) is inappropriate in all the circumstances of the case, direct that in place of that requirement there shall be substituted such other requirement as to the giving of notice to the rating authority affected as the Secretary of State considers appropriate; and the said subsection (6) shall not have effect in a case where the Secretary of State has given such a direction.

(5) Where by any enactment a date is prescribed by which any one of the bodies mentioned in subsection (3)(*b*) above must cause any requisition to be sent to a local authority, the Secretary of State may in any particular case, if he considers that in all the circumstances of that case a later date should be substituted for the date so prescribed, direct that such later date as he considers appropriate be substituted for that date; and in relation to that case the said enactment shall have effect subject to that direction.

(6) Where at any time an authority to which this section applies have—

    (*a*) made a rate for the financial year 1973-74 or 1974-75 or any part of either of those years, or

    (*b*) issued a precept or requisition in respect of any such period,

and subsequently it appears to them that the amount of that rate, precept or requisition, as the case may be, exceeds the amount which they require in respect of that period they may, by way of substitution for that rate, precept or requisition, make a new rate or issue a new precept or requisition, as the case may be.

(7) Where, by virtue of subsection (6) above, an authority have substituted a lower rate for a rate made earlier, section 5 of the General Rate Act 1967 and section 237 of the said Act of 1947 shall not apply to the substituted rate, but the authority shall take such steps as they consider appropriate— 1967 c. 9.

    (*a*) to draw to the attention of any person on whom a rate demand has been served under either of those sections details of the consequential alteration in the amount due from that person, and

    (*b*) to ensure that any resulting overpayment made to the authority is refunded.

(8) If the Secretary of State is satisfied that an authority have failed to discharge any duty imposed on them by an order under this section, he may make a further order declaring the authority to be in default in respect of that duty, and giving such directions for the purpose of enforcing the execution of that duty as appear to him to be expedient.

(9) Any directions given in an order under subsection (8) above shall be enforceable, on an application made on behalf of the Secretary of State, by mandamus ; and, in Scotland, shall be enforceable by order of the Court of Session on an application

by the Lord Advocate under section 91 of the Court of Session Act 1868.

(10) An order or direction under this section may vary or revoke any previous order or direction thereunder.

(11) In this section as it applies in Scotland " financial year " has the same meaning as in section 174 of the said Act of 1947.

17.—(1) If a person contravenes any of the provisions of Part II or Part III of this Act, or of any order or notice under Part II or Part III of this Act, he shall be liable—

(a) on summary conviction to a fine not exceeding £400, and

(b) on conviction on indictment to a fine.

(2) If an organisation of workers, or any other organisation or other person, by taking any action described in subsection (3) below, exercises any pressure on an employer to contravene section 5 or 7 of this Act, that person shall be liable—

(a) on summary conviction to a fine not exceeding £400, and

(b) on conviction on indictment to a fine.

(3) The action referred to in subsection (2) above is—

(a) calling, organising, procuring or financing a strike, or threatening to do so, or

(b) organising, procuring or financing any irregular industrial action short of a strike, or threatening to do so.

(4) Where, under subsection (4) of section 7 of this Act, the Pay Board have given notice of their intention to make or give an order or notice under that section then, for the purposes of subsection (2) above, the giving of the notice under the said subsection (4) shall be treated as if it constituted the making or giving of the order or notice to which it relates.

(5) A person who—

(a) refuses or wilfully neglects to comply with an order or notice under section 15 of this Act, or

(b) in furnishing any estimate or other information in compliance with such an order or notice, makes any statement which he knows to be false in a material particular, or recklessly makes any statement which is false in a material particular, or

(c) with intent to deceive, produces in compliance with such an order or notice a document which is false in a material particular, or

(d) in keeping any records in compliance with an order under section 15 of this Act makes an entry which he knows to be false in a material particular, or recklessly makes any entry which is false in a material particular, or

(e) in furnishing information in connection with an application for approval under Schedule 2 to this Act, or for consent under any provision of this Act, makes any statement, or produces or makes use of any document, which to his knowledge is or may be misleading, false or deceptive in a material particular,

shall be liable on summary conviction to a fine not exceeding £400.

(6) Subject to subsection (7) below, where an offence under this Act committed by a body corporate is proved to have been committed with the consent or connivance of, or to be attributable to any neglect on the part of, any director, manager, secretary or other similar officer of the body corporate or any person who was purporting to act in any such capacity, he as well as the body corporate shall be guilty of the offence and shall be liable to be proceeded against and punished accordingly.

(7) In proceedings for an offence under subsection (2) or paragraph (a) of subsection (5) above against an official of a trade union in respect of action taken by him in his capacity as such an official it shall be a defence to show that he was acting within the scope of his authority on behalf of the trade union.

This subsection shall have effect in relation to an organisation which is for the time being entered in the special register under section 84 of the Industrial Relations Act 1971 as it has effect in relation to a trade union. 1971 c. 72.

(8) Nothing contained in or having effect under this Act, and nothing made illegal by this section, shall give rise to any criminal or tortious liability for conspiracy, or to any other liability in tort ; and nothing which is made illegal by this Act shall constitute an unfair industrial practice within the meaning of the Industrial Relations Act 1971.

(9) Proceedings for an offence under this Act shall not be instituted in England or Wales except by or with the consent of the Attorney General, or in Northern Ireland except by or with the consent of the Attorney General for Northern Ireland.

(10) In this section—

(a) " irregular industrial action short of a strike " has the meaning given by section 33(4) of the Industrial Relations Act 1971.

(*b*) " strike " has the meaning given by section 167(1) of
          that Act, and
     (*c*) " within the scope of his authority " shall be construed
          in accordance with section 167(9) of that Act.

Offences by   **18.**—(1) This section has effect as respects any organisation
unincorporated of workers or organisation of employers, or any other organisa-
bodies.   tion, where the organisation of workers or employers or other
          organisation is an unincorporated body.

     (2) If anything which is made illegal by or under any provi-
     sion of this Act, or which would be illegal but for the provisions
     of subsection (3) below, is done by a person within the scope of
     his authority on behalf of such an unincorporated body, that
     body shall be guilty of an offence under that provision, and shall
     be liable to be proceeded against and punished as if the illegal
     action had been taken by that body.

     (3) In proceedings for an offence under subsection (2), or para-
     graph (*a*) of subsection (5), of section 17 of this Act against an
     official of an unincorporated organisation of workers in respect
     of action taken by him in his capacity as such an official it
     shall be a defence to show that he was acting within the scope
     of his authority on behalf of the unincorporated organisation of
     workers.

     (4) Where an offence is alleged to have been committed
     under this Act by an unincorporated body within subsection (1)
     above—
     (*a*) proceedings for the offence shall be brought in the name
          of that body (and not in that of any of its members),
     (*b*) for the purpose of any such proceedings any rules of
          court relating to the service of documents shall have
          effect as if that body were a corporation, and
     (*c*) any fine imposed on conviction shall be enforceable,
          by way of execution, diligence or otherwise, against the
          funds of that body.

     (5) Where an offence mentioned in subsection (4) above is an
     offence punishable on conviction on indictment, section 33 of
1925 c. 86.   the Criminal Justice Act 1925 and Schedule 2 to the Magistrates'
1952 c. 55.   Courts Act 1952 shall have effect as if the said body were a
     corporation.

     (6) In subsection (2) above the expression " within the scope
     of his authority " shall be construed in accordance with section
1971 c. 72.   167(9) of the Industrial Relations Act 1971.

Application   **19.**—(1) The provisions of this section shall have effect for
to Scotland.   the application of this Act to Scotland.

     (2) (*a*) Where an offence mentioned in section 18(4) of this
          Act is an offence punishable on conviction on indict-
1949 c. 94.   ment section 40 of the Criminal Justice (Scotland) Act

1949 (proceedings on indictment against bodies corporate) shall have effect as if the said body were a body corporate.

(b) Section 17(8) of this Act shall not apply but nothing contained in, or having effect under, this Act or made illegal by that section shall be relevant for the purposes of any proceedings in reparation; and nothing which is made illegal by this Act shall constitute an unfair industrial practice within the meaning of the Industrial Relations Act 1971.

20.—(1) The provisions of this section shall have effect for the application of this Act to Northern Ireland.

(2) A Minister of Northern Ireland may in relation to an Act of the Parliament of Northern Ireland exercise the power of making an order which is conferred by section 8 of this Act; and subsection (2) of that section and paragraph 1(8) of Schedule 3 to this Act shall not apply to an order so made but such an order shall be subject to negative resolution within the meaning of section 41(6) of the Interpretation Act (Northern Ireland) 1954 as if it were a statutory instrument within the meaning of that Act.

(3) In section 16(7) of this Act—

(a) the reference to section 5 of the General Rate Act 1967 and section 237 of the Local Government (Scotland) Act 1947 shall be construed as a reference to Article 9(4) and (5) and Article 32(4) of the Rates (Northern Ireland) Order 1972;

(b) the reference to either of those sections shall be construed as a reference to the said Article 9(4); and

(c) any reference to an authority, except the first such reference, shall be construed as a reference to the Ministry of Finance for Northern Ireland.

(4) Where an offence mentioned in section 18(4) of this Act is an offence punishable on conviction on indictment, section 18 of the Criminal Justice Act (Northern Ireland) 1945 and Schedule 5 to the Magistrates' Court Act (Northern Ireland) 1964 (procedure on charge of an offence against a corporation) shall have effect as if the body there mentioned were a corporation.

(5) It shall be the duty of the Ministry of Commerce for Northern Ireland to enforce in Northern Ireland the provisions of—

(a) any order or notice under section 6 of this Act; and

(b) any order or notice under section 12 of this Act;

and Schedule 4 to this Act shall apply as if—

(i) for references to a local weights and measures authority and to an inspector or chief inspector appointed under the Weights and Measures Act 1963 there were

Marginal notes:

Application to Northern Ireland.

1954 c. 33 (N.I.).

1967 c. 9.
1947 c. 43.

1945 c. 15 (N.I.).
1964 c. 21 (N.I.).

1963 c. 31.

PART V

substituted respectively references to the Ministry of Commerce for Northern Ireland and any of its officers ;

(ii) paragraphs 1(3) and 5 were omitted ; and

(iii) references in paragraph 4 to a Minister of the Crown included references to a Minister of Northern Ireland and to a department of the Government of Northern Ireland.

(6) The Secretary of State shall for each financial year pay into the Exchequer of Northern Ireland such sum as the Secretary of State and the Ministry of Commerce for Northern Ireland may agree to be appropriate as representing the expenses incurred by that Ministry under this Act.

(7) The Parliament of Northern Ireland shall have the same power to pass Acts with respect to any matter as they would have had if this Act had not been passed ; and, in the event of any inconsistency between any Act of the Parliament of Northern Ireland passed after the passing of this Act and any provision of this Act or any order or other instrument having effect by virtue of this Act, the Act of the Parliament of Northern Ireland shall, in Northern Ireland, prevail.

(8) Any expression defined for the purposes of this Act by reference to an Act which does not extend to Northern Ireland shall, unless the context otherwise requires, apply, subject to any necessary modifications, in relation to Northern Ireland as so defined.

Interpretation.

21.—(1) In this Act, unless the context otherwise requires—

" the Minister " means the Minister for the Civil Service, the Treasury, the Secretary of State, the Minister of Agriculture, Fisheries and Food or the Minister of Posts and Telecommunications ;

" Act " and " enactment " include respectively an Act and enactment of the Parliament of Northern Ireland ;

" business " includes any trade, profession or vocation, and the expression " in the course of business " shall be construed accordingly ;

" charge " includes a charge for the performance of services, including any charge for the application of any process to goods ;

" the code " means the code for the time being contained in an order under section 2 of this Act ;

" goods " includes ships and aircraft, minerals, substances and animals (including fish) ;

" official " has the meaning given by section 167(1) of the Industrial Relations Act 1971 ;

1971 c. 72.

" organisation of workers " and " organisation of employers " have the meanings given by sections 61(1) and 62(1) of the Industrial Relations Act 1971 ;

" prescribed ", in relation to publication by the Agencies or by a Minister, means a manner of publication prescribed under paragraph 5(2) of Schedule 3 to this Act ;

" price " means any price or charge for the sale of goods ;

" trade union " has the meaning given by section 61(3) of the Industrial Relations Act 1971.

(2) Any reference in this Act to anything contravening this Act, or any provision of this Act, shall include a reference to a failure to comply with the provision in question.

(3) Any reference in this Act to an offence under this Act, or under any provision of this Act, includes a reference to an offence under an order or notice made or given under this Act, or under that provision, and any reference in this Act to anything contravening, or made illegal by, this Act or any provision of this Act shall be construed accordingly.

(4) Any reference in this Act to any other enactment shall, except so far as the context otherwise requires, be construed as a reference to that enactment as amended or applied by or under any other enactment, including this Act.

(5) This Act shall apply in relation to—

(*a*) a conditional sale agreement, and

(*b*) a hire-purchase agreement,

as if the agreement were a sale of the goods to which the agreement relates for an amount equal to the total purchase price or hire-purchase price, with a fair reduction where the consideration for receipt of that price includes the installation, maintenance or repair of the goods or the performance of other services apart from the giving of credit.

This subsection shall be construed in accordance with the Hire-Purchase Act 1965, the Hire-Purchase (Scotland) Act 1965 or the Hire Purchase Act (Northern Ireland) 1966, as the case may be.

(6) In this Act " Gazette " means, in relation to a matter relating exclusively to England and Wales, or exclusively to Scotland, or exclusively to Northern Ireland, the London Gazette, the Edinburgh Gazette and the Belfast Gazette, respectively, similarly for matters to be published or notified in any two of those Gazettes, and, subject to that, all three of those Gazettes.

22. There shall be paid out of money provided by Parliament—

  (*a*) any administrative expenses incurred by a Government department in consequence of the provisions of this Act, and

  (*b*) any increase in the sums so payable under any other Act which is attributable to this Act.

Short title,
supplemental
provisions
and repeals.
23.—(1) This Act may be cited as the Counter-Inflation Act 1973.

(2) Schedules 3 and 4 to this Act (provisions about orders and notices, and about enforcement) shall have effect for supplementing this Act.

(3) The Acts and instruments specified in Schedule 6 to this Act shall be repealed to the extent set out in the third column of that Schedule.

SCHEDULES

SCHEDULE 1

THE AGENCIES

PART I

AGENCIES' FUNCTIONS UNDER PART II

1.—(1) Each Agency shall in accordance with this paragraph make reports to the Secretary of State on the way they have discharged their functions under Part II of this Act.

(2) Each report shall be submitted to the Secretary of State not later than thirty days after the end of the period covered by the report, and the Secretary of State shall lay the report before Parliament.

(3) The first two months during which Part II of this Act is in force shall be covered by a separate report, and separate reports shall be made covering each subsequent period of three months during which Part II of this Act is in force (on the first or any subsequent occasion); and a separate report shall be made covering any terminal period short of three months.

(4) This paragraph shall have effect in relation to the Price Commission as if references to the Secretary of State were references to the Secretary of State and the Minister of Agriculture, Fisheries and Food, acting jointly.

PART II

ADVISORY ROLE OF THE AGENCIES

References and instructions

2.—(1) The Minister may refer to the appropriate Agency any question relating to prices, charges, remuneration or company dividends, and the Agency shall examine the question and report to the Minister.

(2) The Minister may instruct the appropriate Agency to keep under continuous review any question concerning all or any of the matters mentioned in sub-paragraph (1) above ; and—

   (*a*) the Agency shall from time to time as they think fit, report to the Minister on the matters to which the instruction relates ;

   (*b*) the Minister may at any time require the Agency to make to him a report on those matters, or on any question relating to them.

Supplemental provisions

3.—(1) For the purposes of paragraph 2 above " the appropriate Agency " means the Agency which in the opinion of the Minister is, in the circumstances of the case, the Agency which should consider the reference or, as the case may be, carry out the instruction.

(2) A question referred, or instruction given, to one of the Agencies under paragraph 2 above may be framed in any way whatsoever, and

SCH. 1   in particular may be concerned with a specified region or locality or with named persons.

(3) The Minister referring any question, or giving an instruction, to one of the Agencies under paragraph 2 above may at any time—

(*a*) withdraw the question or instruction, or

(*b*) vary it by referring a further question or, as the case may be, by giving a further instruction, under paragraph 2 above.

(4) In framing any report under paragraph 2 above the Agency concerned shall have regard to the need for excluding, so far as that is practicable, matter which relates to the private affairs of a person and the publication of which would or might in the opinion of the Agency prejudicially affect the interests of that person ; but for the purposes of the law relating to defamation, absolute privilege shall attach to any report made by either Agency.

PART III

INCIDENTAL PROVISIONS HAVING EFFECT IN RELATION TO EACH AGENCY

4. The Agency shall be a body corporate with perpetual succession and a common seal.

Appointment of members

5.—(1) The Secretary of State may appoint persons to the Agency either as full-time members or as part-time members and may appoint any person to be a part-time member of both Agencies.

(2) The Agency shall have a chairman and one or more, as the Secretary of State thinks fit, deputy chairman or deputy chairmen appointed by the Secretary of State from among the members of the Agency (including any part-time members).

Tenure of office, etc., of members

6.—(1) Subject to the following provisions of this paragraph, a member of the Agency shall hold and vacate office as such in accordance with the terms of his appointment.

(2) A person shall not be appointed to the Agency for a term exceeding three years, but previous membership thereof shall not affect eligibility for re-appointment.

(3) The Secretary of State may, with the consent of the member concerned, vary the terms of appointment of any member of the Agency, so far as they relate to his service as a full-time or part-time member.

(4) A member of the Agency may at any time resign his membership by notice in writing addressed to the Secretary of State.

(5) The Secretary of State may, by notice in writing addressed to the member in question, terminate the appointment of any member of the Agency who is, in his opinion, unfit to continue in office or incapable of performing his duties as a member.

Tenure of office of chairman and deputies

7.—(1) Subject to the following provisions of this paragraph, the chairman and any deputy chairman of the Agency shall hold and vacate office as such in accordance with the terms of his appointment.

(2) The chairman or a deputy chairman of the Agency may at any time resign his office as such by notice in writing addressed to the Secretary of State.

(3) If the chairman or a deputy chairman of the Agency ceases to be a member of the Agency, he shall also cease to be chairman or, as the case may be, a deputy chairman.

Remuneration and expenses of members

8. The Secretary of State shall, out of money provided by Parliament—

(a) pay to the members of the Agency such remuneration, and such travelling or other allowances as he may with the approval of the Minister for the Civil Service determine, and

(b) in the case of any member of the Agency to whom he may, with the approval of the said Minister, determine that this paragraph applies, pay such pension, allowance or gratuity to or in respect of the member on his retirement or death, or make such payments towards the provision of such a pension, allowance or gratuity, as he may, with the like approval, determine ;

and if a person ceases to be a member of the Agency and it appears to the Secretary of State that there are special circumstances which make it right that that person should receive compensation he may, with the approval of the said Minister, pay to that person out of money provided by Parliament a sum of such amount as he may, with the like approval, determine.

Application of House of Commons Disqualification Act

9. In Part II of Schedule 1 to the House of Commons Disqualifica- 1957 c. 20. tion Act 1957 (bodies of which all members are disqualified under that Act), there shall (at the appropriate place in alphabetical order) be inserted the following entries :—

" The Price Commission "

" The Pay Board " ;

and the like amendment shall be made in the Part substituted for the said Part II by Schedule 3 to that Act in its application to the Senate and House of Commons of Northern Ireland.

Officers and servants

10. The Agency—

(a) shall have a secretary, to be appointed by them after consultation with the Secretary of State and with the consent of the Minister for the Civil Service, and

(b) may, after such consultation and with the consent of the said Minister, appoint such other officers and servants as they think fit.

11.—(1) The Agency shall pay to their officers and servants such remuneration, and such travelling and other allowances, as the Secretary of State may with the approval of the Minister for the Civil Service determine.

(2) The Agency shall, in the case of such persons engaged in its business as may be determined by them with the approval of the Minister for the Civil Service (not being members of the Agency), pay such pensions, allowances or gratuities to or in respect of them as may be so determined, make such payments towards the provision of such pensions, allowances or gratuities as may be so determined or provide and maintain such schemes (whether contributory or not) for the payment of such pensions, allowances or gratuities as may be so determined.

(3) Where a participant in such a scheme as is mentioned in sub-paragraph (2) above becomes a member of the Agency, he may be treated for the purposes of the scheme as if his service as a member of the Agency were service as a person engaged in their business otherwise than as such a member, and his rights under the scheme shall not be affected by paragraph 8(*b*) above.

General provisions with respect to the Agency's proceedings

12. The validity of any proceedings of the Agency shall not be affected by any vacancy among the members of the Agency, or by any defect in the appointment of any such member.

13. Subject to paragraph 18 below, the Agency may determine their own procedure, including the quorum necessary for their meetings.

Exercise of chairman's functions during absence, incapacity etc.

14.—(1) At any time when the chairman of the Agency is absent or otherwise incapable of acting, or there is a vacancy in the office of chairman—

> (*a*) such one of the Agency's deputy chairmen as the Secretary of State may direct or, in default of any such direction, such one of them as the Agency may determine, or
>
> (*b*) if there is then only one deputy chairman of the Agency, the deputy chairman,

may exercise any of the functions of chairman of the Agency.

(2) At any time when every person who is chairman or deputy chairman of the Agency is absent or otherwise incapable of acting, or there is no such person, such member of the Agency as the Secretary of State may direct or, in default of any such direction, such member of the Agency as the Agency may determine, may exercise any of the functions of chairman of the Agency.

Inquiries

15.—(1) The Agency may hold such inquiries as they consider necessary or desirable for the discharge of their functions under this Act ; and the chairman of the Agency, or other member of the Agency presiding in his stead, may at any such inquiry direct that any person appearing as a witness be examined on oath, and administer an oath accordingly, or, instead of so directing, require the person examined to make and subscribe a declaration of the truth of the matter respecting which he is examined.

(2) If any person who is to give evidence at any such inquiry so requests at the hearing, or by a notice in writing served on the Agency's secretary before the date of the hearing, the Agency may direct that the public shall be excluded from the hearing while that person gives his evidence.

16.—(1) For the purposes of any inquiry under this Act, the chairman of the Agency or any other member of the Agency authorised by the chairman (whether generally or in connection with the particular inquiry) to exercise the powers conferred by this sub-paragraph, may by summons require any person to attend, at such time and place as is specified in the summons, to give evidence on any matter so specified, being a matter in question at the inquiry.

(2) No person shall be compelled for the purposes of any such inquiry to give any evidence which he could not be compelled to give in proceedings before the High Court.

(3) No person shall be required, in obedience to a summons under this paragraph, to go more than ten miles from his place of residence unless the necessary expenses of his attendance are paid or tendered to him.

(4) A person who refuses or wilfully neglects to attend in obedience to a summons issued under this paragraph or to give evidence as required by such a summons shall be liable on summary conviction to a fine not exceeding £400.

(5) In the application of this paragraph to Scotland, for any reference to a summons there shall be substituted a reference to a notice in writing, and for the reference to the High Court there shall be substituted a reference to the Court of Session ; and in the application of this paragraph to Northern Ireland, for the reference to the High Court there shall be substituted a reference to the High Court in Northern Ireland.

Publication of information and advice

17. The Agency may arrange for the publication, in such form and in such manner as they may consider appropriate, of such information and advice with respect to the application of any provisions of the code, or the discharge of any of the Agency's functions, as may appear to them to be expedient.

Power of Secretary of State to give directions

18. In determining any matter of procedure (including the quorum necessary for their meetings) and in exercising their powers under paragraph 17 above, the Agency shall act in accordance with any general directions which may from time to time be given with respect thereto by the Secretary of State.

Expenses of the Agency

19. The expenses incurred by the Agency under paragraph 11 above and, to such amount as the Secretary of State may with

Sch. 1 the approval of the Minister for the Civil Service determine, any other expenses of the Agency shall be paid out of money provided by Parliament.

Interpretation

20. This Part of this Schedule shall have effect in relation to the Price Commission as if references to the Secretary of State were references to the Secretary of State and the Minister of Agriculture, Fisheries and Food, acting jointly.

Section 5(4).

SCHEDULE 2

APPROVALS AND CONSENTS

Procedure for approving proposed increases

1.—(1) The Minister may by order establish procedures by which, in cases prescribed by the order, either Agency will be required—

(a) to entertain proposals for increases of prices, charges or remuneration, and

(b) where satisfied that the increases ought to be allowed, to approve the proposals.

(2) An order under this paragraph—

(a) shall prescribe the time within which an Agency are to give their decision whether or not to approve the proposal, and

(b) may provide that, in circumstances specified in the order, the Agency shall be deemed to have given their approval for the purposes of any provision of this Schedule so specified if they have not duly notified the applicant of their decision within the time prescribed under paragraph (a) above, and

(c) may prescribe some earlier time limit by which the Agency are to be deemed to have given their approval if they have not given notice to the applicant that the application is still under consideration, and

(d) may make it a contravention of the order to implement the increase before the time limit under paragraph (a) above, or (where the application is then no longer under consideration) before such earlier time as is specified in the order.

(3) A proposal for an increase which an Agency are required to entertain under this Schedule shall be made to the Agency in such form and manner as may be prescribed by the Agency.

2.—(1) Where an Agency approve proposals for an increase in accordance with an order under paragraph 1 above, the Agency shall not exercise their powers under Part II of this Act so as to restrict any price or charge, or any kind of remuneration, where the price or charge or remuneration is duly authorised by the approval.

(2) In exercising their powers under an order under paragraph 1 above, an Agency may frame an approval of proposals for an increase in such way as appears to them appropriate for the purpose of ensuring that the provisions of the code are implemented.

(3) In acting under sub-paragraph (2) above an Agency may—

(a) attach any conditions to an approval, and

(*b*) limit or qualify an approval to allow for any change in circumstances, and

(*c*) limit the duration of an approval.

(4) An order under paragraph 1 above which provides that an Agency shall be deemed to have given their approval in any circumstances may impose any such conditions, limitations or qualifications as might have been imposed by the Agency under the preceding provisions of this paragraph.

3. Where notice of an increase is given under section 5 of this Act, an order under paragraph 1 above may treat that notice as an application for approval of the increase.

4.—(1) Any reference in this Act to an order under Part II of this Act shall include a reference to an order under paragraph 1 above.

(2) An order under paragraph 1 above shall be subject to annulment in pursuance of a resolution of either House of Parliament.

Consents by Agencies

5.—(1) There is no contravention of an order or notice under section 6 or section 7 of this Act if what has been done is authorised by the consent in writing of the Agency making or giving the order or notice.

(2) An application for consent under this paragraph shall be made to the Agency in such form and manner as may be prescribed by the Agency.

Consents by the Minister

6.—(1) If, after consultation with the Agency, the Minister is satisfied that there are exceptional circumstances which justify an intervention by him in any case where the Agency have imposed a restriction under section 6 or section 7 of this Act, or are considering whether to do so, he may give his consent in writing to anything which is, or would be, subject to the restriction.

(2) Where the Minister gives his consent, the Agency shall not at any time exercise their powers under Part II of this Act so as to prevent the doing of anything covered by the consent, and if the Agency have already imposed a restriction, the consent shall be equivalent to consent granted by the Agency.

Terms of consents

7.—(1) Any power of granting a consent conferred by or under any provision of this Act includes a power to attach any conditions or limitations to the consent.

(2) The granting of a consent in exercise of a power conferred by or under any provision of this Act shall not affect liability for any offence committed before the date from which the consent is expressed to take effect or, if it is not expressed to take effect from a specified date, before the time when the consent is received by the person to whom it is given.

(3) Where an Agency, or a Minister, grant a consent under this Act, particulars of the consent shall be published in the Gazette, and in such other ways as may be prescribed.

C

Section 23.

SCHEDULE 3

SUPPLEMENTAL PROVISIONS

PART I

ORDERS AND NOTICES UNDER THIS ACT

1.—(1) An order or notice under Part II of this Act may be framed in any way whatsoever, and may define any expression used in the provisions under which it is made or given (other than an expression defined by section 21(1) of this Act) both for the purposes of the order or notice, and for the purposes of the said provision as it applies in relation to the order or notice.

(2) An order or notice under Part II of this Act may prescribe any method of comparing prices, charges, rates of remuneration or rents.

(3) Any such order or notice concerning remuneration may take account of any terms or conditions of employment, and may determine, whether remuneration becoming payable after the period for which it is payable is to be taken into account in making any comparison.

(4) An order made by a Minister under Part II of this Act may contain any kind of supplemental or incidental provisions, including, in the case of an order concerning rents, provisions for the recovery of rent overpaid.

(5) Any provisions made in pursuance of sub-paragraph (4) above shall, if the order so provides, continue in force after Part II of this Act ceases to have effect.

(6) Any order or notice under any provision of Part II of this Act may be varied or revoked by a subsequent order or notice under the same provision.

(7) The variation or revocation of an order or notice under Part II of this Act shall not affect liability for any offence committed before the variation or revocation takes effect.

(8) An order made by a Minister under Part II of this Act shall be contained in a statutory instrument.

(9) An order made by an Agency under Part II of this Act shall be published in the Gazette, and in such other ways as may be prescribed.

(10) Where a notice is given by an Agency or a Minister under any of the following provisions of this Act, that is—

> section 6(3),
> section 7(3),
> section 9(2),
> section 10, or
> section 12,

particulars of the notice shall be published in the Gazette, and in such other ways as may be prescribed.

Identification of two or more different persons　　　　Sch. 3

2.—(1) For the purposes of sections 5 to 7 of this Act, and of any provision made under those sections, the following shall be treated as one person, that is—

(*a*) all the persons who successively carry on any business ;

(*b*) the person having control of any company, and all the companies controlled by that person ;

(*c*) where any companies are amalgamated or reconstructed, the companies wound up in the course of the amalgamation or reconstruction, and the companies resulting from the amalgamation or reconstruction.

(2) An order or notice under sections 5 to 7 of this Act may exclude any of the provisions of sub-paragraph (1) above as they apply to, or in relation to, the order or notice.

Validity of transactions

3.—(1) The Minister may by order made at any time during a period when Part II of this Act is in force prescribe the degree to which anything made illegal by any order or notice made or given under Part II during that period, or anything otherwise affected by any such provision, is to be valid or invalid either during that period or later.

(2) In the case of an order or notice restricting any price or charge, an order under this paragraph may make the excess of any price or charge over the restriction recoverable by the person paying the price or charge.

(3) Where in accordance with an order under this paragraph a contract to pay any remuneration remains invalid (in whole or in part) after the date when section 7 of this Act ceases to be in force, the order may further provide that the provisions of sections 17 and 18 of this Act (offences) shall continue to apply in relation to the implementation of the contract as if section 7 of this Act was still in force.

(4) An order made under this paragraph—

(*a*) may be varied or revoked by a subsequent order so made, and

(*b*) shall be contained in a statutory instrument.

Application of provisions of the Interpretation Act 1889　　1889 c. 63.

4. On the expiration of Part II of this Act (whether on the first or any subsequent occasion), section 38(2) of the Interpretation Act 1889 (effect of repeals) shall apply as if Part II of this Act had been repealed by another Act.

Notices and orders

5.—(1) The Minister may by regulations prescribe the manner in which any notice is to be given under this Act, and the evidence which is to be sufficient evidence of its having been given, and of its contents and authenticity.

SCH. 3

(2) The Minister may by regulations—

(a) prescribe the manner in which any order, notice or consent under this Act is to be published, or the manner in which particulars of any such order, notice or consent are to be published, and

(b) in the case of an order made under this Act by either Agency, prescribe the evidence which is to be sufficient evidence of its having been published, and of its contents and authenticity.

(3) In any proceedings against any person for an offence consisting of a contravention of an order made by either Agency under this Act, it shall be a defence to prove that the order had not been published at the date of the alleged contravention, unless it is proved that at that date reasonable steps had been taken for the purpose of bringing the purport of the order to the notice of the public, or of persons likely to be affected by it, or of the person charged.

(4) The power of making regulations under this paragraph shall be exercisable by statutory instrument subject to annulment in pursuance of a resolution of either House of Parliament.

Crown servants

6.—(1) Although this Act does not bind the Crown an order or notice may be made or given under section 7 of this Act, or under this Schedule, so as, without imposing any obligation on the Crown as an employer or otherwise, to apply (either expressly or impliedly) to persons employed by or under the Crown, and section 17(2) of this Act shall apply accordingly.

1965 c. 62.

(2) For the purposes of this Act employment by any such body as is specified in Schedule 3 to the Redundancy Payments Act 1965 (national health service employers) and corresponding employments in Northern Ireland shall (if they would not otherwise be so regarded) be regarded as employment by or under the Crown.

(3) In the application of this paragraph to Northern Ireland references to the Crown include references to the Crown in right of the Government of Northern Ireland.

Consultations by Ministers before the passing of this Act

7. A provision of this Act which imposes on a Minister a duty to consult any person shall not be taken as implying that further consultation is required by the provision where the Minister is satisfied that there was consultation before the passing of this Act which in his opinion was sufficient for the purpose.

PART II

1972 c. 74.

ORDERS AND NOTICES UNDER THE COUNTER-INFLATION (TEMPORARY PROVISIONS) ACT 1972

Orders and notices about prices, charges and remuneration

8.—(1) Any order or notice which was made or given in exercise of the powers in paragraph (a) or paragraph (b) of subsection (5) of section 2 of the Counter-Inflation (Temporary Provisions) Act

1972 (whether or not also in exercise of other powers in that Act), and which was in force immediately before the relevant date, shall have effect as if it, with the provisions of section 2 which it applies, had been made or given under section 6 or, as the case may be, section 7 of this Act, and the powers of varying or revoking orders and notices under the said sections 6 and 7 may be exercised accordingly.

(2) In this paragraph " the relevant date " means—

   (a) in relation to an order or notice made or given in exercise of the powers in the said paragraph (a) (prices and charges), 29th April 1973, and

   (b) in relation to an order or notice made or given in exercise of the powers in the said paragraph (b) (remuneration), the date when Part II of this Act first comes into force.

Adaptations of the Temporary Provisions Act

9. The references in section 3 of the said Act of 1972 to the time when section 2 of that Act is in force shall be taken as references to a period ending when Part II of this Act first comes into force.

10.—(1) The reference in paragraph 1(4) of the Schedule to the said Act of 1972 (supplemental and incidental provisions continuing in force after the time when section 2 of that Act ceases to have effect) to that time is a reference to the time when any of the provisions of that section have ceased to have effect, and the reference in paragraph 3 of that Schedule to the expiration of section 2 is a reference to the expiration of any provision of section 2.

(2) The reference in paragraph 4(2) of the said Schedule (adaptation of existing legislation about prices, charges, remuneration, dividends or rents) to the time when the said section 2 is in force shall include a reference to any time before 29th April 1973.

(3) An order under the said paragraph 4(2) may contain any kind of supplemental or incidental provisions, and any such supplemental or incidental provisions shall, if the order so provides, continue in force, or take effect, on or after 29th April 1973.

SCHEDULE 4

ENFORCEMENT

Enforcement by local weights and measures authorities

1.—(1) Every local weights and measures authority may within their area enforce the provisions of—

   (a) any order or notice under section 6 of this Act, and

   (b) any order or notice under Part III of this Act.

(2) For the purpose of determining—

   (a) whether to recommend that any such order or notice should be made or given, or

   (b) whether the provisions of any such order or notice are being complied with,

a local weights and measures authority may make, or may authorise any of their officers to make on their behalf, any purchases of goods, and may authorise any of their officers to obtain any services.

(3) Nothing in this Schedule shall confer on any person authorised to enforce any provision of this Act mentioned in this Schedule any power to institute proceedings in Scotland for an offence.

(4) In acting under this paragraph an authority shall conform with such directions, if any, as the Minister may give, either generally to all authorities, or to that particular authority.

Power of Minister to designate officers for purposes of enforcement

2.—(1) The Minister may by order designate—

    (*a*) any inspectors or chief inspectors appointed under the Weights and Measures Act 1963, or

    (*b*) any officers of either Agency,

as persons to execute this Act in accordance with this paragraph by doing what may be done by his officers.

(2) Where an order is made under this paragraph designating any inspectors or chief inspectors, or any officers of either Agency, it shall be the duty of the local weights and measures authorities, or as the case may be of the Agency, to put the services of the persons so designated at the disposal of the Minister making the order.

(3) A person designated by an order under this paragraph shall act in accordance with directions given by the Minister in the same way as would one of his officers, but shall be deemed, while so acting, to continue to be employed by the authority or Agency putting his services at the disposal of the Minister.

(4) An order made under this paragraph—

    (*a*) may be varied or revoked by a subsequent order so made, and

    (*b*) shall be contained in a statutory instrument.

(5) Any reference in this Act to an officer, or a duly authorised officer, of the Minister shall include a reference to a person who is designated under this paragraph, and who is acting in accordance with directions given by the Minister and duly authorised for the purpose.

Powers of inspection and entry

3.—(1) A duly authorised officer of the Minister, or of a local weights and measures authority, may at all reasonable hours, and on production, if required, of his credentials, exercise the following powers for the purpose of determining whether the provisions of—

    (*a*) any order or notice under section 6 of this Act, or

    (*b*) any order or notice under Part III of this Act,

are being complied with.

(2) The said powers are—

    (*a*) a power to inspect any goods and to enter any land or any premises, other than premises used only as a dwelling, and (*b*) a power to require any person carrying on a business, or employed in connection with a business, to produce any documents relating to the business, and a power of making extracts from, or making copies of, the documents.

(3) A person who wilfully obstructs an officer acting under this paragraph shall be liable on summary conviction to a fine not exceeding £400.

(4) A person who, with intent to deceive, produces, in compliance with a requirement under this paragraph, a document which to his knowledge is or may be misleading, false or deceptive in a material particular shall be liable on summary conviction to a fine not exceeding £400.

(5) In this paragraph " premises " includes any stall, vehicle or vessel.

Restriction on disclosure of information obtained under this Act

4.—(1) This paragraph applies to information given or supplied pursuant to Part V of this Act, or obtained in the course of exercising the powers conferred by paragraph 3 above.

(2) No such information shall be disclosed except—

(*a*) with the consent of the person by whom or on whose behalf the information was given or supplied, or as the case may be the owner of the goods or the occupier of the land or premises, or

(*b*) to members of either Agency, or to the officers or servants of either Agency, or

(*c*) to any Minister of the Crown, or an officer or servant appointed by, or person exercising functions on behalf of, a Minister of the Crown, or

(*d*) in the case of information obtained by a person acting on behalf of a local weights and measures authority, to any officer of that authority, or

(*e*) with a view to the institution of, or otherwise for the purpose of, any criminal proceedings pursuant to or arising out of this Act, or the Counter-Inflation (Temporary 1972 c. **74**. Provisions) Act 1972.

(3) Sub-paragraph (2) above does not apply to information given or supplied to either Agency in proceedings to which the public are admitted, or contained in any report of either Agency.

(4) If a person contravenes the provisions of this paragraph he shall be liable—

(*a*) on summary conviction to a fine not exceeding £400, and

(*b*) on conviction on indictment to a fine.

Expenses to be treated as special expenses of county councils

5.—(1) In respect of any period during which a district council in Wales are the local weights and measures authority for their district, any expenditure incurred in enforcing the provisions of Part

SCH. 4
II or Part III of this Act by the council of the county in which that district is situate shall be treated as incurred for special expenses of the county council, and that district shall not be chargeable therewith.

1972 c. 70.

1963 c. 31.

(2) Before the coming into force of the Local Government Act 1972 sub-paragraph (1) above shall not apply, but in respect of any period during which the council of any non-county borough or urban or rural district in England or Wales are acting as a local weights and measures authority, or are a party to any agreement made or deemed to have been made under section 37 of the Weights and Measures Act 1963, any expenditure incurred in enforcing the provisions of Part II or Part III of this Act by the council of the county in which that borough or district is situated shall be treated as incurred for special county purposes, and that borough or district shall not be chargeable therewith.

Section 14.

SCHEDULE 5

RENT RESTRICTION

Special rent limit for existing tenancies brought within the Rent Act

1.—(1) This paragraph applies to a regulated tenancy—

(a) which was granted before 8th March 1973, and

(b) which would not have been a regulated tenancy but for the provisions of subsection (1) of the principal section.

(2) Subject to the provisions of this Schedule, the recoverable rent for any contractual period of a tenancy to which this paragraph applies shall not exceed the limit specified in paragraph 2 below, and the amount of any excess shall, notwithstanding anything in any agreement, be irrecoverable from the tenant.

1968 c. 23.

(3) Where a rent for the dwelling-house is registered under Part IV of the Rent Act 1968 which is less than the limit specified in paragraph 2 below, neither section 20(2) (registered rent as limit for contractual periods) nor section 22(2) (corresponding provision for statutory periods) of that Act shall apply to a tenancy to which this paragraph applies.

1972 c. 47.

(4) Sub-paragraphs (2) and (3) above shall cease to apply if the landlord and the tenant so provide by an agreement conforming with the requirements of section 43(3) of the Housing Finance Act 1972 (agreement to explain the nature of the tenant's security of tenure).

(5) Sub-paragraph (2) above shall not apply where a rent for the dwelling-house is registered under Part IV of the Rent Act 1968 which is not less than the limit specified in paragraph 2 below.

(6) Section 33 of the Rent Act 1968 (enforcement provisions) shall apply as if any amount made irrecoverable by this paragraph were irrecoverable by virtue of Part III of that Act, and section 36 of

that Act (adjustment for differences in lengths of rental periods) shall apply for the purposes of this paragraph.

2.—(1) Where at the date of the passing of this Act Article 10 of the Counter-Inflation (Rents) (England and Wales) Order 1972 applied to the rent under the tenancy (to which paragraph 1 applies), the said limit is the rent payable under the tenancy as limited by the said Article 10 immediately before that date.

(2) In any other case the said limit is the rent payable under the terms of the tenancy (to which paragraph 1 applies) at the passing of this Act.

Adjustment for repairs, services or rates

3.—(1) This paragraph applies to a contractual period the rent for which is subject to paragraph 1(2) of this Schedule.

(2) In this paragraph " the previous terms " means the terms of the tenancy (to which paragraph 1 applies) as at the passing of this Act.

(3) Where under the terms of the tenancy there is with respect to—

    (*a*) the responsibility for any repairs, or

    (*b*) the provision of services by the landlord or any superior landlord, or

    (*c*) the use of furniture by the tenant,

any difference compared with the previous terms, such as to affect the amount of the rent which it is reasonable to charge, the limit in paragraph 2 above shall be increased or decreased by an appropriate amount.

(4) Where for the contractual period there is a difference between the amount (if any) of the rates borne by the landlord or a superior landlord in respect of the dwelling-house and the amount (if any) so borne during the first rental period for which the previous terms were agreed, the limit in paragraph 2 above shall be increased or decreased by the difference.

(5) Where for the contractual period there is an increase in the cost of the provision of the services (if any) provided for the tenant by the landlord or a superior landlord compared with that cost at the time when the previous terms were agreed, such as to affect the amount of the rent which it is reasonable to charge, the limit in paragraph 2 above shall be increased by an appropriate amount.

(6) Where the previous terms provide for a variation of the rent in any of the circumstances mentioned in this paragraph, the limit shall not be further varied under this paragraph by reason of the same circumstances.

(7) Any question whether, or by what amount, the limit is increased or decreased by sub-paragraph (3) or sub-paragraph (5) of this paragraph shall be determined by the county court, and any such determination—

    (*a*) may be made so as to relate to past rental periods, and

    (*b*) shall have effect with respect to rental periods subsequent to the periods to which it relates until revoked or varied by a subsequent determination.

Statutory period of tenancy: no adjustment for improvements

4. Section 25 of the Rent Act 1968 (increase for improvements) shall not apply to a tenancy to which paragraph 1 of this Schedule applies.

Premiums

5.—(1) This paragraph has effect where a premium was lawfully required and paid on the grant of a tenancy to which paragraph 1 of this Schedule applies.

(2) Nothing in section 86 of the Rent Act 1968 (prohibition of premiums on assignment of protected tenancies) shall prevent any person from requiring or receiving, on an assignment of the tenancy, the fraction of the premium specified below (without prejudice, however, to his requiring or receiving a greater sum in a case where he may lawfully do so under Schedule 11 to the Rent Act 1968).

(3) If there was more than one premium, sub-paragraph (2) above applies to the last of them.

(4) The said fraction is $\frac{X}{Y}$ where—

    (*a*) X is the residue of the term of the tenancy at the date of the assignment, and

    (*b*) Y is the term for which the tenancy was granted.

(5) Sub-paragraph (1) of this paragraph shall apply where a tenancy has been assigned as it applies where a tenancy has been granted, and then Y in the said fraction shall be the residue, at the date of that assignment, of the term for which the tenancy was granted.

(6) In this and the next following paragraph " grant " includes continuance and renewal.

6.—(1) Where the tenancy to which paragraph 5(1) above applies was granted on the surrender of a previous tenancy, and a premium had been lawfully required and paid on the grant, or an assignment, of the previous tenancy, the surrender value of the previous tenancy shall be treated, for the purposes of paragraph 5 above as a premium, or as the case may be as part of the premium, paid on the said grant of the tenancy.

(2) For the purposes of sub-paragraph (1) above the surrender value of the previous tenancy shall be taken to be the amount which—

    (*a*) if the previous tenancy had been assigned instead of being surrendered, and (*b*) if this paragraph had applied to it,

would have been the amount which could have been required and received on the assignment in pursuance of paragraph 5 above and this paragraph.

(3) In determining for the purposes of paragraph 5 above, or of this paragraph, the amount which may be or could have been required and received on the assignment of a tenancy terminable, before the end of the term for which it was granted, by a notice to the tenant, that term shall be taken to be a term expiring at the earliest date on which such a notice, given after the date of the assignment, would have been capable of taking effect.

Tenancies ending before passing of this Act

7.—(1) This paragraph applies where the tenancy of a dwelling-house has come to an end at a time before the passing of this Act, and the tenancy would have been a regulated tenancy if the principal section had been in force at that time.

(2) No order for possession of the dwelling-house shall be made which would not be made if the principal section had been in force at the said time.

(3) Where a court has made an order for possession of the dwelling-house before the passing of this Act, but the order has not been executed, the court, if of opinion that the order would not have been made if this Act had come into force before the tenancy came to an end may, on the application of the person against whom it was made, rescind or vary it in such manner as the court thinks fit for the purpose of giving effect to the principal section.

(4) If the tenant under the tenancy which has come to an end duly retains possession of the dwelling-house after the passing of this Act (without any order for possession having been made, or after the rescission of such an order) he shall be deemed to do so under a statutory tenancy arising on the termination of the tenancy which has come to an end, and, subject to sub-paragraph (7) below, the terms of that tenancy (including the rent) shall be deemed to have been the same as those of the tenancy which has come to an end.

(5) Where Article 10 of the Counter-Inflation (Rents) (England and Wales) Order 1972 applied to the rent under the tenancy, the rent under the tenancy imposed by sub-paragraph (4) above shall be the rent as limited by the said Article 10.

S.I. 1972/1851

(6) Paragraphs 1 to 4 of this Schedule shall not apply to a statutory tenancy arising under sub-paragraph (4) above.

(7) The High Court or the county court may by order vary all or any of the terms of the tenancy imposed by sub-paragraph (4) above in any way appearing to the court to be just and equitable (and whether or not in a way authorised by the provisions of sections 23 and 24 of the Rent Act 1968).

1968 c. 23.

(8) If at the passing of this Act the dwelling-house is occupied by a person who would, if the tenancy had been a regulated tenancy, have been the " first successor " within the meaning of paragraph 4 of Schedule 1 to the Rent Act 1968—

(a) an application under sub-paragraph (3) above may be made by that person, and

(b) sub-paragraphs (4), (5) and (6) above shall apply where that person retains possession as they apply where the tenant retains possession.

Mortgages

8. At the end of section 93 of the Rent Act 1968 (mortgages to which Part VIII of that Act applies) there shall be inserted the following subsection—

" (5) If at the date of the passing of the Counter-Inflation Act 1973 land consisting of or including a dwelling-house was subject to a tenancy which becomes a regulated tenancy by virtue of section 14 of that Act, then in relation to that dwelling-house (and any land including that dwelling-house)—

(a) sections 94 and 95 below shall have effect as if for the reference in subsection (1)(a) above to 8th December 1965 there were substituted a reference to the date of the passing of the said Act ;

(b) subsection (2)(a) of the said section 94 shall have effect as if for the reference to the appropriate day there were substituted a reference to 7th March 1973, and

(c) subsection (1)(b) of the said section 95 shall not apply."

Grounds for possession of dwelling-house

9. If at the date of the passing of this Act a dwelling-house was subject to a tenancy which becomes a regulated tenancy by virtue of the principal section, then, in relation to that tenancy—

(a) Case 5, paragraph (b) of Case 10, and paragraph 2(a) of Part III, of Schedule 3 to the Rent Act 1968 shall have effect as if for the references in those provisions to 8th December 1965 there were substituted references to the date of the passing of this Act,

(b) Case 8 of the said Schedule 3 shall have effect as if for the reference to 23rd March 1965 there were substituted a reference to 8th March 1973, and

(c) the said paragraph 2(a) of Part III of Schedule 3 shall have effect as if for 7th June 1966 there were substituted a reference to the expiration of a period of six months beginning with the passing of this Act.

Reserve and Auxiliary Forces (Protection of Civil Interests Act) 1951

10. In section 16(2)(a) of the Reserve and Auxiliary Forces (Protection of Civil Interests) Act 1951 (protection of premises by extension of the Rent Acts) the words " on the appropriate

day " shall cease to have effect, and for the words " in subsection SCH. 5 (1)(*a*) of section 1 " there shall be substituted the words " in paragraphs (*a*), (*aa*) or (*aaa*) of subsection (1) of section 1 ".

Tenancies at a low rent

11.—(1) At the end of section 2(1) of the Rent Act 1968 there 1968 c. 23. shall be inserted the following proviso :—

" Provided that paragraph (*a*) of this subsection shall apply in relation to a dwelling-house—

(i) in relation to which the appropriate day fell before the passing of the Counter-Inflation Act 1973, and

(ii) which had on the said appropriate day a rateable value exceeding, if it is in Greater London, £400 or, if it is elsewhere, £200,

as if for the reference in the said paragraph (*a*) to the appropriate day there were substituted a reference to the date of passing of the Counter-Inflation Act 1973.".

(2) In section 2(5) of the Landlord and Tenant Act 1954 (as 1954 c. 56. originally enacted) for paragraphs (*a*) and (*b*) there shall be substituted the words "for the purposes of this subsection the rateable value of the property is that which would be taken as its rateable value for the purposes of section 2(1)(*a*) of the Rent Act 1968."

Construction

12. In this Schedule—

(*a*) " rates " includes water rates and charges,

(*b*) other expressions shall be construed as in the Rent Act 1968.

SCHEDULE 6   Section 23.

REPEALS

Chapter	Short Title	Extent of Repeal
14 & 15 Geo. 6. c. 65.	The Reserve and Auxiliary Forces (Protection of Civil Interests) Act 1951.	In section 16(2)(*a*) the words " on the appropriate day ".
5 & 6 Eliz. 2. c. 20.	The House of Commons Disqualification Act 1957.	In Part II of Schedules 1 and 3, the entry relating to the National Board for Prices and Incomes.
1966 c. 33.	The Prices and Incomes Act 1966.	The whole Act, so far as unrepealed.
1967 c. 53.	The Prices and Incomes Act 1967.	The whole Act, except sections 4(2) and 5.
1967 c. 88.	The Leasehold Reform Act 1967.	Section 39(1)(*b*).

Chapter	Short Title	Extent of Repeal
1968 c. 23.	The Rent Act 1968.	In Schedule 15, in the paragraph amending section 2 of the Landlord and Tenant Act 1954 the words (amending section 2(5)) from " and in " to the end of the paragraph.
1968 c. 42.	The Prices and Incomes Act 1968.	The whole Act, except section 12.
1968 c. 73.	The Transport Act 1968.	Section 30(9).
1972 c. 47.	The Housing Finance Act 1972.	In section 89, in sub-section (1) the words " (6) and ", in subsection (2) the words " (6) and " and " 1 and ", and subsection (6).

Statutory Instrument

Chapter	Short Title	Extent of Repeal
S.I.1972/1851	The Counter-Inflation (Rents) (England and Wales) Order 1972.	In article 9(5) the words from " and this paragraph " to the end of article 9(5). Article 10, except as respects rent for a period before the passing of this Act.

Consolidated Fund (No. 2) Act 1973

1973 CHAPTER 10

Apply certain sums out of the Consolidated Fund to the service of the years ending on 31st March 1972, 1973 and 1974.   [29th March 1973]

Most Gracious Sovereign,

WE, Your Majesty's most dutiful and loyal subjects, the Commons of the United Kingdom in Parliament assembled, towards making good the supply which we have cheerfully granted to Your Majesty in this Session of Parliament, have resolved to grant unto Your Majesty the sums hereinafter mentioned; and do therefore most humbly beseech Your Majesty that it may be enacted, and be it enacted by the Queen's most Excellent Majesty, by and with the advice and consent of the Lords Spiritual and Temporal, and Commons, in this present Parliament assembled, and by the authority of the same, as follows:—

1. The Treasury may issue out of the Consolidated Fund of the United Kingdom and apply towards making good the supply granted to Her Majesty for the service of the years ending on 31st March 1972 and 1973, the sum of £303,435,096·23. *Issue out of the Consolidated Fund for the years ending 31st March 1972 and 1973.*

2. The Treasury may issue out of the Consolidated Fund of the United Kingdom and apply towards making good the supply granted to Her Majesty for the service of the year ending on 31st March 1974, the sum of £1,150,000,000. *Issue out of the Consolidated Fund for the year ending 31st March 1974.*

3. This Act may be cited as the Consolidated Fund (No. 2) Act 1973. *Short title.*

Fire Precautions (Loans) Act 1973

1973 CHAPTER 11

An Act to provide for the making of loans by local authorities to meet certain expenditure occasioned by the Fire Precautions Act 1971.　　[29th March 1973]

B E IT ENACTED by the Queen's most Excellent Majesty, by and with the advice and consent of the Lords Spiritual and Temporal, and Commons, in this present Parliament assembled, and by the authority of the same, as follows:—

Loans to meet certain expenditure occasioned by Fire Precautions Act 1971.
1971 c. 40.

1.—(1) Where—

　(a) a fire certificate required by virtue of section 1 of the Fire Precautions Act 1971 has been applied for or issued in respect of premises of a description specified in an order made by the Secretary of State under this section, and

　(b) a notice has been served under section 5(4) or 12(8)(b) of that Act in connection with the premises,

any person proposing to incur or liable to meet expenditure in making to any part of the relevant building any structural or other alterations the making of which is requisite as being a step mentioned in the notice may apply to the local authority in whose area the premises are situated for a loan under the following provisions of this section.

(2) If the local authority consider that the applicant—

　(a) can reasonably be expected to meet obligations assumed by him in pursuance of this section in respect of a loan of the amount of the expenditure to which the application relates, or

(b) cannot reasonably be expected to meet obligations so assumed by him in respect of a loan of that amount, but can reasonably be expected to meet obligations so assumed by him in respect of a loan of a smaller amount,

the local authority may, if they think fit, offer to make to the applicant a loan of the appropriate amount on such terms (including terms as to the provision of security or guarantees) as may be specified in the offer.

In this subsection " the appropriate amount ", in a case falling within paragraph (a) above, means the amount of the expenditure to which the application relates, and in a case falling within paragraph (b) above means the smaller amount there referred to.

(3) Subject to subsection (4) below, a loan under this section shall bear interest either—

(a) at the rate which, on the date of acceptance of the offer to make the loan, is the rate for the time being determined by the Treasury in accordance with section 5 of the National Loans Act 1968 in respect of local loans 1968 c. 13. made on the security of local rates on that date and for the same period as that loan, or

(b) if the local authority so determine, at a rate higher by one quarter per cent. than that rate.

In this subsection " local loans " and " made on the security of local rates " have the same meanings as in section 6(2) of the National Loans Act 1968.

(4) Where, on the date of acceptance of an offer to make a loan under this section, there are two or more rates of interest for the time being determined by the Treasury as mentioned in subsection (3) above, the reference in that subsection to the rate so determined shall be read as a reference to such one of those rates as may be specified in a direction given by the Treasury for the purposes of this section ; and the Treasury shall cause any such direction to be published in the London and Edinburgh Gazettes as soon as may be after giving it.

(5) An order under this section—

(a) may describe premises by reference to their rateable value, the purpose for which they are used, the number of persons who may be accommodated in them, or the size or type of the building constituting or comprising the premises, or by reference to any other circumstances whatsoever;

(b) may include such supplementary and incidental provisions as appear to the Secretary of State to be necessary or expedient for the purposes of the order;

(*c*) may be varied or revoked by a subsequent order.

(6) The power to make orders under this section shall be exercisable by statutory instrument, which shall be subject to annulment in pursuance of a resolution of either House of Parliament.

1960 c. 58.

(7) Section 29 of the Charities Act 1960 (which restricts dealings with charity property) shall not apply to the mortgage of an interest as security for a loan under this section.

1971 c. 40.

(8) In this section expressions used in the Fire Precautions Act 1971 have the same meanings as in that Act.

Short title and extent

2.—(1) This Act may be cited as the Fire Precautions (Loans) Act 1973.

(2) This Act does not extend to Northern Ireland.

Gaming (Amendment) Act 1973

1973 CHAPTER 12

An Act to extend section 40 of the Gaming Act 1968 to gaming at clubs other than members' clubs, and to amend the provisions of that section relating to the sums which may be charged for taking part in gaming.   [18th April 1973]

BE IT ENACTED by the Queen's most Excellent Majesty, by and with the advice and consent of the Lords Spiritual and Temporal, and Commons, in this present Parliament assembled, and by the authority of the same, as follows:—

1.—(1) Section 40 of the Gaming Act 1968 (which authorises the making of special charges for the right to take part in certain gaming) shall be amended in accordance with subsections (2) and (3) below.

Amendment of s. 40 of Gaming Act 1968.
1968 c. 65.

(2) In subsection (1)(*a*) (under which the gaming must be carried on as an activity of a members' club or a miners' welfare institute), the word " members " is hereby repealed; and (consequentially) in subsection (4), paragraph (*a*) and the word " members " preceding that paragraph are hereby repealed.

(3) In subsection (2) (under which the charge on any one day may not exceed 2½p. or such other sum as the Secretary of State may by order specify)—

    (*a*) after the words " the charge " there shall be inserted the words " or (if more than one) the aggregate amount of the charges ", and (*b*) the following paragraph shall be added at the end—

" The power of the Secretary of State under this subsection includes power to specify—

(*a*) in the case of gaming carried on as an activity of a members' club or a miners' welfare institute, a sum different from that applicable in the case of gaming carried on as an activity of any other club; and

(*b*) in the case of gaming which consists exclusively of playing bridge or whist, or bridge and whist, and takes place on a day on which the premises used therefor are not used for any other gaming, or for any other gaming except gaming by means of a machine to which Part III of this Act applies, a sum greater than that applicable in all other cases."

Short title.   **2.** This Act may be cited as the Gaming (Amendment) Act 1973.

Supply of Goods (Implied Terms) Act 1973

1973 CHAPTER 13

An Act to amend the law with respect to the terms to be implied in contracts of sale of goods and hire-purchase agreements and on the exchange of goods for trading stamps, and with respect to the terms of conditional sale agreements; and for connected purposes.

[18th April 1973]

BE IT ENACTED by the Queen's most Excellent Majesty, by and with the advice and consent of the Lords Spiritual and Temporal, and Commons, in this present Parliament assembled, and by the authority of the same, as follows:—

Sale of Goods

1. For section 12 of the principal Act (implied conditions as to title, and implied warranties as to quiet possession and freedom from encumbrances) there shall be substituted the following section:—

Implied undertakings as to title, etc.

" Implied undertakings as to title, etc.   12.—(1) In every contract of sale, other than one to which subsection (2) of this section applies, there is—

(a) an implied condition on the part of the seller that in the case of a sale, he has a right to sell the goods, and in the case of an agreement to sell, he will have a right to sell the goods at the time when the property is to pass ; and

(b) an implied warranty that the goods are free, and will remain free until the time when the property is to pass, from any charge or encumbrance not disclosed or known to the buyer before the contract is made and that the buyer will enjoy quiet possession of the goods except so far as it may be disturbed by the owner or other person entitled to the benefit of any charge or encumbrance so disclosed or known.

(2) In a contract of sale, in the case of which there appears from the contract or is to be inferred from the circumstances of the contract an intention that the seller should transfer only such title as he or a third person may have, there is—

(a) an implied warranty that all charges or encumbrances known to the seller and not known to the buyer have been disclosed to the buyer before the contract is made; and

(b) an implied warranty that neither—

(i) the seller; nor

(ii) in a case where the parties to the contract intend that the seller should transfer only such title as a third person may have, that person; nor

(iii) anyone claiming through or under the seller or that third person otherwise than under a charge or encumbrance disclosed or known to the buyer before the contract is made;

will disturb the buyer's quiet possession of the goods."

Sale by description.

2. Section 13 of the principal Act (sale by description) shall be renumbered as subsection (1) of that section, and at the end there shall be inserted the following subsection:—

" (2) A sale of goods shall not be prevented from being a sale by description by reason only that, being exposed for sale or hire, they are selected by the buyer."

Implied undertakings as to quality or fitness.

3. For section 14 of the principal Act (implied undertakings as to quality or fitness) there shall be substituted the following section:—

" Implied under-takings as to quality or fitness.

14.—(1) Except as provided by this section, and section 15 of this Act and subject to the provisions of any other enactment, there is no implied condition or warranty as to the quality or fitness for any particular purpose of goods supplied under a contract of sale.

(2) Where the seller sells goods in the course of a business, there is an implied condition that the goods supplied under the contract are of merchantable quality, except that there is no such condition—

 (*a*) as regards defects specifically drawn to the buyer's attention before the contract is made ; or

 (*b*) if the buyer examines the goods before the contract is made, as regards defects which that examination ought to reveal.

by examination

(3) Where the seller sells goods in the course of a business and the buyer, expressly or by implication, makes known to the seller any particular purpose for which the goods are being bought, there is an implied condition that the goods supplied under the contract are reasonably fit for that purpose, whether or not that is a purpose for which such goods are commonly supplied, except where the circumstances show that the buyer does not rely, or that it is unreasonable for him to rely, on the seller's skill or judgment.

(4) An implied condition or warranty as to quality or fitness for a particular purpose may be annexed to a contract of sale by usage.

(5) The foregoing provisions of this section apply to a sale by a person who in the course of a business is acting as agent for another as they apply to a sale by a principal in the course of a business, except where that other is not selling in the course of a business and either the buyer knows that fact or reasonable steps are taken to bring it to the notice of the buyer before the contract is made.

(6) In the application of subsection (3) above to an agreement for the sale of goods under which the purchase price or part of it is payable by instalments any reference to the seller shall include a reference to the person by whom any antecedent negotiations are conducted ; and section 58(3) and (5) of the Hire-Purchase Act 1965, section 54(3) and (5) of the Hire-Purchase (Scotland) Act 1965 and section 65(3) and (5) of the Hire-Purchase Act (Northern Ireland) 1966 (meaning of antecedent negotiations and related expressions) shall apply in relation to this subsection as they apply in relation to each of those Acts, but as if a reference to any such agreement were included in the references in subsection (3) of each of those sections to the agreements there mentioned."

1965 c. 66.
1965 c. 67.
1966 c. 42, (N.I.).

Exclusion of
implied
terms and
conditions.

4. For section 55 of the principal Act (exclusion of implied terms and conditions) there shall be substituted the following section:—

"Exclusion
of implied
terms and
conditions.

55.—(1) Where any right, duty or liability would arise under a contract of sale of goods by implication of law, it may be negatived or varied by express agreement, or by the course of dealing between the parties, or by usage if the usage is such as to bind both parties to the contract, but the foregoing provision shall have effect subject to the following provisions of this section.

(2) An express condition or warranty does not negative a condition or warranty implied by this Act unless inconsistent therewith.

(3) In the case of a contract of sale of goods, any term of that or any other contract exempting from all or any of the provisions of section 12 of this Act shall be void.

(4) In the case of a contract of sale of goods, any term of that or any other contract exempting from all or any of the provisions of section 13, 14 or 15 of this Act shall be void in the case of a consumer sale and shall, in any other case, not be enforceable to the extent that it is shown that it would not be fair or reasonable to allow reliance on the term.

(5) In determining for the purposes of subsection (4) above whether or not reliance on any such term would be fair or reasonable regard shall be had to all the circumstances of the case and in particular to the following matters—

(a) the strength of the bargaining positions of the seller and buyer relative to each other, taking into account, among other things, the availability of suitable alternative products and sources of supply;

(b) whether the buyer received an inducement to agree to the term or in accepting it had an opportunity of buying the goods or suitable alternatives without it from any source of supply;

(c) whether the buyer knew or ought reasonably to have known of the existence and extent of the term (having regard, among other things, to any custom of the trade and any previous course of dealing between the parties);

(d) where the term exempts from all or any of the provisions of section 13, 14 or 15 of this Act if some condition is not complied with, whether it was reasonable at the time of the contract to expect that compliance with that condition would be practicable ;

(e) whether the goods were manufactured, processed, or adapted to the special order of the buyer.

(6) Subsection (5) above shall not prevent the court from holding, in accordance with any rule of law, that a term which purports to exclude or restrict any of the provisions of section 13, 14 or 15 of this Act is not a term of the contract.

(7) In this section " consumer sale " means a sale of goods (other than a sale by auction or by competitive tender) by a seller in the course of a business where the goods—

(a) are of a type ordinarily bought for private use or consumption ; and

(b) are sold to a person who does not buy or hold himself out as buying them in the course of a business.

(8) The onus of proving that a sale falls to be treated for the purposes of this section as not being a consumer sale shall lie on the party so contending.

(9) Any reference in this section to a term exempting from all or any of the provisions of any section of this Act is a reference to a term which purports to exclude or restrict, or has the effect of excluding or restricting, the operation of all or any of the provisions of that section, or the exercise of a right conferred by any provision of that section, or any liability of the seller for breach of a condition or warranty implied by any provision of that section.

(10) It is hereby declared that any reference in this section to a term of a contract includes a reference to a term which although not contained in a contract is incorporated in the contract by another term of the contract.

(11) This section is subject to section 61(6) of this Act."

5.—(1) After section 55 of the principal Act there shall be inserted the following section :— Conflict of laws.

" Conflict of laws. 55A. Where the proper law of a contract for the sale of goods would, apart from a term that it should be the law of some other country or a term to the like effect, be the law of any part of the United Kingdom, or where any such contract contains a term which purports to substitute, or has the effect of substituting, provisions of the law of some other country for all or any of the provisions of sections 12 to 15 and 55 of this Act, those sections shall, notwithstanding that term but subject to section 61(6) of this Act, apply to the contract."

1967 c. 45.

(2) In section 1(4) of the Uniform Laws on International Sales Act 1967 (which provides that no provision of the law of any part of the United Kingdom shall be regarded as a mandatory provision for the purposes of the Uniform Law on the International Sale of Goods so as to override the choice of the parties) for the words from " no provision " to the end of the subsection there shall be substituted the words " no provision of the law of any part of the United Kingdom, except sections 12 to 15, 55 and 55A of the Sale of Goods Act 1893, shall be regarded as a mandatory provision within the meaning of that Article."

56 & 57 Vict.
c. 71.

International sales.

6. In section 61 of the principal Act (savings) there shall be inserted after subsection (5) thereof the following subsection—

" (6) Nothing in section 55 or 55A of this Act shall prevent the parties to a contract for the international sale of goods from negativing or varying any right, duty or liability which would otherwise arise by implication of law under sections 12 to 15 of this Act."

Interpretation.

7.—(1) In section 62(1) of the principal Act (definitions) at the appropriate points in alphabetical order there shall be inserted the following definitions:

" business " includes a profession and the activities of any government department (including a department of the Government of Northern Ireland), local authority or statutory undertaker;

" contract for the international sale of goods " means a contract of sale of goods made by parties whose places of business (or, if they have none, habitual residences) are in the territories of different States (the Channel Islands and the Isle of Man being treated for this purpose as different States from the United Kingdom) and in the case of which one of the following conditions is satisfied, that is to say—

(a) the contract involves the sale of goods which are at the time of the conclusion of the contract in the course of carriage or will be carried from the territory of one State to the territory of another ; or

    (*b*) the acts constituting the offer and acceptance have been effected in the territories of different States ; or

    (*c*) delivery of the goods is to be made in the territory of a State other than that within whose territory the acts constituting the offer and the acceptance have been effected."

(2) After section 62(1) of the principal Act there shall be inserted the following subsection : —

" (1A) Goods of any kind are of merchantable quality within the meaning of this Act if they are as fit for the purpose or purposes for which goods of that kind are commonly bought as it is reasonable to expect having regard to any description applied to them, the price (if relevant) and all the other relevant circumstances ; and any reference in this Act to unmerchantable goods shall be construed accordingly."

Hire-purchase agreements

8.—(1) In every hire-purchase agreement, other than one to which subsection (2) below applies, there is—

    (*a*) an implied condition on the part of the owner that he will have a right to sell the goods at the time when the property is to pass ; and

    (*b*) an implied warranty that the goods are free, and will remain free until the time when the property is to pass, from any charge or encumbrance not disclosed or known to the hirer before the agreement is made and that the hirer will enjoy quiet possession of the goods except so far as it may be disturbed by any person entitled to the benefit of any charge or encumbrance so disclosed or known.

Implied terms as to title.

(2) In a hire-purchase agreement, in the case of which there appears from the agreement or is to be inferred from the circumstances of the agreement an intention that the owner should transfer only such title as he or a third person may have, there is—

    (*a*) an implied warranty that all charges or encumbrances known to the owner and not known to the hirer have been disclosed to the hirer before the agreement is made ; and

    (*b*) an implied warranty that neither—

        (i) the owner ; nor

(ii) in a case where the parties to the agreement intend that any title which may be transferred shall be only such title as a third person may have, that person ; nor

(iii) anyone claiming through or under the owner or that third person otherwise than under a charge or encumbrance disclosed or known to the hirer before the agreement is made ;

will disturb the hirer's quiet possession of the goods.

Letting by description.
9.—(1) Where under a hire purchase agreement goods are let by description, there is an implied condition that the goods will correspond with the description ; and if under the agreement the goods are let by reference to a sample as well as a description, it is not sufficient that the bulk of the goods corresponds with the sample if the goods do not also correspond with the description.

(2) Goods shall not be prevented from being let by description by reason only that, being exposed for sale or hire, they are selected by the hirer.

Implied undertakings as to quality or fitness.
10.—(1) Except as provided by this section and section 11 below and subject to the provisions of any other enactment, including any enactment of the Parliament of Northern Ireland, there is no implied condition or warranty as to the quality or fitness for any particular purpose of goods let under a hire-purchase agreement.

(2) Where the owner lets goods under a hire purchase agreement in the course of a business, there is an implied condition that the goods are of merchantable quality, except that there is no such condition—

(a) as regards defects specifically drawn to the hirer's attention before the agreement is made ; or

(b) if the hirer examines the goods before the agreement is made, as regards defects which that examination ought to reveal.

(3) Where the owner lets goods under a hire purchase agreement in the course of a business and the hirer, expressly or by implication, makes known to the owner or the person by whom any antecedent negotiations are conducted, any particular purpose for which the goods are being hired, there is an implied condition that the goods supplied under the agreement are reasonably fit for that purpose, whether or not that is a purpose for which such goods are commonly supplied, except where the

circumstances show that the hirer does not rely, or that it is unreasonable for him to rely, on the skill or judgment of the owner or that person.

(4) An implied condition or warranty as to quality or fitness for a particular purpose may be annexed to a hire-purchase agreement by usage.

(5) The foregoing provisions of this section apply to a hire-purchase agreement made by a person who in the course of a business is acting as agent for the owner as they apply to an agreement made by the owner in the course of a business, except where the owner is not letting in the course of a business and either the hirer knows that fact or reasonable steps are taken to bring it to the notice of the hirer before the agreement is made.

(6) Section 58(3) and (5) of the Hire-Purchase Act 1965, section 54(3) and (5) of the Hire-Purchase (Scotland) Act 1965 and section 65(3) and (5) of the Hire-Purchase Act (Northern Ireland) 1966 (meaning of antecedent negotiations and related expressions) shall apply in relation to subsection (3) above as they apply in relation to each of those Acts. *1965 c. 66.* *1965 c. 67.* *1966 c. 42 (N.I.).*

11. Where under a hire-purchase agreement goods are let by reference to a sample, there is an implied condition— Samples.

    (*a*) that the bulk will correspond with the sample in quality ; and

    (*b*) that the hirer will have a reasonable opportunity of comparing the bulk with the sample ; and

    (*c*) that the goods will be free from any defect, rendering them unmerchantable, which would not be apparent on reasonable examination of the sample.

12.—(1) An express condition or warranty does not negative a condition or warranty implied by this Act unless inconsistent therewith. Exclusion of implied terms and conditions.

(2) A term of a hire purchase agreement or any other agreement exempting from all or any of the provisions of section 8 above shall be void.

(3) A term of a hire purchase agreement or any other agreement exempting from all or any of the provisions of section 9, 10 or 11 above shall be void in the case of a consumer agreement and shall, in any other case, not be enforceable to the extent that it is shown that it would not be fair or reasonable to allow reliance on the term.

(4) In determining for the purpose of subsection (3) above whether or not reliance on any such term would be fair or

reasonable regard shall be had to all the circumstances of the case and in particular to the following matters—

  (*a*) the strength of the bargaining positions of the owner and hirer relative to each other, taking into account, among other things, the availability of suitable alternative products and sources of supply ;

  (*b*) whether the hirer received an inducement to agree to the term or in accepting it had an opportunity of acquiring the goods or suitable alternatives without it from any source of supply ;

  (*c*) whether the hirer knew or ought reasonably to have known of the existence and extent of the term (having regard, among other things, to any custom of the trade and any previous course of dealing between the parties) ;

  (*d*) where the term exempts from all or any of the provisions of section 9, 10 or 11 above if some condition is not complied with, whether it was reasonable at the time of the agreement to expect that compliance with that condition would be practicable ;

  (*e*) whether the goods were manufactured, processed or adapted to the special order of the hirer.

(5) Subsection (4) above shall not prevent the court from holding, in accordance with any rule of law, that a term which purports to exclude or restrict any of the provisions of section 9, 10 or 11 above is not a term of the hire-purchase agreement.

(6) In this section " consumer agreement " means a hire-purchase agreement where the owner makes the agreement in the course of a business and the goods to which the agreement relates—

  (*a*) are of a type ordinarily supplied for private use or consumption ; and

  (*b*) are hired to a person who does not hire or hold himself out as hiring them in the course of a business.

(7) The onus of proving that a hire-purchase agreement falls to be treated for the purposes of this section as not being a consumer agreement shall lie on the party so contending.

(8) Any reference in this section to a term exempting from all or any of the provisions of any section of this Act is a reference to a term which purports to exclude or restrict, or has the effect of excluding or restricting, the operation of all or any of the provisions of that section, or the exercise of a right conferred by any provision of that section, or any liability of the owner for breach of a condition or warranty implied by any provision of that section.

(9) It is hereby declared that any reference in this section to a term of an agreement includes a reference to a term which although not contained in an agreement is incorporated in the agreement by another term of the agreement.

13. Where the proper law of a hire purchase agreement would, apart from a term that it should be the law of some other country or a term to the like effect, be the law of any part of the United Kingdom, or where any such agreement contains a term which purports to substitute, or has the effect of substituting, provisions of the law of some other country for all or any of the provisions of sections 8 to 12 above, those sections shall, notwithstanding that term, apply to the agreement.

Conflict of laws.

14.—(1) Section 11(1)(c) of the principal Act (whereby in certain circumstances a breach of a condition in a contract of sale is treated only as a breach of warranty) shall not apply to conditional sale agreements which are agreements for consumer sales.

Special provisions as to conditional sale agreements.

(2) In England and Wales and Northern Ireland a breach of a condition (whether express or implied) to be fulfilled by the seller under any such agreement shall be treated as a breach of warranty, and not as grounds for rejecting the goods and treating the agreement as repudiated, if (but only if) it would have fallen to be so treated had the condition been contained or implied in a corresponding hire-purchase agreement as a condition to be fulfilled by the owner.

15.—(1) In sections 8 to 14 above and this section—
"conditional sale agreement", "hire-purchase agreement", "hirer" and "owner" have the same meanings respectively as in the Hire-Purchase Act 1965 or, as the case may be, the Hire-Purchase (Scotland) Act 1965;
"business" includes a profession and the activities of any government department (including a department of the Government of Northern Ireland), local authority or statutory undertaker;
"consumer sale" has the same meaning as in section 55 of the principal Act, as amended by section 4 above; and
"condition" and "warranty", in relation to Scotland, mean stipulation, and any stipulation referred to in sections 8(1)(a) 9, 10 and 11 above shall be deemed to be material to the agreement.

Supplementary.

1965 c. 66.
1965 c. 67.

(2) In the application of subsection (1) above to Northern Ireland—
(a) "hirer" has the same meaning as in section 65(1) of the Hire Purchase Act (Northern Ireland) 1966; and

1966 c. 42 (N.I.).

(*b*) subject to paragraph (*a*) above, for the reference to the Hire-Purchase Act 1965 there shall be substituted a reference to the Hire-Purchase Act (Northern Ireland) 1966.

(3) Goods of any kind are of merchantable quality within the meaning of section 10(2) above if they are as fit for the purpose or purposes for which goods of that kind are commonly bought as it is reasonable to expect having regard to any description applied to them, the price (if relevant) and all the other relevant circumstances; and in section 11 above " unmerchantable " shall be construed accordingly.

(4) In section 14(2) above " corresponding hire-purchase agreement " means, in relation to a conditional sale agreement, a hire-purchase agreement relating to the same goods as the conditional sale agreement and made between the same parties and at the same time and in the same circumstances and, as nearly as may be, in the same terms as the conditional sale agreement.

(5) Nothing in sections 8 to 13 above shall prejudice the operation of any other enactment including any enactment of the Parliament of Northern Ireland or any rule of law whereby any condition or warranty, other than one relating to quality or fitness, is to be implied in any hire-purchase agreement.

Trading Stamps

Terms to be implied on redemption of trading stamps for goods.
1964 c. 71.

16.—(1) For section 4 of the Trading Stamps Act 1964 (warranties to be implied on redemption of trading stamps for goods) there shall be substituted the following section:—

" Warranties to be implied on redemption of trading stamps for goods.

4.—(1) In every redemption of trading stamps for goods, notwithstanding any terms to the contrary on which the redemption is made, there is—

(*a*) an implied warranty on the part of the promoter of the trading stamp scheme that he has a right to give the goods in exchange;

(*b*) an implied warranty that the goods are free from any charge or encumbrance not disclosed or known to the person obtaining the goods before, or at the time of, redemption and that that person will enjoy quiet possession of the goods except so far as it may be disturbed by the owner or other person entitled to the benefit of any charge or encumbrance so disclosed or known;

(c) an implied warranty that the goods are of merchantable quality, except that there is no such warranty—

(i) as regards defects specifically drawn to the attention of the person obtaining the goods before or at the time of redemption; or

(ii) if that person examines the goods before or at the time of redemption, as regards defects which that examination ought to reveal.

(2) Goods of any kind are of merchantable quality within the meaning of this section if they are as fit for the purpose or purposes for which goods of that kind are commonly bought as it is reasonable to expect having regard to any description applied to them and all the other relevant circumstances.

(3) In the application of this section to Scotland for any reference to a warranty there shall be substituted a reference to a stipulation."

(2) The section so substituted, without subsection (3) thereof, shall be substituted for section 4 of the Trading Stamps Act 1965 c. 6 (Northern Ireland) 1965 (warranties to be implied on redemption (N.I.). of trading stamps for goods).

Miscellaneous

17.—(1) It is hereby declared that this Act extends to Northern Northern Ireland. Ireland.

(2) For the purposes of section 6 of the Government of Ireland 1920 c. 67. Act 1920 this Act shall, so far as it relates to matters within the powers of the Parliament of Northern Ireland, be deemed to be an Act passed before the appointed day within the meaning of that section.

18.—(1) This Act may be cited as the Supply of Goods Short title, (Implied Terms) Act 1973. citation, interpretation,

(2) In this Act " the principal Act " means the Sale of Goods commence- Act 1893. ment, repeal and saving.

(3) This Act shall come into operation at the expiration of a 56 & 57 Vict. period of one month beginning with the date on which it is c. 71. passed.

D

1965 c. 66.
1965 c. 67.
1966 c. 42
(N.I.).

(4) Sections 17 to 20 and 29(3)(c) of each of the following Acts, that is to say, the Hire-Purchase Act 1965, the Hire-Purchase (Scotland) Act 1965 and the Hire Purchase Act (Northern Ireland) 1966 (provisions as to conditions, warranties and stipulations in hire-purchase agreements) shall cease to have effect.

(5) This Act does not apply to contracts of sale or hire-purchase agreements made before its commencement.

Costs in Criminal Cases Act 1973

1973 CHAPTER 14

An Act to consolidate certain enactments relating to costs in criminal cases. [18th April 1973]

B E IT ENACTED by the Queen's most Excellent Majesty, by and with the advice and consent of the Lords Spiritual and Temporal, and Commons, in this present Parliament assembled, and by the authority of the same, as follows:—

Awards by magistrates' courts

1.—(1) A magistrates' court dealing summarily with an indictable offence, or inquiring into any offence as examining justices, may, subject to the provisions of this section, order the payment out of central funds of the costs of the prosecution.

(2) A magistrates' court dealing summarily with an indictable offence and dismissing the information, or inquiring into any offence as examining justices and determining not to commit the accused for trial, may, subject to the provisions of this section, order the payment out of central funds of the costs of the defence.

(3) The costs payable out of central funds under the preceding provisions of this section shall be such sums as appear to the court reasonably sufficient to compensate the prosecutor, or as the case may be the accused, for the expenses properly incurred by him in carrying on the prosecution or the defence, and to compensate any witness for the prosecution, or as the case may be for the defence, for the expense, trouble or loss of time properly incurred in or incidental to his attendance.

(4) Notwithstanding that the court makes no order under subsection (2) above for the payment out of central funds of the costs of the defence, it may order the payment out of those funds of such sums as appear to the court reasonably sufficient to compensate any witness for the defence for the expense, trouble or loss of time properly incurred in or incidental to his attendance.

Awards by magistrates' courts out of central funds.

D 2

(5) References in subsections (3) and (4) above to a witness include any person who is a witness to character only and in respect of whom the court certifies that the interests of justice required his attendance, but no sums shall be payable in pursuance of an order made under this section to or in respect of any witness who is a witness to character only and in respect of whom no such certificate is given.

(6) The amount of costs ordered to be paid under this section shall be ascertained as soon as practicable by the proper officer of the court.

(7) In this section the expression " witness " means a person properly attending to give evidence, whether or not he gives evidence ; and a person who, at the instance of the court, is called or properly attends to give evidence may be made the subject of an order under subsection (4) above whether or not he is a witness for the defence.

Awards by magistrates' courts as between parties.

2.—(1) On the summary trial of an information a magistrates' court shall, on dismissal of the information, have power to make such order as to costs to be paid by the prosecutor to the accused as it thinks just and reasonable.

(2) On the summary trial of an information a magistrates' court shall, on conviction, have power to make such order as to costs to be paid by the accused to the prosecutor as it thinks just and reasonable, but—

(a) where under the conviction the court orders payment of any sum as a fine, penalty, forfeiture or compensation, and the sum so ordered to be paid does not exceed 25p, the court shall not order the accused to pay any costs under this subsection unless in any particular case it thinks fit to do so ;

(b) where the accused is under seventeen years old, the amount of the costs ordered to be paid by the accused himself under this subsection shall not exceed the amount of any fine ordered to be so paid.

(3) A court shall specify in the order of dismissal, or as the case may be the conviction, the amount of any costs that it orders to be paid under subsection (1) or (2) above.

(4) Where examining justices determine not to commit the accused for trial on the ground that the evidence is not sufficient to put him upon his trial, and are of opinion that the charge was not made in good faith, they may order the prosecutor to pay the whole or any part of the costs incurred in or about the defence.

(5) If the amount ordered to be paid under subsection (4) above exceeds £25, the prosecutor may appeal to the Crown Court ; and no proceedings shall be taken upon the order until the time allowed for giving notice of appeal has elapsed, or, if within that time notice of appeal is given, until the appeal is determined or ceases to be prosecuted.

Awards by Crown Court

3.—(1) Subject to the provisions of this section, where a person is prosecuted or tried on indictment before the Crown Court, the court may— Awards by Crown Court out of central funds.

    (*a*) order the payment out of central funds of the costs of the prosecution ;

    (*b*) if the accused is acquitted, order the payment out of central funds of the costs of the defence.

(2) Subject to the provisions of this section, where an appeal is brought to the Crown Court against a conviction by a magistrates' court of an indictable offence, or against the sentence imposed on such a conviction, the court may—

    (*a*) order the payment out of central funds of the costs of the prosecution ;

    (*b*) if the appeal is against a conviction, and the conviction is set aside in consequence of the decision on the appeal, order the payment out of central funds of the costs of the defence.

(3) The costs payable out of central funds under the preceding provisions of this section shall be such sums as appear to the Crown Court reasonably sufficient—

    (*a*) to compensate the prosecutor, or as the case may be the accused, for the expenses properly incurred by him in carrying on the proceedings, and

    (*b*) to compensate any witness for the prosecution, or as the case may be for the defence, for the expense, trouble or loss of time properly incurred in or incidental to his attendance.

(4) Notwithstanding that the court makes no order under this section as respects the costs of the defence, it may order the payment out of central funds of such sums as appear to the court reasonably sufficient to compensate any witness for the defence for the expense, trouble or loss of time properly incurred in or incidental to his attendance.

(5) References in subsections (3) and (4) above to a witness include any person who is a witness to character only and in respect of whom the court certifies that the interests of justice required his attendance, but no sums shall be payable in

pursuance of an order made under this section to or in respect of any witness who is a witness to character only and in respect of whom no such certificate is given.

(6) The amount of costs ordered to be paid under this section shall be ascertained as soon as practicable by the appropriate officer of the Crown Court.

1959 c. 72.

(7) In subsection (2) above, " sentence " includes any order made by a court when dealing with an offender, including a hospital order under Part V of the Mental Health Act 1959 and a recommendation for deportation.

(8) In this section the expression " witness " means a person properly attending to give evidence, whether or not he gives evidence ; and a person who, at the instance of the court, is called or properly attends to give evidence may be made the subject of an order under subsection (4) above whether or not he is a witness for the defence.

(9) The costs of carrying on the defence that may be awarded to any person under this section may include the costs of carrying on the defence before the examining justices who committed him for trial, or as the case may be before the magistrates' court who convicted him.

Awards by Crown Court as between parties.

4.—(1) Where a person is prosecuted or tried on indictment before the Crown Court, the court may—

     (*a*) if the accused is convicted, order him to pay the whole or any part of the costs incurred in or about the prosecution and conviction, including any proceedings before the examining justices ;

     (*b*) if the accused is acquitted, order the prosecutor to pay the whole or any part of the costs incurred in or about the defence including any proceedings before the examining justices.

(2) The amount of costs ordered to be paid under this section shall (except where it is a specific amount ordered to be so paid) be ascertained as soon as practicable by the appropriate officer of the Crown Court.

Awards by Divisional Court.

Awards by, and on appeals from, Divisional Court

5.—(1) A Divisional Court of the Queen's Bench Division may order the payment out of central funds of the costs of any party to proceedings before the Divisional Court in a criminal cause or matter.

(2) The costs payable out of central funds under subsection (1) above shall be such sums as appear to the Divisional Court reasonably sufficient to compensate the party concerned for any expenses properly incurred by him in the proceedings or in any court below.

(3) The amount of costs ordered to be paid under this section shall be ascertained by the master of the Crown Office.

6.—(1) The House of Lords on determining an appeal from a decision of a Divisional Court of the Queen's Bench Division in a criminal cause or matter may order the payment out of central funds of the costs of the accused or the prosecutor.

Awards on appeals from Divisional Court.

(2) The costs payable out of central funds under subsection (1) above shall be such sums as appear to the House of Lords reasonably sufficient to compensate the party concerned for any expenses properly incurred by him in the appeal to the House (including any application for leave to appeal) or in any court below.

(3) The amount of costs ordered to be paid under this section shall (except where it is a specific amount ordered to be paid towards a person's expenses as a whole) be ascertained by such officer or officers, and in such manner, as may be prescribed by order of the House of Lords.

Awards by, and on appeals from, Court of Appeal

7.—(1) When the Court of Appeal allow an appeal under Part I of the Criminal Appeal Act 1968 against—

   (*a*) conviction, or

   (*b*) a verdict of not guilty by reason of insanity, or

   (*c*) a finding under section 4 of the Criminal Procedure (Insanity) Act 1964 that the appellant is under disability,

the court may order the payment out of central funds of the costs of the appellant.

Awards by Court of Appeal out of central funds on determining appeals or applications.

1968 c. 19.

1964 c. 84.

(2) On determining an appeal or application for leave to appeal under Part I of the Criminal Appeal Act 1968, the Court of Appeal may order the payment out of central funds of the costs of the prosecutor.

(3) The costs payable out of central funds under subsection (1) or (2) above shall be such sums as appear to the Court of Appeal reasonably sufficient to compensate the party concerned for any expenses properly incurred by him in the appeal or application (including any proceedings preliminary or incidental thereto) or in any court below.

(4) The amount of costs ordered to be paid under this section shall (except where it is a specific amount ordered to be paid towards a person's expenses as a whole) be ascertained as soon as practicable by the registrar of criminal appeals.

Other awards
by Court of
Appeal out of
central funds.
1968 c. 19.

8.—(1) The Court of Appeal may order the payment out of central funds of such sums as appear to the court reasonably sufficient to compensate a person properly attending to give evidence on an appeal under Part I of the Criminal Appeal Act 1968, or any proceedings preliminary or incidental thereto, whether or not he gives evidence, for the expense, trouble or loss of time properly incurred in or incidental to his attendance.

(2) Where an appellant who is not in custody appears before the Court of Appeal, either on the hearing of his appeal under Part I of the Criminal Appeal Act 1968 or in any proceedings preliminary or incidental thereto, the court may direct that there be paid to him out of central funds the expenses of his appearance.

(3) Any amount ordered to be paid under this section shall be ascertained as soon as practicable by the registrar of criminal appeals.

Awards by
Court of
Appeal
against
accused.

9.—(1) When the Court of Appeal dismiss an appeal or application for leave to appeal under Part I of the Criminal Appeal Act 1968, the court may order the appellant to pay to such person as may be named in the order the whole or any part of the costs of the appeal or application.

(2) Costs ordered to be paid under this section may include the cost of any transcript of a record of proceedings made in accordance with rules of court made for the purposes of section 32 of the Criminal Appeal Act 1968.

(3) The amount of costs ordered to be paid under this section shall (except where it is a specific amount ordered to be paid towards the costs of an appeal or application as a whole) be ascertained as soon as practicable by the registrar of criminal appeals.

Awards out of
central funds
on appeals
from Court
of Appeal.

10.—(1) The Court of Appeal on dismissing an application for leave to appeal to the House of Lords under Part II of the Criminal Appeal Act 1968, and that House on determining an appeal or application for leave to appeal under the said Part II, may order the payment out of central funds of the costs of the accused or the prosecutor.

(2) The costs payable out of central funds under subsection (1) above shall be such sums as appear to the Court of Appeal or the House of Lords (as the case may be) reasonably sufficient to compensate the party concerned for any expenses properly incurred by him in the case being—

    (*a*) where the order is made (whether by the Court of Appeal or by the House of Lords) on the dismissal of an application for leave to appeal, any expenses of the application, and (*b*) where the order is made by the House of Lords on the determination of an appeal, any expenses of the appeal (including any application for leave to appeal) or incurred in any court below.

(3) The amount of costs ordered to be paid under this section shall (except where it is a specific amount ordered to be paid towards a person's expenses as a whole) be ascertained as soon as practicable—

(*a*) where the order is made by the Court of Appeal, by the registrar of criminal appeals ; and

(*b*) where it is made by the House of Lords, by such officer or officers, and in such manner, as may be prescribed by order of the House.

11.—(1) Where the Court of Appeal or the House of Lords dismiss an application by the accused for leave to appeal to that House under Part II of the Criminal Appeal Act 1968, the Court of Appeal or the House of Lords may, if they think fit, order him to pay to such person as may be named in the·order the whole or any part of the costs of the application.

Awards against accused applying for leave to appeal from Court of Appeal.
1968 c. 19.

(2) The amount of costs ordered to be paid under this section shall (except where it is a specific amount ordered to be paid towards the costs of the application as a whole) be ascertained as soon as practicable—

(*a*) where the order is made by the Court of Appeal, by the registrar of criminal appeals ;

(*b*) where the order is made by the House of Lords, by such officer or officers, and in such manner, as may be prescribed by order of the House.

Miscellaneous and general

12.—(1) Where an information charging an indictable offence is laid before a justice of the peace for any area but the information is not proceeded with (either by summary trial or by an inquiry by examining justices) a magistrates' court for that area may order the payment out of central funds of—

Awards where prosecution not proceeded with.

(*a*) the costs properly incurred in preparing a defence to the offence charged, and

(*b*) such sums as appear to the court reasonably sufficient to compensate any person attending to give evidence as a witness for the defence for the expense, trouble or loss of time properly incurred in or incidental to his attendance.

(2) The amount of costs ordered to be paid under subsection (1) above shall be ascertained as soon as practicable by the proper officer of the court.

(3) Where an information is laid before a justice of the peace for any area but the information is not proceeded with (either by summary trial or by an inquiry by examining magistrates), a magistrates' court for that area may make such order as to costs to be paid by the prosecutor to the accused as it thinks just and reasonable.

(4) An order under subsection (3) above shall specify the amount of the costs ordered to be paid.

(5) Where a person committed for trial is not ultimately tried, the Crown Court shall have the same power to order payment of costs under this Act as if the accused had been tried and acquitted.

Central funds.

13.—(1) In this Act and in any other enactment providing for payment of costs out of central funds " central funds " means money provided by Parliament.

(2) The Secretary of State shall, out of money so provided, pay to the persons charged with the duty of making the payments concerned all sums required to meet payments ordered to be made out of central funds under this Act or any other such enactment as is referred to in subsection (1) above.

Payment of costs ordered by superior courts to be paid out of central funds.

14.—(1) As soon as there has been ascertained the amount due to any person as costs ordered (under this or any other Act) by the Crown Court to be paid out of central funds, the appropriate officer of the Crown Court shall pay the amount so ascertained to that person, or to any person appearing to him to be acting on behalf of that person.

(2) As soon as there has been ascertained the amount due to any person as costs ordered (under this or any other Act) to be paid out of central funds by a Divisional Court, by the Court of Appeal or by the House of Lords,—

     (a) the master of the Crown Office, in the case of a Divisional Court, and

     (b) the registrar of criminal appeals, in the case of the Court of Appeal or the House of Lords,

shall pay the amount so ascertained to that person, or to any person appearing to him to be acting on behalf of that person.

Payment of costs ordered by magistrates' courts to be paid out of central funds.

15.—(1) As soon as there has been ascertained the amount due to any person as costs ordered to be paid out of central funds by a magistrates' court—

     (a) dealing summarily with an indictable offence, or

     (b) inquiring into an offence as examining justices and determining not to commit the accused for trial, or

     (c) where an information is not proceeded with, as mentioned in section 12(1) above, the justices' clerk shall pay to that person the amount so ascertained.

(2) As soon as there has been ascertained the amount due to any person as costs ordered to be paid out of central funds by a magistrates' court otherwise than as mentioned in sub-section (1) above, the justices' clerk shall—

(a) so far as the amount is due for travelling or personal expenses in respect of that person's attendance, pay to him the amount due forthwith, and

(b) so far as the amount is not due for such expenses, send a certificate of the amount to the Crown Court, in accordance with arrangements made by the Lord Chancellor.

(3) Where a certificate is sent to the Crown Court under sub-section (2) above the appropriate officer of the Crown Court shall pay to the person to whom the certificate relates, or to any person appearing to him to be acting on behalf of that person, the amount certified or any less amount which the Crown Court considers should have been allowed under this Act.

(4) The appropriate officer of the Crown Court shall, when practicable, include the amount payable as costs certified under this section in any order for payment of costs made by that court.

16.—(1) Where a court orders the payment of costs by the accused or the prosecutor and also orders the payment of costs out of central funds, the costs, so far as they are payable under both orders, shall be primarily payable out of central funds ; and the court shall give notice to the Secretary of State of the order for the payment of costs by the accused or the prosecutor. Payment of costs ordered to be paid out of central funds, and by accused or prosecutor.

(2) To the extent that any costs are primarily payable out of central funds by an order (under this or any other Act) and have been paid out of those funds, the Secretary of State shall be entitled to be reimbursed out of any money due under any other court order for the payment of those costs, and to take any proceedings for the enforcement of any such other order providing for payment of costs by the prosecutor.

17.—(1) The Secretary of State may by statutory instrument make regulations generally for carrying this Act into effect and in particular may by regulations so made prescribe— Regulations.

(a) rates or scales of payments of any costs payable out of central funds under this Act and the conditions under which such costs may be allowed ;

> (b) the manner in which an officer of the court making a payment to any person in respect of his attendance to give evidence is to be repaid out of central funds;
>
> (c) the form of orders, certificates and notices under this Act, and the giving of information when certificates are sent under this Act by the officer of any magistrates' court;

and any provision of this Act enabling any sum to be paid out of central funds shall have effect subject to the regulations.

(2) Regulations under this section may, as respects costs payable out of central funds under any enactment, or as respects other costs payable under this Act, provide a right of appeal from any decision on taxation, or ascertainment of the amount, of the costs, whether to a Taxing Master of the Supreme Court or to any other officer or authority.

Miscellaneous applications of Act.

1948 c. 58

18.—(1) This Act shall apply where a person is committed by a magistrates' court to the Crown Court—

> (a) with a view to his being sentenced to Borstal training under section 20 of the Criminal Justice Act 1948, or
>
> (b) with a view to his being sentenced for an indictable offence under section 29 of that Act, or
>
> (c) with a view to the making of a hospital order with an order restricting his discharge under Part V of the Mental Health Act 1959,

1959 c. 72.

as it applies where a person is convicted before the Crown Court.

1824 c. 83.

(2) This Act shall apply to a person committed by a magistrates' court as an incorrigible rogue under the Vagrancy Act 1824 as if he were committed for trial before the Crown Court and as if the committing court were examining justices.

(3) This Act shall apply to an appeal to the Crown Court under the Vagrancy Act 1824 as if the hearing of the appeal were a trial on indictment and as if the magistrates' court from which the appeal was brought were examining justices.

(4) This Act shall apply to—

> (a) proceedings for dealing with an offender under section 6, 8 or 9 of the Criminal Justice Act 1948 (probation orders and orders for conditional discharge),

1967 c. 80.

> (b) proceedings under section 40(1) of the Criminal Justice Act 1967 for dealing with an offender in respect of a suspended sentence, and

1972 c. 71.

> (c) proceedings under section 13, 17 or 18 of the Criminal Justice Act 1972 (suspended sentence supervision orders and community service orders),

as if the offender had been tried in those proceedings for the offence for which the order was made or the sentence passed.

(5) The provisions of this Act, except those relating to costs as between parties, shall apply with all necessary modifications to proceedings in which it is alleged that an offender required on conviction of an indictable offence to enter into a recognizance to keep the peace or be of good behaviour has failed to comply with a condition of that recognizance, as if that failure were an indictable offence.

19.—(1) Except as provided by sections 7 to 9 of this Act, no costs shall be allowed on the hearing or determination of an appeal to the Court of Appeal under Part I of the Criminal Appeal Act 1968 or of any proceedings preliminary or incidental to such an appeal.

General provisions as to costs 1968 c. 19.

(2) Except as provided by sections 10 and 11 of this Act, no costs shall be allowed on the hearing or determination of an appeal to the House of Lords under Part II of the Criminal Appeal Act 1968 or of any proceedings preliminary or incidental to such an appeal.

(3) Nothing in this Act shall affect the provision in any enactment for the payment of the costs of the prosecution or defence of any offence out of any assets, money or fund other than central funds, or by any person other than the prosecutor or defendant.

20.—(1) In this Act, except so far as the context otherwise requires, " magistrates' court " means a court of summary jurisdiction or examining justices and includes a single examining justice.

Interpretation.

(2) References in this Act to costs paid or ordered to be paid out of central funds under this Act shall be construed as including references to any sums so paid or ordered to be paid as compensation to or expenses of a witness or other person or as counsel's or solicitor's fees.

(3) In this Act " indictable offence " means an offence—

(a) which if committed by an adult is punishable only on conviction on indictment, or is punishable only on such conviction unless the accused consents to summary trial, or

(b) which by virtue of any enactment is punishable either on summary conviction or on conviction on indictment and which a magistrates' court has begun, in accordance with section 18(1) of the Magistrates' Courts Act 1952, to inquire into as if it were punishable on conviction on indictment only.

1952 c. 55.

(4) Subject to rules of court made under section 1(5) of the Criminal Appeal Act 1966 (distribution of business of Court of Appeal between civil and criminal divisions), all jurisdiction of the Court of Appeal under this Act shall be exercised by the criminal division of the Court ; and references in this Act to the Court of Appeal shall be construed accordingly as references to that division of the Court.

Consequential amendments, repeals and transitional provisions.

21.—(1) Schedule 1 to this Act (which makes consequential amendments of enactments not consolidated) shall have effect.

(2) The enactments specified in Schedule 2 to this Act are repealed to the extent specified in the third column of that Schedule.

(3) In so far as any order, regulation or certificate made or issued, or having effect as if made or issued, under an enactment repealed by this Act, or any other thing done or having effect as if done under such an enactment, could have been made, issued or done under a corresponding provision of this Act, it shall not be invalidated by the repeal but shall have effect as if made, issued or done under that corresponding provision.

(4) Where any Act or document refers, or has effect as if it referred, to an enactment repealed by this Act, the reference shall, except where the context otherwise requires, be construed as, or as including, a reference to the corresponding provision of this Act.

(5) Nothing in the preceding provisions of this section or in Schedule 1 to this Act shall be taken as prejudicing the operation of section 38 of the Interpretation Act 1889 (which relates to the effect of repeals).

Short title, commencement and extent

22.—(1) This Act may be cited as the Costs in Criminal Cases Act 1973.

(2) This Act shall come into force on the expiration of the period of three months beginning with the day on which it is passed.

(3) This Act shall not extend to Scotland or Northern Ireland.

SCHEDULES

SCHEDULE 1

Consequential Amendments

1. In section 26(5) of the Magistrates' Courts Act 1952 (medical 1952 c. 55.
reports), for the words " The Costs in Criminal Cases Act 1952 "
there shall be substituted the words " The Costs in Criminal Cases
Act 1973 " and for the words " section five " there shall be substituted
the words " section 1 ".

2. In section 74(*f*) of the Solicitors Act 1957 (savings), for the 1957 c. 27.
words " the Costs in Criminal Cases Act 1952 " there shall be substituted the words " the Costs in Criminal Cases Act 1973 ".

3. In paragraph 4 of the Schedule to the Backing of Warrants 1965 c. 45.
(Republic of Ireland) Act 1965 (powers as to costs and legal aid),
for the words from " section 5 " to " local funds) " there shall be
substituted the words " section 1 of the Costs in Criminal Cases Act
1973 (award of costs by examining justices out of central funds) ".

4. In section 32(2) of the Criminal Justice Act 1967 (medical reports), 1967 c. 80.
after the words " Courts-Martial Appeal Court) " there shall be
inserted the words " and sections 1, 3 and 8(1) of the Costs in Criminal
Cases Act 1973 (payment of costs out of central funds) "; and for the
words " section 5 " there shall be substituted the words " section 1 ".

5. In the Criminal Appeal Act 1968—

   (*a*) in section 31 (powers of Court of Appeal under Part I
       exercisable by single judge), in subsection (1), after the word
       " below " there shall be inserted the words " and the powers
       to make orders for the payment of costs under sections 7
       and 9 of the Costs in Criminal Cases Act 1973 " ;

   (*b*) in section 44 (powers of Court of Appeal under Part II
       exercisable by single judge), at the beginning, there shall
       be inserted the words " The power of the Court of Appeal
       to make an order for costs under section 10 of the Costs
       in Criminal Cases Act 1973, and " ; and

   (*c*) in paragraph 3 of Schedule 2 (acquittal on retrial), for the
       words from " paid out " to " shall " there shall be substituted
       the words " paid out of central funds under section 3 of the
       Costs in Criminal Cases Act 1973 shall " ; and for the words
       " section 24 or 39 of this Act " there shall be substituted
       the words " section 7 or 10 of the Costs in Criminal Cases
       Act 1973 ".

6. In Schedule 9 to the Administration of Justice Act 1970 (enforce- 1970 c. 31.
ment of orders for costs, compensation, etc.) paragraph 5 shall be
omitted and for paragraph 9 there shall be substituted the following
paragraph : —

   " 9. Where a court makes an order by virtue of section 18 of
       the Costs in Criminal Cases Act 1973 for the payment of
       costs by an offender."

7. In section 50 of the Courts Act 1971 (Crown Court rules relating to costs)—

(*a*) in subsection (3), for the words " the Costs in Criminal Cases Act 1952 " there shall be substituted the words " the Costs in Criminal Cases Act 1973 ", and for the words " section 48 above " there shall be substituted the words " section 4 of that Act (awards by Crown Court as between parties) "; and

(*b*) in subsection (4), for the words from " section 48 " to "Act " there shall be substituted the words " any enactment ", and after the word " Court " there shall be inserted the words " being an enactment passed before this Act or contained in the Costs in Criminal Cases Act 1973 ".

Section 21(2).

SCHEDULE 2

REPEALS

Chapter	Short Title	Extent of Repeal
15 & 16 Geo. 6 & 1 Eliz. 2. c. 48.	The Costs in Criminal Cases Act 1952.	The whole Act.
15 & 16 Geo. 6 & 1 Eliz. 2. c. 55.	The Magistrates' Courts Act 1952.	In Schedule 5, the entry relating to the Costs in Criminal Cases Act 1952.
7 & 8 Eliz. 2. c. 72.	The Mental Health Act 1959.	In Part I of Schedule 7, the entry relating to the Costs in Criminal Cases Act 1952.
1967 c. 80.	The Criminal Justice Act 1967.	Section 31(1) and (2). In section 32(2), the words preceding the words " section 33 ", and the words from " and section 47 " to " Crown Court out of central funds) ". Section 32(4).
1968 c. 19.	The Criminal Appeal Act 1968.	Sections 24 to 28. Section 31(2)(*g*). Sections 39 to 41. Section 44(*d*). In Schedule 5, the entries relating to sections 12 and 17(2) of the Costs in Criminal Cases Act 1952.
1970 c. 31.	The Administration of Justice Act 1970.	In Schedule 9, paragraph 5.
1971 c. 23.	The Courts Act 1971.	Sections 47 to 49. Section 51(1). In section 51(2), the words " the Costs in Criminal Cases Act 1952 and other ". Section 52(1) and (2). In section 52(3), paragraph (*a*) and the words from " by the prosecutor " to " may be ".

Chapter	Short Title	Extent of Repeal

1971 c. 23—
cont.
	The Courts Act 1971—
	cont.
		In section 52(5), the words from " Subsections (1) " to " 1952; and ".
		In Schedule 6—
		  paragraphs 1 to 5;
		  paragraph 8;
		  in paragraph 9(1), the words from " Section 5 " to " appeals out of central funds)," and the words from " and after " onwards;
		  paragraph 9(2);
		  paragraph 11.
		In Schedule 9, the entry relating to the Costs in Criminal Cases Act 1952.

1972 c. 71.	The Criminal Justice Act 1972.	Section 39. Schedule 3. In Schedule 5, the amendments of the Costs in Criminal Cases Act 1952, and the amendment of paragraph 9 of Schedule 9 to the Administration of Justice Act 1970.

Administration of Justice Act 1973

1973 CHAPTER 15

An Act to amend the law relating to justices of the peace and to make further provision with respect to the administration of justice and matters connected therewith. [18th April 1973]

BE IT ENACTED by the Queen's most Excellent Majesty, by and with the advice and consent of the Lords Spiritual and Temporal, and Commons, in this present Parliament assembled, and by the authority of the same, as follows:—

PART I

JUSTICES OF THE PEACE

1.—(1) Subject to the following subsections, there shall in England and Wales be a commission of the peace for the following areas (in this Act referred to as "commission areas") and no others, that is to say any county, any London commission area and the City of London; and the commission for any commission area shall be a commission under the Great Seal addressed generally, and not by name, to all such persons as may from time to time hold office as justices of the peace for the commission area.

Appointment of justices of the peace, and supplemental list.

(2) Justices of the peace for any commission area, other than stipendiary magistrates, shall be appointed on behalf and in the name of Her Majesty by instrument under the hand of the Lord Chancellor, and a justice so appointed may be removed from office in like manner; and in any commission area other than the City of London such one of the justices as may be designated by the Lord Chancellor shall be keeper of the rolls.

(3) There shall be transmitted to the keeper of the rolls for each commission area, and be enrolled in the records of the justices for that area, a copy of any instrument appointing or removing a justice of the peace in that area in accordance with this section ; and the keeper of the rolls shall be notified in such manner as the Lord Chancellor may direct of any resignation or death of a justice so appointed, and shall cause to be kept and from time to time rectified a record of those for the time being holding office by virtue of any such appointment.

(4) There shall be kept in the office of the Clerk of the Crown in Chancery—

    (*a*) a record of all persons for the time being holding office as justice of the peace by virtue of appointments made in accordance with this section, together with the instruments of appointment or removal ; and

    (*b*) a supplemental list for England and Wales as provided for by subsection (5) below.

(5) The supplemental list for England and Wales under this Act shall be in lieu of the supplemental lists provided for by section 4 of the Justices of the Peace Act 1949, but shall include the like names and be of the like effect as those lists, except that—

    (*a*) where a person ceases to be a justice for any commission area and is thereupon appointed a justice for another area the Lord Chancellor may direct that his name shall be entered in the supplemental list ; and

    (*b*) the entry of a person's name in the supplemental list shall not preclude him, if so authorised by the Lord Chancellor, from acting as a judge of the Crown Court so long as he has not attained the age of 72 years.

(6) Subsections (1) to (3) above shall be without prejudice to the position of the Lord Mayor and aldermen as justices for the City of London by virtue of the charters of the City, but so that any of them may be excluded by the Lord Chancellor from the exercise of his functions as a justice ; and in the application of subsection (3) to the City a reference to the Lord Mayor shall be substituted for any reference to the keeper of the rolls.

(7) In relation to the counties of Greater Manchester, Merseyside and Lancashire subsections (1) to (3) above shall have effect with the substitution for references to the Lord Chancellor of references to the Chancellor of the Duchy of Lancaster ; and in subsection (5) the references to the Lord Chancellor shall have effect as references to the Chancellor of the Duchy of Lancaster so far as relates to the entry in or removal from the supplemental list of the name of a person who is a justice of the peace only for any of those counties.

(8) For the purposes of this section the Isles of Scilly shall form part of the county of Cornwall.

(9) There shall cease to have effect—

(a) section 1 of the Metropolitan Police Act 1829 in so 1829 c. 44. far as it regulates the appointment or removal of the Commissioner of Police of the Metropolis ; and

(b) so much of section 2 of the Metropolitan Police Act 1856 c. 2. 1856 as provides for the Assistant Commissioners of Police of the Metropolis to be justices of the peace ;

and the Commissioner of Police shall be appointed in like manner as Assistant Commissioners are under the said section 2 to be appointed.

2.—(1) It shall be lawful for Her Majesty to appoint a barrister Stipendiary or solicitor of not less than seven years standing to be, during magistrates. Her Majesty's pleasure, a whole-time stipendiary magistrate in any commission area or areas outside the Inner London area and the City of London, and to appoint more than one such magistrate in the same area or areas ; and a person so appointed to be a magistrate in any commission area shall by virtue of his office be a justice of the peace for that area.

(2) Any appointment of a stipendiary magistrate under this section shall be of a person recommended to Her Majesty by the Lord Chancellor, and a stipendiary magistrate appointed under this section shall not be removed from office except on the Lord Chancellor's recommendation.

(3) A stipendiary magistrate so appointed in any commission area shall sit at such court houses in the area, on such days and at such times as may be determined by or in accordance with directions given by the Lord Chancellor from time to time.

(4) For purposes of pension and of any derivative benefit under the Administration of Justice (Pensions) Act 1950 service 1950 c. 11 (14 as a stipendiary magistrate under this section shall be treated & 15 Geo. 6.). as service as a metropolitan stipendiary magistrate.

(5) Where a stipendiary magistrate would, apart from this Act, be required by section 2(2) of the Justices of the Peace Act 1968 c. 69. 1968 to vacate his office at the end of the completed year of service in the course of which he attains the age of 70, but the Lord Chancellor considers it desirable in the public interest to retain him in office after that time, the Lord Chancellor may from time to time authorise him to continue in office up to such age not exceeding 72 as the Lord Chancellor thinks fit.

(6) So much of section 10(1) of the Administration of Justice 1964 c. 42. Act 1964 as limits the number of metropolitan stipendiary magistrates to forty shall cease to have effect, but—

(a) the number of metropolitan stipendiary magistrates shall not at any time exceed sixty or such larger number as

Her Majesty may from time to time by Order in Council specify ; and

(b) the number of stipendiary magistrates appointed under this section shall not at any time exceed forty or such larger number as may be so specified ;

and Her Majesty shall not be recommended to make an Order in Council under this subsection unless a draft of the Order has been laid before Parliament and approved by resolution of each House.

1956 c. 34.   (7) Section 16(2) of the Criminal Justice Administration Act 1956 and Schedule 2 to that Act shall cease to have effect, but where it appears to the Lord Chancellor that it is expedient so to do in order to avoid delays in the administration of justice in any commission area in which a stipendiary magistrate may be appointed under this section, he may authorise any person qualified to be so appointed to act as a stipendiary magistrate in that area during such period (not exceeding three months at one time) as the Lord Chancellor thinks fit, and may require so to act any stipendiary magistrate appointed under this section in another commission area ; and while so acting in any area under this subsection, a person shall have the same jurisdiction, powers and duties as if he had been appointed stipendiary magistrate in that area, and were a justice of the peace for that area.

The Lord Chancellor may, out of moneys provided by Parliament, pay to any person authorised to act under this subsection, not being a stipendiary magistrate, such remuneration as he may, with the approval of the Minister for the Civil Service, determine.

Courses of instruction for justices of the peace.   **3.**—(1) There may be paid out of moneys provided by Parliament any expenses incurred by the Lord Chancellor in providing courses of instruction for justices of the peace ; and a justice of the peace following a course of instruction so provided shall be entitled to the like allowances as are payable to justices following a course provided under section 17 of the Justices

1949 c. 101.   of the Peace Act 1949 or section 16(2) of the Administration of
1964 c. 42.   Justice Act 1964, and the enactments relating to allowances so payable shall apply accordingly.

(2) If courses of instruction are not provided for justices of the peace of any area as required by section 17 of the Justices of the Peace Act 1949 or section 16(2) of the Administration of Justice Act 1964, then any expenses incurred by the Lord Chancellor in providing courses of instruction to make good the default shall be recoverable by him from the magistrates' courts committee or committee of magistrates in default, and any sums received by him under this subsection shall be paid into the Consolidated Fund.

4. In section 33 of the Solicitors Act 1957 (which precludes
a solicitor from acting in connection with proceedings before Amendment
justices for any area if he or his partner is a justice for that as to right
area) there shall be inserted after subsection (1) the following to practise of
subsection: — justices of the
peace who
" (1A) Where the area for which a solicitor is a justice are solicitors.
of the peace is divided into petty sessional divisions, his 1957 c. 27.
being a justice for the area shall not subject him or any
partner of his to any disqualification under this section in
relation to proceedings before justices acting for a petty
sessional division for which he does not ordinarily act."

5. The provisions of Parts I to III of Schedule 1 to this Act, Consequential.
which reproduces, with the modifications required by the foregoing sections,—

(a) in Part I the effect of the enactments relating to the
retirement and personal pension of stipendiary
magistrates ; and

(b) in Part II the effect of the enactments and rules relating to supplemental lists kept by virtue of section 4 of
the Justices of the Peace Act 1949 ; and 1949 c. 101.

(c) in Part III the effect of section 8 of the Justices of the
Peace Act 1949 and later enactments with respect to
the allowances payable to justices of the peace ;

shall have effect in place of the enactments and rules referred
to in paragraphs (a) to (c) above ; and any such enactment or
instrument as is referred to in Part IV of that Schedule shall
have effect subject to the amendments there provided for, being
amendments consequential on the foregoing sections of this
Act or on Parts I to III of that Schedule.

PART II

MISCELLANEOUS

6.—(1) In the enactments mentioned in Schedule 2 to this Jurisdiction of
Act (which deal with the jurisdiction of county courts in county courts
actions relating to land, and connected matters) there shall be in relation
made the amendments required by that Schedule, in lieu of any to land.
amendment of the same words made by previous enactments ;
and the county court limit under any of the enactments amended
by an entry in Part I of the Schedule shall be the amount
specified in column 3 in that entry or such greater amount as Her
Majesty may from time to time by Order in Council direct.

(2) No recommendation shall be made to Her Majesty in
Council to make an Order under this section unless a draft of the
Order has been laid before Parliament and approved by
resolution of each House of Parliament.

(3) No provision of this Act or of any Order in Council under this section shall affect the operation of section 49 of the County Courts Act 1959 or that of section 109(2)(*a*), (*b*) or (*c*) of that Act in the case of actions commenced before the coming into force of that provision.

7.—(1) In section 92 of the County Courts Act 1959 (which enables the judge, but not the registrar, of the court to refer proceedings to arbitration with the consent of the parties) there shall be made the following amendments—

(*a*) for subsection (1) there shall be substituted the following—

" (1) A county court may, in such cases as may be prescribed, order any proceedings to be referred to arbitration (whether with or without other matters within the jurisdiction of the court in dispute between the parties) to such person or persons (including the judge or registrar) and in such manner and on such terms as the court thinks just and reasonable." ; and

(*b*) in subsection (2), for the word " judge " there shall be substituted the word " court ".

(2) In section 93 of that Act (which enables the judge to refer proceedings or questions arising in proceedings for inquiry and report) there shall be made the following amendments—

(*a*) in subsection (1), at the end, there shall be inserted the words " and, in such cases as may be prescribed by and subject to county court rules, the registrar may refer to a referee for inquiry and report any question arising in any proceedings." ; and

(*b*) in subsection (2), after the word " judge ", there shall be inserted the words " or, as the case may be, the registrar ".

Extension of powers of court in action by mortgagee of dwelling-house.

1970 c. 31.

8.—(1) Where by a mortgage of land which consists of or includes a dwelling-house, or by any agreement between the mortgagee under such a mortgage and the mortgagor, the mortgagor is entitled or is to be permitted to pay the principal sum secured by instalments or otherwise to defer payment of it in whole or in part, but provision is also made for earlier payment in the event of any default by the mortgagor or of a demand by the mortgagee or otherwise, then for purposes of section 36 of the Administration of Justice Act 1970 (under which a court has power to delay giving a mortgagee possession of the mortgaged property so as to allow the mortgagor a reasonable time to pay any sums due under the mortgage) a court may treat as due under the mortgage on account of the principal sum secured and of interest on it only such amounts

as the mortgagor would have expected to be required to pay   PART II
if there had been no such provision for earlier payment.

(2) A court shall not exercise by virtue of subsection (1)
above the powers conferred by section 36 of the Administration   1970 c. 31.
of Justice Act 1970 unless it appears to the court not only that
the mortgagor is likely to be able within a reasonable period
to pay any amounts regarded (in accordance with subsection (1)
above) as due on account of the principal sum secured, together
with the interest on those amounts, but also that he is likely to
be able by the end of that period to pay any further amounts
that he would have expected to be required to pay by then on
account of that sum and of interest on it if there had been no
such provision as is referred to in subsection (1) above for earlier
payment.

(3) Where subsection (1) above would apply to an action in
which a mortgagee only claimed possession of the mortgaged
property, and the mortgagee brings an action for foreclosure
(with or without also claiming possession of the property), then
section 36 of the Administration of Justice Act 1970 together
with subsections (1) and (2) above shall apply as they would
apply if it were an action in which the mortgagee only claimed
possession of the mortgaged property, except that—

　　(a) section 36(2)(b) shall apply only in relation to any claim
　　　　for possession ; and

　　(b) section 36(5) shall not apply.

(4) For purposes of this section the expressions " dwelling-
house ", " mortgage ", " mortgagee " and " mortgagor " shall
be construed in the same way as for the purposes of Part IV
of the Administration of Justice Act 1970.

(5) This section shall have effect in relation to an action begun
before the date on which this section comes into force if before
that date judgment has not been given, nor an order made, in
that action for delivery of possession of the mortgaged property
and, where it is a question of subsection (3) above, an order *nisi*
for foreclosure has not been made in that action.

(6) In the application of this section to Northern Ireland, subsection (3) shall be omitted.

9.—(1) Subject to the following subsections, there shall be   Judicial
paid to—   salaries.

　　(a) Lords of Appeal in Ordinary ;

　　(b) judges of the Supreme Court in England and Wales
　　　　other than the Lord Chancellor ;

　　(c) judges of the Court of Session ;

PART II

(*d*) judges of the Supreme Court in Northern Ireland ;

(*e*) metropolitan stipendiary magistrates ;

(*f*) stipendiary magistrates appointed under this Act ;

such salaries as may be determined, with the consent of the Minister for the Civil Service, by the Lord Chancellor or, in the case of judges of the Court of Session, by the Secretary of State.

(2) Until otherwise determined under this section, there shall be paid to the holders of judicial office mentioned in paragraphs (*a*) to (*e*) of subsection (1) above the same salaries as at the coming into force of this section.

(3) Any salary payable under this section may be increased, but not reduced, by a determination or further determination under this section.

(4) The salary payable to any holder of judicial office under this section shall in each case be abated by the amount of any pension payable to him in respect of any public office in the United Kingdom or elsewhere to which he had previously been appointed or elected ; but any abatement under this subsection shall be disregarded for the purposes of computing the pension payable to him in respect of that judicial office and any derivative benefit within the meaning of the Administration of Justice (Pensions) Act 1950 which depends upon eligibility for such a pension.

1950 c. 11 (14 & 15 Geo. 6.).

(5) Salaries payable under this section shall be charged on and paid out of the Consolidated Fund of the United Kingdom.

Judicial pensions (increase of widow's and children's pensions).

1950 c. 11 (14 & 15 Geo. 6.).

10.—(1) The annual amount of the widow's pension that may be granted under or by virtue of the Administration of Justice (Pensions) Act 1950 wholly or partly in respect of relevant service after the passing of this Act, and the annual amount of the children's pension that may be so granted, shall be increased in accordance with this section ; and where the widow's pension or children's pension (if any) that may be granted in respect of a person's relevant service is so increased, there shall be made towards the cost of the liability therefor such contributions (in lieu of or in addition to that required by section 8 of the Act of 1950) as may be prescribed, in the form either of a reduction or further reduction of the lump sum pension benefit payable in respect of that service or of deductions from the salary so payable or partly in one of those forms and partly in the other.

(2) In the case of pensions attributable wholly to relevant service after the passing of this Act,—

(*a*) the annual amount of a widow's pension may be one-half of the annual amount of the personal pension of the deceased ; and (*b*) subject to section 7(4) of the Act of 1950 (which makes provision for the case of a widow remarrying), the annual amount of a children's pension, while there is only one person for whose benefit it can enure, may amount—

    (i) where the deceased was a man who left a widow and she is still alive, to one-quarter of the annual amount of the personal pension ; and

    (ii) in any other case, to one-third of the annual amount of the personal pension ;

and while there are two or more persons for whose benefit it can enure, may amount to twice the figure given by whichever is applicable of subparagraphs (i) and (ii) above.

In section 7(4) of the Act of 1950 the reference to subsection (2) of that section shall include paragraph (*b*)(ii) of this subsection.

(3) Subject to subsection (4) below, in the case of pensions payable partly in respect of relevant service after the passing of this Act but not attributable wholly to that service, the annual value of the widow's pension or children's pension that may be granted shall be determined by reference to the proportions which the relevant service before and after that time bear to the whole of the relevant service, and shall be the amount obtained by adding—

(*a*) the part proportionate to the service before that time of the annual amount of the pension that might have been granted if this section had not been passed ; and

(*b*) the part proportionate to the service after that time of the annual amount of the pension that might have been granted if this section had always had effect.

(4) In relation to persons serving at the passing of this Act provision may be made by regulations whereby, subject to any prescribed conditions, an election may be made by or with respect to a person—

(*a*) that subsection (2) above shall apply to him as if the whole of his relevant service were service after the passing of this Act, and subsection (3) shall not apply ;

(*b*) that subsections (1) to (3) above shall not apply to him, and the Act of 1950 shall apply as if this section had not been passed ;

(*c*) in the case of a person who elected under section 11(1) or (2) of the Act of 1950 for his eligibility for pension not to satisfy the conditions for the grant of a widow's or children's pension, that the election under that section shall be revoked.

(5) Where a person's relevant service is partly before and partly after the passing of this Act, then for the purposes of this section any widow's or children's pension payable in respect of that service is to be regarded as attributable wholly to the service after that time if the service before that time does not add to the annual rate of the personal pension, and for the purposes of subsection (3) there shall be left out of account so much (if any) of the service before that time as does not add to the annual amount of the personal pension.

(6) Regulations made for purposes of this section may make provision for consequential or incidental matters, including provision excluding or modifying the operation of any enactment passed before this Act; and in particular any regulations providing for contributions by deduction from salary may make consequential provision as to sections 10 and 11 of the Act of 1950 and any other enactment referring or relating to lump sums payable under that Act.

(7) Regulations for purposes of this section may be made, with the concurrence of the Minister for the Civil Service, by the Lord Chancellor or, in relation to pensions for service in offices existing only in Scotland, by the Secretary of State; and the power to make regulations for purposes of this section shall be exercisable by statutory instrument, which shall be subject to annulment in pursuance of a resolution of either House of Parliament.

(8) The foregoing provisions of this section shall have effect in relation to the enactments mentioned in Schedule 3 to this Act as they have effect in relation to the Act of 1950, but subject to the adaptations provided for by that Schedule; and provision corresponding to that which is made by subsections (1) and (3) above, or which may be made by regulations under this section for purposes of those subsections may, in relation to the pension benefits of any resident magistrate or county court registrar included in Schedule 5 to the Superannuation (Northern Ireland) Order 1972 (persons remaining subject to the Superannuation Acts (Northern Ireland) 1967 and 1969), be made by order of the Ministry of Finance for Northern Ireland.

1920 c. 67.   For the purposes of section 6 of the Government of Ireland Act 1920 this subsection shall be deemed to have been passed before the appointed day within the meaning of that section.

1950 c. 11 (14 & 15 Geo. 6.).   (9) In this section—

    (a) " the Act of 1950 " means the Administration of Justice (Pensions) Act 1950;

    (b) " prescribed " means prescribed by regulations made for purposes of this section.

11.—(1) The provisions of Schedule 4 to this Act (which reproduce for certain judicial pensions the effect of existing enactments, except in providing for pensions to be payable without a grant by Letters Patent and in omitting any express provision as to time of payment) shall, with the savings and consequential amendments there contained, have effect in place of those enactments.

(2) Except as provided by Schedule 4 to this Act, the provisions of that Schedule shall apply in relation to persons who retired or died before this section comes into force.

12.—(1) Where the Lord Chancellor is satisfied by means of a medical certificate that a person holding office as Lord of Appeal in Ordinary, as judge of the Supreme Court in England and Wales or as judge of the Supreme Court in Northern Ireland is disabled by permanent infirmity from the performance of the duties of his office, but is for the time being incapacitated from resigning it, then subject to subsections (2) to (4) below the Lord Chancellor may by instrument under his hand declare that person's office to have been vacated, and the instrument shall have the like effect for all purposes as if that person had on the date of the instrument resigned his office.

(2) A declaration under this section with respect to a Lord of Appeal in Ordinary shall be of no effect unless it is made with the concurrence of the senior of the Lords of Appeal or, if made with respect to him, with that of the next senior of them.

(3) A declaration under this section with respect to a judge of the Supreme Court in England and Wales shall be of no effect unless it is made—

(a) in the case of any of the Lord Chief Justice, the Master of the Rolls, the President of the Family Division and the Vice-Chancellor, with the concurrence of two others of them ;

(b) in the case of a Lord Justice of Appeal, with the concurrence of the Master of the Rolls ;

(c) in the case of a puisne judge of the Queen's Bench Division, with the concurrence of the Lord Chief Justice ;

(d) in the case of a puisne judge of the Chancery Division other than the Vice-Chancellor, with the concurrence of the Vice-Chancellor ;

(e) in the case of a puisne judge of the Family Division, with the concurrence of the President of the Family Division.

(4) A declaration under this section with respect to a judge of the Supreme Court of Northern Ireland shall be of no effect unless it is made with the concurrence of the Lord Chief Justice of Northern Ireland or, if made with respect to him, with that of the senior Lord Justice of Appeal.

PART II
Pension etc.
of president of
pensions
appeal
tribunals.
1943 c. 39.

13.—(1) In the case of any person appointed after the coming into force of this section as president of the pension appeal tribunals established under the Pensions Appeal Tribunals Act 1943—

(*a*) the Lord Chancellor may pay such pension, allowances or gratuity to or in respect of him on his retirement or death, or make such payments towards the provision of such a pension, allowance or gratuity, as the Lord Chancellor with the approval of the Minister for the Civil Service may determine; and

(*b*) if, on his ceasing to hold office as president of the pensions appeal tribunals, it appears to the Lord Chancellor that there are special circumstances which make it right that he should receive compensation, the Lord Chancellor may, with the approval of the Minister for the Civil Service, pay to him a sum of such amount as the Lord Chancellor may, with the like approval, determine.

(2) The expenses of the Lord Chancellor under this section shall be defrayed out of moneys provided by Parliament.

Pensions of
resident
magistrates
in Northern
Ireland.
1960 c. 2
(N.I.).

14.—(1) In the Resident Magistrates' Pensions Act (Northern Ireland) 1960 the definition of " retiring salary " in section 22(1) shall be amended by omitting the word " average " and by substituting for the words " during the three years immediately preceding the date of his retirement " the words " immediately before his retirement ".

(2) This section shall not affect any pension or other benefit payable to or in respect of a person who retired or died before the coming into force of this section.

1920 c. 67.

(3) For the purposes of section 6 of the Government of Ireland Act 1920 this section shall be deemed to have been passed before the appointed day within the meaning of that section.

Qualification
for
appointment
as deputy
Circuit judge.
1971 c. 23.

15. For section 24(2)(*a*) of the Courts Acts 1971 (under which a person is qualified for appointment as deputy Circuit judge if he is a barrister of at least ten years' standing or a Recorder who has held that office for at least five years) there shall be substituted—

" (*a*) any barrister or solicitor of at least ten years' standing ".

Appointment
of deputy
district
registrars of
High Court
and deputy
county court
registrars.

16.—(1) If it appears to the Lord Chancellor that it is expedient as a temporary measure to make an appointment under this subsection in order to facilitate the disposal of business in the High Court, he may appoint a person to be a deputy district registrar in any district registry of the High Court during such period or on such occasions as the Lord Chancellor thinks fit;

and a deputy district registrar, while acting under his appointment, shall have the same powers as if he were the district
registrar.

(2) If it appears to the Lord Chancellor that it is expedient
as a temporary measure to make an appointment under this
subsection in order to facilitate the disposal of business in county
courts, he may appoint a person to be deputy county court
registrar for any county court district during such period or on
such occasions as the Lord Chancellor thinks fit; and a deputy
county court registrar, while acting under his appointment, shall
have the same powers and be subject to the same liabilities as
if he were the registrar.

(3) Any person being a solicitor of not less than seven years'
standing shall be qualified for appointment under this section
as deputy district registrar or deputy county court registrar.   1959 c. 22.

(4) Section 29(1) of the County Courts Act 1959 (which
provides that no officer of a county court shall, either by himself
or his partner be directly or indirectly engaged as a solicitor or
agent for any party in any proceedings in that court) shall not
apply to a deputy county court registrar appointed under this
section; but a deputy district registrar or deputy county court
registrar so appointed shall not act as such in relation to any
proceedings in which he is, either by himself or his partner,
directly or indirectly engaged as a solicitor or agent for any
party.

(5) Notwithstanding the expiry of any period for which a
person is appointed under this section to be deputy district
registrar or deputy county court registrar, he may act as such
for the purpose of continuing to deal with, giving judgment in, or
dealing with any ancillary matter relating to, any case with
which he may have been concerned during the period of his
appointment, and for that purpose shall be treated as acting
under that appointment.

(6) The Lord Chancellor may, out of moneys provided by
Parliament, pay to any person appointed deputy district registrar
or deputy county court registrar under this section such remuneration and allowances as he may, with the approval of
the Minister for the Civil Service, determine.

(7) After the coming into force of this section no further
appointment shall be made of provisional district registrars or 1925 c. 49.
deputy district registrars under section 84 of the Supreme Court 1956 c. 46.
of Judicature (Consolidation) Act 1925 or section 11 of the
Administration of Justice Act 1956, or of deputy county court
registrars under section 27 of the County Courts Act 1959; and
on the coming into force of this section any person then holding
office as deputy district registrar or deputy county court registrar

PART II   shall vacate that office, but so that subsections (4), (5) and (6) above shall thereafter apply to him as if he had been appointed under this section for a period then expiring.

Payment of interpreters in criminal cases (England and Wales).

17.—(1) Where in any criminal proceedings an interpreter is required because of a defendant's lack of English, the expenses properly incurred on his employment shall be ordered by the court to be paid out of central funds ; and—

(*a*) where there is laid before a justice of the peace for any area an information charging with an offence a person who because of his lack of English would require an interpreter on his trial, but the information is not proceeded with, then, if he has incurred expenses on the employment of an interpreter for the proceedings on the information, he may apply to a magistrates' court for that area and the court shall order the payment out of central funds of the expenses properly so incurred by him ; and

(*b*) where such a person is committed for trial but is not ultimately tried, then if he has incurred expenses on the employment of an interpreter for the proceedings in the Crown Court, he may apply to the Crown Court and the court shall order the payment out of central funds of the expenses properly so incurred by him.

(2) In this section " criminal proceedings " means any proceedings in which a court has power under the Costs in
1973 c. 14.   Criminal Cases Act 1973 to make an order for payment of costs out of central funds or would have power to do so if any reference in that Act to an indictable offence were a reference to any offence ; and sections 13 to 17 of that Act (which relate to the procedure for implementing orders under the Act and other supplemental matters) shall apply in relation to this section as they apply in relation to that Act, except that—

(*a*) in section 15 (costs ordered by magistrates' court to be paid out of central funds) subsection (1) shall apply as if the reference in paragraph (*a*) to an indictable offence included any offence, and shall also apply where an order is made by a magistrates' court under subsection (1)(*a*) above ; and

(*b*) section 16(2) (payment of costs ordered to be paid out of central funds and by accused or prosecutor) shall not apply so as to require a defendant to reimburse any costs paid out of central funds by virtue of this section.

(3) In this section " court " includes the House of Lords, and " defendant " means the person (whether convicted or not) who is alleged to be guilty of an offence.

18.—(1) In the Costs in Criminal Cases Act (Northern Ireland) 1968, after section 5 thereof, there shall be inserted the following section—

PART II

Payment of interpreters in criminal cases (Northern Ireland).

"Fees of required interpreter.

5A. Notwithstanding anything to the contrary contained in this Act, where in any criminal proceedings an interpreter is required because of a defendant's lack of English, the expenses properly incurred on his employment shall, in accordance with rules made pursuant to section 7, be defrayed by the Ministry.".

1968 c. 10 (N.I.).

(2) Where in any of the following proceedings, that is to say,—

> (*a*) any proceedings on an appeal to the Court of Criminal Appeal in Northern Ireland, or preliminary or incidental to such an appeal;
>
> (*b*) any proceedings before a divisional court of the Queen's Bench Division of the High Court of Justice in Northern Ireland in a criminal cause or matter;
>
> (*c*) any proceedings on an appeal to the House of Lords from a decision in proceedings within (*a*) or (*b*) above or an application for leave to appeal from such a decision;

an interpreter is required because of a defendant's lack of English, the expenses properly incurred on his employment shall be defrayed by the Ministry of Home Affairs for Northern Ireland, up to an amount allowed by the court or (in the case of proceedings in that House) by the House of Lords.

In this subsection " defendant " means the person (whether convicted or not) who is alleged to be guilty of an offence.

(3) For the purposes of section 6 of the Government of Ireland Act 1920 this section shall, so far as it relates to matters within the powers of the Parliament of Northern Ireland, be deemed to have been passed before the appointed day within the meaning of that section.

1920 c. 67.

PART III
SUPPLEMENTARY

19.—(1) The enactments mentioned in Schedule 5 to this Act (which in Part I includes certain enactments that are to the extent specified in column 3 superseded or otherwise obsolete or unnecessary, or become so with the amendment provided for by subsection (2) below) are to the extent so specified hereby repealed, but subject—

Repeals.

> (*a*) in the case of the repeals made by Part I or Part II of Schedule 5 to this Act, to the saving in section 20(6) below; and
>
> (*b*) in the case of the repeals made by Part V of Schedule 5, to the saving in paragraph 4 of Schedule 4.

E

(2) In the Supreme Court of Judicature (Consolidation) Act 1925, in section 2(1) as amended by subsequent enactments, for the words " and not less than twenty-five puisne judges of that Court " there shall be substituted the words " and the puisne judges of that Court ".

20.—(1) The following provisions shall have effect with respect to the coming into force of this Act:—

(a) Part I of this Act and the repeals made by Part II of Schedule 5 shall not come into force until the 1st April 1974 except in so far as provision to the contrary is made by order of the Lord Chancellor made by statutory instrument ;

(b) sections 8, 17 and 18 shall not come into force until the expiration of one month beginning with the date this Act is passed ; and

(c) section 10 shall come into force on such day as may be appointed by order of the Lord Chancellor and the Secretary of State made by statutory instrument.

(2) Any order of the Lord Chancellor under subsection (1)(a) above may make such consequential or transitional provision as appears to the Lord Chancellor to be necessary by reason of the bringing into force thereby of any provisions before 1st April 1974 (and in particular may make any provision that may be required so that the provisions in force before that date may operate without the provisions not in force, or may operate as regards local government or other matters in conjunction with the law as it is before that date), and may adapt accordingly any reference in this Act to that date or to the beginning of that month.

(3) Notwithstanding subsection (1) above, section 1(1) to (3) of this Act shall apply to any commission of the peace issued or appointment of a justice made before the 1st April 1974 but taking effect only on or after that date ; and, subject to section 217 of the Local Government Act 1972,—

(a) any other commission of the peace issued before that date, unless and until superseded by a commission taking effect on or after that date, shall thenceforth have effect as if addressed generally as required by section 1(1) above ; and

(b) any person holding office as justice of the peace on that date by virtue of any such commission shall thenceforth hold that office as if appointed in accordance with section 1(2), and shall be included accordingly in the records required by section 1(3) and (4).

(4) Where immediately before the 1st April 1974 a person's name is entered in the supplemental list kept in connection with any commission of the peace by virtue of section 4 of the Justices of the Peace Act 1949, his name shall be treated as

included in the supplemental list for England and Wales under this Act.

(5) Any person who immediately before the 1st April 1974 holds office as stipendiary magistrate for any area under section 29 of the Justices of the Peace Act 1949 shall from the beginning of that month become stipendiary magistrate in any commission area comprising that area or part of it, and shall be treated for all purposes as if he had been appointed stipendiary magistrate in that commission area under section 2 above:

Provided that—

(a) his salary shall not be less than that payable to him immediately before that date ; and

(b) contributions to his superannuation allowance under Part I of Schedule 1 to this Act and to any derivative benefit within the meaning of the Administration of Justice (Pensions) Act 1950 shall be paid and borne as if this Act had not been passed and his service as stipendiary magistrate after the beginning of April 1974 had been service as a metropolitan stipendiary magistrate ; and

(c) for the purposes of paragraph 1 of Schedule 1 to this Act the date of his appointment shall be taken to have been that of his appointment to the office held by him immediately before the beginning of that month.

(6) Nothing in Part I of this Act or in any repeal made by Part I or II of Schedule 5 shall affect—

(a) any superannuation or other benefits payable wholly in respect of service ending before 1st April 1974, or the person by whom or manner in which any such benefits are to be paid or borne ; or

(b) the division of any commission area into petty sessional divisions as existing at the beginning of that month ; or

(c) any regulations in force at the beginning of that month under section 8 of the Justices of the Peace Act 1949 ;

but any such regulations shall thereafter have effect as if made under Part III of Schedule 1 to this Act.

21.—(1) This Act may be cited as the Administration of Justice Act 1973.

(2) The foregoing sections of this Act shall not extend to Scotland or to Northern Ireland except to the following extent, that is to say—

(a) sections 9 to 12 of this Act, and the repeals made by Parts IV and V of Schedule 5, shall extend to Scotland or to Northern Ireland in so far as they affect the law of Scotland or of Northern Ireland ; and

(b) sections 8, 14 and 18 of this Act (together with so much of section 20(1) as relates to those sections) shall extend to Northern Ireland.

SCHEDULES

SCHEDULE 1

JUSTICES OF THE PEACE (CONSEQUENTIAL RE-ENACTMENTS AND AMENDMENTS)

PART I

RETIREMENT AND SUPERANNUATION OF STIPENDIARY MAGISTRATES

1.—(1) A stipendiary magistrate appointed on or after the 25th October 1968 shall vacate his office at the end of the completed year of service in the course of which he attains the age of 70:

Provided that where the Lord Chancellor considers it desirable in the public interest to retain him in office after that time, the Lord Chancellor may from time to time authorise him to continue in office up to such age not exceeding 72 as the Lord Chancellor thinks fit.

(2) A stipendiary magistrate appointed before the 25th October 1968 shall vacate his office at the end of the completed year of service in the course of which he attains the age of 72:

Provided that where the Lord Chancellor considers it desirable in the public interest to retain him in office after that time, the Lord Chancellor may from time to time authorise him to continue in office up to such age not exceeding 75 as the Lord Chancellor thinks fit.

2.—(1) Subject to the provisions of this paragraph, where a stipendiary magistrate retires (under paragraph 1 above or otherwise) after not less than five years service as stipendiary magistrate, the Minister for the Civil Service on the recommendation of the Lord Chancellor may grant to him a superannuation allowance at an annual rate not exceeding 15/80ths of his annual salary, together with an addition for each complete year of his service as stipendiary magistrate after the first 5 years equal to 1/80th of the salary or, in the case of a year of service after the first 10 years, to 2/80ths of the salary ; but the allowance shall in no case exceed one half of the salary.

(2) An allowance under this paragraph shall be calculated on the salary the magistrate is receiving immediately before his retirement.

(3) An allowance shall not be granted under this paragraph to a magistrate who has not attained the age of 65 at the time of his retirement, unless the Lord Chancellor is satisfied by means of a medical certificate that by reason of infirmity of mind or body he is incapable of discharging the duties of his office, and that the incapacity is likely to be permanent.

(4) A person to whom an allowance is granted under this paragraph on his retirement on a medical certificate shall, until he attains the age of 65, be liable to be called upon to fill any public office or situation under the Crown in the United Kingdom for which his previous public services may render him eligible ; and if he declines,

when called upon to do so, to take upon him such office or situation,
or declines or neglects to execute the duties thereof satisfactorily,
being in a competent state of health, he shall forfeit his right to
the allowance which has been granted to him.

(5) The decision of the Minister for the Civil Service on any
question which arises as to the application of any provision of this
paragraph to any person, or as to the rate of any superannuation
allowance under this paragraph, or as to the reckoning of any service
for such an allowance, shall be final.

(6) Any sums payable on account of allowances under this paragraph shall be charged on and paid out of the Consolidated Fund,
and shall be paid at such times in every year as the Minister for
the Civil Service may determine.

3. In this Part of this Schedule " stipendiary magistrate " means a
metropolitan or other stipendiary magistrate in England or Wales,
and references to service as a stipendiary magistrate are to be construed accordingly.

PART II

SUPPLEMENTAL LIST FOR ENGLAND AND WALES

4.—(1) Subject to sub-paragraph (6) below there shall be entered
in the supplemental list the name of any justice of the peace who
is of the age of 70 years or over and neither holds nor has held
high judicial office within the meaning of the Appellate Jurisdiction 1876 c. 59.
Act 1876 and the name of any justice of the peace who holds or has
held such office and is of the age of 75 years or over:

Provided that a person who on the date when his name falls
to be entered in the supplemental list in accordance with this sub-
paragraph holds office as chairman of the justices in a petty sessions
area (whether by election under section 13 of the Justices of the 1949 c. 101.
Peace Act 1949 or, in the City of London, as Chief Magistrate or
acting Chief Magistrate) shall have his name so entered on the
expiration or sooner determination of the term for which he holds
office on that date.

(2) The Lord Chancellor may direct that the name of a justice
of the peace for any area shall be entered in the supplemental list
if the Lord Chancellor is satisfied either—

   (a) that by reason of the justice's age or infirmity or other like
       cause it is expedient he should cease to exercise judicial
       functions as a justice for the area ; or

   (b) that the justice declines or neglects to take a proper part
       in the exercise of those functions.

(3) On a person's appointment as a justice of the peace for any
area the Lord Chancellor may direct that his name shall be entered
in the supplemental list, if that person is appointed a justice for
that area on ceasing to be a justice for some other area.

(4) The name of a justice of the peace shall be entered in the supplemental list, if he applies for it to be so entered and the application is approved by the Lord Chancellor.

(5) In relation to the entry in the supplemental list of the name of a person who is a justice of the peace only for any of the counties of Greater Manchester, Merseyside and Lancashire, sub-paragraphs (2) to (4) above shall have effect with the substitution for references to the Lord Chancellor of references to the Chancellor of the Duchy of Lancaster.

(6) Nothing in this paragraph shall apply to a person holding office as stipendiary magistrate.

5.—(1) A person's name shall be removed from the supplemental list if he ceases to be a justice of the peace.

(2) The name of any person, if not required to be entered in the supplemental list by paragraph 4(1) above, shall be removed from the list, if so directed by the Lord Chancellor or, where the person in question is a justice only for any of the counties of Greater Manchester, Merseyside and Lancashire, by the Chancellor of the Duchy of Lancaster.

6.—(1) Subject to the following sub-paragraphs, a justice of the peace for any area, while his name is entered in the supplemental list, shall not by reason of being a justice for that area be qualified as a justice to do any act or to be a member of any committee or other body.

(2) Sub-paragraph (1) above shall not preclude a justice from doing all or any of the following acts as a justice, that is to say—

(*a*) signing any document for the purpose of authenticating another person's signature ;

(*b*) taking and authenticating by his signature any written declaration not made on oath ; and

(*c*) giving a certificate of facts within his knowledge or of his opinion as to any matter.

(3) The entry of a person's name in the supplemental list shall also not preclude him, if so authorised by the Lord Chancellor, from acting as a judge of the Crown Court so long as he has not attained the age of 72 years.

(4) No act or appointment shall be invalidated by reason of the disqualification under this paragraph of the person acting or appointed.

7. Any such act as is mentioned in paragraph 6(2)(*a*) to (*c*) above, where it may be done by a justice of the peace, may, subject to any express provision made to the contrary by any enactment or instrument relating to that act, be done also by any person who is chairman of the Greater London Council, mayor of a London borough or chairman of a county or district council in England or Wales.

Part III

Travelling, Subsistence and Financial Loss Allowances

8.—(1) Subject to the provisions of this paragraph, a justice of the peace shall be entitled to receive payments at the prescribed rates by way of travelling allowance or subsistence allowance where expenditure on travelling or, as the case may be, on subsistence is necessarily incurred by him for the purpose of enabling him to perform any of his duties as a justice, and to receive payments at the prescribed rate by way of financial loss allowance where for that performance there is incurred by him any other expenditure to which he would not otherwise be subject or there is suffered by him any loss of earnings or of benefit under the National Insurance Acts 1965 to 1967 which he would otherwise have made or received.

(2) For purposes of this paragraph, a justice following a course of instruction under a scheme made in accordance with arrangements approved by the Lord Chancellor, or a course of instruction provided by the Lord Chancellor, shall be deemed to be acting in the performance of his duties as a justice.

(3) A justice shall not be entitled to any payment under this paragraph in respect of any duties, if in respect of those duties a payment of the like nature may be paid to him under arrangements made apart from this paragraph or if regulations provide that this paragraph shall not apply ; and a stipendiary magistrate shall not be entitled to any payment under this paragraph in respect of his duties as such.

(4) An allowance payable under this paragraph in respect of duties as a justice in the Crown Court shall be paid by the Lord Chancellor ; and an allowance otherwise payable under this paragraph to a justice for any commission area in respect of his duties as such shall be paid by the appropriate authority in relation to that area, that is to say—

   (a) in relation to the City of London, the Common Council ;

   (b) in relation to the Inner London area, the Receiver for the metropolitan police district ;

   (c) in relation to any of the outer London areas, the Greater London Council ;

   (d) in relation to a non-metropolitan county, the county council ;

   (e) in relation to a metropolitan county, the council of the metropolitan district which is or includes the petty sessions area for which the justice acts.

(5) Regulations may make provision as to the manner in which this paragraph is to be administered, and in particular—

   (a) for prescribing the rates of allowances, and the forms to be used and the particulars to be provided for the purpose of claiming payment thereof ;

   (b) for avoiding duplication between payments under this paragraph and under other arrangements where expenditure is incurred for more than one purpose, and otherwise for preventing abuses.

E 4

SCH. 1   (6) Regulations for the purposes of this paragraph shall be made by the Secretary of State by statutory instrument, which shall be subject to annulment in pursuance of a resolution of either House of Parliament.

PART IV
AMENDMENTS

9.—(1) Subject to any express amendment or repeal made by this Act, any enactment passed or instrument made before the passing of this Act shall have effect from the beginning of April 1974 as if—

> (a) any reference to a person appointed justice by a commission of the peace or to a person being removed from a commission of the peace were a reference to his being appointed or removed from office as a justice of the peace in accordance with section 1 of this Act ; and

1949 c. 101.

> (b) any reference to a supplemental list kept by virtue of section 4 of the Justices of the Peace Act 1949 in connection with the commission of the peace for any area were a reference to the supplemental list for England and Wales kept under section 1 of this Act.

1957 c. 27.

(2) For section 33(2) of the Solicitors Act 1957 (which restricts the right to practise of a solicitor who is a justice of the peace for any area and whose name is not on the supplemental list) there shall be substituted—

> " (2) Where a solicitor is a justice of the peace for any area, that shall not subject him or any partner of his to any disqualification under this section if his name is entered in the supplemental list kept under section 1 of the Administration of Justice Act 1973 ; and where a solicitor is, as being Lord Mayor or alderman, a justice of the peace for the City of London, that shall not subject him or any partner of his to any disqualification under this section, if he is in accordance with section 1(6) of that Act excluded from the exercise of his functions as a justice for the City."

1829 c. 44.

10.—(1) In section 1 of the Metropolitan Police Act 1829 for the words from " and by warrant " to " those several counties " there shall be substituted the words " and from time to time by warrant under his sign manual to appoint during His Majesty's pleasure a Commissioner of Police of the Metropolis to execute the duties of chief officer of the police force hereby established " ; and any person holding office as Commissioner of Police of the Metropolis at the coming into force of this paragraph shall be deemed to have been appointed under that section as so amended.

1856 c. 2.

(2) Subject to any express amendment or repeal made by this Act, any reference in the Metropolitan Police Act 1829 or in any other enactment passed before the Metropolitan Police Act 1856 to the justices appointed under the Metropolitan Police Act 1829 or to the Commissioners of Police of the Metropolis shall continue to have effect as a reference to the Commissioner of Police of the Metropolis.

11.—(1) In Schedule 1 to the Administration of Justice (Pensions)   Sᴄʜ. 1
Act 1950 for the entries relating to metropolitan police magistrates   1950 c. 11
and stipendiary magistrates pensionable under section 33 of the   (14 & 15 Geo. 6).
Justices of the Peace Act 1949 there shall, in relation to persons   1949 c. 101.
serving as stipendiary magistrates after the coming into force of
section 2 of this Act, be substituted—

"Stipendiary magistrate in   Service as stipendiary magistrate
   England or Wales.   in England or Wales ".

(2) In the Pensions (Increase) Act 1971, in Schedule 2, there   1971 c. 56.
shall be added at the end of paragraph 13 the words "or under
Part I of Schedule 1 to the Administration of Justice Act 1973 ".

12. In the Justices of the Peace Act 1949 in section 27 (as amended
by section 61 of the Criminal Justice Act 1972) the reference in   1972 c. 71.
subsection (2)(*b*) to section 8 of the Justices of the Peace Act 1949
shall have effect, in relation to payments made after the beginning of
April 1974, as a reference to Part III of this Schedule.

SCHEDULE 2

Section 6.

Jᴜʀɪsᴅɪᴄᴛɪᴏɴ ᴏꜰ Cᴏᴜɴᴛʏ Cᴏᴜʀᴛs ɪɴ ʀᴇʟᴀᴛɪᴏɴ ᴛᴏ Lᴀɴᴅ

Pᴀʀᴛ I

Aᴍᴇɴᴅᴍᴇɴᴛs ᴀs ᴛᴏ Lɪᴍɪᴛ ᴏɴ Jᴜʀɪsᴅɪᴄᴛɪᴏɴ

Act	*Amendments*	*Limit on jurisdiction*
The Landlord and Tenant Act 1954 (2 & 3 Eliz. 2. c. 56).	In section 63(2) for the words "does not exceed £500 " in paragraph (*a*) there shall be substituted the words " is not over the county court limit ", and for the words "exceeds £500 " in paragraph (*b*) there shall be substituted the words " is over the county court limit ".	£5,000.
The County Courts Act 1959 (7 & 8 Eliz. 2. c. 22).	In sections 48(1), 51(*a*) and (*b*) and 191(3), and in the entries in Schedule 1 relating to sections 146 and 147 of the Law of Property Act 1925, for the words " does not exceed £100 " there shall in each case be substituted the words " is not above the county court limit ".	£1,000.

PART II

RELATED AMENDMENTS

1959 c. 22.   In the County Courts Act 1959—

(*a*) in section 49(1) (transfer to High Court of actions for recovery
of land) for the words " exceeding £100 " there shall be
substituted the words " above the county court limit under
section 51 of this Act ";

(*b*) in section 109(2) (proceedings in which there is an appeal on
questions of fact)—

(i) in paragraph (*a*)(iii) for the words " exceeds £60 "
there shall be substituted the words " is over £500 or such
larger sum not exceeding one half of the county court
limit under section 51 of this Act as may for the time
being be substituted by any Order in Council fixing that
limit "; and

(ii) in paragraph (*b*) for the words " exceeding £60 "
there shall be substituted the words " which is over £500
or such larger sum not exceeding one half of the county
court limit under section 48 of this Act as may for the
time being be substituted by any Order in Council fixing
that limit ";

(*c*) in section 200 (construction of references to net annual value
for rating), in subsection (2), for the words from " shall "
onwards, there shall be substituted—

" (*a*) shall, for the purpose of entitling a county court
to exercise jurisdiction (but not for any other purpose), be
taken to have a net annual value for rating not exceeding
that of any such hereditament of which at the time in
question it forms part ; and

(*b*) subject to paragraph (*a*) above, shall be taken to
have a net annual value for rating equal to its value by
the year."

Section 10.   SCHEDULE 3

INCREASE OF CERTAIN WIDOW'S AND CHILDREN'S PENSIONS
IN NORTHERN IRELAND

1. The enactments in relation to which section 10 of this Act has
effect by virtue of section 10(8) are—

1959 c. 25 (N.I.).   (*a*) Part XIII of the County Courts Act (Northern Ireland) 1959
(relating to county court judges and clerks of the Crown
and peace), in relation to which the references in section 10 of
this Act to section 7(4), section 8 and section 11 (or sections
10 and 11) of the Act of 1950 shall be replaced, respectively,
by references to section 126(4) of the County Courts Act
(Northern Ireland) 1959, section 127 of that Act and
1951 c. 20 (N.I.).   section 13 of the Judicial Pensions Act (Northern Ireland)
1951 ;

(*b*) the Resident Magistrates' Pensions Act (Northern Ireland) 1960, in relation to which—

    (i) subsection (4)(*c*) of section 10 of this Act and the reference in subsection (6) to sections 10 and 11 of the Act of 1950 shall not apply ; and

    (ii) the references in section 10 to section 7(4) and section 8 of the Act of 1950 shall be replaced, respectively, by references to section 8(4) and section 9 of the Resident Magistrates' Pensions Act (Northern Ireland) 1960 ;

(*c*) Part II of the Judicial Pensions Act (Northern Ireland) 1951 (relating, by virtue of later enactments, to the National Insurance Commissioners, the President of the Industrial Court and the President of the Industrial Tribunals), in relation to which—

    (i) subsection (4)(*c*) of section 10 of this Act and the reference in subsection (6) to sections 10 and 11 of the Act of 1950 shall not apply ; and

    (ii) the references in section 10 to section 7(4) and section 8 of the Act of 1950 shall be replaced, respectively, by references to section 10(4) and section 11 of the Judicial Pensions Act (Northern Ireland) 1951.

SCH. 3

1960 c. 2 (N.I.).

1951 c. 20 (N.I.).

2. In relation to the provisions to which section 10 of this Act applies by virtue of paragraph 1(*a*) or of paragraph 1(*b*) above references in section 10 to relevant service shall have effect as references to service within the meaning of those provisions.

3. In relation to any of the provisions to which section 10 of this Act applies by virtue of paragraph 1 above, the expression " enactment " in section 10(6) shall mean enactment of the Parliament of Northern Ireland or amendable by Act of that Parliament ; and section 10(7) shall not apply, but regulations for purposes of section 10 may be made with the consent of the Ministry of Finance for Northern Ireland by the Ministry of Home Affairs for Northern Ireland or, in relation to the Judicial Pensions Act (Northern Ireland) 1951, the Ministry of Health and Social Services for Northern Ireland, and shall be subject to negative resolution within the meaning of section 41(6) of the Interpretation Act (Northern Ireland) 1954 as if they were a statutory instrument within the meaning of that Act.

1954 c. 33 (N.I.).

SCHEDULE 4

PENSIONS OF HIGHER JUDICIARY

Sections 11 and 19.

1.—(1) Any Lord of Appeal in Ordinary, any Judge of the Supreme Court in England and Wales other than the Lord Chancellor, and any Judge of the Supreme Court in Northern Ireland, on retirement from that office shall be entitled during his life to a pension at the annual rate provided by this Schedule, if he retires after fifteen years relevant service or after he has attained the age of seventy years, or if at the time of his retirement he is disabled by permanent infirmity from the performance of the duties of his office.

(2) A pension payable under this Schedule shall be charged on and paid out of the Consolidated Fund of the United Kingdom.

SCH. 4

2.—(1) Subject to paragraph 4 below, the annual rate of the pension payable under this Schedule to a person retiring from any office after fifteen or more years relevant service shall be one half of his last annual salary.

(2) Subject as aforesaid, the annual rate of the pension payable under this Schedule to a person retiring from any office after less than fifteen years relevant service shall be as follows, that is to say—

    (*a*) if the period of relevant service does not amount to six years or more, one quarter of his last annual salary ;

    (*b*) if the period amounts to six years or more, one quarter of that salary plus one fortieth of that salary for each completed year of service exceeding five.

1971 c. 56.

(3) This paragraph shall be without prejudice to the operation of the Pensions (Increase) Act 1971.

1950 c. 11
(14 & 15 Geo. 6).

(4) In relation to any person in whose case an election is in force under section 11(1) of the Administration of Justice (Pensions) Act 1950 (which enabled persons serving at the commencement of that Act to opt out of the provisions of that Act for the grant of lump sums and widow's and children's pensions) this paragraph shall have effect as if for any reference to his last annual salary there were substituted a reference to the amount of that salary increased by one third.

3. The relevant service for purposes of this Schedule is—

    (*a*) in relation to the pension of a Lord of Appeal in Ordinary, any service as Lord of Appeal in Ordinary, as Judge of the Supreme Court in England and Wales, as Judge of the Court of Session or as Judge of the Supreme Court in Northern Ireland ; and

    (*b*) in relation to the pension of a Judge of the Supreme Court in England and Wales, any service as a judge of that Court or as Lord of Appeal in Ordinary ; and

    (*c*) in relation to the pension of a Judge of the Supreme Court in Northern Ireland, any service as a judge of that Court or as Lord of Appeal in Ordinary.

1959 c. 9
(8 & 9 Eliz. 2).

4.—(1) Neither this Schedule nor any repeal made by Part V of Schedule 5 to this Act shall affect the rate or amount of any pension or benefit payable to or in respect of a person who retired or died before the 17th December 1959 (being the date of commencement of the Judicial Pensions Act 1959) or who at that time held any of the offices mentioned in paragraph 3 above and did not elect that sections 1 and 2 of that Act should apply to him.

(2) This Schedule shall have effect subject to the provisions of sections 4 and 6 of the Judicial Pensions Act 1959 (which allow for a special rate of pension in certain cases and make provision against double pensions) ; but in that Act " the relevant pension enactments " in relation to pensions payable in respect of the offices

mentioned in paragraph 1 above shall mean this Schedule, and in   Sᴄʜ. 4
section 4(2) of that Act for the words " by virtue of subsection
(2) of section 2 of this Act " there shall be substituted the words
" by retirement after attaining the age of seventy years ".

(3) Subject to sub-paragraph (1) above, the Pensions (Increase) 1971 c. 56.
Act 1971 shall have effect as if in Schedule 2 there were substituted
for paragraph 5—

> " 5. A pension payable under Schedule 4 to the Administration
> of Justice Act 1973 or under the Judges' Pensions (Scotland) 1808 c. 145.
> Act 1808 ".

Sections 19, 20
and 21.

SCHEDULE 5

REPEALS

PART I

OBSOLETE ETC. ENACTMENTS

Chapter	Short Title	Extent of Repeal
45 & 46 Vict. c. 50.	The Municipal Corporations Act 1882.	In section 7, in subsection (1), the definitions of " corporate seal ", " parliamentary election", "county" and "borough civil court ", and subsection (3). Section 31. Section 231. Section 237. Section 241. Section 242(2). In section 255, the words from " the authority " to " Kingdom or ". In Schedule 9, the entry in Part II relating to the Criminal Justice Administration Act 1851.
7 & 8 Geo. 5. c. 49.	The Supreme Court of Judicature (Consolidation) Act 1925.	In section 11(1), in the proviso inserted by the Supreme Court of Judicature (Amendment) Act 1944, the words from " except " to " twenty-five ".
7 & 8 Geo. 6. c. 9.	The Supreme Court of Judicature (Amendment) Act 1944.	Section 1(2), (3), (4) and (6), and in section 1(5) the words from the beginning down to " this section ". In the Schedule, in the last entry in column 2, the words from " except " to " twenty-five ".
12, 13 & 14 Geo. 6. c. 101.	The Justices of the Peace Act 1949.	Section 6. In section 15, in subsection (5), the words " after the establishment of the rule committee ". Section 37(1) from " and " onwards. In section 44(1), the definition of " justices clerk " from " and " onwards. Schedule 2 (but without prejudice to any continuing effect of provisions relating to a person's office or employment or to superannuation in respect of an office or employment).

Chapter	Short Title	Extent of Repeal
14 & 15 Geo. 6. c. 39.	The Common Informers Act 1951.	In the Schedule, the entry for the Justices' Clerks Act 1877.
1964 c. 42.	The Administration of Justice Act 1964.	Section 25.
1968 c. 69.	The Justices of the Peace Act 1968.	In section 1, subsection (3) from " and in " onwards, and subsection (7) from " but " onwards. In section 7, in subsection (2) the words from " and in particular " to " is to act " and subsection (3) (but without prejudice to any Order in Council made before the coming into force of this repeal). In section 8, subsection (2) and in subsection (3) the words from the first " except " onwards. In Schedule 3, paragraph 2(1) from " and section 1(4) " onwards, paragraph 9 and paragraph 10(1). Schedule 5.

PART II

JUSTICES OF THE PEACE

Chapter	Short Title	Extent of Repeal
10 Geo. 4. c. 44.	The Metropolitian Police Act 1829.	Section 1 from " and His Majesty may remove " onwards. Section 2.
2 & 3 Vict. c. 47.	The Metropolitan Police Act 1839.	Section 4.
19 & 20 Vict. c. 2.	The Metropolitan Police Act 1856.	The preamble. Section 1. Section 2 from " and every " onwards. Section 5.
40 & 41 Vict. c. 41.	The Crown Office Act 1877.	In section 3, proviso (2) from " in particular " onwards. In section 5, paragraph (1).

Chapter	Short Title	Extent of Repeal
45 & 46 Vict. c. 50.	The Municipal Corporations Act 1882.	Sections 105, 154, 156, 157, 158, 159(3) to (5), 187, 234, 250(4) and (5) and 258. In Schedule 5, paragraph 3 of Part II from "including" onwards.
6 Edw. 7. c. 16.	The Justices of the Peace Act 1906.	The whole Act so far as unrepealed.
5 & 6 Geo. 5. c. 74.	The Police Magistrates Superannuation Act 1915.	The whole Act.
19 & 20 Geo. 5. c. 37.	The Police Magistrates Superannuation (Amendment) Act 1929.	The whole Act.
12, 13 & 14 Geo. 6. c. 101.	The Justices of the Peace Act 1949.	In section 1, in subsections (1), (2) and (3) the words "by the commission of the peace". Section 4. Section 8. Section 10. Sections 29, 32, 33 and 34. Section 43(2) and (3)(*b*). In section 44(1), in the definition of "magistrate" the words from "kept" to the following "commission", the definition of "metropolitan stipendiary magistrate" and the two following definitions, and the definition of "stipendiary magistrate".
14 & 15 Geo. 6. c. 11.	The Administration of Justice (Pensions) Act 1950.	Section 1, so far as relates to pensions for service as stipendiary magistrate in England or Wales. Section 14. Schedule 2, except the entry for the County Courts Act 1924. In Schedule 3 paragraphs 5 and 6.
14 & 15 Geo. 6. c. 39.	The Common Informers Act 1951.	In the Schedule, the entry for the Municipal Corporations Act 1882, except as respects offences committed before the coming into force of this repeal.
15 & 16 Geo. 6 & 1 Eliz. 2. c. 12.	The Judicial Offices (Salaries, etc.) Act 1952.	Section 1(4).
4 & 5 Eliz. 2. c. 34.	The Criminal Justice Administration Act 1956.	The whole Act, so far as unrepealed.
9 & 10 Eliz. 2. c. 3.	The Administration of Justice (Judges and Pensions) Act 1960.	Section 2.

Chapter	Short Title	Extent of Repeal
1964 c. 42.	The Administration of Justice Act 1964.	In section 2, in subsection (1), the words from " there shall " to " each of " and the words following paragraph (*e*); in subsection (2) the words from the beginning to " section " and the words " of that subsection "; and subsection (4). In section 3, the words " in subsection (1) of " and the words " under the said subsection (1) ". Section 10(1), from " but " onwards. In section 31(1), the words " section 8 of ", the words from " (travelling " to " peace) and ", the words " of that Act " and in paragraph (*b*) the words " of each of those sections ". In Schedule 3, paragraph 6, paragraph 7 and paragraph 20(1) and (8).
1967 c. 28.	The Superannuation (Miscellaneous Provisions) Act 1967.	Section 3(4)(*a*)(iv).
1968 c. 69.	The Justices of the Peace Act 1968.	In section 1, subsection (1); in subsection (2) the words from " notwithstanding " to " itself, and ", and in paragraph (*a*) the words from " by virtue " to " respectively "; and subsections (4), (5), (6) and (8). Section 2. Section 4(1) to (4), but without prejudice to subsection (5). Schedule 1. In Schedule 2, in paragraph 1 the words " by the commission of the peace " and the words " by the commission "; paragraph 3 from the beginning to " and accordingly "; and paragraph 4 from " but " onwards. In Schedule 3, Part II. Schedule 4.
1972 c. 70.	The Local Government Act 1972.	In section 217, subsection (1) from the beginning to "county and ", subsections (4) and (6), and in subsection (7) the words from " and to transfer " to " Crown Court ". In Schedule 27, paragraphs 2, 3, 4 and 11.

PART III

COUNTY COURT JURISDICTION

Chapter	Short Title	Extent of Repeal
7 & 8 Eliz. 2. c. 22.	The County Courts Act 1959.	In section 192(2) (as substituted by the Administration of Justice Act 1969) paragraph (*a*) from " except " onwards.
1963 c. 5.	The County Courts (Jurisdiction) Act 1963.	The whole Act.
1969 c. 58.	The Administration of Justice Act 1969.	In section 10(2), in section 192(2) of the County Courts Act 1959 as there set out, paragraph (*a*) from " except " onwards.

PART IV

JUDICIAL SALARIES

Chapter	Short Title	Extent of Repeal
5 & 6 Eliz. 2. c. 46.	The Judicial Offices (Salaries and Pensions) Act 1957.	The whole Act.
1965 c. 61.	The Judges' Remuneration Act 1965.	The whole Act.
1967 c. 28.	The Superannuation (Miscellaneous Provisions) Act 1967.	Section 3(4)(*a*)(i).
1970 c. 31.	The Administration of Justice Act 1970.	In Schedule 2, paragraph 25.

PART V
JUDICIAL PENSIONS

Chapter	Short Title	Extent of Repeal
39 & 40 Vict. c. 59.	The Appellate Jurisdiction Act 1876.	Section 7.
40 & 41 Vict. c. 57.	The Supreme Court of Judicature Act (Ireland) 1877.	Sections 19 and 20.
15 & 16 Geo. 5. c. 49.	The Supreme Court of Judicature (Consolidation) Act 1925.	Sections 14 and 15.
15 & 16 Geo. 6 and 1 Eliz. 2. c. 12.	The Judicial Offices (Salaries, etc.) Act 1952.	Section 5(1)(*a*) and (*c*).
8 & 9 Eliz. 2. c. 9.	The Judicial Pensions Act 1959.	Section 1, except as regards pensions payable under the Judges' Pensions (Scotland) Act 1808. Section 2(2) except as aforesaid. In Schedule 1 the entries in column 2, except that for the Judges' Pensions (Scotland) Act 1808. Schedule 2, except the entry for the Judges' Pensions (Scotland) Act 1808.

PART VI
DEPUTY DISTRICT AND COUNTY COURT REGISTRARS

Chapter	Short Title	Extent of Repeal
15 & 16 Geo. 5. c. 49.	The Supreme Court of Judicature (Consolidation) Act 1925.	In section 84, subsection (4), in subsection (5) the words "and provisional district registrar", subsection (6) and in subsection (7) the words "and provisional district registrar" and the words "or the provisional district registrar".
4 & 5 Eliz. 2. c. 46.	The Administration of Justice Act 1956.	In section 11, subsection (1) from "but" onwards and subsections (2) to (7).
7 & 8 Eliz. 2. c. 22.	The County Courts Act 1959.	Section 27. In section 29, the subsection (1A) inserted by the Administration of Justice Act 1970.
1970 c. 31.	The Administration of Justice Act 1970.	Section 46.

ELIZABETH II

Education Act 1973

1973 CHAPTER 16

An Act to make provision for terminating and in part replacing the powers possessed by the Secretary of State for Education and Science and the Secretary of State for Wales under the Charities Act 1960 concurrently with the Charity Commissioners or under the Endowed Schools Acts 1869 to 1948, and enlarging certain other powers of modifying educational trusts, and for supplementing awards under section 1 and restricting awards under section 2 of the Education Act 1962, and for purposes connected therewith. [18th April 1973]

B E IT ENACTED by the Queen's most Excellent Majesty, by and with the advice and consent of the Lords Spiritual and Temporal, and Commons, in this present Parliament assembled, and by the authority of the same, as follows:—

Educational trusts

General provisions as to educational trusts.

1960 c. 58.

1.—(1) There shall cease to have effect—

(*a*) section 2 of the Charities Act 1960 (by which, as originally enacted, the powers of the Charity Commissioners were made exercisable concurrently by the Minister of Education) ; and

(*b*) the Endowed Schools Acts 1869 to 1948 (which made provision for the modernisation of educational trusts by schemes settled and approved in accordance with those Acts).

(2) The Secretary of State may by order—

(a) make such modifications of any trust deed or other instrument relating to a school as, after consultation with the managers, governors or other proprietor of the school, appear to him to be requisite in consequence of any proposals approved or order made by him under section 13 or 16 of the Education Act 1944 (which 1944 c. 31. relate to the establishment of and changes affecting schools) ; and

(b) make such modifications of any trust deed or other instrument relating to a school as, after consultation with the governors or other proprietor of the school, appear to him to be requisite to enable the governors or proprietor to meet any requirement imposed by regulations under section 33 of the Education Act 1944 (which relates in particular to the approval of schools as special schools) ; and

(c) make such modifications of any trust deed or other instrument relating to or regulating any institution that provides or is concerned in the provision of educational services, or is concerned in educational research, as, after consultation with the persons responsible for the management of the institution, appear to him to be requisite to enable them to fulfil any condition or meet any requirement imposed by regulations under section 100 of the Education Act 1944 (which authorises the making of grants in aid of educational services or research) ;

and any modification made by an order under this subsection may be made to have permanent effect or to have effect for such period as may be specified in the order.

This subsection shall be construed, and the Education Acts 1944 to 1971 shall have effect, as if this subsection were contained in the Education Act 1944.

(3) In connection with the operation of this section there shall have effect the transitional and other consequential or supplementary provisions contained in Schedule 1 to this Act.

(4) The enactments mentioned in Schedule 2 to this Act (which includes in Part I certain enactments already spent or otherwise no longer required apart from the foregoing provisions of this section) are hereby repealed to the extent specified in column 3 of the Schedule.

(5) Subsection (1)(a) above and Part III of Schedule 2 to this Act shall not come into force until such date as may be appointed by order made by statutory instrument by the Secretary of State.

Special powers as to certain trusts for religious education.

2.—(1) Where the premises of a voluntary school have ceased (before or after the coming into force of this section) to be used for a voluntary school, or in the opinion of the Secretary of State it is likely they will cease to be so used, then subject to subsections (2) to (4) below he may by order made by statutory instrument make new provision as to the use of any endowment shown to his satisfaction to be or have been held wholly or partly for or in connection with the provision at the school of religious education in accordance with the tenets of a particular religious denomination; and for purposes of this section "endowment" includes property not subject to any restriction on the expenditure of capital.

(2) No order shall be made under subsection (1) above except on the application of the persons appearing to the Secretary of State to be the appropriate authority of the denomination concerned; and the Secretary of State shall, not less than one month before making an order under that subsection, give notice of the proposed order and of the right of persons interested to make representations on it, and shall take into account any representations that may be made to him by any person interested therein before the order is made; and the notice shall be given—

(a) by giving to any persons appearing to the Secretary of State to be trustees of an endowment affected by the proposed order a notice of the proposal to make it, together with a draft or summary of the provisions proposed to be included; and

(b) by publishing in such manner as the Secretary of State thinks sufficient for informing any other persons interested a notice of the proposal to make the order and of the place where any person interested may (during a period of not less than a month) inspect such a draft or summary, and by keeping a draft or summary available for inspection in accordance with the notice.

(3) An order under subsection (1) above may require or authorise the disposal by sale or otherwise of any land or other property forming part of an endowment affected by the order, including the premises of the school and any teacher's dwelling-house; and in the case of land liable to revert under the third proviso to section 2 of the School Sites Act 1841 the Secretary of State may by order exclude the operation of that proviso, if he is satisfied either—

1841 c. 38.

(a) that the person to whom the land would revert in accordance with the proviso cannot after due enquiry be found; or

(b) that, if that person can be found, he has consented to relinquish his rights in relation to the land under the proviso and that, if he has consented so to do in consideration of the payment of a sum of money to him, adequate provision can be made for the payment to him of that sum out of the proceeds of disposal of the land.

(4) Subject to subsection (3) above and to any provision affecting the endowments of any public general Act of Parliament, an order under subsection (1) above shall establish and give effect, with a view to enabling the denomination concerned to participate more effectively in the administration of the statutory system of public education, to a scheme or schemes for the endowments dealt with by the order to be used for appropriate educational purposes, either in connection with voluntary schools or partly in connection with voluntary schools and partly in other ways related to the locality served or formerly served by the voluntary school at the premises that have gone or are to go out of use for such a school ; and for this purpose " use for appropriate educational purposes " means use for educational purposes in connection with the provision of religious education in accordance with the tenets of the denomination concerned.

(5) A scheme given effect under this section may provide for the retention of the capital of any endowment and application of the accruing income or may authorise the application or expenditure of capital to such extent and subject to such conditions as may be determined by or in accordance with the scheme ; and any such scheme may provide for the endowments thereby dealt with or any part of them to be added to any existing endowment applicable for any such purpose as is authorised for the scheme by subsection (4) above.

(6) An order under subsection (1) above may include any such incidental or supplementary provisions as appear to the Secretary of State to be necessary or expedient either for the bringing into force or for the operation of any scheme thereby established, including in particular provisions for the appointment and powers of trustees of the property comprised in the scheme or, if the property is not all applicable for the same purposes, of any part of that property, and for the property or any part of it to vest by virtue of the scheme in the first trustees under the scheme or trustees of any endowment to which it is to be added or, if not so vested, to be transferred to them.

(7) Any order under this section shall have effect notwithstanding any Act of Parliament (not being a public general Act), letters patent or other instrument relating to, or trust affecting, the endowments dealt with by the order ; but section 15(3) of the Charities Act 1960 (by virtue of which the court 1960 c. 58. and the Charity Commissioners may exercise their jurisdiction in relation to charities mentioned in Schedule 4 to the Act notwithstanding that the charities are governed by the Acts or

statutory schemes there mentioned) shall have effect as if at the end of paragraph 1 (*b*) of Schedule 4 to the Act there were added the words "or by schemes given effect under section 2 of the Education Act 1973."

(8) This section shall apply where the premises of a non-provided public elementary school ceased before 1st April 1945 to be used for such a school as it applies where the premises of a voluntary school have ceased to be used for a voluntary school.

1944 c. 31.

(9) This section shall be construed, and the Education Acts 1944 to 1971 shall have effect, as if this section were contained in the Education Act 1944.

Awards

Supplementation by Secretary of State, in special cases, of certain awards by local education authority.

1962 c. 12.

3.—(1) The Secretary of State may by regulations make provision for the payment by him, to persons on whom awards have been bestowed by a local education authority under section 1 of the Education Act 1962 (awards for first degree university courses and comparable courses in the United Kingdom), of an allowance in respect of a wife, husband or child for the purpose of enabling those persons to take advantage without hardship of their awards in cases where, in accordance with the regulations having effect under that section, account may not be taken of the wife, husband or child in determining the payments to be made by the authority in pursuance of the award.

(2) The amount of an allowance payable by virtue of this section to the holder of an award in respect of a wife, husband or child shall not exceed the amount by which the payments to be made by the local education authority in pursuance of the award would have been increased if the case had fallen within the provision made with respect to a wife, husband or child by the regulations having effect under section 1 of the Education Act 1962.

(3) Regulations under this section may make different provision for different cases; and the power of the Secretary of State to make regulations under this section shall be exercisable by statutory instrument which shall be subject to annulment in pursuance of a resolution of either House of Parliament.

(4) Any expenses incurred by the Secretary of State in the payment of allowances under this section shall be defrayed out of moneys provided by Parliament.

(5) In this section references to a person's child include that person's stepchild or illegitimate child and a child adopted by that person (alone or jointly with another) in pursuance of an order made by any court in the United Kingdom, the Isle of Man or the Channel Islands or by an adoption specified as an overseas adoption by order of the Secretary of State under

1968 c. 53.

section 4 of the Adoption Act 1968.

4.—(1) Section 2(1) of the Education Act 1962 (powers of local education authorities to bestow awards on persons over compulsory school age attending certain courses in Great Britain or elsewhere) shall not apply to such courses at universities, colleges or other institutions as may for the time being be designated by or under regulations made by the Secretary of State for the purposes of this section as being postgraduate courses or comparable to postgraduate courses.

Exclusion of postgraduate courses from grants under section 2(1) of Education Act 1962.
1962 c. 12.

(2) The power of the Secretary of State to make regulations under this section shall be exercisable by statutory instrument, which shall be subject to annulment in pursuance of a resolution of either House of Parliament.

Supplementary

5.—(1) This Act may be cited as the Education Act 1973, and the Education Acts 1944 to 1971 and this Act may be cited together as the Education Acts 1944 to 1973.

Citation and extent.

(2) Nothing in this Act extends to Scotland or to Northern Ireland.

SCHEDULES

SCHEDULE 1

TRANSITIONAL AND SUPPLEMENTARY PROVISIONS AS TO CHARITIES ETC.

1960 c. 58.

1.—(1) In section 43 of the Charities Act 1960, in its application to regulations made on or after the appointed day, there shall be substituted for subsection (1)—

" (1) Save as otherwise provided by this Act, any power to make regulations which is conferred by this Act shall be exercisable by the Secretary of State " ;

and in subsection (3) for the words (as originally enacted) " the Secretary of State or the Minister of Education " there shall be substituted the words " or the Secretary of State ".

1972 c. 70.

(2) Section 210(3) of the Local Government Act 1972 (which makes special provision for certain charitable property to vest in local education authorities, if it is held for purposes of a charity registered in a part of the charities register maintained by the Secretary of State by virtue of section 2 of the Charities Act 1960) shall have effect, unless the appointed day is later than the end of March 1974, as if the reference to a charity registered in a part of the register which is maintained by the Secretary of State were a reference to a charity so registered immediately before the appointed day.

(3) Any register, books and documents which on the appointed day are in the possession or custody of the Secretary of State for Education and Science, or of the Secretary of State for Wales, and which in his opinion he requires no longer by reason of the repeal of section 2(1) of the Charities Act 1960, shall be transferred to the Charity Commissioners.

(4) The repeal by this Act of section 2(1) of the Charities Act 1960 shall not affect the operation of section 2(1)—

(a) in conferring on the Charity Commissioners functions belonging at the passing of that Act to the Minister of Education ; or

(b) in extending to the Charity Commissioners references to the Secretary of State for Education and Science or the Secretary of State for Wales (or references having effect as if either of them were mentioned) so as to enable the Commissioners to discharge any such functions as aforesaid or to act under or for the purposes of the trusts of a charity ;

but on the appointed day any functions so conferred and any reference so extended shall, subject to sub-paragraph (5) below, cease to be functions of or to extend to either Secretary of State.

(5) Where it appears to the Secretary of State for Education and Science or the Secretary of State for Wales that any reference which, in accordance with sub-paragraph (4) above would on the appointed day cease to extend to him, is not related (or not wholly

related) to the functions ceasing to belong to him by the repeal
of section 2(1) of the Charities Act 1960, he may by order made at 1960 c. 58.
any time, whether before the appointed day or not, exclude the
operation of that sub-paragraph in relation to the reference and make
such modifications of the relevant instrument as appear to him
appropriate in the circumstances.

(6) The repeal of section 2(1) of the Charities Act 1960 shall
not affect the validity of anything done (or having effect as if done)
before the appointed day by or in relation to the Secretary of State
for Education and Science or the Secretary of State for Wales, and
anything so done (or having effect as if so done) in so far as it
could by virtue of section 2(1) have been done by or in relation to
the Charity Commissioners shall thereafter have effect as if done by
or in relation to them.

(7) In this paragraph " appointed day " means the day appointed
under section 1(5) of this Act.

2.—(1) Where before the passing of this Act a scheme under
the Endowed Schools Acts 1869 to 1948 has been published as
required by section 13 of the Endowed Schools Act 1873, the scheme 1873 c. 86.
may be proceeded with as if section 1 of this Act had not been
passed.

(2) Where before the passing of this Act a draft scheme under the
Endowed Schools Acts 1869 to 1948 has been prepared in a case in
which effect might be given to the scheme by order under section
2 of this Act, and the draft scheme has been published as required
by section 33 of the Endowed Schools Act 1869, the scheme may be 1869 c. 56.
proceeded with in pursuance of section 2 of this Act as if section
2(2)(*a*) and (*b*) had been complied with on the date this Act is
passed.

3. The repeals made by this Act in sections 17 and 100 of the
Education Act 1944 shall not affect any order made by virtue of 1944 c. 31.
the provisions repealed, or the operation in relation to any such
order of section 111 of that Act (which relates to the revocation
and variation of orders).

SCHEDULE 2

REPEALS

PART I

REPEALS OF SPENT ETC. ENACTMENTS

Chapter	Short Title	Extent of Repeal
8 & 9 Geo. 5. c. 39.	The Education Act 1918.	Section 14. In section 47, the words from " except " to " direct " and the words from " and the Board " onwards. Section 52(1) from the first " and " onwards.
7 & 8 Geo. 6. c. 31.	The Education Act 1944.	Section 119. Section 121, except proviso (*a*). Schedule 9.
1 & 2 Eliz. 2. c. 33.	The Education (Miscellaneous Provisions) Act 1953.	Section 14. Section 17(2). Schedule 2.
2 & 3 Eliz. 2. c. 70.	The Mines and Quarries Act 1954.	In section 166 the words " section 14 of the Education Act 1918 ", and the words " the said section 14 ". In Schedule 4 the entry relating to the Education Act 1918.
8 & 9 Eliz. 2. c. 58.	The Charities Act 1960.	Section 4(10). Section 38(1) and (2). Section 39(1). Section 44(3). Section 48(2). Section 49(3). In Schedule 1, paragraph 1(6) and paragraph 2(3). Schedule 5. In Schedule 6 the entry for the Reorganisation Areas Measure 1944. Schedule 7.
9 & 10 Eliz. 2. c. 34.	The Factories Act 1961.	In section 167 the words " section 14 of the Education Act 1918 ".
1963 c. 33.	The London Government Act 1963.	In section 81, subsections (1) to (8) (but not so as to alter the charity trustees of any charity) and subsection (10).

PART II

GENERAL

Chapter	Short Title	Extent of repeal
32 & 33 Vict. c. 56.	The Endowed Schools Act 1869.	The whole Act.
36 & 37 Vict. c. 86.	The Endowed Schools Act 1873.	The whole Act.
12 & 13 Geo. 5. c. 50.	The Expiring Laws Continuance Act 1922.	In Schedule 1, the entry for the Endowed Schools Act 1869.
7 & 8 Geo. 6. c. 31.	The Education Act 1944.	In section 17(6) (as added by the Education Act 1968) the words from " or such modifications " to " trust deed ". Section 86. Section 100(4).
11 & 12 Geo. 6. c. 40.	The Education (Miscellaneous Provisions) Act 1948.	Section 2. In section 11(1) the words from the first " and " to the following " Schedule ". In section 14, in subsection (2) the words from " (except " to the following " 1908) " and the words from " and the said " onwards, and in subsection (3) the words from " (other " to the following " provisions) " and the words from " and the said " onwards. In Schedule 1, Part II.
8 & 9 Eliz. 2. c. 58.	The Charities Act 1960.	Section 2(4).
1968 c. 17	The Education Act 1968.	In Schedule 1, in paragraph 2, the words from " or such modifications " to " trust deed ".

Church Assembly Measure

1967 No. 2.	The Extra-Parochial Ministry Measure 1967.	In section 2(5), the words " and section 53 of the Endowed Schools Act 1869 " and the words " and endowed ".

PART III

REPEALS RELATING TO CHARITIES

Chapter	Short Title	Extent of Repeal
10 & 11 Geo. 6. c. 44.	The Crown Proceedings Act 1947.	Section 23(3)(*e*).
8 & 9 Eliz. 2. c. 58.	The Charities Act 1960.	Section 2(1), (2), (3) and (5). Section 3(8). In section 4(8) the words " or of the Minister of Education ". In section 10(6) the words " and to the Minister of Education ". Section 18(13). Section 19(9). Section 20(11). Section 22(12). In section 44, in subsection (1)(*b*) the words " the Minister of Education " and in subsection (2) the words " by the Minister of Education or ". In Schedule 6, in the entry relating to section 31 of the New Parishes Measure 1943 the words " or Minister of Education ".
1969 c. 22.	The Redundant Churches and other Religious Buildings Act 1969.	In section 4, in subsection (3) the words " and the Secretary of State for Education and Science " and in subsection (4) the words " and (13) ".

Church Assembly Measures

6 & 7 Geo. 6. No. 1.	The New Parishes Measure 1943.	In section 31 the words " or of the Board of Education " and the words " or Minister of Education " inserted by the Charities Act 1960.
1968 No. 1.	The Pastoral Measure 1968.	Section 90(3).

Northern Ireland Assembly Act 1973

1973 CHAPTER 17

An Act to establish a Northern Ireland Assembly and to provide for election to that Assembly. [3rd May 1973]

BE IT ENACTED by the Queen's most Excellent Majesty, by and with the advice and consent of the Lords Spiritual and Temporal, and Commons, in this present Parliament assembled, and by the authority of the same, as follows:—

1.—(1) There shall be a Northern Ireland Assembly which shall consist of 78 members.

The Northern Ireland Assembly.

(2) Those members shall be returned for the constituencies in Northern Ireland which would return members to the Parliament of the United Kingdom if a general election were held at the passing of this Act, and the number of members returned by each constituency shall be that specified for the constituency in the second column of the Schedule to this Act.

(3) The first meeting of the Assembly shall be held on such day, and at such time and place, as the Secretary of State may by order direct.

(4) The proceedings of the Assembly shall not be invalid because of any vacancy in their membership.

(5) There shall be paid to each member of the Assembly—

(a) a salary at the rate of £2,500 a year, beginning with the date on which he is returned as a member of the Assembly, and

(b) an allowance to defray expenses incurred by him on secretarial assistance in carrying out his duties as a member.

The said allowance for the twelve months beginning with the date on which the member is returned shall not exceed £600.

(6) For the purposes of subsection (5) above any salary paid for any period to the member in respect of his membership of the House of Commons, or of the Senate, of the Parliament of Northern Ireland shall be treated as if paid on account of any sum due under subsection (5)(*a*) above for the same period.

The election.　2.—(1) The date of the poll for the election of members of the Assembly shall be appointed by the Secretary of State by order contained in a statutory instrument.

(2) The persons entitled to vote on that poll shall be those who would be entitled to vote on polls held on that date at a general election to the Parliament of Northern Ireland.

(3) Each vote in the poll shall be a single transferable vote, that is to say a vote—

 (*a*) capable of being given so as to indicate the voter's order of preference for the candidates for election as members for the constituency, and

 (*b*) capable of being transferred to the next choice—

  (i) when the vote is not required to give a prior choice the necessary quota of votes, or

  (ii) when, owing to the deficiency in the number of votes given for a prior choice, that choice is eliminated from the list of candidates.

(4) Every candidate at the election under this Act shall, in accordance with the provisions of an order under the following provisions of this section, make a deposit of £150, and the deposit shall be forfeited unless the candidate is elected, or the number of votes credited to him at any one or more of the stages of counting the votes exceeds a quarter of the quota needed to elect him.

(5) The Secretary of State shall have power by order to make any provision concerning the election under this Act, or any matter relating to the election, and in particular provision concerning—

 (*a*) the intervals between the stages of the election,

 (*b*) the form of declaration to be made by a candidate, the contents of nomination papers, and the taking of the poll,

 (*c*) the method of voting, and the method of counting and transferring votes,

 (*d*) the procedure on the death of a candidate,

 (*e*) the questioning of elections, and

 (*f*) corrupt and illegal practices, and the disqualifications to be imposed, in any part of the United Kingdom, for a corrupt or illegal practice in the election under this Act.

(6) An order made under subsection (5) above—

(a) may include any supplemental or incidental provisions, including provisions creating criminal offences,

(b) may apply, with any modifications or exceptions specified in the order, any of the provisions of the Electoral Law 1962 c. 14 Act (Northern Ireland) 1962 or of any instrument made (N.I.). or having effect under that Act,

(c) shall be contained in a statutory instrument subject to annulment in pursuance of a resolution of either House of Parliament.

3.—(1) Subject to the provisions of this section, a person is Disqualifica-
disqualified for membership of the Assembly— tion for
membership
(a) if he is disqualified for membership of the Commons of Assembly.
House of the Parliament of the United Kingdom otherwise than by section 1(1)(*f*) of the House of Commons 1957 c. 20.
Disqualification Act 1957, or

(b) if he is disqualified for membership of the Commons House of the Parliament of Northern Ireland by the said section 1(1)(*f*) of the House of Commons Dis-qualification Act 1957 (taken together with section 10 of, and Schedule 3 to, that Act).

(2) A person shall not be disqualified from being a member of the Assembly by reason only that he is a peer, whether of the United Kingdom, Great Britain, England, Scotland or Ireland.

(3) The Secretary of State shall have power by order to make provision—

(a) for the consequences of a disqualification imposed by this section, and

(b) for the circumstances in which such a disqualification may be disregarded, and

(c) for conferring jurisdiction to decide whether a dis-qualification has been imposed by this section.

(4) An order made under subsection (3) above—

(a) may include any supplemental or incidental provisions,

(b) may apply, with any modifications or exceptions specified in the order, any of the provisions of section 6 or section 7 of the House of Commons Disqualification Act 1957,

(c) shall be contained in a statutory instrument subject to annulment in pursuance of a resolution of either House of Parliament.

F

Financial
provisions.

4.—(1) Salaries or allowances payable under this Act for members of the Assembly shall be defrayed out of money provided by Parliament.

(2) Any costs incurred by a government department (including a government department of the Government of Northern Ireland) in connection with the election under this Act shall be paid out of the Consolidated Fund, and any forfeited deposit or other sum received by such a government department in connection with the election under this Act shall be paid into the Consolidated Fund.

Short title and
supplemental
provisions.

5.—(1) This Act may be cited as the Northern Ireland Assembly Act 1973.

(2) Any power of making orders conferred by this Act shall include a power to vary or revoke orders so made.

(3) In this Act—

(*a*) references to any enactment include references to that enactment as amended or extended by or under any enactment, including this Act, and

(*b*) " enactment " includes an Act of the Parliament of Northern Ireland.

SCHEDULE

MEMBERS TO BE RETURNED BY CONSTITUENCIES

Constituency	Number of Members to be returned
East Belfast	6
North Belfast	6
South Belfast	6
West Belfast	6
North Antrim	7
South Antrim	8
Armagh	7
North Down	7
South Down	7
Fermanagh and South Tyrone	5
Londonderry	7
Mid Ulster	6

Matrimonial Causes Act 1973

1973 CHAPTER 18

An Act to consolidate certain enactments relating to matrimonial proceedings, maintenance agreements, and declarations of legitimacy, validity of marriage and British nationality, with amendments to give effect to recommendations of the Law Commission.

[23rd May 1973]

BE IT ENACTED by the Queen's most Excellent Majesty, by and with the advice and consent of the Lords Spiritual and Temporal, and Commons, in this present Parliament assembled, and by the authority of the same, as follows:—

PART I

DIVORCE, NULLITY AND OTHER MATRIMONIAL SUITS

Divorce

1.—(1) Subject to section 3 below, a petition for divorce may be presented to the court by either party to a marriage on the ground that the marriage has broken down irretrievably.

Divorce on breakdown of marriage.

(2) The court hearing a petition for divorce shall not hold the marriage to have broken down irretrievably unless the petitioner satisfies the court of one or more of the following facts, that is to say—

    (*a*) that the respondent has committed adultery and the petitioner finds it intolerable to live with the respondent;

F 3

(b) that the respondent has behaved in such a way that the petitioner cannot reasonably be expected to live with the respondent ;

(c) that the respondent has deserted the petitioner for a continuous period of at least two years immediately preceding the presentation of the petition ;

(d) that the parties to the marriage have lived apart for a continuous period of at least two years immediately preceding the presentation of the petition (hereafter in this Act referred to as " two years' separation ") and the respondent consents to a decree being granted ;

(e) that the parties to the marriage have lived apart for a continuous period of at least five years immediately preceding the presentation of the petition (hereafter in this Act referred to as " five years' separation ").

(3) On a petition for divorce it shall be the duty of the court to inquire, so far as it reasonably can, into the facts alleged by the petitioner and into any facts alleged by the respondent.

(4) If the court is satisfied on the evidence of any such fact as is mentioned in subsection (2) above, then, unless it is satisfied on all the evidence that the marriage has not broken down irretrievably, it shall, subject to sections 3(3) and 5 below, grant a decree of divorce.

(5) Every decree of divorce shall in the first instance be a decree nisi and shall not be made absolute before the expiration of six months from its grant unless the High Court by general order from time to time fixes a shorter period, or unless in any particular case the court in which the proceedings are for the time being pending from time to time by special order fixes a shorter period than the period otherwise applicable for the time being by virtue of this subsection.

Supplemental provisions as to facts raising presumption of breakdown.

2.—(1) One party to a marriage shall not be entitled to rely for the purposes of section 1(2)(a) above on adultery committed by the other if, after it became known to him that the other had committed that adultery, the parties have lived with each other for a period exceeding, or periods together exceeding, six months.

(2) Where the parties to a marriage have lived with each other after it became known to one party that the other had committed adultery, but subsection (1) above does not apply, in any proceedings for divorce in which the petitioner relies

on that adultery the fact that the parties have lived with each other after that time shall be disregarded in determining for the purposes of section 1(2)(*a*) above whether the petitioner finds it intolerable to live with the respondent.

(3) Where in any proceedings for divorce the petitioner alleges that the respondent has behaved in such a way that the petitioner cannot reasonably be expected to live with him, but the parties to the marriage have lived with each other for a period or periods after the date of the occurence of the final incident relied on by the petitioner and held by the court to support his allegation, that fact shall be disregarded in determining for the purposes of section 1(2)(*b*) above whether the petitioner cannot reasonably be expected to live with the respondent if the length of that period or of those periods together was six months or less.

(4) For the purposes of section 1(2)(*c*) above the court may treat a period of desertion as having continued at a time when the deserting party was incapable of continuing the necessary intention if the evidence before the court is such that, had that party not been so incapable, the court would have inferred that his desertion continued at that time.

(5) In considering for the purposes of section 1(2) above whether the period for which the respondent has deserted the petitioner or the period for which the parties to a marriage have lived apart has been continuous, no account shall be taken of any one period (not exceeding six months) or of any two or more periods (not exceeding six months in all) during which the parties resumed living with each other, but no period during which the parties lived with each other shall count as part of the period of desertion or of the period for which the parties to the marriage lived apart, as the case may be.

(6) For the purposes of section 1(2)(*d*) and (*e*) above and this section a husband and wife shall be treated as living apart unless they are living with each other in the same household, and references in this section to the parties to a marriage living with each other shall be construed as references to their living with each other in the same household.

(7) Provision shall be made by rules of court for the purpose of ensuring that where in pursuance of section 1(2)(*d*) above the petitioner alleges that the respondent consents to a decree being granted the respondent has been given such information as will enable him to understand the consequences to him of his consenting to a decree being granted and the steps which he must take to indicate that he consents to the grant of a decree.

PART I
Restriction on
petitions for
divorce
within three
years of
marriage.

3.—(1) Subject to subsection (2) below, no petition for divorce shall be presented to the court before the expiration of the period of three years from the date of the marriage (hereafter in this section referred to as " the specified period ").

(2) A judge of the court may, on an application made to him, allow the presentation of a petition for divorce within the specified period on the ground that the case is one of exceptional hardship suffered by the petitioner or of exceptional depravity on the part of the respondent ; but in determining the application the judge shall have regard to the interests of any child of the family and to the question whether there is reasonable probability of a reconciliation between the parties during the specified period.

(3) If it appears to the court, at the hearing of a petition for divorce presented in pursuance of leave granted under subsection (2) above, that the leave was obtained by the petitioner by any misrepresentation or concealment of the nature of the case, the court may—

    (a) dismiss the petition, without prejudice to any petition which may be brought after the expiration of the specified period upon the same facts, or substantially the same facts, as those proved in support of the dismissed petition ; or

    (b) if it grants a decree, direct that no application to make the decree absolute shall be made during the specified period.

(4) Nothing in this section shall be deemed to prohibit the presentation of a petition based upon matters which occurred before the expiration of the specified period.

Divorce not
precluded
by previous
judicial
separation.

1960 c. 48.

4.—(1) A person shall not be prevented from presenting a petition for divorce, or the court from granting a decree of divorce, by reason only that the petitioner or respondent has at any time, on the same facts or substantially the same facts as those proved in support of the petition, been granted a decree of judicial separation or an order under, or having effect as if made under, the Matrimonial Proceedings (Magistrates' Courts) Act 1960 or any corresponding enactments in force in Northern Ireland, the Isle of Man or any of the Channel Islands.

(2) On a petition for divorce in such a case as is mentioned in subsection (1) above, the court may treat the decree or order as sufficient proof of any adultery, desertion or other fact by reference to which it was granted, but shall not grant a decree of divorce without receiving evidence from the petitioner.

(3) Where a petition for divorce in such a case follows a decree of judicial separation or an order containing a provision exempting one party to the marriage from the obligation to cohabit with the other, for the purposes of that petition a period of desertion immediately preceding the institution of the proceedings for the decree or order shall, if the parties have not resumed cohabitation and the decree or order has been continuously in force since it was granted, be deemed immediately to precede the presentation of the petition.

5.—(1) The respondent to a petition for divorce in which the petitioner alleges five years' separation may oppose the grant of a decree on the ground that the dissolution of the marriage will result in grave financial or other hardship to him and that it would in all the circumstances be wrong to dissolve the marriage.

(2) Where the grant of a decree is opposed by virtue of this section, then—

> (a) if the court finds that the petitioner is entitled to rely in support of his petition on the fact of five years' separation and makes no such finding as to any other fact mentioned in section 1(2) above, and

> (b) if apart from this section the court would grant a decree on the petition,

the court shall consider all the circumstances, including the conduct of the parties to the marriage and the interests of those parties and of any children or other persons concerned, and if of opinion that the dissolution of the marriage will result in grave financial or other hardship to the respondent and that it would in all the circumstances be wrong to dissolve the marriage it shall dismiss the petition.

(3) For the purposes of this section hardship shall include the loss of the chance of acquiring any benefit which the respondent might acquire if the marriage were not dissolved.

6.—(1) Provision shall be made by rules of court for requiring the solicitor acting for a petitioner for divorce to certify whether he has discussed with the petitioner the possibility of a reconciliation and given him the names and addresses of persons qualified to help effect a reconciliation between parties to a marriage who have become estranged.

(2) If at any stage of proceedings for divorce it appears to the court that there is a reasonable possibility of a reconciliation between the parties to the marriage, the court may

PART I   adjourn the proceedings for such period as it thinks fit to enable attempts to be made to effect such a reconciliation.

The power conferred by the foregoing provision is additional to any other power of the court to adjourn proceedings.

Consideration by the court of certain agreements or arrangements.

7. Provision may be made by rules of court for enabling the parties to a marriage, or either of them, on application made either before or after the presentation of a petition for divorce, to refer to the court any agreement or arrangement made or proposed to be made between them, being an agreement or arrangement which relates to, arises out of, or is connected with, the proceedings for divorce which are contemplated or, as the case may be, have begun, and for enabling the court to express an opinion, should it think it desirable to do so, as to the reasonableness of the agreement or arrangement and to give such directions, if any, in the matter as it thinks fit.

Intervention of Queen's Proctor.

8.—(1) In the case of a petition for divorce—

(a) the court may, if it thinks fit, direct all necessary papers in the matter to be sent to the Queen's Proctor, who shall under the directions of the Attorney-General instruct counsel to argue before the court any question in relation to the matter which the court considers it necessary or expedient to have fully argued ;

(b) any person may at any time during the progress of the proceedings or before the decree nisi is made absolute give information to the Queen's Proctor on any matter material to the due decision of the case, and the Queen's Proctor may thereupon take such steps as the Attorney-General considers necessary or expedient.

(2) Where the Queen's Proctor intervenes or shows cause against a decree nisi in any proceedings for divorce, the court may make such order as may be just as to the payment by other parties to the proceedings of the costs incurred by him in so doing or as to the payment by him of any costs incurred by any of those parties by reason of his so doing.

(3) The Queen's Proctor shall be entitled to charge as part of the expenses of his office—

(a) the costs of any proceedings under subsection (1)(a) above ;

(b) where his reasonable costs of intervening or showing cause as mentioned in subsection (2) above are not fully satisfied by any order under that subsection, the amount of the difference ;

(c) if the Treasury so directs, any costs which he pays to any parties under an order made under subsection (2).

9.—(1) Where a decree of divorce has been granted but not made absolute, then, without prejudice to section 8 above, any person (excluding a party to the proceedings other than the Queen's Proctor) may show cause why the decree should not be made absolute by reason of material facts not having been brought before the court ; and in such a case the court may—

(a) notwithstanding anything in section 1(5) above (but subject to sections 10(2) to (4) and 41 below) make the decree absolute ; or

(b) rescind the decree ; or

(c) require further inquiry ; or

(d) otherwise deal with the case as it thinks fit.

(2) Where a decree of divorce has been granted and no application for it to be made absolute has been made by the party to whom it was granted, then, at any time after the expiration of three months from the earliest date on which that party could have made such an application, the party against whom it was granted may make an application to the court, and on that application the court may exercise any of the powers mentioned in paragraphs (a) to (d) of subsection (1) above.

10.—(1) Where in any case the court has granted a decree of divorce on the basis of a finding that the petitioner was entitled to rely in support of his petition on the fact of two years' separation coupled with the respondent's consent to a decree being granted and has made no such finding as to any other fact mentioned in section 1(2) above, the court may, on an application made by the respondent at any time before the decree is made absolute, rescind the decree if it is satisfied that the petitioner misled the respondent (whether intentionally or unintentionally) about any matter which the respondent took into account in deciding to give his consent.

(2) The following provisions of this section apply where—

(a) the respondent to a petition for divorce in which the petitioner alleged two years' or five years' separation coupled, in the former case, with the respondent's consent to a decree being granted, has applied to the court for consideration under subsection (3) below of his financial position after the divorce ; and

(b) the court has granted a decree on the petition on the basis of a finding that the petitioner was entitled to rely in support of his petition on the fact of two years' or five years' separation (as the case may be) and has made no such finding as to any other fact mentioned in section 1(2) above.

(3) The court hearing an application by the respondent under subsection (2) above shall consider all the circumstances, including the age, health, conduct, earning capacity, financial resources and financial obligations of each of the parties, and the financial position of the respondent as, having regard to the divorce, it is likely to be after the death of the petitioner should the petitioner die first; and, subject to subsection (4) below, the court shall not make the decree absolute unless it is satisfied—

    (a) that the petitioner should not be required to make any financial provision for the respondent, or

    (b) that the financial provision made by the petitioner for the respondent is reasonable and fair or the best that can be made in the circumstances.

(4) The court may if it thinks fit makes the decree absolute notwithstanding the requirements of subsection (3) above if—

    (a) it appears that there are circumstances making it desirable that the decree should be made absolute without delay, and

    (b) the court has obtained a satisfactory undertaking from the petitioner that he will make such financial provision for the respondent as the court may approve.

Nullity

Grounds on which a marriage is void.

11. A marriage celebrated after 31st July 1971 shall be void on the following grounds only, that is to say—

    (a) that it is not a valid marriage under the provisions of the Marriages Acts 1949 to 1970 (that is to say where—

        (i) the parties are within the prohibited degrees of relationship;

        (ii) either party is under the age of sixteen; or

        (iii) the parties have intermarried in disregard of certain requirements as to the formation of marriage);

    (b) that at the time of the marriage either party was already lawfully married;

    (c) that the parties are not respectively male and female;

    (d) in the case of a polygamous marriage entered into outside England and Wales, that either party was at the time of the marriage domiciled in England and Wales.

For the purposes of paragraph (d) of this subsection a marriage may be polygamous although at its inception neither party has any spouse additional to the other.

12. A marriage celebrated after 31st July 1971 shall be voidable on the following grounds only, that is to say—

    (*a*) that the marriage has not been consummated owing to the incapacity of either party to consummate it;

    (*b*) that the marriage has not been consummated owing to the wilful refusal of the respondent to consummate it;

    (*c*) that either party to the marriage did not validly consent to it, whether in consequence of duress, mistake, unsoundness of mind or otherwise;

    (*d*) that at the time of the marriage either party, though capable of giving a valid consent, was suffering (whether continuously or intermittently) from mental disorder within the meaning of the Mental Health Act 1959 of such a kind or to such an extent as to be unfitted for marriage;

    (*e*) that at the time of the marriage the respondent was suffering from venereal disease in a communicable form;

    (*f*) that at the time of the marriage the respondent was pregnant by some person other than the petitioner.

13.—(1) The court shall not, in proceedings instituted after 31st July 1971, grant a decree of nullity on the ground that a marriage is voidable if the respondent satisfies the court—

    (*a*) that the petitioner, with knowledge that it was open to him to have the marriage avoided, so conducted himself in relation to the respondent as to lead the respondent reasonably to believe that he would not seek to do so; and

    (*b*) that it would be unjust to the respondent to grant the decree.

(2) Without prejudice to subsection (1) above, the court shall not grant a decree of nullity by virtue of section 12 above on the grounds mentioned in paragraph (*c*), (*d*), (*e*) or (*f*) of that section unless it is satisfied that proceedings were instituted within three years from the date of the marriage.

(3) Without prejudice to subsections (1) and (2) above, the court shall not grant a decree of nullity by virtue of section 12 above on the grounds mentioned in paragraph (*e*) or (*f*) of that section unless it is satisfied that the petitioner was at the time of the marriage ignorant of the facts alleged.

PART I
Marriages
governed by
foreign law or
celebrated
abroad under
English law.

14.—(1) Where, apart from this Act, any matter affecting the validity of a marriage would fall to be determined (in accordance with the rules of private international law) by reference to the law of a country outside England and Wales, nothing in section 11, 12 or 13(1) above shall—

(a) preclude the determination of that matter as aforesaid ; or

(b) require the application to the marriage of the grounds or bar there mentioned except so far as applicable in accordance with those rules.

(2) In the case of a marriage which purports to have been celebrated under the Foreign Marriage Acts 1892 to 1947 or has taken place outside England and Wales and purports to be a marriage under common law, section 11 above is without prejudice to any ground on which the marriage may be void under those Acts or, as the case may be, by virtue of the rules governing the celebration of marriages outside England and Wales under common law.

Application of
ss. 1(5), 8 and
9 to nullity
proceedings.

15. Sections 1(5), 8 and 9 above shall apply in relation to proceedings for nullity of marriage as if for any reference in those provisions to divorce there were substituted a reference to nullity of marriage.

Effect of
decree of
nullity in case
of voidable
marriage.

16. A decree of nullity granted after 31st July 1971 in respect of a voidable marriage shall operate to annul the marriage only as respects any time after the decree has been made absolute, and the marriage shall, notwithstanding the decree, be treated as if it had existed up to that time.

Other matrimonial suits

Judicial
separation.

17.—(1) A petition for judicial separation may be presented to the court by either party to a marriage on the ground that any such fact as is mentioned in section 1(2) above exists, and the provisions of section 2 above shall apply accordingly for the purposes of a petition for judicial separation alleging any such fact, as they apply in relation to a petition for divorce alleging that fact.

(2) On a petition for judicial separation it shall be the duty of the court to inquire, so far as it reasonably can, into the facts alleged by the petitioner and into any facts alleged by the respondent, but the court shall not be concerned to consider whether the marriage has broken down irretrievably, and if it is satisfied on the evidence of any such fact as is mentioned in section 1(2) above it shall, subject to section 41 below, grant a decree of judicial separation.

(3) Sections 6 and 7 above shall apply for the purpose of encouraging the reconciliation of parties to proceedings for judicial separation and of enabling the parties to a marriage to refer to the court for its opinion an agreement or arrangement relevant to actual or contemplated proceedings for judicial separation, as they apply in relation to proceedings for divorce.

18.—(1) Where the court grants a decree of judicial separation it shall no longer be obligatory for the petitioner to cohabit with the respondent.

(2) If while a decree of judicial separation is in force and the separation is continuing either of the parties to the marriage dies intestate as respects all or any of his or her real or personal property, the property as respects which he or she died intestate shall devolve as if the other party to the marriage had then been dead.

(3) Notwithstanding anything in section 2(1)(*a*) of the Matrimonial Proceedings (Magistrates' Courts) Act 1960, a provision in force under an order made, or having effect as if made, under that section exempting one party to a marriage from the obligation to cohabit with the other shall not have effect as a decree of judicial separation for the purposes of subsection (2) above.

19.—(1) Any married person who alleges that reasonable grounds exist for supposing that the other party to the marriage is dead may, subject to subsection (2) below, present a petition to the court to have it presumed that the other party is dead and to have the marriage dissolved, and the court may, if satisfied that such reasonable grounds exist, grant a decree of presumption of death and dissolution of the marriage.

(2) A petition may be presented in pursuance of subsection (1) above—

(*a*) in any case, if the petitioner is domiciled in England and Wales ; and

(*b*) in the case of a petition presented by a wife, if she is resident in England and Wales and has been ordinarily resident there for a period of three years immediately preceding the commencement of the proceedings.

(3) In any proceedings under this section the fact that for a period of seven years or more the other party to the marriage has been continually absent from the petitioner and the petitioner has no reason to believe that the other party has been living within that time shall be evidence that the other party is dead until the contrary is proved.

(4) Sections 1(5), 8 and 9 above shall apply to a petition and a decree under this section as they apply to a petition for divorce and a decree of divorce respectively.

(5) In determining for the purposes of this section whether a woman is domiciled in England and Wales, her husband shall be treated as having died immediately after the last occasion on which she knew or had reason to believe him to be living; and in any proceedings brought in pursuance of subsection (2)(*b*) above the issues shall be determined in accordance with the law which would be applicable thereto if both parties to the marriage were domiciled in England and Wales at the time of the proceedings.

(6) It is hereby declared that neither collusion nor any other conduct on the part of the petitioner which has at any time been a bar to relief in matrimonial proceedings constitutes a bar to the grant of a decree under this section.

General

Relief for respondent in divorce proceedings.

20. If in any proceedings for divorce the respondent alleges and proves any such fact as is mentioned in subsection (2) of section 1 above (treating the respondent as the petitioner and the petitioner as the respondent for the purposes of that subsection) the court may give to the respondent the relief to which he would have been entitled if he had presented a petition seeking that relief.

Part II

Financial Relief for Parties to Marriage and Children of Family

Financial provision and property adjustment orders

Financial provision and property adjustment orders.

21.—(1) The financial provision orders for the purposes of this Act are the orders for periodical or lump sum provision available (subject to the provisions of this Act) under section 23 below for the purpose of adjusting the financial position of the parties to a marriage and any children of the family in connection with proceedings for divorce, nullity of marriage or judicial separation and under section 27(6) below on proof of neglect by one party to a marriage to provide, or to make a proper contribution towards, reasonable maintenance for the other or a child of the family, that is to say—

> (*a*) any order for periodical payments in favour of a party to a marriage under section 23(1)(*a*) or 27(6)(*a*) or in favour of a child of the family under section 23(1)(*d*), (2) or (4) or 27(6)(*d*);
>
> (*b*) any order for secured periodical payments in favour of a party to a marriage under section 23(1)(*b*) or 27(6)(*b*) or in favour of a child of the family under section 23(1)(*e*), (2) or (4) or 27(6)(*e*); and
>
> (*c*) any order for lump sum provision in favour of a party to a marriage under section 23(1)(*c*) or 27(6)(*c*) or in favour of a child of the family under section 23(1)(*f*), (2) or (4) or 27(6)(*f*);

and references in this Act (except in paragraphs 17(1) and 23 of Schedule 1 below) to periodical payments orders, secured periodical payments orders, and orders for the payment of a lump sum are references to all or some of the financial provision orders requiring the sort of financial provision in question according as the context of each reference may require.

(2) The property adjustment orders for the purposes of this Act are the orders dealing with property rights available (subject to the provisions of this Act) under section 24 below for the purpose of adjusting the financial position of the parties to a marriage and any children of the family on or after the grant of a decree of divorce, nullity of marriage or judicial separation, that is to say—

(a) any order under subsection (1)(a) of that section for a transfer of property;

(b) any order under subsection (1)(b) of that section for a settlement of property; and

(c) any order under subsection (1)(c) or (d) of that section for a variation of settlement.

Ancillary relief in connection with divorce proceedings, etc.

22. On a petition for divorce, nullity of marriage or judicial Maintenance separation, the court may make an order for maintenance pend- pending suit. ing suit, that is to say, an order requiring either party to the marriage to make to the other such periodical payments for his or her maintenance and for such term, being a term begin-ning not earlier than the date of the presentation of the petition and ending with the date of the determination of the suit, as the court thinks reasonable.

23.—(1) On granting a decree of divorce, a decree of nullity Financial of marriage or a decree of judicial separation or at any time provision thereafter (whether, in the case of a decree of divorce or of orders in nullity of marriage, before or after the decree is made absolute), connection the court may make any one or more of the following orders, with divorce that is to say— proceedings etc.

(a) an order that either party to the marriage shall make to the other such periodical payments, for such term, as may be specified in the order;

(b) an order that either party to the marriage shall secure to the other to the satisfaction of the court such periodical payments, for such term, as may be so specified;

(c) an order that either party to the marriage shall pay to the other such lump sum or sums as may be so specified;

(d) an order that a party to the marriage shall make to such person as may be specified in the order for the benefit of a child of the family, or to such a child, such periodical payments, for such term, as may be so specified ;

(e) an order that a party to the marriage shall secure to such person as may be so specified for the benefit of such a child, or to such a child, to the satisfaction of the court, such periodical payments, for such term, as may be so specified ;

(f) an order that a party to the marriage shall pay to such person as may be so specified for the benefit of such a child, or to such a child, such lump sum as may be so specified ;

subject, however, in the case of an order under paragraph (d), (e) or (f) above, to the restrictions imposed by section 29(1) and (3) below on the making of financial provision orders in favour of children who have attained the age of eighteen.

(2) The court may also, subject to those restrictions, make any one or more of the orders mentioned in subsection (1)(d), (e) and (f) above—

(a) in any procedings for divorce, nullity of marriage or judicial separation, before granting a decree ; and

(b) where any such proceedings are dismissed after the beginning of the trial, either forthwith or within a reasonable period after the dismissal.

(3) Without prejudice to the generality of subsection (1)(c) or (f) above—

(a) an order under this section that a party to a marriage shall pay a lump sum to the other party may be made for the purpose of enabling that other party to meet any liabilities or expenses reasonably incurred by him or her in maintaining himself or herself or any child of the family before making an application for an order under this section in his or her favour ;

(b) an order under this section for the payment of a lump sum to or for the benefit of a child of the family may be made for the purpose of enabling any liabilities or expenses reasonably incurred by or for the benefit of that child before the making of an application for an order under this section in his favour to be met ; and

(c) an order under this section for the payment of a lump sum may provide for the payment of that sum by instalments of such amount as may be specified in the order and may require the payment of the instalments to be secured to the satisfaction of the court.

(4) The power of the court under subsection (1) or (2)(a) above to make an order in favour of a child of the family shall be

exercisable from time to time ; and where the court makes an order in favour of a child under subsection (2)(*b*) above, it may from time to time, subject to the restrictions mentioned in sub-section (1) above, make a further order in his favour of any of the kinds mentioned in subsection (1)(*d*), (*e*) or (*f*) above.

(5) Without prejudice to the power to give a direction under section 30 below for the settlement of an instrument by con-veyancing counsel, where an order is made under subsection (1)(*a*), (*b*) or (*c*) above on or after granting a decree of divorce or nullity of marriage, neither the order nor any settlement made in pursuance of the order shall take effect unless the decree has been made absolute.

24.—(1) On granting a decree of divorce, a decree of nullity of marriage or a decree of judicial separation or at any time thereafter (whether, in the case of a decree of divorce or of nullity of marriage, before or after the decree is made absolute), the court may make any one or more of the following orders, that is to say—

Property adjustment orders in connection with divorce proceedings, etc.

> (*a*) an order that a party to the marriage shall transfer to the other party, to any child of the family or to such person as may be specified in the order for the benefit of such a child such property as may be so specified, being property to which the first-mentioned party is entitled, either in possession or reversion ;

> (*b*) an order that a settlement of such property as may be so specified, being property to which a party to the marriage is so entitled, be made to the satisfaction of the court for the benefit of the other party to the marriage and of the children of the family or either or any of them ;

> (*c*) an order varying for the benefit of the parties to the marriage and of the children of the family or either or any of them any ante-nuptial or post-nuptial settle-ment (including such a settlement made by will or codicil) made on the parties to the marriage ;

> (*d*) an order extinguishing or reducing the interest of either of the parties to the marriage under any such settlement ;

subject, however, in the case of an order under paragraph (*a*) above, to the restrictions imposed by section 29(1) and (3) below on the making of orders for a transfer of property in favour of children who have attained the age of eighteen.

(2) The court may make an order under subsection (1)(*c*) above notwithstanding that there are no children of the family.

PART II

(3) Without prejudice to the power to give a direction under section 30 below for the settlement of an instrument by conveyancing counsel, where an order is made under this section on or after granting a decree of divorce or nullity of marriage, neither the order nor any settlement made in pursuance of the order shall take effect unless the decree has been made absolute.

Matters to
which court
is to have
regard in
deciding how
to exercise its
powers under
sections 23
and 24.

25.—(1) It shall be the duty of the court in deciding whether to exercise its powers under section 23(1)(*a*), (*b*) or (*c*) or 24 above in relation to a party to the marriage and, if so, in what manner, to have regard to all the circumstances of the case including the following matters, that is to say—

(*a*) the income, earning capacity, property and other financial resources which each of the parties to the marriage has or is likely to have in the foreseeable future ;

(*b*) the financial needs, obligations and responsibilities which each of the parties to the marriage has or is likely to have in the foreseeable future ;

(*c*) the standard of living enjoyed by the family before the breakdown of the marriage ;

(*d*) the age of each party to the marriage and the duration of the marriage ;

(*e*) any physical or mental disability of either of the parties to the marriage ;

(*f*) the contributions made by each of the parties to the welfare of the family, including any contribution made by looking after the home or caring for the family ;

(*g*) in the case of proceedings for divorce or nullity of marriage, the value to either of the parties to the marriage of any benefit (for example, a pension) which, by reason of the dissolution or annulment of the marriage, that party will lose the chance of acquiring ;

and so to exercise those powers as to place the parties, so far as it is practicable and, having regard to their conduct, just to do so, in the financial position in which they would have been if the marriage had not broken down and each had properly discharged his or her financial obligations and responsibilities towards the other.

(2) Without prejudice to subsection (3) below, it shall be the duty of the court in deciding whether to exercise its powers under section 23(1)(*d*), (*e*) or (*f*), (2) or (4) or 24 above in relation to a child of the family and, if so, in what manner, to have regard to all the circumstances of the case including the following matters, that is to say—

(*a*) the financial needs of the child ;

(*b*) the income, earning capacity (if any), property and other financial resources of the child ;

(*c*) any physical or mental disability of the child ;

(*d*) the standard of living enjoyed by the family before the breakdown of the marriage ;

(*e*) the manner in which he was being and in which the parties to the marriage expected him to be educated or trained ;

and so to exercise those powers as to place the child, so far as it is practicable and, having regard to the considerations mentioned in relation to the parties to the marriage in paragraph (*a*) and (*b*) of subsection (1) above, just to do so, in the financial position in which the child would have been if the marriage had not broken down and each of those parties had properly discharged his or her financial obligations and responsibilities towards him.

(3) It shall be the duty of the court in deciding whether to exercise its powers under section 23(1)(*d*), (*e*) or (*f*), (2) or (4) or 24 above against a party to a marriage in favour of a child of the family who is not the child of that party and, if so, in what manner, to have regard (among the circumstances of the case)—

(*a*) to whether that party had assumed any responsibility for the child's maintenance and, if so, to the extent to which, and the basis upon which, that party assumed such responsibility and to the length of time for which that party discharged such responsibility ;

(*b*) to whether in assuming and discharging such responsibility that party did so knowing that the child was not his or her own ;

(*c*) to the liability of any other person to maintain the child.

26.—(1) Where a petition for divorce, nullity of marriage or judicial separation has been presented, then, subject to subsection (2) below, proceedings for maintenance pending suit under section 22 above, for a financial provision order under section 23 above, or for a property adjustment order may be begun, subject to and in accordance with rules of court, at any time after the presentation of the petition.

Commencement of proceedings for ancillary relief, etc.

(2) Rules of court may provide, in such cases as may be prescribed by the rules—

(*a*) that applications for any such relief as is mentioned in subsection (1) above shall be made in the petition or answer ; and

(b) that applications for any such relief which are not so made, or are not made until after the expiration of such period following the presentation of the petition or filing of the answer as may be so prescribed, shall be made only with the leave of the court.

Financial provision in case of neglect to maintain

Financial provision orders, etc., in case of neglect by party to marriage to maintain other party or child of the family.

27.—(1) Either party to a marriage may apply to the court for an order under this section on the ground that the other party to the marriage (in this section referred to as the respondent)—

(a) being the husband, has wilfully neglected—

(i) to provide reasonable maintenance for the applicant, or

(ii) to provide, or to make a proper contribution towards, reasonable maintenance for any child of the family to whom this section applies ;

(b) being the wife, has wilfully neglected to provide, or to make a proper contribution towards, reasonable maintenance—

(i) for the applicant in a case where, by reason of the impairment of the applicant's earning capacity through age, illness or disability of mind or body, and having regard to any resources of the applicant and the respondent respectively which are, or should properly be made, available for the purpose, it is reasonable in all the circumstances to expect the respondent so to provide or contribute, or

(ii) for any child of the family to whom this section applies.

(2) The court shall not entertain an application under this section unless it would have jurisdiction to entertain proceedings by the applicant for judicial separation.

(3) This section applies to any child of the family for whose maintenance it is reasonable in all the circumstances to expect the respondent to provide or towards whose maintenance it is reasonable in all the circumstances to expect the respondent to make a proper contribution.

(4) Where the child of the family to whom the application under this section relates is not the child of the respondent, then, in deciding—

(a) whether the respondent has been guilty of wilful neglect to provide, or to make a proper contribution towards, reasonable maintenance for the child, and (*b*) what order, if any, to make under this section in favour of the child,

the court shall have regard to the matters mentioned in section 25(3) above.

(5) Where on an application under this section it appears to the court that the applicant or any child of the family to whom the application relates is in immediate need of financial assistance, but it is not yet possible to determine what order, if any, should be made on the application, the court may make an interim order for maintenance, that is to say, an order requiring the respondent to make to the applicant until the determination of the application such periodical payments as the court thinks reasonable.

(6) Where on an application under this section the applicant satisfies the court of any ground mentioned in subsection (1) above, the court may make such one or more of the following orders as it thinks just, that is to say—

(*a*) an order that the respondent shall make to the applicant such periodical payments, for such term, as may be specified in the order ;

(*b*) an order that the respondent shall secure to the applicant, to the satisfaction of the court, such periodical payments, for such term, as may be so specified ;

(*c*) an order that the respondent shall pay to the applicant such lump sum as may be so specified ;

(*d*) an order that the respondent shall make to such person as may be specified in the order for the benefit of the child to whom the application relates, or to that child, such periodical payments, for such term, as may be so specified ;

(*e*) an order that the respondent shall secure to such person as may be so specified for the benefit of that child, or to that child, to the satisfaction of the court, such periodical payments, for such term, as may be so specified ;

(*f*) an order that the respondent shall pay to such person as may be so specified for the benefit of that child, or to that child, such lump sum as may be so specified ;

subject, however, in the case of an order under paragraph (*d*), (*e*) or (*f*) above, to the restrictions imposed by section 29(1) and (3) below on the making of financial provision orders in favour of children who have attained the age of eighteen.

(7) Without prejudice to the generality of subsection (6)(*c*) or (*f*) above, an order under this section for the payment of a lump sum—

  (*a*) may be made for the purpose of enabling any liabilities or expenses reasonably incurred in maintaining the applicant or any child of the family to whom the application relates before the making of the application to be met ;

  (*b*) may provide for the payment of that sum by instalments of such amount as may be specified in the order and may require the payment of the instalments to be secured to the satisfaction of the court.

(8) For the purpose of proceedings on an application under this section adultery which has been condoned shall not be capable of being revived, and any presumption of condonation which arises from the continuance or resumption of marital intercourse may be rebutted by evidence sufficient to negative the necessary intent.

Additional provisions with respect to financial provision and property adjustment orders

Duration of continuing financial provision orders in favour of party to marriage, and effect of remarriage.

28.—(1) The term to be specified in a periodical payments or secured periodical payments order in favour of a party to a marriage shall be such term as the court thinks fit, subject to the following limits, that is to say—

  (*a*) in the case of a periodical payments order, the term shall begin not earlier than the date of the making of an application for the order, and shall be so defined as not to extend beyond the death of either of the parties to the marriage or, where the order is made on or after the grant of a decree of divorce or nullity of marriage, the remarriage of the party in whose favour the order is made ; and

  (*b*) in the case of a secured periodical payments order, the term shall begin not earlier than the date of the making of an application for the order, and shall be so defined as not to extend beyond the death or, where the order is made on or after the grant of such a decree, the remarriage of the party in whose favour the order is made.

(2) Where a periodical payments or secured periodical payments order in favour of a party to a marriage is made otherwise than on or after the grant of a decree of divorce or nullity of marriage, and the marriage in question is subsequently dissolved or annulled but the order continues in force, the order shall, notwithstanding anything in it, cease to have effect on

the remarriage of that party, except in relation to any arrears
due under it on the date of the remarriage.

(3) If after the grant of a decree dissolving or annulling a marriage either party to that marriage remarries, that party shall not be entitled to apply, by reference to the grant of that decree, for a financial provision order in his or her favour, or for a property adjustment order, against the other party to that marriage.

29.—(1) Subject to subsection (3) below, no financial pro-Duration of vision order and no order for a transfer of property under continuing section 24(1)(*a*) above shall be made in favour of a child who financial provision has attained the age of eighteen.
orders in
(2) The term to be specified in a periodical payments or favour of secured periodical payments order in favour of a child may children, and begin with the date of the making of an application for the age limit on order in question or any later date but— making certain orders in their
   (*a*) shall not in the first instance extend beyond the date of favour. the birthday of the child next following his attaining the upper limit of the compulsory school age (that is to say, the age that is for the time being that limit by virtue of section 35 of the Education Act 1944 1944 c. 31. together with any Order in Council made under that section) unless the court thinks it right in the circumstances of the case to specify a later date ; and

   (*b*) shall not in any event, subject to subsection (3) below, extend beyond the date of the child's eighteenth birthday.

(3) Subsection (1) above, and paragraph (*b*) of subsection (2), shall not apply in the case of a child, if it appears to the court that—

   (*a*) the child is, or will be, or if an order were made without complying with either or both of those provisions would be, receiving instruction at an educational establishment or undergoing training for a trade, profession or vocation, whether or not he is also, or will also be, in gainful employment ; or

   (*b*) there are special circumstances which justify the making of an order without complying with either or both of those provisions.

(4) Any periodical payments order in favour of a child shall, notwithstanding anything in the order, cease to have effect on the death of the person liable to make payments under the order, except in relation to any arrears due under the order on the date of the death.

PART II
Direction for
settlement of
instrument
for securing
payments or
effecting
property
adjustment.

30. Where the court decides to make a financial provision order requiring any payments to be secured or a property adjustment order—

(a) it may direct that the matter be referred to one of the conveyancing counsel of the court for him to settle a proper instrument to be executed by all necessary parties ; and

(b) where the order is to be made in proceedings for divorce, nullity of marriage or judicial separation it may, if it thinks fit, defer the grant of the decree in question until the instrument has been duly executed.

*Variation, discharge and enforcement of
certain orders, etc.*

Variation,
discharge, etc.,
of certain
orders for
financial
relief.

31.—(1) Where the court has made an order to which this section applies, then, subject to the provisions of this section, the court shall have power to vary or discharge the order or to suspend any provision thereof temporarily and to revive the operation of any provision so suspended.

(2) This section applies to the following orders, that is to say—

(a) any order for maintenance pending suit and any interim order for maintenance ;

(b) any periodical payments order ;

(c) any secured periodical payments order ;

(d) any order made by virtue of section 23(3)(c) or 27(7)(b) above (provision for payment of a lump sum by instalments) ;

(e) any order for a settlement of property under section 24(1)(b) or for a variation of settlement under section 24(1)(c) or (d) above, being an order made on or after the grant of a decree of judicial separation.

(3) The powers exercisable by the court under this section in relation to an order shall be exercisable also in relation to any instrument executed in pursuance of the order.

(4) The court shall not exercise the powers conferred by this section in relation to an order for a settlement under section 24(1)(b) or for a variation of settlement under section 24(1)(c) or (d) above except on an application made in proceedings —

(a) for the rescission of the decree of judicial separation by reference to which the order was made, or

(b) for the dissolution of the marriage in question.

(5) No property adjustment order shall be made on an application for the variation of a periodical payments or secured periodical payments order made (whether in favour of a party

to a marriage or in favour of a child of the family) under PART II
section 23 above, and no order for the payment of a lump sum
shall be made on an application for the variation of a periodical
payments or secured periodical payments order in favour of a
party to a marriage (whether made under section 23 or under
section 27 above).

(6) Where the person liable to make payments under a
secured periodical payments order has died, an application
under this section relating to that order may be made by the
person entitled to payments under the order or by the personal
representatives of the deceased person, but no such application
shall, except with the permission of the court, be made after
the end of the period of six months from the date on which
representation in regard to the estate of that person is first
taken out.

(7) In exercising the powers conferred by this section the
court shall have regard to all the circumstances of the case,
including any change in any of the matters to which the court
was required to have regard when making the order to which
the application relates and, where the party against whom that
order was made has died, the changed circumstances resulting
from his or her death.

(8) The personal representatives of a deceased person against
whom a secured periodical payments order was made shall not
be liable for having distributed any part of the estate of the
deceased after the expiration of the period of six months
referred to in subsection (6) above on the ground that they
ought to have taken into account the possibility that the court
might permit an application under this section to be made
after that period by the person entitled to payments under the
order; but this subsection shall not prejudice any power to recover any part of the estate so distributed arising by virtue of
the making of an order in pursuance of this section.

(9) In considering for the purposes of subsection (6) above
the question when representation was first taken out, a grant
limited to settled land or to trust property shall be left out of
account and a grant limited to real estate or to personal estate
shall be left out of account unless a grant limited to the remainder of the estate has previously been made or is made at
the same time.

32.—(1) A person shall not be entitled to enforce through Payment of cer-
the High Court or any county court the payment of any arrears unenforceable
due under an order for maintenance pending suit, an interim without the
order for maintenance or any financial provision order without leave of the
the leave of that court if those arrears became due more than court.

twelve months before proceedings to enforce the payment of them are begun.

(2) The court hearing an application for the grant of leave under this section may refuse leave, or may grant leave subject to such restrictions and conditions (including conditions as to the allowing of time for payment or the making of payment by instalments) as that court thinks proper, or may remit the payment of the arrears or of any part thereof.

(3) An application for the grant of leave under this section shall be made in such manner as may be prescribed by rules of court.

Orders for
repayment
in certain
cases of
sums paid
under certain
orders.
33.—(1) Where on an application made under this section in relation to an order to which this section applies it appears to the court that by reason of—

> (a) a change in the circumstances of the person entitled to, or liable to make, payments under the order since the order was made, or
>
> (b) the changed circumstances resulting from the death of the person so liable,

the amount received by the person entitled to payments under the order in respect of a period after those circumstances changed or after the death of the person liable to make payments under the order, as the case may be, exceeds the amount which the person so liable or his or her personal representatives should have been required to pay, the court may order the respondent to the application to pay to the applicant such sum, not exceeding the amount of the excess, as the court thinks just.

(2) This section applies to the following orders, that is to say—

> (a) any order for maintenance pending suit and any interim order for maintenance ;
>
> (b) any periodical payments order ; and
>
> (c) any secured periodical payments order.

(3) An application under this section may be made by the person liable to make payments under an order to which this section applies or his or her personal representatives and may be made against the person entitled to payments under the order or her or his personal representatives.

(4) An application under this section may be made in proceedings in the High Court or a county court for—

> (a) the variation or discharge of the order to which this section applies, or

(*b*) leave to enforce, or the enforcement of, the payment of arrears under that order ;

but when not made in such proceedings shall be made to a county court, and accordingly references in this section to the court are references to the High Court or a county court, as the circumstances require.

(5) The jurisdiction conferred on a county court by this section shall be exercisable notwithstanding that by reason of the amount claimed in the application the jurisdiction would not but for this subsection be exercisable by a county court.

(6) An order under this section for the payment of any sum may provide for the payment of that sum by instalments of such amount as may be specified in the order.

Maintenance agreements

34.—(1) If a maintenance agreement includes a provision purporting to restrict any right to apply to a court for an order containing financial arrangements, then—

    (*a*) that provision shall be void ; but

    (*b*) any other financial arrangements contained in the agreement shall not thereby be rendered void or unenforceable and shall, unless they are void or unenforceable for any other reason (and subject to sections 35 and 36 below), be binding on the parties to the agreement.

(2) In this section and in section 35 below—

    " maintenance agreement " means any agreement in writing made, whether before or after the commencement of this Act, between the parties to a marriage, being—

        (*a*) an agreement containing financial arrangements, whether made during the continuance or after the dissolution or annulment of the marriage ; or

        (*b*) a separation agreement which contains no financial arrangements in a case where no other agreement in writing between the same parties contains such arrangements ;

    " financial arrangements " means provisions governing the rights and liabilities towards one another when living separately of the parties to a marriage (including a marriage which has been dissolved or annulled) in respect of the making or securing of payments or the disposition or use of any property, including such rights and liabilities with respect to the maintenance or education of any child, whether or not a child of the family.

Alteration of agreements by court during lives of parties.
35.—(1) Where a maintenance agreement is for the time being subsisting and each of the parties to the agreement is for the time being either domiciled or resident in England and Wales, then, subject to subsection (3) below, either party may apply to the court or to a magistrates' court for an order under this section.

(2) If the court to which the application is made is satisfied either—

(a) that by reason of a change in the circumstances in the light of which any financial arrangements contained in the agreement were made or, as the case may be, financial arrangements were omitted from it (including a change foreseen by the parties when making the agreement), the agreement should be altered so as to make different, or, as the case may be, so as to contain, financial arrangements, or

(b) that the agreement does not contain proper financial arrangements with respect to any child of the family,

then subject to subsections (3), (4) and (5) below, that court may by order make such alterations in the agreement—

(i) by varying or revoking any financial arrangements contained in it, or

(ii) by inserting in it financial arrangements for the benefit of one of the parties to the agreement or of a child of the family,

as may appear to that court to be just having regard to all the circumstances, including, if relevant, the matters mentioned in section 25(3) above ; and the agreement shall have effect thereafter as if any alteration made by the order had been made by agreement between the parties and for valuable consideration.

(3) A magistrates' court shall not entertain an application under subsection (1) above unless both the parties to the agreement are resident in England and Wales and at least one of the parties is resident in the petty sessions area (within the meaning of the Magistrates' Courts Act 1952) for which the court acts, and shall not have power to make any order on such an application except—

1952 c. 55.

(a) in a case where the agreement includes no provision for periodic payments by either of the parties, an order

inserting provision for the making by one of the parties
of periodical payments for the maintenance of the
other party or for the maintenance of any child of the
family;

(b) in a case where the agreement includes provision for
the making by one of the parties of periodical payments, an order increasing or reducing the rate of, or
terminating, any of those payments.

(4) Where a court decides to alter, by order under this section,
an agreement by inserting provision for the making or securing
by one of the parties to the agreement of periodical payments
for the maintenance of the other party or by increasing the rate
of the periodical payments which the agreement provides shall
be made by one of the parties for the maintenance of the other,
the term for which the payments or, as the case may be, the
additional payments attributable to the increase are to be made
under the agreement as altered by the order shall be such term
as the court may specify, subject to the following limits, that
is to say—

(a) where the payments will not be secured, the term shall
be so defined as not to extend beyond the death of
either of the parties to the agreement or the remarriage
of the party to whom the payments are to be made;

(b) where the payments will be secured, the term shall be
so defined as not to extend beyond the death or remarriage of that party.

(5) Where a court decides to alter, by order under this
section, an agreement by inserting provision for the making or
securing by one of the parties to the agreement of periodical
payments for the maintenance of a child of the family or by
increasing the rate of the periodical payments which the agreement provides shall be made or secured by one of the parties
for the maintenance of such a child, then, in deciding the term
for which under the agreement as altered by the order the
payments, or as the case may be, the additional payments
attributable to the increase are to be made or secured for the
benefit of the child, the court shall apply the provisions of
section 29(2) and (3) above as to age limits as if the order in
question were a periodical payments or secured periodical payments order in favour of the child.

(6) For the avoidance of doubt it is hereby declared that
nothing in this section or in section 34 above affects any power
of a court before which any proceedings between the parties to
a maintenance agreement are brought under any other enactment (including a provision of this Act) to make an order

PART II

containing financial arrangements or any right of either party to apply for such an order in such proceedings.

Alteration of agreements by court after death of one party.

36.—(1) Where a maintenance agreement within the meaning of section 34 above provides for the continuation of payments under the agreement after the death of one of the parties and that party dies domiciled in England and Wales, the surviving party or the personal representatives of the deceased party may, subject to subsections (2) and (3) below, apply to the High Court or a county court for an order under section 35 above.

(2) An application under this section shall not, except with the permission of the High Court or a county court, be made after the end of the period of six months from the date on which representation in regard to the estate of the deceased is first taken out.

(3) A county court shall not entertain an application under this section, or an application for permission to make an application under this section, unless it would have jurisdiction by virtue of section 7 of the Family Provision Act 1966 (which confers jurisdiction on county courts in proceedings under the Inheritance (Family Provision) Act 1938 or section 26 of the Matrimonial Causes Act 1965 if the value of the deceased's net estate does not exceed £5,000 or such larger sum as may be fixed by order of the Lord Chancellor) to hear and determine proceedings for an order under section 26 of the Matrimonial Causes Act 1965 (application for maintenance out of deceased's estate by former spouse) in relation to the deceased's estate.

1966 c. 35.

1938 c. 45.
1965 c. 72.

(4) If a maintenance agreement is altered by a court on an application made in pursuance of subsection (1) above, the like consequences shall ensue as if the alteration had been made immediately before the death by agreement between the parties and for valuable consideration.

(5) The provisions of this section shall not render the personal representatives of the deceased liable for having distributed any part of the estate of the deceased after the expiration of the period of six months referred to in subsection (2) above on the ground that they ought to have taken into account the possibility that a court might permit an application by virtue of this section to be made by the surviving party after that period ; but this subsection shall not prejudice any power to recover any part of the estate so distributed arising by virtue of the making of an order in pursuance of this section.

(6) Section 31(9) above shall apply for the purposes of subsection (2) above as it applies for the purposes of subsection (6) of section 31.

(7) Subsection (3) of section 7 of the Family Provision Act 1966 (transfer to county court of proceedings commenced in the High Court) and paragraphs (*a*) and (*b*) of subsection (5) of that section (provisions relating to proceedings commenced in county court before coming into force of order of the Lord Chancellor under that section) shall apply in relation to proceedings consisting of any such application as is referred to in subsection (3) above as they apply in relation to any such proceedings as are referred to in subsection (1) of that section.

PART II

1966 c. 35.

Miscellaneous and supplemental

37.—(1) For the purposes of this section " financial relief " means relief under any of the provisions of sections 22, 23, 24, 27, 31 (except subsection (6)) and 35 above, and any reference in this section to defeating a person's claim for financial relief is a reference to preventing financial relief from being granted to that person, or to that person for the benefit of a child of the family, or reducing the amount of any financial relief which might be so granted, or frustrating or impeding the enforcement of any order which might be or has been made at his instance under any of those provisions.

Avoidance of transactions intended to prevent or reduce financial relief.

(2) Where proceedings for financial relief are brought by one person against another, the court may, on the application of the first-mentioned person—

(*a*) if it is satisfied that the other party to the proceedings is, with the intention of defeating the claim for financial relief, about to make any disposition or to transfer out of the jurisdiction or otherwise deal with any property, make such order as it thinks fit for restraining the other party from so doing or otherwise for protecting the claim ;

(*b*) if it is satisfied that the other party has, with that intention, made a reviewable disposition and that if the disposition were set aside financial relief or different financial relief would be granted to the applicant, make an order setting aside the disposition ;

(*c*) if it is satisfied, in a case where an order has been obtained under any of the provisions mentioned in subsection (1) above by the applicant against the other party, that the other party has, with that intention, made a reviewable disposition, make an order setting aside the disposition ;

and an application for the purposes of paragraph (*b*) above shall be made in the proceedings for the financial relief in question.

(3) Where the court makes an order under subsection (2)(*b*) or (*c*) above setting aside a disposition it shall give such consequential directions as it thinks fit for giving effect to the order

G

(including directions requiring the making of any payments or the disposal of any property).

(4) Any disposition made by the other party to the proceedings for financial relief in question (whether before or after the commencement of those proceedings) is a reviewable disposition for the purposes of subsection (2)(*b*) and (*c*) above unless it was made for valuable consideration (other than marriage) to a person who, at the time of the disposition, acted in relation to it in good faith and without notice of any intention on the part of the other party to defeat the applicant's claim for financial relief.

(5) Where an application is made under this section with respect to a disposition which took place less than three years before the date of the application or with respect to a disposition or other dealing with property which is about to take place and the court is satisfied—

(*a*) in a case falling within subsection (2)(*a*) or (*b*) above, that the disposition or other dealing would (apart from this section) have the consequence, or

(*b*) in a case falling within subsection (2)(*c*) above, that the disposition has had the consequence,

of defeating the applicant's claim for financial relief, it shall be presumed, unless the contrary is shown, that the person who disposed of or is about to dispose of or deal with the property did so or, as the case may be, is about to do so, with the intention of defeating the applicant's claim for financial relief.

(6) In this section " disposition " does not include any provision contained in a will or codicil but, with that exception, includes any conveyance, assurance or gift of property of any description, whether made by an instrument or otherwise.

(7) This section does not apply to a disposition made before 1st January 1968.

Orders for repayment in certain cases of sums paid after cessation of order by reason of remarriage.

38.—(1) Where—

(*a*) a periodical payments or secured periodical payments order in favour of a party to a marriage (hereafter in this section referred to as " a payments order ") has ceased to have effect by reason of the remarriage of that party, and

(*b*) the person liable to make payments under the order or his or her personal representatives made payments in accordance with it in respect of a period after the date of the remarriage in the mistaken belief that the order was still subsisting, the person so liable or his or her personal representatives shall not be entitled to bring proceedings in respect of a cause of action arising out of the circumstances mentioned in paragraphs (*a*) and (*b*) above against the person entitled to payments under the order or her or his personal representatives, but may instead make an application against that person or her or his personal representatives under this section.

(2) On an application under this section the court may order the respondent to pay to the applicant a sum equal to the amount of the payments made in respect of the period mentioned in subsection (1)(*b*) above or, if it appears to the court that it would be unjust to make that order, it may either order the respondent to pay to the applicant such lesser sum as it thinks fit or dismiss the application.

(3) An application under this section may be made in proceedings in the High Court or a county court for leave to enforce, or the enforcement of, payment of arrears under the order in question, but when not made in such proceedings shall be made to a county court; and accordingly references in this section to the court are references to the High Court or a county court, as the circumstances require.

(4) The jurisdiction conferred on a county court by this section shall be exercisable notwithstanding that by reason of the amount claimed in the application the jurisdiction would not but for this subsection be exercisable by a county court.

(5) An order under this section for the payment of any sum may provide for the payment of that sum by instalments of such amount as may be specified in the order.

(6) The clerk of a magistrates' court to whom any payments under a payments order are required to be made, and the collecting officer under an attachment of earnings order made to secure payments under a payments order, shall not be liable—

(*a*) in the case of the clerk, for any act done by him in pursuance of the payments order after the date on which that order ceased to have effect by reason of the remarriage of the person entitled to payments under it, and

(*b*) in the case of the collecting officer, for any act done by him after that date in accordance with any enactment or rule of court specifying how payments made to him in compliance with the attachment of earnings order are to be dealt with,

if, but only if, the act was one which he would have been under a duty to do had the payments order not so ceased to have effect and the act was done before notice in writing of the fact that

G 2

PART II

the person so entitled had remarried was given to him by or on behalf of that person, the person liable to make payments under the payments order or the personal representatives of either of those persons.

(7) In this section " collecting officer ", in relation to an attachment of earnings order, means the officer of the High Court, the registrar of a county court or the clerk of a magistrates' court to whom a person makes payments in compliance with the order.

Settlement, etc., made in compliance with a property adjustment order may be avoided on bankruptcy of settlor. 1914 c. 59.

39. The fact that a settlement or transfer of property had to be made in order to comply with a property adjustment order shall not prevent that settlement or transfer from being a settlement of property to which section 42(1) of the Bankruptcy Act 1914 (avoidance of certain settlements) applies.

Payments, etc., under order made in favour of person suffering from mental disorder. 1959 c. 72.

40. Where the court makes an order under this Part of this Act requiring payments (including a lump sum payment) to be made, or property to be transferred, to a party to a marriage and the court is satisfied that the person in whose favour the order is made is incapable, by reason of mental disorder within the meaning of the Mental Health Act 1959, of managing and administering his or her property and affairs then, subject to any order, direction or authority made or given in relation to that person under Part VIII of that Act, the court may order the payments to be made, or as the case may be, the property to be transferred, to such persons having charge of that person as the court may direct.

PART III

PROTECTION, CUSTODY, ETC., OF CHILDREN

Restrictions on decrees for dissolution, annulment or separation affecting children.

41.—(1) The Court shall not make absolute a decree of divorce or of nullity of marriage, or grant a decree of judicial separation, unless the court, by order, has declared that it is satisfied—

(a) that for the purposes of this section there are no children of the family to whom this section applies ; or

(b) that the only children who are or may be children of the family to whom this section applies are the children named in the order and that—

    (i) arrangements for the welfare of every child so named have been made and are satisfactory or are the best that can be devised in the circumstances ; or

    (ii) it is impracticable for the party or parties appearing before the court to make any such arrangements ; or

(c) that there are circumstances making it desirable that the decree should be made absolute or should be granted, as the case may be, without delay notwithstanding that there are or may be children of the family to whom this section applies and that the court is unable to make a declaration in accordance with paragraph (b) above.

(2) The court shall not make an order declaring that it is satisfied as mentioned in subsection (1)(c) above unless it has obtained a satisfactory undertaking from either or both of the parties to bring the question of the arrangements for the children named in the order before the court within a specified time.

(3) If the court makes absolute a decree of divorce or of nullity of marriage, or grants a decree of judicial separation, without having made an order under subsection (1) above the decree shall be void but, if such an order was made, no person shall be entitled to challenge the validity of the decree on the ground that the conditions prescribed by subsections (1) and (2) above were not fulfilled.

(4) If the court refuses to make an order under subsection (1) above in any proceedings for divorce, nullity of marriage or judicial separation, it shall, on an application by either party to the proceedings, make an order declaring that it is not satisfied as mentioned in that subsection.

(5) This section applies to the following children of the family, that is to say—

(a) any minor child of the family who at the date of the order under subsection (1) above is—

(i) under the age of sixteen, or

(ii) receiving instruction at an educational establishment or undergoing training for a trade, profession or vocation, whether or not he is also in gainful employment ; and

(b) any other child of the family to whom the court by an order under that subsection directs that this section shall apply ;

and the court may give such a direction if it is of opinion that there are special circumstances which make it desirable in the interest of the child that this section should apply to him.

(6) In this section " welfare ", in relation to a child, includes the custody and education of the child and financial provision for him.

G 3

PART III
Orders for
custody and
education of
children in
cases of
divorce, etc.,
and for
custody in
cases of
neglect.

42.—(1) The court may make such order as it thinks fit for the custody and education of any child of the family who is under the age of eighteen—

(*a*) in any proceedings for divorce, nullity of marriage or judicial separation, before or on granting a decree or at any time thereafter (whether, in the case of a decree of divorce or nullity of marriage, before or after the decree is made absolute);

(*b*) where any such proceedings are dismissed after the beginning of the trial, either forthwith or within a reasonable period after the dismissal;

and in any case in which the court has power by virtue of this subsection to make an order in respect of a child it may instead, if it thinks fit, direct that proper proceedings be taken for making the child a ward of court.

(2) Where the court makes an order under section 27 above, the court shall also have power to make such order as it thinks fit with respect to the custody of any child of the family who is for the time being under the age of eighteen; but the power conferred by this subsection and any order made in exercise of that power shall have effect only as respects any period when an order is in force under that section and the child is under that age.

(3) Where the court grants or makes absolute a decree of divorce or grants a decree of judicial separation, it may include in the decree a declaration that either party to the marriage in question is unfit to have the custody of the children of the family.

(4) Where a decree of divorce or of judicial separation contains such a declaration as is mentioned in subsection (3) above, then, if the party to whom the declaration relates is a parent of any child of the family, that party shall not, on the death of the other parent, be entitled as of right to the custody or the guardianship of that child.

(5) Where an order in respect of a child is made under this section, the order shall not affect the rights over or with respect to the child of any person, other than a party to the marriage in question, unless the child is the child of one or both of the parties to that marriage and that person was a party to the proceedings on the application for an order under this section.

(6) The power of the court under subsection (1)(*a*) or (2) above to make an order with respect to a child shall be exercisable from time to time; and where the court makes an order

under subsection (1)(*b*) above with respect to a child it may from time to time until that child attains the age of eighteen make a further order with respect to his custody and education.

(7) The court shall have power to vary or discharge an order made under this section or to suspend any provision thereof temporarily and to revive the operation of any provision so suspended.

43.—(1) Where the court has jurisdiction by virtue of this Part of this Act to make an order for the custody of a child and it appears to the court that there are exceptional circumstances making it impracticable or undesirable for the child to be entrusted to either of the parties to the marriage or to any other individual, the court may if it thinks fit make an order committing the care of the child to the council of a county other than a metropolitan county, or of a metropolitan district or London borough or the Common Council of the City of London (hereafter in this section referred to as " the local authority ") ; and thereupon Part II of the Children Act 1948 (which relates to the treatment of children in the care of a local authority) shall, subject to the provisions of this section, apply as if the child had been received by the local authority into their care under section 1 of that Act.

(2) The authority specified in an order under this section shall be the local authority for the area in which the child was, in the opinion of the court, resident before the order was made to commit the child to the care of a local authority, and the court shall before making an order under this section hear any representations from the local authority, including any representations as to the making of a financial provision order in favour of the child.

(3) While an order made by virtue of this section is in force with respect to a child, the child shall continue in the care of the local authority notwithstanding any claim by a parent or other person.

(4) An order made by virtue of this section shall cease to have effect as respects any child when he becomes eighteen, and the court shall not make an order committing a child to the care of a local authority under this section after he has become seventeen.

(5) In the application of Part II of the Children Act 1948 by virtue of this section—

    (*a*) the exercise by the local authority of their powers under sections 12 to 14 of that Act (which among other

G 4

PART III

things relate to the accommodation and welfare of a child in the care of a local authority) shall be subject to any directions given by the court ; and

(*b*) section 17 of that Act (which relates to arrangements for the emigration of such a child) shall not apply.

(6) It shall be the duty of any parent or guardian of a child committed to the care of a local authority under this section to secure that the local authority are informed of his address for the time being, and a person who knowingly fails to comply with this subsection shall be liable on summary conviction to a fine not exceeding ten pounds.

(7) The court shall have power from time to time by an order under this section to vary or discharge any provision made in pursuance of this section.

1969 c. 54.
1948 c. 43.

(8) So long as by virtue of paragraph 13 of Schedule 4 to the Children and Young Persons Act 1969 sections 15 and 16 of the Children Act 1948 continue to apply in relation to a local authority, subsection (5)(*a*) above shall have effect in relation to that authority as if for the reference to sections 12 to 14 of the last-mentioned Act there were substituted a reference to sections 12 to 16 of that Act.

(9) Subject to the following provisions of this subsection, until 1st April 1974 subsection (1) above shall have effect as if for the words " other than a metropolitan county, or of a metropolitan district " there were substituted the words " county borough ".

1972 c. 70.

An order (or orders) made under section 273(2) of the Local Government Act 1972 (orders bringing provisions of that Act into force before 1st April 1974) may appoint an earlier date (or, as the case may be, different dates for different purposes or areas) on which subsection (1) above shall cease to have effect as mentioned above.

Power to provide for supervision of children.

44.—(1) Where the court has jurisdiction by virtue of this Part of this Act to make an order for the custody of a child and it appears to the court that there are exceptional circumstances making it desirable that the child should be under the supervision of an independent person, the court may, as respects any period during which the child is, in exercise of that jurisdiction, committed to the custody of any person, order that the child be under the supervision of an officer appointed under this section as a welfare officer or under the supervision of a local authority.

(2) Where the court makes an order under this section for supervision by a welfare officer, the officer responsible for carrying out the order shall be such probation officer as may

be selected under arrangements made by the Secretary of State ; PART III
and where the order is for supervision by a local authority,
that authority shall be the council of a county other than a
metropolitan county, or of a metropolitan district or London
borough selected by the court and specified in the order or, if
the Common Council of the City of London is so selected and
specified, that Council.

(3) The court shall not have power to make an order under
this section as respects a child who in pursuance of an order
under section 43 above is in the care of a local authority.

(4) Where a child is under the supervision of any person in
pursuance of this section the jurisdiction possessed by a court
to vary any financial provision order in the child's favour
or any order made with respect to his custody or education
under this Part of this Act shall, subject to any rules of court,
be exercisable at the instance of that court itself.

(5) The court shall have power from time to time by an
order under this section to vary or discharge any provision
made in pursuance of this section.

(6) Subject to the following provisions of this subsection,
until 1st April 1974 subsection (2) above shall have effect as if
for the words " other than a metropolitan county, or of a
metropolitan district " there were substituted the words " county
borough ".

An order (or orders) made under section 273(2) of the Local
Government Act 1972 may appoint an earlier date (or, as the 1972 c. 70.
case may be, different dates for different purposes or areas) on
which subsection (2) above shall cease to have effect as mentioned above.

PART IV

MISCELLANEOUS AND SUPPLEMENTAL

45.—(1) Any person who is a British subject, or whose right Declarations
to be deemed a British subject depends wholly or in part on of legitimacy,
his legitimacy or on the validity of any marriage, may, if he is etc.
domiciled in England and Wales or in Northern Ireland or
claims any real or personal estate situate in England and Wales,
apply by petition to the High Court for a decree declaring that he
is the legitimate child of his parents, or that the marriage of his
father and mother or of his grandfather and grandmother was
a valid marriage or that his own marriage was a valid marriage.

(2) Any person claiming that he or his parent or any remoter
ancestor became or has become a legitimated person may apply

by petition to the High Court, or may apply to a county court in the manner prescribed by county court rules, for a decree declaring that he or his parent or remoter ancestor, as the case may be, became or has become a legitimated person.

In this subsection "legitimated person" means a person legitimated by the Legitimacy Act 1926, and includes a person recognised under section 8 of that Act as legitimated.

(3) Where an application under subsection (2) above is made to a county court, the county court, if it considers that the case is one which owing to the value of the property involved or otherwise ought to be dealt with by the High Court, may, and if so ordered by the High Court shall, transfer the matter to the High Court ; and on such a transfer the proceeding shall be continued in the High Court as if it had been originally commenced by petition to the court.

(4) Any person who is domiciled in England and Wales or in Northern Ireland or claims any real or personal estate situate in England and Wales may apply to the High Court for a decree declaring his right to be deemed a British subject.

(5) Applications to the High Court under the preceding provisions of this section may be included in the same petition, and on any application under the preceding provisions of this section the High Court or, as the case may be, the county court shall make such decree as it thinks just, and the decree shall be binding on Her Majesty and all other persons whatsoever, so however that the decree shall not prejudice any person—

(a) if it is subsequently proved to have been obtained by fraud or collusion ; or

(b) unless that person has been given notice of the application in the manner prescribed by rules of court or made a party to the proceedings or claims through a person so given notice or made a party.

(6) A copy of every application under this section and of any affidavit accompanying it shall be delivered to the Attorney-General at least one month before the application is made, and the Attorney-General shall be a respondent on the hearing of the application and on any subsequent proceedings relating thereto.

(7) Where any application is made under this section, such persons as the court hearing the application thinks fit shall, subject to rules of court, be given notice of the application in the manner prescribed by rules of court, and any such persons may be permitted to become parties to the proceedings and to oppose the application.

(8) No proceedings under this section shall affect any final judgment or decree already pronounced or made by any court of competent jurisdiction.

(9) The court hearing an application under this section may direct that the whole or any part of the proceedings shall be heard in camera, and an application for a direction under this subsection shall be heard in camera unless the court otherwise directs.

46.—(1) Without prejudice to any jurisdiction exercisable by Additional the court apart from this section, the court shall have jurisdiction jurisdiction in to entertain proceedings by a wife, notwithstanding that the proceedings husband is not domiciled in England and Wales,— by a wife.

   (*a*) in the case of any proceedings under this Act (other than proceedings under section 19 or sections 34 to 36), if—

       (i) the wife has been deserted by her husband, or

       (ii) the husband has been deported from the United Kingdom under any law for the time being in force relating to deportation,

   and the husband was immediately before the desertion or deportation domiciled in England and Wales ;

   (*b*) in the case of proceedings for divorce or nullity of marriage, if—

       (i) the wife is resident in England and Wales and has been ordinarily resident there for a period of three years immediately preceding the commencement of the proceedings, and

       (ii) the husband is not domiciled in any other part of the United Kingdom or in the Channel Islands or the Isle of Man.

(2) In any proceedings in which the court has jurisdiction by virtue of subsection (1) above the issues shall be determined in accordance with the law which would be applicable thereto if both parties were domiciled in England and Wales at the time of the proceedings.

47.—(1) A court in England and Wales shall not be precluded Matrimonial from granting matrimonial relief or making a declaration con- relief and cerning the validity of a marriage by reason only that the declarations marriage in question was entered into under a law which of validity permits polygamy. in respect of polygamous

(2) In this section " matrimonial relief " means— marriages.

   (*a*) any decree under Part I of this Act ;

   (*b*) a financial provision order under section 27 above ;

PART IV

(c) an order under section 35 above altering a maintenance agreement;

(d) an order under any provision of this Act which confers a power exercisable in connection with, or in connection with proceedings for, any such decree or order is is mentioned in paragraphs (a) to (c) above;

1960 c. 48.

(e) an order under the Matrimonial Proceedings (Magistrates' Courts) Act 1960.

(3) In this section " a declaration concerning the validity of a marriage " means—

(a) a declaration that a marriage is valid or invalid; and

(b) any other declaration involving a determination as to the validity of a marriage;

being a declaration in a decree granted under section 45 above or a declaration made in the exercise by the High Court of its jurisdiction to grant declaratory relief in any proceedings notwithstanding that a declaration is the only substantive relief sought in those proceedings.

(4) This section has effect whether or not either party to the marriage in question has for the time being any spouse additional to the other party; and provision may be made by rules of court—

(a) for requiring notice of proceedings brought by virtue of this section to be served on any such other spouse; and

(b) for conferring on any such other spouse the right to be heard in any such proceedings,

in such cases as may be prescribed by the rules.

Evidence.

48.—(1) The evidence of a husband or wife shall be admissible in any proceedings to prove that marital intercourse did or did not take place between them during any period.

(2) In any proceedings for nullity of marriage, evidence on the question of sexual capacity shall be heard in camera unless in any case the judge is satisfied that in the interests of justice any such evidence ought to be heard in open court.

Parties to proceedings under this Act.

49.—(1) Where in a petition for divorce or judicial separation, or in any other pleading praying for either form of relief, one party to a marriage alleges that the other has committed adultery, he or she shall make the person alleged to have committed adultery with the other party to the marriage a party to the proceedings unless excused by the court on special grounds from doing so.

(2) Rules of court may, either generally or in such cases
as may be prescribed by the rules, exclude the application of
subsection (1) above where the person alleged to have committed adultery with the other party to the marriage is not
named in the petition or other pleading.

(3) Where in pursuance of subsection (1) above a person is
made a party to proceedings for divorce or judicial separation,
the court may, if after the close of the evidence on the part
of the person making the allegation of adultery it is of opinion
that there is not sufficient evidence against the person so made
a party, dismiss him or her from the suit.

(4) Rules of court may make provision, in cases not falling
within subsection (1) above, with respect to the joinder as
parties to proceedings under this Act of persons involved in
allegations of adultery or other improper conduct made in those
proceedings, and with respect to the dismissal from such proceedings of any parties so joined ; and rules of court made by
virtue of this subsection may make different provision for
different cases.

(5) In every case in which adultery with any party to a
suit is alleged against any person not made a party to the suit
or in which the court considers, in the interest of any person
not already a party to the suit, that that person should be made
a party to the suit, the court may if it thinks fit allow that
person to intervene upon such terms, if any, as the court thinks
just.

50.—(1) The authority having power to make rules of court Matrimonial
for the purposes of—   causes rules.

- (a) this Act, the Matrimonial Causes Act 1967 (which 1967 c. 56.
confers jurisdiction on county courts in certain matrimonial proceedings), section 45 of the Courts Act 1971 c. 23.
1971 (transfer of matrimonial proceedings between
High Court and county court, etc.) and sections 26 to
28A of the Matrimonial Causes Act 1965 (maintenance 1965 c. 72.
of survivor from estate of deceased former spouse) ;

- (b) proceedings in the High Court or a divorce county court
for an order under section 7 of the Matrimonial Homes 1967 c. 75.
Act 1967 (transfer of protected or statutory tenancy
under Rent Act 1968 on dissolution or annulment of 1968 c. 23.
marriage) ;

- (c) certain other proceedings in the High Court, that is to
say—

    (i) proceedings in the High Court under section
    17 of the Married Women's Property Act 1882, not 1882 c. 75.
    being proceedings in the divorce registry treated by

PART IV
1971 c. 23.

1967 c. 75.

1967 c. 56.
1965 c. 72.

1959 c. 22.

1960 c. 48.

virtue of rules made under this section for the purposes of section 45 of the Courts Act 1971 as pending in a county court;

(ii) proceedings in the High Court under section 1 of the Matrimonial Homes Act 1967 (rights of occupation of matrimonial home for spouse not otherwise entitled);

(iii) proceedings in which the only substantive relief sought is a declaration with respect to a person's matrimonial status; or

(d) any enactment passed after this Act which relates to any matter dealt with in this Act, the Matrimonial Causes Act 1967 or sections 26 to 28A of the Matrimonial Causes Act 1965;

shall, subject to the exceptions listed in subsection (2) below, be the Lord Chancellor together with any four or more of the following persons, namely, the President of the Family Division, one puisne judge attached to that division, one registrar of the divorce registry, two Circuit judges, one registrar appointed under the County Courts Act 1959, two practising barristers being members of the General Council of the Bar and two practising solicitors of whom one shall be a member of the Council of the Law Society and the other a member of the Law Society and also of a local law society.

All the members of the authority, other than the Lord Chancellor himself and the President of the Family Division, shall be appointed by the Lord Chancellor for such time as he may think fit.

(2) The following shall be excepted from the purposes mentioned in subsection (1) above—

(a) proceedings in a county court in the exercise of a jurisdiction exercisable by any county court whether or not it is a divorce county court, that is to say, proceedings in a county court under section 32, 33, 36, 38 or 45 above or under section 26 or 27 of the Matrimonial Causes Act 1965;

(b) section 47 above, in so far as it relates to proceedings in a county court under section 45 above or to proceedings for an order under the Matrimonial Proceedings (Magistrates' Courts) Act 1960;

(c) any enactment passed after this Act in so far as it relates to proceedings in a county court in the exercise of any such jurisdiction as is mentioned in paragraph (a) above or to any aspect of section 47 above which is excepted by paragraph (b) above.

(3) Rules of court made under this section may apply, with or without modification, any rules of court made under the Supreme Court of Judicature (Consolidation) Act 1925, the County Courts Act 1959 or any other enactment and—

(*a*) may modify or exclude the application of any such rules or of any provision of the County Courts Act 1959 ;

(*b*) may provide for the enforcement in the High Court of orders made in a divorce county court ;

and, without prejudice to the generality of the preceding provisions, may make with respect to proceedings in a divorce county court any provision regarding the Official Solicitor or any solicitor of the Supreme Court which could be made by rules of court with respect to proceedings in the High Court.

(4) The power to make rules of court by virtue of subsection (1) above shall be exercisable by statutory instrument, which shall be subject to annulment in pursuance of a resolution of either House of Parliament.

(5) In this section " divorce county court " means a county court designated under section 1 of the Matrimonial Causes Act 1967 and " divorce registry " means the principal registry of the Family Division of the High Court.

51. The fees to be taken in any proceedings to which rules under section 50 above apply shall be such as the Lord Chancellor with the concurrence of the Treasury may from time to time by order made by statutory instrument prescribe.

52.—(1) In this Act—

" adopted " means adopted in pursuance of—

(*a*) an adoption order made under the Adoption Act 1958, any previous enactment relating to the adoption of children, the Adoption Act 1968 or any corresponding enactment of the Parliament of Northern Ireland ; or

(*b*) an adoption order made in the Isle of Man or any of the Channel Islands ; or

(*c*) subject to sections 5 and 6 of the Adoption Act 1968, an overseas adoption within the meaning of section 4 of that Act ;

" child ", in relation to one or both of the parties to a marriage, includes an illegitimate or adopted child of that party or, as the case may be, of both parties ;

" child of the family ", in relation to the parties to a marriage, means—

(*a*) a child of both of those parties ; and

PART IV

    (*b*) any other child, not being a child who has been boarded-out with those parties by a local authority or voluntary organisation, who has been treated by both of those parties as a child of their family;

"the court" (except where the context otherwise requires) means the High Court or, where a county court has jurisdiction by virtue of the Matrimonial Causes Act 1967, a county court;

1967 c. 56.

"custody", in relation to a child, includes access to the child;

"education" includes training.

    (2) In this Act—

    (*a*) references to financial provision orders, periodical payments and secured periodical payments orders and orders for the payment of a lump sum, and references to property adjustment orders, shall be construed in accordance with section 21 above; and

    (*b*) references to orders for maintenance pending suit and to interim orders for maintenance shall be construed respectively in accordance with section 22 and section 27(5) above.

    (3) For the avoidance of doubt it is hereby declared that references in this Act to remarriage include references to a marriage which is by law void or voidable.

    (4) Except where the contrary intention is indicated, references in this Act to any enactment include references to that enactment as amended, extended or applied by or under any subsequent enactment, including this Act.

Transitional provisions and savings.

53. Schedule 1 to this Act shall have effect for the purpose of—

    (*a*) the transition to the provisions of this Act from the law in force before the commencement of this Act;

    (*b*) the preservation for limited purposes of certain provisions superseded by provisions of this Act or by enactments repealed and replaced by this Act; and

    (*c*) the assimilation in certain respects to orders under this Act of orders made, or deemed to have been made, under the Matrimonial Causes Act 1965.

1965 c. 72.

Consequential amendments and repeals.

54.—(1) Subject to the provisions of Schedule 1 to this Act—

    (*a*) the enactments specified in Schedule 2 to this Act shall have effect subject to the amendments specified in that Schedule, being amendments consequential on the provisions of this Act or on enactments repealed by this Act; and (*b*) the enactments specified in Schedule 3 to this Act are hereby repealed to the extent specified in the third column of that Schedule.

PART IV

(2) The amendment of any enactment by Schedule 2 to this Act shall not be taken as prejudicing the operation of section 38 of the Interpretation Act 1889 (which relates to the effect of repeals).

1889 c. 63.

55.—(1) This Act may be cited as the Matrimonial Causes Act 1973.

Citation, commencement and extent.

(2) This Act shall come into force on such day as the Lord Chancellor may appoint by order made by statutory instrument.

(3) Subject to the provisions of paragraphs 3(2) and 7(3) of Schedule 2 below, this Act does not extend to Scotland or Northern Ireland.

SCHEDULES

SCHEDULE 1

TRANSITIONAL PROVISIONS AND SAVINGS

PART I

MISCELLANEOUS AND GENERAL

General transitional provisions and savings

1889 c. 63.

1. Without prejudice to the provisions of section 38 of the Interpretation Act 1889 (which relates to the effect of repeals)—

 (*a*) nothing in any repeal made by this Act shall affect any order or rule made, direction given or thing done, or deemed to have been made, given or done, under any enactment repealed by this Act, and every such order, rule, direction or thing shall, if in force at the commencement of this Act, continue in force and, so far as it could have been made, given or done under this Act, be deemed to have been made, given or done under the corresponding provisions of this Act ; and

 (*b*) any reference in any document (including an enactment) to any enactment repealed by this Act, whether a specific reference or a reference to provisions of a description which includes, or apart from any repeal made by this Act includes, the enactment so repealed, shall be construed as a reference to the corresponding enactment in this Act.

2. Without prejudice to paragraph 1 above, but subject to paragraph 3 below, any application made or proceeding begun, or deemed to have been made or begun, under any enactment repealed by this Act, being an application or proceeding which is pending at the commencement of this Act, shall be deemed to have been made or begun under the corresponding provision of this Act.

1965 c. 72.

3. Nothing in Part I of this Act shall apply in relation to any petition for divorce or judicial separation presented before 1st January 1971 and notwithstanding any repeal or amendment made by this Act the Matrimonial Causes Act 1965 (hereafter in this Schedule referred to as the Act of 1965) and any rules of court made for the purposes of that Act shall continue to have effect in relation to proceedings on any such petition which are pending at the commencement of this Act as they had effect immediately before the commencement of this Act.

4. Notwithstanding any repeal or amendment made by this Act, the Act of 1965 and any rules of court made for the purposes of that Act shall continue to have effect in relation to—

 (*a*) any proceedings on a petition for damages for adultery or for restitution of conjugal rights presented before 1st

January 1971 which are pending at the commencement of
this Act, and

(b) any proceedings for relief under section 21 or 34(1)(c) of
the Act of 1965 brought in connection with proceedings
on a petition for restitution of conjugal rights so presented,
being proceedings for relief which are themselves pending
at the commencement of this Act,

as they had effect immediately before the commencement of this
Act ; and nothing in Schedule 2 below shall affect the operation
of any other enactment in relation to any such proceedings.

5. Nothing in any repeal made by this Act shall affect any order
made, or deemed to have been made, under the Act of 1965 which
was continued in force by paragraph 1 of Schedule 1 to the Matri- 1970 c. 45.
monial Proceedings and Property Act 1970 notwithstanding the
repeal by the last-mentioned Act of the provision of the Act of
1965 under which the order had effect, and every such order shall,
if in force at the commencement of this Act, continue in force subject
to the provisions of this Act.

6. Nothing in sections 11 to 14 or 16 of this Act affects any
law or custom relating to the marriage of members of the Royal
Family.

7. Nothing in section 50(1)(a) or (c) above affects—

(a) any rules of court made under the Supreme Court of
Judicature (Consolidation) Act 1925 for the purposes of 1925 c. 49.
proceedings under section 39 of the Act of 1965 and having
effect by virtue of paragraph 1(b) above in relation to
proceedings under section 45 above ;

(b) any rules of court so made for the purposes of proceedings
under section 17 of the Married Women's Property Act 1882 1882 c. 75.
or under section 1 of the Matrimonial Homes Act 1967 ; 1967 c. 75.
or

(c) any rules of court so made for the purposes of the exercise
by the High Court of its jurisdiction to grant declaratory
relief in proceedings in which the only substantive relief
sought is a declaration with respect to a person's matrimonial
status ;

but rules of court made under section 50 may revoke any rules of
court made under the said Act of 1925 in so far as they apply for any
such purposes.

Transitional provisions derived from the Act of 1965

8. Any agreement between the petitioner and the respondent to live
separate and apart, whether or not made in writing, shall be disregarded for the purposes of section 1(2)(c) above (including that
paragraph as it applies, by virtue of section 17 above, to proceedings
for judicial separation) if the agreement was entered into before 1st
January 1938 and either—

(a) at the time when the agreement was made the respondent
had deserted the petitioner without cause ; or

(b) the court is satisfied that the circumstances in which the agreement was made and the parties proceeded to live separate and apart were such as, but for the agreement, to amount to desertion of the petitioner by the respondent.

9. Where the party chargeable under a maintenance agreement within the meaning of section 34 above died before 17th August 1957, then—

(a) subsection (1) of that section shall not apply to the agreement unless there remained undistributed on that date assets of that party's estate (apart from any property in which he had only a life interest) representing not less than four-fifths of the value of that estate for probate after providing for the discharge of the funeral, testamentary and administrative expenses, debts and liabilities payable thereout (other than any liability arising by virtue of that subsection) ; and

(b) nothing in that subsection shall render liable to recovery, or impose any liability upon the personal representatives of that party in respect of, any part of that party's estate which had been distributed before that date.

10. No right or liability shall attach by virtue of section 34(1) above in respect of any sum payable under a maintenance agreement within the meaning of that section in respect of a period before 17th August 1957.

PART II

PRESERVATION FOR LIMITED PURPOSES OF CERTAIN PROVISIONS OF PREVIOUS ENACTMENTS

Nullity

11.—(1) Subject to sub-paragraphs (2) and (3) below, a marriage celebrated before 1st August 1971 shall (without prejudice to any other grounds on which a marriage celebrated before that date is by law void or voidable) be voidable on the ground—

(a) that the marriage has not been consummated owing to the wilful refusal of the respondent to consummate it ; or

(b) that at the time of the marriage either party to the marriage—

(i) was of unsound mind, or

(ii) was suffering from mental disorder within the meaning of the Mental Health Act 1959 of such a kind or to such an extent as to be unfitted for marriage and the procreation of children, or

(iii) was subject to recurrent attacks of insanity or epilepsy; or

(c) that the respondent was at the time of the marriage suffering from venereal disease in a communicable form ; or

(d) that the respondent was at the time of the marriage pregnant by some person other than the petitioner.

(2) In relation to a marriage celebrated before 1st November 1960, for heads (ii) and (iii) of sub-paragraph (1)(*b*) above there shall be substituted the following heads—

" (ii) was a mental defective within the meaning of the Mental Deficiency Acts 1913 to 1938, or

(iii) was subject to recurrent fits of insanity or epilepsy ; or ".

(3) The court shall not grant a decree of nullity in a case falling within sub-paragraph (1)(*b*), (*c*) or (*d*) above unless it is satisfied that—

(*a*) the petitioner was at the time of the marriage ignorant of the facts alleged ; and

(*b*) proceedings were instituted within a year from the date of the marriage ; and

(*c*) marital intercourse with the consent of the petitioner has not taken place since the petitioner discovered the existence of the grounds for a decree ;

and where the proceedings with respect to the marriage are instituted after 31st July 1971 the application of section 13(1) above in relation to the marriage shall be without prejudice to the preceding provisions of this sub-paragraph.

(4) Nothing in this paragraph shall be construed as validating a marriage which is by law void but with respect to which a decree of nullity has not been granted.

12. Where a decree of nullity was granted on or before 31st July 1971 in respect of a voidable marriage, any child who would have been the legitimate child of the parties to the marriage if at the date of the decree it had been dissolved instead of being annulled shall be deemed to be their legitimate child.

Succession on intestacy in case of judicial separation

13. Section 18(2) above shall not apply in a case where the death occurred before 1st August 1970, but section 20(3) of the Act of 1965 (which provides that certain property of a wife judicially separated from her husband shall devolve, on her death intestate, as if her husband had then been dead) shall continue to apply in any such case.

Validation of certain void or voidable decrees

14. Any decree of divorce, nullity of marriage or judicial separation which, apart from this paragraph, would be void or voidable on the ground only that the provisions of section 33 of the Act of 1965 (restriction on the making of decrees of dissolution or separation where children are affected) or of section 2 of the Matrimonial Proceedings (Children) Act 1958 (corresponding 1958 c. 40. provision replaced by section 33) had not been complied with when the decree was made absolute or granted, as the case may be, shall be deemed always to have been valid unless—

(*a*) the court declared the decree to be void before 1st January 1971, or (*b*) in proceedings for the annulment of the decree pending at that date the court has before the commencement of this Act declared or after that commencement declares the decree to be void.

PART III

ASSIMILATION IN CERTAIN RESPECTS TO ORDERS UNDER THIS ACT OF ORDERS MADE, ETC., UNDER THE ACT OF 1965, ETC.

Cesser on remarriage of orders made, etc., under the Act of 1965 and recovery of sums mistakenly paid thereafter

15.—(1) An order made, or deemed to have been made, under section 16(1)(*a*) or (*b*) of the Act of 1965 (including either of those paragraphs as applied by section 16(3) or by section 19) shall, notwithstanding anything in the order, cease to have effect on the remarriage after the commencement of this Act of the person in whose favour the order was made, except in relation to any arrears due under it on the date of the remarriage.

(2) An order for the payment of alimony made, or deemed to have been made, under section 20 of the Act of 1965, and an order made, or deemed to have been made, under section 21 or 22 of that Act shall, if the marriage of the parties to the proceedings in which the order was made was or is subsequently dissolved or annulled but the order continues in force, cease to have effect on the remarriage after the commencement of this Act of the party in whose favour the order was made, except in relation to any arrears due under it on the date of the remarriage.

16. Section 38 above shall apply in relation to an order made or deemed to have been made under section 16(1) (including that subsection as applied by section 16(3) and by section 19), 20(1), 21 or 22 of the Act of 1965 as it applies in relation to a periodical payments or secured periodical payments order in favour of a party to a marriage.

Variation, etc., of certain orders made, etc., under the Act of 1965

17.—(1) Subject to the provisions of this paragraph, section 31 above shall apply, as it applies to the orders mentioned in subsection (2) thereof, to an order (other than an order for the payment of a lump sum) made or deemed to have been made under any of the following provisions of the Act of 1965, that is to say—

(*a*) section 15 (except in its application to proceedings for restitution of conjugal rights);

(*b*) section 16(1) (including that subsection as applied by section 16(3) and by section 19);

(*c*) section 20(1) and section 17(2) as applied by section 20(2);

(*d*) section 22;

(*e*) section 34(1)(*a*) or (*b*), in so far as it relates to the maintenance of a child, and section 34(3).

(2) Subject to the provisions of this paragraph, the court hearing an application for the variation of an order made or deemed to have been made under any of the provisions of the Act of 1965 mentioned in sub-paragraph (1) above shall have power to vary that order in any way in which it would have power to vary it had the order been made under the corresponding provision of Part II of this Act.

(3) Section 31, as it applies by virtue of sub-paragraph (1) above, shall have effect as if for subsections (4), (5) and (6) there were substituted the following subsections—

" (4) The court shall not exercise the powers conferred by this section in relation to an order made or deemed to have been made under section 17(2) of the Act of 1965, as applied by section 20(2) of that Act, in connection with the grant of a decree of judicial separation except on an application made in proceedings—

(*a*) for the rescission of that decree, or

(*b*) for the dissolution of the marriage in question.

(5) No order for the payment of a lump sum and no property adjustment order shall be made on an application for the variation of any order made or deemed to have been made under section 16(1) (including that subsection as applied by section 16(3) or by section 19), 20(1), 22, 34(1)(*a*) or (*b*) or 34(3) of the Act of 1965.

(6) In the case of an order made or deemed to have been made under section 16(1) (including that subsection as applied by section 16(3) or by section 19), 22 or 34(3) of the Act of 1965 and requiring a party to a marriage to secure an annual sum or periodical payments to any other person, an application under this section relating to that order may be made after the death of the person liable to make payments under the order by the person entitled to the payments or by the personal representatives of the deceased person, but no such application shall, except with the permission of the court, be made after the end of the period of six months from the date on which representation in regard to the estate of that person is first taken out " ;

and in that section, as it so applies, the reference in subsection (8) to a secured periodical payments order shall be construed as a reference to any such order as is mentioned in subsection (6).

(4) In relation to an order made before 16th December 1949 on or after granting a decree of divorce or nullity of marriage and deemed, by virtue of paragraph 1 of Schedule 1 to the Act of 1965, to have been made under section 16(1)(*a*) of that Act (secured provision), the powers conferred by this paragraph shall not be exercised unless the court is satisfied that the case is one of exceptional hardship which cannot be met by discharge, variation or suspension of any other order made by reference to that decree, being an order made, or deemed by virtue of that paragraph to have been made, under section 16(1)(*b*) of that Act (unsecured periodical payments).

SCH. 1   18.—(1) Subsections (1) and (3) of section 31 above shall apply to an order made or deemed to have been made under section 15 of the Act of 1965 in its application to proceedings for restitution of conjugal rights, or under section 21 or 34(1)(c) of that Act, as they apply to the orders mentioned in subsection (2) of section 31.

(2) In exercising the powers conferred by virtue of this paragraph the court shall have regard to all the circumstances of the case, including any change in any of the matters to which the court was required to have regard when making the order to which the application relates.

19. Section 42(7) above shall apply in relation to an order for the custody or education of a child made or deemed to have been made under section 34 of the Act of 1965, and in relation to an order for the custody of a child made or deemed to have been made under section 35 of that Act, as it applies in relation to an order made under section 42.

Orders made under the Act of 1965 to count as orders under this Act for certain purposes

20. The power of the court under section 23(1) or (2)(a) or 42(1)(a) above to make from time to time a financial provision order or, as the case may be, an order for custody or education in relation to a child of the family shall be exercisable notwithstanding the making of a previous order or orders in relation to the child under section 34(1)(a) of the Act of 1965 ; and where the court has made an order in relation to a child under section 34(1)(b) of that Act sections 23(4) and 42(6) above shall apply respectively in relation to that child as if the order were an order made under section 23(2)(b) or section 42(1)(b), as the case may be.

21. Where the court has made an order under section 22 of the Act of 1965 the court shall have the like power to make orders under section 42 above with respect to the custody of any child of the family as it has where it makes an order under section 27 above.

Application of provisions of this Act with respect to enforcement of arrears and recovery of excessive payments to certain orders made, etc., under the Act of 1965

22. Section 32 above shall apply in relation to the enforcement, by proceedings begun after 1st January 1971 (whether before or after the commencement of this Act), of the payment of arrears due under an order made, or deemed to have been made, under any of the following provisions of the Act of 1965, that is to say—

(a) section 15 ;

(b) section 16(1) (including that subsection as applied by section 16(3) and by section 19) ;

(c) section 20(1) ;

(d) section 21 ;

(e) section 22 ;

(*f*) section 34(1), in so far as it relates to the maintenance of a child, and section 34(3) ;

as it applies in relation to the enforcement of the payment of arrears due under any such order as is mentioned in that section.

23. Section 33 above shall apply to an order (other than an order for the payment of a lump sum) made or deemed to have been made under any of the provisions of the Act of 1965 mentioned in paragraph 22 above as it applies to the orders mentioned in section 33(2).

Avoidance under this Act of transactions intended to defeat claims for relief and relief granted under the Act of 1965

24.—(1) Section 37 above shall apply in relation to proceedings for relief under section 21 or 34(1)(*c*) of the Act of 1965 continuing by virtue of paragraph 4(*b*) above as it applies in relation to proceedings for relief under any of the provisions of this Act specified in section 37(1).

(2) Without prejudice to sub-paragraph (1) above, section 37 shall also apply where an order has been obtained under any of the following provisions of the Act of 1965, that is to say—

(*a*) section 16(1) (including that subsection as applied by section 16(3) and by section 19) ;

(*b*) section 17(2) (including that subsection as applied by section 20(2)) ;

(*c*) section 20(1) ;

(*d*) section 21 ;

(*e*) section 22 ;

(*f*) section 24 ;

(*g*) section 31 ;

(*h*) section 34(1), in so far as it relates to the maintenance of a child, and section 34(3) ;

(*i*) section 35 ;

as it applies where an order has been obtained under any of the provisions of this Act specified in section 37(1).

Care and supervision of children

25.—(1) Sections 43 and 44 above shall apply where the court has jurisdiction by virtue of paragraph 4(*b*) above to make an order for the custody of a child under section 34(1)(*c*) of the Act of 1965 as they apply where the court has jurisdiction to make an order for custody under Part III of this Act, but as if the reference in section 43(2) to a financial provision order in favour of the child were a reference to an order for payments for the maintenance and education of the child.

(2) Without prejudice to the effect of paragraph 1(*a*) of this Schedule in relation to an order made under section 36 or 37 of the Act of 1965 which could have been made under section 43 or, as the case may be, section 44 above, any order made under section 36

Sch. 1

or 37 of that Act by virtue of the jurisdiction of the court to make an order for the custody of a child under section 34(1)(c) of that Act shall be deemed to have been made under section 43 or 44 above, as the case may require.

26. Section 44(4) above shall apply in relation to the jurisdiction possessed by a court to vary an order made or deemed to have been made with respect to a child's custody, maintenance or education under Part III of the Act of 1965 as it applies in relation to the jurisdiction possessed by a court to vary any financial provision order in a child's favour and any order made with respect to a child's custody or education under Part III of this Act.

SCHEDULE 2

Consequential Amendments

1925 c. 49.

1. In section 225 of the Supreme Court of Judicature (Consolidation) Act 1925 (interpretation), in the definition of "matrimonial cause", for the words from "jactitation" to "rights" there shall be substituted the words "or jactitation of marriage".

1945 c. 16.

2. In section 2(1) of the Limitation (Enemies and War Prisoners) Act 1945, in the definition of "statute of limitation" for the words "subsection (1) of section seven of the Matrimonial Causes Act 1937" there shall be substituted the words "section 13(2) of the Matrimonial Causes Act 1973 and paragraph 11(3) of Schedule 1 to that Act".

1950 c. 37.

3.—(1) In section 16 of the Maintenance Orders Act 1950 (orders enforceable under Part II of that Act)—

   (a) in subsection (2)(a), for sub-paragraph (i) there shall be substituted the following sub-paragraph:—

      " (i) sections 15 to 17, 19 to 22, 30, 34 and 35 of the Matrimonial Causes Act 1965 and sections 22, 23(1), (2) and (4) and 27 of the Matrimonial Causes Act 1973 "; and

   (b) in subsection (2)(c), for sub-paragraph (v) there shall be substituted the following sub-paragraph:—

      " (v) any enactment of the Parliament of Northern Ireland containing provisions corresponding with section 22(1), 34 or 35 of the Matrimonial Causes Act 1965, with section 22, 23(1), (2) or (4) or 27 of the Matrimonial Causes Act 1973, or with section 12(2) of the Guardianship of Minors Act 1971 ".

1970 c. 31.
1971 c. 32.

(2) Sub-paragraph (1) above extends to Scotland and Northern Ireland, and the references to section 16(2)(c) of the Maintenance Orders Act 1950 in paragraph 8 of Schedule 8 to the Administration of Justice Act 1970 and paragraph 9 of Schedule 1 to the Attachment of Earnings Act 1971 shall be construed as references to section 16(2)(c) as amended by sub-paragraph (1)(b) above.

4. In section 109(2) of the County Courts Act 1959 (proceedings in which appeals on questions of fact are to lie) the following paragraph shall be inserted after paragraph (*f*) (in place of the paragraph inserted by section 34(2) of the Matrimonial Proceedings and Property Act 1970) : —

> " (*g*) any proceedings on an application under section 13A of the Matrimonial Proceedings (Magistrates' Courts) Act 1960 or under section 33, 36 or 38 of the Matrimonial Causes Act 1973 ".

5.—(1) In section 26 of the Matrimonial Causes Act 1965 (orders for maintenance of survivor from estate of deceased former spouse)—

> (*a*) in subsection (4) (matters to which the court is to have regard on an application under the section), in paragraph (*c*) the following sub-paragraph shall be inserted after sub-paragraph (ii) (in place of the sub-paragraph inserted by paragraph 1(1) of Schedule 2 to the Matrimonial Proceedings and Property Act 1970) : —
>
> > " (iii) where the survivor is a former wife or a former husband of the deceased, for an order under section 2 or 4 of the Matrimonial Proceedings and Property Act 1970 or under section 23(1)(*a*), (*b*) or (*c*) or 24 of the Matrimonial Causes Act 1973 " ;
>
> (*b*) in subsection (6), the words " means the High Court and " inserted by paragraph 8 of Schedule 1 to the Divorce Reform Act 1969 (after the word " court " where first occurring in the definition of " court " inserted in that subsection by section 7(4) of the Family Provision Act 1966) shall continue to have effect notwithstanding the repeal by this Act of the Divorce Reform Act 1969 ;
>
> (*c*) in subsection (6), in the definition of " former spouse ", for the words " this Act " there shall be substituted the words " the Matrimonial Causes Act 1973 ".

(2) In section 42 of that Act (provisions as to condonation), at the beginning of subsections (1) and (3) there shall be inserted the words " For the purposes of the Matrimonial Proceedings (Magistrates' Courts) Act 1960 ".

6.—(1) In section 2 of the Matrimonial Causes Act 1967 (jurisdiction of divorce county court with respect to ancillary relief and the protection of children)—

> (*a*) in subsection (1), for the words " Part II or Part III of the Matrimonial Causes Act 1965 " there shall be substituted the words " Part II or Part III of the Matrimonial Causes Act 1973 ", and for the words " section 22 or section 24 of that Act " in the subsection as originally enacted there shall be substituted the words " section 27 or 35 of that Act " (in place of the words substituted for the words originally enacted by paragraph 2(1)(*a*) of Schedule 2 to the Matrimonial Proceedings and Property Act 1970) ;

(*b*) for subsection (3) as originally enacted there shall be substituted the following subsection (in place of that substituted by paragraph 2(1)(*b*) of Schedule 2 to the Matrimonial Proceedings and Property Act 1970) : —

" (3) A divorce county court shall not by virtue of this section have jurisdiction to exercise any power under section 32, 33, 36 or 38 of the Matrimonial Causes Act 1973 ; but nothing in this section shall prejudice the exercise by a county court of any jurisdiction conferred on county courts by any of those sections " ; and

(*c*) in subsection (4) as originally enacted, for the words from " section 24 " to the end of the subsection there shall be substituted the words " section 35 of the Matrimonial Causes Act 1973 " (in place of the words substituted for the words originally enacted by paragraph 2(1)(*c*) of Schedule 2 to the Matrimonial Proceedings and Property Act 1970).

(2) In section 3 of that Act (consideration of agreements or arrangements by divorce county courts) for the words " section 5(2) of the Matrimonial Causes Act 1965 " there shall be substituted the words " section 7 of the Matrimonial Causes Act 1973 ".

(3) In section 10 of that Act (interpretation), in the definition of " matrimonial cause " in subsection (1), for the words from " section 2 of the Matrimonial Causes Act 1965 " to " that Act " there shall be substituted the words " section 3 of the Matrimonial Causes Act 1973 ".

7.—(1) In subsection (1) of section 2 of the Domestic and Appellate Proceedings (Restriction of Publicity) Act 1968 (restriction of publicity for certain proceedings) for the words in paragraph (*a*) " section 39 of the Matrimonial Causes Act 1965 " there shall be substituted the words " section 45 of the Matrimonial Causes Act 1973 ", the following paragraph shall be substituted for the paragraph (*c*) inserted in the subsection by paragraph 3 of Schedule 2 to the Matrimonial Proceedings and Property Act 1970 : —

" (*c*) proceedings under section 27 of the Matrimonial Causes Act 1973 (which relates to proceedings by a wife against her husband, or by a husband against his wife, for financial provision) and any proceedings for the discharge or variation of an order made under that section or for the temporary suspension of any provision of any such order or the revival of the operation of any provision so suspended " ;

subsection (2) of that section shall be omitted, and the references in subsection (3) of that section to subsection (1) and to subsection (1)(*a*) thereof shall be construed as references to subsection (1) and to subsection (1)(*a*) as they respectively have effect by virtue of this sub-paragraph.

(2) In section 4(3) of that Act, for the words " or 2(2) of this Act " there shall be substituted the words " of this Act or to section 45(9) of the Matrimonial Causes Act 1973 ".

(3) Sub-paragraph (2) above extends to Northern Ireland.   Sᴄʜ. 2

8. In section 7 of the Family Law Reform Act 1969 (committal 1969 c. 46. of wards of court to care of local authority and supervision of wards of court)—

> (*a*) in subsection (3), for the words " section 36 of the Matrimonial Causes Act 1965 " there shall be substituted the words " section 43 of the Matrimonial Causes Act 1973 " ;
>
> (*b*) in subsection (4), for the words from " subsections (2) " to " 1965 " there shall be substituted the words " section 44(2) of the Matrimonial Causes Act 1973 ".

9. In section 63(6) of the Children and Young Persons Act 1969 1969 c. 54. (local authority functions to be the subject of reports to Parliament by the Secretary of State), in paragraph (*g*), for the words " section 37 of the Matrimonial Causes Act 1965 " there shall be substituted the words " section 44 of the Matrimonial Causes Act 1973 ".

10.—(1) In Schedule 1 to the Administration of Justice Act 1970 1970 c. 31. (High Court business assigned to the Family Division)—

> (*a*) for the words (in the first paragraph) " section 7(1) of the Matrimonial Causes Act 1967 " there shall be substituted the words " section 50(1) of the Matrimonial Causes Act 1973 " ;
>
> (*b*) the paragraphs relating respectively to proceedings for a declaration, to proceedings under section 17 of the Married 1882 c. 75. Women's Property Act 1882, and to proceedings under section 1 of the Matrimonial Homes Act 1967 shall be 1967 c. 75. omitted ; and
>
> (*c*) for the words (in the last paragraph) " section 24 of the Matrimonial Causes Act 1965 " there shall be substituted the words " section 35 of the Matrimonial Causes Act 1973 ".

(2) In Schedule 8 to that Act (as it applies to define maintenance orders both for the purposes of Part II of that Act and for the purposes of the Maintenance Orders Act 1958) the following para- 1958 c. 39. graph shall be inserted after paragraph 2 : —

> " 2A. An order for periodical or other payments made, or having effect as if made, under Part II of the Matrimonial Causes Act 1973 ".

11. In Schedule 1 to the Local Authority Social Services Act 1970 1970 c.42. the entry relating to section 37 of the Matrimonial Causes Act 1965 1965 c. 72. shall be omitted, and the following entry shall be added at the end of the Schedule—

" Matrimonial Causes Act 1973 Section 44	Supervision of child subject to court order in matrimonial proceedings ".

12. In section 45 of the Courts Act 1971 (transfer of matrimonial proceedings between High Court and county court, etc.)—

    (*a*) in subsection (1), for paragraphs (*a*) and (*b*) there shall be substituted the following paragraphs:—

        " (*a*) sections 26 to 28A of the Matrimonial Causes Act 1965 ;

        (*b*) Part II or Part III of the Matrimonial Causes Act 1973 " ;

    (*b*) in subsection (6), after the word " under " there shall be inserted the words " section 50 of the Matrimonial Causes Act 1973 for the purposes of " ; and

    (*c*) subsection (7) shall be omitted.

13. In Schedule 1 to the Attachment of Earnings Act 1971 (maintenance orders to which the Act applies) for paragraph 3 there shall be substituted the following paragraph—

    " 3. An order for periodical or other payments made, or having effect as if made, under Part II of the Matrimonial Causes Act 1973 ".

SCHEDULE 3
ENACTMENTS REPEALED

Chapter	Short Title	Extent of Repeal
1965 c. 72.	The Matrimonial Causes Act 1965.	The whole Act, except: section 8(2); sections 26 to 28A and section 25(4) and (5) as applied by section 28(2); section 42; in section 43(1) the words from " but a husband " to the end of the subsection; in section 46, subsection (1) and in subsection (4) the words from " this Act does not " to the end of the subsection.
1967 c. 56.	The Matrimonial Causes Act 1967.	Sections 7 and 8.
1967 c. 80.	The Criminal Justice Act 1967.	In Part I of Schedule 3, the entry relating to section 36(6) of the Matrimonial Causes Act 1965.
1968 c. 63.	The Domestic and Appellate Proceedings (Restriction of Publicity) Act 1968.	Sections 2(2) and 3(4).
1969 c. 55.	The Divorce Reform Act 1969.	The whole Act.
1970 c. 31.	The Administration of Justice Act 1970.	In Schedule 1, the paragraphs relating respectively to proceedings for a declaration, to proceedings under section 17 of the Married Women's Property Act 1882, and to proceedings under section 1 of the Matrimonial Homes Act 1967. In Schedule 2, paragraph 27.
1970 c. 33.	The Law Reform (Miscellaneous Provisions) Act 1970.	Section 4.
1970 c. 42.	The Local Authority Social Services Act 1970.	In Schedule 1, the entry relating to section 37 of the Matrimonial Causes Act 1965.
1970 c. 45.	The Matrimonial Proceedings and Property Act 1970.	The whole of Part I. Sections 34, 35, 40, 41 and 42. In section 43, subsection (2) and, in subsection (4), the words from the beginning to " of this Act ". The Schedules.
1971 c. 3.	The Guardianship of Minors Act 1971.	In Schedule 1, in the entry relating to section 16(2) of the Maintenance Orders Act 1950, the words from " and " to " 1971 ' ".
1971 c. 23.	The Courts Act 1971.	Section 45(7). In Schedule 8, paragraph 47.

Chapter	Short Title	Extent of Repeal
1971 c. 44.	The Nullity of Marriage Act 1971.	The whole Act.
1972 c. 38.	The Matrimonial Proceedings (Polygamous Marriages) Act 1972.	Sections 1 and 4.
1972 c. 70.	The Local Government Act 1972.	In Schedule 23, paragraph 13.

Independent Broadcasting Authority Act 1973

1973 CHAPTER 19

An Act to consolidate the Television and Sound Broadcasting Acts 1964 and 1972.   [23rd May 1973]

BE IT ENACTED by the Queen's most Excellent Majesty, by and with the advice and consent of the Lords Spiritual and Temporal, and Commons, in this present Parliament assembled, and by the authority of the same, as follows:—

The Independent Broadcasting Authority

1.—(1) There shall be an authority to be called the Independent Broadcasting Authority (in this Act referred to as " the Authority ") which shall consist of a Chairman, a Deputy Chairman and such other members, not being less than five, as the Minister may from time to time determine. <small>Constitution of Authority.</small>

(2) Unless and until the Minister otherwise determines by notice in writing to the Authority, a copy of which shall be laid before each House of Parliament, the number of the said other members shall be eight.

(3) The provisions of Schedule 1 to this Act (which relate to the appointment and remuneration of members of the Authority and to the procedure of and other similar matters concerning the Authority) shall have effect with respect to the Authority.

2.—(1) The function of the Authority shall be to provide in accordance with the provisions of this Act, and until 31st July 1976, television and local sound broadcasting services, additional in each case to those of the British Broadcasting Corporation <small>Function and duties of Authority.</small>

H

and of high quality, both as to the transmission and as to the matter transmitted, for so much of the United Kingdom, the Isle of Man and the Channel Islands as may from time to time be reasonably practicable.

(2) It shall be the duty of the Authority—

(a) to provide the television and local sound broadcasting services as a public service for disseminating information, education and entertainment;

(b) to ensure that the programmes broadcast by the Authority in each area maintain a high general standard in all respects, and in particular in respect of their content and quality, and a proper balance and wide range in their subject-matter, having regard both to the programmes as a whole and also to the days of the week on which, and the times of the day at which, the programmes are broadcast; and

(c) to secure a wide showing or (as the case may be) hearing for programmes of merit.

(3) Without prejudice to the powers conferred on the Authority by this Act, the programmes broadcast by the Authority shall, so far as may be consistently with the observance of the requirements of this Act, be provided not by the Authority but by persons (in this Act referred to as " programme contractors ") who, under contracts with the Authority, have, in consideration of payments to the Authority and subject to the provisions of this Act, the right and the duty to provide programmes or parts of programmes to be broadcast by the Authority, which may include advertisements.

Powers of
Authority.

(4) It is hereby declared that the Authority are not to be treated for the purposes of the enactments and rules of law relating to the privileges of the Crown as a body exercising functions on behalf of the Crown.

3.—(1) The Authority shall, subject to the provisions of this Act, have power to do all such things as are in their opinion necessary for or conducive to the proper discharge of their function as described in section 2(1) of this Act, and, in particular and without prejudice to the generality of the foregoing provision, they shall for the purpose of discharging that function have power—

(a) to establish, install and use stations for wireless telegraphy;

(b) to arrange for the provision and equipment of, or, if need be, themselves to provide and equip, studios and other premises for television and sound broadcasting purposes;

(c) by arrangements made for the purpose with the Post Office and persons carrying on broadcast relay stations, to provide for the distribution from broadcast relay stations of programmes broadcast by the Authority.

(2) Notwithstanding section 2(3) of this Act the Authority may—

(a) arrange for the provision of parts of programmes otherwise than by programme contractors for the purpose of securing the inclusion in the programmes broadcast by the Authority of items of particular classes which in their opinion are necessary for securing a proper balance in the subject-matter of the programmes and cannot, or cannot as suitably, be provided by programme contractors ;

(b) apart from the provision of such items, arrange for the provision (by programme contractors or otherwise) of, or (if need be) themselves provide, programmes or parts of programmes so far as may be necessary by reason of any temporary lack of suitable persons able and willing to become or continue as programme contractors on suitable terms and to perform their obligations as such, or by reason of any interval between the expiration or termination of one contract with a programme contractor and the commencement of another contract with that or another programme contractor ; and

(c) with the consent of the Minister, arrange for the provision, otherwise than by programme contractors, of educational broadcasting services of an experimental nature to be broadcast in addition to education programmes provided for the purpose of the public service referred to in section 2(2)(a) of this Act by programme contractors,

and may, for the purpose of so providing programmes or parts of programmes or putting themselves into a position to do so if necessity arises, make such arrangements for obtaining the necessary material, enter into such contracts, employ such persons, acquire such property and do such things as may appear to them to be necessary or expedient.

(3) Without prejudice to the generality of the preceding provisions of this section, the powers of the Authority shall extend to the carrying on of such businesses and the doing of such things as arise out of the other activities of the Authority or are necessary or expedient for the purpose of turning to account any property or rights of the Authority.

(4) Notwithstanding anything in this section the Authority shall not carry on business as sellers of, or, except with the

approval of the Minister, themselves engage in the manufacture or sale of, apparatus for wireless telegraphy or any other telegraphic equipment.

(5) Notwithstanding anything in this section, the Authority shall not have power to provide broadcasting services other than television services and local sound broadcasting services or (except as provided by this section) to acquire any exclusive or other rights in respect of the broadcasting of any matters in sound only otherwise than as part of a local sound broadcast.

(6) Nothing in subsection (5) of this section shall be construed as precluding the inclusion in any television programme broadcast by the Authority of matter transmitted in sound only—

    (a) by way of relays of any of the British Broadcasting Corporation's party political broadcasts which is so transmitted ;

    (b) in compliance with a notice given to the Authority under section 22(1) of this Act ; or

    (c) by way of news items, announcements or other items incidental or ancillary to the television services provided by the Authority,

or the acquisition by the Authority of rights in respect of any matters to be so transmitted.

(7) Nothing in this section shall be construed as authorising the Authority to do, otherwise than under and in accordance with a licence under section 1 of the Wireless Telegraphy Act 1949 or section 27 of the Post Office Act 1969, anything for the doing of which such a licence is requisite under those Acts respectively, and those Acts shall have effect in relation to the Authority accordingly.

1949 c. 54.
1969 c. 48.

Provisions applying to all programmes

General provisions with respect to content of programmes.

4.—(1) It shall be the duty of the Authority to satisfy themselves that, so far as possible, the programmes broadcast by the Authority comply with the following requirements, that is to say—

    (a) that nothing is included in the programmes which offends against good taste or decency or is likely to encourage or incite to crime or to lead to disorder or to be offensive to public feeling ;

    (b) that a sufficient amount of time in the programmes is given to news and news features and that all news given in the programmes (in whatever form) is presented with due accuracy and impartiality ;

    (c) that proper proportions of the recorded and other matter included in the programmes are of British origin and of British performance ;

(d) that the programmes broadcast from any station or stations contain a suitable proportion of matter calculated to appeal specially to the tastes and outlook of persons served by the station or stations and, where another language as well as English is in common use among those so served, a suitable proportion of matter in that language ;

(e) in the case of local sound broadcasting services, that the programmes broadcast from different stations for reception in different localities do not consist of identical or similar material to an extent inconsistent with the character of the services as local sound broadcasting services ; and

(f) that due impartiality is preserved on the part of the persons providing the programmes as respects matters of political or industrial controversy or relating to current public policy.

In applying paragraph (f) of this subsection, a series of programmes may be considered as a whole.

(2) Without prejudice to the generality of subsection (1) of this section, it shall be the duty of the Authority to secure the exclusion from the programmes broadcast by them of all expressions of their own opinion as to any of the matters referred to in paragraph (f) of that subsection, or of the opinion as to any such matters—

(a) of any of their members or officers, or

(b) of any programme contractor, or

(c) in the case of a programme contractor being a firm, of any partner therein, or

(d) in the case of a programme contractor being a body corporate, of any director or officer thereof or person having control thereof.

(3) It shall be the duty of the Authority to satisfy themselves that the programmes broadcast by the Authority do not include, whether in an advertisement or otherwise, any technical device which, by using images of very brief duration or by any other means, exploits the possibility of conveying a message to, or otherwise influencing the minds of, members of an audience without their being aware, or fully aware, of what has been done.

(4) Nothing shall be included in any programme broadcast by the Authority, whether in an advertisement or not, which offers any prize of significant value, whether competed for or not, or any gift of significant value, being a prize or gift which is available only to persons receiving that programme, or in relation to which any advantage is given to such persons.

H 3

(5) Except with the previous approval of the Authority, there shall not be included in any programme broadcast by the Authority—

(*a*) any religious service or any propaganda relating to matters of a religious nature ;

(*b*) any item, whether an advertisement or not, which gives or is designed to give publicity to the needs or objects of any association or organisation conducted for charitable or benevolent purposes.

(6) For the purpose of maintaining supervision and control over the programmes (including advertisements) broadcast by them the Authority may make visual and sound records of those programmes or any part thereof ; and the making and use by the Authority of any such record exclusively for that purpose—

(*a*) shall not constitute an infringement of the copyright in any work, sound recording or cinematograph film ; and

(*b*) shall not constitute an offence under any of the provisions of the Performers' Protection Acts 1958 and 1963.

Programmes other than advertisements

Code for programmes other than advertisements.

5.—(1) The Authority—

(*a*) shall draw up, and from time to time review, a code giving guidance—

(i) as to the rules to be observed in regard to the showing of violence, and in regard to the inclusion in local sound broadcasts of sounds suggestive of violence, particularly when large numbers of children and young persons may be expected to be watching or listening to the programmes, and

(ii) as to such other matters concerning standards and practice for programmes (other than advertisements) broadcast by the Authority as the Authority may consider suitable for inclusion in the code,

and in considering what other matters ought to be included in the code in pursuance of sub-paragraph (ii) shall have special regard to programmes broadcast when large numbers of children and young persons may be expected to be watching or listening ; and

(*b*) shall secure that the provisions of the code are observed in relation to all programmes (other than advertisements) broadcast by the Authority.

(2) The Authority may, in the discharge of their general responsibility for programmes other than advertisements, impose requirements as to standards and practice for such programmes

which go beyond, or relate to matters not covered by, the provisions of the code; and the methods of control exercisable by the Authority for the purpose of securing that the provisions of the code are observed, and for the purpose of securing compliance with such requirements which go beyond, or relate to matters not covered by, the code, shall include a power to give directions to a programme contractor (or any other person providing such programmes) imposing prohibitions or restrictions as respects items of a specified class or description or as respects a particular item.

6.—(1) In the case of programmes other than advertisements, the methods by which the Authority discharge their duties under section 2(2) and section 5 of this Act in relation to television broadcasts shall, and in relation to local sound broadcasts (to such extent as the Authority consider appropriate) may, include consideration of programme schedules submitted by programme contractors to the Authority for approval in accordance with this section; and, subject to subsection (5) of this section, no such programme provided by a programme contractor—

Submission of programme schedules for Authority's approval.

(a) if it is a television programme, or

(b) if it is a local sound broadcast which the Authority have required to be made in accordance with a programme schedule so approved,

shall be broadcast by the Authority unless it forms part of a programme schedule so approved.

(2) A programme schedule—

(a) shall be drawn up in consultation with the Authority, and

(b) shall be for a period determined by the Authority,

and the Authority may give to programme contractors such directions as appear to the Authority expedient for the purpose of ensuring that the Authority have sufficient time to discharge their responsibilities in the consideration of programme schedules.

(3) The Authority may give directions, which may be, to any degree, either general or specific and qualified or unqualified—

(a) as to the exclusion of any item from a programme schedule;

(b) as to the inclusion in, or in a particular part of, a programme schedule of an item, or items, of a particular category; or

(c) as to the inclusion in a particular part of a programme schedule of a particular item, and the Authority shall not approve a programme schedule until they are satisfied that it conforms with any directions grven under this section.

(4) Without prejudice to the Authority's power to approve for the purposes of this section a revised or amended version of a programme schedule previously approved by them, the Authority may, if they think fit to do so in view of any change of circumstances occurring after a programme schedule has been approved by them, permit the programme contractor to make such alterations in that programme schedule as the Authority may approve, being alterations proposed to them in any convenient manner; and a programme schedule in which alterations have been made by virtue of this subsection shall, as so altered, be treated as having been approved by the Authority in accordance with this section.

(5) The Authority may give directions, which may be, to any degree, either general or specific and conditional or unconditional, authorising the making of alterations in any approved programme schedule without prior reference to the Authority—

(*a*) where it is difficult or impracticable for the programme contractor to communicate with the Authority in the time available, or

(*b*) in the event of a technical breakdown;

and the programmes contained in a programme schedule in which alterations are made by virtue of this subsection may be broadcast by the Authority notwithstanding those alterations.

(6) The Authority's approval under this section may be given subject to such exceptions, reservations and qualifications as the Authority think fit, and the Authority may at any time call for further particulars of a programme schedule submitted to them, or of any item in the programme schedule.

Programme
prizes.

7.—(1) Without prejudice to the provision as to prizes and gifts in section 4(4) of this Act, a programme (other than an advertisement) broadcast by the Authority—

(*a*) shall not include anything which offers any prize of significant value (whether competed for or not) or any gift of significant value unless—

(i) the value of the prize or gift does not exceed an amount previously approved by the Authority for that prize or gift in relation to that programme, and

(ii) the aggregate value of all such prizes and gifts offered in the programme does not exceed an amount previously approved by the Authority for that programme; and

(*b*) shall not include anything which offers any prize or gift of significant value in connection with a game, competition or test of any kind unless the rules governing the conduct of the game, competition or test have been previously approved by the Authority.

(2) Subsection (1) of this section shall not be taken to apply to a programme by reason only that in it there is broadcast a sporting or other event or competition not organised for the purposes of the programme.

Advertisements

8.—(1) The programmes broadcast by the Authority may, so long as the provisions of this Act are complied with in relation thereto, include advertisements inserted therein in consideration of payments to the relevant programme contractor or, in the case of an advertisement included in a programme or part of a programme provided under section 3(2)(*b*) of this Act, to the Authority.

(2) Orders for the insertion of the said advertisements may be received either through advertising or other agents or direct from the advertiser, but neither the Authority nor any programme contractor shall act as an advertising agent.

(3) It shall be the duty of the Authority to secure that the provisions of Schedule 2 to this Act are complied with in relation to the advertisements included in the programmes broadcast by the Authority.

(4) After consultation with the Authority the Minister may make regulations by statutory instrument amending, repealing, or adding to the provisions of the said Schedule.

(5) Without prejudice to any of the duties incumbent on the Authority otherwise than under this subsection in relation to advertisements, it shall be the duty of the Authority to consult from time to time with the Minister as to the classes and descriptions of advertisements which must not be broadcast and the methods of advertising which must not be employed, and to carry out any directions which he may give them in those respects.

(6) Subject to subsections (7) and (8) of this section, nothing shall be included in any programmes broadcast by the Authority, whether in an advertisement or not, which states, suggests or implies, or could reasonably be taken to state, suggest or imply, that any part of any programme broadcast by the Authority which is not an advertisement has been supplied or suggested by any advertiser ; and, except as an advertisement, nothing shall be included in any programme broadcast by the Authority which could reasonably be supposed to have been included therein in return for payment or other valuable consideration to the relevant programme contractor or the Authority.

Advertisements.

(7) Nothing in subsection (6) of this section shall be construed as prohibiting the inclusion, in any part of a programme broadcast by the Authority which is not an advertisement, of any of the following matters, that is to say—

(*a*) items designed to give publicity to the needs or objects of any association or organisation conducted for charitable or benevolent purposes ;

(*b*) reviews of literary, artistic or other publications or productions, including current entertainments ;

(*c*) items consisting of factual portrayals of doings, happenings, places or things, being items which in the opinion of the Authority are proper for inclusion by reason of their intrinsic interest or instructiveness and do not comprise an undue element of advertisement ;

(*d*) announcements of the place of any performance included in the programme, or of the name and description of the persons concerned as performers or otherwise in any such performance, announcements of the number and description of any record so included, and acknowledgments of any permission granted in respect of any such performance, persons or record ;

(*e*) items inserted at the request, or under the authority, of a Minister of the Crown (including a Minister of Northern Ireland) ;

(*f*) such other matters (if any) as may be prescribed by regulations made by the Minister by statutory instrument after consultation with the Authority,

or as prohibiting the inclusion of an advertisement in any programme broadcast by the Authority by reason only of the fact that it is related in subject-matter to any part of that programme which is not an advertisement.

(8) So much of subsection (6) of this section as prohibits the inclusion in programmes (other than advertisements) broadcast by the Authority of anything which could reasonably be supposed to have been included therein in return for payment or other valuable consideration to the Authority shall not apply to any programme so broadcast in an educational service provided under section 3(2)(*c*) of this Act.

(9) Before making any regulations under this section the Minister shall lay a draft thereof before each House of Parliament, and shall not make the regulations until a resolution has been passed by each House of Parliament approving the draft.

9.—(1) It shall be the duty of the Authority—

Code for
advertise-
ments.

    (*a*) to draw up, and from time to time review, a code governing standards and practice in advertising and prescribing the advertisements and methods of advertising to be prohibited, or prohibited in particular circumstances ; and

    (*b*) to secure that the provisions of the code are complied with as regards the advertisements included in the programmes broadcast by the Authority.

(2) The Authority may, in the discharge of their general responsibility for advertisements and methods of advertising, impose requirements as to advertisements and methods of advertising which go beyond the requirements imposed by the code ; and the methods of control exercisable by the Authority for the purpose of securing that the provisions of the code are complied with, and for the purpose of securing compliance with requirements which go beyond the requirements of the code, shall include a power to give directions to a programme contractor with respect to the classes and descriptions of advertisements and methods of advertising to be excluded, or to be excluded in particular circumstances, or with respect to the exclusion of a particular advertisement, or its exclusion in particular circumstances.

(3) The Authority may give directions to a programme contractor with respect to the times when advertisements are to be allowed.

(4) Directions under this section may be, to any degree, either general or specific, and qualified or unqualified, and directions under subsection (3) of this section may, in particular, relate to—

    (*a*) the greatest amount of time to be given to advertisements in any hour or other period ;

    (*b*) the minimum interval which must elapse between any two periods given over to advertisements and the number of such periods to be allowed in any programme or item in a programme or in any hour or day ;

    (*c*) the exclusion of advertisements from a specified broadcast,

and may make different provision for different parts of the day, different days of the week, different types of programmes or for other differing circumstances.

Advisory committees

10.—(1) The Authority may appoint, or arrange for the assistance of, advisory committees to give advice to the Authority and programme contractors on such matters as the Authority may determine ; and a general advisory council may be appointed under this subsection.

(2) Without prejudice to the generality of subsection (1) of this section, the Authority shall in particular appoint, or arrange for the assistance of—

(*a*) a committee representative of the main streams of religious thought in the United Kingdom, the Isle of Man and the Channel Islands, to give advice to the Authority as to the exercise of their functions in relation to any such items as are mentioned in section 4(5)(*a*) of this Act, and on any other matters of a religious nature included in the programmes broadcast by the Authority, or in any publications issued by the Authority ;

(*b*) a committee so constituted as to be representative of both—

(i) organisations, authorities and persons concerned with standards of conduct in the advertising of goods and services (including in particular the advertising of goods or services for medical or surgical purposes), and

(ii) the public as consumers,

to give advice to the Authority with a view to the exclusion of misleading advertisements from the programmes broadcast by the Authority, and otherwise as to the principles to be followed in connection with the advertisements included in such programmes or in any publications issued by the Authority ; and

(*c*) a committee consisting of persons who have, or are representative of authorities or organisations who have, special interest and experience in education, to give advice to the Authority, and in particular advice on the policy for, and planning of, broadcasts intended for reception by schools and other educational establishments.

(3) The functions of the committee referred to in subsection (2)(*b*) of this section shall include the duty of keeping the code referred to in section 9 of this Act under review and submitting to the Authority recommendations as to any alterations which appear to them to be desirable.

(4) Before appointing a person to be the chairman of the committee referred to in subsection (2)(*b*) of this section, the Authority shall satisfy themselves that that person—

    (*a*) will have no financial or other interest in any advertising agency, and

    (*b*) will have no such other financial or other interest in advertising as is in the opinion of the Authority likely to prejudice his independence as chairman ;

and the Authority shall also satisfy themselves from time to time that the chairman of the said committee has no such interest as is described in paragraph (*a*) or (*b*) of this subsection.

(5) The Authority shall, after consultation with such professional organisations as the Minister may require and such other bodies or persons as the Authority think fit, appoint, or arrange for the assistance of, a medical advisory panel to give advice to the Authority as to—

    (*a*) advertisements for medicines and medical and surgical treatments and appliances ;

    (*b*) advertisements for toilet products which include claims as to the therapeutic or prophylactic effects of the products ;

    (*c*) advertisements for medicines and medical and surgical treatments for veterinary purposes,

and such other advertisements as the Authority may think fit to refer to the panel.

(6) The Authority shall consult the panel before drawing up the code referred to in section 9 of this Act and in the course of any review of that code.

(7) The Authority shall ensure that, before the first occasion on which they broadcast an advertisement which in their opinion falls under paragraph (*a*), (*b*) or (*c*) of subsection (5) of this section, the advertisement is, in accordance with arrangements approved by the Authority, referred to a member or members of the panel for advice.

11.—(1) In addition to the committees which are to be, or may be, appointed under section 10 of this Act, the Authority shall appoint local advisory committees in respect of all the localities for which local sound broadcasting services are provided by the Authority; and each such committee shall be appointed for an area consisting either of one such locality or of two or more such localities.

Local advisory committees for local sound broadcasts.

(2) Subject to the next following subsection, each such committee (in this section referred to as a " local committee ")—

    (*a*) shall be so constituted, and

(*b*) shall consist of persons selected by reference to such qualifications,

as in the opinion of the Authority would be appropriate for reflecting, so far as is reasonably practicable, the range of tastes and interests of persons residing in the area for which the committee is appointed (in this section referred to, in relation to a local committee, as its area).

(3) For each local committee the Authority shall invite the appropriate local authorities (either jointly or separately) to nominate persons with a view to their being appointed as members of the committee ; and (unless the number of eligible persons so nominated for a local committee is insufficient for the purpose) the Authority shall appoint at least one-third of the members of each local committee from among persons so nominated.

(4) Before appointing a person to be a member of a local committee the Authority shall satisfy themselves that he—

(*a*) will have no financial or other interest in any advertising agency, and

(*b*) will have no such other financial or other interest in advertising as is in the opinion of the Authority likely to prejudice his independence as a member of that committee,

and the Authority shall also satisfy themselves from time to time that each member of a local committee has no such interest as is described in paragraph (*a*) or (*b*) of this subsection ; and in subsection (3) of this section " eligible persons " means persons in respect of whom the Authority are satisfied that they have no such interest.

(5) The function of a local committee shall be to give to the Authority, with respect to the conduct of their local sound broadcasting services for the area of the committee, such advice as in the opinion of the committee would be appropriate for reflecting, so far as is reasonably practicable, the range of tastes and interests of persons residing in that area.

(6) In this section " appropriate local authority ", in relation to a local committee, means a local authority whose area consists of or includes the whole or part of the area of that committee, and " local authority "—

(*a*) in relation to England and Wales, means, subject to subsection (7) of this section, any of the following, that is to say, the council of a principal area within the meaning of the Local Government Act 1972, the Common Council of the City of London and the Council of the Isles of Scilly ;

(*b*) in relation to Scotland, means the council of a county, county of a city, large burgh or small burgh ; and

1972 c. 70.

(c) in relation to Northern Ireland, means any of the following, that is to say, the council of a county, county or other borough, or urban or rural district, a new town or development commission exercising the functions of any such council and a district council within the meaning of the Local Government Act (Northern Ireland) 1972. 1972 c. 9 (N.I.).

(7) In relation to any time before 1st April 1974, subsection (6)(a) of this section shall have effect as if for the words "the council of a principal area within the meaning of the Local Government Act 1972 " there were substituted the words 1972 c. 70. "the Greater London Council, the council of a county, county borough or county district, the council of a London borough ".

(8) This section shall be treated for the purposes of section 254 of the Local Government Act 1972 (power to make consequential and supplementary provision) as if it were contained in an Act passed in the same session as that Act.

Provisions applying to all contracts for programmes

12.—(1) The Authority shall not enter into any contract with Duties of a programme contractor for the provision of programmes for Authority in relation to a period of more than six years, but that shall not preclude contracts for the Authority from entering into successive contracts with the programmes. same programme contractor.

(2) The Authority shall not enter into any contract with a programme contractor whereby (whether by virtue of that contract alone or by virtue of that contract together with one or more other contracts) the contractor is to provide television programmes for an area and is to provide local sound broadcasts for reception in a locality which, in the opinion of the Authority, is comprised in that area.

(3) It shall be the duty of the Authority to do all that they can to secure—

(a) that persons who are disqualified persons as defined in subsection (5) or (6) of this section do not become or continue as programme contractors, either alone or in partnership with other persons, and

(b) that there is adequate competition to supply programmes between a number of programme contractors independent of each other both as to finance and as to control.

(4) In the performance of their duty under subsection (3)(b) of this section the Authority shall do all that they can to secure—

(a) that no programme contractor with whom the Authority enter into a contract for the provision of television programmes for an area, and no associate of such a programme contractor, has, or during the period of the contract will acquire, control over any programme contractor with whom the Authority enter into a contract for the provision of local sound broadcasts for reception in any locality which in the opinion of the Authority is comprised in that area ; and

(b) that no programme contractor with whom the Authority enter into a contract for the provision of local sound broadcasts for reception in a particular locality, and no associate of such a programme contractor, has, or during the period of contract will acquire, control over any programme contractor for the provision of television programmes for an area which in the opinion of the Authority includes that locality.

(5) In subsection (3)(*a*) of this section " disqualified person ", in relation to contracts for the provision of television programmes, means a person who—

(*a*) being an individual, is not ordinarily resident in the United Kingdom, the Isle of Man or the Channel Islands, or being a body corporate, is incorporated under the laws of any country outside the United Kingdom, the Isle of Man and the Channel Islands ;

(*b*) being an individual or a body corporate, carries on business as an advertising agent (whether alone or in partnership), or has control over any body corporate which carries on business as an advertising agent, or is a director or officer of any such body corporate, or is employed by any person who carries on business as an advertising agent ; or

(*c*) being a body corporate, is under the control of any such person as is mentioned in paragraph (*a*) or (*b*) of this subsection, or of any two or more such persons together, or has among its directors, officers or servants any person who is a disqualified person otherwise than by virtue of paragraph (*a*) of this subsection.

(6) In subsection (3)(*a*) of this section " disqualified person ", in relation to contracts for the provision of local sound broadcasts, means a person who either falls within paragraph (*a*), (*b*) or (*c*) of subsection (5) of this section or, being an individual or body corporate, carries on (whether alone or in partnership) a business which (either wholly, or to an extent which in the opinion of the Authority is substantial)—

(*a*) consists of the manufacture of records or of the publication of musical works, or

(*b*) consists of promoting the broadcasting of sound recordings or of promoting the broadcasting or performance of musical works, or (*c*) consists of obtaining employment for theatrical performers or for persons to take part as performers in programmes broadcast (whether by the Authority or otherwise) by way of television or sound broadcasting,

or has control over any body corporate which carries on such a business, or is a director or officer of any such body corporate, or is employed by any person who carries on such a business.

(7) No contract and no interest in a contract between a programme contractor and the Authority shall be assignable either in whole or in part without the previous consent in writing of the Authority.

(8) In this section—

    (*a*) " record " and " sound recording " have the same meanings as in the Copyright Act 1956, and references 1956 c. 74. to the publication, broadcasting or performance of musical works shall be construed as if they were contained in that Act ; and

    (*b*) " theatrical performer " has the same meaning as in the Theatrical Employers Registration Act 1925.   1925 c. 50.

13.—(1) The contracts between the Authority and the various programme contractors shall contain all such provisions as the Authority think necessary or expedient to be inserted for complying and securing compliance with the provisions of this Act and any restrictions or requirements imposed thereunder in relation to the programmes provided by the programme contractors.

Provisions to be included in contracts for programmes.

(2) Without prejudice to subsection (1) of this section, every contract between the Authority and a programme contractor—

    (*a*) shall, subject to paragraph (*b*) of this subsection, contain a provision reserving to the Authority an absolute right, if, in view of any breaches by the programme contractor of his obligations under his contract with the Authority, the Authority, after giving the programme contractor a reasonable opportunity of making representations with respect to the matter, think it necessary to do so, to serve on the programme contractor a notice in writing, taking effect forthwith or on a date stated in the notice, to determine or suspend for such period as may be specified in the notice, or until a further notice is given, the Authority's obligation to transmit the programmes supplied by the programme contractor (without prejudice, however, to the programme contractor's obligations as to the supply of programmes up to the date when the notice takes effect) ; and (*b*) shall be such as to secure that no notice can be given in pursuance of a right reserved in accordance with the preceding paragraph unless the programme contractor has broken the contract on at least three occasions and, in respect of each of those breaches of contract, has received from the Authority written particulars of the breach within one month from the time when the breach came to the notice of the Authority ;

and where a notice is given in pursuance of a right reserved in accordance with this subsection, the programme contractor shall not be entitled to any compensation from the Authority, or to any refund of any sum previously paid by him, or to any relief from any liability which has accrued at the date when the notice takes effect for any sums payable by him to the Authority.

(3) Without prejudice to the power of the parties to agree upon any wider form of arbitration provision, every such contract shall be such as to secure that any dispute—

(*a*) whether an alleged breach of which the programme contractor has received written particulars is a breach of the contract for the purposes of the provisions included in the contract in pursuance of subsection (2)(*b*) of this section ; or

(*b*) whether the written particulars were received from the Authority within one month from the time when the breach came to the notice of the Authority,

shall be determined by arbitration.

(4) Every contract concluded between the Authority and a programme contractor shall, where the programme contractor is a body corporate, contain all such provisions as the Authority think necessary or expedient to ensure that if any change affecting the nature or characteristics of the body corporate, or any change in the persons having control over or interests in the body corporate, takes place after the conclusion of the contract, which, if it had occurred before the conclusion of the contract, would have induced the Authority to refrain from entering into the contract, the Authority may by notice in writing to the programme contractor, taking effect forthwith or on a date specified in the notice, determine the contract.

(5) Every contract concluded between the Authority and a programme contractor shall contain all such provisions as the Authority for the purposes of the discharge of their functions think necessary or expedient to ensure that the programme contractor—

(*a*) if so required, will provide the Authority in advance with scripts and particulars of the programmes or any

part thereof (including advertisements) and of full
details of the technical arrangements for obtaining
visual images and sounds which are to form the
programmes or any part thereof ;

(b) if so required, will make visual and sound records of
the programmes or any part thereof (including advertisements) and produce them to the Authority for
examination or reproduction ;

(c) will provide the Authority with such declarations,
returns, documents and other information as the
Authority may require ;

(d) in particular, if so required, will provide the Authority
with information as to the costs incurred by the programme contractor in providing the programmes or any
part thereof (including advertisements) and his receipts
from advertisers ;

(e) if so required, will give reasonable facilities to the
Authority for inspecting the books, accounts, records
and other documents kept by the programme contractor for the purposes of any business carried on by
him, and for taking copies of, or of any part of, any
such documents.

(6) The contracts between the Authority and the various programme contractors shall contain all such provisions as the
Authority think necessary or expedient to ensure—

(a) that there is at all times at least one body or organisation effectively equipped and adequately financed to
provide news for broadcasting in the programmes
supplied to the Authority by the respective programme
contractors, and that in so far as any such body or
organisation supplies to programme contractors other
programmes which it can suitably provide, it is effectively equipped and adequately financed for the
purpose ;

(b) that each of the programme contractors with whom the
Authority enter into contracts for the provision of
television programmes is afforded opportunities of
obtaining a financial interest in that body or organisation or, if there are two or more such bodies or
organisations providing news for broadcasting in the
television programmes supplied to the Authority by
those contractors, is afforded opportunities of obtaining
a financial interest in such of those bodies or organisations as the Authority may in his case direct ; and

(c) that the appointment of the manager, editor or other
chief executive of any such body or organisation is
approved by the Authority.

(7) The provisions of this section relating to breaches of contract on the part of programme contractors shall be without prejudice—

> (a) to the right of the Authority to accept as a repudiation by a programme contractor any breach of contract by the programme contractor going to the root of the contract ; and

> (b) to any other remedies of the Authority for the enforcement of their rights in respect of contracts with programme contractors,

and shall not, except as expressly provided therein, affect the jurisdiction of any court in respect of such contracts.

Newspaper
shareholdings
in programme
contractors.

14.—(1) Every contract concluded between the Authority and a programme contractor shall, where the programme contractor is a body corporate, contain all such provisions as the Authority think necessary or expedient to ensure that if at any time there are newspaper shareholdings in the programme contractor, and it appears to the Authority that the existence of those shareholdings has led or is leading to results which are contrary to the public interest, the Authority may, with the consent of the Minister, by notice in writing to the programme contractor, taking effect forthwith or on a date specified in the notice, determine or suspend for such period as may be so specified or until a further notice is given, the Authority's obligation to transmit the programmes supplied by the programme contractor.

(2) Without prejudice to any such provisions contained in a contract between the Authority and a programme contractor, if at any time there are newspaper shareholdings in the programme contractor, and it appears to the Minister that the existence of those shareholdings has led or is leading to results which are contrary to the public interest, he may, after consultation with the Authority, by order made by statutory instrument—

> (a) determine on a date specified in the order the Authority's obligation to transmit the programmes supplied by the programme contractor ; or

> (b) suspend that obligation for such period as may be so specified, or during a period beginning with a date so specified and continuing so long as the order remains in force ; and

> (c) whether or not the order provides for the determination or suspension of the said obligation, direct that, while the order remains in force, the Authority shall not enter into any further contract with the programme contractor for the supply of programmes.

An order under this subsection may be revoked by a subsequent order thereunder.

(3) Before making any order under subsection (2) of this section, other than an order the sole purpose of which is to rescind, postpone commencement of or terminate a period of suspension or to cancel a direction, the Minister shall lay a draft thereof before each House of Parliament, and shall not make the order until a resolution has been passed by each House of Parliament approving the draft.

(4) The determination or suspension in accordance with this section of the Authority's obligation to transmit the programmes supplied by the programme contractor, whether effected by a notice or by an order, shall not affect the programme contractor's obligation as to the supply of programmes up to the date when the determination or suspension takes effect; and where such a determination or suspension takes effect, the programme contractor shall not be entitled to any compensation from the Authority or to any refund of any sum previously paid by the programme contractor or to any relief from any liability which has accrued at the date when the determination or suspension takes effect for any sums payable by the programme contractor to the Authority.

(5) For the purposes of this section there are newspaper shareholdings in a body corporate if shares in that body corporate are held by any individual or body corporate being either—

   (a) the proprietor of any newspaper, whether national or local, or

   (b) a person who has control over any body corporate which is a proprietor of such a newspaper.

15.—(1) The Authority may give directions to any programme contractor requiring him to supply to another programme contractor for inclusion in any comparable programme of his any item supplied or originated by the first programme contractor; and the contracts between the Authority and the various programme contractors shall contain all such provisions as the Authority think necessary or expedient for ensuring— *Buying and selling of programmes by programme contractors.*

   (a) that each programme contractor will take all reasonable steps to put himself in a position to comply with any directions which may be given to him under this subsection and, when any such directions have been given to him, to enable the other programme contractor to include the item to which the directions relate in any comparable programme of his; and

   (b) that if financial and other arrangements for the supply of any item in respect of which directions have been given under this subsection are not agreed between the two programme contractors, or when so agreed do not receive the approval of the Authority required by virtue of subsection (2) of this section, the item will be supplied in accordance with such financial and other arrangements as may be determined by the Authority.

(2) The contracts between the Authority and the various programme contractors shall provide that, where items to be included in the programmes of a programme contractor are not originated by that programme contractor, the financial and other arrangements between the programme contractor and the supplier shall require the approval of the Authority—

(a) in all cases where the supplier is another programme contractor, and

(b) in such other cases as the Authority may from time to time direct ;

and directions given for the purposes of this subsection may apply to programme contractors generally or may be different for different programme contractors.

(3) For the purposes of this section two programmes shall be regarded as being comparable if either—

(a) both are television programmes, or

(b) both are local sound broadcasts.

Wages and conditions of employment of persons employed by programme contractors.

16.—(1) The wages paid by any programme contractor to persons employed by him in connection with his business as such and the conditions of employment of persons so employed shall, unless agreed upon by the programme contractor or any organisations representative of programme contractors and by organisations representative of the persons employed, be no less favourable to the person employed than the wages which would be payable, and the conditions which would have to be observed, under a contract which complies with the requirements of any resolution of the House of Commons for the time being in force applicable to contracts of Government departments ; and if any dispute arises as to what wages ought to be paid, or what conditions ought to be observed, in accordance with this section, it shall, if not otherwise disposed of, be referred by the Secretary of State to the Industrial Arbitration Board for settlement.

(2) Where any award has been made by the Industrial Arbitration Board upon a dispute referred to that Board under this section, then, as from the date of the award or from such other date, not being earlier than the date on which the dispute to which the award relates first arose, as the Board may direct, it shall be an implied term of the contract between the employer and workers to whom the award applies that the rate of wages

to be paid, or the conditions of employment to be observed, under the contract shall, until varied in accordance with the provisions of this section, be in accordance with the award.

(3) In relation to employment in Northern Ireland, the references in this section to the House of Commons, Government departments, the Secretary of State and the Industrial Arbitration Board shall be construed as references to the House of Commons of Northern Ireland, departments of the Government of Northern Ireland, the Ministry of Health and Social Services for Northern Ireland and the Industrial Court in Northern Ireland.

Contracts for local sound broadcasts

17.—(1) Before entering into a sound programme contract the Authority shall seek to ascertain— _{Accumulation of interests in sound programme contracts.}

(a) whether the person or any of the persons with whom the contract is proposed to be made is (either alone or in partnership with one or more other persons) entitled to the benefit of one or more existing sound programme contracts ; and

(b) where the person or any of the persons with whom the contract is proposed to be made is a body corporate, whether that body corporate, or any associate of that body corporate, or any participant in that body corporate or in any such associate, is a person or one of the persons entitled to the benefit of one or more existing sound programme contracts, or is a participant in a body corporate so entitled or included among the persons so entitled or in an associate of a body corporate so entitled or so included ;

and, having regard to any matters ascertained by them under this subsection, the Authority shall consider whether, if the proposed contract were made, any one person would, in any one or more of the capacities mentioned in paragraphs (a) and (b) of this subsection or in any combination of any such capacities, have an aggregate interest in the benefit of two or more sound programme contracts.

(2) If, in the circumstances mentioned in subsection (1) of this section, it appears to the Authority that a person would have such an aggregate interest and that, having regard to—

(a) the nature and extent of that aggregate interest, and

(b) any other circumstances appearing to the Authority to be material,

the existence of that aggregate interest might prejudice the performance by the Authority of any duty imposed on them by this Act in relation to local sound broadcasting services, the Authority shall refrain from entering into the proposed contract.

(3) In this section " sound programme contract " means a contract for the provision of local sound broadcasts, and " existing sound programme contract ", in relation to any contract proposed to be entered into by the Authority, means a sound programme contract which is in force at the time when the Authority are considering entering into the proposed contract ; and " participant ", in relation to a body corporate, means a person who (whether alone or jointly with one or more other persons, and whether directly or through one or more nominees) holds or is beneficially entitled to not less than one-twentieth of the shares in that body corporate.

Special provisions as to newspaper shareholdings in relation to local sound broadcasts.

18.—(1) This section applies to any contract made between the Authority and a programme contractor, where the programme contractor is a body corporate and the contract requires local sound broadcasts to be provided by the contractor and to be transmitted from one or more stations specified in the contract.

(2) Subject to section 19 of this Act, before the Authority enter into a contract to which this section applies—

(*a*) they shall consider, in relation to the locality served or to be served by the station or stations to be specified in the contract (in this section referred to as " the relevant locality "), whether there is any newspaper which circulates wholly or mainly in that locality and is a newspaper in respect of which the appropriate conditions are fulfilled ; and

(*b*) the Authority shall fix a date before which representations may be made to the Authority under subsection (4) of this section and shall cause notice of that date to be given or published as may appear to the Authority to be appropriate for bringing it to the attention of persons who in their opinion are likely to be affected by it.

(3) For the purposes of this section the appropriate conditions shall be taken to be fulfilled in respect of a newspaper if it has in the relevant locality a circulation which, in the opinion of the Authority, represents a substantial proportion of the population of that locality, unless the Authority are satisfied that the broadcasting of the programmes to be provided under the contract in question is unlikely to have a materially adverse effect on the financial position of the newspaper.

(4) The appropriate conditions shall also be taken for the purposes of this section to be fulfilled in respect of a newspaper

if, on representations being made to the Authority by or on behalf of the proprietor of the newspaper before the date fixed under subsection (2)(*b*) of this section, the Authority are satisfied that (notwithstanding that its circulation falls short of the proportion mentioned in subsection (3) of this section) the broadcasting of the programmes to be provided under the contract in question is likely to have a materially adverse effect on the financial position of the newspaper.

(5) Where it appears to the Authority that the appropriate conditions are fulfilled in respect of a newspaper, then, subject to section 19 of this Act, the Authority shall not enter into the contract unless they are satisfied that—

(*a*) arrangements have been made for enabling the proprietor of the newspaper to acquire, on terms approved by the Authority, a shareholding consisting of such number of shares of such descriptions as may be so approved ; and

(*b*) either the acquisition of the shareholding has been completed, or it will be completed within a reasonable time, or the proprietor of the newspaper has declined to acquire it on the terms approved by the Authority.

(6) The number and description of shares to be approved for the purposes of any such arrangements—

(*a*) in the case of a newspaper which is the only local newspaper circulating in the relevant locality, or the only local newspaper having a substantial circulation in that locality, shall not be such as to enable the proprietor of the newspaper to obtain control over the programme contractor ; but

(*b*) in any other case, or (in a case falling within the preceding paragraph) to such extent as is consistent with that paragraph, shall be such as the Authority consider appropriate, having regard to the adverse effect which the broadcasting of the programmes to be provided under the contract in question is likely to have on the financial position of the newspaper.

(7) Any terms approved by the Authority under subsection (5)(*a*) of this section shall be such as, in the opinion of the Authority, will enable the shareholding to be acquired at a price not exceeding its current market value or (if it has no current market value) a price not exceeding a fair valuation of the shareholding.

(8) In this section and section 19 of this Act " newspaper " does not include any publication which is not printed for sale or which is published at intervals of more than seven days, and

" shareholding ", in relation to a programme contractor which is a body corporate, means a holding of shares in that body corporate.

Provisions supplementary to section 18.

19.—(1) Notwithstanding anything in section 18 of this Act, the Authority shall not require arrangements to be made in relation to a newspaper as mentioned in subsection (5) of that section if it is their opinion that it would be contrary to the public interest for the proprietor of that newspaper to acquire a shareholding in accordance with subsection (6) of that section, and the Minister concurs in that opinion.

(2) Every contract to which that section applies shall include provisions whereby, if during the currency of the contract arrangements are made for extending (otherwise than by way of any minor modification) the range of transmission of programmes to be provided under the contract, whether by an alteration in the construction or operation of one or more stations or by the addition of one or more stations or otherwise, subsections (2) to (7) of that section and subsection (1) of this section shall have effect in relation to those arrangements as if they were a contract to which that section applies.

(3) The Authority shall not be required to act in accordance with subsections (2) to (7) of section 18 of this Act in connection with the making of a contract with a programme contractor if—

(a) the contract is to specify the same station as was, or the same stations as were, specified in a previous contract to which that section applied (whether the previous contract was with the same programme contractor or a different programme contractor) ; and

(b) the range or aggregate range of transmission of broadcasts under the new contract is not to be greater (otherwise than by way of any minor modification) than under the previous contract.

(4) Where subsection (3) of this section applies, it shall not be construed as precluding the Authority from requiring such arrangements as are mentioned in subsections (5) to (7) of section 18 of this Act to be made in connection with the new contract in respect of a newspaper whose proprietor acquired a shareholding in accordance with such arrangements in connection with the previous contract, if it appears to the Authority that by reason of special circumstances it would be just and equitable to do so.

20.—(1) Where the Authority enter into a contract with a programme contractor for the provision of local sound broadcasts to be transmitted from one or more stations, the Authority shall, on request made by any person and on payment by him of such sum (if any) as the Authority may reasonably require, furnish to that person such one or more of the following as may be specified in the request, that is to say— Information
as to sound
programme
contracts and
applications
for such
contracts.

   (*a*) a copy of that contract ;

   (*b*) a statement of the number of applications (if any) received by the Authority for a programme contract for the provision of local sound broadcasts to be transmitted from that station or those stations, other than the application received from the contractor with whom the contract is made ; and

   (*c*) subject to the next following subsection, a copy of so much of that contractor's application for such a contract as related to the character of the local sound broadcasts which he proposed to provide if his application were accepted by the Authority.

(2) The Authority shall not be required by virtue of subsection (1) of this section to furnish to any person such a copy as is mentioned in paragraph (*c*) of that subsection until after local sound broadcasts provided by the contractor under the contract in question have begun to be transmitted by the Authority.

Powers of Government in relation to Authority

21.—(1) The Minister may from time to time by notice in writing give directions to the Authority— Government
control over
Authority as
to hours of
broadcasting.

   (*a*) as to the maximum or minimum time, or both the maximum and the minimum time, which is to be given in any day, week or other period to broadcasts from any of the broadcasting stations used by them, and

   (*b*) as to the hours of the day in which such broadcasts are or are not to be given,

and it shall be the duty of the Authority to comply with the notice.

(2) A direction under this section may be framed in any way, and in particular—

   (*a*) may be confined to broadcasts from those broadcasting stations which transmit, or usually transmit, the same programme, or may be different for different broadcasting stations, or for different programmes broadcast from the same station ;

   (*b*) may make special provision for annual holidays and other special occasions ;

(c) may be confined to a specified day in the week, or may be different for different days in the week;

(d) in imposing a maximum number of hours for any purpose, may allow for programmes or items of specified kinds being left out of account in determining the maximum, whether in all circumstances or depending on the fulfilment of specified conditions as regards programmes or items so specified.

(3) The Minister may, whether or not a direction under this section provides for exemptions, exempt the Authority from any requirement of such a direction on any occasion or in any circumstances.

(4) Nothing in the preceding provisions of this section shall be taken as authorising the Minister to give directions which make different provision for the parts of programmes consisting of advertisements and the other parts of programmes.

(5) The powers conferred by this section are in addition to any powers specifically conferred on the Minister by any other provisions of this Act.

Government control over Authority as to certain other matters.

22.—(1) The Minister or any other Minister of the Crown may, if it appears to him to be necessary or expedient to do so in connection with his functions as such, at any time by notice in writing require the Authority to broadcast, at such times as may be specified in the notice and from such of the stations used by them as may be so specified, any announcement so specified, with or without visual images of any picture, scene or object mentioned in the announcement, and it shall be the duty of the Authority to comply with the notice.

(2) Where the Authority broadcast any announcement in pursuance of a notice under the preceding subsection they may, if they think fit, announce that they are doing so in pursuance of such a notice.

(3) Subject to subsection (4) of this section, the Minister may at any time by notice in writing require the Authority to refrain from broadcasting any matter or classes of matter specified in the notice, and it shall be the duty of the Authority to comply with the notice.

(4) If under subsection (3) of this section the Minister by notice in writing requires the Authority to refrain from broadcasting anything, the Authority may, if they think fit, broadcast an announcement of the notice or of the revocation or expiration of the notice.

(5) The Minister may at any time, after consultation with the Authority, by notice in writing require the Authority—

    (*a*) to adopt or use, or refrain from adopting or using, technical measures or processes specified in the notice ;

    (*b*) to install, establish, maintain or use any such additional station, stations or apparatus as may be so specified, situate in such places and complying with such requirements as may be so specified ;

    (*c*) to broadcast such test or experimental transmissions from such station or stations, and at such times and for such periods, as may be so specified,

and it shall be the duty of the Authority to comply with the notice.

(6) A copy of any notice served on the Authority under subsection (5) of this section shall be laid by the Minister before each House of Parliament.

(7) The powers conferred by this section are in addition to any powers specifically conferred on the Minister by any other provisions of this Act.

(8) In relation to any broadcasting station in Northern Ireland, the reference in subsection (1) of this section to a Minister of the Crown shall be deemed to include a reference to any Minister of Northern Ireland.

23.—(1) With a view to preventing the making of exclusive arrangements for the broadcasting of sporting or other events of national interest, the Minister may make regulations as to the grant to the Authority and programme contractors and to the British Broadcasting Corporation respectively of broadcasting facilities in respect of such events. *Prevention of exclusive arrangements for broadcasting events of national interest.*

(2) Regulations made under this section shall not apply to the broadcasting of a record of any event specified therein where the transmission is made more than seven days after that event.

(3) The power to make regulations under this section shall be exercisable by statutory instrument, and before making any such regulations the Minister shall lay a draft thereof before each House of Parliament, and shall not make the regulations until a resolution has been passed by each House of Parliament approving the draft.

Co-operation of Authority with British Broadcasting Corporation in use of broadcasting installations.

24.—(1) The Minister may at any time by notice in writing—

(a) require the Authority to radiate such of their broadcast transmissions as may be specified in the notice from a mast, tower or other installation belonging to the British Broadcasting Corporation (in this section referred to as " the Corporation ") ; or

(b) require the Authority to permit such of the Corporation's broadcast transmissions as may be so specified to be radiated from a mast, tower or other installation belonging to the Authority ; or

(c) require the Authority to co-operate with the Corporation in providing and using an installation and to radiate such of the Authority's broadcast transmissions as may be so specified from that installation,

and it shall be the duty of the Authority to comply with any such notice.

(2) Before giving a notice under this section to the Authority the Minister shall consult the Authority and the Corporation.

(3) If, after a notice is given under this section to the Authority, a dispute between the Authority and the Corporation arising out of the matters to which the notice relates is referred to the Minister by either body, or it appears to the Minister that there is such a dispute, he may give such directions to the Authority as he may think expedient for determining the dispute, and it shall be the duty of the Authority to comply with any such directions.

Finances of Authority

Television and sound broadcasting to be separately financed by Authority.

25.—(1) The provision by the Authority of television broadcasting services, and the provision by them of local sound broadcasting services, shall for financial purposes constitute separate branches of their undertaking ; and references in this Act to a branch of the Authority's undertaking shall be construed accordingly.

(2) For each branch of their undertaking it shall be the duty of the Authority so to conduct their affairs as to secure that their revenues from that branch become at the earliest possible date, and thereafter continue, at least sufficient—

(a) to meet all sums properly chargeable to revenue account in respect of that branch of their undertaking (including sums which, for the purposes of that branch, are required for the repayment of loans and interest thereon, for provision for depreciation and for the establishment and maintenance of the reserve fund for that branch) ; and (*b*) to make provision towards, and as soon as practicable for, necessary capital expenditure for the purposes of that branch of their undertaking.

(3) In the case of that branch of their undertaking which consists of the provision of local sound broadcasting services, subsection (2) of this section shall have effect without prejudice to any duty of the Authority under section 28 of this Act.

(4) For each branch of their undertaking the Authority shall establish and maintain a reserve fund ; and, subject to the following provisions of this section, the management of that fund, the sums to be carried from time to time to the credit of the fund, and the application of the fund, shall be as the Authority may determine.

(5) No part of either of those funds shall be applied otherwise than for the purposes of the branch of the Authority's undertaking for which the fund was established.

(6) The Minister may, with the approval of the Treasury, give to the Authority such directions as he may think fit as to any matter relating to the establishment or management of either of those funds, the carrying of sums to the credit thereof, or the application thereof, and the Authority shall comply with the directions.

26.—(1) The contracts between the Authority and the various programme contractors for the provision of television programmes shall provide for payments to be made by the programme contractors to the Authority under two heads, namely— Rental payments by television programme contractors.

(*a*) payments representing what appear to the Authority, in relation to the branch of their undertaking consisting of the provision of television broadcasting services, to be the appropriate contributions of the respective programme contractors towards meeting the sums which the Authority regard as necessary in order to discharge their duty under section 25(2) of this Act in relation to that branch of their undertaking ; and

(*b*) additional payments (in this and section 27 of this Act referred to as " additional payments ") of amounts determined by reference to advertising receipts as defined in this section.

(2) The additional payments shall not form part of the revenue of the Authority and, when received by the Authority, shall be paid into the Consolidated Fund of the United Kingdom or the Exchequer of Northern Ireland as provided by section 27(4) of this Act.

(3) The additional payments which a programme contractor is to make for any accounting period as defined by this section shall be of an amount which, subject to any order under this section, shall be that determined by subsections (4) and (5) of this section.

(4) If the accounting period is a period of 12 months, the amount of the additional payments for the accounting period shall be that given by the following Table.

TABLE

RATES FOR A 12-MONTH PERIOD

	Appropriate rate for determining amount of additional payment
For the first £2 million of the advertising receipts of the programme contractor for the 12-month accounting period	Nil
For the next £4 million of those advertising receipts	10 per cent.
For the next £3 million of those advertising receipts	17½ per cent.
For the next £3 million of those advertising receipts	20 per cent.
For the next £4 million of those advertising receipts	22½ per cent.
For the amount by which those advertising receipts exceed the aggregate of the said sums of £2 million, £4 million, £3 million, £3 million and £4 million ...	25 per cent.

(5) If the accounting period is a period of less than 12 months, the Table in subsection (4) of this section shall apply with the substitution for the sums specified in column 1 of sums which, to the nearest £100, and ignoring an odd sum of £50 or less, are equal to the sums in the Table multiplied by the fraction represented by the number of whole weeks in the accounting period divided by 52.

(6) The Minister may with the approval of the Treasury, and after consultation with the Authority, by order amend subsection (4) of this section in all or any of the following respects, that is, by increasing or reducing any rate, or the number of different rates, or the amount to which any rate applies ; and the references in this subsection to a rate include the case where the rate is nil.

The power of making orders under this subsection shall include power to vary or revoke a previous order and shall be exerciseable by statutory instrument ; but no such statutory instrument shall be made unless a draft thereof has been laid before Parliament and approved by a resolution of each House.

An order under this subsection shall have effect as respects all additional payments to be computed by reference to advertising receipts for any period after the order comes into force, whether the contracts under which the additional payments are due were executed before or after the making of the order.

(7) In this section and section 27 of this Act—

(*a*) " advertising receipts " means, in relation to a programme contractor, and in relation to any period, the payments received or to be received by the programme contractor in consideration of the insertion of advertisements in programmes provided by the programme contractor and broadcast in the United Kingdom by the Authority in the period ; and

(*b*) " payment " includes any valuable consideration ;

and for the purposes of the definition in paragraph (*a*) of this subsection—

(i) if, in connection with the insertion of advertisements which are paid for by payments constituting advertising receipts, any payments are made to the programme contractor to meet any additional payments due from the programme contractor under this section and section 27 of this Act, those payments shall be regarded as made in consideration of the insertion of the advertisements in question ; and

(ii) in the case of an advertisement inserted in a programme under arrangements made between a programme contractor and a person acting as advertising agent, the amount of any receipt by the programme contractor which represents a payment by the advertiser from which the advertising agent has deducted any amount by way of commission shall be the amount of the payment by the advertiser after the deduction of the commission, so, however, that if the amount so deducted exceeds 15 per cent. of the payment by the advertiser, the amount of the receipt shall be the amount of that payment less 15 per cent.

(8) Subject to subsections (9) and (10) of this section,—

(*a*) each period of 12 months during which a programme contractor provides programmes for broadcasting by the Authority, and

(*b*) where the total period for which a programme contractor provides programmes under any one contract is not an exact number of years, the last part of that total period,

shall be an accounting period for the purposes of this section and section 27 of this Act.

(9) A contract which varies another contract under which a programme contractor provides programmes for broadcasting by the Authority may modify the provisions of subsection (8) of this section, but not so as to create an accounting period of more than 12 months.

(10) If part of an accounting period falls before, and part after, the date on which an order under subsection (6) of this section takes effect, the two parts shall be treated for the purposes of this section and section 27 of this Act as separate accounting periods.

Provisions supplemental to section 26.

27.—(1) The contracts between the Authority and the programme contractors for the provision of television programmes—

(a) shall provide for ascertaining the advertising receipts for any accounting period at monthly intervals in that period, for the computation of the amount, if any, of the additional payments due by reference to the advertising receipts for the part of the accounting period down to the latest date of which account is taken in the computation, and for the making of additional payments in accordance with the computations (and after giving credit for any payments already made) not later than four weeks from the said latest date ; and

(b) shall authorise the Authority, in a case where a programme contractor fails to make a return required by the contract, or makes a return appearing to the Authority to be incomplete or inaccurate, to estimate the amount of the additional payments due, and shall provide that the amount estimated shall be treated as payable, unless the contrary is proved ; and

(c) shall provide that where for any insertion of an advertisement a programme contractor receives or is entitled to an entire consideration not solely referable to that insertion, the advertising receipts shall be calculated by reference to so much only of the consideration as is referable to that insertion according to an apportionment made in such manner as any such contract may provide,

and it shall be the duty of the Authority in framing the contracts with the various programme contractors to include such terms as are in their opinion necessary or expedient to ensure that the amount of the additional payments required under this section and section 26 of this Act are paid promptly and in full.

(2) The contracts between the Authority and the various programme contractors for the provision of television programmes shall include such terms as are in the opinion of

the Authority necessary or expedient to ensure that, except for deduction of commission by persons acting as advertising agents, the amount of the advertising receipts of a programme contractor is not reduced under arrangements by which any part of the consideration for the insertion of advertisements in programmes provided by the programme contractor is receivable by any person other than the programme contractor, whether that person is under the control of the programme contractor or not.

(3) Every contract between the Authority and a programme contractor which provides for the supply of television programmes to be broadcast from stations of which some are in Great Britain and some in Northern Ireland shall provide that, as regards his advertising receipts for any period, the programme contractor shall give to the Authority such information as they may require for the purpose of ascertaining the proportions in which those receipts derive from the broadcasting of advertisements from stations in Great Britain and stations in Northern Ireland respectively.

(4) On receipt of any additional payments the Authority shall deal with them as follows:—

(a) if they were paid under a contract for the supply of programmes to be broadcast from stations all of which are in Great Britain, the Authority shall pay them into the Consolidated Fund of the United Kingdom ;

(b) if they were paid under a contract for the supply of programmes to be broadcast from stations all of which are in Northern Ireland, the Authority shall pay them into the Exchequer of Northern Ireland ;

(c) if they were paid under such a contract as is mentioned in subsection (3) of this section, the Authority shall pay them into that Fund and that Exchequer respectively in the proportions in which, according to the information supplied by the programme contractor, the advertising receipts for the relevant accounting period derive from the broadcasting of advertisements from stations in Great Britain and stations in Northen Ireland respectively, or, if the programme contractor has failed to supply the necessary information, or the payments became due as the result of an estimate made by the Authority, in such proportions as the Authority estimate to be appropriate.

(5) The Authority shall prepare in respect of each financial year an account showing the additional payments received under all their contracts with programme contractors and of the sums paid into the Consolidated Fund of the United Kingdom and the Exchequer of Northern Ireland respectively under subsection (4) of this section and shall send the account to the Comptroller and Auditor General not later than the end of

November following the year; and the Comptroller and Auditor General shall examine, certify and report on the account and lay copies of it, together with his report, before each House of Parliament.

(6) Nothing in this section or section 26 of this Act shall have effect in relation to contracts between the Authority and programme contractors in so far as they relate to local sound broadcasts.

Rental payments by local sound programme contractors.

28.—(1) Where, before the beginning of a financial year, it appears to the Minister, after consultation with the Authority, to be appropriate to do so, having regard—

(a) to the amount which (after making due provision towards or for capital expenditure required for the proper discharge, in relation to local sound broadcasting services, of the duties of the Authority under section 2(1) and (2) of this Act) is likely to be the amount of the relevant expenditure for that year, and

(b) to the need for securing that excessive profits do not accrue to programme contractors for the provision of local sound broadcasts,

the Minister, with the consent of the Treasury, may before the beginning of that year make an order under this subsection in respect of that financial year.

(2) Any such order made in respect of a financial year shall specify an amount (in this subsection referred to as " the specified amount ") by which the relevant revenues for that year ought to exceed the relevant expenditure for that year, and shall require the Authority—

(a) to determine what aggregate amount of relevant revenues for that year they regard as necessary to ensure that those revenues exceed the relevant expenditure by the specified amount ;

(b) to determine, in the case of each programme contractor with whom the Authority enter into a contract for the provision of local sound broadcasts, what amount in the opinion of the Authority represents his appropriate contribution for that year towards meeting that aggregate amount ;

(c) so to exercise their powers under their contract with each such programme contractor as to ensure that the payments made for that year by that contractor are not less than the amount so determined as representing his appropriate contribution, or (if there are circumstances which in the opinion of the Authority make it impracticable for those payments to be equal to the amount so determined) are as near to that amount as in the opinion of the Authority those circumstances permit ; and

(d) to pay into the Consolidated Fund for that year a sum equal to the specified amount or to the amount by which the relevant revenues for that year exceed the relevant expenditure, whichever is the lesser amount.

(3) Any order made under subsection (1) of this section in respect of a financial year may, by a further order made by the Minister after consultation with the Authority, and with the consent of the Treasury,—

(a) be revoked, or

(b) be varied by substituting a lesser amount for the amount specified in the order,

and any such further order may be made either before or after the beginning of the financial year to which it relates.

(4) In making their contracts with programme contractors for the provision of local sound broadcasts, it shall be the duty of the Authority to require these contracts to include such provisions, with respect to the payments to be made by the contractors, as in the opinion of the Authority will ensure that the Authority will be in a position to comply with any order made under this section.

(5) Every such contract as is mentioned in subsection (4) of this section shall impose on the contractor such requirements, with respect to the furnishing of information to the Authority, as appear to the Authority, after consultation with the Minister, to be requisite for enabling the Authority to furnish to the Minister such information as he may require for the purpose of determining at any time—

(a) whether an order should be made under subsection (1) or subsection (3) of this section, and

(b) in the case of an order to be made under subsection (1) or subsection 3 (b) of this section, what amount should be specified in the order,

and for enabling the Authority to comply with any order made under this section ; and the Authority shall furnish to the Minister such information (whether obtained from contractors or otherwise) as is in their possession and is required by the Minister for any such purpose as is mentioned in this subsection.

(6) Any power to make an order under this section shall be exercisable by statutory instrument ; and no such order shall be made unless a draft of the order has been laid before Parliament and approved by a resolution of each House of Parliament.

(7) In this section " the relevant expenditure ", in relation to any financial year, means the aggregate of the sums which, for the purposes of the branch of the Authority's undertaking which

consists of the provision of local sound broadcasting services, are required in respect of that year—

(a) to meet all such sums as are mentioned in section 25(2)(a) of this Act, and

(b) to make such provision towards or for capital expenditure as the Authority propose to make as mentioned in section 25(2)(b),

and " relevant revenues ", in relation to any financial year, means revenues of the Authority for that year which are attributable to that branch of their undertaking.

Application of any excess of revenues over expenditure.
29.—(1) In the case of each branch of the Authority's undertaking (but subject, in the case of the branch consisting of the provision of local sound broadcasting services, to subsection (4) of this section) any excess of the revenues of the Authority for any financial year over the total sums properly chargeable by the Authority to revenue account for that year, including in such sums (without prejudice to the generality of that expression) sums credited under section 25 (4) of this Act to the reserve fund established for that branch, shall be applied by the Authority in such manner as the Minister, with the approval of the Treasury after consultation with the Chairman (or in his absence the Deputy Chairman) of the Authority, may direct.

(2) A direction under subsection (1) of this section may require the whole or any part of any excess of the revenues of the Authority to be paid into the Consolidated Fund.

(3) A direction under subsection (1) of this section shall not require any part of any excess of the revenues of the Authority attributable to one branch of their undertaking to be applied for the purposes of the other branch of their undertaking.

(4) In relation to the branch of the Authority's undertaking which consists of the provision of local sound broadcasting services, subsections (1) and (2) of this section shall have effect in relation only to so much (if any) of any excess as is therein mentioned as is not required for complying with any order made under section 28 of this Act.

Advances to Authority for purposes of local sound broadcasting.
30.—(1) For the purpose of enabling the Authority to defray expenditure properly attributable to capital account in respect of the provision of local sound broadcasting services, and for the purpose of furnishing the Authority with working capital in connection with those services, the Minister may with the consent of the Treasury make advances to the Authority out of moneys provided by Parliament.

(2) The aggregate amount outstanding by way of principal in respect of sums advanced to the Authority under this section shall not at any time exceed £2 million.

(3) Any sums advanced under this section shall be repaid to the Minister at such times and by such methods, and interest on those sums shall be paid to him at such times and at such rates, as he may from time to time direct with the consent of the Treasury.

(4) All sums received by the Minister in pursuance of sub-section (3) of this section shall be paid into the Consolidated Fund.

31.—(1) The Authority shall keep proper accounts and proper records in relation to the accounts, and shall prepare in respect of each financial year a statement of accounts in such form as the Minister with the approval of the Treasury may direct, being a form which shall conform with the best commercial standards.
<small>Accounts, audit and reports.</small>

(2) The accounts of the Authority shall be audited by auditors to be appointed by the Authority with the approval of the Minister, and a person shall not be qualified to be so appointed unless he is a member of one or more of the following bodies—

    the Institute of Chartered Accountants in England and Wales ;

    the Institute of Chartered Accountants of Scotland ;

    the Association of Certified Accountants ;

    the Institute of Chartered Accountants in Ireland ;

    any other body of accountants established in the United Kingdom and for the time being recognised for the purposes of section 161(1)(*a*) of the Companies Act 1948 by the Secretary of State. <small>1948 c. 38.</small>

(3) As soon as may be after the end of every financial year, the Authority shall prepare a general report of their proceedings during that year, and transmit it to the Minister who shall consider it and lay copies of it before each House of Parliament.

(4) The said report shall have attached to it the statement of accounts for the year and a copy of any report made by the auditor on that statement and shall also include such information relating to the plans, and past and present activities, of the Authority, and the financial position of the Authority, as the Minister may from time to time direct.

(5) The Authority shall at all reasonable times upon demand made by the Minister or by any person authorised by him in that behalf—

    (*a*) afford to him or them full liberty to examine the accounts of the Authority, and (*b*) furnish him or them with all forecasts, estimates, information and documents which he or they may require with respect to the financial transactions and engagements of the Authority.

Miscellaneous and general

Machinery for settling terms and conditions of employment of Authority's staff, etc.

32.—(1) Except so far as the Authority are satisfied that adequate machinery exists for achieving the purposes of this section, it shall be the duty of the Authority to seek consultation with any organisation appearing to them to be appropriate with a view to the conclusion between the Authority and that organisation of such agreements as appear to the parties to be desirable with respect to the establishment and maintenance of machinery for—

(*a*) the settlement by negotiation of terms and conditions of employment of persons employed by the Authority, with provision for reference to arbitration, in default of such settlement, of such cases as may be determined by or under the agreements ; and

(*b*) the promotion and encouragement of measures affecting the safety, health, training and welfare of persons employed by the Authority, and the discussion of other matters of mutual interest to the Authority and such persons.

(2) The Authority shall send to the Minister and the Secretary of State copies of any such agreement and of any instrument varying the terms of any such agreement.

(3) In relation to any agreement affecting employment in Northern Ireland, the reference in subsection (2) of this section to the Secretary of State shall be construed as including a reference to the Ministry of Health and Social Services for Northern Ireland.

Audience research.

33. The functions of the Authority shall include the making of arrangements for bringing the programmes (including advertisements) broadcast by the Authority and the other activities of the Authority under constant and effective review, and in particular for ascertaining the state of public opinion concerning the programmes (including advertisements) broadcast by the Authority and for encouraging the making of useful comments and suggestions by members of the public ; and the arrangements shall include provision for full consideration by the Authority of the facts, comments and suggestions so obtained.

34. If at any time the Authority are broadcasting more than one television programme for reception in any one area, the Authority shall in carrying out their duties under this Act ensure that, so far as possible, the same kind of subject-matter is not broadcast at the same time in the different programmes.

35. The Authority may—

(a) for the purposes of any provision in this Act which makes anything subject to the approval of the Authority, or

(b) for the purposes of provisions included in the contracts between the Authority and the various programme contractors in pursuance of section 15(2) of this Act,

give an approval in general terms applying to all cases within the terms in which the approval is given.

36.—(1) Any direction or notice given by the Minister or by the Authority under any provision in this Act may be varied or revoked by a subsequent direction or notice under that provision.

(2) This section shall apply as respects the variation or revocation of directions and notices given at any time before or after the commencement of this Act.

37.—(1) In this Act, unless the context otherwise requires—

" associate ", in relation to a body corporate (including a programme contractor which is a body corporate), means a body corporate which is a member of the same group as that body corporate ; and for this purpose any two bodies corporate are to be treated as members of the same group if one of them is a body corporate of which the other is a subsidiary (within the meaning of section 154 of the Companies Act 1948) or if both of them are subsidiaries (within the meaning of that section) of one and the same body corporate ;

" broadcast relay station " means a station for the re-transmission by cable or wire, to the customers of the persons maintaining the station, of broadcast programmes which those persons receive either by cable or wire or by wireless from the persons who broadcast the programmes ;

" control ", in relation to a body corporate, means the power of a person to secure, by means of the holding of shares or the possession of voting power in or in relation to that or any other body corporate, or by virtue of any powers conferred by the articles of association or other document regulating that or any other body corporate, that the affairs of the first-mentioned body corporate are conducted in accordance with the wishes of that person ;

" financial year " means the twelve months ending with 31st March ;

" local sound broadcast " means a programme which is broadcast (otherwise than as part of a television broadcast) from a station so constructed and operated as to have a range of transmission limited to that which is sufficient, in normal circumstances, to ensure adequate reception throughout a particular locality, or from two or more stations so constructed and operated as to have collectively such a range of transmission, and " local sound broadcasting services " means services consisting of programmes so broadcast ; and, where a programme is so broadcast, the fact that—

(*a*) as so broadcast it is received outside that particular locality, or

(*b*) it is also broadcast (whether simultaneously or not) from one or more other stations for reception in other localities,

shall not prevent it from being regarded as a local sound broadcast within the meaning of this Act ;

" the Minister " means the Minister of Posts and Telecommunications ;

" programme contractor " has the meaning assigned to it by section 2(3) of this Act ;

" wireless telegraphy ", " station for wireless telegraphy " and " apparatus for wireless telegraphy " have the same meanings as in the Wireless Telegraphy Act 1949.

1949 c. 54.

(2) Any reference in this Act to a contract for the provision by a programme contractor of local sound broadcasts shall be construed as including a reference to a contract which is—

(*a*) partly for the provision by that contractor of local sound broadcasts for reception in a particular locality, and

(*b*) partly for the provision of news, information, music or other material to be supplied to other programme contractors for the purposes of local sound broadcasts to be provided by them ;

but, in relation to any such contract, the locality, where the reference is to the provision of local sound broadcasts for reception in a particular locality, shall be taken to be the locality referred to in paragraph (*a*) of this subsection.

(3) For the purposes of this Act—

(*a*) a person shall not be regarded as carrying on business as an advertising agent, or as acting as such an agent, unless he carries on a business involving the selection and purchase of advertising space or time for persons wishing to advertise ;

(*b*) a person who carries on such a business shall be regarded as carrying on business as an advertising agent irrespective of whether he is in law the agent of those for whom he acts ;

(*c*) a person who is the proprietor of a newspaper shall not be regarded as carrying on business as an advertising agent by reason only that he makes arrangements on behalf of advertisers whereby advertisements appearing in the newspaper are also to appear in one or more other newspapers ; and

(*d*) a company or other body corporate shall not be regarded as carrying on business as an advertising agent by reason only that its objects or powers include or authorise that activity ;

and any reference in this Act to an advertising agency shall be construed accordingly.

(4) Any reference in this Act to an enactment shall, except in so far as the context otherwise requires, be construed as a reference to that enactment as amended or extended by or under other enactment.

38. Where in any enactment passed before 12th June 1972, Former or in any statutory instrument having effect by virtue of such name of an enactment, reference is made to the Authority by the name Authority. of the Independent Television Authority, the name " Independent Broadcasting Authority " shall be substituted for that name.

39.—(1) The enactments specified in Part I of Schedule 3 to Repeals, this Act are hereby repealed to the extent specified in the third revocation column of that Part ; and the order specified in Part II of that and savings. Schedule is hereby revoked.

(2) In so far as anything done or deemed to have been done under or in pursuance of any of the enactments repealed by this Act could have been done under or in pursuance of a corresponding provision of this Act, it shall not be invalidated by the repeal effected by subsection (1) of this section but shall have effect as if done under or in pursuance of that corresponding provision ; and anything begun or continued under any of those enactments may be continued under this Act as if begun under this Act.

(3) Subsection (2) of this section applies in particular to any Order in Council, order, regulation, notice, direction, code, programme schedule or other instrument or document whatsoever made, given, drawn up, approved or issued, any contract entered into and any advance made.

(4) So much of any document as refers expressly or by implication to any enactment repealed by this Act, or is to be construed as so referring, shall, if and so far as the context permits, be construed as referring to this Act or the corresponding enactment therein.

1889 c. 63.

(5) Nothing in this section shall be taken as affecting the general application of section 38 of the Interpretation Act 1889 with regard to the effect of repeals.

Short title, extent and commencement.

40.—(1) This Act may be cited as the Independent Broadcasting Authority Act 1973.

(2) It is hereby declared that this Act extends to Northern Ireland.

(3) Her Majesty may by Order in Council direct that all or any of the provisions of this Act shall extend to the Isle of Man or any of the Channel Islands with such adaptations and modifications, if any, as may be specified in the Order: and any Order in Council under this section may be revoked or varied by a subsequent Order in Council.

(4) This Act shall come into operation on 31st July 1973.

SCHEDULES

SCHEDULE 1

PROVISIONS AS TO THE INDEPENDENT BROADCASTING AUTHORITY

Appointment and removal of members

1.—(1) All the members of the Authority (including the Chairman and Deputy Chairman who shall be appointed as such) shall be appointed by the Minister from among persons appearing to him to be qualified for the office, and of the members of the Authority other than the Chairman and Deputy Chairman three shall be persons who appear to the Minister to be suited to make the interests of Scotland, the interests of Wales and Monmouthshire and the interests of Northern Ireland, respectively, their special care.

(2) A person shall be disqualified for being appointed, or being, a member of the Authority so long as he is a Governor of the British Broadcasting Corporation.

(3) Before appointing a person to be a member of the Authority, the Minister shall satisfy himself that that person will have no such financial or other interest (and, in particular, no such financial or other interest in any advertising agency or in any business concerned with the manufacture or sale of apparatus for wireless telegraphy or other telegraphic equipment or in any business consisting or intended to consist in whole or in part in entering into or carrying out contracts with the Authority for the provision of programmes or parts of programmes) as is likely to affect prejudicially the discharge by him of his functions as member of the Authority ; and the Minister shall also satisfy himself from time to time with respect to every member of the Authority that he has no such interest.

(4) Any person who is, or whom the Minister proposes to appoint to be, a member of the Authority shall, whenever requested by the Minister to do so, furnish to him such information as the Minister considers necessary for the performance by the Minister of his duties under sub-paragraph (3) of this paragraph.

(5) Subject to sub-paragraphs (6) and (7) of this paragraph, every member of the Authority shall hold office for such period, not exceeding five years, as may be fixed at the time of his appointment, and shall, on ceasing to be a member, be eligible for re-appointment.

(6) The Minister may at any time direct by notice in writing, a copy of which shall be laid before each House of Parliament, that any member of the Authority shall cease to hold office, and any member of the Authority may at any time by notice in writing to the Minister resign his office.

(7) If any member of the Authority dies or ceases to hold office before the expiration of the term for which he was appointed, the term of office of his successor shall be so fixed as to expire at the end of the first-mentioned term, but the Minister may, if he thinks fit to do so, defer the making of an appointment until the expiration of the said first-mentioned term.

Remuneration of members

2.—(1) The Authority shall pay to each of their members, in respect of his office as such, such remuneration (whether by way of salary or fees) and such allowances as the Minister may, with the approval of the Minister for the Civil Service, determine in the case of those members respectively ; and in determining the remuneration and allowances to be paid under this sub-paragraph, different provision may be made as regards the Chairman, the Deputy Chairman and the other members.

(2) If any member of the Authority, other than the Chairman thereof, is employed about the affairs of the Authority otherwise than as a member thereof, the Authority shall pay to that member such remuneration, if any (in addition to any remuneration to which he may be entitled in respect of his office as a member) as the Minister may, with the approval of the Minister for the Civil Service, determine.

(3) If any determination by the Minister under this paragraph of the remuneration and allowances that are to be paid to the members of the Authority involves any departure from the terms of the original statement of the remuneration and allowances of the members of the Authority laid by the Postmaster General before 1954 c. 55. Parliament under section 1(10) of the Television Act 1954, the Minister shall, as soon as possible after determination, lay a statement thereof before each House of Parliament.

Incorporation and capacity of Authority

3.—(1) The Authority shall be a body corporate with perpetual succession and a common seal.

(2) The Authority may act notwithstanding a vacancy among their members.

(3) It shall be within the capacity of the Authority as a statutory corporation to do such things and enter into such transactions as are incidental or conducive to the exercise and performance of their powers and duties under this Act, including the borrowing of money.

Quorum of Authority

4. The quorum of the Authority shall be four or such number not being less than four as the Authority may from time to time determine.

Duty of members to disclose interest in contracts

5.—(1) A member of the Authority who is in any way directly or indirectly interested in a contract made or proposed to be made by the Authority shall, as soon as possible after the relevant circumstances have come to his knowledge, disclose the nature of his interest at a meeting of the Authority.

(2) Any disclosure made under sub-paragraph (1) of this paragraph shall be recorded in the minutes of the Authority, and the member—

(a) shall not take part after the disclosure in any deliberation or decision of the Authority with respect to that contract, and

(b) shall be disregarded for the purpose of constituting a quoroum of the Authority for any such deliberation or decision.

Power of Authority to regulate own procedure

6. Subject to the preceding provisions of this Schedule, the Authority may regulate their own procedure.

Officers and employees of Authority

7.—(1) The Authority may appoint a secretary and such other officers, and take into their employment such other persons, as they may determine.

(2) The Authority shall, as regards any officers or persons employed in whose case it may be determined by the Authority so to do, pay to or in respect of them such pensions, allowances or gratuities, or provide and maintain for them such pension schemes (whether contributory or not), as may be so determined.

(3) If any officer of or other person employed by the Authority, being a participant in any pension scheme applicable to his office or employment, becomes a member of the Authority, he may be treated for the purposes of the pension scheme as if his service as a member of the Authority were service as an officer of or person employed by the Authority.

Authentication of Authority's seal

8. The application of the seal of the Authority shall be authenticated by the signatures—

(a) of the Chairman or Deputy Chairman of the Authority or some other member of the Authority authorised by the Authority to authenticate the application of the Authority's seal, and

(b) of the secretary of the Authority or some other officer of the authority authorised by the Authority to act in that behalf.

Presumption of authenticity of documents issued by Authority

9. Any document purporting to be an instrument issued by the Authority and to be sealed as aforesaid or to be signed on behalf of the Authority shall be received in evidence and shall be deemed to be such an instrument without further proof unless the contrary is shown.

Section 8.

SCHEDULE 2

RULES AS TO ADVERTISEMENTS

1.—(1) The advertisements must be clearly distinguishable as such and recognisably separate from the rest of the programme.

(2) Successive advertisements must be recognisably separate.

(3) Advertisements must not be arranged or presented in such a way that any separate advertisement appears to be part of a continuous feature.

(4) Audible matter in advertisements must not be excessively noisy or strident.

2. The standards and practice to be observed in carrying out the requirements of the preceding paragraph shall be such as the Authority may determine either generally or in particular cases.

3. The amount of time given to advertising in the programmes shall not be so great as to detract from the value of the programmes as a medium of information, education and entertainment.

4. Advertisements shall not be inserted otherwise than at the beginning or the end of the programme or in natural breaks therein.

5.—(1) Rules (to be agreed upon from time to time between the Authority and the Minister, or settled by the Minister in default of such agreement) shall be observed as to the classes of broadcasts (which shall in particular include the broadcast of any religious service) in which advertisements may not be inserted, and the interval which must elapse between any such broadcast and any previous or subsequent period given over to advertisements.

(2) The Minister may, after consultation with the Authority, impose rules as to the minimum interval which must elapse between any two periods given over to advertisements, and the rules may make different provision for different circumstances.

6. In the acceptance of advertisements there must be no unreasonable discrimination either against or in favour of any particular advertiser.

7.—(1) The charges made by any programme contractor for advertisements shall be in accordance with tariffs fixed by him from time to time, being tariffs drawn up in such detail and published in such form and manner as the Authority may determine.

(2) Any such tariffs may make provision for different circumstances, and, in particular, may provide, in such detail as the Authority may determine, for the making, in special circumstances, of additional special charges.

8. No advertisement shall be permitted which is inserted by or on behalf of any body the objects whereof are wholly or mainly of a religious or political nature, and no advertisement shall be permitted which is directed towards any religious or political end or has any relation to any industrial dispute.

9. If, in the case of any of the broadcasting stations used by the Authority, there appears to the Authority to be a sufficient local demand to justify that course, provision shall be made for a reasonable allocation of time for local advertisements, of which a suitable proportion shall be short local advertisements.

SCHEDULE 3

Section 39.

Repeals and Revocation

Part I

Enactments Repealed

Chapter	Short Title	Extent of Repeal
1964 c. 21	The Television Act 1964.	The whole Act.
1969 c. 48.	The Post Office Act 1969.	In section 3(1), paragraph (b) and the word " and " immediately preceding that paragraph.
1972 c. 11.	The Superannuation Act 1972.	In Schedule 4, the entry relating to the Authority. In Schedule 6, paragraph 44.
1972 c. 31.	The Sound Broadcasting Act 1972.	The whole Act.

Part II

Order Revoked

The Television Act 1964 (Additional Payments) Order 1971 (S.I. 1971/309).

London Cab Act 1973

1973 CHAPTER 20

An Act to amend the London Cab Act 1968.

[23rd May 1973]

B E IT ENACTED by the Queen's most Excellent Majesty, by and with the advice and consent of the Lords Spiritual and Temporal, and Commons, in this present Parliament assembled, and by the authority of the same, as follows:—

Increased penalty for illegal signs, notices and advertisements in connection with private hire-cars.
1968 c. 7.

1. In subsection (3) of section 4 of the London Cab Act 1968 (which prescribes a penalty of £20 for a first offence and £50 for a subsequent offence under provisions of that section prohibiting the display or issue of certain signs, notices and advertisements in connection with private hire-cars) for the words " liable on summary conviction " onwards there shall be substituted the words " liable on summary conviction to a fine not exceeding £200 ".

Power to prohibit signs etc. on private hire-cars.
1869 c. 115.

2. After section 4 of the London Cab Act 1968 there shall be inserted the following section:—

" 4A.—(1) The Secretary of State may, with a view to preventing private hire-cars from competing unfairly with vehicles licensed under section 6 of the Metropolitan Public Carriage Act 1869, by order prohibit the display on or from private hire-cars in the metropolitan police district and the City of London of any sign, notice, mark, illumination or other feature of a description specified in the order.

(2) Any prohibition imposed by an order under this section may be expressed to apply only in circumstances specified in the order or to apply subject to any exceptions so specified.

(3) The power to make orders under this section includes power to vary or revoke a previous order and shall be exercisable by statutory instrument subject to annulment in pursuance of a resolution of either House of Parliament.

(4) Before making any order under this section the Secretary of State shall consult with such bodies appearing to him to represent the owners and drivers of vehicles licensed under section 6 of the said Act of 1869 and the private hire-car trade as he considers appropriate.

(5) This section is without prejudice to subsection (1) of section 4 of this Act and the references in subsection (3)(*a*) of that section to contravention of the said subsection (1) shall include references to contravention of an order under this section.

(6) In this section " private hire-car " has the same meaning as in section 4 of this Act.".

3. This Act may be cited as the London Cab Act 1973; and this Act and the London Cab Act 1968 may be cited together as the London Cab Acts 1968 and 1973.

Short title and citation.

1968 c. 7.

Overseas Pensions Act 1973

1973 CHAPTER 21

An Act to amend the law relating to pensions and other similar benefits payable to or in respect of persons in certain overseas and other employment; and for purposes connected therewith. [23rd May 1973]

B E IT ENACTED by the Queen's most Excellent Majesty, by and with the advice and consent of the Lords Spiritual and Temporal, and Commons, in this present Parliament assembled, and by the authority of the same, as follows:—

Assumption by United Kingdom of responsibility for certain overseas pensions, etc.

1.—(1) The Secretary of State may make any payments falling to be made by Her Majesty's Government in the United Kingdom, or by any Minister of the Crown, in accordance with any agreement between that government and the government of an overseas territory for the assumption by Her Majesty's Government in the United Kingdom of responsibility for the payment of such pensions, allowances or gratuities as the agreement may provide.

(2) Without prejudice to the generality of subsection (1) above, the Secretary of State, for the purposes—

(a) of giving effect to any such agreement ; and

(b) of making such provision as he considers appropriate in consequence of the agreement,

may, with the consent of the Minister for the Civil Service, make, maintain and administer schemes (whether contributory or not) whereby provision is made with respect to the pensions, allowances or gratuities which, subject to the fulfilment of such requirements and conditions as may be prescribed by the schemes, are to be paid, or may be paid, by the Secretary of State to or in respect of—

(i) such of the persons to whom the agreement applies as he may determine ; and

(ii) such other persons for whom it is appropriate, in his opinion, to provide pensions, allowances or gratuities in accordance with any such scheme.

(3) For the purposes of this section " overseas territory " means any territory or country outside the United Kingdom, and " government of an overseas territory " includes a government constituted for two or more overseas territories, and any authority established for the purpose of providing or administering the services which are common to, or relate to matters of any interest to, two or more overseas territories.

2.—(1) The Secretary of State may, with the consent of the Minister for the Civil Service, make, maintain and administer schemes (whether contributory or not) whereby provision is made with respect to the pensions, allowances or gratuities which, subject to the fulfilment of such requirements and conditions as may be prescribed by the schemes, are to be paid, or may be paid, by the Secretary of State to or in respect of such of the persons to whom this section applies as he may determine.

Superannuation schemes as respects certain overseas service and service with the Central Office of the Overseas Audit Department.

(2) This section applies to—

(a) persons who have, whether before or after the passing of this Act, served in any office or employment in respect of which pensions, allowances or gratuities are provided by or under any of the enactments and instruments listed in Schedule 1 to this Act ;

(b) any other persons for whom it is appropriate, in the opinion of the Secretary of State, to provide pensions, allowances or gratuities in accordance with any scheme made under this section superseding or supplementing any provision made by or under any of the said enactments and instruments ;

(c) persons who have served in the Central Office of the Overseas Audit Department (which was wound up on 31st December 1971) ; and

(d) any person to whom section 2 of the Police (Overseas Service) Act 1945 (service overseas by members of home police forces) applies, including any person to whom that section applies by virtue of section 5 of

9 & 10 Geo. 6 c. 17.

the Overseas Service Act 1958 (appointment of certain officers for public service overseas), being a person who is incapacitated or dies as a result of an injury sustained or disease contracted during his overseas service (within the meaning of section 3(1) of the said Act of 1945) or, as the case may be, during his service as an officer to whom the said Act of 1958 applies.

(3) Notwithstanding any repeal made by this Act, the enactments and instruments listed in Schedule 1 to this Act shall, with the necessary adaptations and modifications, have effect as from the commencement of this Act as if they constituted schemes made under this section coming into operation on the said commencement.

(4) The provisions of the pension scheme set out in the departmental instructions in force in relation to the Overseas Audit Department immediately before 31st December 1971 shall, with the necessary adaptations and modifications, have effect as from the commencement of this Act as if they constituted a scheme made under this section coming into operation on the said commencement.

(5) Unless the context otherwise requires, any reference in this or any other Act to a scheme made under this section shall include a reference to a scheme having effect, by virtue of subsection (3) or (4) above, as if made under this section.

Provisions supplementary to sections 1 and 2.
3.—(1) Without prejudice to the generality of section 1 or 2 above, a scheme made under either of those sections—

(a) may provide for the establishment and administration of superannuation funds, the management and application of the assets of such funds, the amalgamation of all or any of such funds and the winding up of, or other dealing with, any such fund ;

(b) may provide for the payment or receipt of transfer values, or in lieu thereof for the transfer or receipt of any fund or part of a fund or policy of insurance ;

(c) may, in such circumstances as the scheme may provide, make provision for payments by way of a return of contributions, with or without interest ;

(d) may provide for the Secretary of State to make such payments as he thinks fit towards the provision of pensions, allowances or gratuities otherwise than by virtue of the scheme ;

(e) may amend or revoke any previous scheme made thereunder ;

(f) may (in the case of a scheme under section 1 above) be framed by reference to the law in force at any time in the overseas territory to which the scheme relates ;

(g) may provide for the amendment or repeal of any provision in any Act of Parliament or in any order or other instrument made under any such Act, where it appears to the Secretary of State that that provision is inconsistent with, or has become unnecessary or requires modification in consequence of, the scheme.

(2) Different schemes may be made under sections 1 and 2 above in relation to different classes of persons to whom each of those sections applies.

(3) The Secretary of State may, to such extent and subject to such conditions as he thinks fit, delegate to any other Minister or officer of the Crown any functions exercisable by him by virtue of section 1 or 2 above or by virtue of any scheme made thereunder.

(4) A scheme made under section 1 or 2 above, or any provision thereof, may be framed—

(a) so as to have effect as from a date earlier than the date on which the scheme is made ; or

(b) so as to apply in relation to the pensions, allowances or gratuities paid or payable to or in respect of persons who, having been persons to whom section 1 or, as the case may be, 2 above applies, have died or ceased to be persons to whom the said section 1 or, as the case may be, 2 applies, before the scheme comes into operation ; or

(c) so as to require or authorise the payment of pensions, allowances or gratuities, to or in respect of such persons.

(5) Any scheme made under section 1 or 2 above may provide for the determination by the Secretary of State of questions arising under the scheme and may provide that the decision of the Secretary of State on any such question shall be final.

(6) Where under any such scheme any question falls to be determined by the Secretary of State, then, at any time before the question is determined, the Secretary of State may (and if so directed by any of the Courts hereinafter mentioned shall) state in the form of a special case for determination by the High Court, the Court of Session or the Court of Appeal in Northern Ireland any question of law arising out of the question which falls to be determined by him.

(7) Where such a case is stated for determination by the High Court, an appeal to the Court of Appeal from the determination by the High Court shall lie only with the leave of the High Court or of the Court of Appeal; and where such a case is stated for determination by the Court of Session then, subject to any rules of court, the Secretary of State shall be entitled to appear and be heard when the case is being considered by that court.

(8) Before a scheme made under section 1 or 2 above comes into operation the Secretary of State shall lay a copy of the scheme before Parliament.

(9) In this section and in sections 1 and 2 above the expression " pensions, allowances or gratuities " includes any compensation payable to or in respect of persons—

> (a) who suffer loss of office or employment, or loss or diminution of emoluments, or
>
> (b) whose office or employment is affected by constitutional changes, or circumstances arising from such changes, in any territory or territories.

Pension increases.
1971 c. 56.

4.—(1) After section 11 of the Pensions (Increase) Act 1971 there shall be inserted the following section—

" 11A.—(1) The Secretary of State, with the approval of the Minister for the Civil Service, may by regulations made as respects any pension to which this section applies—

> (a) direct that the provisions of Part I of this Act shall, with such modifications, adaptations and exceptions as may be specified in the regulations, apply as if the pension were an official pension specified in Part I of Schedule 2, or
>
> (b) authorise the payment by the Secretary of State of supplements to the pension of such amount as may be specified in the regulations.

(2) This section applies to—

> (a) any pension payable under section 1 of the Overseas Pensions Act 1973, and
>
> (b) any pension payable under a scheme made under section 2 of that Act, other than a pension within paragraph 27A of Schedule 2 to this Act.

(3) This section also applies to any derivative pension payable either by the government of an overseas territory or in accordance with an enactment, scheme or other instrument specified in the regulations as being approved

by the Secretary of State for the purpose of this section, where related principal pensions—

    (*a*) are payable under section 1 of the Overseas Pensions Act 1973, or under a scheme made under section 2 of that Act, or

    (*b*) fall within section 10(*b*) or section 11(2)(*c*) above.

(4) The provisions of subsections (4) to (7) of section 11 of this Act (so far as applicable) shall have effect in relation to this section as they have effect in relation to that section.

(5) For the purposes of this section principal pensions are related to a derivative pension if they are payable wholly or partly in respect of the same kind of service as the derivative pension."

(2) For subsection (4) of section 11 of the said Act of 1971 (which requires the Secretary of State to take into account certain matters in determining the amount of any supplement payable under that section) there shall be substituted the following subsection : —

" (4) The supplements which may be authorised by regulations under this section in the case of pensions of any class are supplements, in respect of a period beginning on or after 1st September 1971, of amounts which, when account is taken of—

    (*a*) any increase or supplement payable in respect of the pensions apart from this section ;

    (*b*) any other additions to the value of those pensions ; and

    (*c*) the amount of such other pensions as may be specified by the regulations (being pensions payable to the recipients of the first-mentioned pensions wholly or partly in respect of service in respect of which the first-mentioned pensions are payable) ;

appear to the Secretary of State to correspond as nearly as may be with the increases payable under Part I of this Act on official pensions."

(3) After paragraph 27 of Schedule 2 to the said Act of 1971 there shall be inserted the following paragraph—

" 27A. A pension payable under any scheme or part of a scheme made under section 2 of the Overseas Pensions Act 1973 which incorporates, replaces or amends the provisions of the Governors' Pensions Acts 1957 and 1967

1965 c. 74.

or of the Superannuation Act 1965 so far as it continued to have effect by virtue of section 23(2) of the Superannuation Act 1972."

Financial provisions.

5.—(1) There shall be paid out of moneys provided by Parliament—

(a) any expenses incurred by a Minister of the Crown in the payment of pensions, allowances, gratuities or other sums under section 4 of this Act or in accordance with schemes made under section 1 or 2, or agreements falling within section 1 of this Act ;

(b) any administrative expenses incurred by a government department in consequence of this Act ; and

(c) any increase attributable to the provisions of this Act in the sums payable under any other enactment out of money so provided.

(2) Subject to any scheme made under section 1 or 2 or any agreement falling within section 1 of this Act, there shall be paid into the Consolidated Fund all sums received by a Minister of the Crown by virtue of this Act.

Short title and enactments repealed.

6.—(1) This Act may be cited as the Overseas Pensions Act 1973.

(2) The enactments set out in Schedule 2 to this Act are hereby repealed to the extent specified in column 3 of the Schedule.

SCHEDULES

SCHEDULE 1

Overseas Service Superannuation Provisions

Section 273(1) of the Government of India Act 1935.

The Pensions (India, Pakistan & Burma) Act 1955.

The Governors' Pensions Act 1957.

Sections 2 and 4 of the Overseas Service Act 1958.

The Superannuation Act 1965, so far as it continues to have effect by virtue of section 23(2) of the Superannuation Act 1972.

Section 7 of the Overseas Aid Act 1966.

Sections 4 and 5 of the Superannuation (Miscellaneous Provisions) Act 1967.

Section 4 of the Aden, Perim and Kuria Muria Islands Act 1967.

Section 4 of the Overseas Aid Act 1968.

Section 23(2) of, and paragraphs 36 and 37 of Schedule 6 to, the Superannuation Act 1972.

Any rules, regulations, orders, schemes or warrants made, or having effect as if made, under an enactment listed in this Schedule.

Section 6.

SCHEDULE 2

REPEALS

Chapter	Short Title	Extent of Repeal
26 Geo. 5 & Edw. 8. c. 2.	The Government of India Act 1935.	Section 273(1).
3 & 4 Eliz. 2. c. 22.	The Pensions (India, Pakistan and Burma) Act 1955.	The whole Act.
5 & 6 Eliz. 2. c. 62.	The Governors' Pensions Act 1957.	The whole Act.
6 & 7 Eliz. 2. c. 14.	The Overseas Service Act 1958.	Section 2. In section 3, subsections (1), (3), (6) and (7). Section 4.
1966 c. 21.	The Overseas Aid Act 1966.	Section 7.
1967 c. 28.	The Superannuation (Miscellaneous Provisions) Act 1967.	Sections 4 and 5.
1967 c. 71.	The Aden, Perim and Kuria Muria Islands Act 1967.	Section 4.
1968 c. 57.	The Overseas Aid Act 1968.	Section 4.
1971 c. 56.	The Pensions (Increase) Act 1971.	Section 11(2)(*b*). In Schedule 4, paragraphs 1 and 3.
1972 c. 11.	The Superannuation Act 1972.	Section 23(2). In Schedule 6, paragraphs 36 and 37.

Law Reform (Diligence) (Scotland) Act 1973

1973 CHAPTER 22

An Act to amend the law of Scotland relating to diligence; to exempt from diligence certain household effects and furniture; and for purposes connected with the matters aforesaid.   [23rd May 1973]

B E IT ENACTED by the Queen's most Excellent Majesty, by and with the advice and consent of the Lords Spiritual and Temporal, and Commons, in this present Parliament assembled, and by the authority of the same, as follows:—

1.—(1) An article shall not be liable to be poinded at the instance of a creditor in respect of a debt due to him by a debtor if—

(a) it is an article to which this section applies, and

(b) being at the time of the poinding in a dwellinghouse in which the debtor is residing, it is reasonably necessary to enable him and any person living in family with him in that dwellinghouse to continue to reside there without undue hardship.

Exemption of essential household furniture, etc., from poinding.

(2) This section shall apply to articles of any of the following descriptions, that is to say—

beds or bedding material;
chairs;
tables;
furniture or plenishings providing facilities for cooking, eating or storing food;
furniture or plenishings providing facilities for heating.

(3) The Secretary of State may by order amend subsection (2) above (whether as originally enacted or as amended by an order previously made under this subsection) by adding any item to, or deleting any item from, that subsection or by varying any of the items specified therein; and any order under this subsection shall be made by statutory instrument, which shall be subject to annulment in pursuance of a resolution of either House of Parliament, and may be varied or revoked by a subsequent order made thereunder.

(4) Where any article is poinded in respect of a debt, then, without prejudice to any other remedy available to him, the debtor may within seven days from the date of the poinding appeal to the sheriff on the ground that, by virtue of the foregoing provisions of this section, the said article is not liable to be poinded, and the sheriff shall, if he allows the appeal, order the article to be released from the poinding; and the decision of the sheriff on any such appeal shall not be subject to review.

1947 c. 43.

(5) Section 249(2) of the Local Government (Scotland) Act 1947 (which provides that proceedings under a warrant for the recovery of rates are not to be questioned except in accordance with subsection (1) of that section) shall not prevent the taking of any appeal under subsection (4) above.

1837 c. 41.

(6) Notwithstanding anything contained in section 20 of the Small Debt (Scotland) Act 1837 (which among other things lays down the procedure for poinding and sale on a decree granted in sheriff's small debt court), no article poinded in execution of such a decree, being an article to which this section applies, shall be sold in pursuance of the said section 20 before the expiry of seven days from the date of the poinding or, if an appeal is taken under subsection (4) above in respect of that article, until that appeal is determined or otherwise disposed of.

(7) Nothing in this section shall prejudice the operation of any enactment or rule of law by virtue of which articles of any description are not liable to be poinded in respect of a debt.

1960 c. 62.

(8) In this section "dwellinghouse" includes a caravan as defined in section 29(1) of the Caravan Sites and Control of Development Act 1960.

Short title, commencement and extent.

2.—(1) This Act may be cited as the Law Reform (Diligence) (Scotland) Act 1973.

(2) This Act shall come into operation at the expiration of the period of three months beginning with the day on which it is passed.

(3) This Act shall extend to Scotland only.

Education (Work Experience) Act 1973

1973 CHAPTER 23

An Act to enable education authorities to arrange for children under school-leaving age to have work experience, as part of their education.

[23rd May 1973]

BE IT ENACTED by the Queen's most Excellent Majesty, by and with the advice and consent of the Lords Spiritual and Temporal, and Commons, in this present Parliament assembled, and by the authority of the same, as follows:—

1.—(1) Subject to subsection (2) below, the enactments relating to the prohibition or regulation of the employment of children shall not apply to the employment of a child in his last year of compulsory schooling where the employment is in pursuance of arrangements made or approved by the local education authority or, in Scotland, the education authority with a view to providing him with work experience as part of his education. Work experience in last year of compulsory schooling.

(2) Subsection (1) above shall not be taken to permit the employment of any person in any way contrary to—

(*a*) an enactment which in terms applies to persons of less than, or not over, a specified age expressed as a number of years; or

(*b*) section 1(2) of the Employment of Women, Young Persons and Children Act 1920 or (when it comes into force) section 51(1) of the Merchant Shipping Act 1970 (prohibition of employment of children in ships); 1920 c. 65.
1970 c. 36.

(3) No arrangements shall be made under subsection (1) above for a child to be employed in any way which would be contrary

to an enactment prohibiting or regulating the employment of young persons if he were a young person (within the meaning of that enactment) and not a child; and where a child is employed in pursuance of arrangements so made, then so much of any enactment as regulates the employment of young persons (whether by excluding them from any description of work, or prescribing the conditions under which they may be permitted to do it, or otherwise howsoever) and would apply in relation to him if he were of an age to be treated as a young person for the purposes of that enactment shall apply in relation to him, in and in respect of the employment arranged for him, in all respects as if he were of an age to be so treated.

(4) In this Act—

" enactment " includes any byelaw, regulation or other provision having effect under an enactment;

other expressions which are also used in the Education Acts shall have the same meaning in this section as in those Acts; and

" the Education Acts " means in England and Wales the Education Acts 1944 to 1973 and, in Scotland, the Education (Scotland) Acts 1939 to 1971;

and for the purposes of subsection (1) above a child is in his last year of compulsory schooling at any time during the period of twelve months before he attains the upper limit of compulsory school age or, in Scotland, school age.

Citation and extent.

2.—(1) This Act may be cited as the Education (Work Experience) Act 1973; and—

(a) in relation to England and Wales, this Act shall be included among the Acts which may be cited together as the Education Acts 1944 to 1973; and

(b) in relation to Scotland the Education Acts and this Act may be cited together as the Education (Scotland) Acts 1939 to 1973.

(2) Nothing in this Act extends to Northern Ireland.

Employment of Children Act 1973

1973 CHAPTER 24

An Act to make further provision with respect to restrictions on the employment of persons under the upper limit of school age and to the means of imposing and enforcing such restrictions; and for connected purposes. *[23rd May 1973]*

B E IT ENACTED by the Queen's most Excellent Majesty, by and with the advice and consent of the Lords Spiritual and Temporal, and Commons, in this present Parliament assembled, and by the authority of the same, as follows:— *Regulation of children's employment.*

1.—(1) In this Act, " the Act of 1933 " means the Children and Young Persons Act 1933 and " the Act of 1937 " means the Children and Young Persons (Scotland) Act 1937. *1933 c. 12. 1937 c. 37.*

(2) In section 18(2) of the Act of 1933 and section 28(2) of the Act of 1937, the power of local authorities and, in Scotland, education authorities to make byelaws with respect to the employment of children shall be replaced by a power for the Secretary of State to make regulations for the purposes mentioned in those subsections respectively, any such regulations to be contained in a statutory instrument subject to annulment in pursuance of a resolution of either House of Parliament.

(3) In accordance with subsection (2) above and with a view—
   (a) to making the consequential changes in Part II of the Act of 1933 and Part III of the Act of 1937 which follow from that subsection ;
   (b) to extending the powers exercisable under section 18 of the Act of 1933 and section 28 of the Act of 1937 for regulating the employment of children ; and

K

(*c*) to increasing the penalties for contraventions of those Acts in relation to employment,

the Acts of 1933 and 1937 shall have effect with the amendments shown in Part I of Schedule 1 to this Act.

(4) As amended by subsection (3) above, section 18 of the Act of 1933 is as set out in Part II of Schedule 1 to this Act; and (as so amended) section 28 of the Act of 1937 is also as there set out, but with the differences specified in the note at the end of the Schedule.

(5) Section 19 of the Act of 1933 and section 29 of the Act of 1937 (power of local authorities to make byelaws with respect to the employment of persons under the age of eighteen) shall cease to have effect.

(6) If it appears to the Secretary of State in the case of a local Act that—

(*a*) it contains provisions relating to, or authorising the making of byelaws in respect of, the employment of children ; and

(*b*) those provisions are no longer required having regard to cognate provisions of any public general Act for the time being in force (and in particular the provision made by subsection (2) above),

he may by order amend or repeal those provisions of the local Act ; and an order under this subsection shall be made by statutory instrument subject to annulment in pursuance of a resolution of either House of Parliament.

Supervision by education authorities.

2.—(1) The following powers shall be exercisable in England and Wales by a local education authority and, in Scotland, by an education authority in cases where the authority have reason to suppose that a child is, or is to become, employed (whether or not in the authority's area).

(2) The authority may by a notice served—

(*a*) on the child's parent or guardian or a person who has actual custody of the child ; or

(*b*) on a person appearing to have the child in his employment or to be about to employ him,

require the person served to furnish to the authority, within such period as may be specified in the notice, particulars of how the child is, or is to be, employed and at what times and for what periods.

(3) If it appears to the authority that a child is for the time being, or is to become, employed in ways, or at times or for periods, which are not unlawful apart from this section but

are unsuitable for the child, by reference to his age or state of health, or otherwise prejudicial to his education, they may, by a notice served on any such person as is mentioned in paragraph (a) or (b) of subsection (2) above as one on whom a notice may be served, either—

(a) prohibit the child's employment in any manner specified in the notice; or

(b) require his employment in any manner so specified to be subject to such conditions (specified in the notice and to be complied with by the person served with it) as the authority think fit to impose in the interests of the child.

(4) Any person who—

(a) being served with a notice under subsection (2) above—

(i) fails to furnish the particulars required by the notice within the period specified thereby, or

(ii) in purported compliance with the notice, makes any statement which he knows to be false in a material particular, or recklessly makes any statement which is false in a material particular; or

(b) being served with a notice under subsection (3) prohibiting a child's employment in any manner specified in the notice, employs or causes or permits the child to be employed in that manner contrary to the prohibition; or

(c) being served with such a notice requiring compliance by him with any conditions, wilfully fails to comply with them,

shall be guilty of an offence.

(5) A person guilty of an offence under subsection (4) above shall be liable on summary conviction—

(a) in the case of an offence under paragraph (a) of the subsection, to a fine of not more than £20 or, if he has previously been convicted of an offence under that paragraph, to a fine of not more than £50;

(b) in the case of an offence under paragraph (b) or (c) of the subsection, to a fine of not more than £50, or if he has previously been convicted of an offence under either paragraph, to a fine of not more than £100.

(6) For purposes of this section, a person who assists in a trade or occupation carried on for profit shall be deemed to be employed notwithstanding that he receives no reward for his labour.

K 2

Citation, etc.   **3.**—(1) This Act may be cited as the Employment of Children Act 1973.

(2) In this Act—

    (*a*) " child " means a person who is not for the purposes of the Education Acts over compulsory school age, or in Scotland school age ;

    (*b*) " the Education Acts " means in England and Wales the Education Acts 1944 to 1971 and, in Scotland, the Education (Scotland) Acts 1939 to 1971 ;

and any reference in this Act to an enactment shall, except in so far as the context otherwise requires, be construed as a reference to that enactment as amended by or under any other enactment, including an enactment contained in this Act.

(3) The enactments specified in Schedule 2 to this Act are hereby repealed to the extent specified in column 3 of the Schedule.

(4) This Act shall come into force on such day as the Secretary of State may appoint by order made by statutory instrument and—

    (*a*) different days may be so appointed for different purposes of any one or more provisions of this Act ; and

    (*b*) an order under this subsection bringing section 1(2) or (3) of this Act into force may include such transitional provisions or savings as appear to the Secretary of State to be necessary or expedient for temporarily preserving the power to make, and the effect of, byelaws notwithstanding the coming into force of regulations

(5) Nothing in this Act extends to Northern Ireland.

SCHEDULES

SCHEDULE 1

AMENDMENTS OF ACTS OF 1933 AND 1937: AMENDED TEXT OF 1933 S. 18 AND 1937 S. 28

PART I

AMENDMENTS OF THE TWO ACTS

The Children and Young Persons Act 1933 (c. 12)

1.—(1) In section 18 of the Act of 1933—

(*a*) in subsection (2) for " A local authority may make byelaws " substitute " The Secretary of State may make regulations " ; and

(*b*) in subsections (1), (2) and (3) for " byelaw " and " byelaws " substitute respectively " regulation " and " regulations ".

(2) In section 18(2) of the Act of 1933, after paragraph (*c*) insert—

" (*d*) prohibiting the employment of children otherwise than under and in accordance with a permit to be issued by the local education authority on application made in accordance with the regulations, and imposing on children and others requirements in connection with permits ;

(*e*) requiring employers to furnish particulars with respect to children employed, or proposed to be employed, by them and to keep and produce records."

(3) At the end of section 18 of the Act of 1933, insert—

" (4) Regulations of the Secretary of State under this section shall be made by statutory instrument subject to annulment in pursuance of a resolution of either House of Parliament.".

2. In section 21(1) of the Act of 1933—

(*a*) after " byelaw " insert " or regulation " ; and

(*b*) for " twenty pounds " and " fifty pounds " substitute respectively " £50 " and " £100 ".

3. In section 28(1) of the Act of 1933 after " byelaw " insert " or regulation ".

4. In section 30 of the Act of 1933, after " byelaws " insert " or regulations ".

The Children and Young Persons (Scotland) Act 1937 (c. 37)

5.—(1) In section 28 of the Act of 1937—

(*a*) in subsection (2), for " An education authority may make byelaws " substitute " The Secretary of State may make regulations " ; and

(*b*) in subsections (1), (2) and (3), for " byelaw " and " byelaws " substitute respectively " regulation " and " regulations ".

(2) In section 28(2) of the Act of 1937, after paragraph (*c*) insert—

" (*d*) prohibiting the employment of children otherwise than under and in accordance with a permit to be issued by the education authority on application made in accordance with

K 3

the regulations, and imposing on children and others requirements in connection with permits ;

(*e*) requiring employers to furnish particulars with respect to children employed, or proposed to be employed, by them and to keep and produce records."

(3) At the end of section 28 of the Act of 1937, insert—

" (4) Regulations of the Secretary of State under this section shall be made by statutory instrument subject to annulment in pursuance of a resolution of either House of Parliament.".

6. In section 31(1) of the Act of 1937—

(*a*) after " byelaw " insert " or regulation " ; and

(*b*) for " twenty pounds " and " fifty pounds " substitute respectively " £50 " and " £100 ".

7. In section 36(1) of the Act of 1937, after " byelaw " insert " or regulation ".

8. In section 37 of the Act of 1937, after " byelaws ", insert " or regulations ".

PART II

1933 S. 18 AND 1937 S. 28 AS AMENDED

9.—(1) Subject to the provisions of this section and of any regulations made thereunder no child shall be employed—

(*a*) so long as he is under the age of thirteen years ; or

(*b*) before the close of school hours on any day on which he is required to attend school ; or

(*c*) before seven o'clock in the morning or after seven o'clock in the evening on any day ; or

(*d*) for more than two hours on any day on which he is required to attend school ; or

(*e*) for more than two hours on any Sunday ; or

(*f*) to lift, carry or move anything so heavy as to be likely to cause injury to him.

(2) The Secretary of State may make regulations with respect to the employment of children, and any such regulations may distinguish between children of different ages and sexes and between different localities, trades, occupations and circumstances, and may contain provisions—

(*a*) authorising—

(i) the employment of children under the age of thirteen years (notwithstanding anything in paragraph (*a*) of the last foregoing subsection) by their parents or guardians in light agricultural or horticultural work ;

(ii) the employment of children (notwithstanding anything in paragraph (*b*) of the last foregoing subsection) for

not more than one hour before the commencement of
school hours on any day on which they are required to
attend school ;

(*b*) prohibiting absolutely the employment of children in any
specified occupation ;

(*c*) prescribing—

(i) the age below which children are not to be
employed ;

(ii) the number of hours in each day, or in each week,
for which, and the times of day at which, they may be
employed ;

(iii) the intervals to be allowed to them for meals and
rest ;

(iv) the holidays or half-holidays to be allowed to them ;

(v) any other conditions to be observed in relation to
their employment ;

(*d*) prohibiting the employment of children otherwise than
under and in accordance with a permit to be issued by the
local education authority on application made in accordance
with the regulations, and imposing on children and others
requirements in connection with permits ;

(*e*) requiring employers to furnish particulars with respect to
children employed, or proposed to be employed, by them and
to keep and produce records ;

so, however, that no such regulations shall modify the restrictions
contained in the last foregoing subsection save in so far as is
expressly permitted by paragraph (*a*) of this subsection, and any
restriction contained in any such regulations shall have effect in
addition to the said restrictions.

(3) Nothing in this section, or in any regulation made under this
section, shall prevent a child from taking part in a performance—

(*a*) under the authority of a licence granted under this Part of
this Act ; or

(*b*) in a case where by virtue of section 37(3) of the Children 1963 c. 37.
and Young Persons Act 1963 no licence under that section
is required for him to take part in the performance.

(4) Regulations of the Secretary of State under this section shall
be made by statutory instrument subject to annulment in pursuance
of a resolution of either House of Parliament.

NOTE: Section 28 of the Act of 1937 is to be read as above set
out, except that, in subsection (1)(*b*) and (*d*) and in subsection
(2)(*a*)(ii), for " required " there shall be substituted " under obligation " ; and in subsection (2)(*d*), " local " should be omitted.

SCHEDULE 2

REPEALS

Chapter	Short Title	Extent of Repeal
1933 c. 12.	The Children and Young Persons Act 1933.	Section 19.
1937 c. 37.	The Children and Young Persons (Scotland) Act 1937.	Section 29.
1944 c. 31.	The Education Act 1944.	Section 59.
1962 c. 47.	The Education (Scotland) Act 1962.	Section 137.
1969 c. 49.	The Education (Scotland) Act 1969.	Section 22.

Succession (Scotland) Act 1973

1973 CHAPTER 25

An Act to increase the amounts of the sums payable to a surviving spouse under sections 8 and 9 of the Succession (Scotland) Act 1964 and to empower the Secretary of State by order further to increase such amounts.

[23rd May 1973]

B E IT ENACTED by the Queen's most Excellent Majesty, by and with the advice and consent of the Lords Spiritual and Temporal, and Commons, in this present Parliament assembled, and by the authority of the same, as follows:—

1.—(1) In the case of a person dying after the commencement of this Act—

    (*a*) section 8 of the Succession (Scotland) Act 1964 (prior rights of surviving spouse, on intestacy, in dwelling house and furniture) shall apply as if—

        (i) for the words " £15,000 " in subsection (1)(*a*) and (*b*) there were substituted the words " £30,000 or such larger amount as may from time to time be fixed by order of the Secretary of State ";

        (ii) for the words " £5,000 " in subsection (3)(*a*) and (*b*) there were substituted the words " £8,000 or such larger amount as may from time to time be fixed by order of the Secretary of State ";

    (*b*) section 9 of the said Act of 1964 (prior right of surviving spouse to financial provision on intestacy) shall apply as if—

        (i) for the words " £2,500, or " in subsection (1)(*a*) there were substituted the words " £4,000 or such larger amount as may from time to time be fixed by order of the Secretary of State, or ";

(margin notes) Amendment of sections 8 and 9 of Succession (Scotland) Act 1964.

1964 c. 41.

(ii) for the words " £5,000 " in subsection (1)(*b*) there were substituted the words " £8,000 or such larger amount as may from time to time be fixed by order of the Secretary of State ";

(iii) in the proviso to the said subsection (1) for the words from " of £2,500 " to " £5,000 " there were substituted the words "fixed by virtue of paragraph (*a*) of this subsection or the sum fixed by virtue of paragraph (*b*) of this subsection ".

(2) Any order of the Secretary of State under this section fixing the amount of any sum payable to a surviving spouse shall have effect (and, so far as relates to that sum, shall supersede any previous order) in relation to the estate of any person dying after the coming into force of the order.

(3) Any order of the Secretary of State under this section shall be made by statutory instrument and a draft of the statutory instrument shall be laid before Parliament.

Short title.   **2.** This Act may be cited as the Succession (Scotland) Act 1973.

Land Compensation Act 1973

1973 CHAPTER 26

An Act to confer a new right to compensation for depreciation of the value of interests in land caused by the use of highways, aerodromes and other public works; to confer powers for mitigating the injurious effect of such works on their surroundings; to make new provision for the benefit of persons displaced from land by public authorities; to amend the law relating to compulsory purchase and planning blight; to amend section 35 of the Roads (Scotland) Act 1970; and for purposes connected with those matters.

[23rd May 1973]

B E IT ENACTED by the Queen's most Excellent Majesty, by and with the advice and consent of the Lords Spiritual and Temporal, and Commons, in this present Parliament assembled, and by the authority of the same, as follows:—

PART I

COMPENSATION FOR DEPRECIATION CAUSED BY USE OF PUBLIC WORKS

1.—(1) Where the value of an interest in land is depreciated by physical factors caused by the use of public works, then, if— *Right to compensation.*

    (a) the interest qualifies for compensation under this Part of this Act ; and

    (b) the person entitled to the interest makes a claim within the time limited by and otherwise in accordance with this Part of this Act,

compensation for that depreciation shall, subject to the provisions of this Part of this Act, be payable by the responsible authority to the person making the claim (hereafter referred to as " the claimant ").

(2) The physical factors mentioned in subsection (1) above are noise, vibration, smell, fumes, smoke and artificial lighting and the discharge on to the land in respect of which the claim is made of any solid or liquid substance.

(3) The public works mentioned in subsection (1) above are—

(a) any highway;

(b) any aerodrome; and

(c) any works or land (not being a highway or aerodrome) provided or used in the exercise of statutory powers.

(4) The responsible authority mentioned in subsection (1) above is, in relation to a highway, the appropriate highway authority and, in relation to other public works, the person managing those works.

(5) Physical factors caused by an aircraft arriving at or departing from an aerodrome shall be treated as caused by the use of the aerodrome whether or not the aircraft is within the boundaries of the aerodrome; but, save as aforesaid, the source of the physical factors must be situated on or in the public works the use of which is alleged to be their cause.

(6) Compensation shall not be payable under this Part of this Act in respect of the physical factors caused by the use of any public works other than a highway unless immunity from actions for nuisance in respect of that use is conferred (whether expressly or by implication) by an enactment relating to those works or, in the case of an aerodrome and physical factors caused by aircraft, the aerodrome is one to which section 41(2) of the Civil Aviation Act 1949 (immunity from actions for nuisance) for the time being applies.

1949 c. 67.

(7) Compensation shall not be payable under this Part of this Act in respect of physical factors caused by accidents involving vehicles on a highway or accidents involving aircraft.

(8) Compensation shall not be payable under this Part of this Act on any claim unless the relevant date in relation to the claim falls on or after 17th October 1969.

(9) Subject to section 9 below, "the relevant date" in this Part of this Act means—

(a) in relation to a claim in respect of a highway, the date on which it was first open to public traffic;

(b) in relation to a claim in respect of other public works, the date on which they were first used after completion.

Interests qualifying for compensation.

2.—(1) An interest qualifies for compensation under this Part of this Act if it was acquired by the claimant before the relevant date in relation to the claim and the requirements of subsection

(2) or, as the case may be, subsection (3) below are satisfied on the date on which notice of the claim for compensation in respect of that interest is served.

(2) If and so far as the interest is in land which is a dwelling, the said requirements are—

(a) that the interest is an owner's interest ; and

(b) where the interest carries the right to occupy the land, that the land is occupied by the claimant in right of that interest as his residence.

(3) If and so far as the interest is not in such land as aforesaid, the said requirements are—

(a) that the interest is that of an owner-occupier ; and

(b) that the land is or forms part of either—

(i) a hereditament the annual value of which does not exceed the prescribed amount ; or

(ii) an agricultural unit.

(4) In this section " owner's interest " in relation to any land, means the legal fee simple therein or a tenancy thereof granted or extended for a term of years certain of which, on the date of service of the notice of claim in respect thereof, not less than three years remain unexpired.

(5) In this section " owner-occupier ", in relation to land in a hereditament, means a person who occupies the whole or a substantial part of the land in right of an owner's interest therein and, in relation to land in an agricultural unit, means a person who occupies the whole of that unit and is entitled, while so occupying it, to an owner's interest in the whole or any part of that land.

(6) In this section " the prescribed amount " means the amount for the time being prescribed for the purposes of section 192(4)(a) of the Town and Country Planning Act 1971 1971 c. 78. (interests qualifying for protection under planning blight provisions) and " annual value " and " hereditament " have the meanings given in section 207 of that Act taking references to the date of service of a notice under section 193 of that Act as references to the date on which notice of the claim is served.

(7) This section has effect subject to sections 10(4), 11 and 12 below.

(8) In the application of this section to Scotland—

(a) for subsection (4) there shall be substituted—

" (4) In this section " owner's interest ", in relation to any land, includes the interest of—

(a) the lessee under a lease thereof, being a lease the unexpired period of which on the date

of service of the notice of claim in respect
thereof is not less than three years ; and

(b) a crofter, a landholder, a statutory small
tenant and a cottar in the land ;

(b) in subsection (6) for the references to sections 192(4)(a),
193 and 207 of the Town and Country Planning Act
1971 there shall be substituted respectively references

to sections 181(4)(a), 182 and 196 of the Town and
Country Planning (Scotland) Act 1972.

3.—(1) A claim under this Part of this Act shall be made by
serving on the responsible authority a notice containing particulars of—

(a) the land in respect of which the claim is made ;

(b) the claimant's interest and the date on which, and the
manner in which, it was acquired ;

(c) the claimant's occupation of the land (except where the
interest qualifies for compensation without occupation) ;

(d) any other interests in the land so far as known to the
claimant ;

(e) the public works to which the claim relates ;

(f) the amount of compensation claimed ;

(g) any land contiguous or adjacent to the land in respect
of which the claim is made, being land to which the
claimant was entitled in the same capacity (within the
meaning of section 6 below) on the relevant date.

(2) Subject to the provisions of this section and of sections 12
and 14 below, no claim shall be made otherwise than in the claim
period, that is to say, the period of two years beginning on the
expiration of twelve months from the relevant date.

(3) Subsection (2) above shall not preclude the making of
a claim in respect of an interest in land before the beginning
of the claim period if—

(a) the claimant has during the said twelve months made
a contract for disposing of that interest or (in so far
as the interest is in land which is not a dwelling) for
the grant of a tenancy of that land ; and

(b) the claim is made before the interest is disposed of
or the tenancy is granted ;

but compensation shall not be payable before the beginning of
the claim period on any claim made by virtue of this subsection.

(4) Where notice of a claim has been served on a responsible
authority, any person authorised by that authority may, on giving
reasonable notice, enter the land to which the claim relates for

the purpose of surveying it and ascertaining its value in connection with the claim ; and any person who wilfully obstructs a
person in the exercise of the powers conferred by this subsection
shall be guilty of an offence and liable on summary conviction
to a fine not exceeding £20.

(5) Where compensation is payable by a responsible authority
on a claim there shall be payable by the authority, in addition
to the compensation, any reasonable valuation or legal expenses
incurred by the claimant for the purposes of the preparation and
prosecution of the claim ; but this subsection is without prejudice
to the powers of the Lands Tribunal or the Lands Tribunal for
Scotland in respect of the costs or expenses of proceedings
before the Tribunal by virtue of section 16 below.

4.—(1) The compensations payable on any claim shall be
assessed by reference to prices current on the first day of the
claim period.

(2) In assessing depreciation due to the physical factors caused
by the use of any public works, account shall be taken of the
use of those works as it exists on the first day of the claim
period and of any intensification that may then be reasonably
expected of the use of those works in the state in which they
are on that date.

(3) In assessing the extent of the depreciation there shall be
taken into account the benefit of any relevant works—

(*a*) which have been carried out, or in respect of which a
grant has been paid, under section 20 below, section 15
of the Airports Authority Act 1965 or any corresponding local enactment ;

1965 c. 16.

(*b*) which have been carried out under section 23 or 27
below ;

and it shall be assumed that any relevant works which could be
or could have been carried out, or in respect of which a grant
could be or could have been paid, under any of the provisions
mentioned in paragraph (*a*) above have been carried out but, in a
case where the authority having functions under that provision
have a discretion whether or not to carry out the works or pay
the grant, only if they have undertaken to do so.

(4) The value of the interest in respect of which the claim is
made shall be assessed—

(*a*) subject to subsection (5) below, by reference to the
nature of the interest and the condition of the land as
it subsisted on the date of service of notice of the
claim ;

(b) subject to section 5 below, in accordance with rules (2) to (4) of the rules set out in section 5 of the Land Compensation Act 1961 ;

(c) if the interest is subject to a mortgage or to a contract of sale or to a contract made after the relevant date for the grant of a tenancy, as if it were not subject to the mortgage or contract.

(5) In assessing the value of the interest in respect of which the claim is made there shall be left out of account any part of that value which is attributable to—

(a) any building, or improvement or extension of a building, on the land if the building or, as the case may be, the building as improved or extended, was first occupied after the relevant date ; and

(b) any change in the use of the land made after that date.

(6) In the application of subsection (4) above to Scotland for the references to section 5 of the Land Compensation Act 1961, a mortgage and a contract of sale there shall be substituted

respectively references to section 12 of the Land Compensation (Scotland) Act 1963, a heritable security and missives of sale.

5.—(1) The following assumptions shall be made in assessing the value of the interest in respect of which the claim is made.

(2) Subject to subsection (3) below, it shall be assumed that planning permission would be granted in respect of the land in which the interest subsists (" the relevant land ") or any part thereof for development of any class specified in Schedule 8

to the Town and Country Planning Act 1971.

(3) Notwithstanding subsection (2) above—

(a) it shall not by virtue of that subsection be assumed that planning permission would be granted, in respect of the relevant land or any part thereof, for development of any class specified in Part II of the said Schedule 8 if it is development for which planning permission has been refused and compensation under section 169 of the said Act of 1971 has become payable in respect of that refusal ;

(b) where planning permission has been granted, in respect of the relevant land or any part thereof, for development of any class specified in the said Part II but was so granted subject to conditions, and compensation under the said section 169 has become payable in respect of the imposition of the conditions, it shall not by virtue of the said subsection (2) be assumed that planning permission for that development, in respect of the relevant land or that part thereof, as the case may be, would be granted otherwise than subject to those conditions ;

(c) where an order has been made under section 51 of the said Act of 1971, in respect of the relevant land or any part thereof, requiring the removal of any building or the discontinuance of any use, and compensation has become payable in respect of that order under section 170 of that Act, it shall not by virtue of the said subsection (2) be assumed that planning permission would be granted, in respect of the relevant land or any part thereof, as the case may be, for the rebuilding of that building or the resumption of that use.

(4) It shall be assumed that planning permission would not be granted in respect of the relevant land or any part thereof for any development other than such development as is mentioned in subsection (2) above ; and, if planning permission has been granted in respect of the relevant land or any part thereof for such other development, it shall be assumed that the planning permission has not been granted in so far as it relates to development that has not been carried out.

(5) In this section any expression which is also used in the said Act of 1971 has the same meaning as in that Act and references to any provision of that Act include references to any corresponding provision previously in force.

(6) In the application of this section to Scotland for references in subsections (2) and (3) above to Schedule 8 to the said Act of 1971 and to sections 51, 169 and 170 thereof, there shall be substituted respectively references to Schedule 6 to the Town 1972 c. 52. and Country Planning (Scotland) Act 1972 and to sections 49, 158 and 159 of that Act, and in subsection (5) above for the reference to the said Act of 1971 there shall be substituted a reference to the said Act of 1972.

6.—(1) The compensation payable on a claim shall be reduced Reduction of by an amount equal to any increase in the value of— compensation where land is

(a) the claimant's interest in the land in respect of which benefited. the claim is made ; and

(b) any interest in other land contiguous or adjacent to the land mentioned in paragraph (a) above to which the claimant was entitled in the same capacity on the relevant date,

which is attributable to the existence of or the use or prospective use of the public works to which the claim relates.

(2) Sections 4 and 5 above shall not apply to the assessment, for the purposes of subsection (1) above, of the value of the interest mentioned in paragraph (*a*) of that subsection.

(3) Where, for the purpose of assessing compensation on a claim in respect of any interest in land, an increase in the value of an interest in other land has been taken into account under subsection (1) above, then, in connection with any subsequent acquisition to which this subsection applies, that increase shall not be left out of account by virtue of section 6 of the Land Compensation Act 1961 or taken into account by virtue of section 7 of that Act or any corresponding enactment, in so far as it was taken into account in connection with that claim.

1961 c. 33.

(4) Subsection (3) above applies to any subsequent acquisition, not being an acquisition of the land in respect of which the claim is made, where either—

(*a*) the interest acquired by the subsequent acquisition is the same as the interest previously taken into account (whether the acquisition extends to the whole of the land in which that interest previously subsisted or only to part of that land) ; or

(*b*) the person entitled to the interest acquired is, or directly or indirectly derives title to that interest from, the person who at the time of the claim mentioned in that subsection was entitled to the interest previously taken into account ;

and in this subsection " the interest previously taken into account " means the interest the increased value of which was taken into account as mentioned in the said subsection (3).

(5) For the purposes of this section a person entitled to two interests in land shall be taken to be entitled to them in the same capacity if, but only if, he is entitled—

(*a*) to both of them beneficially ; or

(*b*) to both of them as trustee of one particular trust ; or

(*c*) to both of them as personal representative of one particular person ;

and in this section references to a person deriving title from another person include references to any successor in title of that other person.

(6) In subsection (3) above " corresponding enactment " has the same meaning as in section 8 of the said Act of 1961.

(7) In the application of this section to Scotland, for the references to sections 6, 7 and 8 of the Land Compensation Act 1961 there shall be substituted respectively references to sections 13, 14 and 15 of the Land Compensation (Scotland) Act 1963.

1963 c. 51.

7. Compensation shall not be payable on any claim unless the amount of the compensation exceeds £50.

8.—(1) Where a claim has been made in respect of depreciation of the value of an interest in land caused by the use of any public works and compensation has been paid or is payable on that claim, compensation shall not be payable on any subsequent claim in relation to the same works and the same land or any part thereof (whether in respect of the same or a different interest) except that, in the case of land which is a dwelling, this subsection shall not preclude the payment of compensation both on a claim in respect of the fee simple and on a claim in respect of a tenancy.

(2) Where a person is entitled to compensation in respect of the acquisition of an interest in land by an authority possessing compulsory purchase powers, or would be so entitled if the acquisition were compulsory, and—

(a) the land is acquired for the purposes of any public works ; and

(b) that person retains land which, in relation to the land acquired, constitutes other land or lands within the meaning of section 63 of the Lands Clauses Consolidation Act 1845 or section 7 of the Compulsory Purchase Act 1965 (compensation for acquisition to include compensation for injurious affection of other land retained),

then, whether or not any sum is paid or payable in respect of injurious affection of the land retained, compensation shall not be payable under this Part of this Act on any claim in relation to those works made after the date of service of the notice to treat (or, if the acquisition is by agreement, the date of the agreement) in respect of any interest in the land retained.

(3) Subsection (2) above applies whether the acquisition is before, on or after the date on which this Part of this Act comes into force (hereafter referred to as " the commencement date ") and, where it is on or after that date, the public works for the purposes of which the land is acquired shall be taken to be those specified in the relevant particulars registered under subsection (4) below.

(4) Where on or after the commencement date an authority possessing compulsory purchase powers acquires land for the purposes of any public works and the person from whom the land is acquired retains land which, in relation to the land acquired, constitutes other land or lands within the meaning of the sections mentioned in subsection (2) above, the authority shall deposit particulars of the land retained and the nature

and extent of those works with the council of the district or London borough in which the land retained is situated; and any particulars so deposited shall be registered by the proper officer of the council in the register of local land charges in such manner as may be prescribed by rules made for the purposes of this subsection under section 19 of the Land Charges Act 1925.

(5) In a case in which compensation for injurious affection fell or falls to be assessed otherwise than in accordance with section 44 below, subsection (2) above shall not preclude the payment of compensation under this Part of this Act in respect of depreciation by public works so far as situated elsewhere than on the land acquired.

(6) Where after a claim has been made in respect of any interest in land the whole or part of the land in which that interest subsists is compulsorily acquired, then, if—

    (*a*) the value of that land has been diminished by the public works to which the claim relates; but

    (*b*) the compensation in respect of the compulsory acquisition falls to be assessed without regard to the diminution,

the compensation in respect of the acquisition shall be reduced by an amount equal to the compensation paid or payable on the claim or, if the acquisition extends only to part of the land, to so much of the last-mentioned compensation as is attributable to that part.

(7) Without prejudice to the foregoing provisions of this section, compensation shall not be payable in respect of the same depreciation both under this Part of this Act and under any other enactment.

(8) In the application of this section to Scotland—

    (*a*) in subsection (1) for the words " fee simple " there shall be substituted the words " ownership of the dominium utile ";

    (*b*) in subsection (2)(*b*) for the reference to the sections there mentioned there shall be substituted a reference
          to section 61 of the Lands Clauses Consolidation (Scotland) Act 1845;

    (*c*) in subsection (4) for the words from " the authority shall deposit " to the end there shall be substituted the words " the authority shall cause particulars of the land retained and the nature and extent of those works to be recorded in the Register of Sasines and shall send a copy of those particulars to the local planning authority ".

9.—(1) This section has effect where, whether before, on or after the commencement date—

(*a*) the carriageway of a highway has been altered after the highway has been open to public traffic ;

(*b*) any public works other than a highway have been reconstructed, extended or otherwise altered after they have been first used ; or

(*c*) there has been a change of use in respect of any public works other than a highway or aerodrome.

(2) If and so far as a claim in respect of the highway or other public works relates to depreciation that would not have been caused but for the alterations or change of use, this Part of this Act shall, subject to subsection (3) below, have effect in relation to the claim as if the relevant date (instead of being the date specified in section 1(9) above) were—

(*a*) the date on which the highway was first open to public traffic after completion of the alterations to the carriageway ;

(*b*) the date on which the other public works were first used after completion of the alterations ; or

(*c*) the date of the change of use,

as the case may be.

(3) Subsection (2) above shall not by virtue of any alterations to an aerodrome apply to a claim in respect of physical factors caused by aircraft unless the alterations are runway or apron alterations.

(4) Where a claim relates to such depreciation as is mentioned in subsection (2) above the notice of claim shall specify, in addition to the matters mentioned in section 3 above, the alterations or change of use alleged to give rise to the depreciation ; and if and so far as the claim relates to such depreciation—

(*a*) section 6 above shall have effect as if the increase in value to be taken into account were any increase that would not have been caused but for the alterations or change of use in question ;

(*b*) subsection (1) of section 8 above shall not preclude the payment of compensation unless the previous claim was in respect of depreciation that would not have been caused but for the same alterations or change of use, and subsection (2) of that section shall not preclude the payment of compensation unless the works for which the land was acquired were works resulting from the alterations, or works used for the purpose, to which the claim relates.

(5) For the purposes of this section the carriageway of a highway is altered if, and only if—

   (*a*) the location, width or level of the carriageway is altered (otherwise than by re-surfacing) ; or

   (*b*) an additional carriageway is provided for the highway beside, above or below an existing one ;

and the reference in subsection (2) above to depreciation that would not have been caused but for alterations to the carriageway of a highway is a reference to such depreciation by physical factors which are caused by the use of, and the source of which is situated on, the length of carriageway which has been altered as mentioned in paragraph (*a*) above or, as the case may be, the additional carriageway and the corresponding length of the existing one mentioned in paragraph (*b*) above.

(6) In this section " runway or apron alterations " means—

   (*a*) the construction of a new runway, the major re-alignment of an existing runway or the extension or strengthening of an existing runway ; or

   (*b*) a substantial addition to, or alteration of, a taxiway or apron, being an addition or alteration whose purpose or main purpose is the provision of facilities for a greater number of aircraft.

(7) For the avoidance of doubt it is hereby declared that references in this section to a change of use do not include references to the intensification of an existing use.

Mortgages, trusts for sale and settlements.

10.—(1) Where an interest is subject to a mortgage—

   (*a*) a claim may be made by any mortgagee of the interest as if he were the person entitled to that interest but without prejudice to the making of a claim by that person ;

   (*b*) no compensation shall be payable in respect of the interest of the mortgagee (as distinct from the interest which is subject to the mortgage) ;

   (*c*) any compensation which is payable in respect of the interest which is subject to the mortgage shall be paid to the mortgagee or, if there is more than one mortgagee, to the first mortgagee and shall in either case be applied by him as if it were proceeds of sale.

(2) Where the interest is held on trust for sale the compensation shall be dealt with as if it were proceeds of sale arising under the trust.

1925 c. 18.

(3) Where the interest is settled land for the purposes of the Settled Land Act 1925 the compensation shall be treated as capital money arising under that Act.

(4) Where an interest in land is vested in trustees (other
than a sole tenant for life within the meaning of the Settled
Land Act 1925) and a person beneficially entitled (whether
directly or derivatively) under the trusts is entitled or permitted
by reason of his interest to occupy the land, section 2 above
shall have effect as if occupation by that person were occupation
by the trustees in right of the interest vested in them.

(5) In the application of this section to Scotland—

    (*a*) in subsection (1) for the references to a mortgage and
        a mortgagee there shall be substituted respectively
        references to a heritable security and a heritable
        creditor ;

    (*b*) for subsections (2) and (3) there shall be substituted the
        following subsection—

          " (2) Where the interest is that of any of the
        persons specified in section 67 of the Lands Clauses
        Consolidation (Scotland) Act 1845, that Act shall
        have effect with regard to the application of the
        compensation as it has effect with regard to the
        application of the compensation payable in respect
        of the purchase of land " ;

    (*c*) in subsection (4) the words " (other than a sole tenant
        for life within the meaning of the Settled Land Act
        1925) " shall be omitted.

11.—(1) So much of section 2(1) above as requires an interest
qualifying for compensation under this Part of this Act to
have been acquired by the claimant before the relevant date shall
not apply to any interest acquired by him by inheritance from a
person who acquired that interest, or a greater interest out of
which it is derived, before the relevant date.

(2) For the purposes of this section an interest is acquired by a
person by inheritance if it devolves on him by virtue only of
testamentary dispositions taking effect on, or the law of intestate
succession or the right of survivorship between joint tenants as
applied to, the death of another person or the successive deaths
of two or more other persons.

(3) For the purposes of subsection (2) above a person who
acquires an interest by appropriation of it in or towards satisfaction of any legacy, share in residue or other share in the estate
of a deceased person shall be treated as a person on whom
the interest devolves by direct bequest.

(4) Where an interest is settled land for the purposes of the
Settled Land Act 1925 and on the death of a tenant for life
within the meaning of that Act a person becomes entitled to

the interest in accordance with the settlement, or by any appropriation by the personal representatives in respect of the settled land, subsection (2) above shall apply as if the interest had belonged to the tenant for life absolutely and the trusts of the settlement taking effect after his death had been trusts of his will.

(5) Subsection (4) above shall apply, with any necessary modifications, where a person becomes entitled to an interest on the termination of a settlement as it would apply if he had become entitled in accordance with the terms of the settlement.

(6) In the application of this section to Scotland—

    (*a*) in subsection (2), for the words from " testamentary " to " tenants " there shall be substituted the words—

        " (*a*) a testamentary disposition or any other deed with testamentary effect taking effect on, or

        (*b*) the law of intestate succession " ;

    (*b*) in subsection (3), for the words " by appropriation of it in or towards " there shall be substituted the words " in satisfaction or in partial " ;

    (*c*) subsections (4) and (5) shall be omitted.

Tenants
entitled to
enfranchise-
ment or
extension
under
Leasehold
Reform
Act 1967.
1967 c. 88.

12.—(1) This section has effect where a person is entitled under Part I of the Leasehold Reform Act 1967 to acquire the freehold or an extended lease of a house by virtue of any tenancy (" the qualifying tenancy ") and—

    (*a*) has on or before the relevant date given notice under that Act to the landlord of his desire to have the freehold or an extended lease ; and

    (*b*) has not acquired the freehold or an extended lease before that date.

(2) The qualifying tenancy shall be treated as an owner's interest as defined in section 2(4) above whether or not the unexpired term on the date of service of the notice of claim is of the length there specified.

(3) If no claim is made in respect of the qualifying tenancy before the claimant has ceased to be entitled to it by reason of his acquisition of the freehold or an extended lease he may make a claim in respect of the qualifying tenancy as if he were still entitled to it.

(4) No claim shall be made by virtue of subsection (3) above after the claimant has ceased to be entitled to the freehold or extended lease but such a claim may be made before the beginning of the claim period if it is made before the claimant has disposed of the freehold or extended lease and after he has made a contract for disposing of it.

(5) Compensation shall not be payable before the beginning of the claim period on any claim made by virtue of subsection (4) above.

(6) Any notice of a claim made by virtue of this section shall contain, in addition to the matters mentioned in section 3 above, a statement that it is made in respect of a qualifying tenancy as defined in this section and, if made by virtue of subsection (3) or (4) above, sufficient particulars to show that it falls within that subsection.

(7) In relation to a claim made by virtue of subsection (3) above section 4(4)(*a*) above shall have effect as if the reference to the date of service of notice of the claim were a reference to the relevant date.

13.—(1) Any compensation payable under this Part of this Act in respect of land which is ecclesiastical property shall be paid to the Church Commissioners to be applied for the purposes for which the proceeds of a sale by agreement of the land would be applicable under any enactment or Measure authorising, or disposing of the proceeds of, such a sale.

Ecclesiastical property.

(2) In this section "ecclesiastical property" means land belonging to an ecclesiastical benefice of the Church of England, or being or forming part of a church subject to the jurisdiction of a bishop of any diocese of the Church of England or the site of such a church, or being or forming part of a burial ground subject to such jurisdiction.

14.—(1) Where the whole of the claim period for a claim has expired before the commencement date, or less than two years of that period remains unexpired on that date, that period shall be treated as continuing until the end of two years from the commencement date.

Special provisions for claims arising before commencement date.

(2) Where on or after 17th October 1972 and before the commencement date a person—

(*a*) has disposed of an interest in land which would have qualified for compensation under this Part of this Act if it had then been in force and a notice of claim had been served in respect of the interest immediately before the disposal ; or

(*b*) being entitled to such an interest as is mentioned in paragraph (*a*) above in land which is not a dwelling, has granted a tenancy thereof so that the interest remaining to him is not such an interest as aforesaid,

this Part of this Act shall have effect in relation to any claim made before the end of one year from the commencement date (being a claim in relation to which the relevant date falls before the disposal or the grant of the tenancy) as if that person were still entitled to the interest disposed of or the interest to which he was entitled prior to the grant of the tenancy.

(3) Any notice of a claim made by virtue of subsection (2) above shall specify, in addition to the matters mentioned in section 3 above, the date on which the interest was disposed of or, as the case may be, the date on which the tenancy was granted.

(4) A claim may be made by virtue of subsection (2) above notwithstanding that the claim period has not begun but compensation shall not be payable on the claim before the beginning of that period.

(5) In relation to a claim made by virtue of subsection (2) above section 4(4)(a) above shall have effect as if the reference to the date of service of notice of the claim were a reference to the date immediately preceding that on which the claimant disposed of the interest or granted the tenancy.

Information for ascertaining relevant date.

15.—(1) The responsible authority in relation to a highway or other public works shall keep a record and, on demand, furnish a statement in writing of—

> (a) the date on which the highway was first open to public traffic, or was first open to public traffic after completion of any particular alterations to the carriageway of the highway;
>
> (b) the date on which the public works were first used after completion, or were first used after completion of any particular alterations to those works;
>
> (c) in the case of public works other than a highway or aerodrome, the date on which there was a change of use in respect of the public works.

(2) A certificate by the Secretary of State stating that runway or apron alterations have or have not been carried out at an aerodrome and the date on which an aerodrome at which any such alterations have been carried out was first used after completion of the alterations shall be conclusive evidence of the facts stated.

(3) In this section references to alterations to the carriageway of a highway, to runway or apron alterations and to a change of use shall be construed in the same way as in section 9 above; and subsection (1) above shall not apply unless the date in question falls on or after the commencement date.

Disputes.

16.—(1) Any question of disputed compensation under this Part of this Act shall be referred to and determined by the Lands Tribunal or, in Scotland, the Lands Tribunal for Scotland.

(2) No such question arising out of a claim made before PART I
the beginning of the claim period shall be referred to either of
those Tribunals before the beginning of that period.

17. Where, in resisting a claim under this Part of this Act, Action for
a responsible authority contend that no enactment relating to the nuisance
works in question confers immunity from actions for nuisance following
in respect of the use to which the claim relates, then if— unsuccessful
claim where
   (a) compensation is not paid on the claim ; and responsible
authority have
   (b) an action for nuisance in respect of the matters which disclaimed
       were the subject of the claim is subsequently brought statutory
       by the claimant against the authority, immunity.

no enactment relating to those works, being an enactment in
force when the contention was made, shall afford a defence
to that action in so far as it relates to those matters.

18.—(1) Compensation under this Part of this Act shall carry Interest on
interest, at the rate for the time being prescribed under section compensation.
32 of the Land Compensation Act 1961, from— 1961 c. 33.

   (a) the date of service of the notice of claim ; or

   (b) if that date is before the beginning of the claim period,
       from the beginning of the claim period,

until payment.

(2) In the application of this section to Scotland for the
reference to section 32 of the said Act of 1961 there shall be
substituted a reference to section 40 of the Land Compensation 1963 c. 51.
(Scotland) Act 1963.

19.—(1) In this Part of this Act— Interpretation
   " the appropriate highway authority " means— of Part I.

          (a) except where paragraph (b) below applies, the
          highway authority who constructed the highway to
          which the claim relates ;

          (b) if and so far as the claim relates to depreciation
          that would not have been caused but for alterations
          to the carriageway of a highway, the highway
          authority who carried out the alterations ;

   " claim " means a claim under this Part of this Act and
       " the claimant " means the person making such a
       claim ;

   " the claim period " has the meaning given in section 3(2)
       above but subject to section 14(1) above and subsection
       (3) below ;

   " commencement date " means the date on which this Part
       of this Act comes into force ;

" highway " includes part of a highway and, in relation to England and Wales, means a highway or part of a highway maintainable at the public expense as defined in section 295(1) of the Highways Act 1959 and, in relation to Scotland, means a highway or part of a highway within the meaning of the Roads (Scotland) Act 1970 ;

" highway authority ", in relation to Scotland, has the meaning assigned to it in the said Act of 1970 ;

" land ", in relation to Scotland, includes salmon fishings ;

" public works " and " responsible authority " have the meaning given in section 1 above ;

" the relevant date " has the meaning given in sections 1(9) and 9(2) above.

(2) For the purposes of sections 2(1), 11(1) and 14(2) above an interest acquired or disposed of, or a tenancy granted, pursuant to a contract shall be treated as acquired, disposed of or granted when the contract was made.

(3) In the application of this Part of this Act to a highway which has not always since 17th October 1969 been a highway maintainable at the public expense as defined above—

(a) references to its being open to public traffic shall be construed as references to its being so open whether or not as a highway so maintainable ;

(b) for references to the highway authority who constructed it there shall be substituted references to the highway authority for the highway ;

and no claim shall be made if the relevant date falls at a time when the highway was not so maintainable and the highway does not become so maintainable within three years of that date but, if it does, the claim period shall be treated as continuing until the end of one year from the date on which it becomes so maintainable if, apart from this provision, that period would end earlier.

(4) In the application of subsection (3) above to Scotland—

(a) for the words from " highway which " to " defined above " and " highway so maintainable " there shall be substituted respectively the words " road which has not always since 17th October 1969 been a highway " and " highway " ;

(b) for the words " the highway was not so maintainable and the highway does not become so maintainable " there shall be substituted the words " the road was not a highway and the road does not become a highway " ;

(c) for the words " it becomes so maintainable " there shall be substituted the words " it becomes a highway ".

PART II

MITIGATION OF INJURIOUS EFFECT OF PUBLIC WORKS

Insulation against noise

20.—(1) The Secretary of State may make regulations impos- *Sound-*
ing a duty or conferring a power on responsible authorities *proofing of*
to insulate buildings against noise caused or expected to be *buildings*
caused by the construction or use of public works or to make *affected by*
grants in respect of the cost of such insulation. *public works.*

(2) Regulations under this section may—

   (a) make provision as to the level of noise giving rise to a
      duty or power under the regulations and the area in
      which a building must be situated if a duty or power is
      to arise in respect of it ;

   (b) specify the classes of public works and of buildings in
      respect of which a duty or power is to arise, and the
      classes of persons entitled to make claims, under the
      regulations ;

   (c) specify the nature and extent of the work which is to be
      undertaken under the regulations and the expenditure
      in respect of which and the rate at which grants are
      to be made under the regulations ;

   (d) make the carrying out of work or the making of grants
      under the regulations dependent upon compliance with
      conditions ;

   (e) make provision as to the funds out of which expenses
      incurred by responsible authorities under the regulations
      are to be defrayed ;

   (f) make provision for the settlement of disputes arising
      under the regulations.

(3) Without prejudice to the generality of paragraph (a) of
subsection (2) above, regulations made by virtue of that paragraph may provide for the relevant level of noise or the relevant
area in a particular case to be determined by reference to a
document published by or on behalf of the Secretary of State or
by any other authority or body or in such other manner as may
be provided in the regulations.

(4) If regulations under this section impose a duty or confer
a power to carry out, or make a grant in respect of the cost of,
work in respect of a building which is subject to a tenancy on
a claim in that behalf made by the landlord or the tenant,
provision may also be made by the regulations for enabling
the work to be carried out notwithstanding the withholding of
consent by the other party to the tenancy.

(5) Regulations under this section may authorise or require
local authorities to act as agents for responsible authorities in

PART II

1967 c. 76.

1959 c. 25.
1909 c. 47.

1968 c. 23.
1971 c. 28.

1965 c. 16.

Sound-
proofing of
buildings
affected by
aerodromes.

dealing with claims and in discharging or exercising the duties or powers of responsible authorities under the regulations, and may provide for the making by responsible authorities of payments to local authorities in respect of anything done by them as such agents.

(6) Regulations under this section may authorise the council of a London borough to contribute towards expenses incurred under the regulations by a responsible authority in respect of the insulation of buildings against noise caused or expected to be caused by the use of any highway in that borough in relation to which an order has been made under section 6 of the Road Traffic Regulation Act 1967 (traffic regulation orders in Greater London).

(7) Regulations under this section may contain such supplementary provisions as appear to the Secretary of State to be necessary or expedient and may make different provision with respect to different areas or different circumstances.

(8) The power to make regulations under this section shall be exercisable by statutory instrument.

(9) A draft of any regulations under this section shall be laid before Parliament and the first regulations shall not be made unless the draft has been approved by a resolution of each House of Parliament.

(10) The purposes for which advances may be made by the Secretary of State under section 235(1) of the Highways Act 1959 or section 8 of the Development and Road Improvement Funds Act 1909 shall include the discharge or exercise by a highway authority of any duty or power imposed or conferred on the authority under this section.

(11) In sections 25(4), 31(*a*) and 57(1)(*a*) of the Rent Act 1968 and sections 24(4) and 29(*a*) of the Rent (Scotland) Act 1971 (increase of rent for improvements) after the words " section 15 of the Airports Authority Act 1965 (grants towards cost of sound-proofing) " there shall be inserted the words " or regulations under section 20 of the Land Compensation Act 1973 ".

(12) In this section " public works " and " responsible authority " have the same meaning as in section 1 above except that " public works " does not include an aerodrome and except that " responsible authority ", in relation to a highway, includes any authority having power to make an order in respect of that highway under section 1 or 6 of the Road Traffic Regulation Act 1967 (traffic regulation orders).

21. In section 15 of the Airports Authority Act 1965 (grants towards sound-proofing of dwellings affected by noise from aerodromes) references to dwellings shall include references to

buildings other than dwellings but a scheme under that section   PART II
need apply only to such classes of buildings as the Secretary of
State thinks fit.

Powers of highway authorities

22.—(1) Subject to subsection (3) below, a highway authority Acquisition
may acquire land compulsorily or by agreement for the purpose of land in
of mitigating any adverse effect which the existence or use of a connection
highway constructed or improved by them, or proposed to be with highways.
constructed or improved by them, has or will have on the surroundings of the highway.

(2) Subject to subsection (3) below, a highway authority may
acquire by agreement—

    (*a*) land the enjoyment of which is seriously affected by
        the carrying out of works by the authority for the con-
        struction or improvement of a highway ;

    (*b*) land the enjoyment of which is seriously affected by
        the use of a highway which the authority have con-
        structed or improved,

if the interest of the vendor is one which falls within section
192(3) to (5) of the Town and Country Planning Act 1971 1971 c. 78.
(interests qualifying for protection under blight provisions) taking
references to the date of service of a notice under section 193
of that Act as references to the date on which the purchase
agreement is made.

(3) The powers conferred by subsection (2)(*b*) above shall not
be exercisable unless the date on which the highway or, as the
case may be, the improved highway is first open to public
traffic falls on or after 17th October 1971 and the powers
conferred by subsections (1) and (2)(*a*) above shall not be exercisable unless that date falls on or after 17th October 1972 ; and—

    (*a*) if that date falls not later than one year after the passing
        of this Act—

            (i) the powers conferred by subsection (1) above
            to acquire land compulsorily and the powers con-
            ferred by subsection (2)(*a*) above shall not be exercis-
            able unless the acquisition is begun before the end
            of one year after the passing of this Act ;

            (ii) the powers conferred by subsection (1) above
            to acquire land by agreement and the powers con-
            ferred by subsection (2)(*b*) above shall not be exercis-
            able unless the acquisition is begun before the end
            of one year after the passing of this Act or one year
            after that date, whichever ends later ;

(*b*) if that date falls more than one year after the passing of this Act—

    (i) the powers mentioned in paragraph (*a*)(i) above shall not be exercisable unless the acquisition is begun before that date ;

    (ii) the powers mentioned in paragraph (*a*)(ii) above shall not be exercisable unless the acquisition is begun before the end of one year after that date.

(4) Where under the powers of this section a highway authority have acquired, or propose to acquire, land forming part of a common, open space or fuel or field garden allotment and other land is required for the purpose of being given in exchange for the first-mentioned land, the authority may acquire that other land compulsorily or by agreement.

(5) A power to acquire land compulsorily conferred by this section on a local highway authority shall be exercisable in any particular case on their being authorised by the Secretary of State to exercise it ; and the Acquisition of Land (Authorisation Procedure) Act 1946 shall have effect—

    (*a*) in relation to the compulsory acquisition of land under this section by a local highway authority, as if this section had been in force immediately before the commencement of that Act ;

    (*b*) in relation to the compulsory acquisition of land under this section by the Secretary of State, as if this section had been in force immediately before the commencement of that Act and as if this section were included among the enactments specified in section 1(1)(*b*) of that Act.

(6) For the purposes of subsection (3) above the acquisition of any land is begun—

    (*a*) if it is compulsory, on the date on which the notice required by paragraph 3(1)(*a*) of Schedule 1 to the said Act of 1946 is first published ;

    (*b*) if it is by agreement, on the date on which the agreement is made ;

and where the compulsory acquisition of any land under subsection (1) is begun within the time limited by subsection (3) above but is not proceeded with, any subsequent compulsory acquisition of that land under subsection (1) above shall be treated for the purposes of this section as begun within that time.

(7) For the purpose of assessing the compensation payable on the compulsory acquisition of land under this section—

    (*a*) the land shall be treated as if it were being acquired for the construction of the highway or, as the case may be, the improvement in question ;

(*b*) section 222(6) of the Highways Act 1959 (matters to be   PART II
taken into account by Lands Tribunal) shall, so far as 1959 c. 25.
applicable, apply as it does in relation to compulsory
acquisition under the provisions there mentioned ;

and in section 222(11) of that Act (application of Compulsory 1965 c. 56.
Purchase Act 1965 to acquisition of land by agreement under
Part X of the said Act of 1959) the reference to the said Part X
shall include a reference to this section.

(8) Section 214(5) and (6) of the said Act of 1959 (acquisition
of land for preserving view from or other amenities of a highway) shall cease to have effect ; and in section 10(1) of that Act
(delegation of functions relating to trunk roads) for the words
" under subsection (5) or subsection (6) of section two hundred
and fourteen of this Act or under section two hundred and
fifteen thereof " there shall be substituted the words " under
section 215 of this Act or under section 22 of the Land Compensation Act 1973 ".

(9) References in the Highways Act 1971 to highway land
acquisition powers shall include references to the powers exer- 1971 c. 41.
cisable under this section.

(10) In this section references to the construction or improvement of a highway include references to the construction or
improvement of a highway by virtue of an order under section
9 or 13 of the Highways Act 1959 or section 1 of the Highways
Act 1971.

(11) In the application of this section to Scotland—

(*a*) for the references to sections 192(3) to (5) and 193 of
the Town and Country Planning Act 1971 there shall
be substituted respectively references to sections 181(3)
to (5) and 182 of the Town and Country Planning 1972 c. 52.
(Scotland) Act 1972 ;

(*b*) in subsection (4) for the words " open space or fuel or
field garden allotment " there shall be substituted the
words " or open space " ;

(*c*) for references to the Acquisition of Land (Authorisa- 1946 c. 59.
tion Procedure) Act 1946 there shall be substituted
references to the Acquisition of Land (Authorisation 1947 c. 42.
Procedure) (Scotland) Act 1947 ;

(*d*) for the reference to section 222(6) of the Highways Act
1959 there shall be substituted a reference to section
35(3) of the Roads (Scotland) Act 1970 ;   1970 c. 20.

(*e*) for subsection (8) there shall be substituted—

" (8) In section 5(2) of the Trunk Roads Act 1946 1946 c. 30.
(delegation of functions relating to trunk roads) after

L

1970 c. 20.

the words "section 29(4) of the Roads (Scotland) Act 1970" there shall be inserted the words "or under section 22 of the Land Compensation Act 1973." ";

1949 c. 32.
1970 c. 20.

(f) in subsection (10) for the words from "9" to the end there shall be substituted "3 or 14 of the Special Roads Act 1949 or section 15 of the Roads (Scotland) Act 1970".

Execution
of works
in connection
with highways.

23.—(1) A highway authority may carry out—

(a) on land acquired by them under section 22 above ;

(b) on any other land belonging to them ;

(c) on any highway for which they are the highway authority ;

(d) on any highway which they have been authorised to improve or construct by virtue of an order under section 9 or 13 of the Highways Act 1959, section 1 of the Highways Act 1971, section 3 or 14 of the Special Roads Act 1949 or section 15 of the Roads (Scotland) Act 1970,

1959 c. 25.
1971 c. 41.

works for mitigating any adverse effect which the construction, improvement, existence or use of a highway has or will have on the surroundings of the highway.

(2) Without prejudice to the generality of subsection (1) above, the works that may be carried out under that subsection include the planting of trees, shrubs or plants of any other description and the laying out of any area as grassland.

(3) A highway authority may develop or redevelop any land acquired by them under section 22 above, or any other land belonging to them, for the purpose of improving the surroundings of a highway in any manner which they think desirable by reason of its construction, improvement, existence or use.

Agreements
as to use of
land near
highways.

24.—(1) For the purpose of mitigating any adverse effect which the construction, improvement, existence or use of a highway has or will have on the surroundings of the highway, the highway authority may enter into an agreement with any person interested in land adjoining or in the vicinity of the highway for restricting or regulating the use of the land either permanently or during such period as may be specified in the agreement ; and any such agreement may, in particular, make provision for the planting and maintenance of trees, shrubs or plants of any other description on the land and for restricting the lopping or removal of trees, shrubs or other plants on the land.

(2) An agreement under this section may contain such inci- PART II
dental and consequential provisions (including provisions of a
financial character) as appear to the highway authority to be
necessary or expedient for the purposes of the agreement.

(3) Subject to subsection (4) below, the provisions of any agreement made under this section with any person interested in land
shall be binding on persons deriving title from that person in
respect of the land.

(4) No provision shall be enforceable by virtue of subsection
(3) above against a purchaser for money or money's worth of a
legal estate in the land unless before completion of the purchase
the agreement has been registered in the register of local land
charges by the proper officer of the council of the district or
London borough in which the land is situated in such manner as
may be prescribed by rules made for the purposes of this subsection under section 19 of the Land Charges Act 1925 ; and 1925 c. 22.
in this subsection " purchaser " and " purchase " have the same
meaning as in that Act.

(5) This section is without prejudice to section 52 of the Town 1971 c. 78.
and Country Planning Act 1971 (agreements regulating development or use of land).

(6) In the application of this section to Scotland—

    (*a*) for subsection (4) there shall be substituted—

> " (4) No provision shall be enforceable by virtue
> of subsection (3) above against a third party who
> shall have in good faith and for value acquired right
> (whether completed by infeftment or not) to land
> prior to the agreement being recorded in the Register
> of Sasines, or against any person deriving title from
> such third party " ;

    (*b*) for the reference to section 52 of the said Act of 1971
    there shall be substituted a reference to section 50 of
    the Town and Country Planning (Scotland) Act 1972. 1972 c. 52.

25. The purposes for which advances may be made by the Advances for
Secretary of State under section 235(1) of the Highways Act exercise of
1959 or section 8 of the Development and Road Improvement powers by
Funds Act 1909 shall include the exercise by a highway authority highway
of any powers conferred by sections 22 to 24 above. authorities.
1959 c. 25.
1909 c. 47.

Powers of authorities responsible for other public works

26.—(1) Subject to the provisions of this section, a responsible Acquisition of
authority may acquire land by agreement for the purpose of land in
mitigating any adverse effect which the existence or use of connection
any public works has or will have on the surroundings of the with public
works. works.

L 2

(2) Subject to the provisions of this section, a responsible authority may acquire by agreement—

    (*a*) land the enjoyment of which is seriously affected by the carrying out of works by the authority for the construction or alteration of any public works ;

    (*b*) land the enjoyment of which is seriously affected by the use of any public works,

if the interest of the vendor is of the kind mentioned in section 22(2) above.

(3) The powers conferred by subsection (2)(*b*) above shall not be exercisable unless the date on which the public works or, as the case may be, the altered public works, are first used falls on or after 17th October 1971 and the powers conferred by subsections (1) and (2)(*a*) above shall not be exercisable unless that date falls on or after 17th October 1972 ; and—

    (*a*) if that date falls not later than one year after the passing of this Act—

        (i) the powers conferred by subsections (1) and (2)(*b*) above shall not be exercisable unless the acquisition is begun before the end of one year after the passing of this Act or one year after that date, whichever ends later ;

        (ii) the powers conferred by subsection (2)(*a*) above shall not be exercisable unless the acquisition is begun before the end of one year after the passing of this Act ;

    (*b*) if that date falls more than one year after the passing of this Act—

        (i) the powers mentioned in paragraph (*a*)(i) above shall not be exercisable unless the acquisition is begun before the end of one year after that date ;

        (ii) the powers mentioned in paragraph (*a*)(ii) above shall not be exercisable unless the acquisition is begun before that date.

(4) For the purposes of subsection (3) above the acquisition of any land shall be treated as begun when the agreement for its acquisition is made.

(5) This section applies only where the responsible authority have statutory powers to acquire land (whether compulsorily or by agreement) for the purposes of their functions but would not, apart from this section, have power to acquire land as mentioned in subsections (1) and (2) above.

(6) In this section " public works " and " responsible authority " have the same meaning as in section 1 above except that

" public works " does not include a highway or in Scotland a PART II
road or any works forming part of a statutory undertaking as
defined in section 290(1) of the Town and Country Planning Act 1971 c. 78.
1971 or, as respects Scotland, section 275(1) of the Town and 1972 c. 52.
Country Planning (Scotland) Act 1972.

27.—(1) A responsible authority may carry out— Execution of

works etc. in
connection

    (a) if they have power to acquire land under section 26
        above, on any land acquired by them under that section ; with public

    (b) on any other land belonging to them, works.

works for mitigating any adverse effect which the construction,
alteration, existence or use of any public works has or will have
on the surroundings of the works.

(2) Without prejudice to the generality of subsection (1) above,
the works that may be carried out under that subsection include
the planting of trees, shrubs or plants of any other description
and the laying out of any area as grassland.

(3) A responsible authority may—

    (a) develop or redevelop any land acquired by them under
        section 26 above, or any other land belonging to them,
        for the purpose of improving the surroundings of
        public works in any manner which they think desirable
        by reason of the construction, alteration, existence or
        use of the works ;

    (b) dispose of any land acquired by them under section 26
        above.

(4) This section applies only where the responsible authority
are a body incorporated by or under any enactment and has
effect only for extending the corporate powers of any such
authority.

(5) In this section " public works " and " responsible authority " have the same meaning as in section 1 above except that
" public works " does not include a highway or in Scotland a
road.

Expenses of persons moving temporarily
during construction works etc.

28.—(1) This section has effect where works are carried out— Power to pay

expenses of
persons

    (a) by a highway authority for the construction or improve-
        ment of a highway ; or moving

    (b) by a responsible authority for the construction or altera- temporarily
        tion of any public works other than a highway, during

construction

and the carrying out of those works affects the enjoyment of a works etc.
dwelling adjacent to the site on which they are being carried out

L 3

PART II   to such an extent that continued occupation of the dwelling is not reasonably practicable.

(2) Subject to subsection (3) below, the highway authority or responsible authority, as the case may be, may pay any reasonable expenses incurred by the occupier of the dwelling in providing suitable alternative residential accommodation for himself and members of his household for the whole or any part of the period during which the works are being carried out.

(3) No payment shall be made to any person under this section in respect of any expenses except in pursuance of an agreement made between that person and the authority concerned before the expenses are incurred ; and no payment shall be so made except in respect of the amount by which the expenses exceed those which that person would have incurred if the dwelling had continued to be occupied.

(4) In this section " public works " and " responsible authority " have the same meaning as in section 1 above.

1970 c. 20.   (5) In the application of this section to Scotland " highway authority " has the same meaning as in the Roads (Scotland) Act 1970, and in subsection (1) for any reference to a highway there shall be substituted a reference to a road.

PART III

PROVISIONS FOR BENEFIT OF PERSONS DISPLACED FROM LAND

Home loss payments

Right to home loss payment where person displaced from dwelling.
29.—(1) Where a person is displaced from a dwelling on any land in consequence of—

(a) the compulsory acquisition of an interest in the dwelling ;

(b) the making, passing or acceptance of a housing order, resolution or undertaking in respect of the dwelling ;

(c) where the land has been previously acquired by an authority possessing compulsory purchase powers or appropriated by a local authority and is for the time being held by the authority for the purposes for which it was acquired or appropriated, the carrying out of redevelopment on the land,

he shall, subject to the provisions of this section and section 32 below, be entitled to receive a payment (hereafter referred to as a " home loss payment ") from the acquiring authority, the authority who made the order, passed the resolution or accepted the undertaking or the authority carrying out the redevelopment, as the case may be.

(2) A person shall not be entitled to a home loss payment unless throughout a period of not less than five years ending with the date of displacement—

(a) he has been in occupation of the dwelling, or a substantial part of it, as his only or main residence ; and

(b) he has been in occupation as aforesaid by virtue of an interest or right to which this section applies.

(3) For the purposes of this section a person shall not be treated as displaced from a dwelling in consequence of the compulsory acquisition of an interest therein if he gives up his occupation thereof before the date on which the acquiring authority were authorised to acquire that interest, but, subject to that, it shall not be necessary for the acquiring authority to have required him to give up his occupation of the dwelling.

(4) This section applies to the following interests and rights—

(a) any interest in the dwelling ;

(b) a right to occupy the dwelling as a statutory tenant within the meaning of the Rent Act 1968 or under a contract to which Part VI of that Act (furnished lettings) applies or would apply if the contract or dwelling were not excluded by section 70(3)(a) or 71 of that Act ;

1968 c. 23.

(c) a right to occupy the dwelling as a statutory tenant within the meaning of the Rent (Scotland) Act 1971 or under a contract to which Part VII of that Act (furnished lettings) applies or would apply if the contract or dwelling were not excluded by section 85(3)(a) or 86 of that Act ;

1971 c. 28.

(d) a right to occupy the dwelling under a contract of employment.

(5) No home loss payment shall be made to any person displaced from a dwelling in consequence of the compulsory acquisition of an interest therein if the acquisition is in pursuance of the service by him of a blight notice within the meaning of section 192 of the Town and Country Planning Act 1971 or section 181 of the Town and Country Planning (Scotland) Act 1972 or of a notice under section 11 of the New Towns Act 1965 or section 11 of the New Towns (Scotland) Act 1968.

1971 c. 78.
1972 c. 52.
1965 c. 59.
1968 c. 16.

(6) Where an authority possessing compulsory purchase powers acquire the interest of any person in a dwelling by agreement, then, in relation to any other person who is displaced from the dwelling in consequence of the acquisition, subsections (1) to (4) above shall have effect as if the acquisition were

L 4

compulsory and the authority (if not authorised to acquire the interest compulsorily) had been so authorised on the date of the agreement.

(7) In this section " a housing order, resolution or undertaking " means—

(*a*) a demolition, closing or clearance order under Part II or III of the Housing Act 1957, section 60 of the Housing Act 1969 or Part II of the Housing (Scotland) Act 1966 ;

(*b*) a resolution under section 56 of the said Act of 1966 ; or

(*c*) an undertaking accepted under section 16(4) of the said Act of 1957, section 60(2) of the said Act of 1969 or section 15(4)(i) of the said Act of 1966 ;

and " redevelopment " includes a change of use.

(8) Where an interest in a dwelling is vested in trustees (other than a sole tenant for life within the meaning of the Settled Land Act 1925) and a person beneficially entitled (whether directly or derivatively) under the trusts is entitled or permitted by reason of his interest to occupy the dwelling, he shall be treated for the purposes of this section as occupying it by virtue of an interest in the dwelling.

In the application of this subsection to Scotland the words " (other than a sole tenant for life within the meaning of the Settled Land Act 1925 ") shall be omitted.

(9) This section applies if the date of displacement is on or after 17th October 1972.

Amount of home loss payment in England and Wales.

30.—(1) Subject to subsection (2) below, the amount of a home loss payment in England and Wales shall be—

(*a*) where the date of displacement is before 1st April 1973, an amount equal to the rateable value of the dwelling multiplied by seven ;

(*b*) where the date of displacement is on or after 1st April 1973, an amount equal to the rateable value of the dwelling multiplied by three ;

subject, in either case, to a maximum of £1,500 and a minimum of £150.

(2) The Secretary of State may from time to time by order prescribe different multipliers and a different maximum or minimum for the purposes of subsection (1) above ; and the power to make orders under this subsection shall be exercisable by statutory instrument subject to annulment in pursuance of a resolution of either House of Parliament.

(3) For the purposes of this section the rateable value of a
dwelling shall be determined as follows—

    (*a*) if the dwelling is a hereditament for which a rateable value is shown in the valuation list in force on the date of displacement, it shall be that rateable value ;

    (*b*) if the dwelling forms part only of such a hereditament or consists of or forms part of more than one such hereditament, an apportionment or aggregation of the rateable value or values so shown shall be made by the valuation officer and the rateable value of the dwelling shall be taken to be the amount certified by him as being the amount which, on such an apportionment or aggregation, is properly attributable to the dwelling ;

    (*c*) if neither paragraph (*a*) nor paragraph (*b*) of this subsection applies to the dwelling, its rateable value shall be determined by the valuation officer in accordance with the General Rate Acts 1967 and 1970.

(4) In this section " valuation officer " has the same meaning as in the General Rate Act 1967.

31.—(1) Subject to subsection (2) below, the amount of a home loss payment in Scotland shall be an amount equal to the rateable value of the dwelling multiplied by six, subject to a maximum of £1,500 and a minimum of £150.

(2) The Secretary of State may from time to time by order prescribe a different multiplier and a different maximum or minimum for the purposes of subsection (1) above ; and the power to make orders under this subsection shall be exercisable by statutory instrument subject to annulment in pursuance of a resolution of either House of Parliament.

(3) For the purposes of this section the rateable value of a dwelling shall be determined as follows—

    (*a*) if the dwelling consists of lands and heritages for which a rateable value is shown in the valuation roll in force on the date of displacement, it shall be that rateable value ;

    (*b*) if the dwelling forms part only of such lands and heritages or consists or forms part of more than one unit of such lands and heritages, an apportionment or aggregation of the rateable value or values so shown shall be made by the assessor and the rateable value of the dwelling shall be taken to be the amount certified by him as being the amount which, on such an apportionment or aggregation, is properly attributable to the dwelling ;

(c) if neither paragraph (*a*) nor paragraph (*b*) of this sub-section applies to the dwelling, its rateable value shall be determined by the assessor in accordance with the Valuation Acts.

1956 c. 60.

(4) This section shall be construed as one with the Valuation and Rating (Scotland) Act 1956.

Supplementary provisions about home loss payments.

32.—(1) Subject to subsection (8) below, no home loss payment shall be made except on a claim in that behalf made by the person entitled thereto (" the claimant ") before the expiration of the period of six months beginning with the date of displacement ; and any such claim shall be in writing and shall be accompanied or supplemented by such particulars as the authority responsible for making the payment may reasonably require to enable them to determine whether the claimant is entitled to a payment and, if so, its amount.

(2) A home loss payment shall be made not later than three months after the date on which a claim for the payment is made in accordance with subsection (1) above or, if those three months end before the date of displacement, on the date of displacement.

(3) Where the claimant has been in occupation of a dwelling or a substantial part of it as mentioned in paragraphs (*a*) and (*b*) of section 29(2) above for any period (" the claimant's own qualifying period ") and has also for an immediately preceding period resided in the dwelling, or a substantial part of it, as his only or main residence but without being in occupation as required by those paragraphs then, if another person was, or other persons successively were, in occupation thereof as mentioned in those paragraphs throughout that preceding period, the claimant's own qualifying period shall be treated for the purposes of section 29(2) above as including that preceding period.

(4) Where a person (" the deceased ") dies before the expiration of the period for making a claim to a home loss payment and would have been entitled to such a payment if he had made a claim within that period, a claim to that payment may be made, before the expiration of that period, by any person, not being a minor, who—

(a) throughout a period of not less than five years ending with the date of displacement of the deceased, has resided in the dwelling, or a substantial part of it, as his only or main residence ; and

(b) is entitled to benefit by virtue of testamentary dispositions taking effect on, or the law of intestate succession or the right of survivorship between joint tenants as applied to, the death of the deceased.

(5) Where the claimant has successively been in occupation of or resided in different dwellings in the same building, being dwellings consisting of a room or rooms not constructed or structurally adapted for use as a separate dwelling, section 29(2) above and subsections (3) and (4) above shall have effect as if those dwellings were the same dwelling.

(6) Where there are two or more persons entitled to make a claim to a home loss payment in respect of the same dwelling (whether by virtue of joint occupation or of subsection (4) above) the payment to be made on each claim shall be equal to the whole amount of the home loss payment divided by the number of such persons.

(7) Where an interest in a dwelling is acquired by agreement by an authority possessing compulsory purchase powers, the authority may, in connection with the acquisition, make to the person from whom the interest is acquired a payment corresponding to any home loss payment which they would be required to make to him if the acquisition were compulsory and the authority had been authorised to acquire that interest before he gave up occupation of the dwelling.

(8) Where the date of displacement is before the passing of this Act the period within which a claim to a home loss payment can be made shall be the period of six months beginning with the date of the passing of this Act.

(9) In the application of subsection (4) above to Scotland—

(a) for the word " minor " there shall be substituted the words " person under the age of eighteen " ;

(b) in paragraph (b)—

(i) for the words from " testamentary " to " tenants " there shall be substituted the words " a testamentary disposition or any other deed with testamentary effect taking effect on, or the law of intestate succession ", and

(ii) at the end there shall be added the following words—" or a right to *jus relicti, jus relictae* or *legitim* out of the deceased's estate.".

33.—(1) Sections 29 to 32 above shall, so far as applicable, have effect in relation to a person residing in a caravan on a caravan site who is displaced from that site as they have effect in relation to a person displaced from a dwelling on any land but shall so have effect subject to the following modifications.

Home loss payments for certain caravan dwellers.

(2) No home loss payment shall be made to any person by virtue of this section except where no suitable alternative site for stationing a caravan is available to him on reasonable terms.

(3) Subsection (1) of section 29 above shall have effect as if for the words preceding paragraph (*a*) there were substituted the words " Where a person residing in a caravan on a caravan site is displaced from that site in consequence of " and subsection (2) of that section shall have effect as if for paragraphs (*a*) and (*b*) there were substituted—

" (*a*) he has been in occupation of the caravan site by using a caravan stationed on it as his only or main residence ; and

(*b*) he has been in occupation of the site as aforesaid by virtue of an interest or right to which this section applies."

(4) Sections 30(3) and 31(3) above shall have effect as if—

(*a*) paragraph (*b*) were omitted ; and

(*b*) in paragraphs (*a*) and (*c*) for the word " dwelling " there were substituted the words " caravan site together with a caravan ".

(5) Section 32 above shall have effect—

(*a*) as if in subsection (3) for the words " in occupation of a dwelling or a substantial part of it ", " resided in the dwelling, or a substantial part of it " and " in occupation thereof " there were substituted respectively the words " in occupation of a caravan site ", " resided in a caravan on that site " and " in occupation of that site " ;

(*b*) as if in subsection (4) for the words " resided in the dwelling, or a substantial part of it " there were substituted the words " resided in a caravan on the caravan site " ; and

(*c*) as if for subsection (5) there were substituted—

" (5) Where any land comprises two or more caravan sites and the claimant has successively been in occupation of or resided in a caravan on different caravan sites on that land, section 29(2) above and subsections (3) and (4) above shall have effect as if those sites were the same site."

(6) Sections 29 to 32 above shall have effect as if in any provision not modified as aforesaid for any reference to a dwelling or land there were substituted a reference to a caravan site.

(7) In this section " caravan site " means land on which a caravan is stationed for the purpose of human habitation and land which is used in conjunction with land on which a caravan is so stationed.

Farm loss payments

34.—(1) Where land constituting or included in an agricultural unit is land in respect of which the person in occupation of the unit has an owner's interest, then if—

PART III
Right to farm
loss payment
where person
displaced from
agricultural
unit.

    (*a*) in consequence of the compulsory acquisition of his interest in the whole of that land (" the land acquired ") he is displaced from the whole of that land ; and

    (*b*) not more than three years after the date of displacement he begins to farm another agricultural unit (" the new unit ") elsewhere in Great Britain,

he shall, subject to the provisions of this section and section 36 below, be entitled to receive a payment (hereafter referred to as a " farm loss payment ") from the acquiring authority.

(2) In subsection (1) above " owner's interest " means a freehold interest or a tenancy granted or extended for a term of years certain of which not less than three years remain unexpired on the date of displacement.

(3) For the purposes of this section a person is displaced from land in consequence of the compulsory acquisition of his interest therein if, and only if, he gives up possession thereof—

    (*a*) on being required to do so by the acquiring authority ;

    (*b*) on completion of the acquisition ; or

    (*c*) where the acquiring authority permit him to remain in possession of the land under a tenancy or licence of a kind not making him a tenant as defined in the Agricultural Holdings Act 1948, on the expiration of that tenancy or licence ;

and references in this section and section 35 below to the date of displacement are references to the date on which the person concerned gives up possession as aforesaid.

(4) No farm loss payment shall be made to any person unless on the date on which he begins to farm the new unit he is in occupation of the whole of that unit in right of a freehold interest therein or a tenancy thereof, not having been entitled to any such interest or tenancy before the date on which the acquiring authority were authorised to acquire his interest in the land acquired.

(5) No farm loss payment shall be made by virtue of the displacement of a person from any land if he is entitled to a payment under section 12 of the Agriculture (Miscellaneous Provisions) Act 1968 in consequence of the acquisition of an interest in, or the taking of possession of, that land.

(6) No farm loss payment shall be made to any person displaced from land in consequence of the compulsory acquisition of his interest therein if the acquisition of his interest in the whole or any part of that land is in pursuance of the service by him of a blight notice within the meaning of section 192 of the Town and Country Planning Act 1971 or a notice under section 11 of the New Towns Act 1965.

1971 c. 78.
1965 c. 59.

(7) In the application of this section to Scotland—

(a) for subsection (2) there shall be substituted—

" (2) In subsection (1) above " owner's interest " means the interest of an owner or a lessee under a lease, being a lease the unexpired period of which on the date of displacement is not less than three years or the interest of a crofter or a landholder ; "

(b) for any reference to a tenancy or licence there shall be substituted respectively a reference to a lease or a right or permission relating to land but not amounting to an estate or interest therein ;

(c) in subsection (3)(c) for the words " Agricultural Holdings Act 1948 " there shall be substituted the words " Agricultural Holdings (Scotland) Act 1949 " ;

1948 c. 63.
1949 c. 75.

(d) in subsection (4) for the words " a freehold interest " there shall be substituted the words " an interest as owner thereof ";

(e) in subsection (6) for the words " section 192 of the Town and Country Planning Act 1971 " and " the New Towns Act 1965 " there shall be substituted respectively the words " section 181 of the Town and Country Planning (Scotland) Act 1972 " and " the New Towns (Scotland) Act 1968 ".

1972 c. 52.
1968 c. 16.

(8) This section applies if the date of displacement is on or after 17th October 1972.

Amount of farm loss payment.

35.—(1) Subject to the provisions of this section, the amount of any farm loss payment shall be equal to the average annual profit derived from the use for agricultural purposes of the agricultural land comprised in the land acquired ; and that profit shall be computed by reference to the profits for the three years ending with the date of displacement or, if the person concerned has then been in occupation for a shorter period, that period.

(2) Where accounts have been made up in respect of the profits of the person concerned for a period or consecutive periods of twelve months and that period or the last of them

ends not more than one year before the date of displacement, subsection (1) above shall have effect as if the date on which that period or the last of those periods ends were the date of the displacement.

(3) Where the date of displacement is determined in accordance with section 34(3)(*c*) above and the person concerned has on that date been in occupation for more than three years, he may elect that the average annual profit shall, instead of being computed by reference to the profits for the years mentioned in subsection (1) above, be computed by reference to the profits for—

(*a*) any three consecutive periods of twelve months for which accounts in respect of his profits have been made up, being periods for which he has been in occupation and the last of which ends on or after the date of completion of the acquisition ; or

(*b*) if there are no such periods as aforesaid, any three consecutive years for which he has been in occupation and the last of which ends on or after the date mentioned in paragraph (*a*) above.

(4) In calculating the profits mentioned in subsection (1) above there shall be deducted a sum equal to the rent that might reasonably be expected to be payable in respect of the agricultural land comprised in the land acquired if it were let for agricultural purposes to a tenant responsible for rates, repairs and other outgoings ; and that deduction shall be made whether or not the land is in fact let and, if it is, shall be made to the exclusion of any deduction for the rent actually payable.

(5) In calculating the profits mentioned in subsection (1) above there shall be left out of account profits from any activity if a sum in respect of loss of profits from that activity would fall to be included in the compensation, so far as attributable to disturbance, for the acquisition of the interest in the land acquired.

(6) Where the value of the agricultural land comprised in the land acquired exceeds the value of the agricultural land comprised in the new unit the amount of the farm loss payment shall be proportionately reduced.

(7) For the purposes of subsection (6) above the value of any land shall be assessed—

(*a*) on the basis of its value as land used solely for agriculture and as for a freehold interest therein (or, in Scotland, an interest as owner thereof) with vacant possession ;

(*b*) by reference to the condition of the land and its surroundings and to prices current—

> (i) in the case of the land comprised in the land acquired, on the date of displacement;
>
> (ii) in the case of land comprised in the new unit, on the date on which the person concerned begins to farm the new unit;

1961 c. 33.   (*c*) in accordance with rules (2) to (4) of the rules set out
1963 c. 51.   in section 5 of the Land Compensation Act 1961 or section 12 of the Land Compensation (Scotland) Act 1963;

(*d*) without regard to the principal dwelling, if any, comprised in the same agricultural unit as that land.

(8) The amount of a farm loss payment shall not be greater than the amount, if any, by which—

(*a*) that payment, calculated apart from this subsection, together with compensation for the acquisition of the interest in the land acquired assessed on the assumptions mentioned in section 5(2), (3) and (4) above (including any sum included as compensation for disturbance), exceeds

(*b*) the compensation actually payable for the acquisition of that interest.

(9) Any dispute as to the amount of a farm loss payment shall be referred to and determined by the Lands Tribunal or, in Scotland, the Lands Tribunal for Scotland.

Supplementary   **36.**—(1) Subject to subsection (7) below, no farm loss pay-
provisions   ment shall be made except on a claim in that behalf made by
about farm   the person entitled thereto before the expiration of the period
loss payments.   of one year beginning with the date on which the requirement
in section 34(1)(*b*) above is complied with, and any such claim shall be in writing and shall be accompanied or supplemented by such particulars as the acquiring authority may reasonably require to enable them to determine whether that person is entitled to a payment and, if so, its amount.

(2) Where the agricultural unit containing the land acquired is occupied for the purposes of a partnership firm sections 34 and 35 above shall have effect in relation to the firm and not the partners individually (any interest of a partner in the land acquired being treated as an interest of the firm) except that the requirements in section 34 as to the new unit shall be treated as complied with in relation to the firm as soon as they are complied with by any one of the persons who were members of the firm.

(3) Where a person dies before the expiration of the period
for making a claim to a farm loss payment and would have been
entitled to such a payment if he had made a claim within that
period, a claim to that payment may be made, before the expiration of that period, by his personal representative.

(4) Where an interest in land is acquired by agreement by
an authority possessing compulsory purchase powers, the
authority may, in connection with the acquisition, make to the
person from whom the interest is acquired a payment corresponding to any farm loss payment which they would be required
to make to him if the acquisition were compulsory and the
authority (if not authorised to acquire the interest compulsorily)
had been so authorised on the date of the agreement.

(5) Where a farm loss payment is made to any person the
authority making the payment shall also pay any reasonable
valuation or legal expenses incurred by that person for the
purposes of the preparation and prosecution of his claim to the
payment ; but this subsection is without prejudice to the powers
of the Lands Tribunal or the Lands Tribunal for Scotland in
respect of the costs or expenses of proceedings before the
Tribunal by virtue of section 35(9) above.

(6) A farm loss payment shall carry interest, at the rate
for the time being prescribed under section 32 of the Land 1961 c. 33.
Compensation Act 1961 or, in Scotland, section 40 of the Land 1963 c. 51.
Compensation (Scotland) Act 1963, from the date mentioned in
subsection (1) above until payment.

(7) Where the date mentioned in subsection (1) above is before
the passing of this Act the period within which a claim to a
farm loss payment can be made shall be the period of one year
beginning with the date of the passing of this Act.

Disturbance payments

37.—(1) Where a person is displaced from any land in con-   Disturbance
sequence of—   payments
                 for persons
  (a) the acquisition of the land by an authority possessing without
      compulsory purchase powers ;   compensa-
                                        table interests.
  (b) the making, passing or acceptance of a housing order,
      resolution or undertaking in respect of a house or
      building on the land ;
  (c) where the land has been previously acquired by an
      authority possessing compulsory purchase powers or
      appropriated by a local authority and is for the time
      being held by the authority for the purposes for which

it was acquired or appropriated, the carrying out of redevelopment on the land,

he shall, subject to the provisions of this section, be entitled to receive a payment (hereafter referred to as a " disturbance payment ") from the acquiring authority, the authority who made the order, passed the resolution or accepted the undertaking or the authority carrying out the redevelopment, as the case may be.

(2) A person shall not be entitled to a disturbance payment—

  (*a*) in any case, unless he is in lawful possession of the land from which he is displaced ;

  (*b*) in a case within subsection (1)(*a*) above, unless either—

      (i) he has no interest in the land for the acquisition or extinguishment of which he is (or if the acquisition or extinguishment were compulsory would be) entitled to compensation under any other enactment ; or

      (ii) he has such an interest as aforesaid but the compensation is subject to a site value provision and he is not (or if the acquisition were compulsory would not be) entitled in respect of that acquisition to an owner-occupier's supplement ;

  (*c*) in a case within subsection (1)(*b*) above, if he is entitled to an owner-occupier's supplement by reference to the order, resolution or undertaking.

In this subsection " site value provision " means section 29(2) or 59(2) of the Housing Act 1957, section 20 of the Housing (Scotland) Act 1966 or section 10 of the Housing (Scotland) Act 1969 and " owner-occupier's supplement " means a payment under Part II of Schedule 2 to the said Act of 1957, Schedule 5 to the Housing Act 1969 or sections 18 to 20 of the Housing (Scotland) Act 1969.

(3) For the purposes of subsection (1) above a person shall not be treated as displaced in consequence of any such acquisition or redevelopment as is mentioned in paragraph (*a*) or (*c*) of that subsection unless he was in lawful possession of the land—

  (*a*) in the case of land acquired under a compulsory purchase order, at the time when notice was first published of the making of the compulsory purchase order prior to its submission for confirmation or, where the order did not require confirmation, of the preparation of the order in draft ;

  (*b*) in the case of land acquired under an Act specifying the land as subject to compulsory acquisition, at the time when the provisions of the Bill for that Act specifying the land were first published ;

(c) in the case of land acquired by agreement, at the time when the agreement was made ;

and a person shall not be treated as displaced in consequence of any such order, resolution or undertaking as is mentioned in paragraph (b) of that subsection unless he was in lawful possession as aforesaid at the time when the order was made, the resolution was passed or the undertaking was accepted.

(4) Where a person is displaced from land in circumstances such that, apart from this subsection, he would be entitled to a disturbance payment from any authority and also to compensation from that authority under section 37 of the Landlord and Tenant Act 1954 (compensation from landlord where order for new tenancy of business premises precluded on certain grounds) he shall be entitled, at his option, to one or the other but not to both.

1954 c. 56.

(5) Where a person is displaced from any land as mentioned in subsection (1) above but is not entitled, as against the authority there mentioned, to a disturbance payment or to compensation for disturbance under any other enactment, the authority may, if they think fit, make a payment to him determined in accordance with section 38(1) to (3) below.

(6) A disturbance payment shall carry interest, at the rate for the time being prescribed under section 32 of the Land Compensation Act 1961 or, in Scotland, section 40 of the Land Compensation (Scotland) Act 1963, from the date of displacement until payment.

1961 c. 33.
1963 c. 51.

(7) This section does not apply to any land which is used for the purposes of agriculture.

(8) In section 71(4) of the Housing (Financial Provisions) (Scotland) Act 1972 (financial assistance towards tenants' removal expenses) for the words from " 160 " to the end there shall be substituted the words " 37 of the Land Compensation Act 1973 (disturbance payments for persons without compensatable interests) ".

1972 c. 46.

(9) In this section " a housing order, resolution or undertaking " and " redevelopment " have the same meaning as in section 29 above.

(10) This section applies if the date of displacement is on or after 17th October 1972.

38.—(1) The amount of a disturbance payment shall be equal to—

> (*a*) the reasonable expenses of the person entitled to the payment in removing from the land from which he is displaced ; and
>
> (*b*) if he was carrying on a trade or business on that land, the loss he will sustain by reason of the disturbance of that trade or business consequent upon his having to quit the land.

(2) In estimating the loss of any person for the purposes of subsection (1)(*b*) above, regard shall be had to the period for which the land occupied by him may reasonably have been expected to be available for the purposes of his trade or business and to the availability of other land suitable for that purpose.

This subsection has effect subject to section 46(7) below.

(3) Where the displacement is from a dwelling in respect of which structural modifications have been made for meeting the special needs of a disabled person (whether or not the person entitled to the disturbance payment) then, if—

> (*a*) a local authority having functions under section 29 of the National Assistance Act 1948, or having duties under section 12 of the Social Work (Scotland) Act 1968, provided assistance, or
>
> (*b*) such an authority would, if an application had been made, have provided assistance,

for making those modifications, the amount of the disturbance payment shall include an amount equal to any reasonable expenses incurred by the person entitled to the payment in making, in respect of a dwelling to which the disabled person removes, comparable modifications which are reasonably required for meeting the disabled person's special needs.

(4) Any dispute as to the amount of a disturbance payment shall be referred to and determined by the Lands Tribunal or, in Scotland, the Lands Tribunal for Scotland.

Rehousing

39.—(1) Where a person is displaced from residential accommodation on any land in consequence of—

> (*a*) the acquisition of the land by an authority possessing compulsory purchase powers ;
>
> (*b*) the making, passing or acceptance of a housing order, resolution or undertaking in respect of a house or building on the land ;

(c) where the land has been previously acquired by an
authority possessing compulsory purchase powers or
appropriated by a local authority and is for the time
being held by the authority for the purposes for which
it was acquired or appropriated, the carrying out of
redevelopment on the land,

and suitable alternative residential accommodation on reasonable
terms is not otherwise available to that person, then, subject to
the provisions of this section, it shall be the duty of the relevant
authority to secure that he will be provided with such other
accommodation.

(2) Subsection (1) above shall not by virtue of paragraph (a)
thereof apply to a person if the acquisition is in pursuance of
the service by him of a blight notice within the meaning of
section 192 of the Town and Country Planning Act 1971 or 1971 c. 78.
section 181 of the Town and Country Planning (Scotland) Act 1972 c. 52.
1972.

(3) Subsection (1) above shall not apply to any person who is
a trespasser on the land or who has been permitted to reside in
any house or building on the land pending its demolition.

(4) Subsection (1) above shall not apply to any person to whom
money has been advanced—

(a) under section 41 below ;

(b) under the Small Dwellings Acquisition Acts 1899 to
1923 or section 43 of the Housing (Financial Provisions) 1958 c. 42.
Act 1958 ;

(c) under the Small Dwellings Acquisition (Scotland) Acts
1899 to 1923 or section 49 of the Housing (Financial 1968 c. 31.
Provisions) (Scotland) Act 1968 ; or

(d) by a development corporation or the Commission for
the New Towns otherwise than under section 41 below,

for the purpose of enabling him to obtain accommodation in
substitution for that from which he is displaced as mentioned in
that subsection.

(5) Subsection (1)(a) above shall not apply to any acquisition of
land in relation to which the Secretary of State has before the
passing of this Act decided under paragraph 1 of Schedule 9
to the Housing Act 1957 or paragraph 1 of Schedule 8 to the 1957 c. 56.
Housing (Scotland) Act 1966 that a housing scheme is not 1966 c. 49
necessary.

(6) For the purposes of subsection (1) above a person shall not
be treated as displaced in consequence of any such acquisition
or redevelopment as is mentioned in paragraph (a) or (c) of that

subsection unless he was residing in the accommodation in question—

(*a*) in the case of land acquired under a compulsory purchase order, at the time when notice was first published of the making of the order prior to its submission for confirmation or, where the order did not require confirmation, of the preparation of the order in draft ;

(*b*) in the case of land acquired under an Act specifying the land as subject to compulsory acquisition, at the time when the provisions of the Bill for the Act specifying the land were first published ;

(*c*) in the case of land acquired by agreement, at the time when the agreement was made ;

and a person shall not be treated as displaced in consequence of any such order, resolution or undertaking as is mentioned in paragraph (*b*) of that subsection unless he was residing in the accommodation in question at the time when the order was made, the resolution was passed or the undertaking was accepted.

(7) Subject to subsection (8) below, " the relevant authority " for the purposes of this section is—

(*a*) where the land is in a London borough, the council of that borough or the Greater London Council if they have agreed with that council to discharge the functions of the latter under this section ;

(*b*) where the land is in any other area or district, the local authority having functions in relation to that area under Part V of the Housing Act 1957 or that district under Part VII of the Housing (Scotland) Act 1966.

1957 c. 56.
1966 c. 49.

(8) Where the land is in an area designated as the site of a new town—

(*a*) paragraph (*c*) of subsection (1) above shall apply if the land on which the redevelopment is carried out has been previously acquired by the development corporation and is for the time being held either by that corporation or by the Commission for the New Towns ;

(*b*) if the authority by whom the land is acquired or redeveloped is the development corporation, that corporation shall, in a case falling within paragraph (*a*) or (*c*) of that subsection, be the relevant authority for the purposes of this section ;

(*c*) if the authority by whom the land is redeveloped is the Commission for the New Towns, the Commission shall, in a case falling within paragraph (*c*) of that subsection, be the relevant authority for the purposes of this section.

(9) In this section " a housing order, resolution or under- PART III
taking " and " redevelopment " have the same meaning as in
section 29 above.

40.—(1) Section 39 above shall, so far as applicable, have Duty to
effect in relation to a person residing in a caravan on a caravan rehouse
site who is displaced from that site as it has effect in relation to certain
a person displaced from residential accommodation on any land caravan
but shall so have effect subject to the following modifications. dwellers.

(2) Subsection (1) of the said section 39 shall have effect—

(*a*) as if for the words preceding paragraph (*a*) there were
substituted the words " Where a person residing in a
caravan on a caravan site is displaced from that site in
consequence of " ; and

(*b*) as if for the words following paragraph (*c*) there were
substituted the words " and neither suitable residential
accommodation nor a suitable alternative site for
stationing a caravan is available to that person on
reasonable terms, then, subject to the provisions of
this section, it shall be the duty of the relevant authority to secure that he will be provided with suitable
residential accommodation ".

(3) Subsection (6) of the said section 39 shall have effect as if
in the words preceding paragraph (*a*) for the words " unless he
was residing in the accommodation in question " there were
substituted the words " unless he was residing in a caravan on
the caravan site in question ".

(4) The said section 39 shall have effect as if in any provision
not modified as aforesaid for any reference to land there were
substituted a reference to a caravan site.

(5) In this section " caravan site " has the same meaning as in
section 33 above.

41.—(1) Where a person displaced from a dwelling in conse- Power of
quence of any of the matters mentioned in subsection (1)(*a*), relevant
(*b*) or (*c*) of section 39 above— authority to
make advances
(*a*) is an owner-occupier of the dwelling ; and repayable on

(*b*) wishes to acquire or construct another dwelling in sub- maturity to
stitution for that from which he is displaced, displaced
the relevant authority for the purposes of that section may owner-
advance money to him for the purpose of enabling him to occupiers.
acquire or construct the other dwelling.

(2) The power conferred by this section shall be exercisable
subject to such conditions as may be approved by the Secretary
of State and the following provisions shall apply with respect to
any advance made in the exercise of that power.

(3) The advance shall be made—

    (*a*) on terms providing for the payment of the principal—

        (i) at the end of a fixed period, with or without a provision allowing the authority to extend that period ; or

        (ii) upon notice given by the authority,

    subject, in either case, to a provision for earlier repayment on the happening of a specified event ;

    (*b*) on such other terms as the authority may think fit having regard to all the circumstances.

(4) An advance for the construction of a dwelling may be made by instalments from time to time as the works of construction progress.

(5) The principal of the advance, together with interest thereon, shall be secured by a mortgage of the borrower's interest in the dwelling, and the amount of the principal shall not exceed the value which, in accordance with a valuation duly made on behalf of the relevant authority, it is estimated that the borrower's interest will bear or, as the case may be, will bear when the dwelling has been constructed.

(6) Before advancing money under this section the relevant authority shall satisfy themselves that the dwelling to be acquired is or will be made, or that the dwelling to be constructed will on completion be, in all respects fit for human habitation.

(7) While the payment of the principal of an advance made by a local authority under this section is not required in accordance with the terms of the advance, the local authority may suspend, with respect to so much of any sum borrowed by them as is referable to the advance or with respect to any sum paid in respect of the advance out of their Consolidated Loans Fund, any periodical provision for repayment that may be required by any enactment or by any scheme (whether made under section 55 of the Local Government Act 1958 or under any local enactment) by which the Fund was established.

1958 c. 55.

(8) The power conferred by this section on a relevant authority is without prejudice to any power to advance money exercisable by the authority under any other enactment.

(9) In this section " owner-occupier ", in relation to any dwelling, means a person who occupies it on the date of displacement and either—

    (*a*) occupies it on that date in right of a freehold interest therein or a tenancy thereof granted or extended for a term of years certain of which not less than three years remain unexpired ; or

(*b*) if the displacement is in consequence of the matters PART III
mentioned in paragraph (*c*) of section 39(1) above,
occupied it in right of such an interest or tenancy on
the date on which the land was acquired or appropriated as mentioned in that paragraph.

(10) In this section references to the construction of a dwelling
include references to the acquisition of a building and its conversion into a dwelling and to the conversion into a dwelling
of a building previously acquired.

(11) In the application of this section to Scotland—

(*a*) in subsection (5) for the reference to a mortgage there
shall be substituted a reference to a heritable security ;

(*b*) in subsection (6) for the words from " is or will " to
the end there shall be substituted the words " meets or
will meet the tolerable standard as determined for the
purposes of the Housing (Scotland) Act 1969 by section 1969 c. 34.
2 of that Act " ;

(*c*) in subsection (7) for the words from " or with respect "
to the end there shall be substituted the words " any
periodical provision for repayment that may be
required by any enactment " ;

(*d*) in subsection (9)—

(i) in paragraph (*a*) for the words from " a freehold interest " to " certain " there shall be substituted the words " an owner's interest or a lease ",
and at the end there shall be added the following
words " or by virtue of a tenancy or other interest to
which the Crofters (Scotland) Acts 1955 and 1961 or
the Small Landholders (Scotland) Acts 1886 to 1931
apply ;

(ii) in paragraph (*b*) for the word " tenancy "
there shall be substituted the words " lease or by
virtue of such a tenancy or interest ".

42.—(1) Where a relevant authority within the meaning of Duty of
section 39 above provide or secure the provision of accommoda- displacing
tion for any person in pursuance of subsection (1)(*a*) or (*c*) authority to
of that section, then, if— indemnify
rehousing
or lending
(*a*) the authority providing the accommodation (" the re- authority for
housing authority ") are not the same as the authority net losses.
by whom the land in question is acquired or redeveloped
(" the displacing authority ") ; and

(*b*) the displacing authority are not an authority having
functions under Part V of the Housing Act 1957 or 1957 c. 56.
Part VII of the Housing (Scotland) Act 1966, 1966 c. 49.

the displacing authority shall make to the rehousing authority periodical payments, or if the rehousing authority so require a lump sum payment, by way of indemnity against any net loss in respect of the rehousing authority's provision of that accommodation which may be incurred by that authority in any year during the period of ten years commencing with the year in which the accommodation is first provided.

(2) For the purposes of subsection (1) above a local authority incur a net loss in respect of their provision of accommodation for a person whom they are rehousing—

    (a) if they rehouse him in a dwelling provided by them under Part V of the said Act of 1957, or a house provided by them under Part VII of the said Act of 1966, for the purpose of rehousing him ; or

    (b) if—

        (i) they rehouse him in a Housing Revenue Account dwelling not so provided or (in Scotland) a house to which the housing revenue account relates not so provided, and

        (ii) provide under the said Part V or the said Part VII in the year immediately preceding that in which he first occupies it, or in the period of three years commencing with the year in which he first occupies it, a dwelling or house of a similar type or size.

(3) Where money has been advanced to a person as mentioned in section 39(4) above, then if—

    (a) the authority making the advance (" the lending authority ") are not the same as the displacing authority ; and

    (b) the lending authority incur a net loss in respect of the making of the advance,

the displacing authority shall make to the lending authority a lump sum payment by way of indemnity against that loss.

(4) For the purposes of subsection (3) above, a lending authority incur a net loss in respect of the making of an advance to any person if—

    (a) he does not fully discharge his liability to the authority in respect of principal, interest and costs or expenses in accordance with the terms on which the advance is made ; and

    (b) the deficiency exceeds the net proceeds arising to the authority on a sale of the interest on which the principal and interest is secured.

(5) The Secretary of State may—

    (*a*) for the purposes of subsection (1) above from time to time determine a method to be used generally in calculating net losses incurred by rehousing authorities;

    (*b*) for the purposes of that subsection or subsection (3) above, determine the net loss incurred by a rehousing authority or lending authority in any particular case;

    (*c*) give directions as to the manner in which any payment under this section is to be made.

(6) Subsection (2) above shall be construed as one with the Housing Finance Act 1972 or, in relation to Scotland, the Housing (Financial Provisions) (Scotland) Act 1972.

1972 c. 47.
1972 c. 46.

43.—(1) Where a person displaced from a dwelling in consequence of any such acquisition as is mentioned in section 39(1)(*a*) above—

Power of relevant authority to defray expenses in connection with acquisition of new dwellings.

    (*a*) has no interest in the dwelling or no greater interest therein than as tenant for a year or from year to year; and

    (*b*) wishes to acquire another dwelling in substitution for that from which he is displaced,

the acquiring authority may pay any reasonable expenses incurred by him in connection with the acquisition, other than the purchase price.

(2) No payment shall be made under this section in respect of expenses incurred by any person in connection with the acquisition of a dwelling unless the dwelling is acquired not later than one year after the displacement and is reasonably comparable with that from which he is displaced.

(3) For the purposes of subsection (2) above a dwelling acquired pursuant to a contract shall be treated as acquired when the contract is made.

(4) Subsections (3) and (6) of section 39 above shall have effect in relation to subsection (1) above and to subsection (1)(*a*) of that section as applied thereby.

PART IV

COMPULSORY PURCHASE

Assessment of compensation

44.—(1) Where land is acquired or taken from any person for the purpose of works which are to be situated partly on that land and partly elsewhere, compensation for injurious affection of land retained by that person shall be assessed by reference to the whole of the works and not only the part situated on the land acquired or taken from him.

Compensation for injurious affection.

(2) In this section "compensation for injurious affection" means compensation for injurious affection under section 63 or
121 of the Lands Clauses Consolidation Act 1845 or section 7 or 20 of the Compulsory Purchase Act 1965, and subsection (1) above shall apply with the necessary modifications to such compensation under the said section 7 as substituted by paragraph 7 of Schedule 6 to the Highways Act 1971, paragraph 13 of Schedule 2 to the Gas Act 1972 (compulsory acquisition of rights over land) or any corresponding enactment, including (except where otherwise provided) an enactment passed after this Act.

(3) In this section "compensation for injurious affection", in relation to Scotland, means compensation for injurious affection
under section 61 or 114 of the Lands Clauses Consolidation (Scotland) Act 1845, and subsection (1) above shall apply with the necessary modifications to such compensation under the said section 61 as substituted by paragraph 26 of Schedule 2 to the Gas Act 1972 (compulsory acquisition of rights over land) or any corresponding enactment extending to Scotland, including (except where otherwise provided) an enactment passed after this Act.

Compensation
for acquisition
of dwelling
specially
adapted for
disabled
person.
45.—(1) This section applies to the assessment of compensation in respect of the compulsory acquisition of an interest in a dwelling which—

   (a) has been constructed or substantially modified to meet the special needs of a disabled person ; and

   (b) is occupied by such a person as his residence immediately before the date when the acquiring authority take possession of the dwelling or was last so occupied before that date.

(2) The compensation shall, if the person whose interest is acquired so elects, be assessed as if the dwelling were land which is devoted to a purpose of such a nature that there is no general demand or market for land for that purpose.

Compensation
for
disturbance
where
business
carried on
by person
over sixty.
46.—(1) Where a person is carrying on a trade or business on any land and, in consequence of the compulsory acquisition of the whole of that land, is required to give up possession thereof to the acquiring authority, then if—

   (a) on the date on which he gives up possession as aforesaid he has attained the age of sixty ; and

   (b) on that date the land is or forms part of a hereditament the annual value of which does not exceed the prescribed amount ; and

(c) that person has not disposed of the goodwill of the
whole of the trade or business and gives to the acquiring authority the undertakings mentioned in subsection
(3) below,

the compensation payable to that person in respect of the
compulsory acquisition of his interest in the land or, as the
case may be, under section 121 of the Lands Clauses Consolida- 1845 c. 18.
tion Act 1845 or section 20 of the Compulsory Purchase Act 1965 c. 56.
1965 (tenants from year to year etc.) shall, so far as attributable
to disturbance, be assessed on the assumption that it is not
reasonably practicable for that person to carry on the trade or
business or, as the case may be, the part thereof the goodwill of
which he has retained, elsewhere than on that land.

(2) In subsection (1) above " the prescribed amount " means
the amount which on the date mentioned in that subsection
is the amount prescribed for the purposes of section 192(4)(a)
of the Town and Country Planning Act 1971 (interests qualifying 1971 c. 78
for protection under planning blight provisions) and " annual
value " and " hereditament " have the meanings given in section
207 of that Act taking references to the date of service of a
notice under section 193 of that Act as references to the date
mentioned in subsection (1) above.

(3) The undertakings to be given by the person claiming compensation are—

(a) an undertaking that he will not dispose of the goodwill
of the trade or business, or, as the case may be, of the
part thereof the goodwill of which he has retained ; and

(b) an undertaking that he will not, within such area and for
such time as the acquiring authority may require,
directly or indirectly engage in or have any interest in
any other trade or business of the same or substantially the same kind as that carried on by him on the
land acquired.

(4) If an undertaking given by a person for the purposes of this
section is broken the acquiring authority may recover from him
an amount equal to the difference between the compensation paid
and the compensation that would have been payable if it had
been assessed without regard to the provisions of this section.

(5) This section shall apply to a trade or business carried on by
two or more persons in partnership as if references to the person
by whom it is carried on were references to all the partners and
as if the undertakings mentioned in subsection (3) above were
required to be given by all the partners.

(6) This section shall apply to a trade or business carried on by a company—

    (*a*) as if subsection (1)(*a*) above required—

        (i) each shareholder, other than a minority shareholder, to be an individual who has attained the age of sixty on the date there mentioned ; and

        (ii) each minority shareholder to be an individual who either has attained that age on that date or is the spouse of a shareholder who has attained that age on that date ; and

    (*b*) as if the undertakings mentioned in subsection (3)(*b*) above were required to be given both by the company and by each shareholder.

In this subsection " shareholder " means a person who is beneficially entitled to a share or shares in the company carrying voting rights and " minority shareholder " means a person who is so entitled to less than 50 per cent. of those shares.

(7) This section shall apply in relation to any disturbance payment assessed in accordance with section 38(1)(*b*) above as it applies in relation to the compensation mentioned in subsection (1) above, and shall so apply subject to the necessary modifications and as if references to the giving up of possession of land to the acquiring authority in consequence of its compulsory acquisition were references to displacement as mentioned in section 37 above.

(8) In the application of this section to Scotland for the reference to the sections mentioned in subsection (1) above there shall be substituted a reference to section 114 of the Lands Clauses Consolidation (Scotland) Act 1845 and for the references to sections 192(4)(*a*), 193 and 207 of the Town and Country Planning Act 1971 there shall be substituted respectively references to sections 181(4)(*a*), 182 and 196 of the Town and Country Planning (Scotland) Act 1972.

1845 c. 19.

1971 c. 78.

1972 c. 52.

Compensation in respect of land subject to business tenancy.

1954 c. 56.

47.—(1) Where in pursuance of any enactment providing for the acquisition or taking of possession of land compulsorily an acquiring authority—

    (*a*) acquire the interest of the landlord in any land subject to a tenancy to which Part II of the Landlord and Tenant Act 1954 (security of tenure for business tenants) applies ; or

    (*b*) acquire the interest of the tenant in, or take possession of, any such land,

the right of the tenant to apply under the said Part II for the grant of a new tenancy shall be taken into account in assessing

the compensation payable by the acquiring authority (whether to
the landlord or the tenant) in connection with the acquisition of
the interest or the taking of possession of the land ; and in
assessing that compensation it shall be assumed that neither the
acquiring authority nor any other authority possessing compulsory purchase powers have acquired or propose to acquire
any interest in the land.

(2) Subsection (1) of section 39 of the said Act of 1954 (right
of tenant to apply under the said Part II for a new tenancy to be
disregarded in assessing compensation for compulsory taking of
possession of land subject to short tenancy) shall cease to have
effect.

(3) In subsection (2) of the said section 39 for the words
" the compensation assessed in accordance with the last foregoing subsection " there shall be substituted the words " the
compensation payable under section 121 of the Lands Clauses 1845 c. 19.
Consolidation Act 1845 or section 20 of the Compulsory Pur- 1965 c. 56.
chase Act 1965 in the case of a tenancy to which this Part of
this Act applies ".

48.—(1) This section has effect where in pursuance of any Compensation
enactment providing for the acquisition or taking of possession in respect of
of land compulsorily an acquiring authority—   agricultural
                                                                  holdings.
(a) acquire the interest of the landlord in an agricultural
     holding or any part of it ; or

(b) acquire the interest of the tenant in, or take possession
     of, an agricultural holding or any part of it.

(2) In assessing the compensation payable by the acquiring
authority to the landlord in connection with any such acquisition
of an interest as is mentioned in subsection (1)(a) above—

(a) there shall be disregarded any right of the landlord to
     serve a notice to quit, and any notice to quit already
     served by the landlord, which would not be or would
     not have been effective if—

(i) in section 24(2)(b) of the Agricultural Holdings 1948 c. 63.
Act 1948 (land required for non-agricultural use for
which planning permission has been granted etc.) the
reference to the land being required did not include
a reference to its being required by an acquiring
authority ; and

(ii) in section 25(1)(e) of that Act (proposed termination of tenancy for purpose of land's being used
for non-agricultural use not falling within section
24(2)(b)) the reference to the land's being used did
not include a reference to its being used by an
acquiring authority ; and

(*b*) if the tenant has quitted the holding or any part of it by reason of a notice to quit which is to be so disregarded, it shall be assumed that he has not done so.

(3) In assessing the compensation payable by the acquiring authority to the tenant in connection with any such acquisition of an interest or taking of possession of land as is mentioned in subsection (1)(*b*) above (hereafter referred to as " the tenant's compensation "), there shall be disregarded any right of the landlord to serve a notice to quit, and any notice to quit already served by the landlord, which would not be or would not have been effective if the said sections 24(2)(*b*) and 25(1)(*e*) were construed in accordance with subsection (2)(*a*)(i) and (ii) above.

1968 c. 34.   (4) Section 42 of the Agriculture (Miscellaneous Provisions) Act 1968 (tenant's compensation to be assessed without regard to his prospects of remaining in possession after contractual date) and section 15(1) of that Act (effect on tenant's compensation of provision enabling landlord to resume possession for non-agricultural use) shall cease to have effect.

(5) The tenant's compensation shall be reduced by an amount equal to any payment which the acquiring authority are liable to make to him, in respect of the acquisition or taking of possession in question, under section 12 of the said Act of 1968 (additional payments by acquiring authority in circumstances described in subsection (1)(*b*) above).

(6) If the tenant's compensation as determined in accordance with subsections (3) to (5) above is less than it would have been if those subsections had not been enacted, it shall be increased by the amount of the deficiency.

(7) In the application of this section to Scotland—

    (*a*) in subsections (2) and (3), for the references to sections 24(2)(*b*) and 25(1)(*e*) of the Agricultural Holdings Act 1948 there shall be substituted respectively references to

1949 c. 75.   sections 25(2)(*c*) and 26(1)(*e*) of the Agricultural Holdings (Scotland) Act 1949 ;

    (*b*) after subsection (2)(*a*) there shall be inserted the following—

        " (*aa*) there shall be disregarded any entitlement of the landlord to resume land comprised in the holding by virtue of a stipulation in the lease, and any notice already given in pursuance of such a stipulation which would not be or would not have been effective if the stipulation were construed as not including authority to resume the land for the purpose of its being required by the acquiring authority ; and "

(c) at the end of subsection (2)(*b*) there shall be inserted the PART IV following—

"and

(c) if land comprised in the holding has been resumed by reason of such an entitlement or notice which is to be so disregarded that land shall be assumed not to have been so resumed.";

(*d*) in subsection (3), after the word "disregarded" there shall be inserted the word "(*a*)", and at the end there shall be added the words—

"and

(*b*) any entitlement of the landlord to resume land comprised in the holding by virtue of a stipulation in the lease, and any notice already given in pursuance of such a stipulation which would not be or would not have been effective if the stipulation were construed in accordance with subsection (2)(*aa*) above.";

(*e*) after subsection (6) there shall be inserted the following subsection—

"(6A) This section shall not apply to an agricultural holding which is a croft or the holding of a landholder or a statutory small tenant.".

49.—(1) This section has effect where in pursuance of any Compensation in respect of crofts, etc. enactment providing for the acquisition or taking of possession of land compulsorily an acquiring authority—

(*a*) acquire the interest of the landlord in an agricultural holding which is a croft; or

(*b*) take possession of a croft.

(2) In assessing the compensation payable by the acquiring authority to the landlord of a croft in connection with any such acquisition of an interest as is mentioned in subsection (1)(*a*) above—

(*a*) there shall be disregarded any right of the landlord to apply to the Scottish Land Court under section 12 of the Crofters (Scotland) Act 1955 for authority to resume 1955 c. 21. the croft and any such authority already granted which would not be or would not have been effective if in that section the reference to resuming the croft did not include a reference to its being resumed for the purpose of its being required by the acquiring authority; and

(*b*) if the crofter has surrendered his croft under the said section 12 by reason of an authority which is to be so disregarded it shall be assumed that he has not done so.

M

PART IV

(3) In assessing the compensation payable by the acquiring authority to the crofter in connection with any such taking of possession of a croft as is mentioned in subsection (1)(*b*) above, there shall be disregarded any right of the landlord to apply to the Scottish Land Court under the said section 12 for authority to resume the croft or any such authority already granted which would not be or would not have been effective if the said section 12 were construed in accordance with subsection (2)(*a*) above.

(4) If the compensation payable to the crofter as determined in accordance with subsection (3) above is less than it would have been if that subsection had not been enacted, it shall be increased by the amount of the deficiency.

(5) This section shall apply to part of a croft as it applies to an entire croft.

(6) This section shall apply to the holding or part of the holding of a landholder as it applies to a croft or part of a croft except that for any reference to a croft, crofter or section 12 of the Crofters (Scotland) Act 1955 there shall be substituted respectively a reference to a holding, landholder or section 2 of the Crofters Holdings (Scotland) Act 1886.

1955 c. 21.

1886 c. 29.

(7) This section shall apply to the holding or part of the holding of a statutory small tenant as it applies to a croft or part of a croft except that—

(*a*) for any reference to a croft, crofter or section 12 of the Crofters (Scotland) Act 1955 there shall be substituted respectively a reference to a holding, statutory small tenant or section 32(15) of the Small Landholders (Scotland) Act 1911;

1911 c. 49.

(*b*) in subsection (2)(*b*), for the words " crofter has surrendered his croft under the said section 12 " there shall be substituted the words " landlord has resumed the holding under the said section 32(15) ";

(*c*) after subsection (3) there shall be inserted the following subsection—

" (3A) The compensation payable to the statutory small tenant shall be reduced by an amount equal to any payment which the acquiring authority are liable to make to him, in respect of the taking of possession in question, under section 12 of the Agriculture (Miscellaneous Provisions) Act 1968 (additional payments by acquiring authority in circumstances described in subsection (1)(*b*) above).";

1968 c. 34.

(*d*) in subsection (4), for the words " subsection (3) " there shall be substituted the words " subsections (3) and (3A) ".

50.—(1) The amount of compensation payable in respect of the compulsory acquisition of an interest in land shall not be subject to any reduction on account of the fact that the acquiring authority have provided, or undertake to provide or arrange for the provision of, or another authority will provide, residential accommodation under any enactment for the person entitled to the compensation.

(2) In assessing the compensation payable in respect of the compulsory acquisition of an interest in land which on the date of service of the notice to treat is subject to a tenancy, there shall be left out of account any part of the value of that interest which is attributable to, or to the prospect of, the tenant giving up possession after that date in consequence of being provided with other accommodation by virtue of section 39(1)(*a*) above ; and for the purpose of determining the date by reference to which that compensation is to be assessed the acquiring authority shall be deemed, where the tenant gives up possession as aforesaid, to have taken possession on the date on which it is given up by the tenant.

(3) Subsection (1) above shall apply in relation to any payment to which a person is entitled under Part III of this Act as it applies in relation to the compensation mentioned in that subsection taking references to the acquiring authority as references to the authority responsible for making that payment.

(4) Subsection (2) above shall apply in relation to a case where a notice to treat is deemed to have been served by virtue of Schedule 3 to the Town and Country Planning Act 1968 or 1968 c. 72. Schedule 24 to the Town and Country Planning (Scotland) Act 1972 c. 52. 1972 (general vesting declarations) as it applies in relation to a case where a notice to treat is actually served.

51.—(1) Where the Secretary of State proposes to make an order under section 1 of the New Towns Act 1965 designating any area as—

(*a*) the site of a new town ; or

(*b*) an extension of the site of a new town,
and the purpose or main purpose, or one of the main purposes, for which the order is proposed to be made is the provision of housing or other facilities required in connection with or in consequence of the carrying out of any public development, he may, before making the order, give a direction specifying that development for the purposes of this section in relation to that area.

(2) Where the area mentioned in paragraph 3 or 3A in the first column of Schedule 1 to the Land Compensation Act 1961 1961 c. 33. (cases where land acquired forms part of site of new town or

extension of site of new town) is an area to which a direction under this section relates, then, in the circumstances described in that paragraph—

> (*a*) the increase or diminution in value to be left out of account by virtue of section 6 of that Act (compensation to be assessed without regard to development attributable to designation of new town) or any rule of law relating to the assessment of compensation in respect of compulsory acquisition ; and
>
> (*b*) the increase in value to be taken into account by virtue of section 7 of that Act (reduction of compensation where other land benefited by such development),

shall respectively include any increase or diminution in value, and any increase in value, which is attributable to the carrying out or the prospect of the public development specified in the direction.

(3) No direction shall be given under this section in relation to any area until the Secretary of State has prepared a draft of the order under section 1 of the said Act of 1965 in respect of that area and has published the notice required by paragraph 2 of Schedule 1 to that Act.

(4) Any direction under this section shall be given by order ; and any order containing such a direction may be varied or revoked by a subsequent order.

(5) The power to make orders under this section shall be exercisable by statutory instrument subject to annulment in pursuance of a resolution of either House of Parliament.

(6) In this section " public development " means development (whether or not in the area designated under section 1 of the said Act of 1965) in the exercise of statutory powers by—

> (*a*) a government department ;
>
> (*b*) any statutory undertakers within the meaning of the
1971 c. 78. Town and Country Planning Act 1971 or any body deemed by virtue of any enactment to be statutory undertakers for the purposes of, or of any provision of, that Act ; or
>
> (*c*) without prejudice to paragraph (*b*) above, any body having power to borrow money with the consent of a Minister,

and includes such development which has already been carried out when the direction in respect of it is given as well as such development which is then proposed.

(7) In the application of this section to Scotland—

> 1965 c. 59. (*a*) for any reference to section 1 of the New Towns Act 1965 and for the reference in subsection (3) to paragraph 2 of Schedule 1 to that Act there shall be substituted respectively a reference to section 1 of the

New Towns (Scotland) Act 1968 and to paragraph 2   PART IV
of Schedule 1 to that Act;   1968 c. 16.

(*b*) in subsection (2), for the references to sections 6 and 7
of the Land Compensation Act 1961 and to paragraphs 1961 c. 33.
3 and 3A in the first column of Schedule 1 to that Act
there shall be substituted respectively references to
sections 13 and 14 of the Land Compensation 1963 c. 51.
(Scotland) Act 1963 and to paragraphs 3 and 3A in the
first column of Schedule 1 to that Act;

(*c*) in subsection (6)(*b*), for the reference to the Town and 1971 c. 78.
Country Planning Act 1971 there shall be substituted
a reference to the Town and Country Planning 1972 c. 52.
(Scotland) Act 1972.

Advance payment of compensation

52.—(1) Where an acquiring authority have taken possession Right to
of any land the authority shall, if a request in that behalf is made advance
in accordance with subsection (2) below, make an advance pay- payment of
ment on account of any compensation payable by them for the compensation.
compulsory acquisition of any interest in that land.

(2) Any request under this section shall be made by the person
entitled to the compensation (hereafter referred to as " the
claimant "), shall be in writing, shall give particulars of the
claimant's interest in the land (so far as not already given
pursuant to a notice to treat) and shall be accompanied or
supplemented by such other particulars as the acquiring authority
may reasonably require to enable them to estimate the amount
of the compensation in respect of which the advance payment
is to be made.

(3) Subject to subsection (6) below, the amount of any advance
payment under this section shall be equal to 90 per cent. of the
following amount, that is to say—

(*a*) if the acquiring authority and the claimant have agreed
on the amount of the compensation, the agreed
amount;

(*b*) in any other case, an amount equal to the compensation as estimated by the acquiring authority.

(4) Any advance payment under this section shall be made
not later than three months after the date on which a request
for the payment is made in accordance with subsection (2) above
or, if those three months end before the date on which the
acquiring authority take possession of the land to which the
compensation relates, on the date on which they take possession
as aforesaid.

M 3

(5) Where an advance payment is made on the basis of an estimate under subsection (3)(*b*) above and the amount of that payment exceeds the compensation as finally determined or agreed, the excess shall be repaid ; and if after an advance payment has been made to any person it is discovered that he was not entitled to it the amount of the payment shall be recoverable by the acquiring authority.

(6) No advance payment shall be made on account of compensation payable in respect of any land which is subject to a mortgage the principal of which exceeds 90 per cent. of the amount mentioned in subsection (3) above ; and where the land is subject to a mortgage the principal of which does not exceed 90 per cent. of that amount, the advance payment shall be reduced by such sum as the acquiring authority consider will be required by them for securing the release of the interest of the mortgagee.

(7) Any advance payment on account of compensation in respect of an interest which is settled land for the purposes of the Settled Land Act 1925 shall be made to the persons entitled to give a discharge for capital money and shall be treated as capital money arising under that Act.

(8) Where an acquiring authority make an advance payment under this section on account of compensation in respect of any interest in land they shall deposit with the council of the district or London borough in which the land is situated particulars of the payment, the compensation and the interest in land to which it relates ; and any particulars so deposited shall be registered by the proper officer of the council in the register of local land charges in such manner as may be prescribed by rules made for the purposes of this subsection under section 19 of the Land Charges Act 1925.

(9) Where after particulars of the advance payment made to any claimant have been registered as aforesaid the claimant disposes of the interest in the land to, or creates an interest in the land in favour of, a person other than the acquiring authority, the amount of the advance payment shall be set off against any sum payable by the authority to that other person in respect of the compulsory acquisition of the interest disposed of or the compulsory acquisition or release of the interest created.

(10) Where an advance payment has been made under this section on account of any compensation—

(*a*) section 76 of the Lands Clauses Consolidation Act 1845 and section 9 of the Compulsory Purchase Act 1965 (refusal of owner to convey on tender of compensation) shall have effect as if references to the compensation were references to the balance thereof remaining unpaid ; and (*b*) neither section 11(1) of the said Act of 1965 nor any bond under Schedule 3 to that Act or under section 85 of the said Act of 1845 (interest on compensation where possession is taken before payment) shall require the acquiring authority to pay interest, in respect of any time after the date of the advance payment, on so much of the compensation as corresponds to that payment.

(11) Where the acquiring authority, instead of taking possession of any land, serve a notice in respect of that land under section 98 of the Housing Act 1957 or under paragraph 3 of Schedule 1 or paragraph 10 of Schedule 3 to that Act (notice authorising existing occupier to continue in occupation where house acquired for housing purposes) this section shall have effect as if they had taken possession of the land on the date on which the notice is served.   1957 c. 56

(12) This section shall apply to compensation for the compulsory acquisition of a right over land as it applies to compensation for the compulsory acquisition of an interest in land, and shall so apply with the necessary modifications and as if references to taking possession of the land were references to first entering it for the purpose of exercising the right.

(13) In the application of this section to Scotland—

(*a*) in subsection (6) for any reference to a mortgage or mortgagee there shall be substituted respectively a reference to a heritable security or a heritable creditor ;

(*b*) subsections (7) and (11) shall be omitted ;

(*c*) for subsection (8) there shall be substituted the following subsection—

"(8) Where an acquiring authority make an advance payment under this section on account of compensation in respect of any interest in land, the authority shall cause notice of that fact, specifying particulars of the payment, the compensation and the interest in land to which it relates, to be recorded in the Register of Sasines and shall send a copy of the notice to the local planning authority." ;

(*d*) in paragraph (*a*) of subsection (10) for the words from the beginning to " 1965 " there shall be substituted the words " section 75 of the Lands Clauses Consolidation (Scotland) Act 1845 " and in paragraph (*b*) of that subsection for the words from the beginning to " section 85 " there shall be substituted the words " no bond under section 84 " ;   1845 c. 19.

(*e*) in subsection (12) after the words " a right " there shall be inserted the words " in or ".

PART IV
Notice to
treat in
respect of
part of
agricultural
land.

Severance of land

53.—(1) Where an acquiring authority serve notice to treat in respect of any agricultural land on a person (whether in occupation or not) having a greater interest in the land than as tenant for a year or from year to year, and that person has such an interest in other agricultural land comprised in the same agricultural unit as that to which the notice relates, the person on whom the notice is served (hereafter referred to as " the claimant ") may, within the period of two months beginning with the date of service of the notice to treat, serve on the acquiring authority a counter-notice—

(a) claiming that the other land is not reasonably capable of being farmed, either by itself or in conjunction with other relevant land, as a separate agricultural unit; and

(b) requiring the acquiring authority to purchase his interest in the whole of the other land.

(2) Where a counter-notice is served under subsection (1) above the claimant shall also, within the period mentioned in that subsection, serve a copy thereof on any other person who has an interest in the land to which the requirement in the counter-notice relates, but failure to comply with this subsection shall not invalidate the counter-notice.

(3) Subject to subsection (4) below, " other relevant land " in subsection (1) above means—

(a) land comprised in the same agricultural unit as the land to which the notice to treat relates, being land in which the claimant does not have such an interest as is mentioned in that subsection; and

(b) land comprised in any other agricultural unit occupied by him on the date of service of the notice to treat, being land in respect of which he is then entitled to a greater interest than as tenant for a year or from year to year.

(4) Where an acquiring authority have served a notice to treat in respect of any of the other agricultural land mentioned in subsection (1) above or in respect of other relevant land as defined in subsection (3) above, then, unless and until that notice to treat is withdrawn, this section and section 54 below shall have effect as if that land did not form part of that other agricultural land or did not constitute other relevant land, as the case may be.

(5) This section shall have effect in relation to a case where a notice to treat is deemed to have been served by virtue of any of the provisions of sections 180 to 189 of the Town and Country Planning Act 1971 or sections 169 to 177 of the Town

and Country Planning (Scotland) Act 1972 (purchase notices)   PART IV
or Schedule 3 to the Town and Country Planning Act 1968 or 1968 c. 72.
Schedule 24 to the said Act of 1972 (general vesting declarations)
as it has effect in relation to a case where a notice to treat is
actually served, and section 54 below shall have effect
accordingly.

(6) This section is without prejudice to the rights conferred by
sections 93 and 94 of the Lands Clauses Consolidation Act 1845, 1845 c. 18.
sections 91 and 92 of the Lands Clauses Consolidation (Scotland) 1845 c. 19.
Act 1845 or section 8(2) and (3) of the Compulsory Purchase 1965 c. 56.
Act 1965 (provisions as to divided land).

54.—(1) If the acquiring authority do not within the period Effect of
of two months beginning with the date of service of a counter- counter-notice
notice under section 53 above agree in writing to accept the under
counter-notice as valid, the claimant or the authority may, section 53.
within two months after the end of that period, refer it to the
Lands Tribunal; and on any such reference the Tribunal shall
determine whether the claim in the counter-notice is justified and
declare the counter-notice valid or invalid in accordance with
its determination of that question.

(2) Where a counter-notice is accepted as, or declared to be,
valid under subsection (1) above the acquiring authority shall
be deemed—

  (*a*) to be authorised to acquire compulsorily, under the
       enactment by virtue of which they are empowered to
       acquire the land in respect of which the notice to
       treat was served, the claimant's interest in the
       land to which the requirement in the counter-notice
       relates; and

  (*b*) to have served a notice to treat in respect of that land
       on the date on which the first-mentioned notice to treat
       was served.

(3) A claimant may withdraw a counter-notice at any time
before the compensation payable in respect of a compulsory
acquisition in pursuance of the counter-notice has been determined by the Lands Tribunal or at any time before the end of
six weeks beginning with the date on which the compensation
is so determined; and where a counter-notice is withdrawn by
virtue of this subsection any notice to treat deemed to have been
served in consequence thereof shall be deemed to have been
withdrawn.

(4) Without prejudice to subsection (3) above, the power conferred by section 31 of the Land Compensation Act 1961 to 1961 c. 53.
withdraw a notice to treat shall not be exerciseable in the case
of a notice to treat which is deemed to have been served by
virtue of this section.

(5) The compensation payable in respect of the acquisition of an interest in land in pursuance of a notice to treat deemed to have been served by virtue of this section shall be assessed on the assumptions mentioned in section 5(2), (3) and (4) above.

(6) Where by virtue of this section the acquiring authority become, or will become, entitled to a lease of any land but not to the interest of the lessor—

(a) the authority shall offer to surrender the lease to the lessor on such terms as the authority consider reasonable ;

(b) the question of what terms are reasonable may be referred to the Lands Tribunal by the authority or the lessor and, if at the expiration of three months after the date of the offer mentioned in paragraph (a) above, the authority and the lessor have not agreed on that question and that question has not been referred to the Tribunal by the lessor, it shall be so referred by the authority ;

(c) if that question is referred to the Tribunal, the lessor shall be deemed to have accepted the surrender of the lease at the expiration of one month after the date of the determination of the Tribunal or on such other date as the Tribunal may direct and to have agreed with the authority on the terms of surrender which the Tribunal has held to be reasonable.

For the purposes of this subsection any terms as to surrender contained in the lease shall be disregarded.

(7) Where the lessor refuses to accept any sum payable to him by virtue of subsection (6) above, or refuses or fails to make out his title to the satisfaction of the acquiring authority, they may pay into court any sum payable to the lessor by virtue of that subsection ; and subsections (2) and (5) of section 9 of the Compulsory Purchase Act 1965 (deposit of compensation in cases of refusal to convey etc.) shall apply to that sum with the necessary modifications.

1965 c. 56.

(8) Where an acquiring authority who become entitled to the lease of any land as mentioned in subsection (6) above are a body incorporated by or under any enactment the corporate powers of the authority shall, if they would not otherwise do so, include power to farm that land.

(9) In the application of this section to Scotland—

(a) for any reference to the Lands Tribunal there shall be substituted a reference to the Lands Tribunal for Scotland ;

(b) in subsection (4), for the words " section 31 of the Land
Compensation Act 1961 " there shall be substituted
the words " section 39 of the Land Compensation
(Scotland) Act 1963 " ;

(c) in subsection (6), in paragraph (*a*), for the word " surrender " there shall be substituted the word
" renounce ", and in paragraph (c) for the word " surrender " there shall be substituted the word
" renunciation " ;

(d) in subsection (7), for the word " court " and for the
words from " subsections (2) " to the end there shall be
substituted respectively the words " the Bank within the
meaning of section 3 of the Lands Clauses Consolidation (Scotland) Act 1845 " and the words " the
following provisions of the said Act of 1845 shall
apply to that sum with the necessary modifications—

    (i) section 75 so far as it relates to the opening of
an account,

    (ii) section 76 so far as it relates to the giving of
a receipt,

    (iii) section 77,

    (iv) section 79 ".

55.—(1) Where an acquiring authority serve notice of entry Notice of
under section 11(1) of the Compulsory Purchase Act 1965 on the entry in
person in occupation of an agricultural holding, being a person respect of
having no greater interest therein than as tenant for a year agricultural
or from year to year, and the notice relates to part only of that holding.
holding, the person on whom the notice is served (hereafter 1965 c. 56.
referred to as " the claimant ") may, within the period of two
months beginning with the date of service of the notice of entry,
serve on the acquiring authority a counter-notice—

(a) claiming that the remainder of the holding is not
reasonably capable of being farmed, either by itself or
in conjunction with other relevant land, as a separate
agricultural unit ; and

(b) electing to treat the notice of entry as a notice relating
to the entire holding.

(2) Where a counter-notice is served under subsection (1)
above the claimant shall also, within the period mentioned in
that subsection, serve a copy thereof on the landlord of the
holding, but failure to comply with this subsection shall not
invalidate the counter-notice.

(3) Subject to subsection (4) below, " other relevant land "
in subsection (1) above means—

(a) land comprised in the same agricultural unit as the agricultural holding ; and

(*b*) land comprised in any other agricultural unit occupied by the claimant on the date of service of the notice of entry, being land in respect of which he is then entitled to a greater interest than as tenant for a year or from year to year.

(4) Where an acquiring authority have served a notice to treat in respect of land in the agricultural holding other than that to which the notice of entry relates or in respect of other relevant land as defined in subsection (3) above, then, unless and until that notice to treat is withdrawn, this section and section 56 below shall have effect as if that land did not form part of the holding or did not constitute other relevant land, as the case may be.

(5) In the application of this section to Scotland, in subsection (1) for the words " section 11(1) of the Compulsory Purchase Act 1965 " there shall be substituted the words " paragraph 3 of Schedule 2 to the Acquisition of Land (Authorisation Procedure) (Scotland) Act 1947 or paragraph 8 of Schedule 24 to the Town and Country Planning (Scotland) Act 1972 ".

1947 c. 42.

1972 c. 52.

Effect of counter-notice under section 55.

56.—(1) If the acquiring authority do not within the period of two months beginning with the date of service of a counter-notice under section 55 above agree in writing to accept the counter-notice as valid, the claimant or the authority may, within two months after the end of that period, refer it to the Lands Tribunal ; and on any such reference the Tribunal shall determine whether the claim in the counter-notice is justified and declare the counter-notice valid or invalid in accordance with its determination of that question.

(2) Where a counter-notice is accepted as, or declared to be, valid under subsection (1) above then, if before the end of twelve months after it has been so accepted or declared the claimant has given up possession of every part of the agricultural holding to the acquiring authority—

(*a*) the notice of entry shall be deemed to have extended to the part of the holding to which it did not relate ; and

(*b*) the acquiring authority shall be deemed to have taken possession of that part in pursuance of that notice on the day before the expiration of the year of the tenancy which is current when the counter-notice is so accepted or declared.

(3) Where the claimant gives up possession of an agricultural holding to the acquiring authority as aforesaid but the authority have not been authorised to acquire the landlord's interest in, or in any of, the part of the holding to which the

notice of entry did not relate ("the land not subject to compulsory purchase ")—

(a) neither the claimant nor the authority shall be under
any liability to the landlord by reason of the claimant
giving up possession of the land not subject to compulsory purchase or the authority taking or being in
possession of it ;

(b) immediately after the date on which the authority take
possession of the land not subject to compulsory purchase they shall give up to the landlord, and he shall
take, possession of that land ;

(c) the tenancy shall be treated as terminated on the date
on which the claimant gives up possession of the
holding to the acquiring authority or (if he gives up
possession of different parts at different times) gives
up possession as aforesaid of the last part, but without prejudice to any rights or liabilities of the landlord
or the claimant which have accrued before that date ;

(d) any rights of the claimant against, or liabilities of the
claimant to, the landlord which arise on or out of the
termination of the tenancy by virtue of paragraph (c)
above (whether under the contract of tenancy, under
the Agricultural Holdings Act 1948 or otherwise) shall 1948 c. 63.
be rights and liabilities of the authority, and any question as to the payment to be made in respect of any
such right or liability shall be referred to and determined by the Lands Tribunal ;

(e) any increase in the value of the land not subject to
compulsory purchase which is attributable to the landlord's taking possession of it under paragraph (b) above
shall be deducted from the compensation payable in
respect of the acquisition of his interest in the remainder
of the holding.

(4) Where a tenancy is terminated by virtue of subsection
(3)(c) above, section 58 of the Agricultural Holdings Act 1948
(landlord's right to compensation for deterioration of holding)
shall have effect as if the proviso required the landlord's notice
of intention to claim compensation to be served on the acquiring
authority and to be so served within three months after the
termination of the tenancy.

(5) In the application of this section to Scotland—

(a) for any reference to the Lands Tribunal there shall be
substituted a reference to the Lands Tribunal for Scotland ;

(b) in subsection (3)(d) for the words from "contract" to
"1948" there shall be substituted the words "lease,

the Agricultural Holdings (Scotland) Act 1949, the Crofters (Scotland) Acts 1955 and 1961, the Small Landholders (Scotland) Acts 1886 to 1931 " ;

(c) in subsection (4), for the reference to section 58 of the Agricultural Holdings Act 1948 there shall be substituted a reference to section 59(1) of the Agricultural Holdings (Scotland) Act 1949 and for the word " proviso " there shall be substituted the words " said section 59(1) ".

Other
procedures
for taking
possession
of part of
agricultural
holding.
1845 c. 18.
1965 c. 56.
1968 c. 72.

57.—(1) Before taking possession of part only of an agricultural holding under section 85 of the Lands Clauses Consolidation Act 1845, under Schedule 3 to the Compulsory Purchase Act 1965 or under Schedule 3 to the Town and Country Planning Act 1968 (alternative procedures for taking possession of land) the acquiring authority shall serve notice of their intention to do so on the person in occupation of the holding, and sections 55 and 56 above shall have effect, subject to any necessary modifications, as if possession were being obtained pursuant to a notice of entry under section 11(1) of the said Act of 1965.

(2) Sections 55 and 56 above shall have effect, subject to any necessary modifications, in relation to a notice of entry under paragraph 4 of Schedule 6 to the New Towns Act 1965 (provisions applicable to compulsory acquisitions under that Act) as they have effect in relation to a notice of entry under section 11(1) of the said Act of 1965.

(3) Sections 55 and 56(1) and (2) above shall have effect, subject to any necessary modifications, in relation to a notice under section 101 of the Housing Act 1957 (dispossession of tenant where local authority have agreed to purchase or have appropriated land for purposes of Part V of that Act) as they have effect in relation to a notice of entry under section 11(1) of the said Act of 1965.

(4) Before taking possession of part only of an agricultural holding under section 84 or 114 of the Lands Clauses Consolidation (Scotland) Act 1845 (alternative procedures for taking possession of land) the acquiring authority shall serve notice of their intention to do so on the person in occupation of the holding, and sections 55 and 56 above shall have effect, subject to any necessary modifications, as if possession were being obtained pursuant to a notice of entry under paragraph 3 of

Schedule 2 to the Acquisition of Land (Authorisation Procedure) (Scotland) Act 1947.

(5) Sections 55 and 56 above shall have effect, subject to any necessary modifications, in relation to a notice of entry under paragraph 4 of Schedule 6 to the New Towns (Scotland) Act

1968 (provisions applicable to compulsory acquisitions under PART IV
that Act) as they have effect in relation to a notice of entry
under paragraph 3 of Schedule 2 to the Acquisition of Land 1947 c. 42.
(Authorisation Procedure) (Scotland) Act 1947.

(6) Sections 55 and 56(1), (2) and (5)(*a*) above shall have effect,
subject to any necessary modifications, in relation to a notice
under section 114 of the Housing (Scotland) Act 1966 (disposses- 1966 c. 49.
sion of tenant where local authority have agreed to purchase or
have appropriated land for purposes of Part VII of that Act)
as they have effect in relation to a notice of entry under paragraph 3 of Schedule 2 to the said Act of 1947.

58.—(1) In determining under section 8(1) or 34(2) of the Determination
Compulsory Purchase Act 1965, paragraph 10 of Schedule 3A of material
to the Town and Country Planning Act 1968 or section 202(2) detriment
of the Town and Country Planning Act 1971 whether— where part
of house etc.
    (*a*) part of a house, building or manufactory can be taken proposed for
        without material detriment or damage to the house, compulsory
        venience of the house, acquisition.
    (*b*) part of a park or garden belonging to a house can be 1965 c. 56.
        taken without seriously affecting the amenity or con- 1968 c. 72.
        venience of the house, 1971 c. 78.
the Lands Tribunal shall take into account not only the effect
of the severance but also the use to be made of the part
proposed to be acquired and, in a case where the part is proposed to be acquired for works or other purposes extending to
other land, the effect of the whole of the works and the use
to be made of the other land.

(2) Subsection (1) above shall apply with the necessary modifications to any determination—
    (*a*) under the said section 8(1) as substituted by paragraph
        8 of Schedule 6 to the Highways Act 1971 or paragraph 1971 c. 41.
        14 of Schedule 2 to the Gas Act 1972 (compulsory 1972 c. 60.
        acquisition of rights over land) ; or
    (*b*) under any provision corresponding to or substituted for
        the said section 8(1) which is contained in, or in an
        instrument made under, any other enactment including
        (except where otherwise provided) an enactment passed
        after this Act.

(3) In the application of this section to Scotland—
    (*a*) for the reference in subsection (1) to the provisions
        there mentioned there shall be substituted a reference to
        paragraph 4 of Schedule 2 to the Acquisition of Land 1947 c. 42.
        (Authorisation Procedure) (Scotland) Act 1947 and
        section 191(2) of, and paragraph 26 of Schedule 24 to,
        the Town and Country Planning (Scotland) Act 1972 ; 1972 c. 52.

(*b*) for the reference to the said section 8(1) as substituted by the provisions mentioned in subsection (2)(*a*) above there shall be substituted a reference to the said paragraph 4 as substituted by paragraph 24 of Schedule 2 to the Gas Act 1972 ;

(*c*) for the reference to the Lands Tribunal there shall be substituted a reference to the Lands Tribunal for Scotland.

Miscellaneous

59.—(1) This section has effect where the person in occupation of an agricultural holding, being a person having no greater interest therein than as tenant for a year or from year to year, is served with a notice to quit the holding, and—

(*a*) the notice is served after an acquiring authority have served notice to treat on the landlord of the holding or, being an authority possessing compulsory purchase powers, have agreed to acquire his interest in the holding ; and

(*b*) either—

(i) subsection (1) of section 24 of the Agricultural Holdings Act 1948 does not apply to the notice by virtue of subsection (2)(*b*) of that section (land required for non-agricultural use for which planning permission has been granted etc.) ; or

(ii) the Agricultural Land Tribunal have consented to the operation of the notice and stated in the reasons for their decision that they are satisfied as to the matter mentioned in section 25(1)(*e*) of that Act (land required for non-agricultural use not falling within section 24(2)(*b*)).

(2) If the person served with the notice to quit elects that this subsection shall apply to the notice and gives up possession of the holding to the acquiring authority on or before the date on which his tenancy terminates in accordance with the notice—

(*a*) section 20 of the Compulsory Purchase Act 1965 (compensation for tenants from year to year etc.) and section 12 of the Agriculture (Miscellaneous Provisions) Act 1968 shall have effect as if the notice to quit had not been served and the acquiring authority had taken possession of the holding in pursuance of a notice of entry under section 11(1) of the said Act of 1965 on the day before that on which the tenancy terminates in accordance with the notice to quit ; and (*b*) the provisions of the Agricultural Holdings Act 1948 relating to compensation to a tenant on the termina- tion of his tenancy and sections 9 and 15(2) of the Agriculture (Miscellaneous Provisions) Act 1968 (addi- tional payment and compensation in cases of notice to quit) shall not have effect in relation to the termination of the tenancy by reason of the notice to quit.

(3) No election under subsection (2) above shall be made or, if already made, continue to have effect in relation to any land (whether the whole or part of the land to which the notice to quit relates) if, before the expiration of that notice, an acquiring authority take possession of that land in pursuance of an enactment providing for the taking of possession of land compulsorily.

(4) Any election under subsection (2) above shall be made by notice in writing served on the acquiring authority not later than the date on which possession of the holding is given up.

(5) This section shall have effect in relation to a notice to quit part of an agricultural holding as it has effect in relation to a notice to quit an entire holding and references to a holding and the termination of the tenancy shall be construed accordingly.

(6) A person served with a notice to quit part of an agricultural holding shall not be entitled, in relation to that notice, both to make an election under this section and to give a counter-notice under section 32 of the Agricultural Holdings Act 1948 (tenant's right to cause notice to quit part of holding to operate as notice to quit entire holding).

(7) The reference in subsection (1)(*a*) above to a notice to treat served by an acquiring authority includes a reference to a notice to treat deemed to have been so served under any of the provisions mentioned in section 53(5) above.

(8) In the application of this section to Scotland—

(*a*) for subsection (1)(*b*) there shall be substituted the following paragraph—

" (*b*) either—

(i) subsection (1) of section 25 of the Agricultural Holdings (Scotland) Act 1949 does not apply to the notice by virtue of subsection (2)(*c*) of that section (land required for non-agricultural use for which planning permission has been granted, etc) ; or

(ii) the Scottish Land Court have consented to the operation of the notice and stated in the reasons for their decision that they are satisfied as to the matter mentioned in section 26(1)(e) of that Act (land required for non-agricultural use not falling within section 25(2)(c)) ; " ;

1965 c. 56.

1845 c. 19.

1947 c. 42.

(b) in subsection (2)(a), for the references to section 20 of the Compulsory Purchase Act 1965 and 11(1) of that Act there shall be substituted respectively references to section 114 of the Lands Clauses Consolidation (Scotland) Act 1845 and paragraph 3 of Schedule 2 to the Acquisition of Land (Authorisation Procedure) (Scotland) Act 1947 ;

1948 c. 63.
1968 c. 34.

1949 c. 75.

(c) in subsection (2)(b), for the references to the Agricultural Holdings Act 1948 and section 15(2) of the Agriculture (Miscellaneous Provisions) Act 1968 there shall be substituted respectively references to the Agricultural Holdings (Scotland) Act 1949 and section 15(3) of the said Act of 1968 ;

(d) in subsection (6), for the reference to section 32 of the Agricultural Holdings Act 1948 there shall be substituted a reference to section 33 of the Agricultural Holdings (Scotland) Act 1949 ;

(e) after subsection (7) there shall be inserted the following subsections—

" (7A) This section and section 61 below shall have effect in relation to a notice given in pursuance of a stipulation in a lease entitling the landlord to resume land for building, planting, feuing or other purposes (not being agricultural purposes) as it has effect in relation to a notice to quit as if, in this section, subsections (1)(b) and (6) were omitted ; and references in this section to the termination of the tenancy shall be construed accordingly.

(7B) This section shall not apply where the person in occupation of an agricultural holding is a crofter, landholder or statutory small tenant.".

Requirement to surrender croft, etc.: right to opt for notice of entry compensation.

1955 c. 21.

60.—(1) This section has effect where—

(a) the person in occupation of an agricultural holding is a crofter and is required by an order of the Scottish Land Court under section 12 of the Crofters (Scotland) Act 1955 to surrender his croft ; and

(b) the crofter is so required—

(i) after an acquiring authority have served notice to treat on the landlord of the croft or, being an authority possessing compulsory purchase powers, have agreed to acquire his interest in the croft, and

(ii) where the Court have been satisfied under the said section 12 that the landlord desires to resume the croft for a reasonable purpose which is a purpose other than an agricultural purpose. PART IV

(2) If the crofter required by such an order to surrender his croft elects that this subsection shall apply to the order and gives up possession of the croft to the acquiring authority on or before the date on which the croft is required to be surrendered in accordance with the order—

(a) section 114 of the Lands Clauses Consolidation (Scotland) Act 1845 (compensation for tenants from year to year, etc.) shall have effect as if the crofter had not been so required to surrender his croft and the acquiring authority had taken possession of the croft in pursuance of a notice of entry under paragraph 3 of Schedule 2 to to Acquisition of Land (Authorisation Procedure) (Scotland) Act 1947 on the day before that on which the croft is required to be surrendered in accordance with the order ; and 1845 c. 19.

1947 c. 42.

(b) any provision of an order under section 12 of the Crofters (Scotland) Act 1955 relating to the compensation to a crofter shall not have effect in relation to the surrender of the croft by reason of the order. 1955 c. 21.

(3) No election under subsection (2) above shall be made or, if already made, continue to have effect in relation to any land to which such an order relates if, before the date on which the croft is required to be surrendered in accordance with the order, an acquiring authority take possession of that land in pursuance of an enactment providing for the taking of possession of land compulsorily.

(4) Any election under subsection (2) above shall be made by notice in writing served on the acquiring authority not later than the date on which possession of the croft is given up.

(5) This section shall have effect in relation to an order to surrender part of a croft as it has effect in relation to an order to surrender an entire croft and references to a croft shall be construed accordingly.

(6) The reference in subsection (1)(b)(i) above to a notice to treat served by an acquiring authority includes a reference to a notice to treat deemed to have been so served under any of the provisions mentioned in section 53(5) above.

(7) This section shall apply to a landholder as it applies to a crofter except that for any reference to a croft, crofter or section 12 of the Crofters (Scotland) Act 1955 there shall be substituted

respectively a reference to a holding, landholder or section 2 of the Crofters Holdings (Scotland) Act 1886.

(8) This section shall apply to a statutory small tenant subject to the modifications set out in Part I of Schedule 1 to this Act ; and in accordance with this subsection this section shall have effect in relation to a statutory small tenant as set out in Part II of that Schedule.

Notice to
quit part of
agricultural
holding: right
to claim
notice of entry
compensation
for remainder
of holding.
61.—(1) Where a notice to quit in respect of which a person is entitled to make an election under section 59 above relates to part only of an agricultural holding and that person makes such an election within the period of two months beginning with the date of service of that notice, or, if later, the decision of the Agricultural Land Tribunal, he may also within that period serve a notice on the acquiring authority claiming that the remainder of the holding is not reasonably capable of being farmed, either by itself or in conjunction with other relevant land, as a separate agricultural unit.

(2) If the acquiring authority do not within the period of two months beginning with the date of service of a notice under subsection (1) above agree in writing to accept the notice as valid, the claimant or the authority may, within two months after the end of that period, refer it to the Lands Tribunal, and on any such reference the Tribunal shall determine whether the claim in the notice is justified and declare the notice valid or invalid in accordance with its determination of that question.

(3) Where a notice under subsection (1) above is accepted as, or declared to be, valid under subsection (2) above then, if before the end of twelve months after it has been so accepted or declared the claimant has given up to the acquiring authority possession of the part of the holding to which the notice relates, section 20 of the Compulsory Purchase Act 1965 and section 12 of the Agriculture (Miscellaneous Provisions) Act 1968 shall have effect as if the acquiring authority had taken possession of that part in pursuance of a notice of entry under section 11(1) of the said Act of 1965 on the day before the expiration of the year of the tenancy which is current when the notice is so accepted or declared.

(4) Subsections (2) to (4) of section 55 and subsection (3) of section 56 above shall apply in relation to subsections (1) to (3) above and to a notice under subsection (1) above as they apply in relation to those sections and a counter-notice under subsection (1) of section 55, and shall so apply with the necessary modifications and as if any reference to the notice of entry were a reference to the notice to quit.

(5) Where an election under section 59 above ceases to have effect in relation to any land by virtue of subsection (3) of that section any notice served by virtue of this section shall also cease to have effect in relation thereto.

(6) In the application of this section to Scotland—

(*a*) in subsection (1) for the reference to the Agricultural Land Tribunal there shall be substituted a reference to the Scottish Land Court ;

(*b*) in subsection (2) for any reference to the Lands Tribunal there shall be substituted a reference to the Lands Tribunal for Scotland ;

(*c*) in subsection (3) for the references to sections 11(1) and 20 of the Compulsory Purchase Act 1965 there shall be 1965 c. 56. substituted respectively references to paragraph 3 of Schedule 2 to the Acquisition of Land (Authorisation 1947 c. 42. Procedure) (Scotland) Act 1947 and section 114 of the 1845 c. 19. Lands Clauses Consolidation (Scotland) Act 1845.

62.—(1) Where an order of the Scottish Land Court in respect Requirement of which a person is entitled to make an election under section to surrender 60 above relates to part only of a croft or holding and that person part of croft, makes such an election within the period of two months begin- claim notice ning with the date of the making of the order, he may also of entry within that period serve a notice on the acquiring authority compensation claiming that the remainder of the croft or holding is not reason- for remainder. ably capable of being farmed, either by itself or in conjunction with other relevant land, as a separate agricultural unit.

(2) If the acquiring authority do not within the period of two months beginning with the date of service of a notice under subsection (1) above agree in writing to accept the notice as valid, the claimant or the authority may, within two months after the end of that period, refer it to the Lands Tribunal for Scotland, and on any such reference the Tribunal shall determine whether the claim in the notice is justified and declare the notice valid or invalid in accordance with its determination of that question.

(3) Where a notice under subsection (1) above is accepted as, or declared to be valid under subsection (2) above then, if before the end of twelve months after it has been so accepted or declared the claimant has given up to the acquiring authority possession of the part of the croft or holding to which the notice relates, section 114 of the Lands Clauses Consolidation (Scotland) Act 1845 shall have effect as if the acquiring authority had taken possession of that part in pursuance of a notice of entry under paragraph 3 of Schedule 2 to the Acquisition of

Land (Authorisation Procedure) (Scotland) Act 1947 on the day before the expiration of the year of the tenancy which is current when the notice is so accepted or declared.

(4) Subsections (2) to (4) of section 55 and subsection (3) of section 56 above shall apply in relation to subsections (1) to (3) above and to a notice under subsection (1) above as they apply in relation to those sections and a counter-notice under subsection (1) of section 55, and shall so apply with the necessary modifications and as if in section 55(3)(*b*) for the words " service of the notice of entry " and in section 56(3) for the words " the notice of entry " there were substituted the words " the order of the Scottish Land Court ".

(5) Where an election under section 60 above ceases to have effect in relation to any land by virtue of subsection (3) of that section any notice served by virtue of this section shall cease to have effect in relation thereto.

1968 c. 34.

(6) Subsection (3) above shall apply in the case of the holding of a statutory small tenant as if after the word " 1845 " there were inserted the words " and section 12 of the Agriculture (Miscellaneous Provisions) Act 1968 ".

Interest on
compensation
for injurious
affection
where no
land taken.
1845 c. 18.
1965 c. 56.
1961 c. 33.
1845 c. 33.
1963 c. 51.

63.—(1) Compensation under section 68 of the Lands Clauses Consolidation Act 1845 or section 10 of the Compulsory Purchase Act 1965 (compensation for injurious affection where no land taken) shall carry interest, at the rate for the time being prescribed under section 32 of the Land Compensation Act 1961, from the date of the claim until payment.

(2) Compensation under section 6 of the Railways Clauses Consolidation (Scotland) Act 1845 (compensation for injurious affection where no land taken) shall carry interest, at the rate for the time being prescribed under section 40 of the Land Compensation (Scotland) Act 1963, from the date of the claim until payment.

Extension
of grounds for
challenging
validity of
compulsory
purchase
order.
1946 c. 49.
1947 c. 42.
1971 c. 62.

64. In paragraph 15 of Schedule 1 to the Acquisition of Land (Authorisation Procedure) Act 1946 and paragraph 15 of Schedule 1 to the Acquisition of Land (Authorisation Procedure) (Scotland) Act 1947 (which enable an aggrieved person to challenge the validity of a compulsory purchase order on the ground that certain requirements have not been complied with) references to those requirements shall include references to any requirements of the Tribunals and Inquiries Act 1971 or of any rules made, or having effect as if made, under that Act.

65. At the end of section 6 of the Railways Clauses Con- PART IV
solidation (Scotland) Act 1845 (construction of railway to be Construction
subject to that Act and Lands Clauses Consolidation (Scotland) of section 6 of
Act 1845) there shall be added the following subsection— Railways

" (2) For the avoidance of doubt it is hereby declared Clauses
that in this section the reference to the construction of the Consolidation
railway includes a reference to the execution of works in Act 1845.
connection therewith."
1845 c. 33.
1845 c. 19.

66. Section 35 of the Roads (Scotland) Act 1970 (general Amendment
provisions as to acquisition of land) shall have effect as if— of section 35
of Roads
(*a*) after subsection (1) there were inserted the following (Scotland)
subsection— Act 1970.

" (1A) Any power to acquire land compulsorily 1970 c. 20.
conferred by any of the said sections or by section 22
of the Land Compensation Act 1973 shall include
power to acquire a servitude or other right in or
over land by the creation of a new right." ;

(*b*) at the end there were added the following subsection—

" (5) Where under section 29, 30, 31, 32 or 33 of
this Act or section 22 of the Land Compensation Act
1973 a highway authority are authorised to acquire
land by agreement, the Lands Clauses Acts (except
the provisions relating to the purchase of land otherwise than by agreement and the provisions relating
to access to the special Act, and except sections 120
to 125 of the Lands Clauses Consolidation (Scotland)
Act 1845) and sections 6 and 70 of the Railways
Clauses Consolidation (Scotland) Act 1845, and sections 71 to 78 of that Act, as originally enacted and
not as amended for certain purposes by section 15
of the Mines (Working Facilities and Support) Act 1923 c. 20.
1923, shall be incorporated with this Act, and in
construing those Acts for the purposes of this subsection this Act shall be deemed to be the special
Act, and the highway authority to be the promoters
of the undertaking or company, as the case may
require, and the word ' land ' shall have the meaning
assigned to it by section 50(1) of this Act ".

67.—(1) Subject to the provisions of this section, the Lands Provisions
Clauses Consolidation (Scotland) Act 1845 and the Acquisition relating to
of Land (Authorisation Procedure) (Scotland) Act 1947 shall acquisition of
apply subject to any necessary modifications to the compulsory Scotland.
acquisition under any enactment of a right in or over land by
the creation of a new right as they apply to the compulsory 1947 c. 42.
acquisition of land under the enactment in question.

PART IV

(2) Section 61 of the said Act of 1845 (estimation of purchase money and compensation) shall apply to the compulsory acquisition of such a right as if for the words from " value " to " undertaking " there were substituted the words " extent (if any) to which the value of the land in or over which the right is to be acquired is depreciated by the acquisition of the right ".

(3) Paragraph 4 of Schedule 2 to the said Act of 1947 (protection for vendor against severance of house, garden, etc.) shall apply to the compulsory acquisition of such a right as if at the end there were added the following sub-paragraph—

" (2) In considering the extent of any material detriment to a house, building or manufactory or any extent to which the amenity or convenience of a house is affected, the Lands Tribunal for Scotland shall have regard not only to the right which is to be acquired in or over the land, but also to any adjoining or adjacent land belonging to the same owner and subject to compulsory purchase."

(4) Nothing in this section shall affect the operation of any enactment which makes specific provision to the like effect as the provisions of this section.

PART V

PLANNING BLIGHT

Extension of classes of blighted land

Land affected by proposed structure and local plans etc.

68.—(1) In para graph (*a*) of section 192(1) of the Act of 1971 (land indicated in a structure plan in force for the relevant district as land which may be required for the purposes of functions of public authorities or as land which may be included in an action area) the reference to a structure plan in force shall include a reference to—

(*a*) a structure plan which has been submitted to the Secretary of State under section 7 of that Act ;

(*b*) proposals for alterations to a structure plan which have been submitted to the Secretary of State under section 10 of that Act ;

(*c*) modifications proposed to be made by the Secretary of State in any such plan or proposals as are mentioned in the preceding paragraphs, being modifications of which he has given notice in accordance with regulations under Part II of that Act.

(2) In paragraph (*b*) of the said section 192(1) (land allocated for the purposes of functions of public authorities by a local plan in force for the relevant district and land defined in such

a plan as the site of proposed development for the purposes of any such functions) the reference to a local plan in force shall include a reference to—

    (*a*) a local plan of which copies have been made available for inspection under section 12(2) of the Act of 1971 ;

    (*b*) proposals for alterations to a local plan of which copies have been made available for inspection under section 15(3) of that Act ;

    (*c*) modifications proposed to be made by the local planning authority or the Secretary of State in any such plan or proposals as are mentioned in the preceding paragraphs, being modifications of which notice has been given by the authority or the Secretary of State in accordance with regulations under Part II of that Act.

(3) In section 138(1)(*b*) of the Town and Country Planning Act 1962 as it has effect by virtue of paragraph 58 of Schedule 24 to the Act of 1971 (provisions corresponding to section 192(1)(*b*) of the Act of 1971 pending coming into force of local plans) the reference to a development plan shall include a reference to— 1962 c. 38.

    (*a*) proposals for alterations to a development plan submitted to the Secretary of State under paragraph 3 or 9 of Schedule 5 to the Act of 1971 ;

    (*b*) modifications proposed to be made by the Secretary of State in any such proposals, being modifications of which notice has been given by the Secretary of State by advertisement.

(4) No blight notice shall be served by virtue of subsection (1) or (2) above at any time after the copies of the plan or proposals made available for inspection have been withdrawn under—

    (*a*) section 8(6) or 12(5) of the Act of 1971 (directions by Secretary of State requiring further publicity) ; or

    (*b*) section 10B of that Act (withdrawal of structure plans) ;

but so much of the said section 10B as provides that a structure plan which has been withdrawn shall be treated as never having been submitted shall not invalidate any blight notice served by virtue of subsection (1)(*a*) above before the withdrawal of the structure plan.

(5) No blight notice shall be served by virtue of this section after the relevant plan or alterations have come into force (whether in their original form or with modifications) or the Secretary of State has decided to reject or, in the case of a local plan, the local planning authority have decided to abandon the plan or alterations and notice of the decision has been given by advertisement.

(6) Where an appropriate authority have served a counter-notice objecting to a blight notice served by virtue of this section, then, if the relevant plan or alterations come into force (whether in their original form or with modifications) the appropriate authority may serve on the claimant, in substitution for the counter-notice already served, a further counter-notice specifying different grounds of objection, and section 195 of the Act of 1971 (reference of objections to Lands Tribunal) shall have effect in relation to the further counter-notice as it has effect in relation to the counter-notice already served:

Provided that a further counter-notice under this subsection shall not be served—

(a) at any time after the end of the period of two months beginning with the date on which the relevant plan or alterations come into force ; or

(b) if the objection in the counter-notice already served has been withdrawn or the Lands Tribunal has already determined whether or not to uphold that objection.

(7) References in subsections (1) to (3) above to anything done under any of the provisions there mentioned include references to anything done under those provisions as they apply by virtue of section 17 of, or paragraph 4 of Schedule 5 to, the Act of 1971 (default powers of Secretary of State).

(8) In the application of this section to Greater London—

(a) the reference to section 10 of the Act of 1971 shall include a reference to paragraph 6 of Schedule 4 to that Act ;

(b) for the reference to section 12(2) of that Act there shall be substituted a reference to paragraphs 12(2) and 13(2) of that Schedule ;

(c) for the reference to section 12(5) of that Act there shall be substituted a reference to paragraph 14(3) of that Schedule ;

(d) for the reference to section 15(3) of that Act there shall be substituted a reference to the said section 15(3) as substituted by paragraph 16(1), and to paragraph 16(4), of that Schedule.

(9) In this section references to alterations to a local plan include references to its replacement, and references to alterations to a development plan include references to additions to it.

(10) In relation to land falling within section 192(1)(b) of the Act of 1971 or section 138(1)(b) of the Town and Country Planning Act 1962, as extended by this section, " the appropriate enactment " for the purposes of sections 192 to 207 of the Act of 1971 shall be determined in accordance with section 206(2)

1962 c. 38.

of that Act as if references therein to the development plan were references to any such plan, proposal or modifications as are mentioned in subsection (2)(*a*), (*b*) or (*c*) and subsection (3)(*a*) or (*b*) above.

69.—(1) In section 192(1)(*d*) of the Act of 1971 (land on Land affected or adjacent to line of highway proposed to be constructed etc. by proposed as indicated in an order or scheme which has come into opera- highway tion under the provisions of Part II of the Highways Act 1959 orders. relating to trunk roads or special roads or in an order which 1959 c. 25. has come into operation under section 1 of the Highways Act 1971 c. 41. 1971) the reference to an order or scheme which has come into operation as aforesaid shall include a reference to—

(*a*) an order or scheme which has been submitted for confirmation to, or been prepared in draft by, the Secretary of State under the provisions of Part II of the said Act of 1959 relating to trunk roads or special roads and in respect of which a notice has been published under paragraph 1, 2 or 7 of Schedule 1 to that Act ;

(*b*) an order which has been submitted for confirmation to the Secretary of State under the said section 1 and in respect of which a notice has been published under paragraph 2 of that Schedule.

(2) No blight notice shall be served by virtue of this section at any time after the relevant order or scheme has come into operation (whether in its original form or with modifications) or the Secretary of State has decided not to confirm or make the order or scheme.

(3) Subsection (6) of section 68 above shall have effect in relation to a blight notice served by virtue of this section as it has effect in relation to a blight notice served by virtue of that section taking references to the relevant plan or alterations as references to the relevant order or scheme.

70.—(1) Section 192(1)(*g*) and (*j*) of the Act of 1971 (land Land affected in respect of which a compulsory purchase order is in force by proposed where a notice to treat has not been served) shall apply also compulsory to land in respect of which a compulsory purchase order has purchase orders. been submitted for confirmation to, or been prepared in draft by, a Minister and in respect of which a notice has been published under paragraph 3(1)(*a*) of Schedule 1 to the Acquisition of Land (Authorisation Procedure) Act 1946 or 1946 c. 49. under any corresponding enactment applicable thereto.

(2) No blight notice shall be served by virtue of this section at any time after the relevant compulsory purchase order has

PART V   come into force (whether in its original form or with modifications) or the Minister concerned has decided not to confirm or make the order.

(3) In relation to land falling within the said section 192(1)(*g*) or (*j*) by virtue of this section " the appropriate enactment " for the purposes of sections 192 to 207 of the Act of 1971 shall be the enactment which would provide for the compulsory acquisition of the land or of the rights over the land if the relevant compulsory purchase order were confirmed or made.

Land affected by resolution of planning authority or directions of Secretary of State.

71.—(1) Section 192(1) of the Act of 1971 shall have effect as if the land specified therein included land which—

(*a*) is land indicated in a plan (not being a development plan) approved by a resolution passed by a local planning authority for the purpose of the exercise of their powers under Part III of that Act as land which may be required for the purposes of any functions of a government department, local authority or statutory undertakers ; or

(*b*) is land in respect of which a local planning authority have resolved to take action to safeguard it for development for the purposes of any such functions or been directed by the Secretary of State to restrict the grant of planning permission in order to safeguard it for such development.

(2) Paragraph (*a*) of the said section 192(1) shall not apply to land within subsection (1) above.

(3) In relation to land falling within subsection (1) above " the appropriate enactment " for the purposes of sections 192 to 207 of the Act of 1971 shall be determined in accordance with section 206(2) of that Act as if references therein to the development plan were references to the resolution or direction in question.

Land affected by orders relating to new towns.

1965 c. 59.

72.—(1) Section 192(1) of the Act of 1971 shall have effect as if the land specified therein included land which—

(*a*) is land within an area described as the site of a proposed new town in the draft of an order in respect of which a notice has been published under paragraph 2 of Schedule 1 to the New Towns Act 1965 ; or

(*b*) is land within an area designated as the site of a proposed new town by an order which has come into operation under section 1 of the said Act of 1965.

(2) No blight notice shall be served by virtue of subsection (1)(*a*) above at any time after the order there mentioned has come

into operation (whether in the form of the draft or with modifications) or the Secretary of State has decided not to make the order.

(3) Until such time as a development corporation is established for the new town, sections 192 to 207 of the Act of 1971 shall have effect in relation to land within subsection (1) above as if " the appropriate authority " and " the appropriate enactment " were the Secretary of State and subsection (4) below respectively.

(4) Until such time as aforesaid the Secretary of State shall have power to acquire compulsorily any interest in land in pursuance of a blight notice served by virtue of subsection (1) above ; and where he acquires an interest as aforesaid, then—

(a) if the land is or becomes land within subsection (1)(b) above, the interest shall be transferred by him to the development corporation established for the new town ; and

(b) in any other case, the interest may be disposed of by him in such manner as he thinks fit.

(5) The Land Compensation Act 1961 shall have effect in 1961 c. 33. relation to the compensation payable in respect of the acquisition of an interest by the Secretary of State under subsection (4) above as if the acquisition were by a development corporation under the New Towns Act 1965 and as if, in the case of land within 1965 c. 59. subsection (1)(a) above, the land formed part of an area designated as the site of a new town by an order which has come into operation under section 1 of the said Act of 1965.

(6) Section 11 of the said Act of 1965 (right to require development corporation to acquire land within area designated as the site of a new town) shall cease to have effect except in relation to any notice served under that section before the coming into force of this section.

73.—(1) Section 192(1) of the Act of 1971 shall have effect as Land affected if the land specified therein included land which— by slum
clearance
(a) is land within an area declared to be a clearance area resolution. by a resolution under section 42 of the Housing Act 1957 c. 56. 1957 ; or

(b) is land surrounded by or adjoining an area declared as aforesaid to be a clearance area, being land which a local authority have determined to purchase under section 43 of that Act.

(2) The grounds on which objection may be made in a counter-notice to a blight notice served by virtue of subsection (1) above shall not include those specified in section 194(2)(b) or (c) of the Act of 1971 (no intention to acquire the land).

(3) In relation to land within subsection (1) above " the appropriate enactment " for the purposes of sections 192 to 207 of the Act of 1971 shall be section 43 of the Housing Act 1957.

(4) Where an interest in land is acquired in pursuance of a blight notice served by virtue of subsection (1)(*a*) above the compensation payable for the acquisition shall be assessed in accordance with section 59(2) of the said Act of 1957 (site value) and paragraph 2 of Schedule 2 to the Land Compensation Act 1961 shall not apply.

(5) Where the land in which an interest is acquired as afore-said comprises a house—

(*a*) section 60 of, and Part I of Schedule 2 to, the said Act of 1957 (payments in respect of well-maintained houses) shall have effect as if the house had been made the subject of a compulsory purchase order under Part III of that Act as being unfit for human habitation ;

(*b*) Part II of Schedule 2 to the said Act of 1957 and Schedule 5 to the Housing Act 1969 (payments to owner-occupiers) shall have effect as if the house had been purchased at site value in pursuance of a com-pulsory purchase order made by virtue of the said Part III ;

and references in the said Schedules 2 and 5 to the date of the making of the compulsory purchase order and the date when the house was purchased compulsorily shall be respectively construed as references to the date of service of the blight notice and the date of acquisition in pursuance of that notice.

74.—(1) In section 192(1)(*d*) of the Act of 1971—

(*a*) the reference to a power of compulsory acquisition con-ferred by any of the provisions there mentioned shall include a reference to the power of compulsory acquisi-tion conferred by section 22(1) above ;

(*b*) the reference to land required for purposes of con-struction, improvement or alteration as indicated in an order or scheme there mentioned shall include a refer-ence to land required for the purposes of the said section 22(1).

(2) Section 192(1) of the Act of 1971 shall have effect as if the land specified therein included land which—

(*a*) is land shown on plans approved by a resolution of a local highway authority as land proposed to be acquired by them for the purposes of the said section 22(1) ; or (*b*) is land shown in a written notice given by the Secretary of State to the local planning authority as land proposed to be acquired by him for those purposes in connection with a trunk road or special road which he proposes to provide.

Part V

75.—(1) Section 192(1)(*g*) of the Act of 1971 (land in respect of which there is in force a compulsory purchase order made by a highway authority in the exercise of highway land acquisition powers and providing for the acquisition of rights over land) shall apply generally to land in respect of which there is in force a compulsory purchase order providing for the acquisition of a right or rights over that land, and the provisions of that Act mentioned in subsections (2) and (3) below shall accordingly be amended in accordance with those subsections.

Land affected by compulsory purchase orders providing for acquisition of rights over land.

(2) In the said section 192(1)(*g*)—

(*a*) in sub-paragraph (i) for the words from " made by " to " 1971 " there shall be substituted the word " providing " ;

(*b*) in sub-paragraph (ii) for the words " highway authority " there shall be substituted the words " appropriate authority ".

(3) In section 194—

(*a*) in subsection (4) for the words " is one of the enactments conferring highway land acquisition powers " there shall be substituted the words " confers power to acquire rights over land " ;

(*b*) in subsection (6), in paragraphs (*a*) and (*b*), after the word " acquire " there shall be inserted the words " or to acquire any rights over " and the words following paragraph (*b*) as far as the semi-colon shall be omitted.

76.—(1) Section 192(1) of the Act of 1971 shall have effect as if the land specified therein included land which—

(*a*) either—

Land affected by new street orders.

(i) is within the outer lines prescribed by an order under section 159 of the Highways Act 1959 (orders prescribing minimum width of new streets) ; or 1959 c. 25.

(ii) has a frontage to a highway declared to be a new street by an order under section 30 of the Public Health Act 1925 and lies within the minimum width of the street prescribed by any byelaws or local Act applicable by virtue of the order ; and 1925 c. 71.

PART V

    (*b*) is, or is part of—

      (i) a dwelling erected before, or under construction on, the date on which the order is made ; or

      (ii) the curtilage of any such dwelling.

(2) The grounds on which objection may be made in a counter-notice to a blight notice served by virtue of subsection (1) above shall not include those specified in section 194(2)(*b*) or (*c*) of the Act of 1971.

(3) In relation to land within subsection (1) above " the appropriate authority " and " the appropriate enactment " for the purposes of sections 192 to 207 of the Act of 1971 shall be the highway authority for the highway in relation to which the order mentioned in that subsection was made and section 214(8) of the said Act of 1959 respectively.

(4) This section shall not enable a blight notice to be served in respect of any land in which the appropriate authority have previously acquired an interest either in pursuance of a blight notice served by virtue of this section or by agreement in circumstances such that they could have been required to acquire it in pursuance of such a notice.

Attempts to sell blighted property

Amended requirements about attempts to sell blighted property.

77.—(1) In section 193(1)(*c*) and section 201(1)(*b*) of the Act of 1971 (which require a person serving a blight notice to have made reasonable endeavours to sell his interest since the relevant date, that is to say, the date on which the land became blighted) the words " since the relevant date " and " since the relevant date (within the meaning of section 193 of this Act) " shall be omitted.

(2) In sections 193(1)(*d*) and 201(1)(*c*) of the Act of 1971 (which require a person serving a blight notice to have been unable to sell his interest except at a price lower than if the land had not been blighted) for the words from " he has been unable to sell " onwards there shall be substituted the words " in consequence of the fact that the hereditament or unit or a part of it was, or was likely to be, comprised in land of any of the specified descriptions, he has been unable to sell that interest except at a price substantially lower than that for which it might reasonably have been expected to sell if no part of the hereditament or unit were, or were likely to be, comprised in such land ".

(3) This section does not affect any blight notice served before the passing of this Act.

Blight notices by personal representatives

78.—(1) Where the whole or part of a hereditament or agricultural unit is comprised in land of any of the specified descriptions,
and a person claims that—

> (a) he is the personal representative of a person (" the
> deceased ") who at the date of his death was entitled
> to an interest in that hereditament or unit ; and

> (b) the interest was one which would have qualified for
> protection under sections 192 to 207 of the Act of 1971
> if a notice under section 193 of that Act had been
> served in respect thereof on that date ; and

> (c) he has made reasonable endeavours to sell that interest ;
> and

> (d) in consequence of the fact that the hereditament or
> unit or a part of it was, or was likely to be, comprised
> in land of any of the specified descriptions, he has been
> unable to sell that interest except at a price sub-
> stantially lower than that for which it might reasonably
> have been expected to sell if no part of the heredita-
> ment or unit were, or were likely to be, comprised in
> such land ; and

> (e) one or more individuals are (to the exclusion of any
> body corporate) beneficially entitled to that interest,

he may serve on the appropriate authority a notice in the
prescribed form requiring that authority to purchase that interest
to the extent specified in, and otherwise in accordance with, the
said sections 192 to 207.

(2) Subsection (1) above shall apply in relation to an interest
in part of a hereditament or agricultural unit as it applies in
relation to an interest in the entirety of a hereditament or
agricultural unit :

Provided that this subsection shall not enable any person—

> (a) if the deceased was entitled to an interest in the entirety
> of a hereditament or agricultural unit, to make any
> claim or serve any notice under this section in respect
> of the deceased's interest in part of the hereditament or
> unit ; or

> (b) if the deceased was entitled to an interest only in part
> of the hereditament or agricultural unit, to make or
> serve any such claim or notice in respect of the
> deceased's interest in less than the entirety of that part.

(3) Subject to sections 73(2) and 76(2) above and 80(2)
below, the grounds on which objection may be made in a
counter-notice under section 194 of the Act of 1971 to a notice
under this section are those specified in paragraphs (a) to (c) of

N

subsection (2) of that section and, in a case to which it applies, the grounds specified in paragraph (*d*) of that subsection and also the following grounds—

    (*a*) that the claimant is not the personal representative of the deceased or that, on the date of the deceased's death, the deceased was not entitled to an interest in any part of the hereditament or agricultural unit to which the notice relates;

    (*b*) that (for reasons specified in the counter-notice) the interest of the deceased is not such as is specified in subsection (1)(*b*) above;

    (*c*) that the conditions specified in subsection (1)(*c*), (*d*) or (*e*) above are not fulfilled.

(4) For the purpose of section 201(4) and (5) of the Act of 1971 (which prevent the service of concurrent blight notices under sections 193 and 201 of that Act) a notice served under this section shall be treated as a notice served under the said section 193.

1968 c. 73.   (5) In section 139(1)(*c*) of the Transport Act 1968 (compensation where land acquired for special road service area) the reference to a notice under section 193 of the Act of 1971 shall include a reference to a notice under this section.

Blight notices in respect of agricultural units

Blight notice requiring purchase of whole agricultural unit.   **79.**—(1) Where a blight notice is served in respect of an interest in the whole or part of an agricultural unit and on the date of service that unit or part contains land (hereafter referred to as " the unaffected area ") which does not fall within any of the specified descriptions as well as land (hereafter referred to as " the affected area ") which does so, the claimant may include in the notice—

    (*a*) a claim that the unaffected area is not reasonably capable of being farmed, either by itself or in conjunction with other relevant land, as a separate agricultural unit; and

    (*b*) a requirement that the appropriate authority shall purchase his interest in the whole of the unit or, as the case may be, in the whole of the part of it to which the notice relates.

(2) Subject to section 80(3) below, " other relevant land " in subsection (1) above means—

    (*a*) land comprised in the remainder of the agricultural unit if the blight notice is served only in respect of part of it;

(*b*) land comprised in any other agricultural unit occupied   PART V
    by the claimant on the date of service, being land in
    respect of which he is then entitled to an owner's
    interest as defined in section 203(4) of the Act of 1971.

80.—(1) The grounds on which objection may be made in a Objection
counter-notice to a blight notice served by virtue of section 79 to blight notice
above shall include the grounds that the claim made in the requiring pur-
notice is not justified.   chase of whole
                                                              agricultural
                                                              unit.
(2) Objection shall not be made to a blight notice served
by virtue of section 79 above on the grounds mentioned in
section 194(2)(*c*) of the Act of 1971 (part only of affected area
proposed to be acquired) unless it is also made on the grounds
mentioned in subsection (1) above ; and the Lands Tribunal
shall not uphold an objection to any such notice on the grounds
mentioned in the said section 194(2)(*c*) unless it also upholds
the objection on the grounds mentioned in subsection (1) above.

(3) Where objection is made to a blight notice served by
virtue of section 79 above on the grounds mentioned in subsection (1) above and also on those mentioned in the said section
194(2)(*c*), the Lands Tribunal, in determining whether or not
to uphold the objection, shall treat that part of the affected
area which is not specified in the counter-notice as included in
" other relevant land " as defined in section 79(2) above.

(4) If the Lands Tribunal upholds an objection but only on
the grounds mentioned in subsection (1) above, the Tribunal
shall declare that the blight notice is a valid notice in relation
to the affected area but not in relation to the unaffected area.

(5) If the Tribunal upholds an objection both on the grounds
mentioned in subsection (1) above and on the grounds mentioned in the said section 194(2)(*c*) (but not on any other grounds)
the Tribunal shall declare that the blight notice is a valid
notice in relation to the part of the affected area specified in
the counter-notice as being the part which the appropriate
authority propose to acquire as therein mentioned but not in
relation to any other part of the affected area or in relation to
the unaffected area.

(6) In a case falling within subsection (4) or (5) above, the
Tribunal shall give directions specifying a date on which notice
to treat (as mentioned in section 81 below and section 196
of the Act of 1971) is to be deemed to have been served.

(7) Section 195(5) of the Act of 1971 shall not apply to any
blight notice served by virtue of section 79 above.

PART V
Effect of
blight notice
requiring pur-
chase of whole
agricultural
unit.

81.—(1) In relation to a blight notice served by virtue of section 79 above, subsection (1) of section 196 of the Act of 1971 shall have effect as if for the words " or (in the case of an agricultural unit) the interest of the claimant in so far as it subsists in the affected area " there were substituted the words " or agricultural unit " and subsection (3) of that section shall not apply to any such blight notice.

(2) Where the appropriate authority have served a counter-notice objecting to a blight notice on the grounds mentioned in section 80(1) above, then if either—

    (*a*) the claimant, without referring that objection to the Lands Tribunal, and before the time for so referring it has expired, gives notice to the appropriate authority that he withdraws his claim as to the unaffected area : or

    (*b*) on a reference to the Tribunal, the Tribunal makes a declaration in accordance with section 80(4) above,

the appropriate authority shall be deemed to be authorised to acquire compulsorily under the appropriate enactment the interest of the claimant in so far as it subsists in the affected area (but not in so far as it subsists in the unaffected area) and to have served a notice to treat in respect thereof on the date mentioned in subsection (3) below.

(3) The said date—

    (*a*) in a case falling within paragraph (*a*) of subsection (2) above, is the date on which notice is given in accordance with that paragraph ; and

    (*b*) in a case falling within paragraph (*b*) of that subsection, is the date specified in directions given by the Tribunal in accordance with section 80(6) above.

(4) Where the appropriate authority have served a counter-notice objecting to a blight notice on the grounds mentioned in section 80(1) above and also on the grounds mentioned in section 194(2)(*c*) of the Act of 1971 then if either—

    (*a*) the claimant, without referring that objection to the Lands Tribunal, and before the time for so referring it has expired, gives notice to the appropriate authority that he accepts the proposal of the authority to acquire the part of the affected area specified in the counter-notice, and withdraws his claim as to the remainder of that area and as to the unaffected area ; or

    (*b*) on a reference to the Tribunal, the Tribunal makes a declaration in accordance with section 80(5) above in respect of that part of the affected area,

the appropriate authority shall be deemed to be authorised to acquire compulsorily under the appropriate enactment the interest of the claimant in so far as it subsists in the part of the affected area specified in the counter-notice (but not in so far as it subsists in any other part of that area or in the unaffected area) and to have served a notice to treat in respect thereof on the date mentioned in subsection (5) below.

PART V

(5) The said date—

(a) in a case falling within paragraph (a) of subsection (4) above, is the date on which notice is given in accordance with that paragraph ; and

(b) in a case falling within paragraph (b) of that subsection, is the date specified in directions given by the Tribunal in accordance with section 80(6) above.

(6) The compensation payable in respect of the acquisition by virtue of this section of an interest in land comprised in—

(a) the unaffected area of an agricultural unit ; or

(b) if the appropriate authority have served a counter-notice objecting to the blight notice on the grounds mentioned in the said section 194(2)(c), so much of the affected area of the unit as is not specified in the counter-notice,

shall be assessed on the assumptions mentioned in section 5(2), (3) and (4) above.

(7) In relation to a blight notice served by virtue of section 79 above references to " the appropriate authority " and " the appropriate enactment " shall be construed as if the unaffected area of an agricultural unit were part of the affected area.

(8) The provisions mentioned in section 200(2) of the Act of 1971 (operation of blight provisions where claimant dies after serving blight notice) shall include subsections (2) and (4) above.

Supplementary

82.—(1) In this Part of this Act " the Act of 1971 " means the Town and Country Planning Act 1971.

Supplementary provisions for Part V. 1971 c. 78.

(2) In section 192(6) of the Act of 1971 (definition of " blight notice ") there shall be added at the end the words " or section 78 of the Land Compensation Act 1973 ".

(3) In section 194(5) of the Act of 1971 (which requires a counter-notice to state the grounds of objection) after the words " section 201(6) of this Act " there shall be inserted the words " or section 78(3) or 80(1) of the Land Compensation Act 1973 ".

(4) In sections 192 to 207 of the Act of 1971 references to " these provisions " shall include references to this Part of this

N 3

PART V

Act, and references to " the specified descriptions " shall include references to the descriptions contained in section 192(1)(a), (b), (d), (g) and (j) of that Act as extended by this Part of this Act and to the descriptions contained in sections 71, 72, 73, 74(2) and 76 above.

(5) The Act of 1971 shall have effect as if this Part of this Act were included in the said sections 192 to 207.

Application of Part V to Scotland.

83. This Part of this Act shall have effect in relation to Scotland as set out in Schedule 2 to this Act.

PART VI

SUPPLEMENTARY PROVISIONS

Application to Crown.

84.—(1) Part I of this Act does not apply to any aerodrome in the occupation of a government department but, subject to that, references in that Part and in Part II of this Act to public works and responsible authorities include references to any works or authority which, apart from any Crown exemption, would be public works or a responsible authority.

(2) Parts III and IV of this Act apply in relation to the acquisition of interests in land (whether compulsorily or by agreement) by government departments being authorities possessing compulsory purchase powers, as they apply in relation to the acquisition of interests in land by such authorities who are not government departments.

Financial provisions.

85. There shall be paid out of moneys provided by Parliament—

(a) any expenses incurred under this Act by any government department ;

(b) any increase attributable to this Act in the sums payable out of such moneys under any other Act.

Repeals.

86. The enactments specified in Schedule 3 to this Act are hereby repealed to the extent specified in the third column of that Schedule.

General interpretation.

1947 c. 48.

1948 c. 45.

87.—(1) In this Act—

" agriculture ", " agricultural " and " agricultural land " have the meaning given in section 109 of the Agriculture Act 1947 or, in relation to Scotland, section 86 of the Agriculture (Scotland) Act 1948, and references

to the farming of land include references to the PART VI
carrying on in relation to the land of any agricultural
activities ;

" agricultural holding " has the meaning given in section 1
of the Agricultural Holdings Act 1948 or, in relation 1948 c. 63.
to Scotland, section 1 of the Agricultural Holdings 1949 c. 75.
(Scotland) Act 1949 and " landlord ", " tenant " and
" notice to quit ", in relation to an agricultural holding, have the same meaning as in those Acts respectively ;

" agricultural unit " has the meaning given in section 207(1)
of the Town and Country Planning Act 1971 or, in 1971 c. 78.
relation to Scotland, section 196(1) of the Town and 1972 c. 52.
Country Planning (Scotland) Act 1972 ;

" acquiring authority " and " authority possessing compulsory purchase powers " have the same meaning as in
the Land Compensation Act 1961 or, in relation to 1961 c. 33.
Scotland, the Land Compensation (Scotland) Act 1963 ; 1963 c. 51.

" aerodrome " has the meaning given in section 63(1) of
the Civil Aviation Act 1949 ; 1949 c. 67.

" cottar " has the same meaning as in section 28(4) of the
Crofters (Scotland) Act 1955 ; 1955 c. 21.

" croft ", " crofter " and " landlord ", in relation to a croft,
have the same meanings respectively as in the Crofters
(Scotland) Act 1955 ;

" disabled person " means a person who is substantially
and permanently handicapped by illness, injury or
congenital infirmity, or, in relation to Scotland, means
a person in need under section 12 of the Social Work 1968 c. 49.
(Scotland) Act 1968 as read with section 1 of the
Chronically Sick and Disabled Persons (Scotland) Act 1972 c. 51.
1972 ;

" dwelling " means a building or part of a building occupied
or (if not occupied) last occupied or intended to be
occupied as a private dwelling or, in relation to
Scotland, a private house, and (except in section 29)
includes any garden, yard, outhouses and
appurtenances belonging to or usually enjoyed with
that building or part ;

" heritable security " means any security capable of being
constituted over any interest in land by a disposition
or assignation of that interest in security of any debt
and of being recorded in the Register of Sasines ;

" holding ", in relation to a landholder and a statutory
small tenant, has the same meaning as in section 2(1)
of the Small Landholders (Scotland) Act 1911 and 1911 c. 49.
" landlord ", in relation to such a holding, has the same

N 4

PART VI
1949 c. 75.
1911 c. 49.

1963 c. 51.

1970 c. 20.

1954 c. 56.

meaning as in the Agricultural Holdings (Scotland) Act 1949 ;

" landholder " has the same meaning as in section 2(2) of the Small Landholders (Scotland) Act 1911 ;

" owner ", in relation to Scotland, has the same meaning as in section 45(1) of the Land Compensation (Scotland) Act 1963 ;

" road " has the meaning assigned to it in the Roads (Scotland) Act 1970 ;

" statutory small tenant " has the same meaning as in section 32(1) of the Small Landholders (Scotland) Act 1911 ;

" tenancy ", in relation to England and Wales and otherwise than in relation to an agricultural holding, has the same meaning as in the Landlord and Tenant Act 1954.

1972 c. 70.

(2) In this Act references to the council of a district are, until 1st April 1974, references to the council of a county district or county borough and, thereafter, to the council of a district within the meaning of the Local Government Act 1972 ; and references to a London borough and the council of a London borough include references to the City of London and the Common Council.

1959 c. 25.

(3) Sections 22 to 25 above shall be construed as one with the Highways Act 1959 or, in relation to Scotland, the Roads (Scotland) Act 1970.

(4) Except where the context otherwise requires, references in this Act to any enactment are references to that enactment as amended, and include references to that enactment as extended or applied, by any other enactment, including this Act.

Northern
Ireland.

88.—(1) Her Majesty may by Order in Council—

(a) extend this Act (other than Part V thereof), with such additions, exceptions and modifications as appear to Her Majesty to be expedient, to—

(i) the provision, operation, management or use of public works in Northern Ireland under any enactment relating to a matter in respect of which the Parliament of Northern Ireland does not have power to make laws (in this section referred to as " a reserved enactment ") ; and

(ii) acquisitions of land in Northern Ireland by any department or body exercising powers of acquisition under a reserved enactment ;

(b) apply, with such additions, exceptions and modification as appear to Her Majesty to be expedient, the

provisions of Schedules 5 and 6 to the Roads Act
(Northern Ireland) 1948 or Schedule 6 to the Local 1948 c. 28.
Government Act (Northern Ireland) 1972 to the (N.I.)
acquisition, otherwise than by agreement, of land in 1972 c. 9 (N.I.).
Northern Ireland by any department or body exercis-
ing powers of acquisition under a reserved enactment.

(2) An Order in Council under this section may include such
provisions as appear to Her Majesty to be incidental to or consequential on any provision contained in such an Order by virtue
of subsection (1) above.

(3) An Order in Council under this section may be varied
or revoked by a further Order in Council made thereunder.

89.—(1) This Act may be cited as the Land Compensation Short title,
Act 1973. commence-
ment and
(2) Part I of this Act shall not come into force until the extent.
expiration of the period of one month beginning with the date
on which this Act is passed.

(3) Section 48 above does not affect any compensation which
fell or falls to be assessed by reference to prices current on a
date before the passing of this Act, and the other provisions
of Part IV of this Act relating to the assessment of compensation
do not affect any compensation which fell or falls to be
assessed by reference to prices current on a date before 17th
October 1972.

(4) This Act, except section 88, does not extend to Northern
Ireland.

SCHEDULES

SCHEDULE 1

APPLICATION OF SECTION 60 TO STATUTORY SMALL TENANTS

PART I

Modification of section 60

Section 60 above shall apply to a statutory small tenant subject to the following modifications—

1955 c. 21.

1911 c. 49.

(*a*) for any reference to a croft, crofter or section 12 of the Crofters (Scotland) Act 1955 there shall be substituted respectively a reference to a holding, statutory small tenant or section 32(15) of the Small Landholders (Scotland) Act 1911;

(*b*) in subsection (1), for the words from " crofter " in paragraph (*a*) to " so required " in paragraph (*b*) there shall be substituted the words " statutory small tenant and resumption of the holding is authorised by an order of the Scottish Land Court under section 32(15) of the Small Landholders (Scotland) Act 1911; and (*b*) the resumption is so authorised ";

(*c*) in subsection (2), for the words " crofter required by such an order to surrender his croft " there shall be substituted the words " statutory small tenant, resumption of whose holding is authorised by such an order ";

(*d*) in subsections (2) and (3), for the words " croft is required to be surrendered ", wherever they occur, there shall be substituted the words " holding is authorised to be resumed ";

1968 c. 34.

(*e*) in subsection (2)(*a*), after the words " year, etc.) " there shall be inserted the words " and section 12 of the Agriculture (Miscellaneous Provisions) Act 1968 " and for the words " the crofter had not been so required to surrender his croft " there shall be substituted the words " resumption of the holding had not been so authorised ";

(*f*) for subsection (2)(*b*) there shall be substituted the following paragraph—

"(*b*) any provision of the said section 32(15) relating to compensation to a statutory small tenant shall not have effect in relation to the resumption of the holding by reason of the order.";

(*g*) in subsection (5), for the words " to surrender ", wherever they occur, there shall be substituted the words " authorising resumption of ".

PART II   SCH. 1

Section 60 *as modified, in its application to statutory small tenants*

(1) This section has effect where—

(*a*) the person in occupation of an agricultural holding is a Resumption of statutory small tenant and resumption of the holding is holding of authorised by an order of the Scottish Land Court under statutory section 32(15) of the Small Landholders (Scotland) Act small tenant: right to opt 1911 ; and for notice of entry
(*b*) the resumption is so authorised— compensation.

(i) after an acquiring authority have served notice to 1911 c. 49. treat on the landlord of the holding or, being an authority possessing compulsory purchase powers, have agreed to acquire his interest in the holding ; and

(ii) where the Court have been satisfied under the said section 32(15) that the landlord desires to resume the holding for a reasonable purpose which is a purpose other than an agricultural purpose.

(2) If the statutory small tenant, resumption of whose holding is authorised by such an order, elects that this subsection shall apply to the order and gives up possession of the holding to the acquiring authority on or before the date on which the holding is authorised to be resumed in accordance with the order—

(*a*) section 114 of the Lands Clauses Consolidation (Scotland) 1845 c. 19. Act 1845 (compensation for tenants from year to year, etc.) and section 12 of the Agriculture (Miscellaneous Provisions) 1968 c. 34. Act 1968 shall have effect as if resumption of the holding had not been so authorised and the acquiring authority had taken possession of the holding in pursuance of a notice of entry under paragraph 3 of Schedule 2 to the Acquisition of Land (Authorisation Procedure) (Scotland) 1947 c. 42. Act 1947 on the day before that on which the holding is authorised to be resumed in accordance with the order ; and

(*b*) any provision of the said section 32(15) relating to compensation to a statutory small tenant shall not have effect in relation to the resumption of the holding by reason of the order.

(3) No election under subsection (2) above shall be made or, if already made, continue to have effect in relation to any land to which such an order relates if, before the date on which the holding is authorised to be resumed in accordance with the order, an acquiring authority take possession of that land in pursuance of an enactment providing for the taking of possession of land compulsorily.

(4) Any election under subsection (2) above shall be made by notice in writing served on the acquiring authority not later than the date on which possession of the holding is given up.

SCH. 1   (5) This section shall have effect in relation to an order authorising resumption of part of a holding as it has effect in relation to an order authorising resumption of an entire holding and references to a holding shall be construed accordingly.

(6) The reference in subsection (1)(*b*)(i) above to a notice to treat served by an acquiring authority includes a reference to a notice to treat deemed to have been so served under any of the provisions mentioned in section 53(5) above.

Section 83.

SCHEDULE 2

APPLICATION OF PART V TO SCOTLAND

PLANNING BLIGHT

Extension of classes of blighted land

Land affected by proposed structure and local plans etc.

68.—(1) In paragraph (*a*) of section 181(1) of the Act of 1972 (land indicated in a structure plan in force as land which may be required for the purposes of functions of public authorities or as land which may be included in an action area) the reference to a structure plan in force shall include a reference to—

(*a*) a structure plan which has been submitted to the Secretary of State under section 5 of that Act ;

(*b*) proposals for alterations to a structure plan which have been submitted to the Secretary of State under section 8 of that Act ;

(*c*) modifications proposed to be made by the Secretary of State in any such plan or proposals as are mentioned in the preceding paragraphs, being modifications of which he has given notice in accordance with regulations under Part II of that Act.

(2) In paragraph (*b*) of the said section 181(1) (land allocated for the purposes of functions of public authorities by a local plan in force and land defined in such a plan as the site of proposed development for the purposes of any such functions) the reference to a local plan in force shall include a reference to—

(*a*) a local plan of which copies have been made available for inspection under section 10(2) of the Act of 1972 ;

(*b*) proposals for alterations to a local plan of which copies have been made available for inspection under section 13(2) of that Act ;

(*c*) modifications proposed to be made by the local planning authority or the Secretary of State in any such plan or proposals as are mentioned in the preceding paragraphs, being modifications of which notice has been given by the authority or the Secretary of State in accordance with regulations under Part II of that Act.

(3) In section 38(1)(*b*) of the Town and Country Planning (Scotland) Act 1959 as it has effect by virtue of paragraph 49 of Schedule 22 to the Act of 1972 (provisions corresponding to section 181(1)(*b*) of the Act of 1972 pending coming into force of local plans) the reference to a development plan shall include a reference to—

(*a*) proposals for alterations to a development plan submitted to the Secretary of State under paragraph 3 of Schedule 3 to the Act of 1972 ;

(*b*) modifications proposed to be made by the Secretary of State in any such proposals, being modifications of which notice has been given by the Secretary of State by advertisement.

(4) No blight notice shall be served by virtue of subsection (1) or (2) above at any time after the copies of the plan or proposals made available for inspection have been withdrawn under section 6(6) or 10(5) of the Act of 1972 (directions by Secretary of State requiring further publicity).

(5) No blight notice shall be served by virtue of this section after the relevant plan or alterations have come into force (whether in their original form or with modifications) or the Secretary of State has decided to reject or, in the case of a local plan, the local planning authority have decided to abandon the plan or alterations and notice of the decision has been given by advertisement.

(6) Where an appropriate authority have served a counter-notice objecting to a blight notice served by virtue of this section, then, if the relevant plan or alterations come into force (whether in their original form or with modifications) the appropriate authority may serve on the claimant, in substitution for the counter-notice already served, a further counter-notice specifying different grounds of objection, and section 184 of the Act of 1972 (reference of objections to Lands Tribunal for Scotland) shall have effect in relation to the further counter-notice as it has effect in relation to the counter-notice already served :

Provided that a further counter-notice under this subsection shall not be served—

(*a*) at any time after the end of the period of two months beginning with the date on which the relevant plan or alterations come into force ; or

(*b*) if the objection in the counter-notice already served has been withdrawn or the Lands Tribunal for Scotland has already determined whether or not to uphold that objection.

(7) References in subsections (1) to (3) above to anything done under any of the provisions there mentioned include references to anything done under those provisions as they apply by virtue of section 15 of, or paragraph 4 of Schedule 3 to, the Act of 1972 (default powers of Secretary of State).

(8) In this section references to alterations to a local plan include references to its replacement, and references to alterations to a development plan include references to additions to it.

SCH. 2
1959 c. 70.

(9) In relation to land falling within section 181(1)(*b*) of the Act of 1972 or section 38(1)(*b*) of the Town and Country Planning (Scotland) Act 1959, as extended by this section, " the appropriate enactment " for the purposes of sections 181 to 196 of the Act of 1972 shall be determined in accordance with section 195(2) of the Act of 1972 as if references therein to the development plan were references to any such plan, proposals or modifications as are mentioned in subsection (2)(*a*), (*b*) or (*c*) and subsection (3)(*a*) or (*b*) above.

Land affected by proposed highway orders.
1946 c. 30.
1949 c. 32.

1970 c. 20.

1935 c. 47.

69.—(1) In section 181(1)(*e*) of the Act of 1972 (land on or adjacent to line of road proposed to be constructed etc. as indicated in an order or scheme which has come into operation under the provisions of the Trunk Roads Act 1946 or Special Roads Act 1949)—

(*a*) the reference to such an order or scheme which has come into force as aforesaid shall include a reference to an order or scheme proposed to be made or confirmed under section 1(2) of the Trunk Roads Act 1946, section 1, 3 or 14 of the Special Roads Act 1949 or section 15 of the Roads (Scotland) Act 1970 in respect of which a notice has been published under Schedule 2 to the said Act of 1946 or Schedule 1 to the said Act of 1949 ; and

(*b*) for the reference to section 13 of the Restriction of Ribbon Development Act 1935 there shall be substituted a reference to sections 29 to 33 of the Roads (Scotland) Act 1970 as read with, in addition to the enactments specified in the said section 181(1)(*e*), section 15 of the said Act of 1970.

(2) No blight notice shall be served by virtue of this section at any time after the relevant order or scheme has come into operation (whether in its original form or with modifications) or the Secretary of State has decided not to confirm or make the order or scheme.

(3) Subsection (6) of section 68 above shall have effect in relation to a blight notice served by virtue of this section as it has effect in relation to a blight notice served by virtue of that section taking references to the relevant plan or alterations as references to the relevant order or scheme.

Land affected by proposed compulsory purchase orders.

1947 c. 42.

70.—(1) Section 181(1)(*g*) and (*i*) of the Act of 1972 (land in respect of which a compulsory purchase order is in force where a notice to treat has not been served) shall apply also to land in respect of which a compulsory purchase order has been submitted for confirmation to, or been prepared in draft by, a Minister and in respect of which a notice has been published under paragraph 3(1)(*a*) of Schedule 1 to the Acquisition of Land (Authorisation Procedure) (Scotland) Act 1947 or under any corresponding enactment applicable thereto.

(2) No blight notice shall be served by virtue of this section at any time after the relevant compulsory purchase order has come into force (whether in its original form or with modifications) or the Minister concerned has decided not to confirm or make the order.

(3) In relation to land falling within the said section 181(1)(*g*) or (*i*) by virtue of this section " the appropriate enactment " for the

purposes of sections 181 to 196 of the Act of 1972 shall be the enactment which would provide for the compulsory acquisition of the land or of the rights in or over the land if the relevant compulsory purchase order were confirmed or made.

SCH. 2

71.—(1) Section 181(1) of the Act of 1972 shall have effect as if the land specified therein included land which—

Land affected by resolution of planning authority or directions of Secretary of State.

> (a) is land indicated in a plan (not being a development plan) approved by a resolution passed by a local planning authority for the purpose of the exercise of their powers under Part III of that Act as land which may be required for the purposes of any functions of a government department, local authority or statutory undertakers ; or

> (b) is land in respect of which a local planning authority have resolved to take action to safeguard it for development for the purposes of any such functions or been directed by the Secretary of State to restrict the grant of planning permission in order to safeguard it for such development.

(2) Paragraph (a) of the said section 181(1) shall not apply to land within subsection (1) above.

(3) In relation to land falling within subsection (1) above " the appropriate enactment " for the purposes of sections 181 to 196 of the Act of 1972 shall be determined in accordance with section 195(2) of that Act as if references therein to the development plan were references to the resolution or direction in question.

72.—(1) Section 181(1) of the Act of 1972 shall have effect as if the land specified therein included land which—

Land affected by orders relating to new towns.

> (a) is land within an area described as the site of a proposed new town in the draft of an order in respect of which a notice has been published under paragraph 2 of Schedule 1 to the New Towns (Scotland) Act 1968 ; or

1968 c. 16.

> (b) is land within an area designated as the site of a proposed new town by an order which has come into operation under section 1 of the said Act of 1968.

(2) No blight notice shall be served by virtue of subsection (1)(a) above at any time after the order there mentioned has come into operation (whether in the form of the draft or with modifications) or the Secretary of State has decided not to make the order.

(3) Until such time as a development corporation is established for the new town, sections 181 to 196 of the Act of 1972 shall have effect in relation to land within subsection (1) above as if " the appropriate authority " and the " appropriate enactment " were the Secretary of State and subsection (4) below respectively.

(4) Until such time as aforesaid the Secretary of State shall have power to acquire compulsorily any interest in land in pursuance of a blight notice served by virtue of subsection (1) above ; and where he acquires an interest as aforesaid, then—

> (a) if the land is or becomes land within subsection (1)(b) above, the interest shall be transferred by him to the development corporation established for the new town ; and

SCH. 2

(b) in any other case, the interest may be disposed of by him in such manner as he thinks fit.

1963 c. 51.

(5) The Land Compensation (Scotland) Act 1963 shall have effect in relation to the compensation payable in respect of the acquisition of an interest by the Secretary of State under subsection (4) above as if the acquisition were by a development corporation under the New Towns (Scotland) Act 1968 and as if, in the case of land within subsection (1)(a) above, the land formed part of an area designated as the site of a new town by an order which has come into operation under section 1 of the said Act of 1968.

(6) Section 11 of the said Act of 1968 (right to require development corporation to acquire land within area designated as the site of a new town) shall cease to have effect except in relation to any notice served under that section before the coming into force of this section.

Land affected by housing treatment resolution.

1969 c. 34.

73.—(1) Section 181(1) of the Act of 1972 shall have effect as if the land specified therein included land which—

(a) is land within an area declared to be a housing treatment area by a resolution under section 4 of the Housing (Scotland) Act 1969 where the resolution provides that any of the buildings in that area are to be demolished ; or

(b) is land surrounded by or adjoining an area declared as aforesaid to be a housing treatment area, whether or not the resolution provides that any of the buildings in that area are to be demolished.

(2) The grounds on which objection may be made in a counter-notice to a blight notice served by virtue of subsection (1) above shall not include those specified in section 183(2)(b) or (c) of the Act of 1972 (no intention to acquire the land).

(3) In relation to land within subsection (1) above " the appropriate enactment " for the purposes of sections 181 to 196 of the Act of 1972 shall be section 5 of the Housing (Scotland) Act 1969.

Land affected by proposed exercise of powers under section 22.

1959 c. 25.

74.—(1) In section 181(1)(e) of the Act of 1972—

(a) the reference to a power of compulsory acquisition conferred by any of the provisions there mentioned shall include a reference to the power of compulsory acquisition conferred by section 22(1) above ;

(b) the reference to land required for purposes of construction, improvement or alteration as indicated in an order or scheme there mentioned shall include a reference to land required for the purposes of the said section 22(1).

(2) Section 181(1) of the Act of 1972 shall have effect as if the land specified therein included land which—

(a) is land shown on plans approved by a resolution of a local highway authority as land proposed to be acquired by them for the purposes of the said section 22(1) ; or

(b) is land shown in a written notice given by the Secretary of State to the local planning authority as land proposed to be acquired by him for those purposes in connection with a trunk road or special road which he proposes to provide.

75.—(1) Section 181(1) of the Act of 1972 (which sets out the classes of blighted land) shall apply to land in the case of which there is in force a compulsory purchase order providing for the acquisition of a right in or over that land, and the appropriate authority have power to serve, but have not served, notice to treat in respect of the right ; and the provisions of that Act mentioned in subsections (2) to (4) below shall accordingly be amended in accordance with those subsections.

Sch. 2
Land affected
by compulsory
purchase orders
providing for
acquisition of
rights in or
over land.

(2) In section 181—

    (*a*) at the end of subsection (1) there shall be added the follow-ing paragraph—

        " (*i*) is land in the case of which there is in force a compulsory purchase order providing for the acquisition of a right in or over that land, and the appropriate authority have power to serve, but have not served, notice to treat in respect of the right." ;

    (*b*) in subsection (6), for the word " (*h*) " there shall be sub-stituted the word " (*i*) ".

(3) In section 183—

    (*a*) after subsection (3) there shall be inserted the following subsection—

        " (3A) Where the appropriate enactment confers power to acquire a right in or over land, subsection (2) of this section shall have effect as if—

            (*a*) in paragraph (*b*), after the word ' acquire ' there were inserted the words ' or to acquire any right in or over ' ;

            (*b*) in paragraph (*c*), for the words ' do not propose to acquire ' there were substituted the words ' pro-pose neither to acquire nor to acquire any right in or over ' ;

            (*c*) in paragraph (*d*), after the words ' affected area ' there were inserted the words ' or to acquire any right in or over any part thereof ' ;

    (*b*) in subsection (5), in paragraphs (*a*) and (*b*), after the word ' acquire ' there shall be inserted the words ' or to acquire any right in or over ' ".

(4) At the end of section 195(1) there shall be added the following words " or, as respects the description contained in paragraph (*i*) of section 181(1) of this Act, the enactment under which the com-pulsory purchase order referred to in that paragraph was made.".

Attempts to sell blighted property

76.—(1) In sections 182(1)(*c*) and 190(1)(*b*) of the Act of 1972 (which require a person serving a blight notice to have made reason-able endeavours to sell his interest since the relevant date, that is to say, the date on which the land became blighted) the words " since the relevant date " and " since the relevant date (within the meaning of section 182 of this Act) " shall be omitted.

Amended
requirements
about attempts
to sell blighted
property.

Sch. 2

(2) In sections 182(1)(*d*) and 190(1)(*c*) of the Act of 1972 (which require a person serving a blight notice to have been unable to sell his interest except at a price lower than if the land had not been blighted) for the words from " he has been unable to sell " onwards there shall be substituted the words " in consequence of the fact that the hereditament or unit or a part of it was, or was likely to be, comprised in land of any of the specified descriptions, he has been unable to sell that interest except at a price substantially lower than that for which it might reasonably have been expected to sell if no part of the hereditament or unit were, or were likely to be, comprised in such land ".

(3) This section does not affect any blight notice served before the passing of this Act.

Blight notices by personal representatives

Power of personal representative to serve blight notice.

77.—(1) Where the whole or part of a hereditament or agricultural unit is comprised in land of any of the specified descriptions, and a person claims that—

(*a*) he is the personal representative of a person (" the deceased ") who at the date of his death was entitled to an interest in that hereditament or unit ; and

(*b*) the interest was one which would have qualified for protection under sections 181 to 196 of the Act of 1972 if a notice under section 182 of that Act had been served in respect thereof on that date ; and

(*c*) he has made reasonable endeavours to sell that interest ; and

(*d*) in consequence of the fact that the hereditament or unit or a part of it was, or was likely to be, comprised in land of any of the specified descriptions, he has been unable to sell that interest except at a price substantially lower than that for which it might reasonably have been expected to sell if no part of the hereditament or unit were, or were likely to be, comprised in such land ; and

(*e*) one or more individuals are (to the exclusion of any body corporate) beneficially entitled to that interest,

he may serve on the appropriate authority a notice in the prescribed form requiring that authority to purchase that interest to the extent specified in, and otherwise in accordance with, the said sections 181 to 196.

(2) Subsection (1) above shall apply in relation to an interest in part of a hereditament or agricultural unit as it applies in relation to an interest in the entirety of a hereditament or agricultural unit :

Provided that this subsection shall not enable any person—

(*a*) if the deceased was entitled to an interest in the entirety of a hereditament or agricultural unit, to make any claim or serve any notice under this section in respect of the deceased's interest in part of the hereditament or unit ; or

(*b*) if the deceased was entitled to an interest only in part of the hereditament or agricultural unit, to make or serve any such claim or notice in respect of the deceased's interest in less than the entirety of that part.

(3) Subject to sections 73(2) above and 79(2) below, the grounds on which objection may be made in a counter-notice under section 183 of the Act of 1972 to a notice under this section are those specified in paragraphs (*a*) to (*c*) of subsection (2) of that section and, in a case to which it applies, the grounds specified in paragraph (*d*) of that subsection and also the following grounds—

(*a*) that the claimant is not the personal representative of the deceased or that, on the date of the deceased's death, the deceased was not entitled to an interest in any part of the hereditament or agricultural unit to which the notice relates ;

(*b*) that (for reasons specified in the counter-notice) the interest of the deceased is not such as is specified in subsection (1)(*b*) above ;

(*c*) that the conditions specified in subsection (1)(*c*), (*d*) or (*e*) above are not fulfilled.

(4) For the purpose of section 190(4) and (5) of the Act of 1972 (which prevent the service of concurrent blight notices under sections 182 and 190 of that Act) a notice served under this section shall be treated as a notice served under the said section 182.

(5) In section 139(1)(*c*) of the Transport Act 1968 (compensation 1968 c. 73. where land acquired for special road service area) the reference to a notice under section 182 of the Act of 1972 shall include a reference to a notice under this section.

Blight notices in respect of agricultural units

78.—(1) Where a blight notice is served in respect of an interest in the whole or part of an agricultural unit and on the date of service that unit or part contains land (hereafter referred to as "the unaffected area ") which does not fall within any of the specified descriptions as well as land (hereafter referred to as "the affected area ") which does so, the claimant may include in the notice—

Blight notice requiring purchase of whole agricultural unit.

(*a*) a claim that the unaffected area is not reasonably capable of being farmed, either by itself or in conjunction with other relevant land, as a separate agricultural unit ; and

(*b*) a requirement that the appropriate authority shall purchase his interest in the whole of the unit or, as the case may be, in the whole of the part of it to which the notice relates.

(2) Subject to section 79(3) below, " other relevant land " in subsection (1) above means—

(*a*) land comprised in the remainder of the agricultural unit if the blight notice is served only in respect of part of it ;

(*b*) land comprised in any other agricultural unit occupied by the claimant on the date of service, being land in respect of which he is then entitled to an owner's interest as defined in section 192(4) of the Act of 1972.

SCH. 2
Objection to
blight notice
requiring pur-
chase of whole
agricultural
unit.

79.—(1) The grounds on which objection may be made in a counter-notice to a blight notice served by virtue of section 78 above shall include the grounds that the claim made in the notice is not justified.

(2) Objection shall not be made to a blight notice served by virtue of section 78 above on the grounds mentioned in section 183(2)(c) of the Act of 1972 (part only of affected area proposed to be acquired) unless it is also made on the grounds mentioned in subsection (1) above ; and the Lands Tribunal for Scotland shall not uphold an objection to any such notice on the grounds mentioned in the said section 183(2)(c) unless it also upholds the objection on the grounds mentioned in subsection (1) above.

(3) Where objection is made to a blight notice served by virtue of section 78 above on the grounds mentioned in subsection (1) above and also on those mentioned in the said section 183(2)(c), the Lands Tribunal for Scotland, in determining whether or not to uphold the objection, shall treat that part of the affected area which is not specified in the counter-notice as included in " other relevant land " as defined in section 78(2) above.

(4) If the Lands Tribunal for Scotland upholds an objection but only on the grounds mentioned in subsection (1) above, the Tribunal shall declare that the blight notice is a valid notice in relation to the affected area but not in relation to the unaffected area.

(5) If the Tribunal upholds an objection both on the grounds mentioned in subsection (1) above and on the grounds mentioned in the said section 183(2)(c) (but not on any other grounds) the Tribunal shall declare that the blight notice is a valid notice in relation to the part of the affected area specified in the counter-notice as being the part which the appropriate authority propose to acquire as therein mentioned but not in relation to any other part of the affected area or in relation to the unaffected area.

(6) In a case falling within subsection (4) or (5) above, the Tribunal shall give directions specifying a date on which notice to treat (as mentioned in section 80 below and section 185 of the Act of 1972) is to be deemed to have been served.

(7) Section 184(5) of the Act of 1972 shall not apply to any blight notice served by virtue of section 78 above.

Effect of
blight notice
requiring pur-
chase of whole
agricultural
unit.

80.—(1) In relation to a blight notice served by virtue of section 78 above, subsection (1) of section 185 of the Act of 1972 shall have effect as if for the words " or (in the case of an agricultural unit) the interest of the claimant in so far as it subsists in the affected area " there were substituted the words " or agricultural unit " and subsection (3) of that section shall not apply to any such blight notice.

(2) Where the appropriate authority have served a counter-notice objecting to a blight notice on the grounds mentioned in section 79(1) above, then if either—

(a) the claimant, without referring that objection to the Lands Tribunal for Scotland, and before the time for so referring it

has expired, gives notice to the appropriate authority that he
withdraws his claim as to the unaffected area ; or

(*b*) on a reference to the Tribunal, the Tribunal makes a
declaration in accordance with section 79(4) above,

the appropriate authority shall be deemed to be authorised to acquire
compulsorily under the appropriate enactment the interest of the
claimant in so far as it subsists in the affected area (but not in so far
as it subsists in the unaffected area) and to have served a notice to
treat in respect thereof on the date mentioned in subsection (3) below.

(3) The said date—

(*a*) in a case falling within paragraph (*a*) of subsection (2) above,
is the date on which notice is given in accordance with that
paragraph ; and

(*b*) in a case falling within paragraph (*b*) of that subsection, is the
date specified in directions given by the Tribunal in
accordance with section 79(6) above.

(4) Where the appropriate authority have served a counter-notice
objection to a blight notice on the grounds mentioned in section 79(1)
above and also on the grounds mentioned in section 183(2)(*c*) of the
Act of 1972, then if either—

(*a*) the claimant, without referring that objection to the Lands
Tribunal for Scotland, and before the time for so referring it
has expired, gives notice to the appropriate authority that
he accepts the proposal of the authority to acquire the part
of the affected area specified in the counter-notice, and
withdraws his claim as to the remainder of that area and as
to the unaffected area ; or

(*b*) on a reference to the Tribunal, the Tribunal makes a declaration in accordance with section 79(5) above in respect of
that part of the affected area,

the appropriate authority shall be deemed to be authorised to acquire
compulsorily under the appropriate enactment the interest of the
claimant in so far as it subsists in the part of the affected area specified
in the counter-notice (but not in so far as it subsists in any other part
of that area or in the unaffected area) and to have served a notice
to treat in respect thereof on the date mentioned in subsection (5)
below.

(5) The said date—

(*a*) in a case falling within paragraph (*a*) of subsection (4) above,
is the date on which notice is given in accordance with that
paragraph ; and

(*b*) in a case falling within paragraph (*b*) of that subsection, is
the date specified in directions given by the Tribunal in
accordance with section 79(6) above.

(6) The compensation payable in respect of the acquisition by
virtue of this section of an interest in land comprised in—

(*a*) the unaffected area of an agricultural unit ; or

(*b*) if the appropriate authority have served a counter-notice objecting to the blight notice on the grounds mentioned in the said section 183(2)(*c*), so much of the affected area of the unit as is not specified in the counter-notice,

shall be assessed on the assumptions mentioned in section 5(2), (3) and (4) above.

(7) In relation to a blight notice served by virtue of section 78 above references to " the appropriate authority " and " the appropriate enactment " shall be construed as if the unaffected area of an agricultural unit were part of the affected area.

(8) The provisions mentioned in section 189(2) of the Act of 1972 (operation of blight provisions where claimant dies after serving blight notice) shall include subsections (2) and (4) above.

Supplementary

Supplementary provisions for Part V.

1972 c. 52.

81.—(1) In this Part of this Act " the Act of 1972 " means the Town and Country Planning (Scotland) Act 1972.

(2) In section 181(6) of the Act of 1972 (definition of " blight notice ") there shall be added at the end the words " or section 77 of the Land Compensation Act 1973 ".

(3) In section 183(4) of the Act of 1972 (which requires a counter-notice to state the grounds of objection) after the words " section 190(6) of this Act ", there shall be inserted the words " or section 77(3) or 79(1) of the Land Compensation Act 1973 ".

(4) In sections 181 to 196 of the Act of 1972 references to " these provisions " shall include references to this Part of this Act, and references to " the specified descriptions " shall include references to the descriptions contained in section 181(1)(*a*), (*b*), (*e*), (*g*) and (*i*) of that Act as extended by this Part of this Act and to the descriptions contained in sections 71, 72, 73 and 74(2) above.

(5) The Act of 1972 shall have effect as if this Part of this Act were included in the said sections 181 to 196.

SCHEDULE 3

REPEALS

Chapter	Short Title	Extent of Repeal
49 & 50 Vict. c. 22.	The Metropolitan Police Act 1886.	Section 5.
12, 13 & 14 Geo. 6 c. 67.	The Civil Aviation Act 1949.	Section 31(3).
2 & 3 Eliz. 2. c. 56.	The Landlord and Tenant Act 1954.	Section 39(1).
5 & 6 Eliz. 2. c. 56.	The Housing Act 1957.	Section 32. Section 42(3). Section 63(1). Section 100. Section 144. Schedule 9.
7 & 8 Eliz. 2. c. 25.	The Highways Act 1959.	In section 82(2) the words " subsection (5), or subsection (6) ". In section 214, subsections (5), (6) and (7) and the proviso to subsection (8). Section 222(5) and (10). Section 225(1) and (2). In section 238(3) the words " (5) and (6) ".
9 & 10 Eliz. 2. c. 33.	The Land Compensation Act 1961.	Section 30.
1963 c. 33.	The London Government Act 1963.	In Schedule 6 paragraph 58· In Schedule 8 paragraphs 12 and 13.
1963 c. 51.	The Land Compensation (Scotland) Act 1963.	Section 38 except so far as relating to land used for the purposes of agriculture.
1965 c. 16.	The Airports Authority Act 1965.	In Schedule 4 paragraph 2(3).
1965 c. 56.	The Compulsory Purchase Act 1965.	In Schedule 7 the entry relating to the Landlord and Tenant Act 1954.
1965 c. 59.	The New Towns Act 1965.	Section 11 and paragraph 7 of Schedule 6 except in relation to any notice served under section 11 before the passing of this Act. Section 22(1), (2), (5) and (6).
1966 c. 49.	The Housing (Scotland) Act 1966.	Section 160(1) and (2). Section 168. Schedule 8.
1968 c. 16.	The New Towns (Scotland) Act 1968.	Section 11 and paragraph 8 of Schedule 6 except in relation to any notice served under section 11 before the passing of this Act. Section 22(1), (2), (5) and (6).

Chapter	Short Title	Extent of Repeal
1968 c. 34.	The Agriculture (Miscellaneous Provisions) Act 1968.	Sections 15(1) and 42 except in relation to compensation falling to be assessed by reference to prices current on a date before the passing of this Act and except for the purposes of section 48(6) of this Act.
1969 c. 33.	The Housing Act 1969.	Section 32(3) and (4).
1969 c. 34.	The Housing (Scotland) Act 1969.	Sections 63 and 64.
1971 c. 78.	The Town and Country Planning Act 1971.	Section 130(1), (2), (4) and (5). In section 193, in subsection (1)(c) the words " since the relevant date " and subsection (3) except in relation to a blight notice served before the passing of this Act. In section 194(6) the words following paragraph (b) as far as the semi-colon. In section 201(1)(b) the words " since the relevant date (within the meaning of section 193 of this Act) " except in relation to a blight notice served before the passing of this Act. In section 207(1) the definition of " highway land acquisition powers".
1972 c. 47.	The Housing Finance Act 1972.	Section 94.
1972 c. 52.	The Town and Country Planning (Scotland) Act 1972.	Section 120(5) and (6). In section 182, in subsection (1)(c) the words " since the relevant date " and subsection (3) except in relation to a blight notice served before the passing of this Act. In section 190(1)(b) the words " since the relevant date (within the meaning of section 182 of this Act) " except in relation to a blight notice served before the passing of this Act.

Bahamas Independence Act 1973

1973 CHAPTER 27

An Act to make provision for, and in connection with, the attainment by the Bahamas of fully responsible status within the Commonwealth.   [14th June 1973]

BE IT ENACTED by the Queen's most Excellent Majesty, by and with the advice and consent of the Lords Spiritual and Temporal, and Commons, in this present Parliament assembled, and by the authority of the same, as follows:—

1.—(1) On and after 10th July 1973 (in this Act referred to as "the appointed day") Her Majesty's Government in the United Kingdom shall have no responsibility for the government of the Bahamas.

Fully responsible status of Bahamas.

(2) No Act of the Parliament of the United Kingdom passed on or after the appointed day shall extend, or be deemed to extend, to the Bahamas as part of their law; and on and after that day the provisions of Schedule 1 to this Act shall have effect with respect to the legislative powers of the Bahamas.

2.—(1) On and after the appointed day the British Nationality Acts 1948 to 1965 shall have effect as if in section 1(3) of the British Nationality Act 1948 (Commonwealth countries having separate citizenship) there were added at the end the words " and the Bahamas ".

Consequential modifications of British Nationality Acts.

1948 c. 56.

(2) Except as provided by section 3 of this Act, any person who immediately before the appointed day is a citizen of the United Kingdom and Colonies shall on that day cease to be such a citizen if he becomes on that day a citizen of the Bahamas.

(3) Except as provided by section 3 of this Act, any person who immediately before the appointed day—

(a) is a citizen of the United Kingdom and Colonies by virtue of a certificate of naturalisation granted or registration effected by the Governor or Government of the Bahamas ; and

(b) is also a citizen or national of another country,

shall on that day cease to be a citizen of the United Kingdom and Colonies whether or not he becomes on that day a citizen of the Bahamas.

(4) Except as provided by section 3 of this Act and without prejudice to subsection (3) of this section, any person who—

(a) immediately before the appointed day is a citizen of the United Kingdom and Colonies by virtue of any such certificate or registration as is mentioned in sub-section (3)(a) of this section ; and

(b) after that day becomes a citizen of the Bahamas under any such provisions as are mentioned in subsection (5) of this section,

shall cease to be a citizen of the United Kingdom and Colonies on the date on which he becomes a citizen of the Bahamas under those provisions.

(5) The provisions mentioned in subsection (4)(b) of this section are any provisions of an Order in Council made after the passing of this Act under the Bahama Islands (Constitution) Act 1963 whereby a person becomes, or is entitled to become, a citizen of the Bahamas after the appointed day by reason of his being immediately before that day a citizen of the United Kingdom and Colonies by virtue of any such certificate or registration as is mentioned in subsection (3)(a) of this section or by reason of his possessing immediately before that day Bahamian status as defined in section 128 of the Constitution set out in the Schedule to the Bahama Islands (Constitution) Order 1969.

1963 c. 56.

S.I. 1969/590.

1948 c. 56.

(6) Section 6(2) of the British Nationality Act 1948 (registration as citizens of the United Kingdom and Colonies of women who have been married to such citizens) shall not apply to a woman by virtue of her marriage to—

(a) a person who on the appointed day ceases to be such a citizen under subsection (2) or (3) of this section or who would have done so if living on the appointed day ; or (*b*) a person who after the appointed day ceases to be such a citizen under subsection (4) of this section.

(7) The references in this section to a person who is a citizen of the United Kingdom and Colonies by virtue of any such certificate as is mentioned in subsection (3)(*a*) of this section shall include references to a person who has become a person naturalised in the United Kingdom and Colonies by virtue of section 32(6) of the British Nationality Act 1948 (persons given 1948 c. 56. local naturalisation in a colony or protectorate before the commencement of that Act) in its application to the Bahamas.

3.—(1) Subject to subsection (5) of this section, a person Retention of shall not cease to be a citizen of the United Kingdom and citizenship Colonies under section 2 of this Act if he, his father or his of United father's father— Kingdom and Colonies

(*a*) was born in the United Kingdom or in a colony or by certain an associated state ; or persons connected

(*b*) is or was a person naturalised in the United Kingdom with the and Colonies ; or Bahamas.

(*c*) was registered as a citizen of the United Kingdom and Colonies ; or

(*d*) became a British subject by reason of the annexation of any territory included in a colony.

(2) A person shall not cease to be a citizen of the United Kingdom and Colonies under the said section 2 if either—

(*a*) he was born in a protectorate or protected state ; or

(*b*) his father or his father's father was so born and is or at any time was a British subject.

(3) A woman who immediately before the appointed day is the wife of a citizen of the United Kingdom and Colonies—

(*a*) shall not cease to be such a citizen under the said section 2 unless her husband either does so at the same time or has already done so ; and

(*b*) if she would, apart from paragraph (*a*) of this sub-section, have ceased to be such a citizen under that section at any time and her husband subsequently ceases to be such a citizen under that section, she shall cease to be such a citizen when her husband does so.

(4) Subject to subsection (5) of this section, the reference in subsection (1)(*b*) of this section to a person naturalised in the United Kingdom and Colonies shall include a reference to a person who would, if living immediately before the commencement of the British Nationality Act 1948, have

become a person naturalised in the United Kingdom and Colonies by virtue of section 32(6) of that Act.

(5) In this section—

1948 c. 56.

    (*a*) references to a colony shall be construed as not including references to any territory which, on the appointed day, is not a colony for the purposes of the British Nationality Act 1948 as that Act has effect on that day, and accordingly do not include references to the Bahamas, and

    (*b*) references to a protectorate or protected state shall be construed as not including references to any territory which, on the appointed day, is not a protectorate or a protected state (as the case may be) for the purposes of that Act as it has effect on that day ;

and subsection (1) of this section shall not apply to a person by virtue of any certificate of naturalisation granted or registration effected by the Governor or Government of a territory which by virtue of this subsection is excluded from references in this section to a colony, protectorate or protected state.

Consequential modifications of other enactments.
1889 c. 63.

4.—(1) Notwithstanding anything in the Interpretation Act 1889, the expression " colony " in any Act of the Parliament of the United Kingdom passed on or after the appointed day shall not include the Bahamas.

(2) On and after the appointed day—

1955 c. 18.
1955 c. 19.
1957 c. 53.

    (*a*) the expression " colony " in the Army Act 1955, the Air Force Act 1955 and the Naval Discipline Act 1957 shall not include the Bahamas, and

    (*b*) in the definitions of " Commonwealth force " in section 225(1) and 223(1) respectively of the said Acts of 1955, and in the definition of " Commonwealth country " in section 135(1) of the said Act of 1957, at the end there shall be added the words " or the Bahamas " ;

1971 c. 33.

and no Order in Council made on or after the appointed day under section 1 of the Armed Forces Act 1971 which continues either of the said Acts of 1955 or the said Act of 1957 in force for a further period shall extend to the Bahamas as part of their law.

(3) On and after the appointed day the provisions specified in Schedule 2 to this Act shall have effect subject to the amendments specified respectively in that Schedule.

(4) Subsection (3) of this section, and Schedule 2 to this Act, shall not extend to the Bahamas as part of their law.

5.—(1) The Board of Trade may on the appointed day trans- Transfer of
fer to the Government of the Bahamas all the interest of the colonial
Board in, and in the appurtenances to, the lighthouses in the lighthouses.
Bahamas which immediately before that day are colonial lights
within the meaning of the Merchant Shipping (Mercantile Marine 1898 c. 44.
Fund) Act 1898.

(2) On the appointed day those lighthouses shall cease to be
colonial lights within the meaning of the said Act of 1898, and
accordingly on that day—

 (*a*) the entry relating to the Bahamas in Schedule 3 to that
    Act shall be repealed ; and
 (*b*) section 670 of the Merchant Shipping Act 1894 (power 1894 c. 60.
    to fix colonial light dues) shall cease to have effect in
    relation to those lighthouses.

(3) Notwithstanding subsection (2) of this section there shall
be paid out of the General Lighthouse Fund any expenses
incurred by the Secretary of State in respect of those lighthouses
after the appointed day under any agreement made before that
day between him and the Government of the Bahamas.

6.—(1) In this Act, and in any amendment made by this Act Interpretation.
in any other enactment, " the Bahamas " means the territories
which immediately before the appointed day constitute the
Colony of the Commonwealth of the Bahama Islands and which
on and after that day are to be called the Commonwealth of
the Bahamas.

(2) Part III of the British Nationality Act 1948 (interpretation 1948 c. 56.
etc.) as in force at the passing of this Act shall have effect for
the purposes of sections 2 and 3 of this Act as if they were
included in that Act.

(3) References in this Act to any enactment are references
to that enactment as amended or extended by or under another
enactment.

7.—(1) This Act may be cited as the Bahamas Independence Short title,
Act 1973.   repeal and
                                                             extent.
(2) The Bahama Islands (Constitution) Act 1963 is hereby 1963 c. 56.
repealed as from the appointed day but not so as to affect the
operation as part of the law of the Bahamas of any Order in
Council made by virtue of that Act before that day.

(3) In accordance with section 3(3) of the West Indies Act 1967 c. 4.
1967, it is hereby declared that sections 2, 3 and 6(2) of this
Act extend to all associated states.

SCHEDULES

Section 1.

SCHEDULE 1

LEGISLATIVE POWERS OF BAHAMAS

1865 c. 63.

1. The Colonial Laws Validity Act 1865 shall not apply to any law made on or after the appointed day by the legislature of the Bahamas.

2. No law and no provision of any law made on or after the appointed day by that legislature shall be void or inoperative on the ground that it is repugnant to the law of England, or to the provisions of any Act of the Parliament of the United Kingdom, including this Act, or to any order, rule or regulation made under any such Act, and accordingly the powers of that legislature shall include the power to repeal or amend any such Act, order, rule or regulation in so far as it is part of the law of the Bahamas.

3. The legislature of the Bahamas shall have full power to make laws having extra-territorial operation.

4. Without prejudice to the generality of the preceding provisions of this Schedule—

1894 c. 60.

    (*a*) sections 735 and 736 of the Merchant Shipping Act 1894 shall be construed as if references therein to the legislature of a British possession did not include references to the legislature of the Bahamas ; and

1890 c. 27.

    (*b*) section 4 of the Colonial Courts of Admiralty Act 1890 (which requires certain laws to be reserved for the signification of Her Majesty's pleasure or to contain a suspending clause) and so much of section 7 of that Act as requires the approval of Her Majesty in Council to any rules of court for regulating the practice and procedure of a Colonial Court of Admiralty shall cease to have effect in the Bahamas.

Section 4.

SCHEDULE 2

AMENDMENTS NOT AFFECTING THE LAW OF THE BAHAMAS

Diplomatic immunities

1961 c. 11.

1. In section 1(5) of the Diplomatic Immunities (Conferences with Commonwealth Countries and Republic of Ireland) Act 1961, before the word " and " in the last place where it occurs there shall be inserted the words " the Bahamas ".

Financial

1958 c. 6.

2. In section 2(4) of the Import Duties Act 1958, before the words " together with " there shall be inserted the words " the Bahamas ".

Visiting forces

3. In the Visiting Forces (British Commonwealth) Act 1933, 1933 c. 6.
section 4 (attachment and mutual powers of command) shall apply
in relation to forces raised in the Bahamas as it applies to forces
raised in Dominions within the meaning of the Statute of West- 1931 c. 4 (22 &
minster 1931. 23 Geo. 5.).

4. In the Visiting Forces Act 1952— 1952 c. 67.

(*a*) in section 1(1)(*a*) (countries to which the Act applies) at
the end there shall be added the words " the Bahamas or " ;

(*b*) in section 10(1)(*a*), the expression " colony " shall not include
the Bahamas ;

and, until express provision with respect to the Bahamas is made by
an Order in Council under section 8 of that Act (application to
visiting forces of law relating to home forces), any such Order for
the time being in force shall be deemed to apply to visiting forces
of the Bahamas.

Ships and aircraft

5. In section 427(2) of the Merchant Shipping Act 1894, as set 1894 c. 60.
out in section 2 of the Merchant Shipping (Safety Convention)
Act 1949, before the words " or in any " there shall be inserted the 1949 c. 43.
words " or the Bahamas ".

6. The Ships and Aircraft (Transfer Restriction) Act 1939 shall 1939 c. 70.
not apply to any ship by reason only of its being registered in, or
licensed under the law of, the Bahamas ; and the penal provisions
of that Act shall not apply to persons in the Bahamas (but without
prejudice to the operation with respect to any ship to which that
Act does apply of the provisions thereof relating to the forfeiture
of ships).

7. In the Whaling Industry (Regulation) Act 1934, the expression 1934 c. 49.
" British ship to which this Act applies " shall not include a British
ship registered in the Bahamas.

8. The Bahamas shall not be a relevant overseas territory for the
purposes of sections 21(2) and 22(3) of the Civil Aviation Act 1971. 1971 c. 75.

Colonial stock

9. Section 20 of the Colonial Stock Act 1877 (which relates to the 1877 c. 59.
jurisdiction of courts in the United Kingdom as to colonial stock)
shall, in its application to stock of the Bahamas, have effect as if
for the second paragraph there were substituted—

" (2) Any person claiming to be interested in colonial stock
to which this Act applies, or in any dividend thereon, may
institute civil proceedings in the United Kingdom against the
registrar in relation to that stock or dividend.

(3) Notwithstanding anything in the foregoing provisions of
this section, the registrar shall not by virtue of an order made
by any court in the United Kingdom in any such proceedings
as are referred to in this section be liable to make any payment
otherwise than out of moneys in his possession in the United
Kingdom as registrar."

Commonwealth Institute

1925 ch. xvii.
1958 c. 16.

10. In section 8(2) of the Imperial Institute Act 1925, as amended by the Commonwealth Institute Act 1958, (power to vary the provisions of the said Act of 1925 if an agreement for the purpose is made with the governments of certain territories which for the time being are contributing towards the expenses of the Commonwealth Institute) at the end there shall be added the words " and the Bahamas ".

Rate Rebate Act 1973

1973 CHAPTER 28

An Act to exclude payments of attendance allowances
from calculations of gross income when assessing
eligibility for rate rebates under the General Rate Act
1967 and (as respects Scotland) the Rating Act 1966.

[*14th June 1973*]

BE IT ENACTED by the Queen's most Excellent Majesty, by and
with the advice and consent of the Lords Spiritual and
Temporal, and Commons, in this present Parliament
assembled, and by the authority of the same, as follows:—

1. At the end of paragraph 11 of Schedule 9 to the General
Rate Act 1967 and (as respects Scotland) of section 7(3) of the
Rating Act 1966 (which provide for certain income to be left out
of account when calculating the reckonable income of an
applicant for a rate rebate under those Acts) there shall be added
the following—

> " (*c*) any income by way of payments of any attendance
> allowance within the meaning of any regulations for the
> time being in force under the Family Income Supplements
> Act 1970."

*Exclusion of
attendance
allowance
when
calculating
reckonable
income for
rate rebate.*
1967 c. 9.
1966 c. 9.
1970 c. 55.

2.—(1) Section 1 of this Act shall have effect for the purpose
of determining the right of any person to a rate rebate and the
amount of rate rebate to which any person is entitled in relation
to the rebate period beginning on 1st October 1973 and to each
subsequent rebate period.

*Application of
section 1.*

(2) Section 1 of this Act shall also have effect in relation to the
current rebate period for the purpose of determining the right of
any person to a rate rebate and the amount of rate rebate to
which any person is entitled if, in either case, he makes an application for the rebate after the passing of this Act.

O

(3) A rebate application in respect of the current rebate period may be made after the passing of this Act by any person notwithstanding that he has made a rebate application in respect of that period which has either been granted, or refused, or has not been dealt with, before the passing of this Act, but where a second application is made in respect of that period, the rating authority, in determining the amount of rebate payable in respect of the later application, shall take into account the amount of rebate payable, if any, in respect of the earlier application.

1967 c. 9.

(4) Without prejudice to subsection (4) of section 49 of the General Rate Act 1967 (rebate applications to be made before the end of a rebate period) subsection (2) of that section (reduction of rebates in case of delayed applications) shall not apply in relation to any application made after the passing of this Act in respect of the current rebate period by a person whose reckonable income for the purposes of that application is reduced by reason of this Act.

(5) Except in so far as the context otherwise requires, expressions used in this section and in the General Rate Act 1967 have the same meanings in this section as in that Act, and " the current rebate period " means the rebate period beginning on 1st April 1973.

(6) In the application of this section to Scotland—

1966 c. 9.

(*a*) for the reference to the General Rate Act 1967 there shall be substituted a reference to the Rating Act 1966;

(*b*) for the reference to section 49 of the said Act of 1967 there shall be substituted a reference to section 5 of the said Act of 1966;

(*c*) for the references to 1st October and 1st April there shall be substituted the references relative to the said dates respectively contained in section 5(10)(*a*) of the said Act of 1966.

Expenses.

3. There shall be paid out of money provided by Parliament any increase attributable to this Act in the sums payable out of money so provided under any other Act.

Citation.

4. This Act may be cited as the Rate Rebate Act 1973; and this Act, in its application to England and Wales, may be cited together with the General Rate Acts 1967 and 1970 as the General Rate Acts 1967 to 1973.

Guardianship Act 1973

1973 CHAPTER 29

An Act to amend the law of England and Wales as to the guardianship of minors so as to make the rights of a mother equal with those of a father, and so as to make further provision with respect to applications and orders under section 9 of the Guardianship of Minors Act 1971 and with respect to the powers of a guardian under that Act in relation to the minor's property, and to amend section 4(2) of the Matrimonial Proceedings (Magistrates' Courts) Act 1960; to make provision in relation to like matters for Scotland; and for purposes connected therewith.   [5th July 1973]

BE IT ENACTED by the Queen's most Excellent Majesty, by and with the advice and consent of the Lords Spiritual and Temporal, and Commons, in this present Parliament assembled, and by the authority of the same, as follows: —

PART I

ENGLAND AND WALES

1.—(1) In relation to the custody or upbringing of a minor, Equality of and in relation to the administration of any property belonging parental rights. to or held in trust for a minor or the application of income of any such property, a mother shall have the same rights and authority as the law allows to a father, and the rights and authority of mother and father shall be equal and be exercisable by either without the other.

O 2

(2) An agreement for a man or woman to give up in whole or in part, in relation to any child of his or hers, the rights and authority referred to in subsection (1) above shall be unenforceable, except that an agreement made between husband and wife which is to operate only during their separation while married may, in relation to a child of theirs, provide for either of them to do so ; but no such agreement between husband and wife shall be enforced by any court if the court is of opinion that it will not be for the benefit of the child to give effect to it.

(3) Where a minor's father and mother disagree on any question affecting his welfare, either of them may apply to the court for its direction, and (subject to subsection (4) below) the court may make such order regarding the matters in difference as it may think proper.

(4) Subsection (3) above shall not authorise the court to make any order regarding the custody of a minor or the right of access to him of his father or mother.

(5) An order under subsection (3) above may be varied or discharged by a subsequent order made on the application of either parent or, after the death of either parent, on the application of any guardian under the Guardianship of Minors Act 1971, or (before or after the death of either parent) on the application of any other person having the custody of the minor.

1971 c. 3.   (6) Section 15(1) to (3) and section 16 of the Guardianship of Minors Act 1971 (jurisdiction and procedure) shall apply for the purposes of subsections (3) to (5) above as if they were contained in section 9 of that Act, except that section 15(3) shall not exclude any jurisdiction of a county court or a magistrates' court in proceedings against a person residing in Scotland or Northern Ireland for the revocation, revival or variation of any order under subsection (3) above.

(7) Nothing in the foregoing provisions of this section shall affect the operation of any enactment requiring the consent of both parents in a matter affecting a minor, or be taken as applying in relation to a minor who is illegitimate.

1956 c. 69.

959 c. 72.   (8) In the Sexual Offences Act 1956 there shall be substituted for section 38 the provisions set out in Schedule 1 to this Act, and in the Mental Health Act 1959 in section 49(4)(*d*) (under which for purposes of that Act a man deprived under the said section 38 of authority over a patient is not to be treated as the patient's nearest relative) for the word " man " there shall be substituted the word " person " ; but, save as aforesaid, nothing in this section shall be taken to affect the provisions of the Mental Health Act 1959 as to the person who is " the nearest relative " for purposes of the Act.

2.—(1) In sections 9, 13, 15 and 16 of the Guardianship of Minors Act 1971 there shall be made the amendments provided for by Part I of Schedule 2 to this Act (being amendments providing for mother and father to be treated alike in relation to applications under section 9 of that Act, and amendments relating to cases in which custody is given to an individual other than one of the parents) ; and accordingly section 9 and section 15(3) to (6) shall have effect as they are set out in Part II of that Schedule with the amendments required by this subsection.

PART I
Jurisdiction
and orders on
applications
under s. 9
of
Guardianship
of Minors
Act 1971.
1971 c. 3.

(2) Where an application made under section 9 of the Guardianship of Minors Act 1971 relates to the custody of a minor under the age of sixteen, then subject to sections 3 and 4 below—

(a) if by an order made on that application any person is given the custody of the minor, but it appears to the court that there are exceptional circumstances making it desirable that the minor should be under the super-vision of an independent person, the court may order that the minor shall be under the supervision of a specified local authority or under the supervision of a probation officer ;

(b) if it appears to the court that there are exceptional circumstances making it impracticable or undesirable for the minor to be entrusted to either of the parents or to any other individual, the court may commit the care of the minor to a specified local authority.

(3) Where the court makes an order under subsection (2)(b) above committing the care of a minor to a local authority, the court may make a further order requiring the payment by either parent to that authority while it has the care of the minor of such weekly or other periodical sum towards the maintenance of the minor as the court thinks reasonable having regard to the means of that parent.

(4) On an application under section 9 of the Guardianship of Minors Act 1971 the court may, in any case where it adjourns the hearing of the application for more than seven days, make an interim order, to have effect until such date as may be specified in the order and containing—

(a) provision for payment by either parent to the other, or to any person given the custody of the minor, of such weekly or other periodical sum towards the maintenance of the minor as the court thinks reason-able having regard to the means of the parent on whom the requirement is imposed ; and

(b) where by reason of special circumstances the court thinks it proper, any provision regarding the custody

O 3

PART I

of the minor or the right of access to the minor of the mother or father;

but an interim order under this subsection shall not be made to have effect after the end of the three months beginning with the date of the order or of any previous interim order made under this subsection with respect to the application, and shall cease to have effect on the making of a final order or on the dismissal of the application.

1971 c. 3.

(5) A magistrates' court may also make such an interim order where under section 16(4) of the Guardianship of Minors Act 1971 it refuses to make an order on an application under section 9 on the ground that the matter is one that would more conveniently be dealt with by the High Court; but an interim order under this subsection shall not be made so as to have effect after the end of the three months beginning with the date of the order.

(6) Where an application under section 9 of the Guardianship of Minors Act 1971 relates to a minor who is illegitimate, references in subsections (2) and (4)(b) above and in sections 3 and 4 below to the father or mother or parent of the minor shall be construed accordingly (but subsections (3) and (4)(a) above shall not apply).

(7) In section 16(2) of the Guardianship of Minors Act 1971 (which provides for appeals from orders made by a county court under that Act) for the words " made by a county court under this Act " there shall be substituted the words " made on an application under this Act by a county court ".

(8) For purposes of this section " local authority " means the council of a non-metropolitan county or a metropolitan district or London borough, or the Common Council of the City of London, and, until the coming into force of the Local Government Act 1972, includes the council of any county or county borough; and the matters which under section 2 of the Local Authority Social Services Act 1970 are to stand referred to an authority's social services committee shall include all matters relating to the discharge by the authority of functions under this section.

1972 c. 70.

1970 c. 42.

Additional provisions as to supervision orders.

3.—(1) Where the court makes an order under section 2(2)(a) above (in this section referred to as a " supervision order "), and the order provides for supervision by a probation officer, then—

    (a) if it is an order of the High Court, the officer responsible for carrying out the order shall be such probation officer as may be selected under arrangements made by the Secretary of State; and (*b*) in any other case the order shall be for supervision by a probation officer appointed for or assigned to the petty sessions area in which, in the opinion of the court, the minor is or will be resident, and the officer responsible for carrying out the order shall be selected in like manner as if the order were a probation order.

(2) A supervision order shall cease to have effect when the minor attains the age of 16 ; and where a supervision order is made at a time when the parents of the minor are residing together—

(*a*) the order may direct that it is to cease to have effect if for a period of three months after it is made they continue to reside together ; and

(*b*) the order (whether or not it includes a direction under paragraph (*a*) above) may direct that it is not to operate while they are residing together.

(3) A supervision order may be varied or discharged by a subsequent order made on the application of either parent or after the death of either parent, on the application of any guardian under the Guardianship of Minors Act 1971, or (before 1971 c. 3. or after the death of either parent) on the application of any other person having the custody of the minor by virtue of an order under section 9(1) of that Act or on that of the probation officer or local authority having the supervision of the minor by virtue of the order ; and section 16 of that Act shall have effect in relation to applications under this subsection as it has effect in relation to applications under that Act, and section 16(5) shall apply as it applies in relation to the applications there mentioned.

(4) Without prejudice to subsection (3) above, in relation to supervision orders of magistrates' courts the rules made under section 15 of the Justices of the Peace Act 1949 may make pro- 1949 c. 101. vision for substituting from time to time a probation officer appointed for or assigned to a different petty sessions area or, as the case may be, a different local authority, if in the opinion of the court the minor is or will be resident in that petty sessions area or, as the case may be, in the area of that authority.

(5) Section 15(4) to (6), except section 15(5)(*a*), of the Guardianship of Minors Act 1971 shall apply in relation to supervision orders as they apply in relation to orders under section 9(2) of that Act.

4.—(1) An order under section 2(2)(*b*) above committing the Additional care of a minor to a local authority shall commit him to the provisions care (while a minor) of the authority in whose area he is, in as to order committing the opinion of the court, resident immediately before being so care of minor committed. to local

O 4   authority.

(2) Before making an order under section 2(2)(*b*) above the court shall inform the local authority of the court's proposal to make the order, and shall hear any representations from the authority, including any representations as to the making also of an order under section 2(3) above for payments to the authority.

(3) In relation to an order under section 2(2)(*b*) above committing the care of a minor to a local authority, or to an order under section 2(3) requiring payments to be made to an authority to whom the care of a minor is so committed, the following provisions of the Guardianship of Minors Act 1971, that is to say, sections 9(3) and (4), 12(2), 13, 15(4) to (6) and 16(5), shall apply as if the order under section 2(2)(*b*) above were an order under section 9 of that Act giving custody of the minor to a person other than one of the parents (and the local authority were lawfully given that custody by the order), and any order for payment to the local authority were an order under section 9(2) requiring payment to be made to them as a person so given that custody.

1971 c. 3.

(4) On the making of an order under section 2(2)(*b*) above with respect to a minor, Parts II and III of the Children Act 1948 together with sections 30, 47 and 58 of the Children and Young Persons Act 1963 (which relate to the treatment of children in the care of a local authority and to contributions towards their maintenance) shall apply as if the minor had been received by the local authority into their care under section 1 of the Children Act 1948, except that—

1948 c. 43.
1963 c. 37.

    (*a*) the exercise by the local authority of their powers under sections 12 and 13 of that Act shall, where the order is made by the High Court, be subject to any directions given by the court ; and

    (*b*) section 17 of that Act (which relates to arrangements for emigration) shall not apply ; and

    (*c*) section 24(2) of that Act (which provides for a child's father and mother to be liable to make contributions in respect of him) shall not apply, but so that references to the local authority who are entitled to receive contributions shall be construed as if section 24(2) did apply.

(5) While an order under section 2(2)(*b*) above remains in force with respect to a minor, the minor shall continue in the care of the local authority notwithstanding any claim by a parent or other person.

(6) Each parent or guardian of a child for the time being in the care of a local authority by virtue of an order under section 2(2)(*b*) above shall give notice to the authority of any change of address of that parent or guardian, and any person who without reasonable excuse fails to comply with this subsection shall be liable on summary conviction to a fine not exceeding £10.

5.—(1) There shall be no appeal under section 16 of the Guardianship of Minors Act 1971 from an interim order under section 2(4) or (5) above if the appeal relates only to a provision requiring payments to be made towards the maintenance of a minor.

PART I
Additional
provisions
as to interim
orders.
1971 c. 3.

(2) Section 9(3) and (4) and section 13 of the Guardianship of Minors Act 1971 shall apply to any such interim order as they apply to an order under section 9(1) or (2).

(3) Where in the case of an application under section 9 of the Guardianship of Minors Act 1971 the applicant or the respondent (or any of the respondents) resides in Scotland or Northern Ireland, then—

(a) a county court or magistrates' court may exercise the jurisdiction to make, vary or discharge interim orders requiring payments to be made towards the maintenance of the minor or interim orders relating to the custody of the minor in any case in which, in accordance with section 15(4) or (5) of the Guardianship of Minors Act 1971, the court could make an order under section 9 of that Act relating to the custody of the minor or, as the case may be, could vary or discharge such an order ; and

(b) a magistrates' court shall have jurisdiction to make an interim order on the application of the respondent in any case in which, in accordance with section 15(6) of that Act, the court could make an order under section 9 of that Act.

6.—(1) If the court dealing with an application under section 9 of the Guardianship of Minors Act 1971 or section 3(3) of this Act requests a local authority to arrange for an officer of the authority to make to the court a report, orally or in writing, with respect to any specified matter (being a matter appearing to the court to be relevant to the application), or requests a probation officer to make such a report to the court, it shall be the duty of the local authority or probation officer to comply with the request.

Evidence on
applications
under s. 9 of
Guardianship
of Minors
Act 1971.

(2) Any statement which is or purports to be a report in pursuance of subsection (1) above shall be made, or if in writing be read aloud, before the court at a hearing of the application, and immediately after it has been so made or read aloud the court shall ask whether any party to the proceedings who is present or represented by counsel or solicitor at the hearing objects to anything contained therein ; and where objection is made—

(a) the court shall require the officer by whom the statement was or purported to be made to give evidence on or with respect to the matters referred to therein ; and

(b) any party to the proceedings may give or call evidence with respect to any matter referred to in the statement or in any evidence given by the officer.

(3) The court may take account of any statement made or read aloud under subsection (2) above and of any evidence given under paragraph (a) of that subsection, so far as that statement or evidence relates to the matters specified by the court under subsection (1), notwithstanding any enactment or rule of law relating to the admissibility of evidence.

(4) Where for the purpose of subsection (1) above a magistrates' court adjourns the hearing of an application, then, subject to section 46(2) of the Magistrates' Courts Act 1952 (which provides for the notice required of a resumed hearing), the court may resume the hearing at the time and place appointed notwithstanding the absence of both or all of the parties.

1952 c. 55.

(5) Section 2(8) above shall apply in relation to this section as it applies in relation to section 2.

Powers of guardians.
1971 c. 3.

7.—(1) Subject to subsection (2) below, a guardian under the Guardianship of Minors Act 1971, besides being guardian of the person of the minor, shall have all the rights, powers and duties of a guardian of the minor's estate, including in particular the right to receive and recover in his own name for the benefit of the minor property of whatever description and wherever situated which the minor is entitled to receive or recover.

(2) Nothing in subsection (1) above shall restrict or affect the power of the High Court to appoint a person to be, or to act as, the guardian of a minor's estate either generally or for a particular purpose ; and subsection (1) above shall not apply to a guardian under the Guardianship of Minors Act 1971 so long as there is a guardian of the minor's estate alone.

Amendment of Matrimonial Proceedings (Magistrates' Courts) Act 1960 s. 4(2).
1960 c. 48.
1948 c. 43.

8. Section 4(2) of the Matrimonial Proceedings (Magistrates' Courts) Act 1960 (under which a magistrates' court has power in certain proceedings under that Act to call for a report by a probation officer or by an officer of a local authority employed in connection with functions specified in the now repealed section 39(1) of the Children Act 1948) shall be amended by omitting the words " or by such an officer of a local authority as is mentioned in subsection (7) of section 3 of this Act ", and by adding at the end the words " or for such a report by an officer of a local authority employed in connection with functions of the authority under the Children and Young Persons Acts 1933 to 1969 ".

9.—(1) In the enactments mentioned in the following subsections there shall be made the amendments there provided for (being amendments consequential on the foregoing provisions of this Act) ; and the enactments mentioned in Schedule 3 to this Act are hereby repealed to the extent specified in column 3 of that Schedule.

PART I
Consequential
amendments,
and repeals.

(2) The words " the Guardianship of Minors Acts 1971 and 1973 " shall be substituted for the words " the Guardianship of Infants Acts 1886 and 1925 " wherever they occurred in any of the following enactments as originally enacted, that is to say—

(a) in the Legal Aid and Advice Act 1949, in Schedule 1, in paragraph 3(b) of Part I (the proceedings for which legal aid may be given in magistrates' courts) ;

1949 c. 51.

(b) in the Magistrates' Courts Act 1952, in sections 52(2), 56(1) and 57(4) (periodical payments through justices' clerk, and definition of " domestic proceedings ") ;

1952 c. 55.

(c) in the Administration of Justice Act 1970, in Schedule 1 (High Court business assigned to Family Division).

1970 c. 31.

(3) The following enactments, as amended by the Guardianship of Minors Act 1971 (which as so amended relate to the enforcement of orders under that Act for the payment of money) shall be further amended as follows :—

1971 c. 3.

(a) in the Reserve and Auxiliary Forces (Protection of Civil Interests) Act 1951, in section 2(1)(d), after the words " the Guardianship of Minors Act 1971 " there shall be inserted the words " or under section 2(4)(a) of the Guardianship Act 1973 " ;

1951 c. 65.

(b) in the Maintenance Orders Act 1950, in section 16(2)(a)(iii), and in the Administration of Justice Act 1970, in Schedule 8, in paragraph 4(a), and in the Attachment of Earnings Act 1971, in Schedule 1, in paragraph 5(a), after the words " the Guardianship of Minors Act 1971 " there shall in each case be inserted the words " or section 2(3) or 2(4)(a) of the Guardianship Act 1973 " ;

1950 c. 37.

1971 c. 32.

PART II

SCOTLAND

10.—(1) In relation to a pupil or minor, and to the administration of any property belonging to or held in trust for a pupil or minor or the application of income of any such property, a mother shall have the same rights and authority as the law

Equality of
parental
rights.

allows to a father (and shall accordingly hold the office of tutor to a pupil or, as the case may be, curator to a minor) and the rights and authority of mother and father shall be equal and be exercisable by either without the other.

(2) An agreement for a man or woman to give up in whole or in part, in relation to any child of his or hers, the rights and authority referred to in subsection (1) above shall be unenforceable, except that an agreement made between husband and wife which is to operate only during their separation while married may, in relation to a child of theirs, provide for either of them to do so; but no such agreement between husband and wife shall be enforced by any court if the court is of the opinion that it will not be for the benefit of the child to give effect to it.

(3) Where a father and mother of a pupil or minor disagree on any question affecting his welfare, either of them may apply to the Court of Session or to any sheriff court, having jurisdiction under the Guardianship of Infants Act 1886, for the court's direction, and (subject to subsection (4) below) the court may make such order regarding the matters in difference as it may think proper.

1886 c. 27.

(4) Subsection (3) above shall not authorise the court to make any order regarding the custody of a pupil or minor or the right of access to him of his father or mother.

(5) An order under subsection (3) above may be varied or discharged by a subsequent order made on the application of either parent or, after the death of either parent, on the application of any guardian under the Guardianship of Infants Acts 1886 and 1925, or (before or after the death of either parent) on the application of any person having the custody of the pupil or minor; and the power conferred on the court by this subsection may be exercised in proceedings by or against a person residing in England or Wales or Northern Ireland.

(6) Nothing in the foregoing provisions of this section shall affect the operation of any enactment requiring the consent of both parents in a matter affecting a pupil or minor or be taken as applying in relation to a pupil or minor who is illegitimate.

1960 c. 61.

(7) Nothing in the said provisions shall be taken to affect the provisions of the Mental Health (Scotland) Act 1960 as to the person who is " the nearest relative " for the purposes of that Act.

1925 c. 45.

(8) In the Guardianship of Infants Act 1925 in section 1 the words " or any right at common law possessed by the father " and section 2 are hereby repealed.

11.—(1) Where an application made under section 5 of the
Guardianship of Infants Act 1886, as read with section 3 of the
Guardianship of Infants Act 1925, section 16 of the Administration of Justice Act 1928 and section 1 of the Custody of
Children (Scotland) Act 1939, or under section 2(1) of the
Illegitimate Children (Scotland) Act 1930 relates to the custody
of a child— PART II
Jurisdiction
and orders
relating to care
and custody
of children.
1886 c. 27.
1925 c. 45.
1928 c. 26.
1939 c. 4.
1930 c. 33.

(a) if it appears to the court that there are exceptional
circumstances making it impracticable or undesirable
for the child to be entrusted to either of the parents
or to any other individual, the court may commit the
care of the child to a specified local authority;

(b) if by an order made on that application either parent or
any other person (other than a local authority) is
given the custody of the child, but it appears to the
court that there are exceptional circumstances making
it desirable that the child should be under the supervision of a local authority, the court may order that
the child shall be under the supervision of a specified
local authority, subject to any directions given by the
court;

but any order made by virtue of the above paragraphs shall
cease to have effect when the child attains the age of sixteen.

(2) While an order made by virtue of this section committing
the care of a child to a local authority is in force with respect
to any child the child shall continue in the care of the local
authority notwithstanding any claim by a parent or other person.

(3) Where the court makes an order by virtue of subsection
(1)(a) above committing the care of a child to a local authority, the
court may make a further order requiring the payment by either
parent to that authority while it has the care of the child of
such weekly or other periodical sum towards the maintenance
of the child as the court thinks reasonable having regard to
the means of that parent.

(4) Before making an order by virtue of subsection (1)(a)
above, the court shall hear any representations from the local
authority, including any representations as to the making of an
order under subsection (3) above for payments to the authority.

(5) On the making of an order by virtue of this section
committing the care of a child to a local authority Part II of
the Social Work (Scotland) Act 1968 (which relates to the treat- 1968 c. 49.
ment of children in care of local authorities) shall, subject to the
provisions of this section, apply as if the child had been received

PART II   by the local authority into their care under section 15 of that
Act, so however that—

> (*a*) the exercise by the local authority of their powers under
> or by virtue of sections 20 to 22 of that Act shall
> be subject to any directions given by the court ; and
>
> (*b*) section 23 of that Act (which relates to arrangements
> for the emigration of a child under the care of a local
> authority) shall not apply.

1925 c. 45.   (6) In section 3 of the Guardianship of Infants Act 1925
1950 c. 37.   and in section 7 of the Maintenance Orders Act 1950 there shall
be made the amendments provided for in Part I of Schedule 4
to this Act (being amendments providing for mother and father
to be treated alike for the purposes of the said section 3 and
amendments relating to cases in which custody is given to an
individual other than one of the parents) ; and accordingly
section 3 and section 7 shall have effect as they are set out in
Part II of the Schedule with the amendments required by this
subsection.

Provisions   **12.**—(1) Any order made by virtue of section 11 above may
supplementary from time to time be varied or may be discharged by a sub-
to section 11.   sequent order on the application of—

> (*a*) either parent, or
>
> (*b*) (after the death of either parent) any guardian under
1886 c. 27.   > the Guardianship of Infants Act 1886, or
>
> (*c*) any other person having custody of the child, or
>
> (*d*) the specified local authority having the care or super-
> vision of the child.

(2)(*a*) Where an application is made under section 5 of the
Guardianship of Infants Act 1886 or under section 2(1) of the
1930 c. 33.   Illegitimate Children (Scotland) Act 1930 or for the variation
or discharge of any order made under the said Acts or by
virtue of section 11 of this Act, the court shall have power
to appoint a specified local authority or an individual not being
an officer of the local authority to investigate and report to the
court on all the circumstances of the child and on the proposed
arrangements for the care and upbringing of the child.

(*b*) If on consideration of a report furnished in pursuance of
this subsection the court, either ex proprio motu or on the
application of any person concerned, thinks it expedient to do
so, it may require the person who furnished the report to appear
and be examined on oath regarding any matter dealt with in the
report, and such person may be examined or cross-examined
accordingly.

(*c*) Any expenses incurred in connection with the preparation
of a report by a local authority or other person appointed under
this subsection shall form part of the expenses of the action and

be defrayed by such party to the action as the court may direct, and the court may certify the amount of the expenses so incurred.

(3) Each parent or guardian of a child for the time being in the care of a local authority by virtue of an order under section 11(1)(*a*) above shall give notice to the authority of any change of address of that parent or guardian and any person who without reasonable excuse fails to comply with this subsection shall be liable on summary conviction to a fine not exceeding £10.

13.—(1) In this Part of this Act—

" child " means a child under sixteen years of age ;

" specified local authority " means a local authority within the meaning of the Social Work (Scotland) Act 1968.

Interpretation of Part II.

1968 c. 49.

14. The enactments specified in Schedule 5 to this Act shall have effect subject to the amendments set out in the Schedule, being amendments consequential on the foregoing provisions of this Part of this Act.

Consequential amendments.

PART III

GENERAL

15.—(1) This Act may be cited as the Guardianship Act 1973 ; and—

(*a*) Part I of this Act and the Guardianship of Minors Act 1971 may be cited together as the Guardianship of Minors Acts 1971 and 1973 ; and

(*b*) Part II of this Act and the Guardianship of Infants Acts 1886 and 1925 may be cited together as the Guardianship of Children (Scotland) Acts 1886 to 1973.

Short title, citation, extent and commencement.

1971 c. 3.

(2) Part I of this Act shall not extend to Scotland or to Northern Ireland, and Part II shall not extend to England and Wales or to Northern Ireland, except that each Part shall extend throughout the United Kingdom in so far as it amends section 16 of the Maintenance Orders Act 1950.

1950 c. 37.

(3) This Act shall come into force on such day as the Secretary of State may appoint by order made by statutory instrument, and different days may be appointed for the coming into force of different provisions.

SCHEDULES

SCHEDULE 1

PROVISIONS SUBSTITUTED FOR SEXUAL OFFENCES ACT 1956 S. 38

(1) On a person's conviction of an offence under section 10 of this Act against a girl under the age of eighteen, or of an offence under section 11 of this Act against a boy under that age, or of attempting to commit such an offence, the court may by order divest that person of all authority over the girl or boy.

(2) An order divesting a person of authority over a girl or boy under the foregoing subsection may, if that person is the guardian of the girl or boy, remove that person from the guardianship.

(3) An order under this section may appoint a person to be the guardian of the girl or boy during his or her minority or any less period.

(4) An order under this section may be varied from time to time or rescinded by the High Court and, if made on conviction of an offence against a girl or boy who is a defective, may, so far as it has effect for any of the purposes of the Mental Health Act 1959, be rescinded either before or after the girl or boy has attained the age of eighteen.

SCHEDULE 2

AMENDMENTS OF GUARDIANSHIP OF MINORS ACT 1971 SS. 9, 13, AND 16, AND AMENDED TEXT OF S. 9 AND S. 15(3)—(6)

PART I

AMENDMENTS

1.—(1) Section 9 of the Guardianship of Minors Act 1971 is to be amended in accordance with sub-paragraphs (2) to (4) below.

(2) In section 9(2) there shall be substituted—

(a) for the words " the mother ", where they first occur, the words " any person (whether or not one of the parents) " ; and

(b) for the words " the father to pay to the mother " the words " payment to that person by the parent or either of the parents excluded from having that custody of " ; and

(c) for the words " the father ", where they last occur, the words " that parent ".

(3) At the end of section 9(3) there shall be added—

" Provided that, unless the court in making the order directs otherwise, paragraphs (a) and (b) above shall not apply to any provision of the order giving the custody of the minor to a person other than one of the parents or made with respect to a minor of whom custody is so given ".

(4) In section 9(4) the words "(in the case of an order under SCH. 2 subsection (1))" shall be omitted, and at the end of section 9(4) there shall be added the words "or (before or after the death of either parent) on the application of any other person having the custody of the minor by virtue of an order under subsection (1) of this section ".

2. In section 13(1) of the Guardianship of Minors Act 1971 (which 1971 c. 3. provides for the enforcement of orders of a magistrates' court committing to the applicant the legal custody of a minor) for the words " the applicant " there shall be substituted the words " any person " ; at the first place where the applicant is mentioned, and the words " the person given the custody " at the other two places ; and for the words " that person " there shall be substituted the words " the person so served.

3.—(1) Section 15 of the Guardianship of Minors Act 1971 is to be amended in accordance with sub-paragraphs (2) to (4) below.

(2) In section 15(4) there shall be substituted—

    (*a*) for the words " to the mother " where they first occur, the words " to a person resident in England or Wales " ; and

    (*b*) for the words " requiring the father to make payments to the mother " the words " requiring payments to be made " ; and

    (*c*) for the words " the father ", where they last occur, the words " one parent " and for the words " the mother ", in the last two places where they occur, the words " the other parent ".

(3) In section 15(5) the words " in the case of proceedings by the mother " shall be omitted, and for the words " requiring the father to make payments to the mother " there shall be substituted the words " requiring payments to be made ".

(4) In section 15(6) for the words " a woman " there shall be substituted the words " a person ", and for the words " that subsection " there shall be substituted the words " that section ".

4. At the end of section 16 of the Guardianship of Minors Act 1971 there shall be added as subsection (5)—

" (5) In relation to applications made to a magistrates' court under section 9 of this Act for the discharge or variation of an order giving the custody of a minor to a person other than one of the parents or made with respect to a minor of whom custody is so given, rules made under section 15 of the Justices of the Peace Act 1949 may make provision as to 1949 c. 101. the persons who are to be made defendants on the application ; and if on any such application there are two or more defendants, the power of the court under section 55(1) of the Magistrates' 1952 c. 55. Courts Act 1952 shall be deemed to include power, whatever adjudication the court makes on the complaint, to order any of the parties to pay the whole or part of the costs of all or any of the other parties."

Part II
Text of s. 9 and s. 15(3) to (6), as Amended

Section 9, as amended

9.—(1) The court may, on the application of the mother or father of a minor (who may apply without next friend), make such order regarding—

    (*a*) the custody of the minor ; and

    (*b*) the right of access to the minor of his mother or father,

as the court thinks fit having regard to the welfare of the minor and to the conduct and wishes of the mother and father.

(2) Where the court makes an order under subsection (1) of this section giving the custody of the minor to any person (whether or not one of the parents), the court may make a further order requiring payment to that person by the parent or either of the parents excluded from having that custody of such weekly or other periodical sum towards the maintenance of the minor as the court thinks reasonable having regard to the means of that parent.

(3) An order may be made under subsection (1) or (2) of this section notwithstanding that the parents of the minor are then residing together, but—

    (*a*) no such order shall be enforceable, and no liability thereunder shall accrue, while they are residing together ; and

    (*b*) any such order shall cease to have effect if for a period of three months after it is made they continue to reside together:

Provided that, unless the court in making the order directs otherwise, paragraphs (*a*) and (*b*) above shall not apply to any provision of the order giving the custody of the minor to a person other than one of the parents or made with respect to a minor of whom custody is so given.

(4) An order under subsection (1) or (2) of this section may be varied or discharged by a subsequent order made on the application of either parent or after the death of either parent on the application of any guardian under this Act, or (before or after the death of either parent) on the application of any other person having the custody of the minor by virtue of an order under subsection (1) of this section.

Section 15(3) to (6), as amended

(3) A county court or magistrates' court shall not have jurisdiction under this Act in any case where the respondent or any of the respondents resides in Scotland or Northern Ireland—

    (*a*) except in so far as such jurisdiction may be exercisable by virtue of the following provisions of this section ; or

    (*b*) unless a summons or other originating process can be served and is served on the respondent or, as the case may be, on the respondents in England or Wales.

(4) An order under this Act giving the custody of a minor to a person resident in England or Wales, whether with or without an order requiring payments to be made towards the minor's maintenance, may be made, if one parent resides in Scotland or Northern Ireland and the other parent and the minor in England or Wales, by a magistrates' court having jurisdiction in the place in which the other parent resides.

(5) It is hereby declared that a magistrates' court has jurisdiction—

(a) in proceedings under this Act by a person residing in Scotland or Northern Ireland against a person residing in England or Wales for an order relating to the custody of a minor (including an order requiring payments to be made towards the minor's maintenance) ;

(b) in proceedings by or against a person residing in Scotland or Northern Ireland for the revocation, revival or variation of any such order.

(6) Where proceedings for an order under subsection (1) of section 9 of this Act relating to the custody of a minor are brought in a magistrates' court by a person residing in Scotland or Northern Ireland, the court shall have jurisdiction to make any order in respect of the minor under that section on the application of the respondent in the proceedings.

SCHEDULE 3

Section 9.

REPEALS UNDER PART I OF THIS ACT

Chapter	Short Title	Extent of Repeal
12 Chas. 2. c. 24.	The Tenures Abolition Act 1660.	Section 9.
36 & 37 Vict. c. 12.	The Custody of Infants Act 1873.	The preamble, and section 2.
7 & 8 Eliz. 2. c. 72.	The Mental Health Act 1959.	Section 127(2).
1969 c. 46.	The Family Law Reform Act 1969.	In Part I of Schedule 1 the entry relating to the Sexual Offences Act 1956 and that relating to the Mental Health Act 1959.
1971 c. 3.	The Guardianship of Minors Act 1971.	In section 1 the words " or any right at common law possessed by the father ". Section 2. Section 8. In Schedule 1 the entry relating to the Legal Aid and Advice Act 1949 and that relating to the Magistrates' Courts Act 1952, and in the entry relating to the Administration of Justice Act 1970 the words from " for " where first occurring to " 1971 " where next occurring.

SCHEDULE 4

AMENDMENTS OF GUARDIANSHIP OF INFANTS ACT 1925 S. 3, AND OF
MAINTENANCE ORDERS ACT 1950 S. 7, AND TEXTS AS AMENDED

PART I

Guardianship of Infants Act 1925, s. 3

1925 c. 45.

1.—(1) Section 3 of the Guardianship of Infants Act 1925 is to be amended in accordance with sub-paragraphs (2) to (6) below.

(2) In section 3(1) for the words " mother of the infant is then residing with the father of the infant ", there shall be substituted the words " parents are then residing together ".

(3) In section 3(2) there shall be substituted—
  (a) for the words " the mother ", where they first occur, the words " any person (whether or not one of the parents) " ; and
  (b) for the words " the mother is then residing with the father ", the words " the parents are residing together " ; and
  (c) for the words " the father shall pay to the mother " the words " the parent or either of the parents excluded from having that custody shall pay to that person " ; and
  (d) for the words " the father ", where they last occur, the words " that parent ".

(4) In section 3(3) there shall be substituted—
  (a) for the words " mother resides with the father ", the words " parents are residing together " ; and
  (b) for the words " the mother of the infant continues to reside with the father ", the words " they continue to reside together ".

(5) At the end of section 3(3) there shall be added—
  " Provided that unless the court in making the order directs otherwise, this subsection shall not apply to any provisions of the order giving the custody of the child to a person other than one of the parents or made with respect to a child of whom custody is so given."

1886 c. 27.

(6) In section 3(4), for the words " either of the father or the mother of the infant " there shall be substituted the words " of either parent or of any other person having the custody of the child by virtue of an order made under section 5 of the Guardianship of Infants Act 1886.".

Maintenance Orders Act 1950, s. 7

1950 c. 37.

2. In section 7 of the Maintenance Orders Act 1950 there shall be substituted—
  (a) for the words " to the mother ", where they first occur, the words " to a person resident in Scotland " ; and

(*b*) for the words "requiring the father to make payments to the mother" the words "requiring payments to be made";
and

(*c*) for the words "the father", where they last occur, the words "one parent" and for the words "the mother", in the last two places where they occur, the words "the other parent".

PART II

Texts of s. 3 and s. 7 as amended

Guardianship of Infants Act 1925, s. 3, *as amended*

3.—(1) The power of the court under section five of the Guardian- 1886 c. 27. ship of Infants Act 1886 to make an order as to the custody of an infant and the right of access thereto may be exercised notwithstanding that the parents are then residing together.

(2) Where the court under the said section as so amended makes an order giving the custody of the infant to any person (whether or not one of the parents), then, whether or not the parents are residing together, the court may further order that the parent or either of the parents excluded from having that custody shall pay to that person towards the maintenance of the infant such weekly or other periodical sum as the court, having regard to the means of that parent, may think reasonable.

(3) No such order, whether for custody or maintenance, shall be enforceable and no liability thereunder shall accrue while the parents are residing together, and any such order shall cease to have effect if for a period of three months after it is made they continue to reside together:

Provided that unless the court in making the order directs otherwise, this subsection shall not apply to any provisions of the order giving the custody of the child to a person other than one of the parents or made with respect to a child of whom custody is so given.

(4) Any order so made may, on the application of either parent or of any other person having the custody of the child by virtue of an order made under section five of the Guardianship of Infants Act 1886, be varied or discharged by a subsequent order.

Maintenance Orders Act 1950, s. 7, *as amended*

7. An order under the Guardianship of Infants Acts 1886 and 1925, giving the custody of a pupil child to a person resident in Scotland, whether with or without an order requiring payments to be made towards the maintenance of the pupil child, may be made, if one parent resides in England or Northern Ireland and the other parent and the pupil child in Scotland, by the sheriff within whose jurisdiction the other parent resides.

Section 14.

SCHEDULE 5

CONSEQUENTIAL AMENDMENTS RELATING TO SCOTLAND

1886 c. 27.

1. In section 5 of the Guardianship of Infants Act 1886, at the end there shall be added—

> " or (whether before or after the death of either parent) of any other person having the custody of the child by virtue of an order made under this section ".

1925 c. 45.

2. In section 8 of the Guardianship of Infants Act 1925, for the words " as amended by this Act " there shall be substituted the words " by virtue of section 3 of this Act or under section 11(3) of the Guardianship Act 1973 ".

1930 c. 33.

3. In section 2(1) of the Illegitimate Children (Scotland) Act 1930, after the words " either parent ", where they last occur, there shall be inserted the words " or of any other person having the custody of the child by virtue of an order made under this section ".

1950 c. 37.

4. In section 16(2)(*b*) of the Maintenance Orders Act 1950, after sub-paragraph (vi) there shall be inserted the following sub-paragraph—

> " (vii) an order for the payment of weekly or other periodical sums under subsection (3) of section 11 of the Guardianship Act 1973 ; ".

1951 c. 65.

5. In section 8(1)(*d*) of the Reserve and Auxiliary Forces (Protection of Civil Interests) Act 1951, after " 1925 " there shall be inserted the words " or under subsection (3) of section 11 of the Guardianship Act 1973 ".

1966 c. 19.

6. In section 8(1)(*d*) of the Law Reform (Miscellaneous Provisions) (Scotland) Act 1966, after " 1958 " there shall be inserted the words " or by virtue of Part II of the Guardianship Act 1973 ".

1968 c. 49.

7. In section 2(2) of the Social Work (Scotland) Act 1968, in sub-paragraph (*c*), at the end there shall be added " and sections 11 and 12 of the Guardianship Act 1973 ".

Sea Fisheries (Shellfish) Act 1973

1973 CHAPTER 30

An Act to amend the Sea Fisheries (Shellfish) Act 1967. [5th July 1973]

BE IT ENACTED by the Queen's most Excellent Majesty, by and with the advice and consent of the Lords Spiritual and Temporal, and Commons, in this present Parliament assembled, and by the authority of the same, as follows:—

1. At the end of section 16(2) of the Sea Fisheries (Shellfish) Act 1967 (which makes certain exemptions in respect of the closed season for the sale of oysters) there shall be added the following— *Amendment of s. 16(2) of 1967 c. 83.*

" , or

(*e*) were Pacific or Japanese oysters (*Crassostrea gigas*), Portuguese oysters (*Crassostrea angulata*) or other members of the genus *Crassostrea* ".

2.—(1) This Act may be cited as the Sea Fisheries (Shellfish) Act 1973; and this Act and the Sea Fisheries (Shellfish) Act 1967 may be cited together as the Sea Fisheries (Shellfish) Acts 1967 and 1973. *Citation, commencement and extent.*

(2) This Act shall come into force on 1st May 1974.

(3) This Act shall not extend to Northern Ireland.

Dentists (Amendment) Act 1973

1973 CHAPTER 31

An Act to amend the Dentists Act 1957.   [5th July 1973]

BE IT ENACTED by the Queen's most Excellent Majesty, by and with the advice and consent of the Lords Spiritual and Temporal, and Commons, in this present Parliament assembled, and by the authority of the same, as follows:—

Amendments of Dentists Act 1957.
1957 c. 28.

1.—(1) Section 10 of the Dentists Act 1957 (which provides for the remedy where qualifying courses of study or examinations are inadequate) shall be read and have effect as if in place of subsection (2) thereof there were inserted the following subsections:

" (1A) The powers respectively conferred by the foregoing subsection upon the General Dental Council to make representations and upon the Privy Council to make orders may be exercised in respect of a specifically described degree or licence in dentistry granted by a dental authority.

(2) If an order is made under this section in respect of any degree or licence in dentistry granted by a dental authority, no person shall be entitled to be registered under this Act in respect of such degree or licence in dentistry granted after the time mentioned in the order."

(2) Section 17 of the said Act (which relates to the procedure for registration) shall be read and have effect as if in subsection (3) thereof in place of the words " the registrar on receipt of any such lists shall duly register those persons " there were inserted the words " the registrar on receipt of any such lists shall, subject to the provisions of this Act, duly register those persons ".

2. This Act may be cited as the Dentists (Amendment) Act Short title and 1973 and this Act and the Dentists Act 1957 may be cited together citation. as the Dentists Acts 1957 and 1973.

National Health Service Reorganisation Act 1973

1973 CHAPTER 32

An Act to make further provision with respect to the national health service in England and Wales and amendments of the enactments relating to the national health service in Scotland; and for purposes connected with those matters.   [5th July 1973]

B E IT ENACTED by the Queen's most Excellent Majesty, by and with the advice and consent of the Lords Spiritual and Temporal, and Commons, in this present Parliament assembled, and by the authority of the same, as follows:—

PART I

ADMINISTRATION

Functions of Secretary of State

1. It shall be the duty of the Secretary of State to arrange for the reorganisation in accordance with this Act of the national health service established in pursuance of section 1 of the National Health Service Act 1946.

Reorganisation of national health service.
1946 c. 81.

2.—(1) Without prejudice to his powers apart from this subsection, the Secretary of State shall have power—

    (a) to provide such services as he considers appropriate for the purpose of discharging any duty imposed on him by the Health Service Acts; and

    (b) to do any other thing whatsoever which is calculated to facilitate, or is conducive or incidental to, the discharge of such a duty.

General powers and duties of Secretary of State to provide services.

(2) It shall be the duty of the Secretary of State to provide throughout England and Wales, to such extent as he considers necessary to meet all reasonable requirements,—

   (a) hospital accommodation;

   (b) other accommodation for the purpose of any service provided under the Health Service Acts;

   (c) medical, dental, nursing and ambulance services;

   (d) such other facilities for the care of expectant and nursing mothers and young children as he considers are appropriate as part of the health service;

   (e) such facilities for the prevention of illness, the care of persons suffering from illness and the after-care of persons who have suffered from illness as he considers are appropriate as part of the health service in place of arrangements of a kind which immediately before the passing of this Act it was the function of local health authorities to make in pursuance of section 12

1968 c. 46.
   of the Health Services and Public Health Act 1968;

   (f) such other services as are required for the diagnosis and treatment of illness;

and regulations may provide for the making and recovery of charges in respect of facilities designated by the regulations as facilities provided in pursuance of paragraph (d) or (e) of this subsection.

(3) The functions exercisable by local health authorities and the Greater London Council by virtue of sections 21 and 24 to 27 of the principal Act and sections 10 and 11 of the said Act of 1968 (which relate to the provision of certain health services by those bodies) shall cease to be exercisable by those bodies; but nothing in this section affects the provisions of Part IV of the principal Act (which relates to arrangements with practitioners for the provision of medical, dental, ophthalmic and pharmaceutical services).

Medical and dental service for pupils.
3.—(1) It shall be the duty of the Secretary of State to make provision for the medical and dental inspection at appropriate intervals of pupils in attendance at schools maintained by local education authorities and for the medical and dental treatment of such pupils.

(2) Without prejudice to the powers of the Secretary of State apart from this subsection, he may—

   (a) by arrangement with any local education authority, make provision for any medical or dental inspection or treatment of—

      (i) senior pupils in attendance at any educational establishment, other than a school, which is maintained by the authority and at which full-time further education is provided, or

(ii) any child or young person who, in pursuance
of special arrangements made for him by the authority by virtue of section 56 of the Education Act 1944 c. 31.
1944, is receiving primary or secondary education
otherwise than at a school ;

(b) by arrangement with the proprietor of any educational
establishment which is not maintained by a local
education authority, make any such provision in respect
of junior or senior pupils in attendance at the
establishment.

(3) A local education authority shall not make an arrangement in pursuance of the preceding subsection in respect of
such an establishment as is mentioned in paragraph (a)(i) of
that subsection except by agreement with the governors of the
establishment ; and an arrangement made in pursuance of
paragraph (b) of the preceding subsection may include provision
for the making of payments by the proprietor in question.

(4) It shall be the duty of the local education authorities by
which schools (other than voluntary schools) are maintained and
of the managers or governors of voluntary schools to make available to the Secretary of State such accommodation as is appropriate for the purpose of assisting him to make such provision
as is mentioned in subsection (1) of this section for pupils in
attendance at the schools.

(5) In this section expressions to which meanings are assigned
by section 114(1) of the Education Act 1944 have those meanings.

4. It shall be the duty of the Secretary of State to make Family
arrangements, to such extent as he considers necessary to meet planning
all reasonable requirements in England and Wales, for the giving service.
of advice on contraception, the medical examination of persons
seeking advice on contraception, the treatment of such persons
and the supply of contraceptive substances and appliances ;
and it is hereby declared that the power conferred by section
1(1) of the National Health Service Act 1952 to provide for the 1952 c. 25.
making and recovery of charges includes power to provide for
the making and recovery of charges for the supply of any such
substances or appliances.

Local administration

5.—(1) It shall be the duty of the Secretary of State to estab- Regional and
lish by order in accordance with Part I of Schedule 1 to this Area Health
Act—   Authorities,
                                                                 Family
(a) authorities, to be called Regional Health Authorities, Practitioner
for such regions in England as he may by order Committees
determine ; and   and special
                                                                 health
                                                                 authorities.

(*b*) authorities, to be called either Area Health Authorities or Area Health Authorities (Teaching) in accordance with the following subsection, for such areas in Wales and the said regions as he may by order determine;

and orders determining regions or areas in pursuance of this subsection shall be separate from orders establishing authorities for the regions or areas.

(2) An order establishing an Authority in pursuance of paragraph (*b*) of the preceding subsection may provide for it to be called an Area Health Authority (Teaching) if and only if the Secretary of State is satisfied that the Authority is to provide for a university or universities substantial facilities for undergraduate or post-graduate clinical teaching; and where the Secretary of State is satisfied that an Area Health Authority is to provide or is providing such facilities he may provide by order for the Authority to be called an Area Health Authority (Teaching) and where he is satisfied that an Area Health Authority (Teaching) no longer provides such facilities he may provide by order for the Authority to be called an Area Health Authority.

(3) It shall be the duty of the Secretary of State, before providing that an Authority shall be called or cease to be called an Area Health Authority (Teaching), to consult the university or universities concerned with the facilities in question.

(4) Any reference in the following provisions of this Act to an Area Health Authority includes a reference to an Area Health Authority (Teaching) unless the context otherwise requires.

(5) It shall be the duty of each Area Health Authority to establish for its area, in accordance with Part II of Schedule 1 to this Act, a body which shall be called a Family Practitioner Committee.

(6) If the Secretary of State considers that a special body should be established for the purpose of performing any functions which he may direct the body to perform on his behalf, or on behalf of an Area Health Authority or a Family Practitioner Committee, he may by order establish a body for that purpose and, subject to the provisions of Part III of Schedule 1 to this Act, make such further provision relating to the body as he thinks fit; and a body established in pursuance of this subsection shall, without prejudice to the power conferred by subsection (3) of the following section to allocate a particular name to the body, be called a special health authority.

6.—(1) It shall be the duty of the Secretary of State to exercise the powers conferred on him by subsection (1) of the preceding section and the following subsection so as to secure—

- (*a*) that the regions determined in pursuance of those subsections together comprise the whole of England, that the areas so determined together comprise the whole of Wales and those regions and that no region includes part only of any area ; and

- (*b*) that the provision of health services in each region can conveniently be associated with a university which has a school of medicine or with two or more such universities.

(2) The Secretary of State may by order vary the region of a Regional Health Authority or the area of an Area Health Authority whether or not the variation entails the determination of a new or the abolition of an existing region or area, and an order made by virtue of this subsection may (without prejudice to the generality of section 56(4) of this Act) contain such provisions for the transfer of officers, property, rights and liabilities as the Secretary of State thinks fit ; but it shall be the duty of the Secretary of State before he makes an order in pursuance of this subsection to consult with respect to the order such bodies as he may recognise as representing officers who in his opinion are likely to be transferred or affected by transfers in pursuance of the order and such other bodies as he considers are concerned with the order.

(3) Without prejudice to the generality of the said section 56(4) or of the power to make an order conferred by subsection (6) of the preceding section, an order made in pursuance of that subsection may in particular contain provisions as to the membership of the body established by the order, the transfer to the body of officers, property, rights and liabilities and the name by which the body is to be known ; but it shall be the duty of the Secretary of State before he makes such an order to consult with respect to the order such bodies as he may recognise as representing officers who in his opinion are likely to be transferred or affected by transfers in pursuance of the order.

(4) The provisions of Part III of Schedule 1 to this Act shall, so far as applicable, have effect in relation to an Authority or other body established in pursuance of the preceding section.

7.—(1) The Secretary of State may direct a Regional Health Authority, an Area Health Authority of which the area is in Wales or a special health authority to exercise on his behalf such of his functions relating to the health service as are specified in the directions (including any of his functions under enactments relating to mental health and nursing homes but excluding the duty imposed on him by section 1(1) of the principal Act to secure the effective provision of the services mentioned in subsection (3) of this section); and subject to the following subsection it shall be the duty of the body in question to comply with the directions.

(2) A Regional Health Authority may direct any Area Health Authority of which the area is included in its region to exercise such of the functions exercisable by the Regional Health Authority by virtue of the preceding subsection as are specified in the directions and it shall be the duty of the Area Health Authority to comply with the directions ; but if the Secretary of State directs a Regional Health Authority to secure that any of those functions specified in his directions are or are not exercisable by an Area Health Authority it shall be the duty of the Regional Health Authority to comply with his directions.

(3) It shall be the duty of each Family Practitioner Committee in accordance with regulations—

    (*a*) to administer, on behalf of the Area Health Authority by which the Committee was established, the arrangements made in pursuance of the Health Service Acts for the provision of general medical services, general dental services, general ophthalmic services and pharmaceutical services for the area of the Authority; and

    (*b*) to perform such other functions relating to those services as may be prescribed ;

and if it appears to the Secretary of State that, in consequence of regulations made by virtue of the preceding provisions of this subsection, references to an Area Health Authority in particular provisions of the Health Service Acts should be construed as references to a Family Practitioner Committee, he may by regulations provide accordingly.

(4) Regulations may provide for functions exercisable by virtue of the preceding provisions of this section by a body other than an Area Health Authority, or exercisable by virtue of any provisions of the Health Service Acts by an Area Health Authority, to be exercisable on behalf of the body in question—

    (*a*) by an equivalent body or by another body of which the members consist only of the body and equivalent bodies ;

    (*b*) by a committee, sub-committee or officer of the body or an equivalent body or such another body as aforesaid ;

(c) in the case of functions exercisable by an Area Health Authority, by a special health authority, an officer of such an authority or a Family Practitioner Committee;

(d) in the case of functions exercisable by a Family Practitioner Committee, by a special health authority, an officer of such an authority or an officer of an Area Health Authority;

and for the purposes of this subsection a Regional or Area Health Authority or a Family Practitioner Committee is equivalent to another body of the same name and a special health authority is equivalent to another such authority; but nothing in this subsection shall be construed as precluding any body from acting by an agent where it is entitled so to act apart from this subsection.

(5) The Secretary of State may give directions with respect to the exercise of any functions exercisable by any body by virtue of the preceding provisions of this section or by an Area Health Authority by virtue of Part IV of the principal Act; and subject to any directions given by the Secretary of State by virtue of this subsection—

(a) a Regional Health Authority may give directions with respect to the exercise, by an Area Health Authority of which the area is included in its region, of any functions exercisable by the Area Health Authority by virtue of subsection (2) of this section;

(b) an Area Health Authority may give directions with respect to the exercise by the Family Practitioner Committee established by it of any functions which are exercisable by the Committee by virtue of subsection (3) of this section and are prescribed for the purposes of this paragraph;

and it shall be the duty of the body in question to comply with the directions.

(6) Any directions given by the Secretary of State in pursuance of this section shall be given either by regulations or by an instrument in writing except that any such directions in respect of functions conferred on the Secretary of State by section 9(1) or (2) of this Act and any such directions in pursuance of subsection (1) of this section in respect of functions relating to special hospitals shall only be given by regulations, and any directions given by an Authority in pursuance of this section shall be given by an instrument in writing.

(7) Directions given and regulations made in pursuance of this section in respect of a function—

(a) shall not, except in prescribed cases, preclude a body or person by whom the function is exercisable apart from

PART I

1889 c. 63.

the directions or regulations from exercising the function; and

(b) may in the case of directions given by an instrument in writing be varied or revoked by subsequent directions given in pursuance of this section (without prejudice to the operation of section 32(3) of the Interpretation Act 1889 in the case of directions given by regulations);

so however that an Area Health Authority shall not be entitled to exercise any function which by virtue of subsection (3) of this section is exercisable by the Family Practitioner Committee established by the Authority.

Local advisory committees.

8.—(1) Where the Secretary of State is satisfied that a committee formed for the region of a Regional Health Authority is representative of persons of any of the following categories, namely—

(a) the medical practitioners of the region; or

(b) the dental practitioners of the region; or

(c) the nurses and midwives of the region; or

(d) the registered pharmacists of the region; or

(e) the ophthalmic and dispensing opticians of the region,

then, subject to the following subsection, it shall be the duty of the Secretary of State to recognise the committee; and a committee recognised in pursuance of this subsection shall be called the Regional Medical, Dental, Nursing and Midwifery, Pharmaceutical or Optical Committee, as the case may be, for the region in question.

(2) Where the Secretary of State is satisfied that a committee formed for the region of a Regional Health Authority is representative of—

(a) any category of persons (other than a category mentioned in the preceding subsection) who provide services forming part of the health service; or

(b) two or more of any of the categories of persons mentioned in the preceding subsection and the preceding paragraph,

and that it is in the interests of the health service to recognise the committee, it shall be the duty of the Secretary of State to recognise it in pursuance of this subsection and determine that it shall be known by a name specified in the determination; and where a committee recognised in pursuance of this subsection appears to the Secretary of State to represent categories of persons which include a category mentioned in the preceding subsection, he shall not be required by virtue of that subsection to recognise a committee representing persons of that category.

(3) The Secretary of State may, by notice in writing served on any member of a committee recognised in pursuance of this section, withdraw his recognition of the committee if he considers it expedient to do so—

(a) where the committee is recognised in pursuance of subsection (1) or (2)(a) of this section, with a view to recognising in pursuance of subsection (2)(b) of this section another committee representing categories of persons which include the category represented by the recognised committee ;

(b) where the committee is recognised in pursuance of the said subsection (2)(b), with a view to recognising in pursuance of any of the provisions of subsection (1) or (2) of this section other committees which together are representative of the categories in question.

(4) It shall be the duty of a committee recognised by reference to the region of a Regional Health Authority in pursuance of subsection (1) or (2) of this section—

(a) to advise the Authority on the provision by the Authority of services of the kind provided by the categories of persons of whom the committee is representative ; and

(b) to perform such other functions as may be prescribed ;

and it shall be the duty of the Authority to consult the committee with respect to such matters and on such occasions as may be prescribed.

(5) A Regional Health Authority may defray such expenses incurred by such a committee in performing the duty imposed on the committee by the preceding subsection as the Authority considers reasonable (which may include travelling and other allowances and compensation for loss of remunerative time for members of the committee at such rates as the Secretary of State may determine with the approval of the Minister for the Civil Service).

(6) The preceding provisions of this section shall have effect in relation to Wales as if—

(a) for references to a region of an Authority there were substituted references to Wales ;

(b) for the words " Regional Medical " in subsection (1) there were substituted the words " Welsh Medical " ;

(c) for the words " the Authority " in both places in subsection (4)(a) and for those words and the words " A Regional Health Authority " in subsection (5) there were substituted the words " the Secretary of State " ; and (*d*) in subsection (4) the words following paragraph (*b*) were omitted.

(7) Subsections (1) to (5) of this section shall have effect in relation to an Area Health Authority of which the area is in England or Wales with the substitution for the word " Regional " of the word " Area " and for the word " region " of the word " area ".

Community
Health
Councils etc.

9.—(1) It shall be the duty of the Secretary of State to establish in accordance with this section a Council for the area of each Area Health Authority or separate Councils for such separate parts of the areas of those Authorities as he thinks fit ; and such a council shall be called a Community Health Council (and is hereafter in this section referred to as a " Council ").

(2) The Secretary of State may if he thinks fit discharge the duty aforesaid by establishing a Council for a district which includes the areas or parts of the areas of two or more Area Health Authorities ; but the Secretary of State shall be treated as not having discharged that duty unless he secures that there is no part of the area of an Area Health Authority which is not included in some Council's district.

(3) It shall be the duty of a Council—
  (*a*) to represent the interests in the health service of the public in its district ; and
  (*b*) to perform such other functions as may be conferred on it by virtue of the following subsection.

(4) Provision may be made by regulations as to—
  (*a*) the membership of Councils (including the election by members of a Council of a chairman of the Council) ;
  (*b*) the proceedings of Councils ;
  (*c*) the staff, premises and expenses of Councils ;
  (*d*) the consultation of Councils by Area Health Authorities with respect to such matters and on such occasions as may be prescribed ;
  (*e*) the furnishing of information to Councils by Area Health Authorities and the rights of members of Councils to enter and inspect premises controlled by Area Health Authorities ;
  (*f*) the consideration by Councils of matters relating to the operation of the health service within their districts and the giving of advice by Councils to Area Health Authorities on such matters ;
  (*g*) the preparation and publication of reports by Councils on such matters and the furnishing and publication by

Area Health Authorities of comments on the reports; and

(*h*) the functions to be exercised by Councils in addition to the functions exercisable by them by virtue of paragraph (*a*) of the preceding subsection and the preceding provisions of this subsection;

and the Secretary of State may pay to members of Councils such travelling and other allowances (including compensation for loss of remunerative time) as he may determine with the consent of the Minister for the Civil Service.

(5) It shall be the duty of the Secretary of State to exercise his power to make regulations in pursuance of paragraph (*a*) of the preceding subsection so as to secure as respects each Council that—

(*a*) at least one member of the Council is appointed by each local authority of which the area or part of it is included in the Council's district and at least half of the members of the Council consist of persons appointed by those local authorities;

(*b*) at least one third of the members of the Council are appointed in a prescribed manner by bodies (other than public or local authorities) of which the activities are carried on otherwise than for profit;

(*c*) the other members of the Council are appointed by such bodies, in such manner and after such consultations as may be prescribed; and

(*d*) no member of the Council is also a member of a Regional Health Authority or Area Health Authority;

but nothing in this subsection shall affect the validity of anything done by or in relation to a Council during any period during which, by reason of a vacancy in the membership of the Council or a defect in the appointment of a member of it, a requirement included in regulations in pursuance of this subsection is not satisfied.

(6) The Secretary of State may by regulations—

(*a*) provide for the establishment of a body—

(i) to advise Councils with respect to the performance of their functions and to assist Councils in the performance of their functions, and

(ii) to perform such other functions as may be prescribed; and

(*b*) make provision as to the membership, proceedings, staff, premises and expenses of the said body;

and the Secretary of State may pay to members of the said body such travelling and other allowances (including compensation for loss of remunerative time) as he may determine with the consent of the Minister for the Civil Service.

(7) In this section—

" local authority " means the council of a London borough
or of a county or district as defined in relation to
England in section 270(1) of the Local Government
Act 1972 or of a county or district mentioned in section
20(3) of that Act (which relates to Wales) or the Common Council of the City of London ; and

" district ", in relation to a Council, means the locality
for which it is established, whether that locality consists
of the area or part of the area of an Area Health
Authority or such an area or part together with the
areas or parts of the areas of other Area Health
Authorities ;

and the district of a Council must be such that no part of it
is separated from the rest of it by territory not included in the
district.

Co-operation and assistance

Co-operation
between Health
Authorities
and local
authorities.

10.—(1) In exercising their respective functions Health
Authorities and local authorities shall co-operate with one
another in order to secure and advance the health and welfare
of the people of England and Wales.

(2) There shall be committees, to be called joint consultative
committees, who shall advise Area Health Authorities and the
authorities in column 2 of the Table below on the performance
of their duties under the preceding subsection and on the planning and operation of services of common concern to those
authorities.

TABLE

1 *Area Health Authority*	2 *Associated authorities*
An Area Health Authority in a metropolitan county in England.	The local authority for each district wholly or partly in the area of the Authority.
An Area Health Authority in a non-metropolitan county in England, or an Area Health Authority in Wales.	The local authority for each county, and also for each district, wholly or partly in the area of the Authority.
An Area Health Authority in Greater London.	The local authority for each London borough wholly or partly in the area of the Authority. Also the Inner London Education Authority, if wholly or partly in the area of the Authority. Also the Common Council of the City of London, if in the area of the Authority.

(3) Except as provided by an order under the following provisions of this section, each joint consultative committee shall
represent one or more Area Health Authorities together with one

or more of the authorities in column 2 of the Table above, and an Area Health Authority shall be represented together with each of the authorities associated with that Authority in column 2 of the said Table in one or other of the committees (but not necessarily the same committee).

(4) The Secretary of State shall have power by order to provide for any matter relating to joint consultative committees, and such an order may in particular—

    (*a*) provide for the way in which the provisions of subsections (2) and (3) of this section are to be carried out, or provide for varying the arrangements set out in those subsections ;

    (*b*) provide, where it appears to the Secretary of State appropriate, for an Area Health Authority to be represented on a joint consultative committee together with a local or other authority whose area is not within the area of the Area Health Authority ;

    (*c*) afford a choice to any authorities as to the number of joint consultative committees on which they are to be represented, and provide for the case where the authorities cannot agree on the choice ;

    (*d*) authorise or require a joint consultative committee to appoint any sub-committee or to join with another joint consultative committee or other joint consultative committees in appointing a joint sub-committee ;

    (*e*) authorise or require the appointment to a joint consultative committee, or to any sub-committee, of persons who are not members of the authorities represented by the joint consultative committee ;

    (*f*) require the authorities represented on a joint consultative committee to defray the expenses of the committee, and of any sub-committee, in such shares as may be determined by or under the order, and provide for the way in which any dispute between those authorities concerning the expenses is to be resolved ; and

    (*g*) require those authorities to make reports to the Secretary of State on the work of the joint consultative committee and of any sub-committee.

(5) Before making an order under this section the Secretary of State shall consult with such associations of local authorities as appear to him to be concerned, and with any local authority with whom consultation appears to him to be desirable.

(6) In this and the three next following sections " Health Authority " means a Regional or Area Health Authority or a special health authority.

PART I
Supply of
goods and
services by
Secretary of
State.

11.—(1) The Secretary of State may—

    (*a*) supply to local authorities, and to such public bodies or classes of public bodies as may be determined by the Secretary of State, any goods or materials of a kind used in the health service ;

    (*b*) make available to local authorities, and to such bodies or classes of bodies as aforesaid, any facilities (including the use of any premises and the use of any vehicle, plant or apparatus) provided by him for any service under the Health Service Acts and the services of persons employed by the Secretary of State or by a Health Authority ;

    (*c*) carry out maintenance work in connection with any land or building for the maintenance of which a local authority is responsible.

(2) The Secretary of State may supply or make available to persons providing general medical services, general dental services, general ophthalmic services or pharmaceutical services such goods, materials or other facilities as may be prescribed.

(3) The Secretary of State shall make available to local authorities—

    (*a*) any services or other facilities (excluding the services of any person but including goods or materials, the use of any premises and the use of any vehicle, plant or apparatus) provided under the Health Service Acts ;

    (*b*) the services provided as part of the health service by any person employed by the Secretary of State or a Health Authority ; and

    (*c*) the services of any medical practitioner, dental practitioner or nurse employed by the Secretary of State or a Health Authority otherwise than to provide services which are part of the health service,

so far as is reasonably necessary and practicable to enable local authorities to discharge their functions relating to social services, education and public health.

(4) It shall be the duty of the Secretary of State, before he makes the services of any officer of a Health Authority available in pursuance of subsection (1)(*b*) or subsection (3)(*b*) or (*c*) of this section, to consult the officer or a body recognised by the Secretary of State as representing the officer about the matter or to satisfy himself that the Health Authority has consulted the officer about the matter ; but the Secretary of State shall be entitled to disregard the preceding provisions of this subsection in a case where he considers it necessary to make the services of an officer available as aforesaid for the purpose of dealing

temporarily with an emergency and has previously consulted such a body about the making available of services in an emergency.

(5) For the purposes of subsection (1)(*b*) or subsection (3)(*b*) or (*c*) of this section the Secretary of State may give such directions to Health Authorities to make services of their officers available as he considers appropriate; and it shall be the duty of a Health Authority to comply with any such directions.

(6) The powers conferred by this section may be exercised on such terms as may be agreed, including terms as to the making of payments to the Secretary of State, and such charges may be made by the Secretary of State in respect of services or facilities provided under subsection (3) of this section as may be agreed between the Secretary of State and the local authority or, in default of agreement, as may be determined by arbitration.

(7) The Secretary of State may by order provide that, in relation to a vehicle which is made available by him in pursuance of this section and is used in accordance with the terms on which it is so made available, the Vehicles (Excise) Act 1971 and Part VI of the Road Traffic Act 1972 shall have effect with such modifications as are specified in the order.

(8) Any power to supply goods or materials conferred by this section includes a power to purchase and store them and a power to make arrangements with third parties for the supply of the goods or materials by those third parties.

(9) In subsection (1) of this section—
" maintenance work " includes minor renewals, minor improvements and minor extensions ; and
" public bodies " includes public bodies in Northern Ireland.

12.—(1) In the Local Authorities (Goods and Services) Act 1970 (supply of goods or services to public bodies) the expression " public body " shall include any Health Authority and, so far as relates to his functions under the Health Service Acts, shall include the Secretary of State.

Supply of goods and services by local authorities.
1970 c. 39.

The preceding provisions of this subsection shall have effect as if made by an order under section 1(5) of the said Act of 1970 and accordingly may be varied or revoked by such an order.

(2) Every local authority shall make available to Health Authorities acting in the area of the local authority the services of persons employed by the local authority for the purposes of the authority's functions under the Local Authorities Social Services Act 1970 so far as is reasonably necessary and prac-

1970 c. 42.

PART I ticable to enable Health Authorities to discharge their functions under the Health Service Acts.

(3) Such charges may be made by a local authority for acting under the preceding subsection as may be agreed between the local authority and the Secretary of State or, in default of agreement, as may be determined by arbitration.

Voluntary organisations and other bodies.

13.—(1) The Secretary of State may, where he considers it appropriate, arrange with any person or body (including a voluntary organisation) for that person or body to provide, or assist in providing, any service under the Health Service Acts.

(2) The Secretary of State may make available—

(a) to any person or body (including a voluntary organisation) carrying out any arrangements under the preceding subsection ; or

1968 c. 46.

(b) to any voluntary organisation eligible for assistance under section 64 or section 65 of the Health Services and Public Health Act 1968 (assistance made available by the Secretary of State or local authorities),

any facilities (including goods or materials, or the use of any premises and the use of any vehicle, plant or apparatus) provided by him for any service under the Health Service Acts and, where anything is so made available, the services of persons employed by the Secretary of State or by a Health Authority in connection with it.

(3) The powers conferred by this section may be exercised on such terms as may be agreed, including terms as to the making of payments by or to the Secretary of State, and any goods or materials may be made available either temporarily or permanently ; and subsection (7) of section 11 of this Act shall have effect in relation to a vehicle made available in pursuance of this section as if for the reference to that section there were substituted a reference to this section.

(4) Any power to supply goods or materials conferred by this section includes a power to purchase and store them and includes a power to make arrangements with third parties for the supply of goods or materials by those third parties.

(5) In this section " voluntary organisation " means a body the activities of which are carried on otherwise than for profit, but does not include any public or local authority.

PART II

ABOLITION OF CERTAIN AUTHORITIES AND TRANSFER OF PROPERTY, STAFF AND ENDOWMENTS ETC.

Abolition of certain authorities

Abolition of authorities.

14.—(1) All Regional Hospital Boards, Hospital Management Committees and Executive Councils, the Joint Pricing Committee for England, the Welsh Joint Pricing Committee and, except as

provided by the following section, all Boards of Governors shall
cease to exist on the appointed day; and on that day any
authority which is a local health authority by virtue of section
19 of the principal Act shall cease to be a local health authority
and all joint boards constituted in pursuance of that section shall
cease to exist.

(2) The Secretary of State may by order make such provision
as he considers appropriate in anticipation or in consequence of
the abolition by the preceding subsection of any body or in
connection with the winding up of the body's affairs; and if a
body abolished by that subsection has, as respects a period before
the appointed day, not performed a duty imposed on the body
by subsection (2) or (3) of section 55 of the principal Act (which
relate to accounts), then—

(a) it shall be the duty of the Secretary of State to secure
that the duty so imposed is performed by a Regional
or Area Health Authority or special health authority
determined by him; and

(b) that section shall have effect in relation to the body and
period in question as if for references to each financial
year in subsections (3) and (4) there were substituted
references to that period and as if the word " annual "
in subsection (3) were omitted.

15.—(1) The Secretary of State may by order provide that Preservation
the preceding section shall, while the order is in force, not of certain
apply to any body specified in the order which is the Board of Boards of
Governors of a teaching hospital mentioned in Schedule 2 to Governors.
this Act.

(2) An order made by virtue of the preceding subsection—

(a) must be made before the appointed day except in a
case falling within paragraph (c) of this subsection;

(b) shall provide for the order to cease to have effect, unless
it is previously revoked, on the expiration of a period
specified in the order (which shall not be longer than
five years beginning with the date on which the order
is made);

(c) may be made after the appointed day in respect of a
preserved Board for the purpose of securing that the
Board continues to be a preserved Board for a further
period; and

(d) may at any time be revoked by order by the Secretary
of State;

and it shall be the duty of the Secretary of State, before he
makes an order in pursuance of the preceding subsection or
paragraph (d) of this subsection, to consult the University of
London and the Board of Governors in question about the
order.

(3) The Secretary of State may by order provide that, in relation to a preserved Board and any person, thing, right, liability or other matter whatsoever connected with the Board,—

(a) any provision of this Act which repeals or amends any enactment and is specified in the order shall not apply ;

(b) any enactment which, apart from any provision made by virtue of the preceding paragraph, is repealed or amended by this Act shall have effect with such modifications as are specified in the order ; and

(c) such provisions of this Act and any instrument in force by virtue of this Act as are specified in the order shall have effect with such modifications as are so specified ;

but nothing in this Act, and in particular nothing in any provision of this Act amending section 55 of the principal Act (which relates to accounts), shall affect the application of that section to a preserved Board.

(4) The Secretary of State may by order—

(a) provide that a preserved Board shall cease to exercise functions with respect to the administration of any hospital specified in the order ;

(b) confer on a preserved Board such functions as are specified in the order with respect to the administration of a hospital so specified (whether or not apart from the order the Board has functions with respect to the administration of that hospital) ; and

(c) provide that this Act and any instrument in force by virtue of this Act shall, in relation to any person, thing, right, liability or other matter whatsoever connected with the hospital in question, have effect with such modifications as are specified in the order.

(5) Where a Board of Governors ceases to be a preserved Board this Act and any instrument in force by virtue of this Act shall, in relation to the Board and any person, thing, right, liability and other matter whatsoever connected with the Board, have effect with the substitution of a reference to the date of the cesser for the first reference in subsection (1) of the preceding section and the reference in subsection (2) of that section to the appointed day and with such further modifications as the Secretary of State may by order specify.

(6) In this Act " preserved Board " means a Board of Governors to which by virtue of this section the preceding section does not for the time being apply ; and any question whether a person, thing, right, liability or other matter whatsoever is for the purposes of this section connected with a Board of Governors or a hospital shall be determined by the Secretary of State.

Transfer of property etc.

16.—(1) Subject to subsection (4) of this section, on the appointed day there shall by virtue of this subsection be trans- ferred to and vest in the Secretary of State—

(*a*) all property which immediately before that day—

(i) was held by a local authority solely for the purposes of one or more of its health functions, or

(ii) was held by a local authority otherwise than as mentioned in the preceding sub-paragraph and was used by the authority wholly or mainly for the purposes there mentioned ; and

(*b*) all rights and liabilities which were acquired or incurred by a local authority wholly or mainly in the performance of its health functions and to which the authority was entitled or subject immediately before the appointed day.

(2) The Secretary of State may by order—

(*a*) make provision for securing that where any property has, at any time during the period beginning with 16th November 1972 and ending immediately before the appointed day—

(i) been held by a local authority as mentioned in paragraph (*a*)(i) of the preceding subsection, or

(ii) been held and used by a local authority as mentioned in paragraph (*a*)(ii) of that subsection,

but in consequence of anything done otherwise than in the ordinary course of business is not so held or, as the case may be, held and used by the authority immediately before the appointed day, the property is treated for the purposes of the preceding subsection as so held or held and used by the authority immediately before the appointed day ;

(*b*) make provision as to the manner of determining, and as to the matters which are to be taken into account or disregarded for the purpose of determining, whether immediately before the appointed day any property was held or held and used as mentioned in the preceding subsection or any local authority was entitled or subject to rights or liabilities acquired or incurred as there mentioned ;

(*c*) make provision for securing that where any premises transferred to the Secretary of State by virtue of this section contain accommodation which was used immediately before the appointed day for the purposes of functions of a local authority other than health functions, the accommodation may continue to be used by the authority for those purposes on such terms and for such period as may be agreed between the Secretary of State and the authority or, in default of agreement, as may be determined in a manner specified in the order ;

(d) make provision for securing that where any premises not transferred to the Secretary of State by virtue of this section contain accommodation which was used immediately before the appointed day for the purposes of health functions of a local authority, the accommodation may be used by the Secretary of State for similar purposes on such terms and for such period as aforesaid ;

(e) provide that such as may be specified in the order of the rights and liabilities transferred to the Secretary of State by virtue of this section shall be enforceable by and against a Regional or Area Health Authority or special health authority so specified instead of by and against the Secretary of State ;

(f) make provision as to the persons on whom shall lie the burden of proving, for the purposes of provision made by virtue of paragraph (a) of this subsection, that a particular thing was done in the ordinary course of business.

(3) The preceding provisions of this section shall have effect in relation to a local education authority as if for any reference to a local authority and health functions there were substituted respectively a reference to a local education authority and functions under the following enactments (which relate to medical and dental inspection and treatment) namely, section 48(1) and (3) of the Education Act 1944, section 78 of that Act so far as that section relates to such inspection and treatment and section 4 of the Education (Miscellaneous Provisions) Act 1953.

(4) The Secretary of State may at any time before the appointed day provide by order that property, rights or liabilities specified in the order shall not be transferred to him by virtue of this section ; and nothing in subsections (1) to (3) of this section applies to property, rights or liabilities to which section 25 of this Act applies.

(5) Where any property transferred from a local authority or a local education authority to the Secretary of State by virtue of this section consists of uncompleted buildings which were being constructed by the authority, the authority may complete the buildings on such terms as it may agree with the Secretary of State.

(6) In this section—

" health functions " means—

> (a) functions under Part III and section 65 of the principal Act and sections 10 to 12 of the Health Services and Public Health Act 1968 so far as those functions do not stand referred to social services committees by virtue of section 2 of the Local Authority Social Services Act 1970 ;

1968 c. 46.

1970 c. 42.

> (b) functions under the National Health Service (Family Planning) Act 1967 and the National Health Service (Family Planning) Amendment Act 1972 ;

1967 c. 39.
1972 c. 72.

> (c) functions under section 196 of the Public Health Act 1936 so far as those functions relate to the diagnosis and treatment of diseases ; and

1936 c. 49.

> (d) functions under the enactments mentioned in section 41(1) of this Act ; and

" local authority " means—

> (a) except in relation to functions mentioned in paragraph (d) above and functions of the Greater London Council, any authority which immediately before the passing of this Act was a local health authority ;
> (b) in relation to functions mentioned in paragraph (d) above, a local authority within the meaning of section 41 of this Act ;
> (c) in relation to functions of the Greater London Council, that Council,

and in relation to functions mentioned in paragraph (c) of the preceding definition includes any authority, in addition to an authority or body mentioned in paragraph (a) of this definition, on which functions are conferred by the said section 196.

17.—(1) All property, rights and liabilities which immediately before the appointed day were property, rights and liabilities of an Executive Council or either of the pricing committees mentioned in section 14(1) of this Act shall by virtue of this subsection be transferred to and vest in the Secretary of State on that day ; and the Secretary of State may by order provide for such of those rights and liabilities as are specified in the order to be enforceable by and against an Area Health Authority or special health authority or Family Practitioner Committee so specified instead of by and against the Secretary of State.

Transfers from Executive Councils and pricing committees.

(2) The Secretary of State may by order make such provision as he considers is appropriate in anticipation or in consequence of any transfer which is to be or has been made by virtue of the preceding subsection.

PART II

Transfers to
employment
by new
authorities
and social
service
authorities.

Transfer of staff

18.—(1) The Secretary of State may by order make provision—

    (*a*) for the transfer on the appointed day to the employment of new health authorities designated by or under the order of persons so designated who immediately before that day were—

        (i) employed by old health authorities so designated, or

        (ii) employed by local health authorities or by the Greater London Council and so employed wholly or mainly for the purposes of functions mentioned in paragraphs (*a*) and (*b*) of the definition of health functions in section 16(6) of this Act, or

        (iii) employed by local education authorities wholly or mainly for the purposes of functions under the enactments mentioned in section 16(3) of this Act, or

        (iv) employed as relevant staff or speech therapists by local education authorities wholly or mainly for the purposes of providing special educational treatment in pursuance of section 34 of the Education Act 1944 and ascertaining whether children require such treatment, or

        (v) employed by local authorities within the meaning of section 41 of this Act wholly or mainly for the purposes of functions under the enactments mentioned in subsection (1) of that section ;

    (*b*) for requiring any such authority, body or Council as is mentioned in sub-paragraphs (i) to (v) of the preceding paragraph and is designated by or under the order to make, after consulting new health authorities so designated if the order requires them to be consulted, schemes for the transfer on the appointed day to the employment of new health authorities designated by or under the schemes of persons designated by or under the schemes who were employed as mentioned in the preceding paragraph ;

    (*c*) for any scheme made in pursuance of the preceding paragraph to be varied or revoked, at any time before the appointed day, by a subsequent scheme so made ;

    (*d*) for requiring an authority or other person by whom a scheme is made in pursuance of this subsection to

submit the scheme or provisions of it to the Secretary
of State for his approval, and for requiring the
authority or other person to make, before the appointed
day, such changes in the scheme as the Secretary of
State may direct.

(2) The Secretary of State may by order make provision—

  (a) for the transfer on the appointed day to the employment
  of new health authorities of persons to whom this
  subsection applies;

  (b) for requiring public health authorities designated by
  or under the order to make schemes for the transfer
  on the appointed day, to the employment of new health
  authorities designated by or under the schemes, of
  persons to whom this subsection applies;

  (c) as to the manner of determining whether an individual
  is a person to whom this subsection applies and which
  authority is the new health authority to whose employment such a person is to be transferred;

  (d) for determining, in the case of a person who apart from
  provision made by virtue of this paragraph falls to be
  transferred to the same employment or different
  employments by virtue of this subsection and any other
  provision of this Act, which of the provisions in question are not to apply in his case;

and it shall be the duty of the Secretary of State, before he
makes an order in pursuance of this subsection, to consult with
respect to the order such bodies as appear to him to represent
public health authorities and to be concerned with the order
and any other body which he considers it desirable to consult
about the order.

(3) The persons to whom the preceding subsection applies
are—

  (a) relevant staff employed immediately before the
  appointed day—

    (i) by public health authorities wholly or mainly
    for the purposes of any functions of such authorities
    under sections 143, 147, 153 and 166 to 170 of the
    Public Health Act 1936, sections 40 and 41 of the 1936 c. 49.
    Public Health Act 1961 and sections 49 to 52 of 1961 c. 64.
    the Health Services and Public Health Act 1968 1968 c. 46.
    (which relate to the control of infectious disease and
    food poisoning) and Part IX of the Public Health
    Act 1936 (which relates to common lodging houses),
    or

    (ii) by public health authorities, in their capacities
    as food and drugs authorities within the meaning

PART II
1955 c. 16
(4 Eliz. 2.).

of the Food and Drugs Act 1955, wholly or mainly for the purposes of any functions of food and drugs authorities under that Act ; and

1936 c. 49.

(b) persons employed immediately before the appointed day wholly or mainly in premises provided in pursuance of section 196 of the Public Health Act 1936 (which relates to laboratories) and transferred to the Secretary of State by section 16 of this Act.

(4) The Secretary of State may by order make provision for the transfer—

1970 c. 42.

(a) to the employment of bodies who are local authorities for the purposes of the Local Authority Social Services Act 1970 of persons of descriptions specified in the order who are for the time being employed by old health authorities or new health authorities wholly or mainly for the purposes of functions which stand referred to social services committees by virtue of section 2 of that Act ;

(b) to the employment of new health authorities of relevant staff and speech therapists who are for the time being employed wholly or mainly for the purposes mentioned in the preceding paragraph by bodies who are such local authorities as are there mentioned ;

and an order made by virtue of this subsection may include provision—

(i) for transfers in pursuance of the order to be made on such days as may be determined by or under the order ; and

(ii) as to the manner of determining whether an individual is a person liable to be transferred by virtue of this subsection and which authority is the authority to whose employment such a person is to be transferred.

(5) A person transferred by virtue of paragraph (a) of the preceding subsection to the employment of such a body as is mentioned in that paragraph shall not be required in the course of that employment to perform duties otherwise than at or in connection with a hospital unless he has consented to perform such duties.

(6) The Secretary of State may by order make provision for the transfer to the employment of any new health authorities, with effect from such dates (whether before or after the making of the order) as may be specified in the order, of persons who—

(a) were employed by an old health authority, or by another authority in its capacity as a local health authority, immediately before the date when the authority ceased to exist or to be a local health authority ; and

(b) are not on that date transferred to the employment of a new health authority by virtue of any provision of subsections (1) to (4) of this section.

(7) In this section—

" new health authority " means any Regional or Area Health Authority and any special health authority ;

" old health authority " means any Regional Hospital Board, Board of Governors or Executive Council and any pricing committee mentioned in section 14(1) of this Act ;

" public health authority " means the council of a county, borough (including a London borough), urban district and rural district, the Common Council of the City of London and a port health authority constituted in pursuance of section 2 of the Public Health Act 1936 ; 1936 c. 49. and

" relevant staff " means persons of any of the following categories, namely, medical practitioners, persons registered or enrolled within the meaning of the Nurses Act 1957 and persons registered by 1957 c. 15. a board in respect of a profession in pursuance of the Professions Supplementary to Medicine Act 1960. 1960 c. 66.

19.—(1) Without prejudice to the duty imposed on the Secre- Provisions tary of State by subsection (2) of the preceding section, it shall supple- be the duty of the Secretary of State, before he makes an order mentary to in pursuance of that section or the following subsection, to s. 18. consult with respect to the order such bodies as he may recognise as representing persons who in his opinion are likely to be transferred or affected by transfers in pursuance of the order.

(2) It shall be the duty of the Secretary of State by order to make provision for securing, in the case of a person transferred to the employment of any body by virtue of the preceding section,—

(a) that, while he is in the employment of that body and has not been served with a notice in writing stating that it is served for the purposes of this subsection and specifying such new terms and conditions of employment as are mentioned in the following paragraph, the scale of his remuneration and, taken as a whole, the other terms and conditions of his employment by that body are not less favourable to him than were immediately before the transfer those of the employment from which the transfer was made;

(b) that any new terms and conditions determined by that body for his employment by that body are such that—

(i) so long as he is engaged in duties reasonably comparable to the duties in which immediately before the transfer he was engaged in the employment from which the transfer was made, the scale of his remuneration and, taken as a whole, the other terms and conditions of his employment by that body are not less favourable to him than were, immediately before the transfer, those of the employment from which the transfer was made, and

(ii) so long as he is engaged in duties not so comparable, the terms and conditions of his employment by that body (excluding terms as to remuneration) are, taken as a whole, not less favourable than as mentioned in the preceding sub-paragraph;

(c) that for the purposes of any enactment specified in the order the employments from which and to which he was transferred by virtue of the preceding section are treated as one continuous employment;

and an order made in pursuance of this subsection may contain provision for the determination of questions arising with respect to the effect in relation to any person of provision made by virtue of paragraphs (a) to (c) of this subsection.

(3) An order or scheme made by virtue of any provision of the preceding section except subsection (4)(a) may include provision for securing that, in determining whether a person was at a particular time employed by an authority wholly or mainly for the purposes of functions of the authority of a particular kind mentioned in that section, any functions of that authority which are of a different kind so mentioned and for the purposes of which the person was at that time also employed by the authority may be treated as functions of the particular kind in question; and it is hereby declared that, in determining in pursuance of the preceding section whether a person was at any time employed by an authority wholly or mainly for the purposes of functions of the authority, any employment of his at that time which was not employment by the authority is to be disregarded.

(4) An order made by virtue of the preceding section may include provision—

(a) for the determination of any question arising in connection with the order as to whether a person is or

was employed in a particular capacity or wholly or
mainly for particular purposes ;

(b) for enabling any person who objects, on such grounds
as may be specified in the order, to his transfer in
pursuance of the order or a scheme made by virtue
of the order to make in respect of the transfer representations to whichever of the two Commissions appointed
in pursuance of the following section is appropriate
in his case, and for requiring the Commission to advise
the person who made the order or scheme or, if that
person has ceased to exist, to advise the Secretary of
State on whether it would be appropriate in consequence of the representations to amend the order or
scheme before the day when transfers take effect in
pursuance of it or to transfer a person on or after that
day from the employment to which he is transferred in
pursuance of the order or scheme ;

(c) for the transfer of a person in consequence of such
representations—

(i) from the employment of a new health authority
to the employment of a different new health authority
or, except where the person in question was transferred in pursuance of the order or scheme from
the employment of an old health authority, to the
employment of an authority established by or under
the Local Government Act 1972 or a London autho- 1972 c. 70.
rity, or

(ii) from the employment of a body to which the
person in question was transferred by virtue of paragraph (a) of subsection (4) of the preceding section to
the employment of a different body which is such a
local authority as is mentioned in that paragraph ;

and in this subsection " old health authority " and " new health
authority " have the same meanings as in the preceding section
and " London authority " means the Greater London Council, a
London borough council and the Common Council of the City
of London.

20.—(1) It shall be the duty of the Secretary of State to Health
appoint, within one month beginning with the date of the Service Staff
passing of this Act, two Commissions to be called the National Commissions
Health Service Staff Commission and the Welsh National
Health Service Staff Commission ; and the Commissions—

(a) shall consist respectively of such persons as the Secretary of State may from time to time appoint as members

of the Commission after consulting any bodies appearing to him to represent persons employed in England or, as the case may be, employed in Wales who are liable to transfer in pursuance of section 18 of this Act and any other bodies appearing to him to be concerned with transfers of such persons in pursuance of that section ; and

(b) shall in the case of the National Health Service Staff Commission exercise its functions in relation to England and in the case of the other Commission exercise its functions in relation to Wales.

(2) It shall be the duty of each Commission—

(a) to keep under review the arrangements made by relevant bodies for recruiting and engaging employees and the arrangements made for transfers in pursuance of section 18 of this Act and to give advice to the Secretary of State and the relevant bodies with respect to the arrangements ;

(b) to consider and advise the Secretary of State on any matter which he refers to the Commission as being a matter which in his opinion arises in connection with persons liable to transfer in pursuance of section 18 of this Act ;

(c) to consider and advise the Secretary of State on the steps required to safeguard the interests of persons liable as aforesaid ; and

(d) to arrange for the consideration of representations made to the Commission in pursuance of provision made by virtue of paragraph (b) of subsection (4) of the preceding section and for the giving of advice in pursuance of provision so made ;

and each Commission shall have power to take any steps which it considers are appropriate for the purpose of selecting and recommending to Regional or Area Health Authorities and special health authorities persons whom it considers are suitable for employment by any of those authorities.

(3) The Secretary of State may—

(a) give directions to each Commission with respect to its procedure ;

(b) give directions to relevant bodies with respect to the furnishing by them of information requested by the appropriate Commission and with respect to the action to be taken by them in consequence of advice given by that Commission ;

(c) pay to any member of either Commission such remuneration as the Secretary of State may determine with the approval of the Minister for the Civil Service ;

(d) defray any expenses incurred with his approval by either Commission in the performance of its functions; and

(e) wind up either Commission in such manner and at such time as he thinks fit;

and it shall be the duty of a body to which directions are given in pursuance of this subsection to comply with the directions.

(4) In this section " relevant bodies " means bodies from and to whose employment persons are liable to be transferred by virtue of section 18 of this Act.

Hospital endowments etc.

21. A Health Authority shall have power to accept, hold and administer any property on trust for all or any purposes relating to the health service.

Power of Health Authorities to accept gifts.

22.—(1) Where the terms of a trust instrument authorise or require the trustees, whether immediately or in the future, to apply any part of the capital or income of the trust property for the purposes of any hospital vested in the Secretary of State, the trust instrument shall be construed as authorising or, as the case may be, requiring the trustees to apply the trust property to the like extent, and at the like times, for the purpose of making payments, whether of capital or income, to the appropriate hospital authority.

Private trusts for hospitals: payments to Health Authorities.

(2) Any sum so paid to the appropriate hospital authority shall, so far as practicable, be applied by them for the purpose specified in the trust instrument.

(3) In this section " the appropriate hospital authority " means—

(a) where Special Trustees are appointed for the hospital, those trustees,

(b) in any other case, the Area Health Authority exercising functions on behalf of the Secretary of State in respect of the hospital.

(4) Nothing in this section shall apply—

(a) to a trust for a special hospital ; or

(b) to property transferred under section 24 of this Act.

23.—(1) The Hospital Endowments Fund shall be wound up by the Secretary of State, and the winding up shall be completed by 31st March 1974 or as soon after as is practicable.

Winding-up of Hospital Endowments Fund.

PART II

(2) The Secretary of State shall by order provide for the distribution of the assets of the Hospital Endowments Fund among the following authorities and bodies, that is—

> Regional Health Authorities,
> Area Health Authorities, and
> Special Trustees,

or among such of those authorities or trustees as are specified in the order, in such proportions or up to such amounts as may be so specified.

Transfer of trust property from abolished authorities.

24.—(1) Subject to the following subsection, property held immediately before the appointed day on trust by a body specified in column 1 of the Table below (excluding a preserved Board) shall on the appointed day be transferred to and vest in the person specified in the relevant entry in column 2 of that Table.

TABLE

1. Existing trustees	2. New trustees
A regional hospital board in England.	Such one or more of the Regional Health Authorities as may be specified by an order made by the Secretary of State.
The Welsh Hospital Board ...	Such one or more Area Health Authorities or special health authorities in Wales as may be specified by an order made by the Secretary of State.
A Hospital Management Committee (other than a University Hospital Management Committee) holding any property on trust for one or more hospitals.	The Area Health Authority or Authorities responsible for the administration of the hospitals.
A University Hospital Management Committee.	The Special Trustees appointed for the university hospital.
A Board of Governors	The Special Trustees appointed for the teaching hospital.

(2) If after the passing of this Act and before 31st October 1973 a University Hospital Management Committee or Board of Governors requests the Secretary of State in writing to secure that property held immediately before the appointed day by the Committee or Board is not transferred to and vested in Special Trustees by virtue of the preceding subsection, he may by an order made before the appointed day provide that the property shall be treated for the purposes of that subsection as if it were held immediately before that day by a Hospital Management Committee which is not a University Hospital Management Committee.

(3) Where the Secretary of State has arranged before the
appointed day for an Area Health Authority (Teaching) established before that day—

> (*a*) to become responsible for the administration of a
> hospital or group of hospitals controlled and managed
> by a Hospital Management Committee which is not a
> University Hospital Management Committee ; and

> (*b*) not to become responsible on that day for the adminis-
> tration of any hospital which immediately before that
> day was controlled and managed by a University Hos-
> pital Management Committee or a Board of Governors,

he may by an order made before that day specify the hospital or
group in question and provide that for the purposes of subsection
(1) of this section and section 29(1) of this Act the Hospital
Management Committee shall be deemed to be a University
Hospital Management Committee and the hospital or group
shall be deemed to be designated as a university hospital.

25.—(1) Any property held immediately before the appointed   Transfer of
day by a local health authority on trust for purposes which are   trust property
wholly or mainly the same as those of any part of the health   held for
service shall on the appointed day be transferred to and vest   health services
in such one or more Health Authorities as may be specified by   health
an order made by the Secretary of State.   authorities.

(2) Any property held immediately before the appointed day
by the Greater London Council on trust for the purpose of its
functions under section 27 of the principal Act (ambulance
services) shall on the appointed day be transferred to and vest
in such Health Authority as may be specified by an order made
by the Secretary of State.

(3) The Secretary of State may by order provide for determining whether immediately before the appointed day any
property was held as mentioned in the preceding provisions of
this section.

(4) Nothing in section 210 of the Local Government Act 1972   1972 c. 70.
(charities) shall apply to property to be transferred under this
section.

26.—(1) The Secretary of State may, having regard to any   Power to
change or proposed change in the arrangements for the adminis-   make further
tration of a hospital or in the area or functions of any Health   transfers of
Authority, by order provide for the transfer of any trust property   trust property.

from any Health Authority or Special Trustees to any other Health Authority or Special Trustees.

(2) If it appears to the Secretary of State at any time that all the functions of any Special Trustees should be discharged by one or more Health Authorities then, whether or not there has been any such change as is mentioned in the preceding subsection, he may by order provide for the transfer of all trust property from the Special Trustees to the Health Authority or, in such proportions as he may specify in the order, to those Health Authorities.

(3) Before acting under this section the Secretary of State shall consult the Health Authorities and Special Trustees concerned.

Application
of trust
property
previously
held for
general
hospital
purposes.

27.—(1) This section applies—

    (*a*) to property which is transferred under section 23 of this Act ; and

    (*b*) to property which is transferred under section 24 of this Act and which immediately before the appointed day was, in accordance with any provision contained in or made under section 7 of the principal Act, applicable for purposes relating to hospital services or relating to some form of research,

and this section shall continue to apply to the property after any further transfer under the preceding section.

(2) The person holding the property after the transfer or last transfer shall secure, so far as is reasonably practicable, that the objects of any original endowment and the observance of any conditions attached thereto, including in particular conditions intended to preserve the memory of any person or class of persons, are not prejudiced by the provisions of this Part of this Act.

In this subsection "original endowment" means a hospital endowment which was transferred under section 7 of the principal Act and from which the property in question is derived.

(3) Subject to the preceding subsection, the property shall be held on trust for such purposes relating to hospital services (including research), or to any other part of the health service associated with any hospital, as the person holding the property thinks fit.

(4) Where the person holding the property is a body of Special Trustees, the power conferred by the preceding subsection shall be exercised as respects the hospitals for which they are appointed.

28.—(1) Any discretion given by a trust instrument to the trustees of property transferred under section 24, 25 or 26 of this Act shall be exercisable by the person to whom the property is so transferred and, subject to the preceding section and subject to the following provisions of this section, the transfer shall not affect the trusts on which the property is held.

PART II
Application of trust property: further provisions.

(2) Where property is transferred under section 24 of this Act and any discretion is given by a trust instrument to the trustees to apply the property, or income arising from the property, to such hospital services (including research) as the trustees think fit without any restriction on the kinds of hospital services and without any restriction to one or more specified hospitals, the discretion shall be enlarged so as to allow the application of the property, or as the case may be of the income arising from the property, to such extent as the trustees think fit, for any other part of the health service associated with any hospital.

(3) The preceding subsection shall apply on any subsequent transfer of the property under section 26 of this Act.

29.—(1) The Secretary of State shall appoint bodies of trustees (in this Act referred to as Special Trustees) for the hospital or hospitals which, immediately before the appointed day, were controlled and managed by any University Hospital Management Committee or Board of Governors (excluding any body on whose request an order was made in pursuance of section 24(2) of this Act and any preserved Board), and those trustees shall hold and administer the property transferred to them under this Act.

Special Trustees for a university or teaching hospital.

(2) Special Trustees shall have power to accept, hold and administer any property on trust for all or any purposes relating to hospital services (including research), or to any other part of the health service associated with hospitals, being a trust which is wholly or mainly for hospitals for which the Special Trustees are appointed.

(3) The number of trustees for any hospital or hospitals shall be such as the Secretary of State may from time to time determine after consultation with such bodies and persons as he considers appropriate.

(4) The term of office of any Special Trustee shall be fixed by the Secretary of State, but a Special Trustee may be removed by the Secretary of State at any time during his term of office.

30.—(1) Where by section 24, 25 or 26 of this Act, or by an order under any of those sections, property is transferred to two or more authorities, it shall be apportioned by them in such

Endowments: supplementary provisions.

PART II proportions as they may agree or as may in default of agreement be determined by the Secretary of State:

Provided that where the property is transferred pursuant to an order, the order may provide for the way in which the property is to be apportioned.

(2) Where property is so apportioned, the Secretary of State may by order make any consequential amendments of the trust instrument relating to the property.

(3) In sections 21 to 29 of this Act, unless the context otherwise requires—

" Health Authority " means a Regional or Area Health Authority or a special health authority ; and

" University Hospital Management Committee " means a Hospital Management Committee of a hospital or group of hospitals designated as a university hospital under 1968 c. 46. section 5(1) of the Health Services and Public Health Act 1968.

(4) Any provision in the said sections for the transfer of any property includes provision for the transfer of any rights and liabilities arising from that property.

1960 c. 58. (5) Nothing in the said sections shall affect any power of Her Majesty, the court (as defined in the Charities Act 1960) or any other person to alter the trusts of any charity.

PART III

THE HEALTH SERVICE COMMISSIONERS FOR ENGLAND AND FOR WALES

Appointment and tenure of office.
31.—(1) For the purpose of conducting investigations in accordance with this Part of this Act, there shall be appointed a Commissioner to be known as the Health Service Commissioner for England and a Commissioner to be known as the Health Service Commissioner for Wales.

(2) Her Majesty may by Letters Patent from time to time appoint a person to be a Commissioner, and a person so appointed shall, subject to the following subsection, hold office during good behaviour.

(3) A person appointed to be a Commissioner may be relieved of office by Her Majesty at his own request or may be removed from office by Her Majesty in consequence of Addresses from both Houses of Parliament, and shall in any case vacate office on completing the year of service in which he attains the age of sixty-five years.

(4) A person who is a member of a relevant body shall not be appointed to be a Commissioner, and a Commissioner shall not become a member of a relevant body.

32.—(1) Subject to subsections (3) and (4) of this section, there shall be paid to the holder of the office of a Commissioner such salary as the House of Commons may by resolution from time to time determine, and any such resolution may take effect from the date on which it is passed or from another date specified in the resolution.

(2) Subject to subsections (5) and (6) of this section, Schedule 1 to the Parliamentary Commissioner Act 1967 (which relates to pensions and other benefits) shall have effect with respect to persons who have held office as a Commissioner as it has effect with respect to persons who have held office as the Parliamentary Commissioner for Administration.

1967 c. 13.

(3) The salary payable to a holder of the office of a Commissioner shall be abated by the amount of any pension payable to him in respect of any public office in the United Kingdom or elsewhere to which he has previously been appointed or elected ; but any such abatement shall be disregarded in computing that salary for the purposes of the said Schedule 1.

(4) A person holding the office of Parliamentary Commissioner for Administration and one or more of the offices of Health Service Commissioner for England, Health Service Commissioner for Scotland and Health Service Commissioner for Wales shall so long as he does so be entitled only to the salary pertaining to the first-mentioned office ; and a person holding two or more of those offices other than that of Parliamentary Commissioner for Administration shall so long as he does so be entitled only to the salary pertaining to such one of those offices as he selects.

(5) A person—

(a) shall not be entitled to make simultaneously different elections in pursuance of paragraph 1 of the said Schedule 1 in respect of different offices mentioned in the preceding subsection ; and

(b) shall, if he has made or is treated as having made an election in pursuance of that paragraph in respect of such an office, be deemed to have made the same election in respect of all such other offices to which he is or is subsequently appointed ;

and no account shall be taken for the purposes of that Schedule of a period of service in such an office if salary in respect of the office was not paid for that period.

(6) Subject to the preceding subsection, the Minister for the Civil Service may by regulations provide that the said Schedule 1 shall have effect, in relation to persons who have held more than one of the offices mentioned in subsection (4) of this section, with such modifications as the said Minister considers

PART III

necessary in consequence of their having held more than one of those offices ; and it is hereby declared that different regulations may be made in pursuance of paragraph 4 of that Schedule in relation to different offices so mentioned.

(7) Any salary, pension or other benefit payable by virtue of this section shall be charged on and issued out of the Consolidated Fund.

Administrative provisions.

33.—(1) A Commissioner may appoint such officers as he may determine with the approval of the Minister for the Civil Service as to numbers and conditions of service ; and it shall be the duty of the Health Service Commissioner for Wales to include among his officers such persons having a command of the Welsh language as he considers are needed to enable him to investigate complaints in Welsh.

(2) Any function of a Commissioner under this Part of this Act may be performed by any officer of the Commissioner authorised for that purpose by him or by any officer so authorised of another Commissioner mentioned in subsection (4) of the preceding section.

(3) To assist him in any investigation a Commissioner may obtain advice from any person who in his opinion is qualified to give it and may pay such fees or allowances to any such person as he may determine with the approval of the said Minister.

(4) The expenses of a Commissioner under this Part of this Act, to such amount as may be sanctioned by the said Minister, shall be defrayed out of money provided by Parliament.

Matters subject to investigation.

34.—(1) In this Part of this Act " relevant body " means any of the following bodies, namely—

(a) Regional Hospital Boards ;

(b) Boards of Governors ;

(c) Hospital Management Committees ;

(d) Executive Councils ;

(e) Regional Health Authorities ;

(f) Area Health Authorities ;

(g) any special health authority established on or before the appointed day ;

(h) any special health authority which is established after that day and is designated by Order in Council as an authority to which this paragraph applies ;

(i) Family Practitioner Committees ; and

(j) the Public Health Laboratory Service Board ;

and, except where the context otherwise requires, any reference in this Part of this Act to a relevant body includes a reference to an officer of the body.

(2) The Health Service Commissioner for England shall not conduct an investigation under this Part of this Act in respect of the Welsh Hospital Board, any Hospital Management Committee responsible for hospitals in Wales, any Executive Council or Area Health Authority of which the area is in Wales, the Family Practitioner Committee established by such an Authority, or a special health authority exercising functions only or mainly in Wales, and the Health Service Commissioner for Wales shall not conduct such an investigation in respect of a relevant body other than one of the bodies aforesaid.

(3) Subject to the provisions of this section, a Commissioner may investigate—

(a) an alleged failure in a service provided by a relevant body ; or

(b) an alleged failure of a relevant body to provide a service which it was a function of the body to provide ; or

(c) any other action taken by or on behalf of a relevant body,

in a case where a complaint is duly made by or on behalf of any person that he has sustained injustice or hardship in consequence of the failure or in consequence of maladministration connected with the other action.

(4) Except as hereafter provided, a Commissioner shall not conduct an investigation under this Part of this Act in respect of any of the following matters—

(a) any action in respect of which the person aggrieved has or had a right of appeal, reference or review to or before a tribunal constituted by or under any enactment or by virtue of Her Majesty's prerogative ;

(b) any action in respect of which the person aggrieved has or had a remedy by way of proceedings in any court of law :

Provided that a Commissioner may conduct an investigation notwithstanding that the person aggrieved has or had such a right or remedy, if satisfied that in the particular circumstances it is not reasonable to expect him to resort or have resorted to it.

(5) Without prejudice to the preceding subsection, a Commissioner shall not conduct an investigation under this Part of this Act in respect of any such action as is described in Schedule 3 to this Act ; and nothing in this section shall be construed as authorising such an investigation in respect of action taken in connection with any general medical services, general dental services, general ophthalmic services or pharmaceutical services by a person providing the services.

(6) Her Majesty may by Order in Council amend the said Schedule 3 so as to exclude from the provisions of that Schedule action described in paragraph 3 or 4 of the Schedule.

PART III

(7) In determining whether to initiate, continue or discontinue an investigation under this Part of this Act, a Commissioner shall, subject to the preceding provisions of this section, act in accordance with his own discretion ; and any question whether a complaint is duly made to a Commissioner under this Part of this Act shall be determined by the Commissioner.

Provisions
relating to
complaints.

35.—(1) A complaint under this Part of this Act may be made by any individual, or by any body of persons whether incorporated or not, not being—

  (a) a local authority or other authority or body constituted for purposes of the public service or of local government or for the purposes of carrying on under national ownership any industry or undertaking or part of an industry or undertaking ;

  (b) any other authority or body whose members are appointed by Her Majesty or any Minister of the Crown or government department, or whose revenues consist wholly or mainly of money provided by Parliament.

(2) Where the person by whom a complaint might have been made under the preceding provisions of this Part of this Act has died or is for any reason unable to act for himself, the complaint may be made by his personal representative or by a member of his family or by some body or individual suitable to represent him ; but except as aforesaid and as provided by subsection (5) of this section a complaint shall not be entertained under this Part of this Act unless made by the person aggrieved himself.

(3) A complaint shall not be entertained under this Part of this Act by a Commissioner unless it is made in writing to him by or on behalf of the person aggrieved not later than one year from the day on which the person aggrieved first had notice of the matters alleged in the complaint ; but a Commissioner may conduct an investigation pursuant to a complaint not made within that period if he considers it reasonable to do so.

(4) Before proceeding to investigate a complaint a Commissioner shall satisfy himself that the complaint has been brought by or on behalf of the person aggrieved to the notice of the relevant body in question and that that body has been afforded a reasonable opportunity to investigate and reply to the complaint ; but a Commissioner shall disregard the preceding provisions of this subsection in relation to a complaint made by an officer of the relevant body in question on behalf of the person aggrieved if the officer is authorised by virtue of subsection (2) of this section to make the complaint and the Commissioner is satisfied that in the particular circumstances those provisions ought to be disregarded.

(5) Notwithstanding anything in the preceding provision of this section, a relevant body—

(a) may itself (excluding its officers) refer to a Commissioner a complaint that a person has, in consequence of a failure or maladministration for which the body is responsible, sustained such injustice or hardship as is mentioned in section 34(3) of this Act if the complaint—

(i) is made in writing to the relevant body by that person or by a person authorised by virtue of subsection (2) of this section to make the complaint to the Commissioner on his behalf, and

(ii) is so made not later than one year from the day mentioned in subsection (3) of this section or within such other period as the Commissioner considers appropriate in any particular case; but

(b) shall not be entitled to refer a complaint in pursuance of the preceding paragraph after the expiration of three months beginning with the day on which the body received the complaint;

and a complaint referred to a Commissioner in pursuance of this subsection shall, subject to section 34(7) of this Act, be deemed to be duly made to him under this Part of this Act.

36. The following provisions of the Parliamentary Commissioner Act 1967 shall, with any necessary modifications, apply to the Commissioners, their officers and a relevant body as they apply to the Parliamentary Commissioner for Administration, his officers and a department concerned, namely—

Application of certain provisions of Parliamentary Commissioner Act 1967.
1967 c. 13.

(a) section 7 (procedure in respect of investigations);

(b) section 8 (evidence);

(c) section 9 (obstruction and contempt);

(d) section 11 (secrecy of information), except subsection (4);

but in sections 7(1) and 8(1) of that Act as applied by this section the words " the principal officer of " and " Minister " shall be omitted.

37.—(1) In any case where a Commissioner conducts an investigation under this Part of this Act, he shall send a report of the results of his investigation—

Reports by Commissioners.

(a) to the person who made the complaint;

(b) to the relevant body in question;

(c) to any person who is alleged in the complaint to have taken or authorised the action complained of;

Q

(*d*) if the relevant body in question is not an Area Health Authority for an area in England, a Hospital Management Committee or a Family Practitioner Committee, to the Secretary of State ;

(*e*) if that body is an Area Health Authority for an area in England, to the Regional Health Authority of which the region includes that area ;

(*f*) if that body is a Hospital Management Committee, to the Regional Hospital Board by which the Committee was appointed ; and

(*g*) if that body is a Family Practitioner Committee, to the Area Health Authority by which the Committee was established.

(2) In any case where a Commissioner decides not to conduct an investigation under this Part of this Act, he shall send a statement of his reasons for doing so to the person who made the complaint and to the relevant body in question.

(3) If, after conducting an investigation under this Part of this Act, it appears to a Commissioner that the person aggrieved has sustained such injustice or hardship as is mentioned in section 34(3) of this Act and that the injustice or hardship has not been and will not be remedied, he may if he thinks fit make a special report to the Secretary of State who shall, as soon as is reasonably practicable, lay a copy of the report before each House of Parliament.

(4) Each of the Commissioners shall annually make to the Secretary of State a report on the performance of his functions under this Part of this Act and may from time to time make to the Secretary of State such other reports with respect to those functions as the Commissioner thinks fit, and the Secretary of State shall lay a copy of every such report before each House of Parliament.

(5) For the purposes of the law of defamation, the publication of any matter by a Commissioner in sending or making a report in pursuance of subsection (1), (3) or (4) of this section or in sending a statement in pursuance of subsection (2) of this section shall be absolutely privileged.

Transitional provisions.

38. Regulations may provide that, where a relevant body is abolished in pursuance of this Act, any prescribed provisions of this Part of this Act and Schedule 3 to this Act shall apply, with or without prescribed modifications, in relation to a complaint in respect of the body which was duly made to a Commissioner under this Part of this Act before the date of the abolition or is made in accordance with the regulations within the period of one year beginning with that date.

39.—(1) In this Part of this Act and Schedule 3 to this Act—　PART III
"action" includes failure to act, and other expressions Interpretation
　　connoting action shall be construed accordingly;　of Part III.
"a Commissioner" means the Health Service Commissioner
　　for England or the Health Service Commissioner for
　　Wales and "the Commissioners" means both those
　　persons;
"person aggrieved" means the person who claims or is
　　alleged to have sustained such injustice or hardship
　　as is mentioned in section 34(3) of this Act; and
"relevant body" has the meaning assigned to it by section
　　34(1) of this Act.

(2) It is hereby declared that nothing in this Part of this Act
authorises or requires a Commissioner to question the merits
of a decision taken without maladministration by a relevant
body in the exercise of a discretion vested in that body.

PART IV

MISCELLANEOUS AND GENERAL

Miscellaneous

40.—(1) The duty imposed on the Secretary of State by Special
section 1 of the principal Act to provide services for the hospitals.
purposes of the health service shall include a duty to provide
and maintain establishments (in this Act referred to as "special
hospitals") for persons subject to detention under the Mental 1959 c. 72.
Health Act 1959 who in his opinion require treatment under
conditions of special security on account of their dangerous,
violent or criminal propensities.

(2) Any institution provided under section 97 of the Mental
Health Act 1959 or deemed to be so provided when that
section came into force shall be deemed to be provided in
pursuance of the preceding subsection.

41.—(1) There are hereby transferred to the Secretary of Nursing
State the functions which, immediately before this subsection homes and
comes into force, were exercisable by local authorities by virtue mental
of any provision of the following enactments (which relate to nursing
the supervision of nursing homes and mental nursing homes), homes.
namely, sections 187 and 188 of the Act of 1936 (and section
298 of that Act so far as it relates to those sections) and
sections 14 to 18 of the Act of 1959 (and section 23 of that
Act so far as it relates to those sections); and any reference
in any of the said sections to a local authority shall be construed
accordingly.

(2) The Secretary of State may make regulations—

> (*a*) with respect to the registration of persons under Part VI of the Act of 1936 in respect of nursing homes and mental nursing homes (and in particular, without prejudice to the generality of the preceding provisions of this paragraph, with respect to the making of applications for registration, the refusal and cancellation of registration and appeals to magistrates' courts against refusals and cancellations of registration);
>
> (*b*) with respect to the keeping of records relating to nursing homes and mental nursing homes and with respect to the notification of events occurring in such homes;
>
> (*c*) with respect to entry into and the inspection of premises used or reasonably believed to be used as a nursing home;
>
> (*d*) containing such provisions (including provisions for the transfer of staff and provisions applying with prescribed modifications any provision made by virtue of section 19(2) of this Act) as the Secretary of State considers appropriate for the purpose of securing continuity between the system of supervising nursing homes and mental nursing homes which was in operation before the coming into force of the preceding subsection and the system of supervising such homes thereafter;
>
> (*e*) providing that a contravention or failure to comply with any specified provisions of the regulations shall be an offence against the regulations.

1963 c. 13.   (3) Subsections (2) and (3) of section 1 of the Nursing Homes Act 1963 (which provide for an offence against regulations under that section to be punishable on summary conviction with a fine not exceeding £20, for cancellation of a person's registration in respect of a nursing home if he has been convicted of such an offence and for making officers of a body corporate which is guilty of such an offence also guilty of the offence) shall apply to an offence against regulations made by virtue of the preceding subsection as they apply to an offence against regulations under that section; and the said subsection (3) shall apply to an offence under section 187 of the Act of 1936 as it applies to an offence against regulations under the said section 1.

(4) In this section—

1936 c. 49.   "the Act of 1936" means the Public Health Act 1936;
1959 c. 72.   "the Act of 1959" means the Mental Health Act 1959;

> "local authority" means the council of a county, county borough, county district or London borough, the

Common Council of the City of London, the Sub-
Treasurer of the Inner Temple and the Under
Treasurer of the Middle Temple;

" mental nursing home " has the same meaning as in Part
III of the Act of 1959; and

" nursing home " has the same meaning as in the Act of
1936.

(5) Sections 189 to 191, 194 and 195 of the Act of 1936
(which contain provisions which are superseded by subsections
(2) and (3) of this section) shall cease to have effect.

42. For subsection (1) of section 38 of the principal Act (which   Pharma-
relates to arrangements for pharmaceutical services) there shall   ceutical
be substituted the following subsection—   services.

(1) It shall be the duty of every Area Health Authority
to make in accordance with regulations arrangements as
respects its area for the supply to persons who are in that
area of—

(*a*) proper and sufficient drugs and medicines and
listed appliances which are ordered for those
persons by a medical practitioner in pursuance of
his functions in the health service, the Scottish
health service, the Northern Ireland health service
or the armed forces of the Crown (excluding forces
of a Commonwealth country and forces raised in
a colony); and

(*b*) listed drugs and medicines which are ordered for
those persons by a dental practitioner in pursuance
of such functions;

and the services provided in accordance with the arrangements are in this Act referred to as " pharmaceutical
services ".

In this subsection—

" the health service " means the service established by
section 1 of this Act;

" listed " means included in a list for the time being
approved by the Secretary of State for the
purposes of this subsection; and

" the Scottish health service " and " the Northern Ire
land health service " mean respectively the health
service established in pursuance of section 1 of the
National Health Service (Scotland) Act 1947 or
any service provided in pursuance of Article 4(*a*)
of the Health and Personal Social Services
(Northern Ireland) Order 1972.

PART IV

and in subsection (2) of the said section 38 for the words from " receiving general medical services " to " dental practitioner rendering those services " there shall be substituted the words " for whom they are ordered as mentioned in the last foregoing subsection to receive the drugs, medicines and appliances there mentioned ".

Miscellaneous functions of Secretary of State.

43.—(1) If the Secretary of State considers that any accommodation provided by him by virtue of the Health Service Acts is suitable for use in connection with the provision of general medical services, general dental services, general ophthalmic services or pharmaceutical services he may make the accommodation available on such terms as he thinks fit to persons providing any of those services.

(2) The Secretary of State may permit any person who is a medical or dental practitioner, a registered pharmacist, an ophthalmic or dispensing optician or a person of any other description determined by him and who provides services under the Health Service Acts to use for the purpose of private practice, on such terms as the Secretary of State may determine, facilities available at accommodation provided by the Secretary of State by virtue of the Health Service Acts.

(3) Where the Secretary of State makes arrangements with medical practitioners for the vaccination or immunisation of persons against disease, he shall so far as reasonably practicable give every medical practitioner providing general medical services an opportunity to participate in the arrangements.

(4) It shall be the duty of the Secretary of State to make available, in premises provided by him by virtue of the Health Service Acts, such facilities as he considers are reasonably required, by any university which has a medical or dental school, in connection with clinical teaching and with research connected with clinical medicine or, as the case may be, clinical dentistry.

(5) Nothing in this section shall be construed as prejudicing any powers exercisable by the Secretary of State apart from this section.

Provision for early retirement in lieu of compensation for loss of office.

44.—(1) In order to facilitate the early retirement of certain persons who might otherwise suffer, in consequence of this Act, loss of employment or loss or diminution of emoluments, any person who—

    (a) is in any such employment as may be prescribed for the purposes of this subsection ; and

    (b) attains or has attained the age of fifty on or before a prescribed date ; and (*c*) fulfils such other conditions as may be prescribed ; may by notice given before a prescribed date and in the prescribed manner elect that this section shall apply to him.

(2) Where any person has made an election under the preceding subsection, then, unless within a prescribed period notice of objection to the election is given to him by a prescribed person, this section shall apply to him on his retirement within a prescribed period and before attaining the normal retiring age and compensation on his retirement shall not be payable to or in respect of him in pursuance of section 24 of the Super- 1972 c. 11. annuation Act 1972 (which among other things relates to compensation for loss of office).

(3) Subject to the following subsection, the Secretary of State shall by regulations provide for the payment by him to or in respect of a person to whom this section applies of benefits corresponding, as near as may be, to those which would have been paid to or in respect of that person under the relevant superannuation scheme if—

　(*a*) at the date of his retirement he had attained the normal retiring age ; and

　(*b*) the actual period of his reckonable service were increased by such period as may be prescribed, not exceeding the period beginning on the date of his retirement and ending on the date on which he would attain the normal retiring age.

(4) Regulations in pursuance of the preceding subsection shall be so framed as to secure that the sums which would otherwise be payable under the regulations in accordance with that subsection to or in respect of any person are reduced to take account of any benefits payable to or in respect of him under the relevant superannuation scheme.

(5) Any sums payable under regulations made in pursuance of subsection (3) of this section shall be treated for the purposes of section 73 of the Finance Act 1972 (under which com- 1972 c. 41. pensation for loss of office or employment is chargeable to tax as a payment made on retirement or removal from office or employment) in like manner as compensation paid in pursuance of the said section 24.

(6) In this section—

　" normal retiring age " means—

　　(*a*) in relation to any person to whom an age of compulsory retirement applies by virtue of the relevant superannuation scheme, that age ; and

　　(*b*) in relation to any other person, the age of sixty-five in the case of a man and sixty in the case of

PART IV
a woman or, in either case, such other age as may be prescribed;

" reckonable service ", in relation to any person, means service in respect of which benefits are payable under the relevant superannuation scheme; and

" relevant superannuation scheme ", in relation to any person, means the instrument which is applicable in the case of his employment and which makes provision with respect to the pensions, allowances or gratuities which, subject to the fulfilment of certain requirements and conditions, are to be, or may be, paid to or in respect of persons in that employment.

Overseas aid.
45. Each Regional and Area Health Authority, each special health authority and the Public Health Laboratory Service Board shall have power—

(a) with the consent of the Secretary of State, to enter into and carry out agreements with the relevant Minister under which, at the expense of that Minister, the authority or board acts as the instrument by means of which he furnishes technical assistance in the exercise of the power conferred on him by section 1(1) of the

1966 c. 21.
Overseas Aid Act 1966;

(b) with the consent of the Secretary of State and the relevant Minister, to enter into and carry out agreements under which the authority or board furnishes, for any purpose specified in the said section 1(1), technical assistance (excluding financial assistance) in any country or territory outside the United Kingdom against reimbursement to the authority or board of the cost of furnishing the assistance;

and in this section " the relevant Minister " means the Minister of the Crown by whom is exercisable the power conferred on the Minister for Overseas Development by the said section 1(1) as originally enacted.

Notices of births and deaths.
46.—(1) It shall be the duty of each registrar of births and deaths to furnish, to the prescribed medical officer of the Area Health Authority of which the area includes the whole or part of the sub-district of the registrar, such particulars of each birth and death which occurred in the area of the Authority as are entered after this subsection comes into force in a register of births or deaths kept for that sub-district; and regulations may make provision as to the manner in which and the times at which particulars are to be furnished in pursuance of this subsection.

(2) In section 203 of the Public Health Act 1936 (which among other things provides for the notification of births to medical officers of health of welfare authorities), in subsections (1) and (2) for references to the medical officer of health of the welfare authority there shall be substituted references to the prescribed medical officer of the Area Health Authority, and in subsection (2) for the reference to a welfare authority there shall be substituted a reference to an Area Health Authority and references to a residence shall be omitted.

Financial provisions

47.—(1) It shall be the duty of the Secretary of State to *Expenses of* pay— *new health authorities.*

- (*a*) to each Area Health Authority in Wales and each Regional Health Authority the sums needed to defray such expenditure of the Authority as the Secretary of State approves in the prescribed manner ;

- (*b*) to each Family Practitioner Committee sums equal to the expenses which the Secretary of State determines are incurred by the Committee for the purpose of performing the functions conferred on the Committee by virtue of this Act ; and

- (*c*) to each special health authority sums equal to such of the expenses of the authority as are not defrayed by payments made to the authority in pursuance of subsection (3) of this section.

(2) It shall be the duty of each Regional Health Authority to pay to each Area Health Authority of which the area is included in the region of the Regional Health Authority the sums needed to defray such expenses of the Area Health Authority as the Regional Health Authority approves in the prescribed manner.

(3) Where an order establishing a special health authority provides for any expenses of the authority to be defrayed by a Regional or Area Health Authority or by two or more such Authorities in portions determined by or in accordance with the order, it shall be the duty of each Authority in question to pay to the special health authority sums equal to, or to the appropriate portion of, those expenses.

(4) Sums falling to be paid in pursuance of the preceding provisions of this section shall be payable subject to compliance with such conditions as to records, certificates or otherwise as the Secretary of State may determine.

PART IV
Expenses and
receipts of
Secretary of
State etc.

48. There shall be paid out of money provided by Parliament—

(*a*) any expenses incurred by the Secretary of State for the purposes of this Act ; and

(*b*) any increase attributable to the provisions of this Act in the sums payable under any other Act out of money so provided ;

and any sums received by the Secretary of State by virtue of this Act shall be paid into the Consolidated Fund.

Stamp duty.
1895 c. 16.

49. Nothing in section 12 of the Finance Act 1895 (which requires certain Acts and certain instruments relating to the vesting of property by virtue of an Act to be stamped as conveyances on sale) shall apply to this Act or an order made in pursuance of this Act ; and stamp duty shall not be payable on such an order.

Remission of
charges, and
consequential
adaptation of
1966 c. 20 s. 6.
1951 c. 31.
1952 c. 25.

1966 c. 20.

50.—(1) Regulations may provide for the remission or repayment of any charges which, in pursuance of section 1 of the National Health Service Act 1951 or section 2 of the National Health Service Act 1952, are payable apart from this section, by a person whose income as calculated in accordance with regulations is at less than the prescribed rate, in respect of the supply or replacement of dental or optical appliances or in respect of services provided as part of the general dental services ; and accordingly in section 6 of the Ministry of Social Security Act 1966 (which specifies the medical, dental and similar requirements which are and are not to be taken into account for the purposes of that Act) the words from " include any requirement " to " but " and the word " other " shall be omitted.

1947 c. 27.

(2) In the application of the preceding subsection to Scotland the reference to general dental services shall be construed as a reference to general dental services provided under Part IV of the National Health Service (Scotland) Act 1947.

Compensation
for loss of
rights to sell
medical
practices.

51. In section 36(3)(*c*) of the principal Act and 37(3)(*c*) of the National Health Service (Scotland) Act 1947 (under which regulations must secure that, except in prescribed circumstances, compensation for loss of the right to sell a medical practice is not paid until the retirement or death of the medical practitioner concerned, whichever first occurs), the words from " and secure " to " occurs " shall be omitted.

52.—(1) If the Secretary of State considers it appropriate for remuneration in respect of services provided by any person in pursuance of Part IV of the principal Act to be paid by a particular body and apart from this subsection the functions of the body do not include the function of paying the remuneration, the Secretary of State may by order confer that function on the body ; and any sums required to enable any body having that function to pay remuneration in respect of such services shall, if apart from this subsection there is no provision authorising the payment of the sums by the Secretary of State or out of money provided by Parliament, be paid by him.

(2) In deciding whether to make an order under subsection (1) of section 3 of the Local Government Act 1966 (which relates to the variation of rate support grant orders) in respect of the year beginning with 1st April 1974 or 1st April 1975 and what order to make under that subsection in respect of either year, the Secretary of State shall have regard to any relief in respect of the year in question which he considers has been or is likely to be obtained by local authorities in consequence of this Act and was not taken into account in making the relevant rate support grant order.

Supplemental

53.—(1) In section 58(1) of the principal Act (which enables the Secretary of State to acquire by agreement or compulsorily any land required by him for the purposes of that Act), for the words " this Act " there shall be substituted the words " the National Health Service Acts 1946 to 1973 " and for the words " at any hospital vested in the Minister " there shall be substituted the words " for any purposes of those Acts " ; and the Secretary of State may acquire any property, other than land, required by him for the purposes of the Health Service Acts.

(2) Section 128 of the Town and Country Planning Act 1971 (which among other things provides that where a Minister acquires consecrated land or land comprised in a burial ground compulsorily he may, subject to the safeguards provided by that section, use the land for the purpose for which he acquired it notwithstanding any obligation or restriction imposed by ecclesiastical law or anything in any enactment relating to burial grounds) shall apply to consecrated land and land comprised in a burial ground within the meaning of that section which is held by the Secretary of State for any of the purposes of the health service and has not been acquired by him as mentioned in subsection (1) of that section as if the land had been so acquired for those purposes.

(3) The Secretary of State may use, for the purposes of any of the functions conferred on him by the Health Service Acts,

PART IV

any property belonging to him by virtue of any of those Acts; and it is hereby declared that the Secretary of State has power to maintain all such property.

General
ancillary
provisions.

54.—(1) If the Secretary of State considers that by reason of an emergency it is necessary, in order to ensure that a service falling to be provided in pursuance of the Health Service Acts is provided, to direct that during a period specified in the directions a function conferred on any body or person by virtue of those Acts shall to the exclusion of or concurrently with that body or person be performed by another body or person, he may give directions accordingly and it shall be the duty of the bodies or persons in question to comply with the directions; and the powers conferred on the Secretary of State by this subsection are in addition to any other powers exercisable by him.

(2) The Secretary of State may by order make such incidental, supplemental, transitional or consequential provision (including provision making modifications of enactments) as he considers appropriate for any of the purposes of this Act or in consequence of or for giving full effect to any provision of this Act; and nothing in the following subsection or any other provision of this Act shall be construed as prejudicing the generality of the power conferred by this subsection.

(3) An order made by virtue of the preceding subsection may include provision—

(a) for any thing duly done by a body in the exercise of functions which by virtue of this Act become functions of another body to be deemed to have been duly done by the other body; and

(b) without prejudice to the generality of the preceding paragraph, for any instrument, in so far as it was made in the exercise of such functions, to continue in force until varied or revoked by the other body.

(4) In so far as—

(a) any apportionment, agreement, order or regulation made by virtue of an enactment repealed by this Act; or

(b) any approval, consent, direction or notice given by virtue of such an enactment; or

(c) any proceedings begun or thing done by virtue of such an enactment,

could, if a corresponding enactment which is contained in this Act had been in force at the relevant time, have been made, given, begun or done by virtue of the corresponding enactment,

it shall, if effective immediately before the relevant correspond-   PART IV
ing enactment comes into force, continue to have effect
thereafter as if made, given, begun or done by virtue of that
corresponding enactment.

(5) The Secretary of State may by order provide that any right
which a Regional Hospital Board, a Board of Governors or a
Hospital Management Committee was entitled to enforce by
virtue of section 13 of the principal Act immediately before
the appointed day and any liability in respect of which such
a board or committee was liable by virtue of that section
immediately before that day shall, on and after that day, be
enforceable by or as the case may be against a Regional Health
Authority, Area Health Authority or special health authority
specified in the order as if the authority so specified were concerned as a principal with the matter in question and did not
exercise functions on behalf of the Secretary of State.

55.—(1) Except where the contrary intention appears, in Interpretation
this Act the following expressions have the following meanings— etc.

" the appointed day " means such day as the Secretary of
State may by order appoint ;

" Board of Governors " means a body constituted in pursuance of section 11 of the principal Act as the Board
of Governors of a teaching hospital ;

" functions " includes powers and duties ;

" the health service " means the health service established
in pursuance of section 1 of the principal Act ;

" the Health Service Acts " means the National Health
Service Acts 1946 to 1968 and this Act ;

" local health authority " includes a joint board constituted
in pursuance of section 19 of the principal Act and a
body exercising delegated functions of such an
authority in pursuance of section 46 of the Local Gov- 1958 c. 55.
ernment Act 1958 ;

" modifications " includes additions, omissions and
amendments ;

" prescribed " means prescribed by regulations ;

" preserved Board " has the meaning assigned to it by
section 15(6) of this Act ;

" the principal Act " means the National Health Service Act 1946 c. 81.
1946 ;

" regulations " means, subject to subsection (2) of the following section, regulations made by the Secretary of State ;

" special hospital " has the meaning assigned to it by section
40(1) of this Act ; and

PART IV

"Special Trustees" has the meaning assigned to it by section 29(1) of this Act;

and any other expression to which a meaning is assigned by Part IV or section 79(1) of the principal Act has that meaning in this Act.

1972 c. 70.

(2) Section 269 of the Local Government Act 1972 (which relates to the meaning of "England" and "Wales" in Acts passed after 1st April 1974) shall apply to this Act as if this Act had been passed after that date; and it is hereby declared that in this Act "property" includes land.

(3) Any reference in this Act to any enactment is a reference to it as amended or applied by or under any other enactment including this Act.

Orders and regulations etc.

56.—(1) Any power to make orders or regulations conferred by this Act shall be exercisable by statutory instrument; and

> (a) a statutory instrument made by virtue of this subsection, except an instrument containing only such orders as are mentioned in the following paragraph, or by virtue of section 34 (1)(*h*) or (6) of this Act or subsection (6) of the following section shall be subject to annulment in pursuance of a resolution of either House of Parliament;
>
> (b) a statutory instrument containing only orders made by virtue of section 14(2), 24(2) or (3) or 54 of this Act or orders appointing a day in pursuance of this Act shall be laid before Parliament after being made.

(2) Any power to make regulations conferred on the Secretary of State by this Act shall, if the Treasury so directs, be exercisable by the Treasury and the Secretary of State acting jointly.

(3) Any power to make an order conferred by this Act, except sections 15(2)(*d*), 23(2) and 24(2) and (3), includes power to vary or revoke the order by a subsequent order made in the exercise of that power; but provisions of an order which appoint a day or provide for an enactment to come into force on a specified day shall not by virtue of this subsection be revoked or varied on or after that day.

1963 c. 13.

(4) Any power conferred by the Health Service Acts or the Nursing Homes Act 1963 to make orders, regulations or schemes, and any power conferred by section 7 of this Act to give directions by an instrument in writing, may unless the contrary intention appears be exercised—

> (a) either in relation to all cases to which the power extends, or in relation to all those cases subject to specified

exceptions, or in relation to any specified cases or classes of case ; and

(b) so as to make, as respects the cases in relation to which it is exercised,—

(i) the full provision to which the power extends or any less provision (whether by way of exception or otherwise) ;

(ii) the same provision for all cases in relation to which the power is exercised, or different provision for different cases or different classes of case, or different provision as respects the same case or class of case for different purposes of those Acts or that section ;

(iii) any such provision either unconditionally or subject to any specified condition,

and includes power to make such incidental or supplemental provision in the orders, regulations, schemes or directions as the persons making or giving them consider appropriate.

(5) Any directions given in pursuance of any provision of this Act other than section 7 may be varied or revoked by subsequent directions given in pursuance of that provision.

57.—(1) The enactments mentioned in Schedule 4 to this Act shall have effect subject to the amendments specified in that Schedule.

(2) The enactments and Order in Council mentioned in the first and second columns of Schedule 5 to this Act are hereby repealed to the extent specified in the third column of that Schedule.

(3) An order bringing any provision of the said Schedule 4 or Schedule 5 into force in pursuance of subsection (3) of the following section may, without prejudice to the generality of that subsection or subsection (4) of the preceding section, provide that the enactment or Order in Council amended or repealed by that provision shall, in such cases and for such periods as are specified in the order, continue to have effect as if the provision were not in force.

(4) An order bringing any provision of the said Schedule 5 into force as mentioned in the preceding subsection may, without prejudice as therein mentioned, provide that any orders, regulations or other instruments in force by virtue of that provision shall continue in force ; and an instrument continued in force in pursuance of this subsection may be varied or revoked by regulations.

(5) The Secretary of State may by order repeal or amend any provision of any local Act passed before this Act (including

Minor and consequential amendments, and repeals.

PART IV   an Act confirming a provisional order) or of any order or other instrument made under an Act so passed if it appears to him that the provision is inconsistent with, or has become unnecessary or requires alteration in consequence of, any provision of this Act or corresponds to any provision repealed by this Act.

(6) Her Majesty may by Order in Council make such modifications of the Health Service Acts as She considers appropriate in connection with the consolidation of those Acts.

Citation, commencement and extent.

58.—(1) This Act may be cited as the National Health Service Reorganisation Act 1973, and—

(a) this Act and the National Health Service Acts 1946 to 1968 may be cited together as the National Health Service Acts 1946 to 1973 ; and

(b) this Act so far as it extends to Scotland and the National Health Service (Scotland) Acts 1947 to 1972 may be cited together as the National Health Service (Scotland) Acts 1947 to 1973.

(2) The following provisions of this Act shall come into force on the passing of this Act, namely sections 1, 5 to 10, 14 to 21, 23 to 26, 29, 30, 41 (so far as it is applied by sections 16 and 18), 44, 47 to 49, 51 to 57 and this section, Schedules 1 and 2, paragraphs 22, 79, 133, 141, 151 and 152 of Schedule 4 and the entry in Schedule 5 relating to section 36(3)(c) of the principal Act.

(3) The provisions of this Act which do not come into force in pursuance of the preceeding subsection shall come into force on such day as the Secretary of State may by order appoint ; and, without prejudice to the generality of section 56(4) of this Act, different days may be appointed in pursuance of this subsection for different provisions of this Act and for different purposes of the same provision of this Act.

(4) The Secretary of State may by order provide that this Act shall extend to the Isles of Scilly with such modifications, if any, as are specified in the order ; and except as provided in pursuance of this subsection this Act shall not extend to the Isles of Scilly.

(5) The following provisions only of this Act shall extend to Scotland, namely, this subsection and subsections (1) to (3) of this section, sections 32(4) to (7), 36, 37(5), section 39(1) so far as it relates to those sections, sections 50, 51 and 57, paragraphs 41, 42, 43, 49, 58(2), 59(1), 67, 77 to 82, 96, 102, 104, 106, 109, 123,

128, 130, 133 to 135 and 138 to 150 of Schedule 4, the entries PART IV
in Schedule 5 relating to the National Health Service (Scotland) 1947 c. 27.
Act 1947, the Dentists Act 1957, the Opticians Act 1958, the 1957 c. 28.
Radioactive Substances Act 1960, the Health Visiting and Social 1958 c. 32.
Working Training Act 1962, the Redundancy Payments Act 1960 c. 34.
1965, (excluding the reference to paragraph 6), the Ministry of 1962 c. 33.
Social Security Act 1966 and the National Health Service (Scot- 1965 c. 62.
land) Act 1972, and section 56 so far as it relates to subsection 1966 c. 20.
(3) of this section, sections 32(6) and 50 and paragraphs 138 and 1972 c. 58.
139 of Schedule 4.

(6) The following provisions only of this Act shall extend to 1947 c. 19.
Northern Ireland, namely, this subsection and subsections (1) to 1957 c. 28.
(3) of this section, sections 36 and 37(5), section 39(1) so far 1958 c. 32.
as it relates to those sections, section 57, paragraphs 40, 69, 79 1960 c. 34.
to 82, 96, 102, 104, 109, 128, 130, 134, 146 and 148 of Schedule 1962 c. 33.
4 and the entries in Schedule 5 relating to the Polish Resettlement Act 1947, the Dentists Act 1957, the Opticians Act 1958,
the Radioactive Substances Act 1960, the Health Visiting and
Social Work (Training) Act 1962 and the Order in Council of
1972.

SCHEDULES

SCHEDULE 1

ADDITIONAL PROVISIONS RELATING TO NEW AUTHORITIES

PART 1

MEMBERSHIP OF REGIONAL AND AREA HEALTH AUTHORITIES

Regional Health Authorities

1.—(1) A Regional Health Authority shall consist of a chairman appointed by the Secretary of State and of such number of other members appointed by him as he thinks fit.

(2) Except in prescribed cases it shall be the duty of the Secretary of State, before he appoints a member of a Regional Health Authority other than the chairman, to consult with respect to the appointment—

(a) subject to sub-paragraph (3) of this paragraph, such of the following bodies of which the areas or parts of them are within the region of the Authority, namely, county councils, metropolitan district councils, the Greater London Council, London borough councils and the Common Council of the City of London ;

(b) the university or universities with which the provision of health services in that region is or is to be associated ;

(c) such bodies as the Secretary of State may recognise as being, either in that region or generally, representative respectively of medical practitioners, dental practitioners, nurses, midwives, registered pharmacists and ophthalmic and dispensing opticians or representative of such other professions as appear to him to be concerned ;

(d) any federation of workers' organisations which appears to the Secretary of State to be concerned and any voluntary organisation within the meaning of section 13 of this Act and any other body which appear to him to be concerned ; and

(e) in the case of an appointment of a member falling to be made after the establishment of the Regional Health Authority, that Authority.

(3) In relation to an appointment of a member falling to be made before the appointed day, the preceding sub-paragraph shall have effect as if for paragraph (a) there were substituted the following paragraph—

(a) such of the following bodies providing services in the region of the Authority as the Secretary of State thinks fit, namely, Regional Hospital Boards, Boards of Governors, Executive Councils, the Greater London Council and local health authorities.

Area Health Authorities

2.—(1) Subject to paragraph 4 below, an Area Health Authority for an area in England shall consist of the following members—

(a) a chairman appointed by the Secretary of State ;

(b) the specified number of members appointed by the relevant Regional Authority after consultation, except in prescribed cases, with the bodies mentioned in sub-paragraph (2) of this paragraph ;

(c) the specified number of members appointed by the relevant Regional Authority on the nomination of the university or universities specified as being associated with the provision of health services in that Authority's region ; and

(d) the specified number (not less than four) of members appointed by the specified local authority or local authorities.

(2) The bodies referred to in paragraph (b) of the preceding sub-paragraph are—

(a) such bodies as the relevant Regional Authority may recognise as being, either in its region or in the area of the Area Health Authority or generally, representative respectively of medical practitioners, dental practitioners, nurses, midwives, registered pharmacists and ophthalmic and dispensing opticians or representative of such other professions as appear to the relevant Regional Authority to be concerned ;

(b) such other bodies (including any federation of workers' organisations) as appear to the relevant Regional Authority to be concerned, excluding any university which has nominated or is entitled to nominate a member and any local authority which has appointed or is entitled to appoint a member ;

(c) in relation to an appointment of a member falling to be made before the appointed day, such of the Regional Hospital Boards, Hospital Management Committees, Boards of Governors and Executive Councils providing services within the area of the Area Health Authority in question as the relevant Regional Authority thinks fit ; and

(d) in relation to an appointment of a member falling to be made after the establishment of the Area Health Authority in question, that Authority.

3. The preceding paragraph shall apply to an Area Health Authority for an area in Wales as if for any reference to the relevant Regional Authority there were substituted a reference to the Secretary of State and for any reference to England or the region of that Authority there were substituted a reference to Wales.

SCH. 1

4. The members of an Area Health Authority (Teaching) shall, in addition to the members appointed in pursuance of paragraph 2 above, include the specified number of members appointed—

    (*a*) in the case of members falling to be appointed before the appointed day, by the Secretary of State from among the members of and after consultation with such as he thinks fit of—

        (i) the Boards of Governors and Hospital Management Committees of teaching hospitals and university hospitals situated wholly or partly within the area of the Authority in question, or

        (ii) if there is no such Board or Committee, the Hospital Management Committees managing hospitals or groups of hospitals situated wholly or partly within that area ;

    (*b*) in the case of members falling to be appointed on or after the appointed day to an Area Health Authority (Teaching) of which the area is in England by the relevant Regional Authority from among persons appearing to that Authority to have knowledge of and experience in the administration of a hospital providing substantial facilities for under-graduate or post-graduate clinical teaching ;

    (*c*) in the case of members falling to be appointed on or after the appointed day to an Area Health Authority (Teaching) of which the area is in Wales, by the Secretary of State from among persons appearing to him to have such knowledge and experience ;

and in this paragraph " university hospital " means a hospital or group of hospitals designated as a university hospital in pursuance of section 5 of the Health Services and Public Health Act 1968.

1968 c. 46.

Supplemental

5.—(1) References in the preceding provisions of this Schedule to the region or area of an Authority shall, in a case where the Authority has not been established or a region or area for it has not been determined, be construed as a reference to the locality which the Secretary of State considers is to be the region or area of the Authority.

(2) For the purposes of paragraphs 2 to 4 above—

    " local authority " means the council of a non-metropolitan county, a metropolitan district and a London borough, the Inner London Education Authority and the Common Council of the City of London ;

    " the relevant Regional Authority " means the Regional Health Authority of which the region includes the area of the Area Health Authority in question ; and

    " specified " means specified in the order establishing the Area Health Authority in question or, where another order provides for it to be called an Area Health Authority or an Area Health Authority (Teaching), in that other order.

(3) Where an order establishing an Area Health Authority or another order providing for it to be called an Area Health Authority

or an Area Health Authority (Teaching) specifies more than one university in pursuance of paragraph 2(1)(c) above, the order may contain provision as to which of the universities shall, either severally or jointly, nominate all or any of the members falling to be nominated in pursuance of the said paragraph 2(1)(c); and where such an order specifies more than one local authority in pursuance of paragraph 2(1)(d) above, the order may provide for each of the local authorities to appoint in pursuance of the said paragraph 2(1)(d) the number of members specified in the order in relation to that local authority.

PART II

MEMBERSHIP OF FAMILY PRACTITIONER COMMITTEES

6.—(1) Subject to paragraph 7 below, a Family Practitioner Committee shall consist of thirty members of whom—

(a) eleven shall be appointed by the Area Health Authority responsible for establishing the Committee and at least one of them must be, but not every one of them shall be, a member of the Authority;

(b) four shall be appointed by the local authority entitled in pursuance of paragraph 2(1)(d) above to appoint members of that Authority or, where two or more local authorities are so entitled, by those authorities acting jointly;

(c) eight shall be appointed by the Local Medical Committee for the area of that Authority and one of them must be, and not more than one shall be, a medical practitioner having the qualifications prescribed in pursuance of section 41 of the principal Act (which relates to ophthalmic services);

(d) three shall be appointed by the Local Dental Committee for that area;

(e) two shall be appointed by the Local Pharmaceutical Committee for that area;

(f) one shall be an ophthalmic optician appointed by such members of the Local Optical Committee for that area as are ophthalmic opticians; and

(g) one shall be a dispensing optician appointed by such members of the said Local Optical Committee as are dispensing opticians;

and the members of a Family Practitioner Committee shall from time to time, in accordance with such procedure as may be prescribed, select one of their members to be the chairman of the Committee.

(2) If any appointment falling to be made in pursuance of the preceding sub-paragraph by or by certain members of a Local Committee is not made before such date as the Area Health Authority in question may determine for that appointment, the appointment shall be made by that Authority to the exclusion of the Committee or members in question.

(3) The members of a Local Committee who are mentioned in paragraphs (f) and (g) of sub-paragraph (1) of this paragraph may if they think fit appoint, in addition to the member of a Family

Practitioner Committee appointed by them, an ophthalmic or, as the case may be, a dispensing optician to be the deputy of the member so appointed, and the Local Committee by which such a practitioner as is mentioned in paragraph (c) of the said sub-paragraph (1) is appointed in pursuance of that paragraph as a member of a Family Practitioner Committee may if it thinks fit appoint another such practitioner to be his deputy ; and a deputy appointed in pursuance of this sub-paragraph may, while the member for whom he is the deputy is absent from any meeting of the relevant Family Practitioner Committee, act as a member of that Committee in the place of the absent member.

(4) If an Area Health Authority proposes to make before the appointed day an appointment in pursuance of paragraph (a) of sub-paragraph (1) of this paragraph, it shall be the duty of the Authority before it makes the appointment to consult such Executive Councils exercising functions in its area as the Authority considers appropriate.

7.—(1) If it appears to the Secretary of State that, by reason of special circumstances affecting the area of an Area Health Authority, it is appropriate that the Family Practitioner Committee established or to be established by the Authority should not be in accordance with the preceding paragraph, he may by order provide that that paragraph shall apply in relation to the Committee with such modifications as are specified in the order.

(2) It shall be the duty of the Secretary of State—

(a) before he makes an order in pursuance of the preceding sub-paragraph in respect of a Family Practitioner Committee which is already established to consult the Committee with respect to the order ; and

(b) in making any such order to have regard to the desirability of maintaining, so far as practicable, the same numerical proportion as between members falling to be appointed by different bodies in pursuance of the preceding paragraph apart from any modification.

Part III

Supplementary Provisions Relating to New Authorities

Corporate status

8. Each Regional Health Authority, Area Health Authority, special health authority and Family Practitioner Committee (hereafter in this Schedule referred to severally as " an authority ") shall be a body corporate with perpetual succession and a common seal.

Pay and allowances

9.—(1) The Secretary of State may pay to the chairman of an authority other than a Family Practitioner Committee such remuneration as he may determine with the approval of the Minister for the Civil Service.

(2) The Secretary of State may make such provision as he may determine as aforesaid for the payment of a pension, allowance or

gratuity to or in respect of the chairman of an authority other than such a Committee.

(3) Where a person ceases to be the chairman of an authority other than such a Committee and it appears to the Secretary of State that there are special circumstances which make it right for him to receive compensation, the Secretary of State may make to him a payment of such amount as the Secretary of State may determine as aforesaid.

(4) The Secretary of State may pay to a member of an authority, or of a committee or sub-committee of an authority, such travelling and other allowances (including attendance allowance or compensation for loss of remunerative time) as he may determine as aforesaid.

(5) Allowances shall not be paid in pursuance of the preceding sub-paragraph except in connection with the exercise, in such circumstances as the Secretary of State may determine as aforesaid, of such functions as he may so determine.

(6) Payments in pursuance of this paragraph shall be made at such times and in such manner and subject to such conditions as the Secretary of State may determine as aforesaid.

Staff

10.—(1) An authority other than a Family Practitioner Committee may employ, on such terms as it may determine in accordance with regulations and such directions as may be given by the Secretary of State, such officers as it may so determine ; and regulations made for the purposes of this sub-paragraph may contain provision—

(a) with respect to the qualifications of persons who may be employed as officers of an authority ;

(b) requiring an authority to employ, for the purpose of performing prescribed functions of the authority or any other body, officers having prescribed qualifications or experience ; and

(c) as to the manner in which any officers of an authority are to be appointed.

(2) Regulations may make provision for the transfer of officers from one authority to another which is not a Family Practitioner Committee and for the making of arrangements under which the services of an officer of an authority are placed at the disposal of another authority or a local authority.

(3) The Secretary of State may direct an authority to place services of any of its officers at the disposal of another authority and, subject to any directions given by the Secretary of State in pursuance of this sub-paragraph, a Regional Health Authority may direct an Area Health Authority of which the area is included in its region to place services of any of its officers at the disposal of another such Area Health Authority ; and it shall be the duty of an authority to which directions are given in pursuance of this sub-paragraph to comply with the directions.

(4) The Secretary of State may direct an authority, other than a Family Practitioner Committee, to employ as an officer of the

SCH. 1   authority any person who is or was employed by another authority and is specified in the direction, and a Regional Health Authority may direct an Area Health Authority of which the area is included in its region to employ as an officer of the Area Health Authority a person who is or was employed by an authority other than the Area Health Authority and is specified in the direction ; and it shall be the duty of an authority to which a direction is given in pursuance of this sub-paragraph to comply with the direction.

(5) Regulations made in pursuance of this paragraph shall not require that all consultants employed by an authority are to be so employed whole-time.

11.—(1) It shall be the duty of the Secretary of State, before he makes regulations in pursuance of the preceding paragraph, to consult such bodies as he may recognise as representing persons who in his opinion are likely to be affected by the regulations.

(2) Subject to the following sub-paragraph, it shall be the duty of the Secretary of State or as the case may be of a Regional Health Authority, before he or the Authority gives directions to an authority in pursuance of sub-paragraph (3) or (4) of the preceding paragraph in respect of any officer of an authority, to consult the officer about the directions or to satisfy himself or itself that the authority of which he is an officer has consulted the officer about the placing or employment in question or (except in the case of a direction in pursuance of the said sub-paragraph (4)) to consult with respect to the directions such body as he or the Authority may recognise as representing the officer.

(3) If the Secretary of State or Regional Health Authority considers it necessary to give directions in pursuance of sub-paragraph (3) of the preceding paragraph for the purpose of dealing temporarily with an emergency and has previously consulted bodies recognised by him or the Authority as representing the relevant officers about the giving of such directions for that purpose, the Secretary of State or the Authority shall be entitled to disregard the preceding sub-paragraph in relation to the directions.

Miscellaneous

12. Provision may be made by regulations as to—
   (a) the appointment and tenure of office of the chairman and members of an authority ;
   (b) the appointment of and the exercise of functions by committees and sub-committees of an authority (including joint committees and joint sub-committees of two or more authorities and committees and sub-committees consisting wholly or partly of persons who are not members of the authority in question) ;
   (c) the procedure of an authority and of such committees and sub-committees as are mentioned in the preceding sub-paragraph.

13. An authority may pay subscriptions, of such amounts as the Secretary of State may approve, to the funds of such bodies as he may approve.

14. The proceedings of an authority shall not be invalidated by any vacancy in its membership or by any defect in the appointment of a member of the authority.

15.—(1) An authority shall, notwithstanding that it is exercising any function on behalf of the Secretary of State or another authority, be entitled to enforce any rights acquired in the exercise of that function, and be liable in respect of any liabilities incurred (including liabilities in tort) in the exercise of that function, in all respects as if it were acting as a principal ; and proceedings for the enforcement of such rights and liabilities shall be brought, and brought only, by or as the case may be against the authority in question in its own name.

(2) An authority shall not be entitled to claim in any proceedings any privilege of the Crown in respect of the discovery or production of documents ; but this sub-paragraph shall not prejudice any right of the Crown to withhold or procure the witholding from production of any document on the ground that its disclosures would be contrary to the public interest.

16. Provision may be made by regulations with respect to the recording of information by an authority and the furnishing of information by an authority to the Secretary of State or another authority.

SCHEDULE 2

Hospitals of which the Boards of Governors may be preserved

The teaching hospitals to which the following names are assigned by orders made by virtue of section 11 of the principal Act before the passing of this Act, that is to say—

The Hospitals for Sick Children

The National Hospitals for Nervous Diseases

The Royal National Throat, Nose and Ear Hospital

The Moorfields Eye Hospital

The Bethlem Royal Hospital and the Maudsley Hospital

St. John's Hospital for Diseases of the Skin

The Royal National Orthopaedic Hospitals

The National Heart and Chest Hospitals

St. Peter's Hospitals

The Royal Marsden Hospital

Queen Charlotte's Hospital for Women

The Eastman Dental Hospital.

SCHEDULE 3

Matters not subject to investigation by Health Service Commissioners

1. Action taken in connection with the diagnosis of illness or the care or treatment of a patient, being action which, in the opinion of the Commissioner in question, was taken solely in consequence of

SCH. 3   the exercise of clinical judgment, whether formed by the person taking the action or by any other person.

2. Action taken by an Executive Council or a Family Practitioner S.I. 1956 No. Committee in the exercise of its functions under the National Health 1077. Service (Service Committees and Tribunal) Regulations 1956 or any instrument amending or replacing those regulations.

3. Action taken in respect of appointments or removals, pay, discipline, superannuation or other personnel matters in relation to service under the Health Service Acts.

4. Action taken in matters relating to contractual or other commercial transactions, other than in matters arising from arrangements between a relevant body and another body which is not a relevant body for the provision of services for patients by that other body; and in determining what matters arise from such arrangements any arrangements for the provision of services at an establishment maintained by a Minister of the Crown for patients who are mainly members of the armed forces of the Crown shall be disregarded.

5. Action which has been or is the subject of an inquiry under section 70 of the principal Act.

Section 57.

SCHEDULE 4

MINOR AND CONSEQUENTIAL AMENDMENTS OF ENACTMENTS

1936 c. 40.   *The Midwives Act* 1936

1. In section 2(3) of the Midwives Act 1936 (which relates to the appointment of midwives), the first reference to that Act shall be construed as including a reference to section 2 of the National Health Service Reorganisation Act 1973.

1936 c. 49.   *The Public Health Act* 1936

2. In section 1(1) of the Public Health Act 1936 (which imposes on local authorities the duty of carrying the Act into execution), after the words " carry this Act " there shall be inserted the words ", excluding Part VI except section 198,".

3. In section 143(3) of that Act (which provides that regulations may be made for the treatment of persons affected with certain diseases and specifies the authorities for the enforcement of the regulations), after the words " port health authorities " there shall be inserted the words " Regional Health Authorities, Area Health Authorities or special health authorities ".

4. In section 169(1) of that Act (which provides that a person suffering from a notifiable disease may be removed to a hospital), for the words " Hospital Management Committee or Board of Governors " there shall be substituted the words " Area Health Authority responsible for the administration ".

5. In section 187(2) of that Act (which requires an application for the registration of a person in respect of a nursing home to be accompanied by a fee of £1), for the words from " fee " onwards

there shall be substituted the words "fee of such amount as the   Secretary of State may prescribe by regulations; and without prejudice to the operation of section 5(2) of the Statutory Instruments Act 1946 any such regulation shall be laid before Parliament ".

6. In section 244 of that Act (which provides that a person living in a common lodging house who is suffering from a notifiable disease may be removed to a hospital), for the words " Hospital Management Committee or Board of Governors " there shall be substituted the words " Area Health Authority responsible for the administration ".

The Education Act 1944   1944 c. 31.

7. In subsection (4) of section 48 of the Education Act 1944 (which requires local education authorities to encourage and assist pupils to take advantage of the facilities for free medical treatment provided in pursuance of that section), for the words " such facilities as aforesaid " there shall be substituted the words " the provision for medical and dental inspection and treatment made for them in pursuance of section 3(1) or 3(2)(a)(i) of the National Health Service Reorganisation Act 1973 " and for the words " medical treatment provided under this section " there shall be substituted the words " of the provision so made ".

8. In section 114(1) of that Act, at the end of the definition of " Medical officer " there shall be inserted the words " or whose services are made available to that authority by the Secretary of State ".

The Education Act 1946   1946 c. 50.

9. In section 4(2)(c) of the Education Act 1946 (which relates to buildings connected with the carrying out by local education authorities of their functions relating to medical inspection or treatment), for the words from " local " to " treatment " there shall be substituted the words " Secretary of State to carry out the functions conferred on him by section 3 of the National Health Service Reorganisation Act 1973 ".

The principal Act

10. In section 1 of the principal Act (which among other things provides for the establishment of the national health service and the provision of services in accordance with the following provisions of that Act), in subsection (1) for the words " the following provisions of this Act " there shall be substituted the words " the National Health Service Acts 1946 to 1973 " and in subsection (2) for the words " this Act " there shall be substituted the words " those Acts ".

11. In section 2 of that Act, in subsection (1) (which among other things provides for the Central Health Services Council to give advice to the Secretary of State about the services provided under that Act and any services provided by local health authorities), for the words from " under this Act " to " such authorities " there shall be substituted the words " under the National Health Service Acts 1946 to 1973 " and in subsection (3) (which among other things provides for standing advisory committees to consist partly of members appointed by the Secretary of State after consultation with that

Council as being persons of experience in relevant services) the words from " after consultation with that Council " to " those services " shall be omitted.

12.—(1) In section 3(2) of that Act (which relates to the supply as part of the hospital and specialist services of appliances of a more expensive type than the prescribed type and the replacement and repair of appliances), for the words " as part of the hospital and specialist services " in paragraph (*a*) and the words " as part of the services aforesaid " in paragraph (*b*) there shall be substituted the words " by him ".

(2) In section 3(3) of that Act (which relates to the payment by the Secretary of State of travelling expenses in connection with hospital and specialist services), for the words " hospital and specialist services " there shall be substituted the words " any services provided under the National Health Service Acts 1946 to 1973 ".

13. In section 4 of that Act (which relates to hospital accommodation available on part payment), for the words from " in any hospital " to " available " there shall be substituted the words ", at any hospital or group of hospitals vested in the Secretary of State or in which patients are treated under arrangements made by virtue of section 13(1) of the National Health Service Reorganisation Act 1973 or at the hospitals in a particular area which are vested in him or in which patients are so treated, accommodation in single rooms or small wards which is not for the time being needed by any patient on medical grounds, the Secretary of State may authorise the accommodation to be made available, to such extent as he may determine,".

14. In section 16(1) of that Act (which relates to research connected with illness), after the word " illness " there shall be inserted the words " and into such other matters connected with any service provided under the National Health Service Acts 1946 to 1973 as the Secretary of State considers appropriate ".

15. In section 17 of that Act (which authorises the Secretary of State to provide a bacteriological service for the control of infectious diseases), for the word " bacteriological " there shall be substituted the word " microbiological ".

16. In section 18 of that Act (which among other things provides that where the Secretary of State has, in providing hospital and specialist services, acquired supplies of human blood for the purpose of carrying out a blood transfusion he may arrange for the supplies to be available to local health authorities and medical practitioners who require them in cases of emergency), for the words from " in providing " to " transfusion " there shall be substituted the words " acquired supplies of human blood for the purposes of any service under the National Health Service Acts 1946 to 1973 " and for the words from " local " to " emergency " there shall be substituted the words " any person " ; and the words " in cases of emergency " where they first occur shall be omitted.

17.—(1) In section 22(1) of that Act (which requires local health authorities to make arrangements for the care, including in particular dental care, of nursing and expectant mothers and young children), the words " including in particular dental care " shall be omitted.

(2) In section 22(2) of that Act (which authorises the making and recovery of certain charges with the approval of the Minister) the words " with the approval of the Minister " shall be omitted.

18. In section 32 of that Act (which relates to local representative committees)—

(a) for the words " Executive Council " in subsection (1) there shall be substituted the words " Area Health Authority " ;

(b) for the words " of that area " in subsection (1)(a) there shall be substituted the words " providing general medical services or general ophthalmic services in that area " and for the words " of that area " in subsection (1)(c) there shall be substituted the words " providing general dental services in that area " ;

(c) for the words " Executive Council " in subsection (2) there shall be substituted the words " Family Practitioner Committee for the area of an Area Health Authority in respect of which Local Committees are recognised in pursuance of the foregoing subsection " ;

(d) for the words " Executive Council " in both places where they occur and the word " Council " in subsection (3) there shall be substituted the words " Family Practitioner Committee " and for the words " that Committee " and " the Committee " wherever they occur in that subsection there shall be substituted the words " the Local Committee " ; and

(e) for the word " Committee " in both places where it occurs in subsection (4) there shall be substituted the words " Local Committee ".

19.—(1) In section 33(1) of that Act (which imposes a duty on Executive Councils to make arrangements for the provision of general medical services), for the words " Executive Council " there shall be substituted the words " Area Health Authority ".

(2) After section 33(2) of that Act there shall be inserted the following subsection—

(3) Regulations under the last foregoing subsection may provide for the personal medical services there mentioned to include the provision of, and of services connected with, any such advice, examination and treatment as are mentioned in section 4 of the National Health Service Reorganisation Act 1973.

20. In section 34 of that Act (which relates to the distribution of medical practitioners providing services), for the words " Executive Councils ", " Executive Council " and " Council " in each place where they occur there shall be substituted respectively the words " Area Health Authorities ", " Area Health Authority " and " Authority ".

21. In section 35(1) of that Act (which prohibits the sale of medical practices where the name of a medical practitioner is entered on any list of medical practitioners), in the proviso after the word " Council " there shall be inserted the words " or Area Health Authority ".

22. After subsection (3) of section 36 of that Act (of which paragraph (*d*) requires the payment of interest on compensation payable in pursuance of that section), there shall be inserted the following subsection—

> (3A) Regulations under subsection (3)(*d*) of this section may provide for the interest payable on any amount of compensation to be paid at a date later than the date on which the compensation is paid.

23. At the end of section 38(3) of that Act (which relates to charges for pharmaceutical services) there shall be inserted the words " ; and it is hereby declared that regulations under this subsection may include provision in respect of charges for the supply of such substances and appliances as are mentioned in section 4 of the National Health Service Reorganisation Act 1973 ".

24. In section 39(1) of that Act (which provides that no medical or dental practitioner may supply pharmaceutical services to a patient except as provided by regulations), for the words " Executive Council " there shall be substituted the words " Area Health Authority ".

25.—(1) In section 40(1) of that Act (which imposes a duty on Executive Councils to make arrangements for the provision of general dental services), for the words " Executive Council " there shall be substituted the words " Area Health Authority ".

(2) In the proviso to section 40(1) of that Act (under which the remuneration of certain dental practitioners must not, except in special circumstances, consist wholly or mainly of a fixed salary), for the words from " except " onwards there shall be substituted the words " consist wholly or mainly of a fixed salary unless either—

> (*a*) the remuneration is paid in pursuance of arrangements made under section 43 of this Act ; or
>
> (*b*) the services are provided in prescribed circumstances and the practitioner consents ;

and it shall be the duty of the Secretary of State, before he prescribes any circumstances for the purposes of paragraph (*b*) above to consult such organisations as appear to him to be representative of the dental profession ".

(3) At the end of section 40(2)(*d*) of that Act (which provides that regulations may prescribe duties of the Dental Estimates Board), there shall be inserted the words " and to the remuneration of dental practitioners providing general dental services ".

(4) In section 40(2)(*e*) of that Act (which provides that regulations may make provision for certain matters in relation to the Board), for the words " Executive Council " there shall be substituted the words " Area Health Authority " and for the words " the supplementary

provisions of the Fifth Schedule to this Act" there shall be substituted the words "Part III of Schedule 1 to the National Health Service Reorganisation Act 1973 ".

26. In section 41(1) of that Act (which imposes a duty on Executive Councils to provide general ophthalmic services), for the words from "Part II" to "specialist services" there shall be substituted the words "section 2 of the National Health Service Reorganisation Act 1973 to provide" and for the words "Executive Council" there shall be substituted the words "Area Health Authority ".

27. In section 42 of that Act (which provides for the constitution of a tribunal to enquire into cases of disqualification of practitioners), for the words "Executive Council" in each place where they occur and for the word "Councils" there shall be substituted respectively the words "Area Health Authority" and "Authorities ".

28. In section 43 of that Act (which provides that the Secretary of State may make arrangements for services where services are inadequate), for the words "Executive Council" in both places where they occur there shall be substituted the words "Area Health Authority ".

29. In section 47 of that Act (which provides for disputes to be referred to the Secretary of State), for the words "Executive Council" where they first occur there shall be substituted the words "Area Health Authority" and the words from "or between" to "health centre" shall be omitted.

30. In section 54(6) of that Act (which provides for payments under the section to be made in accordance with regulations), after the word " otherwise " there shall be inserted the word " as ".

31.—(1) In section 55 of that Act (which relates to the accounts of existing health authorities), in subsection (2) for the words from the beginning to "Council" there shall be substituted the words "Every Regional Health Authority, Area Health Authority, special health authority, all Special Trustees appointed in pursuance of section 29(1) of the National Health Service Reorganisation Act 1973 and the Dental Estimates Board ".

(2) In subsection (3) of that section, for the words "Committee and Council" there shall be substituted the words "Authority, special health authority and all such Special Trustees" and at the end of the subsection there shall be inserted the words " ; and the accounts prepared and transmitted by an Area Health Authority in pursuance of this subsection shall include annual accounts of the Family Practitioner Committees established by the Authority and of any Community Health Council of which the district includes any part of the Authority's area."

(3) In subsection (4) of that section, for the words " Boards, Committees and Councils " there shall be substituted the words " Authorities, special authorities and Special Trustees ".

32. In section 57(1) of that Act (which confers default powers on the Secretary of State), for the words from " Regional Hospital Board " to " Executive Council " there shall be substituted the

words " Regional Health Authority, Area Health Authority, special health authority, Family Practitioner Committee ", and after the words " this Act " there shall be inserted the words " or the National Health Service Reorganisation Act 1973 ".

33. In section 70 of that Act (which provides that the Secretary of State may hold an inquiry in connection with matters arising under that Act), after the words " this Act " there shall be inserted the words " or the National Health Service Reorganisation Act 1973 ".

34. In section 71 of that Act (which provides for the recovery of charges), after the words " this Act " in both places where they occur there shall be inserted the words " or the National Health Service Reorganisation Act 1973 ".

35. In secton 72 of that Act (which applies the provisions of section 265 of the Public Health Act 1875 relating to the protection of members and officers of certain authorities), for the words from " Regional Hospital Board " to " Executive Council " there shall be substituted the words " Regional Health Authority, an Area Health Authority, a special health authority and a Family Practitioner Committee " and for the words " this Act " there shall be substituted the words " the National Health Service Acts 1946 to 1973 ".

36. In section 74 of that Act (which relates to miscellaneous administrative matters), in paragraph (c) after the words " this Act " there shall be inserted the words " or the National Health Service Reorganisation Act 1973 " and the words " local health authorities and " shall be omitted.

37. In section 79(1) of that Act (interpretation), in the definition of " medicine ", for the words " includes any prescribed chemical re-agent " there shall be substituted the words " includes such chemical re-agents as are included in a list for the time being approved by the Secretary of State for the purposes of section 38(1) of this Act ".

38. In Schedule 1 to that Act (which provides for the constitution of the Central Council and advisory committees), in paragraph 3 the words from " and the Central Council " onwards shall be omitted and in paragraph 4 after the word " fit " there shall be inserted the words " and as are approved by the Secretary of State ".

39. In Schedule 7 to that Act, in paragraph 3 (which provides for associations of Executive Councils to be consulted about the appointment of one member of the tribunal concerned with the removal of names from the list of persons undertaking to provide services under Part IV of that Act), for the words " Executive Councils " in both places there shall be substituted the words " Family Practitioner Committees ".

The Polish Resettlement Act 1947

40. In section 4(1) of the Polish Resettlement Act 1947 (which provides that the Secretary of State may provide health services for persons resettled in pursuance of that Act), after the word

"1946" there shall be inserted the words "or the National Health Service Reorganisation Act 1973,", for the words "local health authorities, executive councils" there shall be substituted the words "Area Health Authorities", for the words "that Act" in the second place where they occur there shall be substituted the words "those Acts" and for the words "local health authorities" in the second place where they occur there shall be substituted the words "local social services authorities".

The National Health Service (Scotland) Act 1947

41. After subsection (3) of section 37 of the National Health Service (Scotland) Act 1947 (of which paragraph (*d*) requires the payment of interest on compensation payable in pursuance of that section), there shall be inserted the following subsection—

(3A) Regulations under subsection (3)(*d*) of this section may provide for the interest payable on any amount of compensation to be paid at a date later than the date on which the compensation is paid.

42.—(1) For subsection (1) of section 40 of that Act (which relates to arrangements for pharmaceutical services), there shall be substituted the following subsection—

(1) It shall be the duty of every Health Board to make in accordance with regulations arrangements as respects its area for the supply to persons who are in that area of—

(*a*) proper and sufficient drugs and medicines and listed appliances which are ordered for those persons by a medical practitioner in pursuance of his functions in the health service, the health service for England and Wales, the Northern Ireland health service or the armed forces of the Crown (excluding forces of a Commonwealth country and forces raised in a colony); and

(*b*) listed drugs and medicines which are ordered for those persons by a dental practitioner in pursuance of such functions;

and the services provided in accordance with the arrangements are in this Act referred to as "pharmaceutical services".

In this subsection—

"the health service" means the service established by section 1 of this Act;

"listed" means included in a list for the time being approved by the Secretary of State for the purposes of this subsection; and

"the health service for England and Wales" and "the Northern Ireland health service" mean respectively the health service established in pursuance of section 1 of the National Health Service Act 1946 or any service provided in pursuance of Article 4(*a*) of the Health and Personal Social Services (Northern Ireland) Order 1972.

R

SCH. 4

(2) In subsection (2) of that section for the words from " receiving general medical services " to " dental practitioner rendering those services " there shall be substituted the words " for whom they are ordered as mentioned in the last foregoing subsection to receive the drugs, medicines and appliances there mentioned ".

43. In section 80(1) of that Act (interpretation), in the definition of " medicine ", for the words " includes any prescribed chemical re-agent " there shall be substituted the words " includes such chemical re-agents as are included in a list for the time being approved by the Secretary of State for the purposes of section 40(1) of this Act ".

1948 c. 29.

The National Assistance Act 1948

44. In section 21(7) of the National Assistance Act 1948 (which provides among other things that a local authority may make arrangements for the provision of health services on premises in which accommodation is provided for persons under that section), for paragraph (c) there shall be substituted the following paragraph—

(c) arrange with a Regional Health Authority, Area Health Authority or special health authority for the provision on the premises by the authority of services under the National Health Service Acts 1946 to 1973 ;

and the words from " In this subsection " onwards shall be omitted.

45. In section 24(6) of that Act (which relates to the determination of the ordinary residence of a patient), for the words from " forming " to " 1946 " there shall be substituted the words " vested in the Secretary of State ".

46. In section 29 of that Act (which provides for the local authority to make welfare arrangements for handicapped persons), in subsection (6)(b) after the word " 1946 " there shall be inserted the words " the National Health Service Reorganisation Act 1973 ".

47. In section 47 of that Act (which provides that persons in need of care and attention may be removed to suitable premises), in subsection (8) after the word " 1946 " there shall be inserted the words " or the National Health Service Reorganisation Act 1973 ".

1948 c. 64.

The National Service Act 1948

48. In paragraph 3 of Schedule 1 to the National Service Act 1948 (which includes among the categories of persons not liable for service certain persons suffering from mental disabilities), for the words " Regional Hospital Board " there shall be substituted the words " Regional Health Authority or of an Area Health Authority of which the area is in Wales " and for the words from " local health authority ", where they first occur, onwards there shall be substituted the words " council which is a local authority for the purposes of the Local Authority Social Services Act 1970 and so provided in pursuance of section 12 of the Health Services and Public Health Act 1968 or is otherwise receiving care from such a council in pursuance of that section ".

The Recall of Army and Air Force Pensioners Act 1948

SCH. 4

49. In paragraph 2 of the Schedule to the Recall of Army and Air Force Pensioners Act 1948 (which includes among the categories of persons not liable to be recalled certain persons suffering from mental disabilities), for the words " Regional Hospital Board " there shall be substituted the words " Regional Health Authority, of an Area Health Authority of which the area is in Wales, of a special health authority or of a Health Board,".

1948 c. 8.
(12, 13 and 14 Geo. 6.).

The National Health Service (Amendment) Act 1949

1949 c. 93.

50. In section 8 of the National Health Service (Amendment) Act 1949 (which relates to the removal of doubts as to the operation of section 35 of the principal Act), after the words " Executive Council " there shall be inserted the words " or an Area Health Authority ".

51. In section 13(1) of that Act (which provides for the reference to arbitration of disputes as to conditions of service of persons employed in health services), after the words " the Act of 1946 " there shall be inserted the words " or the National Health Service Reorganisation Act 1973 ".

52.—(1) In section 18(1) of that Act (which provides for the superannuation of offices of voluntary hospitals), for the words " Regional Hospital Boards " there shall be substituted the words " Area Health Authorities ".

(2) In subsection (4) of that section, for the words " a Regional Hospital Board or the Board of Governors of a teaching hospital " there shall be substituted the words " the Secretary of State " and for the words " hospital and specialist services " there shall be substituted the words " services under the National Health Service Acts 1946 to 1973".

53. In section 23(1) of that Act (which provides that voluntary organisations may transfer property to a local health authority), for the words " a local health authority " and the words " the authority " there shall be substituted the words " the Secretary of State".

54. In section 25(2) of that Act (which provides that no payment shall be made under subsection (1) of that section to a medical practitioner in respect of an examination carried out as part of his duty to provide general medical services for the person examined or as part of his duty as an officer of a Regional Hospital Board or a Board of Governors), for the words " Regional Hospital Board or a Board of Governors of a teaching hospital " there shall be substituted the words " Regional Health Authority, an Area Health Authority or a special health authority ".

55. In section 28 of that Act (which relates to the recovery of expenses from in-patients engaged in remunerative employment), for the words " hospital and specialist services " there shall be substituted the words " services under the National Health Service Acts 1946 to 1973 ".

The Shops Act 1950

56. In section 22(1) of the Shops Act 1950 (which specifies requirements to be complied with in respect of the employment of persons in the business of a shop on Sundays), in paragraph (v) of the proviso for the words " Executive Council " there shall be substituted the words " Area Health Authority ".

57. In Schedule 5 to that Act (which specifies transactions for the purposes of which a shop may be open on Sundays), in paragraph 1(g) for the words " Executive Council " there shall be subsituted the words " Area Health Authority ".

1951 c. 31.

The National Health Service Act 1951

58.—(1) In section 1 of the National Health Service Act 1951 (which authorises charges for certain dental and optical appliances), in subsection (1) for the words " Part II or Part IV of those Acts respectively " there shall be substituted the words " the National Health Service Acts 1946 to 1973 ".

(2) In subsection (2) of that section, for the words " under the said Part II " there shall be substituted the words " , otherwise than under Part IV of the said Acts of 1946 and 1947 ".

(3) In subsection (3)(a) of that section, for the words " the said Part II " where they first occur there shall be substituted the words " the National Health Service Acts 1946 to 1973 otherwise than under Part IV of the said Act of 1946 " and for those words in the second place where they occur there shall be substituted the words " those Acts ".

(4) In subsection (4) of that section for the words " Executive Council " there shall be substituted the words " Area Health Authority or Family Practitioner Committee ".

59.—(1) In the Schedule to that Act, at the end of the definition of " children's glasses " there shall be inserted the words " and which are supplied for a person who was, at the time of the examination or testing of sight leading to the supply of the glasses or of the first such examination or testing, under sixteen years of age or receiving full-time instruction in a school within the meaning of the Education Act 1944 or the Education (Scotland) Act 1962 ".

(2) In that Schedule, in the definition of " current specified cost ", for the words " Part II of those Acts respectively " there shall be substituted the words " the National Health Service Acts 1946 to 1973 otherwise than under Part IV of the said Act of 1946 ".

1951 c. 53.

The Midwives Act 1951

60. In section 11 of the Midwives Act 1951 (which prohibits unqualified persons from acting for gain as maternity nurses in any area on and after the date on which that section is applied to the area by an order under subsection (2) of that section), subsection (2) and the words from " on or after " to " therein " in subsection (1) shall cease to have effect.

61. In section 23(2) of that Act (which provides that the Central Midwives Board may apportion between local health authorities any deficit disclosed in its annual accounts), for the words from " the local " to " being " there shall be substituted the words " Regional Health Authorities and Area Health Authorities of which the areas are in Wales, in such proportions as may be determined by the Secretary of State ".

62. Sections 26 and 27 of that Act (which authorise a local supervising authority to aid the training of midwives and to provide residential accommodation for pupil midwives) shall cease to have effect.

63. In section 29(2) of that Act (which provides for the payment of expenses of a prosecution for an offence under the Act), for the words from " council " to " borough " there shall be substituted the words " Regional Health Authority or the Area Health Authority of which the area is in Wales for the region or area respectively ".

64. In section 31 of that Act (which defines local supervising authority for the purposes of the Act), for the words " Every local health authority throughout England and Wales " there shall be substituted the words " A Regional Health Authority and an Area Health Authority of which the area is in Wales ", and for the words " area of the said authority " there shall be substituted the words " region or area of the authority ".

The National Health Service Act 1952

65.—(1) In section 1(1) of the National Health Service Act 1952 (which authorises charges for certain drugs, medicines and appliances), for the words from " as part " to " Part II " there shall be substituted the words " under the National Health Service Acts otherwise than under Part IV ".

(2) In section 1(2)(c) of that Act (which provides that no charge is to be made under that section for the supply of an appliance for a young person), after the word " appliance ", there shall be inserted the words ", otherwise than in pursuance of section 4 of the National Health Service Reorganisation Act 1973 ".

66.—(1) In subsection (4) of section 7 of that Act (which among other things relates to the making of charges for medicines supplied in connection with free medical treatment for certain pupils), for the words from the beginning to " education authorities " there shall be substituted the words " For the purposes of subsections (1) and (2)(a) of section 3 of the National Health Service Reorganisation Act 1973 (which provides for the Secretary of State ".

(2) In subsection (6) of that section (supplementary and consequential provisions), for the words from " Regional " to " Council " there shall be substituted the words " Regional Health Authority, Area Health Authority or Family Practitioner Committee "

67. In section 8(1) of that Act (interpretation), for the word " 1951 " where it first occurs there shall be substituted the word " 1973 ".

The Landlord and Tenant Act 1954

68. In section 57(6) of the Landlord and Tenant Act 1954 (which modifies on grounds of public interest certain rights of a tenant where property belongs to, or is held for the purposes of, a government department or specified other bodies), for the words from " Board of " to " 1946 " there shall be substituted the words " Regional Health Authority, Area Health Authority or special health authority " and for the words " that Act " there shall be substituted the words " the National Health Service Act 1946 and the National Health Service Reorganisation Act 1973 ".

The Medical Act 1956

69.—(1) In section 16 of the Medical Act 1956, in subsection (1) (which provides that the expression " institution " includes a health centre only if it is a centre provided under section 21 of the principal Act, section 15 of the National Health Service (Scotland) Act 1947, or section 17 of the Health Services Act (Northern Ireland) 1948), for the words from " section 21 " onwards there shall be substituted the words " section 2 of the National Health Service Reorganisation Act 1973, section 2 of the National Health Service (Scotland) Act 1972, or Article 5 of the Health and Personal Social Services (Northern Ireland) Order 1972 ".

(2) In subsection (2) of that section (which provides that employment in a health centre shall not be treated as employment for the purposes of section 15 of that Act unless it is employment by a medical practitioner in the provision of general medical services under Part IV of the principal Act, Part IV of the said Act of 1947 or Part II of the said Act of 1948, or employment in the provision of such out-patient services as are mentioned in the sections referred to in subsection (1) of that section), in paragraph (*a*) for the words from " said Act of 1946 " to " 1948 " there shall be substituted the words " National Health Service Act 1946, Part IV of the National Health Service (Scotland) Act 1947 or Part VI of the said Order of 1972 " and in paragraph (*b*) for the words from " such out-patient ", where they first occur, onwards there shall be substituted the words " the services of specialists or other services provided for out-patients in a health centre provided as mentioned in the last foregoing subsection ".

The Nurses Act 1957

70. In the Nurses Act 1957, for the words " area nurse-training committee ", " an area nurse-training committee " and " area nurse-training committees " wherever they occur there shall be substituted respectively the words " regional nurse-training committee ", " a regional nurse-training committee " and " regional nurse-training committees ".

71.—(1) In section 11 of that Act (which establishes nurse-training committees for hospital areas), in subsection (1) for the words " hospital area " there shall be substituted the words " region and for Wales " and for the word " area " in the third place where it occurs there shall be substituted the words " region or to Wales ".

(2) In subsection (2) of that section (which establishes nurse-training committees for hospital areas), for the words "hospital area" there shall be substituted the words "region or for Wales", for the word "area" in paragraphs (*a*), (*b*), (*c*)(iii) and (*d*) there shall be substituted the words "region or in Wales" and for sub-paragraphs (i) and (ii) of paragraph (*c*) there shall be substituted the following sub-paragraph—

(i) Area Health Authorities in the region or in Wales and special health authorities exercising functions there, and.

72. In section 12(1) of that Act (which provides that the General Nursing Council may adopt experimental schemes for the training of nurses), the words "situated in such hospital area" shall be omitted.

73. In section 13(1) of that Act (which provides for expenditure by a Hospital Management Committee or Board of Governors on the training of nurses), for the words from "Hospital Management" to "area" in the second place where it occurs there shall be substituted the words "Regional Health Authority, Area Health Authority or special health authority", for the words from "approved" to "for the area" there shall be substituted the words "approved by a regional nurse-training committee" and for the words "section 54 of the National Health Service Act 1946" there shall be substituted the words "section 47 of the National Health Service Reorganisation Act 1973".

74. In section 14 of that Act (which provides for contributions by a nurse-training committee towards the expenses of an authority or person engaged in the training of nurses), for the words "hospital area" and the word "area" in the third place where it occurs there shall be substituted respectively the words "region or for Wales" and "region or in Wales" and for the words from "Hospital Management Committee" to "teaching hospital" there shall be substituted the words "Regional Health Authority, Area Health Authority or special health authority".

75. In section 16 of that Act (which provides that a dispute between a nurse-training committee and a Hospital Management Committee or Board of Governors shall be determined by the General Nursing Council), for the words "hospital area" there shall be substituted the words "region or for Wales" and for the words from "Hospital Management Committee" to "in the area" there shall be substituted the words "Regional Health Authority, Area Health Authority or special health authority".

76. In section 33 of that Act (interpretation), after the definition of "prescribed" there shall be inserted the following definition—

"region" means a region determined for a Regional Health Authority in pursuance of the National Health Service Reorganisation Act 1973 ;.

77. In Schedule 1 to that Act (which provides for the constitution of the General Nursing Council), in paragraph 3(*e*) for the words "section 25 of the National Health Service Act 1946" there shall

SCH. 4

be substituted the words "section 2 of the National Health Service Reorganisation Act 1973 of attending persons in their homes ".

78.—(1) In Schedule 2 to that Act (which provides for the membership of nurse-training committees), in paragraph 1 for the words " hospital area " there shall be substituted the words " region and the regional nurse-training committee for Wales " and in sub-paragraph (a) of that paragraph for the words " Regional Hospital Board for the area " there shall be substituted the words " Regional Health Authority for the region or in the case of the committee for Wales by the Secretary of State ".

(2) In paragraph 1(b) of that Schedule for the words from " Boards " onwards there shall be substituted the words "Area Health Authorities of which the areas are in the region or, as the case may be, in Wales ; ".

(3) For sub-paragraph (f) of paragraph 1 of that Schedule there shall be substituted the following sub-paragraph—

> (f) persons appointed by the Regional Health Authority after consultation with the local education authorities in the region or, in the case of the committee for Wales, by the Secretary of State after consultation with the local education authorities in Wales ;.

(4) For sub-paragraph (g) of paragraph 1 of that Schedule there shall be substituted the following sub-paragraph—

> (g) persons appointed by the Regional Health Authority after consultation with the university or universities with which the Authority is associated or, in the case of the committee for Wales, by the Secretary of State after consultation with the university or universities with which Wales is associated ;

and paragraph 1(e) of that Schedule shall be omitted.

(5) In paragraph 2(a) of that Schedule for the words " hospital area " there shall be substituted the words " region and the regional nurse-training committee for Wales ".

(6) In paragraph 4(1) of that Schedule for the words " Regional Hospital Board for a hospital area " there shall be substituted the words " Regional Health Authority for a region and in Wales the duty of the Secretary of State ", for the word " area " in the third place where it occurs there shall be substituted the words " region and for Wales, respectively " and for the word " Board " in the second place where it occurs there shall be substituted the word " Authority ".

1957 c. 20.

The House of Commons Disqualification Act 1957

79.—(1) In Part II of Schedule 1 to the House of Commons Disqualification Act 1957 (which specifies bodies of which all members are disqualified under that Act), as it applies to the House of Commons of the Parliament of the United Kingdom, there shall be inserted at the appropriate points in alphabetical order—

> (a) the entry " The National Health Service Staff Commission " ;
> (b) the entry " The Welsh National Health Service Staff Commission ".

(2) In Part III of Schedule 1 to that Act (which specifies offices of which the holders are disqualified under that Act), as it applies to the House of Commons of the Parliament of the United Kingdom, there shall be inserted at the appropriate points in alphabetical order—

(*a*) the entry " Chairman in receipt of remuneration of any Regional Health Authority, Area Health Authority or Area Health Authority (Teaching) or of any special health authority " ;

(*b*) the entry " Health Service Commissioner for England " ;
 and

(*c*) the entry " Health Service Commissioner for Wales " ;

and in the Part substituted for the said Part III by Schedule 3 to that Act in relation to the Senate and House of Commons of Northern Ireland there shall be inserted at the appropriate places in alphabetical order the entries specified in paragraphs (*b*) and (*c*) above.

The Dentists Act 1957

80. In section 42(4) of the Dentists Act 1957 (which relates to the meaning of national and local authority health services), the words " and local authority " shall be omitted and for paragraphs (*a*) to (*d*) there shall be substituted the words " of services under section 2 or 3 of the National Health Service Reorganisation Act 1973 or section 2, 5 or 6 of the National Health Service (Scotland) Act 1972 or Article 5, 8 or 9 of the Health and Personal Social Services (Northern Ireland) Order 1972 and services at health centres provided under the said sections 2 or Article 5 ".

The Opticians Act 1958

81. In section 21(2)(*b*) of the Opticians Act 1958 (which provides that the restrictions on the sale of optical appliances under subsection (1) of that section apply if the supply was effected in pursuance of arrangements made with any body on whom functions are conferred by Parts II or IV of the principal Act, Parts II or IV of the National Health Service (Scotland) Act 1947 or Parts II or III of the Health Services Act (Northern Ireland) 1948), after the word " 1946," there shall be inserted the words " the National Health Service Reorganisation Act 1973," after the word " 1947," there shall be inserted the words " the National Health Service (Scotland) Act 1972," and for the words " Part II or Part III of the Health Services Act (Northern Ireland), 1948 " there shall be substituted the words " the Health and Personal Social Services (Northern Ireland) Order 1972 " ; and the words " Part II or " in both places where they occur shall be omitted.

The Public Records Act 1958

82. In Schedule 1 to the Public Records Act 1958 (which determines what are public records for the purposes of that Act), in Part I of the Table in that Schedule, in the entry relating to the Department

of Health and Social Security (which, before its amendment by Article 5(4)(*b*) of The Secretary of State for Social Services Order 1968, was the entry relating to the Ministry of Health) before the words " Welsh Board of Health " there shall be inserted the words—

" records of property passing to Regional or Area Health Authorities or special health authorities under sections 23 to 26 of the National Health Service Reorganisation Act 1973.

records of property held by a Regional or Area Health Authority or special health authority under section 21 or 22 of the said Act of 1973 ".

The Mental Health Act 1959

83. In section 3(1) of the Mental Health Act 1959 (which provides for the constitution of Mental Health Review Tribunals for areas of Regional Hospital Boards), for the words from " area " to " 1946 " there shall be substituted the words " region for which a Regional Health Authority is established in pursuance of the National Health Service Reorganisation Act 1973, and for Wales ".

84. Without prejudice to the operation of section 41(1) of this Act, in section 14(3) of that Act (under which the registration authority, in relation to a home, is the council of the county or county borough in which the home is situated), for the words from " in relation " to " situated " there shall be substituted the words " means the Minister ".

85. In section 17(1) of that Act (which among other things relates to the inspection of records kept in respect of nursing homes in accordance with byelaws), for the words from " accordance with byelaws " onwards there shall be substituted the words " pursuance of section 41(2)(*b*) of the National Health Service Reorganisation Act 1973 ".

86. In section 28(2) of that Act, for the words " a local health authority " there shall be substituted the words " the Secretary of State ".

87. In section 37(2) of that Act (which provides that where an application is made to a regional hospital board to make an order for the discharge of a patient, certain persons there specified may visit the patient), for the words " regional hospital board " there shall be substituted the words " Regional Health Authority, Area Health Authority or a special health authority ".

88.—(1) In section 47 of that Act, in subsection (3) (which specifies the authorities or persons who may make orders for the discharge of a patient), for the words " regional hospital board " there shall be substituted the words " Regional Health Authority, Area Health Authority or special health authority " and for the word " board " there shall be substituted the word " authority ".

(2) At the end of subsection (4) of that section (which provides that the powers conferred by that section on an authority may be exercised by three or more members of the authority), there shall be inserted the words " or by three or more members of a committee or sub-committee of that authority or body which has been authorised by them in that behalf ".

89. In section 56(3) of that Act (which among other things provides that regulations may determine the manner in which functions of regional hospital boards are to be exercised), for the words " or regional hospital boards " there shall be substituted the words " Regional Health Authorities, Area Health Authorities or special health authorities ".

90. In section 59(1) of that Act, in paragraph (*a*) of the definition of " the managers ", for the words from " for hospital " onwards there shall be substituted the words " as a hospital by or on behalf of the Secretary of State under the National Health Service Acts 1946 to 1973, the Area Health Authority or special health authority responsible for the administration of the hospital ".

91. In sections 62(1) and 72(4) of that Act (which provide that at least one of the medical practitioners giving evidence or making a report under those sections shall be a practitioner approved by a local health authority for the purposes of section 28 of that Act), for the words " a local health authority " there shall be substituted the words " the Secretary of State ".

92. In section 128(1)(*b*) of that Act (which makes it an offence for a man to have sexual intercourse with a woman who is a mentally disordered patient and is in his custody in pursuance of arrangements under the National Health Service Act 1946 or the National Assistance Act 1948), after the word " 1948 " there shall be inserted the words " or the National Health Service Reorganisation Act 1973, ".

93. In section 132 of that Act (which provides that Regional Hospital Boards shall notify local health authorities of hospitals which have arrangements for the reception of urgent cases requiring treatment for mental disorder), for the words " Regional Hospital Board " there shall be substituted the words " Regional Health Authority and, in Wales, every Area Health Authority ", for the word " area " in the second place where it occurs there shall be substituted the words " region or area, as the case may be," and for the word " Board " in both places where it occurs there shall be substituted the word " Authority ".

94. In section 133(2) of that Act (which provides that the making of payments to persons under that section shall be included as services provided under Part II of the National Health Service Act 1946), after the word " 1946 " there shall be inserted the words " and the National Health Service Reorganisation Act 1973 " and for the words " Part II of that Act " there shall be substituted the words " those Acts ".

95. In section 147(1) of that Act (interpretation)—

    (*a*) in the definition of " hospital ", for the words " for hospital and specialist services under Part II of that Act " there shall be substituted the words " as a hospital by or on behalf of the Secretary of State under the National Health Service Acts 1946 to 1973 " ;

    (*b*) in the definition of " mental welfare officer ", for the words " local health authority " there shall be substituted the words " local social services authority " ; and

SCH. 4   (*c*) in the definition of "special hospital", for the words
                "meaning assigned to it by Part VII of this Act" there
                shall be substituted the words "same meaning as in the
                National Health Service Reorganisation Act 1973".

The Radioactive Substances Act 1960

1960 c. 34.   96. In section 14(1) of the Radioactive Substances Act 1960
(which provides that Hospital Management Committees or Boards
of Governors shall be treated as persons for the purposes of provisions of that Act dealing with the disposal of radioactive waste
notwithstanding that their functions are exercised on behalf of the
Secretary of State), for the words "a Hospital Management Committee" and "Hospital Management Committee" there shall be
substituted respectively the words "an Area Health Authority"
and "Area Health Authority"; and the words "or is a teaching
hospital within the meaning of the National Health Service Act,
1946" and the words ", or (in the case of a teaching hospital) the
Board of Governors," shall be omitted.

The Public Health Laboratory Service Act 1960

1960 c. 49.   97. In section 5(2) of the Public Health Laboratory Service Act
1960 (which defines "the public health laboratory service"), for
the word "bacteriological" there shall be substituted the word
"microbiological".

98. In the Schedule to that Act (which provides for the constitution of the Public Health Laboratory Service Board), in paragraph 2 for the word "bacteriological" there shall be substituted
the word "microbiological", in paragraph 3(*b*) for the word
"bacteriologists" there shall be substituted the word "micro-
biologists" and for paragraph 3(*d*) there shall be substituted the
following paragraph—

(*d*) not less than one person with experience of service in
hospitals, and.

The Public Bodies (Admission to Meetings) Act 1960

1960 c. 67.   99. In paragraph 1 of the Schedule to the Public Bodies (Admission to Meetings) Act 1960 (which specifies the bodies in England
and Wales to which that Act applies), for paragraph (*f*) there shall
be substituted the following paragraph—

(*f*) Regional Health Authorities, Area Health Authorities and
Community Health Councils and, if the order establishing
a special health authority so provides, that authority;

and paragraph (*g*) (which relates to Executive Councils) shall be
omitted.

National Health Service Act 1961

1961 c. 19.   100. In section 1(4) of the National Health Service Act 1961 (which
provides for exemption from certain charges for spectacles), for the
words from "Part II" to "1946" there shall be substituted the
words "the National Health Service Acts 1946 to 1973".

101. In section 3(1) of that Act (interpretation), in paragraph (*a*)
of the definition of "the relevant time", for the words "Part II of

the Act of 1946 " there shall be substituted the words " the National   SCH. 4
Health Service Acts 1946 to 1973 otherwise than under Part IV of
the Act of 1946 " and for the words " Part II or Part IV thereof "
there shall be substituted the words " those Acts " ; and in paragraph (b) of that definition for the words " either of the said Acts "
there shall be substituted the words " the Act of 1946 ".

The Health Visiting and Social Work (Training) Act 1962   1962 c. 33.

102.—(1) In paragraph 3 of Schedule 1 to the Health Visiting and
Social Work (Training) Act 1962 (which specifies the persons by
whom members of the Council for Education and Training of
Health Visitors are to be appointed), in sub-paragraph (a) for the
word " fourteen " there shall be substituted the word " twenty ".

(2) For sub-paragraph (c) of paragraph 3 of that Schedule there
shall be substituted the following sub-paragraph—

(c) such number as the Secretary of State may determine by
such bodies as he may think fit, being bodies representative
of local authorities in England and Wales, and in this
sub-paragraph " local authorities " means authorities
established by or under the Local Government Act 1972 or
the London Government Act 1963.

(3) For sub-paragraph (f) of paragraph (3) of that Schedule there
shall be substituted the following sub-paragraph—

(f) such number as the Secretary of State may determine by
such bodies as he may think fit, being bodies representative
of local authorities in Scotland, and in this sub-paragraph
" local authorities " means local authorities within the
meaning of the Local Government (Scotland) Act 1947 ;

and sub-paragraphs (d), (e), (g) and (h) of that paragraph shall be
omitted.

(4) In paragraphs 5(b) and 10 of that Schedule for the words " the
Society of Medical Officers of Health " there shall be substituted
the words " bodies appearing to the Health Ministers to represent
specialists in community medicine ".

The London Government Act 1963   1963 c. 33.

103. Subsections (1) to (6) of section 32 of the London Government
Act 1963 (which relate to the co-ordination of school and other
health services in inner London) shall cease to have effect.

The Emergency Laws (Re-enactment and Repeals) Act 1964   1964 c. 60.

104. In section 15 of the Emergency Laws (Re-enactment and
Repeals) Act 1964 (interpretation), for the words " 1946 to 1961 "
there shall be substituted the words " 1946 to 1973 ".

The Public Health (Notification of Births) Act 1965   1965 c. 42.

105. In section 1(2) of the Public Health (Notification of Births)
Act 1965 (which amends section 203(2) of the Public Health Act
1936 and imposes an obligation on welfare authorities to supply

SCH. 4   pre-paid addressed envelopes containing the form of notice to be given under that section), for the words " welfare authorities " there shall be substituted the words " Area Health Authorities ".

1965 c. 62.

The Redundancy Payments Act 1965

106. In Schedule 3 to the Redundancy Payments Act 1965 (which specifies bodies the employees of which are excluded from the general provisions as to redundancy payments provided for in section 1 of that Act), for paragraph 1 there shall be substituted the following paragraph—

    1. A Regional Health Authority, Area Health Authority, special health authority, Health Board or the Common Services Agency for the Scottish Health Service.

1966 c. 27.

The Building Control Act 1966

107. In section 5(1) of the Building Control Act 1966 (which among other things provides that any work carried out at the expense of any body corporate constituted under section 11 of the principal Act shall be exempt from control under the said Act of 1966), in paragraph (*h*) for the words " constituted under section 11 of the National Health Service Act 1946 " there shall be substituted the words " established in pursuance of section 5 of the National Health Service Reorganisation Act 1973 ".

1967 c. 9

The General Rate Act 1967

108. In section 45 of the General Rate Act 1967 (which provides for relief from rates in respect of facilities for disabled persons), for the words " local health authority " in paragraph (*b*) there shall be substituted the words " local social services authority ".

1967 c. 13.

The Parliamentary Commissioner Act 1967

109. In Schedule 3 to the Parliamentary Commissioner Act 1967 (which specifies matters which are not subject to investigation by the Commissioner under that Act), in paragraph 8 for the words " Regional Hospital Board, Board of Governors of a Teaching Hospital, Hospital Management Committee or Board of Management " there shall be substituted the words " Regional Health Authority, an Area Health Authority, a special health authority, a Family Practitioner Committee, a Health Board or the Common Services Agency for the Scottish Health Service ".

The Superannuation (Miscellaneous Provisions) Act 1967

110. In subsection (1) of section 7 of the Superannuation (Miscellaneous Provisions) Act 1967 (which provides for an extension of superannuation provisions of the National Health Service Acts), in paragraph (*a*) for the words " Act 1946 " there shall be substituted the words " Acts 1946 to 1973 " and in paragraph (*b*) for the words " Act of 1946 " there shall be substituted the words " Acts of 1946 to 1973 ".

The Leasehold Reform Act 1967

111.—(1) In subsection (5) of section 28 of the Leasehold Reform 1967 c. 88.
Act 1967 (which includes Regional Hospital Boards, Hospital
Management Committees and Boards of Governors as bodies to
which the provisions of that section relating to the retention and
resumption of land required for public purposes apply), for paragraph (*d*) there shall be substituted the following paragraph—

> (*d*) to any Regional Health Authority, any Area Health
> Authority and any special health authority ; and.

(2) In subsection (6) of that section (which in the case of a Regional
Hospital Board, Hospital Management Committee or Board of
Governors substitutes the purposes of the National Health Service
Act 1946 for the purposes of any body in the definition of the
expression " relevant development "), for paragraph (*c*) there shall be
substituted the following paragraph—

> (*c*) in the case of a Regional Health Authority, Area Health
> Authority or special health authority, the purposes of the
> National Health Service Acts 1946 to 1973 shall be substi-
> tuted for the purposes of the body.

The Health Services and Public Health Act 1968   **1968 c. 46.**

112.—(1) In sections 1(1) and 2(1) of the Health Services and Public
Health Act 1968 (which relate to the treatment of resident and non-
resident private patients at hospitals providing hospital and specialist
services), for the words " providing hospital and specialist services "
there shall be substituted the words " or group of hospitals vested in
him or of the hospitals vested in him in a particular area " and after
the words " the hospital " there shall be inserted the words " or
hospitals in question ".

(2) In section 1(2) and (3) of that Act, for the words " providing
hospital and specialist services " there shall be substituted the words
" vested in the Secretary of State ".

113. In section 17(1) of that Act (which provides that " supplementary ophthalmic services " shall be referred to as " general ophthalmic
services "), for the words " Executive Councils " there shall be substituted the words " Area Health Authorities ".

114. In section 28(2) of that Act (under which regulations may
make provision generally with respect to audit under section 55(2)
of the principal Act), for the words " the said subsection (2) " there
shall be substituted the words " section 55(2) of the 1946 Act ".

115. In section 29(1) of that Act (which provides for the control of
the making of payments by or on behalf of Regional Hospital Boards
and certain other existing health authorities), for the words from
" Regional " to " 1946 Act " there shall be substituted the words
" Regional Health Authorities, Area Health Authorities, special
health authorities, Family Practitioner Committees, Community
Health Councils ".

116. In section 30(1) of that Act (which provides for the grant of certificates of exemption from prescription charges), for the words from " as part of " to " Part II " there shall be substituted the words " under the National Health Service Acts 1946 to 1973 otherwise than under Part IV ".

117. In section 31 of that Act (under which the Secretary of State may allow persons to use, on terms which may include the payment of charges, any services provided in connection with hospital and specialist services and may for that purpose provide extended services), for the words from " any services the provision " to " services if " there shall be substituted the words " any services provided by virtue of the National Health Service Acts 1946 to 1973 and may provide the services in question to an extent greater than that necessary apart from this section if ".

118. In section 32 of that Act (under which the Secretary of State may sell or otherwise dispose of goods he produces in connection with the hospital and specialist services and may for that purpose produce goods in excess of those needed for those services), for the words " hospital and specialist services " there shall be substituted the words " services under the National Health Service Acts 1946 to 1973 " and for the words " the 1946 Act " in both places where they occur there shall be substituted the words " the National Health Service Acts 1946 to 1973 ".

119. In section 36(1) of that Act (which provides that the Secretary of State may pay allowances and remuneration to members of certain bodies), in paragraph (*b*) for the words " 1946 Act " there shall be substituted the words " National Health Service Acts 1946 to 1973 ".

120. In section 40(1) of that Act (which provides that the Secretary of State may make arrangements for the accommodation of persons displaced in the course of development for purposes of the Acts relating to the national health service or to mental health), after the words " Mental Health Act 1959 " there shall be inserted the words " or the National Health Service Reorganisation Act 1973 ".

121. At the end of section 45(4)(*b*) of that Act (which prohibits a local authority when making arrangements for the welfare of old people from making available accommodation or services required to be provided under the National Health Service Act 1946), after the words " this Act " there shall be added the words " or the National Health Service Reorganisation Act 1973 ".

122.—(1) In section 48 of that Act (which provides for the reporting of cases of notifiable diseases and food poisoning to local authorities), for subsection (2) there shall be substituted the following subsection—

(2) The officer who receives the certificate aforesaid shall, on the day of its receipt (if possible) and in any case within forty-eight hours after its receipt, send a copy of the certificate—

(*a*) to the Area Health Authority within whose area are situate the premises whose address is specified in the certificate by virtue of paragraph (*a*) of the foregoing subsection ; and

   (*b*) if the certificate is given with respect to a patient in a
       hospital who came there from premises outside the
       district of the local authority within whose district the
       hospital is situate and the certificate states that the
       patient did not contract the disease or the poisoning in
       the hospital—

       (i) to the proper officer for the district within
   which the premises from which the patient came are
   situate, and

       (ii) to the Area Health Authority for the area in
   which those premises are situate if that Authority is
   not responsible for the administration of the hospital,
   and

       (iii) to the proper officer of the relevant port health
   authority constituted in pursuance of section 2 of the
   Public Health Act 1936 if those premises were a ship
   or hovercraft situate within the port health district
   for which that authority is constituted.

(2) Subsection (3) of that section shall be omitted.

123. In section 62(1) of that Act (which provides for references
to vessels in the Public Health Act 1936 and references to ships
in the Food and Drugs Act 1955 to include references to hover
vehicles), for the words from " hover vehicles " to " air " there
shall be substituted the words " hovercraft within the meaning
of the Hovercraft Act 1968 ".

124.—(1) In section 63 of that Act (which provides for the instruction of officers of hospital authorities and other persons employed
in activities connected with health welfare), in subsection (1)(*a*)
for the words from " Regional " to " teaching hospital " there shall
be substituted the words " Regional Health Authority, Area Health
Authority or a special health authority ".

(2) In subsection (1)(*b*) of that section for the words from " specified " to " Treasury " there shall be substituted the words " determined by him ".

(3) In subsection (2)(*a*) of that section for the words " county,
county borough " there shall be substituted the words " non-metropolitan county, metropolitan district ".

(4) In subsection (2)(*b*) of that section for the words " Executive
Council " there shall be substituted the words " Area Health
Authority ".

(5) In subsection (8) of that section at the end of the definition
of " the relevant enactments " there shall be inserted the words
" and the National Health Service Reorganisation Act 1973 ".

125.—(1) In section 64 of that Act (which provides that the
Secretary of State may give financial assistance to voluntary organisations), at the end of subsection (3)(*a*) there shall be inserted the
words " the National Health Service Reorganisation Act 1973 ".

SCH. 4   (2) In subsection (3)(*b*) of that section for the words " county, county borough " there shall be substituted the words " non-metropolitan county, metropolitan district " and for the words " Executive Council " there shall be substituted the words " Area Health Authority ".

126. In section 65 of that Act (which provides that local authorities may give financial and other assistance to certain voluntary organisations), at the end of subsection (3)(*b*) there shall be inserted the words " the National Health Service Reorganisation Act 1973 ".

127. In section 70(1) of that Act (which provides that a copy of a notice given by a keeper of a common lodging house under section 242 of the Public Health Act 1936 shall be sent by the local authority to the local health authority), for the words from the beginning to " receives " there shall be substituted the words " The local authority within whose district a common lodging house is situate shall, on the day on which they receive " and for the words " local health authority " in the second place where they occur there shall be substituted the words " Area Health Authority ".

1968 c. 67.   *The Medicines Act* 1968

128.—(1) In section 55(2)(*b*) of the Medicines Act 1968 (which provides that the restrictions imposed by that Act on the supply of a medicinal product do not apply where the product is delivered or administered by a midwife and supplied in pursuance of arrangements made by a local health authority), for the words from " a local health authority " onwards there shall be substituted the words " the Secretary of State or the Ministry of Health and Social Services for Northern Ireland.".

(2) In section 131(5) of that Act (which provides that for the purposes of that section the provision of services by the Secretary of State under the principal Act shall be treated as the carrying on of a business by the Secretary of State), for the words " Act 1946 " there shall be substituted the words " Acts 1946 to 1973 " and for the words " Health Services Acts (Northern Ireland) 1948 to 1967 " there shall be substituted the words " Health and Personal Social Services (Northern Ireland) Order 1972 ".

(3) In section 132(1) of that Act (interpretation), in the definition of " health centre " for the words " section 21 of the National Health Service Act 1946 " there shall be substituted the words " section 2 of the National Health Service Reorganisation Act 1973 " and for the words " section 17 of the Health Services Act (Northern Ireland) 1948 " there shall be substituted the words " Article 5 of the Health and Personal Social Services (Northern Ireland) Order 1972."

The Nurses Act 1969

129. In section 6 of the Nurses Act 1969 (which provides that 1969 c. 47. allowances may be paid to members of an area nurse-training committee or (in Scotland) a regional nurse-training committee), the words from the beginning to " (in Scotland) " shall be omitted.

The Post Office Act 1969

1969 c. 48.

130. In section 86(1) of the Post Office Act 1969 (interpretation), in paragraph (a) of the definition of "national health service authority" for the words from "regional" onwards there shall be substituted the words "Regional Health Authority, Area Health Authority, special health authority or Family Practitioner Committee ; " and in paragraph (c) of that definition for the words from "means" onwards there shall be substituted the words "means a Health and Social Services Board, the Northern Ireland Central Services Agency for the Health and Social Services or the Northern Ireland Staffs Council for the Health and Social Services established under the Health and Personal Social Services (Northern Ireland) Order 1972.".

The Local Authority Social Services Act 1970

1970 c. 42.

131.—(1) In Schedule 1 to the Local Authority Social Services Act 1970 (which specifies the enactments conferring functions assigned to the social services committee of a local authority), at the end of the entry relating to the Health Visiting and Social Work (Training) Act 1962 there shall be inserted the following—

Section 5(1)(c)	Research into matters relating to functions of local authorities.

(2) In that Schedule, at the end of the entry relating to the Health Services and Public Health Act 1968 there shall be inserted the following—

Section 65	Financial and other assistance to voluntary organisations.

The Chronically Sick and Disabled Persons Act 1970

1970 c. 44.

132.—(1) In section 17(1) of the Chronically Sick and Disabled Persons Act 1970 (which provides that Regional Hospital Boards and Boards of Governors shall secure, so far as practicable, that younger patients are separated from older patients), for the words "Every board" to "teaching hospital)" there shall be substituted the words "The Secretary of State".

(2) For subsection (2) of that section (which provides that the Boards shall provide the Secretary of State with information as to

SCH. 4   persons to whom subsection (1) applies and that he shall lay before Parliament a statement of that information), there shall be substituted the following subsection—

> (2) The Secretary of State shall in each year lay before each House of Parliament a statement, in such form as he considers appropriate, of information as to any persons to whom subsection (1) of this section applied who, not being elderly persons, have during the preceding year been cared for in a hospital vested in him and in such part of the hospital as is mentioned in that subsection.

1971 c. 56.

The Pensions (Increase) Act 1971

133. At the end of paragraph 22 of Schedule 2 to the Pensions (Increase) Act 1971 (by virtue of which certain pensions payable by the Secretary of State under enactments relating to the health service are official pensions for the purposes of that Act) there shall be inserted the following sub-paragraph—

> (d) section 44 of the National Health Service Reorganisation Act 1973 or section 34A of the National Health Service (Scotland) Act 1972.

1971 c. 62.

The Tribunals and Inquiries Act 1971

134. In Part I of Schedule 1 to the Tribunals and Inquiries Act 1971 (which among other things provides that Executive Councils and service committees of Executive Councils are tribunals under the direct supervision of the Council on Tribunals), for paragraph 17(a) there shall be substituted the following—

> 17. (a) Family Practitioner Committees established in pursuance of section 5 of the National Health Service Reorganisation Act 1973 ;

and in paragraph 17(c) for the words " an Executive Council " there shall be substituted the words " a Family Practitioner Committee " and for the words " Act 1946 (c. 81) " there shall be substituted the words " Acts 1946 to 1973 ".

1971 c. 72.

The Industrial Relations Act 1971

135.—(1) In section 167 of the Industrial Relations Act 1971 (interpretation), in subsection (2)(a) for the words " Executive Council " there shall be substituted the words " Area Health Authority or Family Practitioner Committee " and after the words " 1946 or " there shall be inserted the words " by a Health Board ".

(2) In subsection (2)(b) of that section for the words " Executive Council " there shall be substituted the words " Area Health Authority, Family Practitioner Committee or Health Board ".

1972 c. 20.

The Road Traffic Act 1972

136.—(1) In section 156 of the Road Traffic Act 1972 (which provides that payment for hospital treatment of a traffic casualty shall be made to a Regional Hospital Board or a Board of Governors of a teaching hospital), in subsection (1)(a) for the words from

"National Health Service Act 1946" onwards there shall be sub-   Sch. 4
stituted the words "National Health Service Acts 1946 to 1973, to
the Area Health Authority or special health authority responsible
for the administration of the hospital or to the Secretary of State if
no such authority is so responsible ".

(2) Paragraphs (*b*) and (*c*) of subsection (1) of that section shall
be omitted.

(3) In subsections (2)(*a*) and (3) of that section for the word
" Board " there shall be substituted the word " Authority ".

The Employment Medical Advisory Service Act 1972   1972 c. 28.

137. In section 1(6) of the Employment Medical Advisory Service
Act 1972 (which imposes on every local education authority the duty
of arranging for one of its officers who is a medical practitioner to
furnish to an employment medical adviser such particulars of the
school medical report and other medical history of a person who is
under eighteen as the adviser requires for the efficient performance of
his functions), for the words from " every " to " officers " there shall
be substituted the words " the Secretary of State to secure that each
Area Health Authority arranges for one of its officers ".

The National Health Service (Scotland) Act 1972   1972 c. 58.

138. In section 22 of the National Health Service (Scotland) Act
1972 (supply of goods and services to local authorities, etc.), after
subsection (2) there shall be added the following subsection—

> (3) The Secretary of State may by order provide that, in
> relation to a vehicle which is made available by him in
> pursuance of this section and is used in accordance with the
> terms on which it is so available, the Vehicles (Excise) Act
> 1971 and Part VI of the Road Traffic Act 1972 shall have effect
> with such modifications as are specified in the order.

139. In section 23 of that Act (assistance to voluntary organisations), after subsection (1) there shall be added the following
subsection—

> (1A) The Secretary of State may by order provide that, in
> relation to a vehicle which is made available by him in
> pursuance of this section and is used in accordance with the
> terms on which it is so available, the Vehicles (Excise) Act
> 1971 and Part VI of the Road Traffic Act 1972 shall have effect
> with such modifications as are specified in the order.

140. In section 34(2) of that Act (transfer of other staff), after
paragraph (*f*) there shall be inserted the following paragraph—

> (*g*) an education authority wholly or mainly as a speech
> therapist for the purposes of providing special education
> in pursuance of sections 1 and 3A of the Education
> (Scotland) Act 1962.

141. After section 34 of that Act there shall be inserted the following section—

Provision for early retirement in lieu of compensation for loss of office.

34A.—(1) In order to facilitate the early retirement of certain persons who might otherwise suffer, in consequence of this Act, loss of employment or loss or diminution of emoluments, any person who—

  (a) is in any such employment as may be prescribed for the purposes of this subsection ; and

  (b) attains or has attained the age of fifty on or before a prescribed date ; and

  (c) fulfils such other conditions as may be prescribed ;

may by notice given before a prescribed date and in the prescribed manner elect that this section shall apply to him.

(2) Where any person has made an election under the preceding subsection, then, unless within a prescribed period notice of objection to the election is given to him by a prescribed person, this section shall apply to him on his retirement within a prescribed period and before attaining the normal retiring age and compensation on his retirement shall not be payable to or in respect of him in pursuance of section 24 of the Superannuation Act 1972 (which among other things relates to compensation for loss of office).

(3) Subject to the following subsection, the Secretary of State shall by regulations provide for the payment by him to or in respect of a person to whom this section applies of benefits corresponding, as near as may be, to those which would have been paid to or in respect of that person under the relevant superannuation scheme if—

  (a) at the date of his retirement he had attained the normal retiring age ; and

  (b) the actual period of his reckonable service were increased by such period as may be prescribed, not exceeding the period beginning on the date of his retirement and ending on the date on which he would attain the normal retiring age.

(4) Regulations in pursuance of the preceding subsection shall be so framed as to secure that the sums which would otherwise be payable under the regulations in accordance with that subsection to or in respect of any person are reduced to take account of any benefits payable to or in respect of him under the relevant superannuation scheme.

(5) Any sums payable under regulations made in pursuance of subsection (3) of this section shall be treated for the purposes of section 73 of the Finance Act 1972 (under

which compensation for loss of office or employment is chargeable to tax as a payment made on retirement or removal from office or employment) in like manner as compensation paid in pursuance of the said section 24.

(6) In this section—

"normal retiring age" means—

 (a) in relation to any person to whom an age of compulsory retirement applies by virtue of the relevant superannuation scheme, that age ; and

 (b) in relation to any other person, the age of sixty-five in the case of a man and sixty in the case of a woman or, in either case, such other age as may be prescribed ;

"reckonable service", in relation to any person, means service in respect of which benefits are payable under the relevant superannuation scheme ; and

"relevant superannuation scheme", in relation to any person, means the instrument which is applicable in the case of his employment and which makes provision with respect to the pensions, allowances or gratuities which, subject to the fulfilment of certain requirements and conditions, are to be, or may be, paid to or in respect of persons in that employment.

142. In section 43(2) of that Act (which provides that, subject to the provisions of that section, Schedule 1 to the Parliamentary Commissioner Act 1967 shall apply to persons who have held office as Health Service Commissioner for Scotland), after the word "section" there shall be inserted the words "and subsection (4) to (6) of section 32 of the National Health Service Reorganisation Act 1973".

143. For subsection (2) of section 44 of that Act (administrative provisions), there shall be substituted the following subsection—

(2) Any function of the Commissioner under this Part of this Act may be performed by any officer of the Commissioner authorised for that purpose by him or by any officer so authorised of another Commissioner mentioned in subsection (4) of section 32 of the National Health Service Reorganisation Act 1973.

144. For subsection (2) of section 45 of that Act (bodies and action subject to investigation), there shall be substituted the following subsection—

(2) Subject to the provisions of this section, the Commissioner may investigate—

 (a) an alleged failure in a service provided by a body subject to investigation ; or

 (b) an alleged failure of a body subject to investigation to provide a service which it was a function of the body to provide ; or

(c) any other action taken by or on behalf of a body subject to investigation,

in a case where a complaint is duly made by or on behalf of any person that he has sustained injustice or hardship in consequence of the failure or in consequence of maladministration connected with the other action.

In this subsection, " function " includes a power and a duty.

145.—(1) In section 46(2) of that Act (provisions relating to complaints), for the word " other " there shall be substituted the words " by some body or ".

(2) In subsection (4) of that section at the end there shall be inserted the words " ; but the Commissioner may disregard the preceding provisions of this subsection in relation to a complaint made by an officer of the body subject to investigation on behalf of the person aggrieved if the officer is authorised by virtue of subsection (2) of this section to make the complaint and the Commissioner is satisfied that in the particular circumstances those provisions ought to be disregarded."

146. In section 47 of that Act (application of certain provisions of the Parliamentary Commissioner Act 1967), the words " except subsection (4) ", where they first occur, shall be omitted ; and at the end there shall be added the words " In sections 7(1) and 8(1) of the said Act of 1967 as applied by this section, the words ' the principal officer of ' and ' Minister ' shall be omitted.".

147. For section 65(3) of that Act (extent), there shall be substituted the following subsection—

(3) The following provisions of this Act shall extend to England and Wales, namely, this subsection, sections 42(4), 47, 48(5), 50(1), paragraphs 104, 128, 130, 143 to 145 and 152 of Schedule 6, Schedule 7 so far as it relates to paragraphs 3 and 5 of Schedule 3 to the Redundancy Payments Act 1965 and subsection (1) of this section so far as it relates to the other provisions mentioned in this subsection.

148. After section 65(3) of that Act there shall be inserted the following subsection—

(4) The following provisions of this Act shall extend to Northern Ireland, namely, this subsection, sections 42(4), 47, 48(5), 50(1), paragraphs 104, 128, 130, 143 to 145 and 152 of Schedule 6 and subsection (1) of this section so far as it relates to the other provisions mentioned in this subsection.

149. In Schedule 6 to that Act (minor and consequential amendments to enactments), after paragraph 20 there shall be inserted the following paragraph—

20A. In section 18(5) (application to Scotland of provisions in respect of superannuation of officers of certain hospitals), at the end there shall be added the words " , for the reference to Regional Hospital Boards or Area Health Authorities of a reference to Health Boards, and for the reference to services under the National Health Service Acts 1946 to 1973 of a

reference to services under the National Health Service   Sᴄʜ. 4
(Scotland) Acts 1947 to 1973 ".

150. In Schedule 6 to that Act (minor and consequential amendments to enactments), after paragraph 156 there shall be inserted the
following paragraph—

The Road Traffic Act 1972

156A.—(1) In section 156(1)(c) of the Road Traffic Act 1972
(which provides that payment for hospital treatment of a traffic
casualty will be made payable to the Secretary of State or to a
Regional Hospital Board or Board of Management), for the
words from " Regional " to " Management " there shall be
substituted the words " Health Board ".

Local Government Act 1972   1972 c. 70.

151.—(1) At the end of section 113(1) of the Local Government
Act 1972 (which gives power to a local authority to place officers at
the disposal of another local authority) there shall be inserted the
following subsection—

(1A) Without prejudice to any powers exercisable apart from
this section, a local authority may enter into an agreement with
a Regional Health Authority, Area Health Authority or special
health authority—

   (a) for the placing at the disposal of the Regional or Area
       Health Authority or special health authority for the
       purposes of their functions, on such terms as may be
       provided by the agreement, of the services of officers
       employed by the local authority ;

   (b) for the placing at the disposal of the local authority
       for the purposes of their functions, on such terms as
       may be provided by the agreement, of the services
       of officers employed by the Regional or Area Health
       Authority or the special health authority ;

but a local authority shall not enter into an agreement in pursuance of paragraph (a) of this subsection in respect of any officer
without consulting him.

(2) After section 113(2) of that Act there shall be inserted the
following subsection—

(3) An officer whose services are placed at the disposal of
a local authority in pursuance of subsection (1A) of this section
shall be treated as an officer of the authority for the purposes
of any enactment relating to the discharge of local authorities'
functions.

152. In section 261(7) of that Act (which relates to the remuneration which officers of local authorities are to be deemed to be
receiving for the purposes of the provisions of that Act relating to the
transfer of officers and compensation for loss of office), after the
words " loss of office " there shall be inserted the words " or for
the purposes of the provisions of the National Health Service
Reorganisation Act 1973 relating to the transfer of officers and the
provisions of section 24 of the Superannuation Act 1972 (which
among other things relate to compensation for loss of office) ".

SCHEDULE 5

REPEALS

Chapter	Short title	Extent of repeal
37 & 38 Vict. c. 88.	The Births and Deaths Registration Act 1874.	Section 28.
26 Geo. 5 and 1 Edw. 8. c. 49.	The Public Health Act 1936.	In section 143(3), the word " or " where it first occurs. Sections 189 to 191 and 194 to 196. In section 203, in subsection (2) the words " or residence " in both places where they occur and in subsection (6) the words " of health ".
7 & 8 Geo. 6. c. 31.	The Education Act 1944.	Sections 48(1), (2), (3) and (5). Section 69(1). In section 78, subsection (1) and in subsection (2) the words from " and may " to " school or establishment ". Section 79. In section 114(1), the definitions of " medical inspection " and " medical treatment ".
9 & 10 Geo. 6. c. 81.	The National Health Service Act 1946.	In section 2(3), the words from " after consultation with that Council " to " those services ". Sections 3(1) and 6 to 14 except section 6(4). Section 16(2). In section 18, the words " in cases of emergency " where they first occur. Sections 19 to 21. In section 22, in subsection (1) the words " including in particular dental care ", in subsection (2) the words " with the approval of the Minister " and subsection (3). Sections 24 to 27, 30 and 31. In section 33, in subsection (1) the words " whether at a health centre or otherwise ". In section 36(3)(c), the words from " and secure " to " occurs ". Section 37. In section 40(1), the words " whether at a health centre or otherwise ". In section 41(1), the words " whether at a health centre or otherwise " in both places where they occur.

Chapter	Short title	Extent of repeal
9 & 10 Geo. 6. c. 81—*cont.*	The National Health Service Act 1946—*cont.*	Section 46. In section 47, the words from " or between " to " health centre ". In section 52(2), the words " except sums required to be transferred to the Hospital Endowment Fund ". Sections 54(1) to (3) and 56. In section 58(3), the words " or a local health authority ". Sections 59(1) and 60. In section 61, the words " and in the making of appointments to the Hospital Management Committee ". Sections 62, 64, 66, 68, 69 and 73. In section 74(*c*), the words " local health authorities and ". In section 75, subsection (1) and in subsection (2) the words " except regulations made under section 68 " and the words from " and such of " to " constituted ". In section 76, the words from " and the enactments " to " that Part " and the words " and repeal ". Section 78. In section 79(1), the definition of " appointed day " and in the definition of " local authority " the words " county borough,". In Schedule 1, in paragraph 3 the words from " and the Central Council " onwards. Schedules 2 and 3. Part I of Schedule 4. Schedule 5. In Schedule 10, the entries relating to the Poor Law Act 1930, the Yarmouth Naval Hospital Act 1931, the Pharmacy and Poisons Act 1933 and the Public Health Act 1936 (except so much of the entry relating to section 244 of that Act as ends with the word " Minister ").
10 & 11 Geo. 6. c. 19.	The Polish Resettlement Act 1947.	In section 4, the words " , on or after the appointed day for the purposes of that Act,".

Chapter	Short title	Extent of repeal
10 & 11 Geo. 6. c. 27.	The National Health Service (Scotland) Act 1947.	In section 37(3)(c), the words from "and secure" to "occurs".
11 & 12 Geo. 6. c. 29.	The National Assistance Act 1948.	In section 21(7), the words from "In this subsection" onwards. Section 47(10). In Schedule 6, paragraph 6(3).
11 & 12 Geo. 6. c. 43.	The Children Act 1948.	In Schedule 3, the entry relating to the National Health Service Act 1946.
12, 13 & 14 Geo. 6. c. 93.	The National Health Service (Amendment) Act 1949.	Sections 3(1), 12, 20(2), 24 and 29(3). In Part I of the Schedule, the entries relating to sections 21, 31(4) and 46 of, and Schedule 3 to, the National Health Service Act 1946.
14 & 15 Geo. 6. c. 31.	The National Health Service Act 1951.	In section 3, the words "as part of the hospital and specialist services under Part II of the National Health Service Act 1946".
14 & 15 Geo. 6. c. 53.	The Midwives Act 1951.	In section 11, in subsection (1) the words from "on or after" to "therein", and subsections (2) and (5). In section 21, the words "local health authority or other". Sections 26, 27 and 33.
1 & 2 Eliz. 2. c. 33.	The Education (Miscellaneous Provisions) Act 1953.	Section 4. In Schedule 1, the entries relating to sections 78, 79 and 114(1) of the Education Act 1944.
5 & 6 Eliz. 2. c. 15.	The Nurses Act 1957.	In section 12(1), the words "situated in such hospital area". In section 33, in subsection (1) the definitions of "Board of Governors", "hospital area" and "teaching hospital", and subsection (2). In Schedule 2, paragraph 1(e) and paragraph 3.
5 & 6 Eliz. 2. c. 28.	The Dentists Act 1957.	In section 36(2)(a), the words "and local authority". In section 42, in subsections (1)(b), (2), (3) and (4) the words "and local authority". In section 43, in subsections (1)(b), (2) and (5) the words "and local authority". In section 50(2), the words "and local authority".

Chapter	Short title	Extent of repeal
5 & 6 Eliz. 2. c. 28—*cont.*	The Dentists Act 1957.	In Schedule 1, in paragraphs 13(3) and 14(3) the words " and local authority ".
5 & 6 Eliz. 2. c. 44.	The National Health Service (Amendment) Act 1957.	The whole Act.
6 & 7 Eliz. 2. c. 32.	The Opticians Act 1958.	In section 21(2)(*b*), the words " Part II or " in both places where they occur.
7 & 8 Eliz. 2. c 72.	The Mental Health Act 1959.	In section 14, in subsection (3) the words from " and the power " onwards, and subsections (4) and (5). Section 16(3). In section 17, in subsection (1) the words " or by the registration authority " and the words " in the area of the authority ", and subsection (5). In section 37(2)(*a*), the words " or board ". In section 56, subsection (2)(*d*). Sections 97 and 98. In section 133(2), the words " and specialist ". In section 135(6), the words " under Part III of the National Health Service Act, 1946, or ".
8 & 9 Eliz. 2. c. 34.	The Radioactive Substances Act 1960.	In section 14, in subsection (1) the words " or is a teaching hospital within the meaning of the National Health Service Act 1946 " and the words " , or (in the case of a teaching hospital) the Board of Governors,".
8 & 9 Eliz. 2. c. 67.	The Public Bodies (Admission to Meetings) Act 1960.	In the Schedule, paragraph 1(*g*).
10 & 11 Eliz. 2. c. 33.	The Health Visiting and Social Work (Training) Act 1962.	In Schedule 1, paragraph 3(*d*), (*e*), (*g*) and (*h*).
1963 c. 13.	The Nursing Homes Act 1963.	In section 1(1), in paragraph (*b*) the word " local " and in paragraph (*c*) the word " and ", and paragraph (*d*). In section 1(2), the words from " in the case of a first offence " to " subsequent offence ".
1963 c. 33.	The London Government Act 1963.	Section 32(1) to (6). In section 45, subsection (3), and in subsection (6) the words from " and in section 20(2)(*c*) " onwards.

Chapter	Short title	Extent of repeal
1964 c. 32.	The National Health Service (Hospital Boards) Act 1964.	The whole Act.
1965 c. 62.	The Redundancy Payments Act 1965.	In Schedule 3, paragraphs 2 and 6, and in paragraph 7 the words " section 31(4) of the said Act of 1946 or ".
1966 c. 20.	The Ministry of Social Security Act 1966.	In section 4(1), the words " 6 or ". In section 6, in subsection (1) the words from " include any requirement " to " but " and the word " other ", and subsection (2). Section 8(4).
1967 c. 28.	The Superannuation (Miscellaneous Provisions) Act 1967.	In section 7, in subsection (1)(*a*) the words " local health authority or other ".
1967 c. 39.	The National Health Service (Family Planning) Act 1967.	The whole Act.
1967 c. 80.	The Criminal Justice Act 1967.	In Part I of Schedule 3, the entries relating to section 48(2) of the Education Act 1944 and the Nursing Homes Act 1963.
1968 c. 14.	The Public Expenditure and Receipts Act 1968.	In Schedule 3, the entry relating to section 28 of the Births and Deaths Registration Act 1874.
1968 c. 46.	The Health Services and Public Health Act 1968.	In section 1, in subsection (3) the words " hospital and specialist " in the second place where they occur in that subsection as originally enacted. Section 3(3). Sections 5 to 8, 9(1), 10, 11 and 16. In section 18, subsections (1) and (3). Sections 21 to 24 and 27(1). In section 28(1), the words from the beginning to " Hospital Board and ". Section 34. In section 36(1)(*a*), paragraphs (ii) and (iii) except the words " the Dental Estimates Board ". In section 39(1), the words " supplied as part of the hospital and specialist services ". In section 48, subsection (3). In section 57, the definition of " local health authority ".

Chapter	Short title	Extent of repeal
1968 c. 46— *cont.*	The Health Services and Public Health Act 1968 —*cont.*	In section 63, subsections (4) and (7) and in subsection (8) the words from " Board of Governors " to " 1946 " where it first occurs and the words from " section 4 " to " 1967 ". In section 64(3)(*a*), the words " the National Health Service (Family Planning) Act 1967 ". In section 65, in subsection (2) the words from " and the Greater London Council " onwards and in subsection (3)(*b*) the words "the National Health Service (Family Planning) Act 1967 ". Sections 67 and 69. In section 70(2), the words from " and ' local health authority ' " onwards. Schedule 1. In Schedule 3, in Part I the entry relating to the Midwives Act 1936, in the entry relating to the National Assistance Act 1948 the words from "In section 21(7)" to the words "under Part I of this Act" where they first occur, the entry relating to the Midwives Act 1951, and in the entry relating to the London Government Act 1963 the word " 10 "; and in Part II, paragraph (*b*).
1969 c. 47.	The Nurses Act 1969.	In section 6, the words from the beginning to " (in Scotland) ".
1970 c. 42.	The Local Authority Social Services Act 1970.	In section 2, subsections (3), (4), (5) and (6). In section 3, subsection (2). In Schedule 1, the entries relating to sections 29 and 20 of the National Health Service Act 1946 and, in the entry relating to the Mental Health Act 1959, paragraphs (*b*), (*c*) and (*d*).
1970 c. 44.	The Chronically Sick and Disabled Persons Act 1970.	Section 19.
1972 c. 11.	The Superannuation Act 1972.	In section 10(1)(*a*), the words " local health authority or other ".

Chapter	Short title	Extent of repeal
1972 c. 20.	The Road Traffic Act 1972.	In section 156, subsection (1)(*b*) and (*c*).
1972 c. 58.	The National Health Service (Scotland) Act 1972.	In section 43, subsection (4). In section 47, the words "except subsection (4)" where they first occur. In Schedule 6, paragraphs 7, 98 to 100, in paragraph 130 the words from "for paragraph 1" to "and", and paragraphs 103, 131, 133, 142 and 153. In Schedule 7, the entries relating to the Dentists Act 1957 and the Opticians Act 1958.
1972 c. 70.	The Local Government Act 1972.	In Schedule 14, paragraphs 17 and 48.
1972 c. 72.	The National Health Service (Family Planning) Amendment Act 1972.	The whole Act.

Order in Council

S.I. 1972 No. 1265.	The Health and Personal Social Services (Northern Ireland) Order 1972.	In Schedule 16, paragraphs 18, 20, 23, 78, 79 and 80.

Protection of Wrecks
Act 1973

1973 CHAPTER 33

An Act to secure the protection of wrecks in territorial
waters and the sites of such wrecks, from interference by
unauthorised persons; and for connected purposes.

[18th July 1973]

B E IT ENACTED by the Queen's most Excellent Majesty, by and
with the advice and consent of the Lords Spiritual and
Temporal, and Commons, in this present Parliament
assembled, and by the authority of the same, as follows:—

1.—(1) If the Secretary of State is satisfied with respect to any Protection of
site in United Kingdom waters that— sites of
historic
(a) it is, or may prove to be, the site of a vessel lying wrecked wrecks.
on or in the sea bed; and

(b) on account of the historical, archaeological or artistic
importance of the vessel, or of any objects contained or
formerly contained in it which may be lying on the sea
bed in or near the wreck, the site ought to be protected
from unauthorised interference,

he may by order designate an area round the site as a restricted
area.

(2) An order under this section shall identify the site where the
vessel lies or formerly lay, or is supposed to lie or have lain, and—

(a) the restricted area shall be all within such distance of
the site (so identified) as is specified in the order, but
excluding any area above high water mark of ordinary
spring tides; and

(b) the distance specified for the purposes of paragraph (a)
above shall be whatever the Secretary of State thinks
appropriate to ensure protection for the wreck.

(3) Subject to section 3(3) below, a person commits an offence if, in a restricted area, he does any of the following things otherwise than under the authority of a licence granted by the Secretary of State—

   (*a*) he tampers with, damages or removes any part of a vessel lying wrecked on or in the sea bed, or any object formerly contained in such a vessel; or

   (*b*) he carries out diving or salvage operations directed to the exploration of any wreck or to removing objects from it or from the sea bed, or uses equipment constructed or adapted for any purpose of diving or salvage operations; or

   (*c*) he deposits, so as to fall and lie abandoned on the sea bed, anything which, if it were to fall on the site of a wreck (whether it so falls or not), would wholly or partly obliterate the site or obstruct access to it, or damage any part of the wreck;

and also commits an offence if he causes or permits any of those things to be done by others in a restricted area, otherwise than under the authority of such a licence.

(4) Before making an order under this section, the Secretary of State shall consult with such persons as he considers appropriate having regard to the purposes of the order; but this consultation may be dispensed with if he is satisfied that the case is one in which an order should be made as a matter of immediate urgency.

(5) A licence granted by the Secretary of State for the purposes of subsection (3) above shall be in writing and—

   (*a*) the Secretary of State shall in respect of a restricted area grant licences only to persons who appear to him either—

      (i) to be competent, and properly equipped, to carry out salvage operations in a manner appropriate to the historical, archaeological or artistic importance of any wreck which may be lying in the area and of any objects contained or formerly contained in a wreck, or

      (ii) to have any other legitimate reason for doing in the area that which can only be done under the authority of a licence;

   (*b*) a licence may be granted subject to conditions or restrictions, and may be varied or revoked by the Secretary of State at any time after giving not less than one week's notice to the licensee; and

   (*c*) anything done contrary to any condition or restriction of a licence shall be treated for purposes of subsection (3) above as done otherwise than under the authority of the licence.

(6) Where a person is authorised, by a licence of the Secretary of State granted under this section, to carry out diving or salvage operations, it is an offence for any other person to obstruct him, or cause or permit him to be obstructed, in doing anything which is authorised by the licence, subject however to section 3(3) below.

2.—(1) If the Secretary of State is satisfied with respect to a vessel lying wrecked in United Kingdom waters that— *Prohibition on approaching dangerous wrecks.*

    (*a*) because of anything contained in it, the vessel is in a condition which makes it a potential danger to life or property; and

    (*b*) on that account it ought to be protected from unauthorised interference,

he may by order designate an area round the vessel as a prohibited area.

(2) An order under this section shall identify the vessel and the place where it is lying and—

    (*a*) the prohibited area shall be all within such distance of the vessel as is specified by the order, excluding any area above high water mark of ordinary spring tides; and

    (*b*) the distance specified for the purposes of paragraph (*a*) above shall be whatever the Secretary of State thinks appropriate to ensure that unauthorised persons are kept away from the vessel.

(3) Subject to section 3(3) below, a person commits an offence if, without authority in writing granted by the Secretary of State, he enters a prohibited area, whether on the surface or under water.

3.—(1) In this Act— *Supplementary provisions.*

    " United Kingdom waters " means any part of the sea within the seaward limits of United Kingdom territorial waters and includes any part of a river within the ebb and flow of ordinary spring tides;

    " the sea " includes any estuary or arm of the sea; and

    references to the sea bed include any area submerged at high water of ordinary spring tides.

(2) An order under section 1 or section 2 above shall be made by statutory instrument subject to annulment in pursuance of a resolution of either House of Parliament and may be varied or revoked by a subsequent order under the section; and the Secretary of State shall revoke any such order if—

    (*a*) in the case of an order under section 1 designating a restricted area, he is of opinion that there is not, or is no longer, any wreck in the area which requires protection under this Act;

S 2

(*b*) in the case of an order under section 2 designating a prohibited area, he is satisfied that the vessel is no longer in a condition which makes it a potential danger to life or property.

(3) Nothing is to be regarded as constituting an offence under this Act where it is done by a person—

(*a*) in the course of any action taken by him for the sole purpose of dealing with an emergency of any description; or

(*b*) in exercising, or seeing to the exercise of, functions conferred by or under an enactment (local or other) on him or a body for which he acts; or

(*c*) out of necessity due to stress of weather or navigational hazards.

(4) A person guilty of an offence under section 1 or section 2 above shall be liable on summary conviction to a fine of not more than £400, or on conviction on indictment to a fine; and proceedings for such an offence may be taken, and the offence may for all incidental purposes be treated as having been committed, at any place in the United Kingdom where he is for the time being.

Citation.   **4.** This Act may be cited as the Protection of Wrecks Act 1973.

Ulster Defence Regiment Act 1973

1973 CHAPTER 34

An Act to enable women to serve in the Ulster Defence Regiment, and for connected purposes.

[18th July 1973]

BE IT ENACTED by the Queen's most Excellent Majesty, by and with the advice and consent of the Lords Spiritual and Temporal, and Commons, in this present Parliament assembled, and by the authority of the same, as follows:—

1.—(1) Women may volunteer and be accepted for service in the Ulster Defence Regiment, and accordingly in section 1(1) of the Ulster Defence Regiment Act 1969 (establishment of the Regiment) for the word " men " there shall be substituted the word " persons ". *Service of women in Ulster Defence Regiment. 1969 c. 65.*

(2) Section 1(6) of that Act (which excludes section 3(1) of the Army and Air Force (Women's Service) Act 1948 in the case of the Ulster Defence Regiment) shall cease to have effect. *1948 c. 21.*

(3) In section 16 of the Disabled Persons (Employment) Act (Northern Ireland) 1945, as amended by section 4 of the Disabled Persons (Employment) Act (Northern Ireland) 1960 (preference for ex-service men and women in selection for training and rehabilitation courses), in paragraph (*b*), after the words " 1948 " there shall be inserted the words " or in the Ulster Defence Regiment ". *1965 c. 6 (N.I.) 1960 c. 4 (N.I.)*

(4) Any increase in the expenditure of any government department under the Ulster Defence Regiment Act 1969 which is attributable to the provisions of this section shall be defrayed out of moneys provided by Parliament.

2. This Act may be cited as the Ulster Defence Regiment Act 1973. *Short title.*

S 3

Employment Agencies Act 1973

1973 CHAPTER 35

An Act to regulate employment agencies and businesses; and for connected purposes. [18th July 1973]

BE IT ENACTED by the Queen's most Excellent Majesty, by and with the advice and consent of the Lords Spiritual and Temporal, and Commons, in this present Parliament assembled, and by the authority of the same, as follows:—

Licences

Employment agencies and businesses to be licensed.

1.—(1) Subject to subsections (2) and (3) of this section, no person shall carry on an employment agency or an employment business at any premises after the date on which this section comes into force unless he is the holder of a current licence from the licensing authority authorising him to carry on such an agency or such a business at those premises.

(2) A person who has duly applied for a licence under this Act before the date mentioned in the foregoing subsection shall not be precluded by that subsection from carrying on an employment agency or an employment business after that date—

(a) until the commencement of the licence ; or

(b) if the application is refused, until the time for appealing against the refusal has expired and, if such an appeal is duly brought, until the time when it is disposed of.

(3) A person who, on the date mentioned in subsection (1) of this section, is carrying on an employment agency or an employment business under the authority of a licence granted under an enactment repealed by or under this Act may, so long as he complies with any conditions subject to which the licence

has been granted, continue to carry on that business under the authority of that licence until the licence expires.

(4) Any person who contravenes subsection (1) of this section shall be guilty of an offence and liable on summary conviction to a fine not exceeding £400.

2.—(1) (*a*) An applicant for a licence under this Act shall, not less than twenty-one days before making his application—

Grant of licences, etc.

> (i) display notice of the application in a place where it can conveniently be read by the public on or near the premises at which the employment agency or employment business is or is to be carried on and take such steps as he reasonably can to keep that notice so displayed for a period of twenty-one days; and

> (ii) advertise notice of the application in a news-paper approved by the licensing authority:

Provided that this paragraph shall not apply where the applicant is the holder of a current licence or a person who is carrying on an employment agency or an employment business under the authority of a licence granted under an enactment repealed by or under this Act and the carrying on of the employment agency or employment business at the premises in question is authorised by that licence.

(*b*) A notice under paragraph (*a*) of this subsection—

> (i) shall state the name and address of the applicant; and

> (ii) shall state the situation of the premises at which the employment agency or employment business is or is to be carried on and the class of business carried on or to be carried on at those premises.

(*c*) An application for a licence shall not be entertained by the licensing authority unless it is made in the prescribed manner and is accompanied—

> (i) by the prescribed particulars; and

> (ii) where paragraph (*a*) of this subsection applies, by a certificate, signed by or on behalf of the applicant, stating that he has complied with that paragraph and a copy of the newspaper containing notice of the application.

(2) **Subject** to the provisions of this section, the licensing authority shall, as soon as reasonably practicable after the receipt of an application for a licence and on payment of the prescribed fee, grant a licence to any person who duly applies for one.

(3) An application for a licence in respect of an employment agency or an employment business may be refused on any of the following grounds, that is to say—

  (a) that the applicant is an individual under the age of twenty-one years ;

  (b) that the applicant is a person who on account of misconduct or for any other sufficient reason is unsuitable to hold a licence in respect of an agency or business of the class in question ;

  (c) that any person (other than the applicant) who is or is to be concerned with the carrying on of the employment agency or employment business is a person who on account of misconduct or for any other sufficient reason is unsuitable to be associated with an agency or business of the class in question ;

  (d) that the premises at which the employment agency or employment business is or is to be carried on are unsuitable in respect of an agency or business of the class in question ;

  (e) that the employment agency or employment business has been or is being improperly conducted.

(4) The licensing authority shall, within seven days after making a decision on an application for a licence, give notice in writing of the decision to the applicant and such notice shall state, in the case of a decision to refuse a licence, the grounds for the refusal.

(5) Unless revoked under the subsequent provisions of this Act, a licence shall continue in force for one year (or such longer period, not exceeding five years, as the licensing authority may specify in any particular case) beginning with the date specified therein for its commencement:

Provided that where the holder of a licence in respect of any premises has duly applied before its expiry for a further licence in respect of those premises, the previous licence shall not expire until the commencement of the further licence or, if the application is refused, until the time for appealing against the refusal has expired and, if such an appeal is duly brought, until it is disposed of.

(6) Where the holder of a licence dies, it shall be deemed to have been transferred on his death, if he was the sole holder, to his personal representatives and, if he was a joint holder, to the surviving holder or holders.

(7) It shall be the duty of the holder of a licence under this Act, within one month of any change in the particulars accompanying the application for that licence under subsection (1) of this section, to give to the licensing authority

notice in writing of the change and any person who fails to comply with this subsection shall be guilty of an offence and liable on summary conviction to a fine not exceeding £100:

Provided that nothing in this subsection shall be taken as authorising the holder of a licence to carry on any business otherwise than in accordance with the provisions of the licence.

(8) Every licence granted under this Act shall be endorsed with notice of the effect of subsection (7) of this section.

3.—(1) A licence under this Act may be revoked by the licensing authority on any of the grounds specified in section 2(3) of this Act. Revocation of licences.

(2) The licensing authority shall not act under subsection (1) of this section unless they have given not less than one month's notice in writing to the holder of the licence of the grounds on which they propose to revoke the licence and, if the holder makes representations in writing to the licensing authority within one month of the date on which the notice is given or such longer period as the licensing authority may allow, the licensing authority shall have regard to those representations.

(3) On deciding to act under subsection (1) of this section the licensing authority shall give notice in writing of their decision to the holder of the licence stating the grounds for the revocation.

(4) The revocation of a licence by the licensing authority shall not take effect until the time for appealing against the decision of the licensing authority has expired and, if such an appeal is duly brought, until it is disposed of.

4.—(1) Any person who is aggrieved by a decision of the licensing authority— Appeals.

(a) refusing to grant him a licence ; or

(b) revoking a licence of which he is the holder,

may appeal in the prescribed manner giving the prescribed particulars, to the Secretary of State.

(2) An appeal under subsection (1) of this section against any decision shall be brought within twenty-one days of the date on which notice of the decision was given in accordance with the foregoing provisions of this Act.

(3) The Secretary of State may, in such cases as he considers it appropriate to do so, having regard to the nature of the questions which appear to him to arise, direct that an appeal under subsection (1) of this section shall be determined on his behalf by a person appointed by him for the purpose.

(4) Before the determination of an appeal the Secretary of State shall ask the appellant and the licensing authority whether they wish to appear and be heard on the appeal and—

>   (a) the appeal may be determined without a hearing of the parties if both of them express a wish not to appear and be heard as aforesaid ;

>   (b) the Secretary of State shall, if either of the parties expresses a wish to appear and be heard, afford to both of them an opportunity of so doing.

1971 c. 62. (5) The Tribunals and Inquiries Act 1971 shall apply to a hearing held by a person appointed in pursuance of subsection (3) of this section to determine an appeal as it applies to a statutory inquiry held by the Secretary of State, but as if in section 12(1) of that Act (statement of reasons for decisions) the reference to any decision taken by the Secretary of State included a reference to a decision taken on his behalf by that person.

(6) A person who determines an appeal under subsection (1) of this section on behalf of the Secretary of State and the Secretary of State, if he determines such an appeal, may give such directions as he considers appropriate to give effect to his determination.

Conduct of employment agencies and employment businesses

General regulations.
5.—(1) The Secretary of State may make regulations to secure the proper conduct of employment agencies and employment businesses and to protect the interests of persons availing themselves of the services of such agencies and businesses, and such regulations may in particular make provision—

>   (a) requiring persons carrying on such agencies and businesses to keep records ;

>   (b) prescribing the form of such records and the entries to be made in them ;

>   (c) prescribing qualifications appropriate for persons carrying on such agencies and businesses ;

>   (d) regulating advertising by persons carrying on such agencies and businesses ;

>   (e) safeguarding clients' money deposited with or otherwise received by persons carrying on such agencies and businesses ;

>   (f) regulating the provision of services by persons carrying on such agencies and businesses in respect of persons who seek employment outside the United Kingdom or of persons normally resident outside the United Kingdom who seek employment in the United Kingdom ;

(*g*) regulating the provision of services by persons carrying on such agencies and businesses in respect of persons who are under the age of eighteen years or are undergoing full-time education:

Provided that regulations under this section shall not make provision for regulating or restricting the charging of fees to employers by persons carrying on such agencies and businesses.

(2) Any person who contravenes or fails to comply with any regulation made under this section shall be guilty of an offence and liable on summary conviction to a fine not exceeding £400.

6.—(1) Except in such cases or classes of case as the Secretary of State may prescribe, a person carrying on an employment agency or an employment business shall not demand or directly or indirectly receive from any person any fee for finding him employment or for seeking to find him employment.

Restriction on charging persons seeking employment, etc.

(2) Any person who contravenes this section shall be guilty of an offence and liable on summary conviction to a fine not exceeding £400.

7.—(1) The holder of a licence under this Act in respect of any employment agency or employment business shall keep displayed on the premises to which the licence relates in such a position that it can be readily seen by persons resorting to those premises—

Display of licences, etc.

(*a*) the licence ; and

(*b*) a copy of any regulations under this Act which apply to the employment agency or employment business.

(2) Any person who fails to comply with this section shall be guilty of an offence and liable on summary conviction to a fine not exceeding £400.

Supplementary provisions

8.—(1) Every licensing authority shall, as soon as practicable after 31st December in each year, send to the Secretary of State a report on the exercise of their functions under this Act during that year, being a report containing particulars with respect to such matters arising thereunder as may be prescribed.

Annual reports and information.

(2) A copy of every report made in pursuance of subsection (1) of this section by a licensing authority shall be kept at their offices, shall be open to inspection by any person at all reasonable hours free of charge and shall be supplied to any person on payment of a reasonable charge therefor.

(3) A licensing authority shall give to the Secretary of State such information with respect to the exercise of their functions under this Act as he may from time to time require.

Inspection.

9.—(1) Any officer of a licensing authority duly authorised by them in that behalf may at all reasonable times on producing, if so required, written evidence of his authority—

(a) enter any premises used or to be used for or in connection with the carrying on of an employment agency or employment business by a person who is the holder of, or who has applied for, a licence under this Act and any other premises which the officer has reasonable cause to believe are used for or in connection with the carrying on of an employment agency or employment business ; and

(b) inspect those premises and any records or other documents kept in pursuance of this Act or of any regulations made thereunder ; and

(c) subject to subsection (2) of this section, require any person on those premises to furnish him with such information as he may reasonably require for the purpose of ascertaining whether the provisions of this Act and of any regulations made thereunder are being complied with or of enabling the licensing authority to exercise their functions under this Act.

(2) A person shall not be required under paragraph (c) of subsection (1) of this section to answer any question tending to incriminate himself or, in the case of a person who is married, his or her wife or husband.

(3) Any person who obstructs an officer in the exercise of his powers under paragraph (a) or (b) of subsection (1) of this section shall be guilty of an offence and liable on summary conviction to a fine not exceeding £50 and any person who, without reasonable excuse, fails to comply with a requirement under paragraph (c) of that subsection shall be guilty of an offence and liable on summary conviction to a fine not exceeding £100.

(4)(a) No information obtained in the course of exercising the powers conferred by subsection (1) of this section shall be disclosed except—

(i) with the consent of the person by whom the information was furnished or, where the information was furnished on behalf of another person, with the consent of that other person or with the consent of the person carrying on or proposing to carry on the employment agency or employment business concerned ; or

(ii) to a licensing authority, or to the officers or servants of a licensing authority, for the purposes of the exercise of their respective functions under this Act ; or

(iii) by the officers of a licensing authority, for the purposes of the exercise of their functions under this Act, to the person carrying on or proposing to carry on the employment agency or employment business concerned, to any person in his employment or, in the case of information relating to a person availing himself of the services of such an agency or business, to that person ; or

(iv) to the Secretary of State, or an officer or servant appointed by, or person exercising functions on behalf of, the Secretary of State for the purposes of the exercise of their respective functions under this Act; or

(v) with a view to the institution of, or otherwise for the purposes of, any criminal proceedings pursuant to or arising out of this Act or for the purposes of any hearing on an appeal brought under subsection (1) of section 4 of this Act.

(*b*) Any person who contravenes paragraph (*a*) of this subsection shall be guilty of an offence and liable on summary conviction to a fine not exceeding £400.

10.—(1) Any person who for the purpose of procuring the grant of a licence under this Act— *Fraudulent applications and entries.*

(*a*) makes a statement which he knows to be false in a material particular or recklessly makes a statement which is false in a material particular ; or

(*b*) produces, furnishes, sends or otherwise makes use of a document which he knows is false in a material particular or recklessly produces, furnishes, sends or otherwise makes use of a document which is false in a material particular,

shall be guilty of an offence.

(2) Any person who makes or causes to be made or knowingly allows to be made any entry in a record or other document required to be kept in pursuance of this Act or of any regulations made thereunder which he knows to be false in a material particular shall be guilty of an offence.

(3) Any person guilty of an offence under this section shall be liable on summary conviction to a fine not exceeding £400.

11. Where an offence under this Act committed by a *Offences by* body corporate is proved to have been committed with the *bodies* consent or connivance of, or to have been attributable to any *corporate.* neglect on the part of, any director, manager, secretary or other similar officer of the body corporate or a person who was purporting to act in any such capacity, he, as well as the body corporate, shall be guilty of the offence and shall be liable to be proceeded against and punished accordingly.

Regulations and orders.

12.—(1) Subject to the next following subsection, the Secretary of State shall have power to make regulations for prescribing anything which under this Act is to be prescribed.

(2) The Secretary of State shall not make any regulations under this Act except after consultation with such bodies as appear to him to be representative of the interests concerned.

(3) Regulations under this Act may make different provision in relation to different cases or classes of case.

(4) The power of the Secretary of State to make regulations and orders under this Act shall be exercisable by statutory instrument.

(5) A statutory instrument containing regulations under this Act, or an order under section 14(3) of this Act, shall be subject to annulment in pursuance of a resolution of either House of Parliament.

Interpretation.

13.—(1) In this Act—

" current licence " means a licence granted under this Act which has not expired and which has not been revoked ;

" employment " includes—

(*a*) employment by way of a professional engagement or otherwise under a contract for services ;

(*b*) the reception in a private household of a person under an arrangement whereby that person is to assist in the domestic work of the household in consideration of receiving hospitality and pocket money or hospitality only ;

and " worker " and " employer " shall be construed accordingly ;

" employment agency " has the meaning assigned by subsection (2) of this section but does not include any arrangements, services, functions or business to which this Act does not apply by virtue of subsection (7) of this section ;

" employment business " has the meaning assigned by subsection (3) of this section but does not include any arrangements, services, functions or business to which this Act does not apply by virtue of subsection (7) of this section ;

" fee " includes any charge however described ;

" holder " in relation to a licence includes a person to whom it is deemed to have been transferred under section 2(6) of this Act ;

" licensing authority " means—

> (a) as respects premises in a London borough, the council of that borough ;

> (b) as respects premises in the City of London, the Inner Temple or the Middle Temple, the Common Council of that City ;

> (c) as respects premises in a metropolitan district, the council of that district ;

> (d) as respects premises in a non-metropolitan county, the council of that county ;

> (e) as respects premises in a county in Wales, the council of that county ;

> (f) in relation to Scotland, as respects premises situated in a large burgh, within the meaning of the Local Government (Scotland) Act 1947, the council 1947 c. 43. of that burgh, and, in any other case, the council of the county in which the premises are situated ;

" local authority ", in relation to England and Wales, means a county council, the Greater London Council, the Common Council of the City of London, a district council or a London borough council and, in relation to Scotland, means a county council, a town council or a district council ;

" organisation " includes an association of organisations ;

" organisation of employers " means an organisation which consists wholly or mainly of employers and whose principal objects include the regulation of relations between employers and workers or organisations of workers ;

" organisation of workers " means an organisation which consists wholly or mainly of workers and whose principal objects include the regulation of relations between workers and employers or organisations of employers ;

" prescribed " means prescribed by regulations made under this Act by the Secretary of State ;

" seaman " has the same meaning as in the Merchant 1894 c. 60. Shipping Act 1894.

(2) For the purposes of this Act " employment agency " means the business (whether or not carried on with a view to profit and whether or not carried on in conjunction with any other business) of providing services (whether by the provision of information or otherwise) for the purpose of finding workers employment with employers or of supplying employers with workers for employment by them.

(3) For the purposes of this Act " employment business " means the business (whether or not carried on with a view to

profit and whether or not carried on in conjunction with any other business) of supplying persons in the employment of the person carrying on the business, to act for, and under the control of, other persons in any capacity.

(4) The reference in subsection (2) of this section to providing services does not include a reference—

(*a*) to publishing a newspaper or other publication unless it is published wholly or mainly for the purpose mentioned in that subsection;

(*b*) to the display by any person of advertisements on premises occupied by him otherwise than for the said purpose; or

1949 c. 54.
(*c*) to broadcasting by wireless telegraphy (within the meaning of the Wireless Telegraphy Act 1949), whether by way of sound broadcasting or of television.

1972 c. 70.
(5) For the purposes of section 269 of the Local Government Act 1972, this Act shall be deemed to have been passed after 1st April 1974.

(6) In this Act, except where the context otherwise requires, references to any enactment shall be construed as references to that enactment as amended, extended or applied by or under any other enactment.

(7) This Act does not apply to—

(*a*) any business which is carried on exclusively for the purpose of obtaining employment for—

(i) persons formerly members of Her Majesty's naval, military or air forces; or

(ii) persons released from a prison, Borstal institution, detention centre or young offenders' institution;

and which is certified annually by or on behalf of the Admiralty Board of the Defence Council, the Army Board of the Defence Council or the Air Force Board of the Defence Council or by the Secretary of State (as the case may be) to be properly conducted;

1957 c. 16.
1951 c. 55.
(*b*) any agency for the supply of nurses as defined in section 8 of the Nurses Agencies Act 1957 or section 32 of the Nurses (Scotland) Act 1951;

(*c*) the business carried on by any county or district nursing association or other similar organisation, being an association or organisation established and existing wholly or mainly for the purpose of providing patients with the services of a nurse to visit them in their own homes without herself taking up residence there;

(*d*) services which are ancillary to the letting upon hire of any aircraft, vessel, vehicle, plant or equipment ;

(*e*) the making of arrangements for finding seamen for persons seeking to employ seamen or for finding employment for seamen ;

(*f*) the exercise by a local authority of any of their functions ;

(*g*) services provided by any organisation of employers or organisation of workers for its members ;

(*h*) services provided by an appointments board or service controlled by—

(i) one or more universities ;

(ii) a central institution as defined in section 145 of the Education (Scotland) Act 1962 or a college of education as defined in the said section 145 ;   1962 c. 47.

(*i*) any business carried on, or any services provided by, such persons or classes of persons as may be prescribed :

Provided that paragraph (*b*) of this subsection shall not be taken as exempting from the provisions of this Act any other business carried on in conjunction with an agency for the supply of nurses.

(8) Subsection (7)(*c*) of this section shall have effect in its application to Scotland as if at the end there were added the words " or mainly or substantially supported by voluntary subscriptions and providing patients with the services of a nurse whether or not the nurse takes up residence in the patient's house ".

14.—(1) This Act may be cited as the Employment Agencies Act 1973. Short title, repeals, commencement and extent.

(2) The enactments specified in the Schedule to this Act are hereby repealed to the extent specified in the third column of that Schedule.

(3) The Secretary of State may, after consultation with such bodies as appear to him to be concerned, by order repeal any provision of any local Act, being a provision which is not specified in Part II of the said Schedule and which appears to him to be unnecessary having regard to the provisions of this Act, or to be inconsistent with the provisions of this Act, and may by that order make such amendments of that or any other local Act as appear to him to be necessary in consequence of the repeal and such transitional provision as appears to him to be necessary or expedient in connection with the matter.

(4) This Act shall come into force on such date as the Secretary of State may by order appoint, and different dates may be appointed for different provisions and for different purposes.

(5) This Act does not extend to Northern Ireland.

SCHEDULE

REPEALS

PART I

PUBLIC GENERAL ACTS

Chapter	Short Title	Extent of Repeal
7 Edw. 7. c. 53.	The Public Health Acts Amendment Act 1907.	Section 85.

PART II

LOCAL ACTS

Chapter	Short Title	Extent of Repeal
11 & 12 Geo. 5. c. 1.	The London County Council (General Powers) Act 1921.	In section 4, the definition of " employment agency " and " licensing authority ". Part III.
14 & 15 Geo. 5. c. xcv.	The Manchester Corporation Act 1924.	Section 91.
15 & 16 Geo. 5. c. cxv.	The Surrey County Council Act 1925.	Part V.
16 & 17 Geo. 5. c. lxxxv.	The Guildford Corporation Act 1926.	Part IX.
17 & 18 Geo. 5. c. lxxxviii.	The Liverpool Corporation Act 1927.	Part XII.
18 & 19 Geo. 5. c. lxxxvii.	The Sheffield Corporation Act 1928.	Part XVI.
20 & 21 Geo. 5. c. cxix.	The Leeds Corporation Act 1930.	Part IX.
20 & 21 Geo. 5. c. clxxiv.	The Cardiff Corporation Act 1930.	Part XI.
20 & 21 Geo. 5. c. clxxxvi.	The Bootle Corporation Act 1930.	Part II.
21 & 22 Geo. 5. c. cix.	The Brighton Corporation Act 1931.	Part XXIV.
22 & 23 Geo. 5. c. lxix.	The Bury Corporation Act 1932.	Part XI.
23 & 24 Geo. 5. c. xlv.	The Essex County Council Act 1933.	Part V.
25 & 26 Geo. 5. c. cxiii.	The Hertfordshire County Council Act 1935.	Part V.
25 & 26 Geo. 5. c. cxxii.	The Birmingham Corporation Act 1935.	Part VIII.
25 & 26 Geo. 5. c. cxxiv.	The Newcastle-upon-Tyne Corporation (General Powers) Act 1935.	Part IV.
1 Edw. 8 & 1 Geo. 6. c. xxxv.	The West Ham Corporation Act 1937.	Part V.
7 & 8 Geo. 6. c. xxi.	The Middlesex County Council Act 1944.	Part XIV.

Chapter	Short Title	Extent of Repeal
10 & 11. Geo. 6. c. xviii.	The Inverness Burgh Order Confirmation Act 1947.	Part II of the Schedule.
11 & 12 Geo. 6. c. xli.	The Ipswich Corporation Act 1948.	Part IX.
7 & 8 Eliz. 2. c. xxxiii.	The Reading and Berkshire Water &c. Act 1959.	Part VIII.
8 & 9 Eliz. 2. c. iii.	The Glasgow Corporation Consolidation (General Powers) Order Confirmation Act 1960.	Sections 53 to 56 of the Schedule.
8 & 9 Eliz. 2. c. xl.	The Croydon Corporation Act 1960.	Part X.
1967 c. v.	The Edinburgh Corporation Order Confirmation Act 1967.	Sections 377 to 381 of the Schedule.
1971 c. xliv.	The Teeside Corporation (General Powers) (No. 2) Act 1971.	Sections 33 to 40.
1971 c. lx.	The Torbay Corporation (No. 2) Act 1971.	Sections 67 to 74.

Northern Ireland Constitution Act 1973

1973 CHAPTER 36

An Act to make new provision for the government of Northern Ireland.   [18th July 1973]

BE IT ENACTED by the Queen's most Excellent Majesty, by and with the advice and consent of the Lords Spiritual and Temporal, and Commons, in this present Parliament assembled, and by the authority of the same, as follows:—

PART I

PRELIMINARY

Status of Northern Ireland

Status of Northern Ireland as part of United Kingdom.

1. It is hereby declared that Northern Ireland remains part of Her Majesty's dominions and of the United Kingdom, and it is hereby affirmed that in no event will Northern Ireland or any part of it cease to be part of Her Majesty's dominions and of the United Kingdom without the consent of the majority of the people of Northern Ireland voting in a poll held for the purposes of this section in accordance with Schedule 1 to this Act.

Devolution orders

Initial devolution of legislative and executive responsibility.

2.—(1) If it appears to the Secretary of State—

    (*a*) that the Northern Ireland Assembly (in this Act referred to as " the Assembly ") has made satisfactory provision by its standing orders for the purposes mentioned in section 25(2) to (5) below ; and

    (*b*) that a Northern Ireland Executive can be formed which, having regard to the support it commands in the Assembly and to the electorate on which that support

is based, is likely to be widely accepted throughout the
community,

and that having regard to those matters there is a reasonable
basis for the establishment in Northern Ireland of government
by consent, he shall lay before Parliament the draft of an Order
in Council appointing a day for the commencement of Part II
of this Act and declaring what matters shall, subject to section
3 below, be transferred matters for the purposes of this Act.

(2) The matters declared by an Order under this section to be
transferred matters shall not include—

   (a) any of the matters specified in Schedule 2 to this Act
       (in this Act referred to as " excepted matters "); or
   (b) any of the matters specified in Schedule 3 to this Act.

(3) If the draft laid before Parliament under subsection (1)
above is approved by resolution of each House of Parliament
the Secretary of State shall submit it to Her Majesty in Council
and Her Majesty in Council may make the Order in terms of
the draft.

(4) On the day appointed by an Order under this section
for the commencement of Part II of this Act (in this Act referred
to as " the appointed day ") section 1 of the Northern Ireland 1972 c. 22.
(Temporary Provisions) Act 1972 shall expire.

3.—(1) If at any time after the appointed day it appears to Alterations in
the Secretary of State— devolved
   (a) that any matter (not being an excepted matter) which responsibilities.
       is not a transferred matter by virtue of an Order under
       section 2 above or a previous Order under this section
       should become a transferred matter; or
   (b) that any matter which by virtue of any such Order is a
       transferred matter should cease to be such a matter,
he may, subject to subsection (2) below, lay before Parliament
the draft of an Order in Council declaring that the matter shall
be or, as the case may be, shall cease to be a transferred matter
with effect from such date as may be specified in the Order.

(2) The Secretary of State shall not lay before Parliament the
draft of an Order in Council declaring that any matter not
specified in Schedule 3 to this Act shall cease to be a transferred
matter unless the Assembly has passed a resolution praying
that it should cease to be a transferred matter.

(3) Subsection (3) of section 2 above shall have effect in
relation to any draft laid before Parliament under this section
as it has effect in relation to a draft laid before Parliament
under that section.

(4) Any matter (not being an excepted matter) which is not
for the time being a transferred matter is in this Act referred
to as a " reserved matter ".

PART II

LEGISLATIVE POWERS AND EXECUTIVE AUTHORITIES

Legislative powers

Measures of
Northern
Ireland
Assembly.

4.—(1) Laws may be made for Northern Ireland by Measures of the Assembly (in this Act referred to as " Measures ").

(2) A Measure shall be enacted by being passed by the Assembly and approved by Her Majesty in Council.

(3) Subject to section 17 below, a Measure shall have the same force and effect as an Act of the Parliament of the United Kingdom.

(4) This section does not affect the power of the Parliament of the United Kingdom to make laws for Northern Ireland but, subject to the said section 17, a Measure may amend or repeal any provision made by or under any Act of Parliament in so far as it is part of the law of Northern Ireland.

(5) It is hereby declared for the avoidance of doubt that a Measure is not invalid by reason of any failure to comply with the provisions of section 5, 6, 14 or 18(2), (5) or (6) below ; and no act or omission under any of those provisions shall be called in question in any legal proceedings.

Secretary of
State's
consent for
proposed
Measures
dealing with
excepted
or reserved
matters.

5.—(1) The consent of the Secretary of State shall be required in accordance with this section in relation to a proposed Measure which contains any provision dealing with an excepted matter or reserved matter ; and the Secretary of State shall not give his consent in relation to a proposed Measure which contains any provision dealing with an excepted matter unless he considers that the provision is ancillary to other provisions (whether in that Measure or previously enacted) dealing with reserved matters or transferred matters.

(2) Every proposed Measure introduced in the Assembly shall be considered by the Clerk to the Assembly on introduction and if—

    (a) he considers that it contains any provision dealing with an excepted matter or reserved matter ; and

    (b) it has not been endorsed with a statement that the Secretary of State has consented to the Assembly considering the proposed Measure,

then, subject to subsection (4) below, the Clerk shall refer the proposed Measure to the Secretary of State and the Assembly shall not proceed with the Measure unless the Secretary of State's consent to the consideration of the Measure by the Assembly is signified or the Assembly is informed that in his opinion the Measure does not contain any such provision as aforesaid.

(3) Before the Assembly enters on the stage in its proceedings
at which a proposed Measure falls finally to be passed or
rejected—

    (*a*) the Clerk to the Assembly shall again consider the
        proposed Measure ; and

    (*b*) if he considers that it contains any provision dealing with
        an excepted matter or reserved matter he shall, subject
        to subsection (4) below, refer it to the Secretary of
        State,

and the Assembly shall not enter on that stage unless the
Secretary of State's consent to the Measure is signified or the
Assembly is informed that in his opinion the Measure does not
contain any such provision as aforesaid.

(4) Neither subsection (2) nor subsection (3) above shall
require the Clerk to the Assembly to refer any proposed
Measure to the Secretary of State, or preclude the Assembly from
proceeding with a proposed Measure, by reason only that it
contains a provision which, in the opinion of the Clerk, is
ancillary to other provisions (whether in that Measure or
previously enacted) dealing with transferred matters only.

(5) Every proposed Measure passed by the Assembly shall be
transmitted to the Secretary of State for submission to Her
Majesty in Council but if—

    (*a*) he considers that it contains any provision dealing with
        an excepted matter or reserved matter ; and

    (*b*) it has not been referred to him under subsection (3)
        above (whether by virtue of subsection (4) above or
        otherwise),

he shall not submit the Measure to Her Majesty in Council
unless he consents to the Measure.

(6) If the Secretary of State withholds his consent to a proposed
Measure passed by the Assembly he shall refer it back to the
Assembly for further consideration ; and, if it is modified by
the Assembly and again transmitted to him, subsection (5) above
shall apply to it as if it were a new proposed Measure transmitted to him after being passed by the Assembly.

(7) For the purposes of this section a provision is ancillary to
other provisions if it is a provision which is necessary or
expedient for making those other provisions effective or which
provides for the enforcement of those other provisions or which
is otherwise incidental to, or consequential on, those provisions ;
and references in this section to provisions previously enacted
are references to provisions contained in, or in any instrument
made under, another Measure, an Act of the Parliament of the
United Kingdom or an Act of the Parliament of Northern
Ireland.

PART II
Parliamentary
control of
Measures
dealing with
excepted or
reserved
matters.

6.—(1) Subject to the provisions of this section, a proposed Measure to which the Secretary of State has consented under section 5(3) or (5) above shall not be submitted by him to Her Majesty in Council unless he has first laid it before Parliament and either—

(a) the period of twenty days beginning with the date on which it is laid has expired without notice having been given in either House of a motion praying that the proposed Measure shall not be submitted to Her Majesty in Council for approval ; or

(b) if notice of such a motion is given within that period the motion has been rejected or withdrawn.

(2) Subsection (1) above shall not apply to a proposed Measure if the Secretary of State considers that it contains no provision dealing with an excepted matter or reserved matter except a provision which is ancillary (within the meaning of section 5 above) to other provisions dealing with transferred matters only.

(3) Subsection (1) above shall not apply to a proposed Measure if the Secretary of State considers that by reason of urgency it should be submitted to Her Majesty in Council without first being laid before Parliament.

(4) Any Measure submitted by virtue of subsection (3) above shall, if approved by Her Majesty in Council, be laid before Parliament by the Secretary of State after approval, and if—

(a) within the period of twenty days beginning with the date on which it is laid notice is given in either House of a motion praying that the Measure shall cease to have effect ; and

(b) that motion is carried,

Her Majesty may by Order in Council repeal that Measure with effect from such date as may be specified in the Order.

(5) An Order in Council under subsection (4) above may make such consequential or transitional provision in connection with the repeal as appears to Her Majesty to be necessary or expedient.

(6) Any notice of motion for the purposes of subsection (1) or (4) above must be signed by not less than twenty members of the House in which it is given ; and any period mentioned in those subsections shall be computed, in relation to each House, by reference only to days on which that House sits.

Executive authorities

7.—(1) The executive power in Northern Ireland shall continue to be vested in Her Majesty.

(2) As respects transferred matters the Secretary of State shall, as Her Majesty's principal officer in Northern Ireland, exercise on Her Majesty's behalf such prerogative or other executive powers of Her Majesty in relation to Northern Ireland as may be delegated to him by Her Majesty.

PART II

(3) The powers so delegated shall be exercised through the members of the Northern Ireland Executive established by this Act and the Northern Ireland departments.

(4) A member of the Northern Ireland Executive who is head of a Northern Ireland department shall, in formulating policy with respect to matters within the responsibilities of that department, consult so far as practicable with the consultative committee established in relation to his department under section 25 below, and where such policy is to be implemented by a proposed Measure he shall consult as aforesaid before the proposed Measure is introduced.

(5) The Ministries of the Government of Northern Ireland existing on the appointed day shall be the Northern Ireland departments for the purposes of this Act (and shall be known as departments instead of Ministries) but provision may be made by Measure for establishing new Northern Ireland departments or dissolving existing ones.

(6) The Secretary of State as Her Majesty's principal officer in Northern Ireland, the members of the Northern Ireland Executive, any other persons appointed under section 8 below and the Northern Ireland departments are in this Act referred to as Northern Ireland executive authorities.

8.—(1) The Northern Ireland Executive shall consist of—
    (a) the chief executive member;
    (b) the persons who are for the time being heads of the Northern Ireland departments; and
    (c) any other person appointed under subsection (3) below to be a member of the Executive.

The Northern Ireland Executive.

(2) The chief executive member shall preside over the Executive and act as Leader of the Assembly.

(3) The chief executive member and the heads of the Northern Ireland departments shall be appointed by the Secretary of State on behalf of Her Majesty and the Secretary of State may likewise appoint such number of additional persons (if any) as he thinks fit to discharge, whether as members of the Executive or otherwise, such functions as he may determine; but the total number of persons at any time holding appointments under this section shall not exceed twelve.

(4) Subject to subsections (5) and (6) below, appointments under this section shall be from among persons who are members

PART II

of the Assembly and shall be such as will in the opinion of the Secretary of State secure that the Executive has the character mentioned in section 2(1)(*b*) above.

(5) Two of the persons at any time holding appointments under this section (other than the chief executive member) may be persons who were not appointed from among members of the Assembly but not more than one of them shall be the head of a Northern Ireland department.

(6) If at any time after the appointed day it appears to the Secretary of State that it is not possible to make an appointment which complies with the requirements of subsection (4) above he may make an appointment which does not comply with those requirements but any person so appointed shall not hold office for more than six months.

(7) Before making any appointment under this section (otherwise than by virtue of subsection (6)) the Secretary of State shall so far as practicable consult with the parties represented in the Assembly.

(8) Persons appointed under this section shall hold office at Her Majesty's pleasure; and a person who is required by this section to be appointed from among members of the Assembly shall not continue in office for more than six months after ceasing to be a member of the Assembly.

(9) A person appointed under this section who is not a member of the Assembly shall be entitled to sit and speak in the Assembly but not to vote.

(10) Every person appointed under this section shall, on appointment, take the oath or make the affirmation set out in Schedule 4 to this Act.

Remuneration and pensions of members of Northern Ireland Executive etc.

9.—(1) There shall be paid to each person appointed under section 8 above such salary and allowances as may be prescribed by Order in Council; and provision may be made by Order in Council for the payment of pensions to or in respect of persons who have held appointments under that section.

(2) Any Order in Council under this section may be varied or revoked by a subsequent Order.

(3) Any salaries or allowances payable by virtue of an Order in Council under this section, and any sums required by any such Order relating to pensions to be paid out of public funds, shall be defrayed out of moneys appropriated for that purpose by Measure.

Attorney General for Northern Ireland.

10.—(1) The Attorney General for England and Wales shall by virtue of that office be Attorney General for Northern Ireland also, and he and the Solicitor General shall by virtue of membership of the bar of England and Wales have in Northern Ireland the same rights of audience as members of the bar of Northern Ireland.

(2) If at any time the office of Attorney General for England and Wales is vacant any functions authorised or required by any enactment or otherwise to be discharged by the Attorney General for Northern Ireland may be discharged by the Solicitor General for England and Wales as his deputy, and any certificate, petition, direction, notice, proceeding or other document, matter or thing whatsoever authorised or required to be given, delivered, served, taken or done to, on or against the Attorney General for Northern Ireland may be given, delivered, served, taken or done to, on or against the Solicitor General for England and Wales.

(3) The Solicitor General for England and Wales may also act as Attorney General for Northern Ireland as deputy for the Attorney General for England and Wales if the Attorney General is unable to act owing to absence or illness, or if the Attorney General authorises the Solicitor General to act in any particular case.

(4) The Attorney General for Northern Ireland shall cease to be a member of the Northern Ireland Supreme Court Rules Committee but the members of that Committee shall include, in addition to those mentioned in section 8 of the Northern Ireland Act 1962, one practising member of the Bar of Northern Ireland nominated by the Attorney General.

1962 c. 30.

11.—(1) Arrangements may be made between any department of the Government of the United Kingdom and any Northern Ireland department for any functions of one of them to be discharged by, or by officers of, the other.

(2) No such arrangements shall affect the responsibility of the department on whose behalf any functions are discharged.

(3) In this section references to a department of the Government of the United Kingdom include references to any Minister of the Crown and references to a Northern Ireland department include references to the head of a Northern Ireland department; and this section shall have effect in relation to the Post Office as it has effect in relation to a department of the Government of the United Kingdom.

Agency arrangements between United Kingdom and Northern Ireland departments.

Relations with Republic of Ireland

12.—(1) A Northern Ireland executive authority may—

    (*a*) consult on any matter with any authority of the Republic of Ireland ;

    (*b*) enter into agreements or arrangements with any authority of the Republic of Ireland in respect of any transferred matter.

Consultation, agreements and arrangements with Republic of Ireland.

PART II

(2) It is hereby declared that provision may be made by Measure for giving effect to any agreement or arrangement made under subsection (1) above, including provision for transferring to any authority designated by or constituted under the agreement or arrangement any function which would otherwise be exercisable by any authority in Northern Ireland or for transferring to an authority in Northern Ireland any functions which would otherwise be exercisable by any authority elsewhere.

(3) Subsection (2) above does not affect the operation of sections 5 and 6 above in relation to the enactment of any Measure.

Financial provisions

Consolidated Fund of Northern Ireland.

13.—(1) The Consolidated Fund of Northern Ireland shall continue to exist but there shall cease to be an Exchequer of Northern Ireland separate from the Consolidated Fund.

(2) Subject to any provision made by or under any Act of the Parliament of the United Kingdom or of Northern Ireland or any Measure charging any sums on the Consolidated Fund of Northern Ireland, all sums forming part of that Fund shall be appropriated to the public service of Northern Ireland by Measure and shall not be applied for any purpose for which they are not so appropriated.

(3) Except as otherwise provided by Act of the Parliament of Northern Ireland or by Measure, the accounts of the Consolidated Fund of Northern Ireland shall be audited by the Comptroller and Auditor-General for Northern Ireland in the manner provided by the Exchequer and Audit Act (Northern Ireland) 1921.

1921 c. 2. (N.I.).

(4) Subsection (2) above is without prejudice to any appropriation made by Order in Council under section 1(3) of the Northern Ireland (Temporary Provisions) Act 1972 ; and if part of a financial year falls before and part after the appointed day the accounts and reports mentioned in section 3 of the Northern Ireland (Financial Provisions) Act 1972 shall be prepared separately in relation to each part and that section (which requires those accounts and reports to be laid before the House of Commons) shall apply to the accounts and reports relating to the part before the appointed day as it applies to the accounts and reports relating to a financial year ending before the appointed day.

1972 c. 22.

1972 c. 76.

Proceedings in Assembly for imposing charge on public funds or for imposing taxation.

14. No vote, resolution or Measure shall be passed by the Assembly for—

(a) charging any sum on the Consolidated Fund of Northern Ireland or appropriating any sum out of that Fund or increasing the sums so charged or appropriated ;

(*b*) releasing or compounding any debt owed to the Crown ;
or

(*c*) imposing or increasing any tax,

except in pursuance of a recommendation from the Head of the Department of Finance for Northern Ireland signified to the Assembly by him or by a member of the Northern Ireland Executive authorised by him for that purpose.

15.—(1) Subject to subsection (4) below, there shall in respect of each year be charged on and paid out of the Consolidated Fund of the United Kingdom into the Consolidated Fund of Northern Ireland a sum equal to the Northern Ireland share of United Kingdom taxes. Payment to Northern Ireland of share of United Kingdom taxes.

(2) The Northern Ireland share of United Kingdom taxes in respect of each year shall be determined by the Treasury ; and that share shall be such amount as, in the opinion of the Treasury, represents the proceeds for that year of the taxes payable into the Consolidated Fund of the United Kingdom which are properly attributable to Northern Ireland after deducting the cost of collection and other appropriate costs.

(3) The Treasury may make regulations with respect to the method by which the proceeds of the taxes, and the costs, mentioned in subsection (2) above are to be attributed to Northern Ireland ; and any determination under that subsection shall be made in accordance with those regulations.

(4) The Treasury may by order direct that there shall be deducted from the sum payable under subsection (1) above in respect of any year such sum as may be specified in the order by way of contribution towards the expenses falling on the Consolidated Fund of the United Kingdom in respect of that year which relate to excepted matters and reserved matters.

(5) The sums payable under subsection (1) above shall be paid at such times and in such manner as the Treasury may determine, and payments may be made on account of sums subsequently so payable.

(6) The power to make regulations or orders under this section shall be exercisable by statutory instrument and—

(*a*) any regulations under subsection (3) shall be subject to annulment in pursuance of a resolution of the House of Commons ;

(*b*) no order shall be made under subsection (4) unless a draft of it has been approved by the House of Commons.

16.—(1) The Secretary of State may from time to time pay out of moneys provided by Parliament into the Consolidated Fund of Northern Ireland such sums by way of grant as he Grants to Northern Ireland out of moneys provided by Parliament.

PART II
may with the consent of the Treasury determine and may, in connection with any such payment, impose such conditions as he may with the like consent determine.

1967 c. 54.
1971 c. 68.
(2) No further payments shall be made under section 26(7) of the Finance Act 1967 or under or by virtue of section 67 of the Finance Act 1971 (payments towards certain expediture in Northern Ireland).

PART III
PREVENTION OF RELIGIOUS AND POLITICAL DISCRIMINATION

Discrimination in legislation.
17.—(1) Any Measure, any Act of the Parliament of Northern Ireland and any relevant subordinate instrument shall, to the extent that it discriminates against any person or class of persons on the ground of religious belief or political opinion, be void.

(2) In this section " relevant subordinate instrument " means an instrument of a legislative character (including a byelaw) made (whether before or after the coming into force of this section) under any Act of the Parliament of the United Kingdom or the Parliament of Northern Ireland or under any Measure and extending only to Northern Ireland or a part of Northern Ireland.

Special procedure for determining validity of legislation.
18.—(1) If it appears to the Secretary of State to be expedient in the public interest that steps should be taken for the speedy decision of any question whether a provision of a Measure, Act of the Parliament of Northern Ireland or relevant subordinate instrument within the meaning of section 17 above is void by virtue of that section, he may recommend to Her Majesty that the question be referred for decision to the Judicial Committee of the Privy Council.

(2) If it appears to the Secretary of State that a proposed Measure transmitted to him after being passed by the Assembly contains a provision which, if the Measure were enacted, might be void by virtue of the said section 17 he shall refer it back to the Assembly for further consideration ; and if—

    (*a*) it is again transmitted to him with or without modification ; and

    (*b*) it still appears to him to contain such a provision as aforesaid,

he shall recommend to Her Majesty that the question whether that provision would be void by virtue of the said section 17 be referred for decision to the Judicial Committee of the Privy Council.

(3) For the purposes of their consideration of any question referred to them under this section the Judicial Committee may hear any person who appears to them to be interested in the determination of that question.

PART III

(4) The decision of the Judicial Committee under this section as to the validity of any provision shall be stated in open court and shall be binding in all subsequent legal proceedings.

(5) Where the Judicial Committee decide that a provision in a proposed Measure would be void the Secretary of State shall not submit the proposed Measure for the approval of Her Majesty in Council ; and where they decide that such a provision would not be void their decision shall be taken as applying also to that provision if contained in the Measure when enacted.

(6) Subsection (6) of section 5 above shall apply where the Secretary of State is precluded by subsection (5) above from submitting a proposed Measure for approval as it applies where he withholds his consent under that section and as if the reference to subsection (5) of that section included a reference to subsections (2) and (5) above.

(7) This section is without prejudice to any power of Her Majesty to refer to the Judicial Committee any questions other than those mentioned in this section.

19.—(1) It shall be unlawful for a Minister of the Crown, a member of the Northern Ireland Executive or other person appointed under section 8 above, the Post Office and any authority or body listed in Schedule 2 to the Parliamentary Commissioner Act 1967, Schedule 1 to the Parliamentary Commissioner Act (Northern Ireland) 1969 or Schedule 1 to the Commissioner for Complaints Act (Northern Ireland) 1969 to discriminate, or aid, induce or incite another to discriminate, in the discharge of functions relating to Northern Ireland against any person or class of persons on the ground of religious belief or political opinion.

Discrimination by public authorities.

1967 c. 13.
1969 c. 10 (N.I.)
1969 c. 25 (N.I.).

(2) The obligation to comply with subsection (1) above is a duty owed to any person who may be adversely affected by a contravention of that subsection, and any breach of that duty is actionable in Northern Ireland accordingly.

(3) Without prejudice to the right of any person apart from this subsection to claim an injunction restraining another from continuing or repeating any act which is unlawful by virtue of subsection (1) above, the plaintiff may in an action in respect of an act alleged to be unlawful as aforesaid claim any such injunction as is mentioned below on the grounds—

(a) that the act was done by the defendant and was unlawful as aforesaid ;

(b) that the defendant had previously done such unlawful acts of the same kind as, or of a similar kind to, that act ; and

(c) that he is likely, unless restrained by order of the court, to do further acts of the same or of a similar kind ;

PART III

and the court may, if satisfied as to those grounds and whether or not damages are awarded, grant such injunction as appears to the court to be proper in all the circumstances, being an injunction restraining the defendant from doing, or causing or permitting others to do, further acts of the same or a similar kind.

The Standing Advisory Commission on Human Rights.

20.—(1) There shall be constituted a Commission to be known as the Standing Advisory Commission on Human Rights (and hereafter in this section referred to as the Advisory Commission) for the purpose of—

(a) advising the Secretary of State on the adequacy and effectiveness of the law for the time being in force in preventing discrimination on the ground of religious belief or political opinion and in providing redress for persons aggrieved by discrimination on either ground ;

(b) keeping the Secretary of State informed as to the extent to which the persons, authorities and bodies mentioned in section 19(1) above have prevented discrimination on either ground by persons or bodies not prohibited from discriminating by that law.

(2) The Advisory Commission shall consist of—

(a) a chairman appointed by the Secretary of State from among the members of the Advisory Commission ;

(b) the chairman of the Northern Ireland Community Relations Commission ;

(c) the Northern Ireland Commissioner for Complaints ;

(d) the Northern Ireland Parliamentary Commissioner for Administration ; and

(e) such other members as may be appointed by the Secretary of State ;

and any member mentioned in paragraphs (b) to (d) above is hereafter in this section referred to as an ex-officio member.

(3) An ex-officio member of the Advisory Commission shall on ceasing to hold the office by virtue of which he is a member of the Commission cease to be a member of the Commission and, if he is the chairman, to be chairman.

(4) The members of the Advisory Commission, other than the ex-officio members, shall hold and vacate office in accordance with the terms of their respective appointments and shall, on ceasing to hold office, be eligible for re-appointment, but any such member may at any time by notice addressed to the Secretary of State resign his office.

(5) The Secretary of State may out of moneys provided by Parliament pay the members of the Advisory Commission, other than the ex-officio members, such remuneration and such

allowances as may be determined by the Secretary of State with the consent of the Minister for the Civil Service. PART III

(6) The Secretary of State shall provide the Advisory Commission with such officers and such accommodation as may be appropriate.

(7) The Advisory Commission shall make annual reports to the Secretary of State with respect to the exercise of their functions and make copies of those reports available to the Assembly; and the Secretary of State shall lay any such report before each House of Parliament.

21.—(1) Subject to subsections (2) and (3) below, it shall be unlawful for an authority or body to which this section applies to require any person to take an oath, make an undertaking in lieu of an oath or make a declaration, as a condition of his being appointed to or acting as a member of that authority or body, or of serving with or being employed under that authority or body. Unlawful oaths, undertakings and declarations.

(2) Subsection (1) above shall not prevent a person being required to take an oath or make an undertaking or a declaration which is specifically required or authorised to be taken or made—

(a) by the law in force immediately before the coming into force of that subsection; or

(b) by or under this Act or by a subsequent Measure for the time being in force;

but, except as aforesaid, has effect notwithstanding anything in any enactment, any Measure or any instrument made under an enactment or a Measure.

(3) Subsection (1) above shall not prevent a person being required to make a declaration of acceptance of office or a declaration that he is qualified to act, serve or be employed, or not disqualified from acting, serving or being employed, in any capacity.

(4) This section applies to the Assembly and to any authority or body listed in Schedule 1 to the Parliamentary Commissioner Act (Northern Ireland) 1969 or Schedule 1 to the Commissioner for Complaints Act (Northern Ireland) 1969. 1969 c. 10 (N.I.). 1969 c. 25 (N.I.).

(5) Subsections (1) to (3) above shall apply with the necessary modifications to a member of the Northern Ireland Executive or other person appointed under section 8 above as they apply to any such authority or body.

(6) Subsections (2) and (3) of section 19 above shall apply in relation to subsection (1) above as they apply in relation to subsection (1) of that section.

T

PART III
Removal of
restrictions on
investigation
into mal-
administration.

22.—(1) The enactments mentioned in subsection (2) below (which preclude a Commissioner appointed under any of the Acts so mentioned from conducting an investigation under the relevant Act when the person aggrieved has or had a remedy by way of proceedings in a court of law) shall not apply to an investigation of a complaint alleging maladministration involving discrimination on the ground of religious belief or political opinion or a requirement in contravention of section 21 above to take an oath or make an undertaking or declaration.

(2) The said enactments are:—

1967 c. 13.

(*a*) section 5(2)(*b*) of the Parliamentary Commissioner Act 1967 ;

1969 c. 10.
(N.I.).

(*b*) section 5(2)(*b*) of the Parliamentary Commissioner Act (Northern Ireland) 1969 ; and

1969 c. 25.
(N.I.).

(*c*) section 5(3)(*b*) of the Commissioner for Complaints Act (Northern Ireland) 1969.

Interpretation
and
supplemental.

23.—(1) For the purposes of this Part of this Act a Measure, an Act of the Parliament of Northern Ireland or any other instrument discriminates against any person or class of persons if it treats that person or that class less favourably in any circumstances than other persons are treated in those circumstances by the law for the time being in force in Northern Ireland.

(2) For those purposes a person discriminates against another person or a class of persons if he treats that other person or that class less favourably in any circumstances than he treats or would treat other persons in those circumstances.

(3) No Measure, Act of the Parliament of Northern Ireland or other instrument and no act done by any person shall be treated for the purposes of this Act as discriminating if the instrument has the effect, or, as the case may be, the act is done for the purpose, of safeguarding national security or protecting public safety or public order.

(4) A certificate purporting to be signed by or on behalf of the Secretary of State and certifying that an act specified in the certificate was done for the purpose of safeguarding national security shall be conclusive evidence that it was done for that purpose.

(5) No provision of this Part of this Act shall affect the operation before the coming into force of that provision of any Measure, Act of the Parliament of Northern Ireland or other instrument.

(6) No provision of this Part of this Act shall render unlawful anything required or authorised to be done by any Act of the Parliament of the United Kingdom, whenever passed.

PART IV

THE NORTHERN IRELAND ASSEMBLY

24.—(1) The Assembly elected under the Northern Ireland Assembly Act 1973, and every Assembly subsequently elected, shall as its first business elect one of its members to be the presiding officer of the Assembly.

Presiding officer and Clerk of the Assembly.
1973 c. 17.

(2) The person so elected shall hold office until the dissolution of the Assembly unless he previously resigns or ceases to be a member of the Assembly or is removed from office by resolution of the Assembly ; and if the presiding officer vacates his office before the expiration of his term of office the Assembly shall elect another person to fill his place for the remainder of that term.

(3) There shall be a Clerk to the Assembly appointed by Her Majesty on the recommendation of the Secretary of State.

(4) The Clerk to the Assembly shall, with the consent of the Ministry of Finance for Northern Ireland as to numbers, appoint such other officers and servants of the Assembly as he considers requisite.

(5) The remuneration of the Clerk to the Assembly shall be such as may be determined by the Ministry of Finance for Northern Ireland ; and the remuneration and conditions of service of the other officers and servants of the Assembly shall be such as may be determined by the Clerk to the Assembly with the consent of that Ministry.

(6) The remuneration of the Clerk to the Assembly shall be charged on and paid out of the Consolidated Fund of Northern Ireland and the remuneration of the other officers and servants of the Assembly shall be defrayed out of moneys appropriated by Measure.

(7) The Clerk to the Assembly shall act as presiding officer while that office is vacant pending an election under subsection (1) or (2) above.

(8) Any functions of the Clerk to the Assembly (including functions under section 5 above or under subsection (7) above) may, if the office of Clerk is vacant or the Clerk is for any reason unable to act, be discharged by any other officer for the time being discharging the duties of the Clerk.

25.—(1) The Assembly shall make standing orders for regulating its procedure.

Procedure.

(2) The standing orders shall include provision—

(*a*) for general debate of a proposed Measure with an opportunity for members to vote on its general principles ;

T 2

(*b*) for the consideration of, and an opportunity for members to vote on, the details of a proposed Measure ; and

(*c*) for a final stage at which a proposed Measure can be passed or rejected but not amended.

(3) The standing orders shall include provision for the procedure to be adopted where the Secretary of State has withheld his consent to a proposed Measure under subsection (3) of section 5 above or has referred a proposed Measure back to the Assembly for further consideration.

(4) The standing orders shall include provision for the establishment of consultative committees to advise and assist the head of each of the Northern Ireland departments in the formulation of policy with respect to matters within the responsibilities of his department, and a committee may be so established either in relation to a single department or in relation to more than one.

(5) Standing orders made by virtue of subsection (4) above shall, subject to subsection (6) below, provide for the head of the department or the heads of departments in relation to which a consultative committee is established to be chairman or joint chairmen of that committee and shall make provision for securing that the balance of parties in the Assembly is, so far as practicable, reflected in the membership of the consultative committees taken as a whole.

(6) Her Majesty may by Order in Council repeal or amend so much of subsection (5) above as relates to the chairmanship of consultative committees and make such consequential or transitional provision in connection with the repeal or amendment as appears to Her Majesty to be necessary or expedient ; but the power to make Orders under this subsection (which includes power to vary or revoke a previous Order) shall not be exercisable before the appointed day and no recommendation shall be made to Her Majesty to make such an Order unless a draft of it has been approved by resolution of each House of Parliament.

(7) The standing orders may provide for enabling a consultative committee to obtain from any department in relation to which it is established such information as the committee may require for the purpose of discharging its functions but shall not enable the committee or any member thereof to have access to any papers of that department.

(8) The standing orders shall include provision for the examination by a committee of the Assembly of the manner in which moneys charged on or appropriated out of the Consolidated Fund of Northern Ireland have been applied.

(9) The Secretary of State may give directions for regulating
the procedure of the Assembly so far as he considers requisite
pending the making of standing orders by the Assembly.

(10) Subsection (8) above does not apply to the application of
moneys before the appointed day.

26.—(1) The powers, privileges and immunities of the Privileges,
Assembly and of the members and committees thereof shall be remuneration,
the same as those for the time being held and enjoyed by the etc.
House of Commons and its members and committees but this
subsection has effect subject to section 25(7) above and to any
provision made by Measure.

(2) There shall be paid to each member of the Assembly such
salary and allowances as may be prescribed by Order in Council ;
and provision may be made by Order in Council for the payment
of pensions to or in respect of persons who have been members
of the Assembly.

(3) Any salary or allowances payable to a member by virtue
of an Order in Council under subsection (2) above shall accrue
from the date on which he is returned as a member but shall
not be payable unless he takes his seat in the manner prescribed
by standing orders.

(4) Special provision may be made by Order in Council under
subsection (2) above in respect of the member who is the
presiding officer of the Assembly and in respect of such other
members (if any) as may be elected by the Assembly to discharge other functions in relation to the Assembly.

(5) Any salaries or allowances payable by virtue of an Order
under subsection (2) above, and any sums required by such an
Order relating to pensions to be paid out of public funds, shall
be defrayed out of moneys appropriated for that purpose by
Measure.

(6) Any Order in Council under subsection (2) above may be
varied or revoked by a subsequent Order.

(7) A member of the Assembly may resign his seat by giving
notice in writing to the presiding officer of the Assembly ; and
if a seat becomes vacant by resignation, death or disqualification
the presiding officer shall as soon as practicable inform the
Assembly thereof.

(8) Provision may be made by Order in Council under subsection (2) above for increasing the salary specified in section
1(5) of the Northern Ireland Assembly Act 1973 or for altering 1973 c. 17.
the allowances there mentioned but, save as aforesaid, neither
that subsection nor subsection (3) above affects any payment to

PART IV

be made under the said section 1(5) to any person by virtue of his membership of the Assembly elected under that Act.

(9) Subsection (5) above shall, as from the appointed day, apply to any salaries or allowances payable under the said section 1(5).

Dissolution
and
prorogation.
1973 c. 17.

27.—(1) The Assembly elected under the Northern Ireland Assembly Act 1973 shall by virtue of this subsection be dissolved—

    (*a*) if an Order in Council is made under section 2 above before 30th March 1974, on the fourth anniversary of the appointed day ;

    (*b*) if no Order in Council is so made, on 30th March 1974.

(2) Any Assembly elected after that mentioned in subsection (1) above shall by virtue of this subsection be dissolved—

    (*a*) except where paragraph (*b*) below applies, on the fourth anniversary of the dissolution of its predecessor ;

    (*b*) if its predecessor was dissolved by virtue of paragraph (*b*) of subsection (1) above and no Order in Council is made under section 2 above before the expiration of the period of six months beginning with the day on which it was elected, at the expiration of that period.

(3) If, apart from this subsection, the date of dissolution under subsection (1)(*a*) or (2) above would fall on a Saturday, Sunday or public holiday it shall fall on the next subsequent day which is not a Saturday, Sunday or public holiday.

(4) The Secretary of State may by order direct that any date of dissolution under paragraph (*a*) of subsection (1) or (2) above shall, instead of being determined in accordance with that paragraph and subsection (3) above, be a date specified in the order, being a date falling not more than two months before or after the date so determined.

(5) If it appears to Her Majesty that the composition of the Assembly is such that it is not possible for the Secretary of State to make appointments under section 8 above which comply with the requirements of subsection (4) of that section and that it is in the public interest that the Assembly should be dissolved, Her Majesty, after taking into account any vote or resolution of the Assembly which appears to Her Majesty to be relevant, may by Order in Council direct that the date of dissolution for the Assembly, instead of being determined in accordance with the foregoing provisions of this section, shall be such earlier date as may be specified in the Order.

(6) In any case in which an Order could be made under subsection (5) above Her Majesty may, instead of or before

making an Order under that subsection, by Order in Council prorogue or further prorogue the Assembly.

(7) If the Assembly is dissolved in accordance with subsection (1)(*b*) or (5) above Her Majesty may by Order in Council appoint a day for the election of members of a new Assembly; and the first meeting of the new Assembly shall be held on such day as the Secretary of State may by order direct.

(8) An Order in Council under this section may be varied or revoked by a subsequent Order and, except in the case of an Order proroguing the Assembly for a period of four months or less and not extending a previous period of prorogation, no recommendation shall be made to Her Majesty to make an Order under this section unless a draft of it has been approved by resolution of each House of Parliament.

(9) Any power of the Secretary of State to make an order under subsection (4) or (7) above includes power to vary or revoke a previous order and, in the case of an order under subsection (4), shall be exercisable by statutory instrument subject to annulment in pursuance of a resolution of either House of Parliament.

(10) An Order in Council under this section proroguing the Assembly shall specify the period of prorogation and the Assembly shall meet at the expiration of that period but without prejudice to the power of Her Majesty to recall it earlier and subject to any further prorogation or any dissolution by or under this section before the expiration of that period.

28.—(1) Section 1(2) of the Northern Ireland Assembly Act 1973 and the Schedule to that Act (which provide for the members of the Assembly to be returned for the constituencies in Northern Ireland which would return members to the Parliament of the United Kingdom if a general election were held at the passing of that Act and specifies the number of members to be returned by each constituency) shall apply also in relation to any subsequent election of members of the Assembly and, subject to subsection (6) below, shall so apply as if for the reference to the passing of that Act there were substituted a reference to the date on which the election is held.

Constituencies and number of members.
1973 c. 17.

(2) Where the Boundary Commission for Northern Ireland submit to the Secretary of State a report under section 2(1) or (3) of the House of Commons (Redistribution of Seats) Act 1949 showing the constituencies into which the whole of, or any area in, Northern Ireland should be divided they shall submit therewith a supplementary report showing the number of members which they recommend should be returned to the Assembly by each of those constituencies.

1949 c. 66.

(3) The recommendations in a supplementary report shall not be such as substantially to alter the number of members specified in section 1(1) of the said Act of 1973 (total number of members of Assembly) ; and those recommendations shall be such as to secure, so far as practicable, that the ratio of the electorate of each constituency to the number of members to be returned by that constituency is the same in every constituency.

In this subsection " the electorate ", in relation to a constituency, means the number of persons whose names appear on the register of electors for that constituency in force on the enumeration date (as defined in Schedule 2 to the said Act of 1949) under section 29 below.

(4) Section 2(4) and (5) and section 3 of the said Act of 1949 (publication of notice of proposed report of Boundary Commission and implementation of recommendations in report) shall apply to a supplementary report under this section as they apply to a report under that Act.

(5) An Order in Council under the said Act of 1949 for giving effect, with or without modifications, to the recommendations contained in a report or supplementary report of the Boundary Commission for Northern Ireland may amend section 1(1) of the said Act of 1973 by altering the number of members there specified and may amend the Schedule to that Act by altering the name of any of the constituencies there mentioned or the number of members there specified in relation to any constituency.

(6) Any provision of an Order in Council under the said Act of 1949 altering the boundaries of any constituency in Northern Ireland or the number of members specified in the said section 1(1) or the said Schedule in relation to any constituency shall not affect any election to the Assembly before the next general election to the Assembly or affect the constitution of the Assembly then in being.

(7) The officers of the Boundary Commission for Northern Ireland shall include the Chief Electoral Officer for Northern Ireland as an additional assessor.

Elections and franchise. 1973 c. 17.

29.—(1) The following provisions of section 2 of the Northern Ireland Assembly Act 1973, that is to say—

(a) subsection (3) (voting in poll for election under that Act to be by single transferable vote) ;

(b) subsection (4) (deposits by candidates at that election) ;

(c) subsection (5) (power of Secretary of State by order to make provision as to the conduct etc. of that election) ;

shall apply also to any subsequent election of members of the Assembly, including bye-elections.

(2) The provision that may be made by an order under subsection (5) of the said section 2 as extended by this section shall include provision for determining, subject to section 27(7) above, the date of the poll for any such subsequent election, provision as to the persons entitled to vote at any such election and the registration of such persons and provision for such other matters relating to any such election as the Secretary of State thinks necessary or expedient.

30.—(1) For section 10 of the House of Commons Disqualification Act 1957 (which applies certain provisions of that Act to the Senate and House of Commons of the Parliament of Northern Ireland) there shall be substituted—

Disqualification for membership of Assembly.
1957 c. 20.

"Provisions relating to Northern Ireland Assembly.

10.—(1) Subject to subsection (2) of this section, the following provisions of this Act, that is to say—

(a) section 1(1), (3) and (4) and sections 3, 5, 8 and 9 ; and

(b) Parts I, II and III of Schedule 1,

shall apply in relation to the Northern Ireland Assembly as they apply in relation to the House of Commons of the Parliament of the United Kingdom, and references in those provisions to the House of Commons shall be construed accordingly.

(2) In relation to the Northern Ireland Assembly for Parts II and III of Schedule 1 to this Act there shall be substituted the Parts set out in Schedule 3 to this Act."

(2) In Schedule 3 to the said Act of 1957 the heading shall be changed to "Provisions substituted for Parts II and III of Schedule 1 in relation to Northern Ireland Assembly" and all the other provisions of that Schedule except the substituted Parts II and III shall be omitted.

(3) In section 3 of the Northern Ireland Assembly Act 1973 (disqualification for membership of Assembly) in subsection (1) for the words from "a person is disqualified for membership of the Assembly" onwards there shall be substituted the words "a person is disqualified for membership of the Assembly if he is disqualified for membership of the Commons House of the Parliament of the United Kingdom otherwise than by the House of Commons Disqualification Act 1957" and in subsection (3) of that section references to a disqualification imposed by that section shall include references to a disqualification imposed by the said Act of 1957 as amended by this section.

1973 c. 17.

PART V

MISCELLANEOUS AND SUPPLEMENTARY

Abolition of Parliament of Northern Ireland.

31.—(1) The Parliament of Northern Ireland shall cease to exist.

(2) Unless and until the Clerk to the Assembly otherwise determines, every person who immediately before the date of the passing of this Act was employed in the service of, or of either House of, the Parliament of Northern Ireland in any office mentioned in subsection (3) below shall as from that date be employed in the service of the Assembly with the same remuneration and conditions of service.

(3) The said offices are Clerk-Assistant of the Parliaments, Second Clerk-Assistant of the Parliaments, Fourth Clerk at the Table, Librarian and Assistant Librarian, Editor and Deputy Editor of Official Reports of Debates and Reporter.

(4) Subject to subsection (5) below, all property which immediately before the date of the passing of this Act was held in trust or used for the purposes of, or either House of, the Parliament of Northern Ireland, or partly for those purposes and partly for other purposes, shall on and after that date be applied for the purposes of the Assembly or such other purposes as the Ministry of Finance for Northern Ireland may determine.

(5) The Secretary of State may require the Ministry to make available to him in any premises comprised in the property mentioned in subsection (4) above (other than the Parliament Buildings at Stormont) such accommodation and facilities as he may specify ; and the Secretary of State shall in consideration of the use thereof after the appointed day make to the Ministry such payments out of moneys provided by Parliament as he and the Ministry may agree.

(6) In so far as any of the property mentioned in subsection (4) above was not immediately before the date of the passing of this Act vested in the Ministry of Finance for Northern Ireland it shall vest in that Ministry on that date ; and subsections (4) and (5) above shall have effect notwithstanding anything in any deed or other instrument relating to the property to which those subsections apply.

Abolition of office of Governor and provisions as to Privy Council of Northern Ireland.

32.—(1) The office of Governor of Northern Ireland shall cease to exist.

(2) There shall be charged on and paid out of the Consolidated Fund of the United Kingdom to the last holder of that office such sum as the Secretary of State may, with the consent of the Minister for the Civil Service, determine to be appropriate.

(3) No further appointments shall be made to the Privy Council of Northern Ireland.

33.—(1) The Secretary of State shall be the sole trustee under Schedule 2 to the Ministerial Salaries and Members' Pensions Act (Northern Ireland) 1965 unless and until he appoints other persons to be trustees under that Schedule; and so long as the Secretary of State is sole trustee paragraphs 1 to 5 of that Schedule shall not apply.

(2) Save as aforesaid and without prejudice to any provision made under this Act, nothing in this Act affects any pension payable under the said Act of 1965 or section 1 of the Ministerial Offices Act (Northern Ireland) 1952 the right to which has accrued before the passing of this Act or accrues upon a person ceasing to be a member of the Parliament of Northern Ireland by reason of section 31 above.

PART V

Preservation of pension rights of former members of Parliament of Northern Ireland and former Ministers.

1965 c. 18 (N.I.).

1952 c. 15 (N.I.).

34.—(1) As from the appointed day the Prosecution of Offences (Northern Ireland) Order 1972 (which establishes and makes provision for the office of Director of Public Prosecutions for Northern Ireland) shall have effect subject to the following provisions of this section.

Director of Public Prosecutions for Northern Ireland.

S.I. 1972/538.

(2) Any appointment to the office of Director or deputy Director of Public Prosecutions for Northern Ireland shall be made by the Attorney General for Northern Ireland; and the Attorney General for Northern Ireland may remove the Director or deputy Director on the ground of inability or misbehaviour.

(3) In Article 4(2)(*b*) and (*c*) (provisions as to resignation and retirement) for references to the Governor of Northern Ireland there shall be substituted references to the Attorney General for Northern Ireland.

(4) Article 3(2) (which places the Director under the superintendence of the Attorney General so long as section 1 of the Northern Ireland (Temporary Provisions) Act 1972 has effect) shall continue to apply after that section ceases to have effect.

1972 c. 22.

(5) Any reference in Article 4 or 8 to the Ministry of Home Affairs or the Ministry of Finance shall, as respects anything falling to be done after the appointed day, be construed as a reference to the Secretary of State.

35.—(1) As from the appointed day there shall be a Crown Solicitor for Northern Ireland appointed by the Attorney General for Northern Ireland.

Crown Solicitor for Northern Ireland.

(2) The Crown Solicitor shall hold office on such terms and conditions as may be determined by the Attorney General for Northern Ireland.

PART V

(3) The services of the Crown Solicitor shall be available to any Minister or department of the Government of the United Kingdom and, with the approval of the Attorney General for Northern Ireland and on such terms as he may determine, to any Northern Ireland executive authority.

(4) The remuneration of, and other expenses incurred in connection with, the Crown Solicitor shall be defrayed out of moneys provided by Parliament.

Provisions as to other Northern Ireland officers.

36.—(1) Any appointment on or after the appointed day to the office of—

  (*a*) Northern Ireland Parliamentary Commissioner for Administration ;

  (*b*) Northern Ireland Commissioner for Complaints ;

  (*c*) Civil Service Commissioner for Northern Ireland ;

  (*d*) Comptroller and Auditor-General for Northern Ireland,

shall be made by Her Majesty.

1969 c. 10 (N.I.).

(2) The Parliamentary Commissioner Act (Northern Ireland) 1969 shall, in relation to any complaint made on or after the date of the passing of this Act, have effect as if for any reference in sections 5 and 6 to a member of the House of Commons there were substituted a reference to a member of the Assembly; and any report to be sent on or after that date under section 10(1) of that Act in respect of a complaint made before that date shall be sent by the Commissioner to such member of the Assembly as he thinks appropriate.

(3) Section 10(3), (4) and (5) of the said Act of 1969 shall, as from the appointed day, have effect as if for any reference to each or either House of Parliament or to a member of the House of Commons there were substituted a reference to the Assembly or a member of the Assembly.

(4) Subsections (2) and (3) above have effect subject to any provision made by Measure.

(5) Her Majesty may by Order in Council make provision with respect to the appointment of lord-lieutenants, lieutenants and deputy lieutenants in Northern Ireland, for conferring on them functions which apart from the Order would be exercisable by lieutenants in Northern Ireland, for altering the designation of vice-lieutenants in Northern Ireland and for matters incidental to or consequential on any provision so made, including the amendment or repeal of any enactment passed before this Act.

(6) An Order in Council under subsection (5) above may be varied or revoked by a subsequent Order.

37.—(1) The functions of the Joint Exchequer Board are hereby transferred to the Treasury and that Board shall cease to exist.

(2) Any sums which, apart from this Act, would be payable into the Consolidated Fund of the United Kingdom by virtue of section 22(1) of the Government of Ireland Act 1920 (reserved taxes) shall continue to be so paid ; and, subject to subsection (3) below, any sums which, apart from this Act, would be payable into the Consolidated Fund of Northern Ireland by virtue of section 21(1) of that Act (transferred taxes) shall continue to be so paid.

(3) There shall be paid into the Consolidated Fund of the United Kingdom, as from such date as the Treasury may by order direct, the proceeds of any tax specified in the order which would otherwise be paid into the Consolidated Fund of Northern Ireland.

(4) The power to make orders under subsection (3) above includes power to vary or revoke a previous order and shall be exercisable by statutory instrument.

38.—(1) Her Majesty may by Order in Council make provision with respect to the following matters—

  (a) elections (but not the franchise) and boundaries in respect of local authorities in Northern Ireland ;

  (b) the constitution of the Police Authority for Northern Ireland.

(2) Her Majesty may by Order in Council make such amendments of the law of any part of the United Kingdom as appear to Her Majesty to be necessary or expedient in consequence of any provision made by or under any Measure or Act of the Parliament of Northern Ireland or Order in Council under section 1(3) of the Northern Ireland (Temporary Provisions) Act 1972 or by or under any Act of the Parliament of the United Kingdom passed before this Act in so far as the provision is part of the law of Northern Ireland.

(3) An Order in Council under subsection (2) above may contain such consequential and supplemental provisions as appear to Her Majesty to be necessary or expedient.

(4) An Order in Council under this section may be varied or revoked by a subsequent Order.

(5) No recommendation shall be made to Her Majesty to make an Order in Council under this section unless a draft of the Order has been approved by resolution of each House of Parliament.

PART V
Provisions as to Joint Exchequer Board and other financial matters.
1920 c. 67.

Power to legislate by Order in Council for certain matters relating to Northern Ireland.

1972 c. 22.

PART V
Power to
legislate by
Order in
Council for
purposes con-
sequential on
this Act or on
Orders under
s. 3.

1972 c. 22.

39.—(1) Her Majesty may by Order in Council make such provision, including provision amending the law of any part of the United Kingdom, as appears to Her Majesty to be necessary or expedient in consequence of, or for giving full effect to, this Act or any Order under section 3 above ; and, without prejudice to the generality of that power, provision may in particular be made by any such Order for any of the matters mentioned in subsections (2) to (7) below.

(2) Provision may be made for transferring, with effect from the appointed day, any functions which immediately before that day are (or but for the Northern Ireland (Temporary Provisions) Act 1972 or section 32 or 37 above would be) exercisable by an existing Northern Ireland authority—

> (a) in so far as those functions appear to Her Majesty to be concerned with an excepted matter or reserved matter, to a United Kingdom authority ;

> (b) in so far as they appear to Her Majesty to be concerned with a transferred matter, to a new Northern Ireland authority.

(3) Provision may be made, with effect from the appointed day, for anything which immediately before that day would, apart from the said Act of 1972 or section 31 above, fall to be done by or to the Parliament of Northern Ireland or either House of that Parliament in connection with any matter (other than the passing of Acts of that Parliament) to be done instead by or to—

> (a) in so far as that matter appears to Her Majesty to be an excepted matter or reserved matter, the Parliament of the United Kingdom or either House of that Parliament ;

> (b) in so far as that matter appears to Her Majesty to be a transferred matter, the Assembly.

(4) Provision may be made for transferring, with effect from any date specified in an Order under section 3 above, any functions which immediately before that date are exercisable by a United Kingdom authority or a new or existing Northern Ireland authority—

> (a) in so far as they appear to Her Majesty to be concerned with a matter which on that date becomes a transferred matter, to a new or existing Northern Ireland authority ;

> (b) in so far as they appear to Her Majesty to be concerned with a matter which on that date ceases to be a transferred matter, to a United Kingdom authority.

(5) Provision may be made, with effect from any date specified in an Order under the said section 3, for anything which immediately before that date falls to be done by or to the Parliament of the United Kingdom or either House of that Parliament or by the Assembly in connection with any matter (other than the passing of Acts of Parliament or Measures) to be done instead by or to—

(a) in so far as that matter appears to Her Majesty to be a matter which on that date becomes a transferred matter, the Assembly ;

(b) in so far as that matter appears to Her Majesty to be a matter which on that date ceases to be a transferred matter, the Parliament of the United Kingdom or either House of that Parliament.

(6) Provision may be made for any sums to be charged on and payable out of, or payable into, the Consolidated Fund of the United Kingdom or the Consolidated Fund of Northern Ireland or for any sums to be paid out of moneys provided by Parliament or out of moneys appropriated by Measure.

(7) Provision may be made, to such extent as may appear to Her Majesty to be necessary or expedient in consequence of, or for giving full effect to, this Act or any Order under section 3 above—

(a) for transferring or apportioning any property, rights or liabilities ;

(b) for substituting any authority for any other authority in any charter, contract or other document or in any legal proceedings ;

(c) for any other transitional or consequential matter.

(8) In this section—

" existing Northern Ireland authority " means the Governor of Northern Ireland, the Privy Council of Northern Ireland, the Governor of Northern Ireland in Council, the Prime Minister and any other Minister of the Government of Northern Ireland, any department of that Government, the Comptroller and Auditor-General for Northern Ireland, the Joint Exchequer Board and the Chief Crown Solicitor in Northern Ireland ;

" new Northern Ireland authority " means any of the Northern Ireland executive authorities ;

" United Kingdom authority " means the Privy Council, any Minister of the Government of the United Kingdom, the Treasury, the Defence Council, the Commissioners of Inland Revenue, the Commissioners of Customs and Excise, the Comptroller and Auditor General and the Crown Solicitor for Northern Ireland appointed under this Act.

PART V

(9) The power to make Orders under this section includes power to vary or revoke a previous Order and no recommendation shall be made to Her Majesty to make an Order under this section unless a draft of it has been approved by resolution of each House of Parliament.

General adaptation of references to institutions and offices abolished by this Act.

40.—(1) Schedule 5 to this Act shall have effect as from the appointed day for adapting references in existing statutory provisions to institutions and offices which cease to exist by virtue of this Act.

(2) Where an existing statutory provision refers (otherwise than for the purpose of extending or restricting the powers of the Parliament of Northern Ireland) to the matters in respect of which that Parliament has or does not have power to make laws, that provision shall be construed as referring to the matters in respect of which that Parliament would or would not have had power to make laws if this Act had not been passed.

(3) In this section " existing statutory provision " means any provision contained in an Act of the Parliament of Northern Ireland or in an Act of the Parliament of the United Kingdom passed before the appointed day or in the Session in which the appointed day falls and any provision contained in an instrument made before the appointed day under any such Act.

(4) Subsection (1) above applies also in relation to any charter, contract or other document (not being a statutory provision) made before the appointed day.

(5) This section and Schedule 5 have effect subject to any provision made by or under this Act or by Measure, and modify references only so far as their context and the nature of the provision or document in question admit.

Repeals.

41.—(1) The enactments specified in Schedule 6 to this Act are hereby repealed to the extent specified in the third column of that Schedule—

(a) in the case of the enactments in Part I of that Schedule, as from the passing of this Act ;

(b) in the case of those in Part II, as from the appointed day.

(2) Without prejudice to the generality of the powers conferred by section 39 above, an Order in Council under that section may repeal or revoke any existing statutory provision (as defined in section 40 above) which appears to Her Majesty to be unnecessary in consequence of, or inconsistent with, any provision of this Act.

42.—(1) Except so far as otherwise provided by or under this **PART V** Act, nothing in this Act shall affect the continued operation in Saving for or in relation to Northern Ireland of any law in force at the existing laws. passing of this Act or on the appointed day.

(2) Without prejudice to subsection (1) above, neither the abolition of the Parliament of Northern Ireland nor the repeal by this Act of any provision relating to that Parliament shall affect the validity or otherwise of any Act of that Parliament.

(3) Neither the abolition of the Parliament of Northern Ireland or of the office of Governor of Northern Ireland nor the repeal by this Act of any provision relating to that Parliament or office shall affect the operation of the Northern Ireland (Tem- 1972 c. 22. porary Provisions) Act 1972 or the validity of any Order in Council made under section 1(3) of that Act ; and any provision of any Act passed in the same Session as this Act which confers powers on the Parliament of Northern Ireland or functions on the Governor or the Governor in Council shall be construed as conferring corresponding powers on Her Majesty to make laws under the said section 1(3) or corresponding functions on the Secretary of State.

43.—(1) This Act may be cited as the Northern Ireland Con- Short title, stitution Act 1973. interpretation
and com-
(2) In this Act— mencement.

> " the appointed day " means the day appointed under sec-
> tion 2 above for the commencement of Part II of this
> Act ;
> " the Assembly " means the Northern Ireland Assembly ;
> " excepted matter " means any matter specified in Schedule
> 2 to this Act ;
> " enactment " includes an enactment of the Parliament of
> Northern Ireland ;
> " functions " includes powers and duties ;
> " Measure " means a Measure of the Northern Ireland
> Assembly ;
> " Northern Ireland " has the same meaning as for the pur-
> poses of the Government of Ireland Act 1920 ;   1920 c. 67.
> " Northern Ireland executive authorities " has the meaning
> given in section 7(6) above ;
> " reserved matter " has the meaning given in section 3(4)
> above ;
> " transferred matter " means any matter which is for the
> time being declared to be such a matter by an order
> under Part I of this Act.

(3) In accordance with section 7(5) above, references in this Act to the Ministry of Finance for Northern Ireland shall from the appointed day be construed as references to the Department of Finance for Northern Ireland.

(4) Any reference in this Act to any enactment is a reference to that enactment as amended by, and includes a reference to that enactment as extended or applied by, any other enactment including this Act.

(5) Part I of this Act and, except where otherwise stated, Parts IV and V of this Act shall come into force at the passing of this Act.

(6) Part III of this Act shall come into force on a day specified in an order made by the Secretary of State by statutory instrument, and different days may be specified under this subsection for different provisions of Part III.

SCHEDULES

SCHEDULE 1

POLLS FOR PURPOSES OF SECTION 1

1. The Secretary of State may by order direct the holding of a poll for the purposes of section 1 of this Act on a date specified in the order, but the date so specified shall not be earlier than 9th March 1983 or earlier than ten years after the date of a previous poll under this Schedule.

2. Any order under this Schedule directing the holding of a poll shall make provision as to the persons entitled to vote on the poll, the question or questions to be asked of the persons so voting and the conduct of the poll, and may make such other provision in connection with the poll as appears to the Secretary of State to be expedient, including provision applying, with or without modifications, any enactment or statutory provision with respect to Parliamentary elections or elections to the Assembly.

3. The power to make orders under this Schedule includes power to vary or revoke a previous order and shall be exercisable by statutory instrument but no such order shall be made unless a draft of the order has been approved by resolution of each House of Parliament.

SCHEDULE 2

EXCEPTED MATTERS

1. The Crown, including the succession to the Crown and a regency, but not—

   (a) functions of Northern Ireland executive authorities or functions in relation to Northern Ireland of any Minister of the Crown ;

   (b) property belonging to Her Majesty in right of the Crown or belonging to a government department or held in trust for Her Majesty for the purposes of a government department ;

   (c) foreshore or the sea bed or subsoil or their natural resources so far as vested in Her Majesty in right of the Crown.

2. The Parliament of the United Kingdom ; parliamentary elections, including the franchise ; disqualifications for membership of that Parliament.

3. International relations, including treaties, the making of peace or war and neutrality, and matters connected therewith but not—

   (a) the surrender of fugitive offenders between Northern Ireland and the Republic of Ireland ;

   (b) the exercise of legislative powers so far as required for giving effect to any agreement or arrangement made under section 12 of this Act ;

(c) the exercise of legislative powers for any of the purposes mentioned in section 2(2)(*a*) or (*b*) of the European Communities Act 1972 or for purposes similar to those of any of sections 5 to 12 of, or any paragraph of Schedule 4 to, that Act.

4. The armed forces of the Crown but not any matter within paragraph 3 of Schedule 3 to this Act.

5. Dignities and titles of honour.

6. Treason and treason felony but not powers of arrest or criminal procedure in respect thereof.

7. Nationality ; immigration ; aliens as such.

8. Taxes for the time being levied under any law applying to the United Kingdom as a whole, existing Northern Ireland taxes and taxes substantially of the same character as any of those taxes.

In this paragraph " existing Northern Ireland taxes " means any of the following taxes levied in Northern Ireland before the appointed day, that is to say, estate duty, stamp duty, general betting duty, pool betting duty, duty on gaming machine licences and duty on licences in respect of mechanically-propelled vehicles.

9. The appointment and removal of judges of the Supreme Court of Judicature of Northern Ireland, county court judges, recorders, resident magistrates, justices of the peace, members of juvenile court panels, coroners, the Chief and other National Insurance Commissioners for Northern Ireland and the President and other members of the Lands Tribunal for Northern Ireland.

10. The appointment and office of the Director and deputy Director of Public Prosecutions for Northern Ireland.

11. Elections, including the franchise, in respect of the Northern Ireland Assembly and local authorities.

12. Coinage, legal tender and bank notes.

13. The National Savings Bank.

14. Special powers and other provisions for dealing with terrorism or subversion.

15. Without prejudice to paragraphs 10 and 11 above, any matter for which provision is made by the Northern Ireland Assembly Act 1973 or this Act but not—

    (*a*) matters in respect of which it is stated by this Act that provision may be made by Measure ; or

    (*b*) matters specified in Schedule 3 to this Act ;

and this paragraph shall not be taken to apply to any matter by reason only that provision is made in respect of it by an Order in Council under section 6(4) or (5), 38 or 39 of this Act.

SCHEDULE 3

MINIMUM RESERVED MATTERS ON APPOINTED DAY

1. Any such property as is mentioned in paragraph 1(*b*) of Schedule 2 to this Act but not as respects any aerodrome or harbour.

2. All matters, other than those specified in paragraph 9 of Schedule 2 to this Act, relating to the Supreme Court of Judicature of Northern Ireland, the Court of Criminal Appeal in Northern Ireland, county courts, courts of summary jurisdiction (including magistrates' courts and juvenile courts) and coroners, including procedure, evidence, appeals, juries, costs, legal aid and the registration, execution and enforcement of judgments and orders but not—

    (*a*) bankruptcy, insolvency, the winding up of corporate and unincorporated bodies or the making of arrangements or compositions with creditors ;

    (*b*) the regulation of the profession of solicitors.

3. Without prejudice to paragraphs 4, 5 and 6 below, the maintenance of public order, including the conferring of powers, authorities, privileges or immunities for that purpose on constables, members of the armed forces of the Crown and other persons, but not any matter within paragraph 14 of Schedule 2 to this Act.

4. The following matters—

    (*a*) the criminal law, including the creation of offences and penalties ;

    (*b*) the prevention and detection of crime and powers of arrest and detention in connection with crime or criminal proceedings ;

    (*c*) prosecutions ;

    (*d*) the treatment of offenders (including children and young persons, and mental health patients, involved in crime) ;

    (*e*) the surrender of fugitive offenders between Northern Ireland and the Republic of Ireland ;

    (*f*) compensation out of public funds for victims of crime.

Sub-paragraph (*d*) of this paragraph includes, in particular, prisons and other institutions for the treatment or detention of persons mentioned in that sub-paragraph.

5. The establishment, organisation and control of the Royal Ulster Constabulary and of any other police force ; the Police Authority for Northern Ireland ; traffic wardens.

6. Firearms and explosives.

7. Disqualification for membership of the Northern Ireland Assembly ; privileges, powers and immunities of the Assembly, its members and committees greater than those conferred by section 26(1) of this Act.

8. The exercise of legislative powers so far as required for giving effect to any agreement or arrangement made under section 12 of this Act.

9. Trade with any place outside the United Kingdom but not—

  (*a*) the furtherance of the trade of Northern Ireland or the protection of traders in Northern Ireland against fraud ;

  (*b*) services in connection with, or the regulation of, the quality, insurance, transport, marketing or identification of agricultural or food products, including livestock ;

  (*c*) the prevention of disease or the control of weeds and pests ;

  (*d*) aerodromes and harbours.

10. Navigation, including merchant shipping, but not harbours or inland waters.

11. The foreshore and the sea bed and subsoil and their natural resources (except so far as affecting harbours) ; submarine pipe-lines ; submarine cables, including any land line used solely for the purpose of connecting one submarine cable with another.

12. Civil aviation but not aerodromes.

13. Postal services, including telecommunications and the issue, transmission and payment of money and postal orders issued by the Post Office ; designs for postage stamps.

14. Wireless telegraphy, including sound broadcasting and television.

15. Domicile.

16. Nuclear installations.

17. Trade marks, designs, copyright and patent rights.

18. Units of measurement and United Kingdom primary standards.

19. Oaths, undertakings in lieu of oaths and declarations other than those excepted from subsection (1) of section 21 of this Act by subsection (3) of that section.

20. Trustee Savings Banks.

21. Civil defence.

1926 c. 8 (N.I.).

22. The Emergency Powers Act (Northern Ireland) 1926 or any enactment for similar purposes.

SCHEDULE 4

Section 8.

FORM OF OATH OR AFFIRMATION UNDER SECTION 8

I swear by Almighty God [*or* affirm] that I will uphold the laws of Northern Ireland and conscientiously fulfil [as a member of the Northern Ireland Executive] my duties under the Northern Ireland Constitution Act 1973 in the interests of Northern Ireland and its people.

SCHEDULE 5

Section 40.

GENERAL ADAPTATION OF REFERENCES TO INSTITUTIONS AND OFFICES ABOLISHED BY THIS ACT

1.—(1) Any reference to an Act or enactment of the Parliament of Northern Ireland shall be construed as including a reference to a Measure.

(2) Sub-paragraph (1) applies whether the reference is express or implied and also where the reference is to a local or private Act of that Parliament or to an order confirmed by that Parliament.

(3) Any reference to Bills in the Parliament of Northern Ireland shall be construed as including a reference to proposed Measures in the Assembly.

2.—(1) Any reference to moneys provided by the Parliament of Northern Ireland shall be construed as a reference to moneys appropriated by Measure.

(2) Any reference to the payment of a sum to, into or out of the Exchequer of Northern Ireland shall be construed as a reference to the payment of that sum to, into or out of the Consolidated Fund of Northern Ireland.

3.—(1) Any reference to a resolution of the Senate or of the House of Commons of the Parliament of Northern Ireland, or of either House of that Parliament, shall be construed as a reference to a resolution of the Assembly.

(2) Any reference to the laying or presenting of any document before or to the Parliament of Northern Ireland or either House of that Parliament shall be construed as a reference to the laying or presenting of the document before or to the Assembly.

4.—(1) Any reference to the Governor of Northern Ireland, as respects functions to be discharged by him, or to the Governor of Northern Ireland in Council shall be construed as a reference to the Secretary of State.

(2) Any reference to the making of an Order in Council by the Governor of Northern Ireland shall be construed as a reference to the making of an order by the Secretary of State.

5. Any reference to the Prime Minister of Northern Ireland shall, as respects functions to be discharged by him, be construed as a reference to the chief executive member.

6. Any reference to the Executive Committee for Northern Ireland shall be construed as a reference to the Northern Ireland Executive.

7.—(1) Any reference to a Minister of Northern Ireland identified by a title corresponding to that of a Ministry of Northern Ireland shall, as respects functions to be discharged by him, be construed as a reference to the head of the Northern Ireland department bearing the name of that Ministry immediately before the appointed day.

(2) Any reference to an unspecified Minister or to unspecified Ministers of Northern Ireland shall, as respects the discharge of functions, be construed as a reference to the head of a Northern Ireland department or the heads of Northern Ireland departments.

8.—(1) Any reference to a specified Ministry of Northern Ireland shall be construed as a reference to that Ministry by its existing name but with the substitution of the word " Department " for the word " Ministry ".

(2) Any reference to an unspecified Ministry or unspecified Ministries of Northern Ireland shall be construed as a reference to a Northern Ireland department or to Northern Ireland departments.

SCHEDULE 6

Repeals

Part I

Enactments Repealed from Passing of this Act

Chapter	Short Title	Extent of Repeal
10 & 11 Geo. 5. c. 67.	The Government of Ireland Act 1920.	Section 1(1). Sections 4 to 6. Section 8(4)(*b*). In section 9(2), in proviso (*b*) the words " Parliament or ". Sections 11 to 19. Section 21(1), (2), (3) and (5). Section 25(1), (3) and (4). Sections 31 and 32. Section 34. Section 37. Section 45. In section 46 the words from " existing judges " to " Court) " and the words " and pending proceedings ". Section 52. In section 61 the words " and subject " onwards. Section 64(1). Section 65(2). Section 67. Sections 69 and 70 (without prejudice to Orders already made). Section 73. In section 74 the definitions of " constituency ", " parliamentary elector ", " parliamentary election ", " election laws " and " submarine cable ". In section 75 the words from " the establishment " to " Ireland or ". Schedules 3 to 5. In Schedule 7, paragraphs 1, 3 and 7 of Part III.
11 & 12 Geo. 5 c. 19.	The Housing Act 1921.	Section 10(6).
13 Geo. 5. Session 2. c. 2.	The Irish Free State (Consequential Provisions) Act 1922 (Session 2).	In Schedule 1, paragraph 1(1) so far as it establishes the office of Governor, paragraph 2(2) except as respects the removal of Privy Councillors, in paragraph 2(3) the words from " and after " onwards and paragraph 5.
15. & 16 Geo. 5. c. 34.	The Northern Ireland Land Act 1925.	Section 36(2).

Chapter	Short Title	Extent of Repeal
16 & 17 Geo. 5. c. 44.	The Supreme Court of Judicature of Northern Ireland Act 1926.	Section 3.
16 & 17 Geo. 5. c. 45.	The Fertilisers and Feeding Stuffs Act 1926.	Section 29(2).
17 & 18 Geo. 5. c. 42.	The Statute Law Revision Act 1927.	Section 4(2).
18 & 19 Geo. 5. c. 24.	The Northern Ireland (Miscellaneous Provisions) Act 1928.	Section 2.
19 & 20 Geo. 5. c. 14.	The Northern Ireland Land Act 1929.	Section 8(2).
21 & 22 Geo. 5. c. 33.	The Architects (Registration) Act 1931.	Section 18(3).
22 & 23 Geo. 5. c. 11.	The Northern Ireland (Miscellaneous Provisions) Act 1932.	Section 3. Section 9(1), (4)(*b*) and (5).
22 & 23 Geo. 5. c. 12.	The Destructive Imported Animals Act 1932.	In section 12(2), the words from " and " onwards.
25 & 26 Geo. 5. c. 21.	The Northern Ireland Land Purchase (Winding Up) Act 1935.	Section 15(4).
26 Geo. 5 & 1 Edw. 8. c. 22.	The Hours of Employment (Conventions) Act 1936.	Section 5(2).
1 Edw. 8 & 1 Geo. 6. c. 14.	The East India Loans Act 1937.	Section 12(4).
1 & 2 Geo. 6. c. 6.	The Air-Raid Precautions Act 1937.	In section 14 the words from " and that " onwards. In section 15(2) the words " except the provisions thereof relating to the power of the Parliament of Northern Ireland to make laws ".
1 & 2 Geo. 6. c. 54.	The Architects Registration Act 1938.	Section 6(2).
2 & 3 Geo. 6. c. 31.	The Civil Defence Act 1939.	Section 92(2).
2 & 3 Geo. 6. c. 72.	The Landlord and Tenant (War Damage) Act 1939.	Section 25. In section 26(2) the words " except the provisions of the last foregoing section ".
2 & 3 Geo. 6. c. 73.	The Housing (Emergency Powers) Act 1939.	Section 5. In section 6(3) the words " except the provisions of the last foregoing section ".
2 & 3 Geo. 6. c. 94.	The Local Government Staffs (War Service) Act 1939.	Section 16. In section 17(3) the words " except the provisions of the last foregoing section ".
2 & 3 Geo. 6. c. 95.	The Teachers Superannuation (War Service) Act 1939.	Section 12. In section 13(4) the words " except the provisions of the last foregoing section ".

Chapter	Short Title	Extent of Repeal
2 & 3 Geo. 6. c. 102.	The Liability for War Damage (Miscellaneous Provisions) Act 1939.	Section 7. In section 8(3) the words " The provisions of the last foregoing section, and ".
2 & 3 Geo. 6. c. 103.	The Police and Firemen (War Service) Act 1939.	Section 15. In section 16(3) the words " except the provisions of the last foregoing section ".
2 & 3 Geo. 6. c. 114.	The Execution of Trusts (Emergency Provisions) Act 1939.	Section 8. In section 9(3) the words " except the provisions of the last foregoing section ".
3 & 4 Geo. 6. c. 10.	The Industrial Assurance and Friendly Societies (Emergency Protection from Forfeiture) Act 1940.	Section 11. In section 12 the words " except for the provisions of the last foregoing section ".
3 & 4 Geo. 6. c. 19.	The Societies (Miscellaneous Provisions) Act 1940.	Section 11. In section 12(2) the words " except the provisions of the last foregoing section ".
3 & 4 Geo. 6. c. 26.	The Superannuation Schemes (War Service) Act 1940.	Section 2. In section 3(2) the words " except the provisions of the last preceding section ".
3 & 4 Geo. 6. c. 31.	The War Charities Act 1940.	Section 13. In section 14(2) the words " except the provisions of the last foregoing section ".
3 & 4 Geo. 6. c. 38.	The Truck Act 1940.	Section 2. In section 3(2) the words " Save as provided in the last foregoing section ".
4 & 5 Geo. 6. c. 41.	The Landlord and Tenant (War Damage) (Amendment) Act 1941.	Section 18.
7 & 8 Geo. 6. c. 10.	The Disabled Persons (Employment) Act 1944.	Section 22(2).
7 & 8 Geo. 6. c. 22.	The Police and Firemen (War Service) Act 1944.	Section 6(1). In section 7(3) the words " save in so far as it amends section fifteen of the principal Act ".
7 & 8 Geo. 6. c. 25.	The Law Officers Act 1944.	Section 3.
7 & 8 Geo. 6. c. 34.	The Validation of War-time Leases Act 1944.	In section 6, in subsection (1) the words " The foregoing provisions of " and subsection (2).
7 & 8 Geo. 6. c. 43.	The Matrimonial Causes (War Marriages) Act 1944.	Section 3.
8 & 9 Geo. 6. c. 10.	The Compensation of Displaced Officers (War Service) Act 1945.	In section 10, subsection (1) and in subsection (2) the words " except the last foregoing subsection ".
8 & 9 Geo. 6. c. 12.	The Northern Ireland (Miscellaneous Provisions) Act 1945.	Sections 1 and 2.

Chapter	Short Title	Extent of Repeal
8 & 9 Geo. 6. c. 44.	The Treason Act 1945.	Section 3(3).
9 & 10 Geo. 6. c. 13.	The Finance (No. 2) Act 1945.	Section 54(4).
9 & 10 Geo. 6. c. 20.	The Building Materials and Housing Act 1945.	Section 11(2).
9 & 10 Geo. 6. c. 28.	The Assurance Companies Act 1946.	The whole Act, so far as unrepealed.
9 & 10 Geo. 6. c. 58.	The Borrowing (Control and Guarantees) Act 1946.	In section 6, in subsection (1) the words " other than the provisions of this section " and subsection (2).
9 & 10 Geo. 6. c. 67.	The National Insurance Act 1946.	Section 70(6).
9 & 10 Geo. 6. c. 80.	The Atomic Energy Act 1946.	In section 20(1) the words from " and notwithstanding " onwards.
10 & 11 Geo. 6. c. 37.	The Northern Ireland Act 1947.	Section 1(1) and (2). Sections 3 to 7. Section 8(2) (without prejudice to Orders already made). In section 9, subsection (2) and (without prejudice to Orders already made) subsection (3). Sections 10 and 11. In section 14(3) the words " or in section two of the Northern Ireland (Miscellaneous Provisions) Act 1945 ".
10 & 11 Geo. 6. c. 44.	The Crown Proceedings Act 1947.	Section 53(6).
11 & 12 Geo. 6. c. 29.	The National Assistance Act 1948.	In section 67, subsection (1) and in subsection (2) the words " other than the last foregoing subsection ".
11 & 12 Geo. 6. c. 39.	The Industrial Assurance and Friendly Societies Act 1948.	Section 17(3). In section 24(2) the words " subsection (3) of section seventeen thereof and ".
11 & 12 Geo. 6. c. 41.	The Law Reform (Personal Injuries) Act 1948.	In section 5, subsection (1) and in subsection (2) the words " except in so far as it enlarges the powers of the Parliament of Northern Ireland ".
11 & 12 Geo. 6. c. 46.	The Employment and Training Act 1948.	Section 20(1).
11 & 12 Geo. 6. c. 52.	The Veterinary Surgeons Act 1948.	Section 30.
11 & 12 Geo. 6. c. 62.	The Statute Law Revision Act 1948.	Section 6(2).
11 & 12 Geo. 6. c. 65.	The Representation of the People Act 1948.	In section 79, in subsection (2) the words " to the Parliament of Northern Ireland or " and subsection (3).
11 & 12 Geo. 6. c. 66.	The Monopolies and Restrictive Practices (Inquiry and Control) Act 1948.	In section 21(1) the words from " but " onwards.

Chapter	Short Title	Extent of Repeal
12, 13 & 14 Geo. 6. c. 5.	The Civil Defence Act 1948.	In section 10, in subsection (1) the words " other than this section " and subsection (2).
12, 13 & 14 Geo. 6. c. 27.	The Juries Act 1949.	Section 34.
12, 13 & 14 Geo. 6. c. 41.	The Ireland Act 1949.	Section 1(2).
12, 13 & 14 Geo. 6. c. 51.	The Legal Aid and Advice Act 1949.	Section 26.
12, 13 & 14 Geo. 6. c. 55.	The Prevention of Damage by Pests Act 1949.	Section 29(2).
12, 13 & 14 Geo. 6. c. 60.	The Housing Act 1949.	In section 43(7) the words following paragraph (c).
12, 13 & 14 Geo. 6. c. 66.	The House of Commons (Redistribution of Seats) Act 1949.	Section 7.
12, 13 & 14 Geo. 6. c. 67.	The Civil Aviation Act 1949.	Section 35(3).
12, 13 & 14 Geo. 6. c. 68.	The Representation of the People Act 1949.	In section 174, in subsection (2) the words " to the Parliament of Northern Ireland or " and subsection (3).
12, 13 & 14 Geo. 6. c. 100.	The Law Reform (Miscellaneous Provisions) Act 1949.	Section 10. In section 11(2) the words " (except section ten) ".
14 Geo. 6. c. 6.	The Statute Law Revision Act 1950.	Section 5(4).
14 Geo. 6. c. 20.	The Colonial and Other Territories (Divorce Jurisdiction) Act 1950.	Section 5.
14 Geo. 6. c. 36.	The Diseases of Animals Act 1950.	In section 87 the second paragraph. Section 88. In section 91(2) the words " and eighty-eight ".
14 Geo. 6. c. 37.	The Maintenance Orders Act 1950.	Section 31(1).
14 & 15 Geo. 6. c. 39.	The Common Informers Act 1951.	Section 2.
14 & 15 Geo. 6. c. 65.	The Reserve and Auxiliary Forces (Protection of Civil Interests) Act 1951.	Section 65(5).
15 & 16 Geo. 6 & 1 Eliz. 2. c. 11.	The Northern Ireland (Foyle Fisheries) Act 1952.	The whole Act.
15 & 16 Geo. 6 & 1 Eliz. 2. c. 39.	The Motor Vehicles (International Circulation) Act 1952.	Section 5.
15 & 16 Geo. 6 & 1 Eliz. 2. c. 44.	The Customs and Excise Act 1952.	In section 314, in subsection (4) the words from the beginning to " power to make laws; and " and subsections (5) and (7).

Chapter	Short Title	Extent of Repeal
15 & 16 Geo. 6 & 1 Eliz. 2. c. 66.	The Defamation Act 1952.	Section 15. In section 18(2) the words " (except section fifteen) ".
2 & 3 Eliz. 2. c. 5.	The Statute Law Revision Act 1953.	Section 4(1).
2 & 3 Eliz. 2. c. 23.	The Hill Farming Act 1954.	Section 2(5).
2 & 3 Eliz. 2. c. 39.	The Agriculture (Miscellaneous Provisions) Act 1954.	Section 10(12). Section 11(4). In section 12(7) the words from " but " onwards. In section 16 the words " sections ten and eleven in so far as they extend the powers of the Parliament of Northern Ireland, and ".
2 & 3 Eliz. 2. c. 58.	The Charitable Trusts (Validation) Act 1954.	Section 5.
3 & 4 Eliz. 2. c. 8.	The Northern Ireland Act 1955.	Section 1. Sections 3 and 5.
4 & 5 Eliz. 2. c. 16.	The Food and Drugs Act 1955.	Section 134(2) and (3).
4 & 5 Eliz. 2. c. 18.	The Aliens' Employment Act 1955.	Section 2(3).
4 & 5 Eliz. 2. c. 25.	The Therapeutic Substances Act 1956.	Section 17(3).
4 & 5 Eliz. 2. c. 46.	The Administration of Justice Act 1956.	Section 55(4).
4 & 5 Eliz. 2. c. 52.	The Clean Air Act 1956.	In section 36 the words "other than this section" and the words from "but" onwards. In section 37(1) the words from " but " onwards.
4 & 5 Eliz. 2. c. 68.	The Restrictive Trade Practices Act 1956.	
4 & 5 Eliz. 2. c. 69.	The Sexual Offences Act 1956.	Section 50(2).
4 & 5 Eliz. 2. c. 76.	The Medical Act 1956.	Section 56(2).
5 & 6 Eliz. 2. c. 20.	The House of Commons Disqualification Act 1957.	In section 14, in subsection (3) the words " and of the Senate and House of Commons of Northern Ireland ". In Schedule 1, in Part III, the words " Crown Solicitor in Northern Ireland ", " Speaker of the Senate or House of Commons of Northern Ireland " and " Standing Counsel to the Speaker of the Senate or House of Commons of Northern Ireland ". In Schedule 3, all the words following the heading and preceding the substituted Parts II and III, and in the substituted Part III the words " Crown Solicitor in Northern

Chapter	Short Title	Extent of Repeal
5 & 6 Eliz. 2. c. 20.—*cont.*	The House of Commons Disqualification Act 1957—*cont.*	Ireland" and "Standing Counsel to the Speaker of the Senate or House of Commons of Northern Ireland ".
5 & 6 Eliz. 2. c. 28.	The Dentists Act 1957.	In section 52 the words from "and " onwards.
5 & 6 Eliz. 2. c. 36.	The Cheques Act 1957.	In section 7 the words from "but " onwards.
6 & 7 Eliz. 2. c. 17.	The Recreational Charities Act 1958.	Section 4.
6 & 7 Eliz. 2. c. 26.	The House of Commons (Redistribution of Seats) Act 1958.	Section 7(3).
6 & 7 Eliz. 2. c. 32.	The Opticians Act 1958.	In section 31(2), the words from "and " onwards.
6 & 7 Eliz. 2. c. 39.	The Maintenance Orders Act 1958.	Section 22. In section 23(2) the words " and the last foregoing section ".
6 & 7 Eliz. 2. c. 46.	The Statute Law Revision Act 1958.	Section 5.
6 & 7 Eliz. 2. c. 47.	The Agricultural Marketing Act 1958.	In section 53, subsection (2) (without prejudice to the power of the Secretary of State to revoke a certificate), subsection (3), in subsection (4) the words "giving or " and subsection (12).
6 & 7 Eliz. 2. c. 51.	The Public Records Act 1958.	Section 12(2).
6 & 7 Eliz. 2. c. 53.	The Variation of Trusts Act 1958.	In section 2(2) the words from "but " onwards.
6 & 7 Eliz. 2. c. 62.	The Merchant Shipping (Liability of Shipowners and Others) Act 1958.	Section 10(3).
7 & 8 Eliz. 2. c. 19.	The Emergency Laws (Repeal) Act 1959.	Section 8(1).
7 & 8 Eliz. 2. c. 56.	The Rights of Light Act 1959.	Section 6. In section 8(4) the words "except section six thereof ".
7 & 8 Eliz. 2. c. 68.	The Statute Law Revision Act 1959.	Section 3.
7 & 8 Eliz. 2. c. 72.	The Mental Health Act 1959.	Section 151. In section 152 the words " section one hundred and fifty-one ".
8 & 9 Eliz. 2. c. 34.	The Radioactive Substances Act 1960.	Section 21(5).
8 & 9 Eliz. 2. c. 37.	The Payment of Wages Act 1960.	Section 8. In section 9(4) the words "except the last preceding section ".
8 & 9 Eliz. 2. c. 44.	The Finance Act 1960.	Section 73(9). Section 74(8).
8 & 9 Eliz. 2. c. 46.	The Corporate Bodies' Contracts Act 1960.	Section 3. In section 4(3) the words "subject to the provisions of section three of this Act ".

Chapter	Short Title	Extent of Repeal
8 & 9 Eliz. 2. c. 56.	The Statute Law Revision Act 1960.	Section 2.
8 & 9 Eliz. 2. c. 57.	The Films Act 1960.	In section 52, subsection (3) and in subsection (4) the words " to the powers of the Parliament of Northern Ireland and ".
8 & 9 Eliz. 2. c. 58.	The Charities Act 1960.	In section 38(5) the words from " but " onwards. Section 47. In section 49(2)(*a*) the words " or extends the powers of the Parliament of Northern Ireland ".
8 & 9 Eliz. 2. c. 61.	The Mental Health (Scotland) Act 1960.	Section 115. In section 116 the words " section one hundred and fifteen ".
8 & 9 Eliz. 2. c. 64.	The Building Societies Act 1960.	Section 75.
8 & 9 Eliz. 2. c. 65.	The Administration of Justice Act 1960.	Section 18(2).
8 & 9 Eliz. 2. c. 66.	The Professions Supplementary to Medicine Act 1960.	In section 14(2) the words from " and " onwards.
9 & 10 Eliz. 2. c. 14.	The Nurses (Amendment) Act 1961.	Section 13. In section 15(3) the words " and section thirteen ".
9 & 10 Eliz. 2. c. 37.	The Small Estates (Representation) Act 1961.	In section 3(5) the words " other than this subsection " and the words from " but " onwards.
9 & 10 Eliz. 2. c. 39.	The Criminal Justice Act 1961.	Section 40(1).
10 & 11 Eliz. 2. c. 21.	The Commonwealth Immigrants Act 1962.	Section 20(3).
10 & 11 Eliz. 2. c. 23.	The South Africa Act 1962.	Section 3(3).
10 & 11 Eliz. 2. c. 27.	The Recorded Delivery Service Act 1962.	Section 3(2).
10 & 11 Eliz. 2. c. 30.	The Northern Ireland Act 1962.	Section 1(8). Section 2(3). Section 7(11). Sections 12 to 18. Section 19(1). Sections 20 and 21. Section 22(1).
10 & 11 Eliz. 2. c. 33.	The Health Visiting and Social Work (Training) Act 1962.	Section 7(5).
10 & 11 Eliz. 2. c. 44.	The Finance Act 1962.	Section 28(6).
10 & 11 Eliz. 2. c. 46.	The Transport Act 1962.	Section 93(2).
1963 c. 18.	The Stock Transfer Act 1963.	Section 5(3).
1963 c. 30.	The Statute Law Revision Act 1963.	Section 2.

Chapter	Short Title	Extent of Repeal
1963 c. 31.	The Weights and Measures Act 1963.	In Schedule 10 paragraphs 3 to 6 and 11.
1963 c. 41.	The Offices, Shops and Railway Premises Act 1963.	Section 87. In section 91(3) the words from " except " onwards.
1963 c. 44.	The Wills Act 1963.	In section 7(5) the words from " and " onwards.
1963 c. 47.	The Limitation Act 1963.	Section 14(2) and (3).
1964 c. 14.	The Plant Varieties and Seeds Act 1964.	In section 39(1) the words from " but " onwards.
1964 c. 24.	The Trade Union (Amalgamations, etc.) Act 1964.	In section 10, in subsection (1) the words " except subsection (4) of this section " and subsection (4).
1964 c. 28.	The Agriculture and Horticulture Act 1964.	In section 26(3) the words from " but " onwards.
1964 c. 29.	The Continental Shelf Act 1964.	Section 12.
1964 c. 30.	The Legal Aid Act 1964.	Section 4. In section 6(5) the words " other than section 4 ".
1964 c. 40.	The Harbours Act 1964.	Section 59. In section 63(2) the words " section 59 and ".
1964 c. 58.	The Resale Prices Act 1964.	In section 12(2) the words from " but " onwards.
1964 c. 60.	The Emergency Laws (Re-enactments and Repeals) Act 1964.	Section 20(5).
1964 c. 72.	The Fishery Limits Act 1964.	Section 4(2) and (3).
1964 c. 79.	The Statute Law Revision Act 1964.	Section 2.
1965 c. 2.	The Administration of Justice Act 1965.	Section 31.
1965 c. 25.	The Finance Act 1965.	In section 92(9) the words from " but " onwards. In section 93(7) the words from " but " onwards.
1965 c. 37.	The Carriage of Goods by Road Act 1965.	Section 11(3).
1965 c. 45.	The Backing of Warrants (Republic of Ireland) Act 1965.	Section 11.
1965 c. 51.	The National Insurance Act 1965.	Section 104(5).
1965 c. 52.	The National Insurance (Industrial Injuries) Act 1965.	Section 83(5). In section 88(2) the words " 83(5) and ".
1965 c. 53.	The Family Allowances Act 1965.	Section 24. In section 25(2) the words " and 24 ".
1965 c. 54.	The National Health Service Contributions Act 1965.	Section 6. In section 9(2) the figure " 6 ".
1965 c. 57.	The Nuclear Installations Act 1965.	Section 27(7).

Chapter	Short Title	Extent of Repeal
1965 c. 62.	The Redundancy Payments Act 1965.	Section 58(4).
1965 c. 69.	The Criminal Procedure (Attendance of Witnesses) Act 1965.	Section 9. In section 10(6) the words " Section 9 extends to Northern Ireland and ".
1965 c. 74.	The Superannuation Act 1965.	Section 39(4).
1966 c. 5.	The Statute Law Revision Act 1966.	Section 2.
1966 c. 18.	The Finance Act 1966.	Section 44(8).
1966 c. 23.	The Botswana Independence Act 1966.	In the Schedule, paragraph 8(3).
1966 c. 24.	The Lesotho Independence Act 1966.	In the Schedule, paragraph 8(3).
1966 c. 30.	The Reserve Forces Act 1966.	In section 18(9) the words following paragraph (d).
1966 c. 34.	The Industrial Development Act 1966.	Section 14. In section 31(7)(a) the words " section 14 and " and " other ".
1966 c. 36.	The Veterinary Surgeons Act 1966.	In section 29(2) the words from " and " onwards.
1966 c. 46.	The Bus Fuel Grants Act 1966.	Section 1(2).
1967 c. 4.	The West Indies Act 1967.	Section 20(2).
1967 c. 22.	The Agriculture Act 1967.	In section 72(1) the words from " but " onwards.
1967 c. 32.	The Development of Inventions Act 1967.	Section 14.
1967 c. 34.	The Industrial Injuries and Diseases (Old Cases) Act 1967.	Section 12 (3). In section 16(2) the words " 12(3) and ".
1967 c. 54.	The Finance Act 1967.	Section 4(6)(a), (c) and (d). In Schedule 6, in paragraph 12, the words from " but " onwards.
1967 c. 58.	The Criminal Law Act 1967.	Section 11(4).
1967 c. 71.	The Aden, Perim and Kuria Muria Islands Act 1967.	Section 8(2).
1967 c. 80.	The Criminal Justice Act 1967.	Section 105(1) and (2).
1967 c. 84.	The Sea Fish (Conservation) Act 1967.	Section 23(3).
1968 c. 2.	The Provisional Collection of Taxes Act 1968.	Section 6(3).
1968 c. 13.	The National Loans Act 1968.	Section 23(2).
1968 c. 21.	The Criminal Appeal (Northern Ireland) Act 1968.	Section 52.
68 c. 29.	The Trade Descriptions Act 1968.	Section 40(2), (3), (4) and (7).
968 c. 32.	The Industrial Expansion Act 1968.	Section 17.

U

Chapter	Short Title	Extent of Repeal
1968 c. 34.	The Agriculture (Miscellaneous Provisions) Act 1968.	Section 49. In section 54(4) the words from " but " onwards.
1968 c. 49.	The Social Work (Scotland) Act 1968.	Section 96. In section 97(2) the words " section 96 ".
1968 c. 53.	The Adoption Act 1968.	Section 13. In section 14(3) the words " and 13 ".
1968 c. 56.	The Swaziland Independence Act 1968.	In the Schedule, paragraph 8(3).
1968 c. 59.	The Hovercraft Act 1968.	Section 5(1).
1968 c. 60.	The Theft Act 1968.	In section 36, subsection (2) and in subsection (3) the words " apart from subsection (2) above ".
1968 c. 61.	The Civil Aviation Act 1968.	Section 13(1).
1968 c. 63.	The Domestic and Appellate Proceedings (Restriction of Publicity) Act 1968.	Section 4(3).
1968 c. 64.	The Civil Evidence Act 1968.	Section 19. In section 20(3) the words " except in so far as it enlarges the powers of the Parliament of Northern Ireland ".
1968 c. 66.	The Restrictive Trade Practices Act 1968.	In section 15 the words from " and " onwards.
1968 c. 67.	The Medicines Act 1968.	Section 134(2).
1968 c. 73.	The Transport Act 1968.	Section 164(2).
1968 c. 77.	The Sea Fisheries Act 1968.	Section 20.
1969 c. 15.	The Representation of the People Act 1969.	In section 26(4) the words " and (3) ".
1969 c. 19.	The Decimal Currency Act 1969.	Section 18(2).
1969 c. 32.	The Finance Act 1969.	Section 16(2).
1969 c. 37.	The Employer's Liability (Defective Equipment) Act 1969.	In section 2, subsection (3) and in subsection (4) the words " except the foregoing subsection ".
1969 c. 40.	The Medical Act 1969.	In section 22 the words from " and " onwards.
1969 c. 42.	The Architects Registration (Amendment) Act 1969.	In section 4(2) the words from " but " onwards.
1969 c. 46.	The Family Law Reform Act 1969.	Section 13. Section 28(4)(f).
1969 c. 48.	The Post Office Act 1969.	Section 139(2).
1969 c. 50.	The Trustee Savings Banks Act 1969.	Section 97(2).

Chapter	Short Title	Extent of Repeal
1969 c. 52.	The Statute Law (Repeals) Act 1969.	In section 5, in subsection (1) the words from " but " onwards and in subsection (2) the words from " and " onwards.
1969 c. 54.	The Children and Young Persons Act 1969.	In section 73(5) the words following paragraph (c).
1969 c. 58.	The Administration of Justice Act 1969.	Section 33. In section 36(3) the figure " 33 ".
1969 c. 63.	The Police Act 1969.	Section 1(4).
1970 c. 2.	The Industrial Development (Ships) Act 1970.	Section 2.
1970 c. 11.	The Sea Fish Industry Act 1970.	Section 43(1).
1970 c. 22.	The Tonga Act 1970.	In the Schedule, paragraph 7(3).
1970 c. 31.	The Administration of Justice Act 1970.	Section 53. In section 54(6) the words " and 53 ".
1970 c. 40.	The Agriculture Act 1970.	Section 109. Section 112.
1970 c. 42.	The Local Authority Social Services Act 1970.	In section 15(7) the words following the semi-colon.
1970 c. 46.	The Radiological Protection Act 1970.	Section 5(3).
1971 c. 11.	The Atomic Energy Authority Act 1971.	Section 17(5) and (7). Section 18(3).
1971 c. 23.	The Courts Act 1971.	Section 58. In section 59(6)(a) the words " and section 58 ".
1971 c. 25.	The Administration of Estates Act 1971.	Section 13.
1971 c. 29.	The National Savings Bank Act 1971.	In Schedule 1, paragraph 4(3).
1971 c. 32.	The Attachment of Earnings Act 1971.	Section 28. In section 29(3) the words " and 28 ".
1971 c. 38.	The Misuse of Drugs Act 1971.	Section 38(3).
1971 c. 40.	The Fire Precautions Act 1971.	Section 42. In section 44(2) the words " except section 42 ".
1971 c. 43.	The Law Reform (Miscellaneous Provisions) Act 1971.	Section 5(3). In section 6(3) the words " Except for section 5(3) ".
1971 c. 47.	The Wild Creatures and Forest Laws Act 1971.	In section 2(3) the words from " and " onwards.
1971 c. 50.	The National Insurance Act 1971.	In section 16(4), paragraph (a) and in paragraph (b) the words " other than paragraph (a) above ".
1971 c. 52.	The Statute Law (Repeals) Act 1971.	Section 2(2).
1971 c. 53.	The Recognition of Divorces and Legal Separations Act 1971.	Section 9.

Chapter	Short Title	Extent of Repeal
1971 c. 60.	The Prevention of Oil Pollution Act 1971.	Section 30(6).
1971 c. 61.	The Mineral Workings (Offshore Installations) Act 1971.	Section 14(3).
1971 c. 66.	The Friendly Societies Act 1971.	Section 12(5). In section 15(3) the words " except subsection (5) of section 12 ".
1971 c. 72.	The Industrial Relations Act 1971.	Section 165(1) and (4).
1971 c. 73.	The Social Security Act 1971.	Section 10(1).
1971 c. 75.	The Civil Aviation Act 1971.	Section 65(2).
1971 c. 80.	The Banking and Financial Dealings Act 1971.	In section 5(2) the words from " but " onwards.
1972 c. 6.	The Summer Time Act 1972.	Section 4(2).
1972 c. 10.	The Northern Ireland Act 1972.	The whole Act.
1972 c. 14.	The Transport Holding Company Act 1972.	In section 3(2) the words from " and " onwards.
1972 c. 18.	The Maintenance Orders (Reciprocal Enforcement) Act 1972.	Section 48(2).
1972 c. 27.	The Road Traffic (Foreign Vehicles) Act 1972.	Section 6. In section 8(3) the words " with the exception of section 6 ".
1972 c. 33.	The Carriage by Railway Act 1972.	Section 10(2).
1972 c. 36.	The National Insurance (Amendment) Act 1972.	Section 2(2)(*b*).
1972 c. 38.	The Matrimonial Proceedings (Polygamous Marriages) Act 1972.	In section 5(3) the words following the semi-colon.
1972 c. 50.	The Legal Advice and Assistance Act 1972.	In section 14(5) the words from the beginning to " this section ".
1972 c. 57.	The National Insurance Act 1972.	Section 7(1)(*b*).
1972 c. 60.	The Gas Act 1972.	In section 33(2) the second paragraph.
1972 c. 63.	The Industry Act 1972.	Section 18(2).
1972 c. 65.	The National Debt Act 1972.	Section 18.
1972 c. 68.	The European Communities Act 1972.	In section 2(5) the words from the beginning as far as the semi-colon. Section 4(3)(*b*).
1972 c. 71.	The Criminal Justice Act 1972.	In section 63, subsection (1) and in subsection (2) the words from the beginning to " but ".

Chapter	Short Title	Extent of Repeal
1972 c. 75.	The Pensioners and Family Income Supplement Payments Act 1972.	Section 5(2).
1972 c. 77.	The Northern Ireland (Border Poll) Act 1972.	The whole Act.
1973 c. 9.	The Counter-Inflation Act 1973.	Section 20(7).
1973 c. 13.	The Supply of Goods (Implied Terms) Act 1973.	Section 17(2).
1973 c. 15.	The Administration of Justice Act 1973.	In section 10(8), the second paragraph. Section 14(3). Section 18(3).

PART II

ENACTMENTS REPEALED FROM APPOINTED DAY

Chapter	Short Title	Extent of Repeal
10 & 11 Geo. 5. c. 67.	The Government of Ireland Act 1920.	Section 8, so far as unrepealed (except subsection (7)). Section 9. Section 20(1), (2) and (4). Sections 22 to 24. Section 25(5). Section 26(4). Section 47. Section 51. Section 53. Sections 62 and 63. In section 74 the definitions of " customs duties ", " excess profits duty " and " postal service ". Schedule 6.
13 Geo. 5. Session 2. c. 2.	The Irish Free State (Consequential Provisions) Act 1922 (Session 2).	In Schedule 1, paragraph 4.
25 & 26 Geo. 5. c. 21.	The Northern Ireland Land Purchase (Winding Up) Act 1935.	Section 1(3). Section 6(4). Section 11(3). Schedule 2.
1 & 2 Geo. 6. c. 6.	The Air Raid Precautions Act 1937.	Section 14, so far as unrepealed.
10 & 11 Geo. 6. c. 37.	The Northern Ireland Act 1947.	Section 1(3).
11 & 12 Geo. 6. c. 64.	The National Service Act 1948.	Section 57(2).
12, 13 & 14 Geo. 6. c. 47.	The Finance Act 1949.	Section 49(2).

U 3

Chapter	Short Title	Extent of Repeal
14 & 15 Geo. 6. c. 25.	The Supplies and Services (Defence Purposes) Act 1951.	In section 2(11)(*d*) the words " without prejudice to section sixty-three of the Government of Ireland Act 1920 ".
9 & 10 Eliz. 2. c. 15.	The Post Office Act 1961.	Section 2(4). Section 27(1).
9 & 10 Eliz. 2. c. 36.	The Finance Act 1961.	In section 9(9) the words from the beginning to "but".
10 & 11 Eliz. 2. c. 30.	The Northern Ireland Act 1962.	In section 8(1) the words " the Attorney General " and the word " other ". Section 19(2). In section 29(1) the definition of " the Attorney General ".
1963 c. 9.	The Purchase Tax Act 1963.	Section 37.
1964 c. 28.	The Agriculture and Horticulture Act 1964.	Section 1(11).
1965 c. 10.	The Superannuation (Amendment) Act 1965.	In Schedule 1 the entry relating to the Government of Ireland Act 1920.
1967 c. 54.	The Finance Act 1967.	Section 4(6)(*b*). Section 26(7).
1968 c. 13.	The National Loans Act 1968.	In Schedule 5 the entry relating to the Government of Ireland Act 1920.
1968 c. 44.	The Finance Act 1968.	In section 41(7) the words from " and " onwards.
1969 c. 48.	The Post Office Act 1969.	Section 139(4). In Schedule 4, paragraph 25. In Schedule 6, in Part III, the entry relating to section 9 of the Government of Ireland Act 1920.
1970 c. 10.	The Income and Corporation Taxes Act 1970.	In Schedule 15, paragraph 2.
1971 c. 29.	The National Savings Bank Act 1971.	In section 21(4) the words from " and those debited " onwards.
1971 c. 68.	The Finance Act 1971.	Section 67(2) and (4).
1972 c. 41.	The Finance Act 1972.	Section 1(4). In Schedule 7, paragraph 2(3).
1972 c. 76.	The Northern Ireland (Financial Provisions) Act 1972.	Section 2.

Water Act 1973

1973 CHAPTER 37

An Act to make provision for a national policy for water, for the conferring and discharge of functions as to water (including sewerage and sewage disposal, fisheries and land drainage) and as to recreation and amenity in connection with water, for the making of charges by water authorities and other statutory water undertakers, and for connected purposes.　　　　[18th July 1973]

BE IT ENACTED by the Queen's most Excellent Majesty, by and with the advice and consent of the Lords Spiritual and Temporal, and Commons, in this present Parliament assembled, and by the authority of the same, as follows:—

PART I

NATIONAL POLICY AND CENTRAL AND LOCAL ORGANISATION

National policy

1.—(1) It shall be the duty of the Secretary of State and the Minister of Agriculture, Fisheries and Food (in this Act referred to as "the Minister") to promote jointly a national policy for water in England and Wales and so to discharge their respective functions under subsections (2) and (3) below as to secure the effective execution of that policy by the bodies responsible for the matters mentioned in those subsections.

National policy for water.

(2) It shall be the duty of the Secretary of State to secure the effective execution of so much of that policy as relates to—

　(a) the conservation, augmentation, distribution and proper use of water resources, and the provision of water supplies;

　(b) sewerage and the treatment and disposal of sewage and other effluents;

U 4

(*c*) the restoration and maintenance of the wholesomeness of rivers and other inland water ;

(*d*) the use of inland water for recreation ;

(*e*) the enhancement and preservation of amenity in connection with inland water ; and

(*f*) the use of inland water for navigation.

(3) It shall be the duty of the Minister to secure the effective execution of so much of that policy as relates to land drainage and to fisheries in inland and coastal waters.

(4) Accordingly in the following provisions of this Act " the appropriate Minister or Ministers " means—

(*a*) in relation to a matter falling exclusively within subsection (2) above, the Secretary of State ;

(*b*) in relation to a matter falling exclusively within subsection (3) above, the Minister ; and

(*c*) in relation to a matter falling partly within one and partly within the other of those subsections, both the Secretary of State and the Minister acting jointly ;

and " the Ministers " means both the Secretary of State and the Minister acting jointly.

(5) It shall be the duty of the Welsh National Water Development Authority established under section 2 below to consider and advise the appropriate Minister or Ministers on any matter concerning that part of the national policy for water which falls to be executed by the Authority and on any other matters (including matters for which the Authority are not responsible) referred to the Authority by the appropriate Minister or Ministers.

(6) It shall be the duty of the Secretary of State to collate and publish information from which assessments can be made of the actual and prospective demand for water, and of actual and prospective water resources, in England and Wales.

(7) The Secretary of State may also (in so far as he considers it appropriate to do so) collaborate with others in collating and publishing the like information relating to the demand for water, and to water resources, whether in England and Wales or elsewhere.

Water authorities

Establishment of water authorities.

2.—(1) For the purpose of exercising functions conferred on them by or by virtue of Part II of this Act, there shall be established in accordance with the following provisions of this section authorities to be known as regional water authorities, being the authorities named in column 1 of Schedule 1 to this Act,

and also an authority to be known as the Welsh National Water
Development Authority (in this Act referred to as "the Welsh
authority ").

(2) Subject to subsection (5) below and Part IV of Schedule 5
to this Act—

(*a*) the regional water authorities shall exercise their functions as respects the existing areas described in
column 2 of Schedule 1 to this Act (being, in general,
areas established for the purposes of functions relating
to water resources or land drainage) ; and

(*b*) the Welsh authority shall exercise their functions as
respects the existing areas of the Dee and Clwyd,
Glamorgan, Gwynedd, South West Wales, Usk and
Wye River Authorities.

In this subsection any reference to an existing area is a
reference to that area as existing immediately before the passing
of this Act except that, in the case of an area which is altered
after the passing of this Act under any enactment other than this
section, it is a reference to the altered area.

(3) In this Act and any other enactment " water authority "
means an authority established in accordance with this section
and " water authority area " means, in relation to any functions
of a water authority, the area as respects which the water
authority are for the time being to exercise those functions.

(4) Each of the authorities mentioned in subsection (1)
above shall be established by an order made by the Ministers
and shall come into existence on a day appointed by the order,
and—

(*a*) the order or orders establishing the regional water
authorities shall be made not later than one month
after the passing of this Act ; and

(*b*) the order establishing the Welsh authority shall be
made in accordance with section 3(10) below.

(5) The Ministers may by order change the name of any water
authority or alter the boundaries of a water authority area for
the purposes of any functions specified in the order.

(6) Without prejudice to any power exercisable by virtue of
section 34 below, an order under this section may contain such
transitional, incidental, supplementary or consequential provision as the Ministers consider necessary or expedient for the
purposes of the order.

(7) Part I of Schedule 2 to this Act shall have effect in
relation to the boundaries of water authority areas, Part II of
that Schedule shall have effect in relation to maps of such areas
and of watercourses in them and Part III shall have effect in
relation to the alteration of such boundaries.

(8) The supplementary provisions contained in Part I of Schedule 3 to this Act and the administrative and financial provisions contained in Part III of that Schedule shall have effect with respect to water authorities.

Members of
water
authorities.

3.—(1) A regional water authority shall consist of the following members, that is to say—

(*a*) a chairman appointed by the Secretary of State ;

(*b*) such number of members appointed by the Minister as may be specified in an order under section 2 above, being not less than two or more than four ;

(*c*) such number of members appointed by the Secretary of State as may be so specified ; and

(*d*) such number of members as may be so specified appointed by local authorities in accordance with subsections (6) to (8) below ;

and any such order shall be so framed that the total number of members appointed by the Secretary of State and the Minister is less than the number of those appointed by local authorities.

(2) The members appointed by the Minister shall be persons who appear to him to have had experience of, and shown capacity in, agriculture, land drainage or fisheries.

(3) The members appointed by the Secretary of State shall be persons who appear to the Secretary of State to have had experience of, and shown capacity in, some matter relevant to the functions of water authorities.

(4) One of the members of the Severn-Trent Water Authority appointed by the Secretary of State shall be a member of the Welsh authority.

(5) In appointing the members of a regional water authority the Minister concerned shall have regard to the desirability of members of the authority being familiar with the requirements and circumstances of the authority's area.

(6) Subject to subsections (8) and (9) below, if a quarter or more of the population of any county is resident within the area of a regional water authority, then,—

(*a*) in the case of a metropolitan county, the county council may appoint two members, and the councils of the districts within the county may between them appoint two members, of the water authority ;

(*b*) in the case of a non-metropolitan county or of a county in Wales, the county council may appoint one member, and the councils of the districts within the county may between them appoint one member, of the water authority ;

and if one-sixth or more, but less than one-fourth, of the population of any county is resident within that area, the county council may, after consultation with the councils of the districts within the county and wholly or partly within that area appoint one member of the water authority.

Where the area of a water authority is different for different functions, that area shall be taken for the purposes of this subsection to be the area as respects which the authority discharge any functions or, as respects the period between the passing of this Act and 1st April 1974, the area as respects which they will discharge any functions as from that date.

(7) In the case of the Thames Water Authority, the Greater London Council may appoint ten members, and the London borough councils and the Common Council of the City of London may between them appoint ten members, of the Authority.

(8) In the case of the South West Water Authority, the Cornwall and Devon county councils may each appoint two members, the councils of the districts in Cornwall may between them appoint two members, and the councils of the districts in Devon may between them appoint two members, of the Authority.

(9) The Ministers may by order vary the membership of any regional water authority, but any such order which makes different provision in relation to a regional water authority from the provision made by this section in relation to that authority shall not be made unless a draft of the order has been laid before, and approved by resolution of, each House of Parliament.

(10) The constitution of the Welsh authority shall be prescribed by the order establishing it under section 2 above, but—

(a) an order establishing that authority or any order varying the constitution of the authority shall not be made unless a draft of the order has been laid before, and approved by resolution of, each House of Parliament; and

(b) a draft of the order establishing that authority shall be so laid not later than one month after the passing of this Act.

In reckoning that period for the purposes of this subsection no account shall be taken of any time during which Parliament is dissolved or prorogued or during which both Houses are adjourned for more than four days.

(11) An order made under or by virtue of this section which is required to be laid before Parliament shall, notwithstanding that it makes different provision in relation to one water authority from the provision made by this section or any order under it in relation to any other water authority or authorities, proceed in Parliament as if its provisions would, apart from this section,

require to be enacted by a public Bill which cannot be referred to a select or other committee of either House under the Standing Orders of either House relating to Private Bills.

(12) Members of a water authority appointed by a local authority or authorities may be members of that authority or one of those authorities or other persons.

(13) Any member of a water authority so appointed who at the time of his appointment was a member of the local authority or of one of the local authorities appointing him shall, if he ceases to be a member of that local authority, cease also to be a member of the water authority at the expiration of the period of three months beginning with the date when he ceases to be a member of the local authority or on the appointment of another person in his place, whichever first occurs; but for the purposes of this subsection a member of a local authority shall not be deemed to have ceased to be a member of the local authority by reason of retirement if he has been re-elected a member thereof not later than the day of his retirement.

National Water Council

Establishment and functions of National Water Council.

4.—(1) There shall be established a Council, to be called the National Water Council, which shall come into existence on such day as may be appointed by order made by the Ministers.

(2) The Council shall consist of—

(a) a chairman appointed by the Secretary of State;

(b) the chairmen of the water authorities; and

(c) not more than ten other members, of whom not more than eight shall be appointed by the Secretary of State and not more than two shall be appointed by the Minister.

(3) The members of the Council other than the chairman of the Council and the chairmen of the water authorities shall be persons appearing to the Secretary of State or the Minister, as the case may be, to have special knowledge of matters relevant to the functions of the water authorities.

(4) Parts II and III of Schedule 3 to this Act shall have effect with respect to the Council.

(5) It shall be the duty of the Council—

(a) to consider, and advise any Minister on, any matter relating to the national policy for water, and to consider and advise any Minister and the water authorities on any other matter of common interest to those authorities, including in either case any such matter as may be referred to the Council by any Minister;

(b) to promote and assist the efficient performance by water authorities of their functions, and in particular their functions relating to research and their functions with respect to the preparation, review and provision of plans under section 24 below ;

(c) to consider and advise any Minister on any matter on which the Council are consulted by him in pursuance of a requirement imposed by this Act ;

(d) with a view to the establishment throughout the United Kingdom of a scheme for the testing and approval of water fittings for ascertaining whether they comply with regulations and byelaws for preventing the waste, misuse or contamination of water, to consult with statutory water companies in England and Wales, regional water boards and water development boards in Scotland, the Ministry of Development in Northern Ireland, the Greater London Council and such associations of manufacturers, professional associations, local authority associations, trades unions and other organisations as the Council think appropriate ;

(e) to prepare, after consultation with statutory water companies and with such associations of employees and such educational and other authorities or bodies (including authorities and bodies in Scotland and Northern Ireland) as the Secretary of State may direct, a scheme for training and education in connection with the services provided in England and Wales by water authorities and the corresponding services provided in Scotland and Northern Ireland and, in so far as appears to the Council after the like consultations to be appropriate, the provision by the Council of facilities or assistance by the Council in the provision of facilities by others.

(6) If the Council establish any such scheme as is mentioned in subsection (5)(d) above, they shall secure that the scheme is administered by a committee of the Council which includes among its members persons representing the interests of regional water boards and water development boards in Scotland and of the Ministry of Development in Northern Ireland.

(7) As soon as may be after preparing a scheme under subsection (5)(e) above the Council shall submit it to the Secretary of State for his approval and—

(a) the Secretary of State may approve the scheme, with or without modifications ; and

(b) the Council shall implement the scheme as so approved.

(8) The Council may from time to time, after the like consultation as is mentioned in subsection (5)(e) above, prepare amendments to any scheme for the time being in force under subsection (7) above, and subsection (7) shall apply to the scheme as amended as it applies to the original scheme.

(9) The Council may furnish to any person or body for the benefit of any country or territory outside the United Kingdom technical assistance in connection with training and education in relation to any services corresponding to those provided in England and Wales by water authorities.

(10) The appropriate Minister or Ministers may, after consultation with the Council, give to the Council—

(*a*) directions of a general character as to the exercise and performance by the Council of their functions in relation to matters which appear to the appropriate Minister or Ministers to affect the execution of the national policy for water or otherwise to affect the national interest ; and

(*b*) directions to discontinue any activity, either wholly or to a specified extent, or not to extend any activity or not to extend it beyond specified limits.

(11) A direction under subsection (10)(*b*) above shall be given by statutory instrument, of which a draft shall be laid before Parliament.

(12) The Council shall have power, if so authorised by any two or more water authorities, to perform services for or to act on behalf of those bodies in relation to matters of common interest to them ; and if the Council perform services on behalf of water authorities, they may perform similar services on behalf of statutory water companies in England and Wales and public authorities and other bodies in Scotland, Northern Ireland, the Channel Islands and the Isle of Man who have functions similar to any of those exercisable in England or Wales by a water authority.

Supplementary provisions as to water authorities

Directions to
water
authorities.

5.—(1) The Minister may give water authorities directions of a general character as to the exercise by such authorities of their functions with respect to fisheries and land drainage, so far as the exercise of those functions appears to the Minister to affect the execution of the national policy for water or otherwise to affect the national interest.

(2) The Secretary of State may give water authorities directions of a general character as to the exercise by such authorities of any other functions of theirs, so far as the exercise of those functions appears to the Secretary of State to affect the execution of the national policy for water or otherwise to affect the national interest.

(3) **A** direction under this section may be given either to a
particular water authority or to water authorities generally, but
before giving a direction to water authorities generally the
appropriate Minister or Ministers shall consult the Council about
the proposed direction.

6.—(1) Subject to any express provision contained in this Act
or any Act passed after this Act, a water authority may arrange
for the discharge of any of their functions—

   (*a*) by a committee, a sub-committee or an officer of the
authority ; or

   (*b*) by any other water authority ;

and two or more water authorities may arrange to discharge
any of their functions jointly or may arrange for the discharge
of any of their functions by a joint committee of theirs.

(2) Where by virtue of this section any functions of a water
authority or two or more water authorities may be discharged
by a committee, then, unless the authority or authorities otherwise direct, the committee may arrange for the discharge of
any of those functions by a sub-committee or by an officer of
the authority or one of those authorities, and where by virtue
of this section any such functions may be discharged by a
sub-committee, then, unless the water authority or authorities
or the committee otherwise direct, the sub-committee may
arrange for the discharge of any of those functions by an officer
of the authority or one of those authorities.

(3) A water authority may not make arrangements under
this section for the discharge of any functions, so far as they
are exercisable by their regional land drainage committee or any
of their local land drainage committees, and may not make any
such arrangements for the discharge of the authority's functions
with respect to issuing precepts, making drainage charges or
borrowing money.

(4) Any arrangements made by a water authority under this
section for the discharge of any functions shall not prevent the
authority from discharging those functions.

(5) References in the foregoing provisions of this section to
the discharge of any functions of a water authority include
references to the doing of anything which is calculated to facilitate, or is conducive or incidental to, the discharge of any of
those functions.

(6) For the purpose of discharging any functions in pursuance
of arrangements under this section—

   (*a*) a water authority may appoint a committee of the
authority ; or

    (*b*) two or more water authorities may appoint a joint committee of those authorities ; or

    (*c*) any such committee may appoint one or more sub-committees ;

and the number of members of any such committee and their term of office shall be fixed by the appointing authority or authorities, or, in the case of a sub-committee, by the appointing committee.

(7) A committee appointed under subsection (6) above may include persons who are not members of the appointing authority or authorities or, in the case of a sub-committee, the authority or authorities of whom they are a sub-committee, but at least two-thirds of the members appointed to any such committee shall be members of that authority or those authorities, as the case may be.

(8) A water authority may appoint a committee, and two or more water authorities may join in appointing a committee, to advise the appointing authority or authorities on any matter relating to the discharge of their functions, and any such committee—

    (*a*) may consist of such persons (whether members of the appointing authority or authorities or not) appointed for such term as may be determined by the appointing authority or authorities ; and

    (*b*) may appoint one or more sub-committees to advise the committee with respect to any such matter.

(9) A person who is disqualified for being a member of a water authority shall be disqualified also for being a member of a committee or sub-committee appointed under this section.

Supply of goods and services, etc. 1970 c. 39.

7.—(1) The powers conferred by section 1 of the Local Authorities (Goods and Services) Act 1970 (supply of goods and services to local authorities and public bodies)—

    (*a*) shall be exercisable by a local authority within the meaning of that section as if a water authority and the Council were each a public body within the meaning of that section ;

    (*b*) shall be exercisable by a water authority as if another water authority, any such local authority or a development corporation, and no other body, were a public body within the meaning of that section ; and

    (*c*) shall, so far as concerns the discharge of sewerage or sewage disposal functions, be exercisable by a development corporation as if a water authority, and no other body, were a public body within the meaning of that section.

(2) A water authority may require an existing local authority who between the passing of this Act and 1st April 1974 are discharging functions transferred by this Act to the water authority or, where that local authority is abolished by the 1972 Act, the local authority or one of the local authorities who replace the abolished authority, to enter into an agreement under section 1(1) of the said Act of 1970 with the water authority for a period of not more than five years from that date, and it shall be the duty of the local authority who have been so required to enter into such an agreement, unless it is determined by the Secretary of State that the requirement is unreasonable having regard to the discharge of those functions immediately before that date and the operation of any enactment which comes into force on that date.

(3) An existing local authority who between the passing of this Act and 1st April 1974 discharge functions transferred by this Act to a water authority, or, where that local authority is abolished by the 1972 Act, the local authority or one of the local authorities who replace the abolished authority, may require the water authority to enter into an agreement under section 1(1) of the said Act of 1970 with the requiring authority for a period of not more than five years from that date, and it shall be the duty of the water authority to enter into such an agreement, unless it is determined by the Secretary of State that the requirement is unreasonable having regard to the circumstances of the existing local authority immediately before that date and the operation of any enactment which comes into force on that date.

(4) If an authority who have required another authority, and an authority who have been required, to enter into an agreement under subsection (2) or (3) above, are unable to agree on all or any of the terms of the agreement, the terms or term may be determined by the Secretary of State ; and any question whether a local authority replace an existing local authority shall also be determined by him.

(5) A water authority and a statutory water company may enter into an agreement providing that either of the parties shall do any of the following things, that is to say—

(a) supply goods or materials to the other party ;

(b) provide administrative, professional or technical services for the other party ;

(c) allow the other party to use any vehicle, plant or apparatus and, without prejudice to paragraph (b) above, place at the disposal of the other party the services of any person employed in connection with the vehicle or other property in question ;

(*d*) carry out works of maintenance in connection with land or buildings for the maintenance of which the other party is responsible ;

and any such agreement may contain such terms as to payment or otherwise as the parties consider appropriate.

(6) Either party to an agreement under subsection (5) above may purchase and store any goods or materials which in their opinion they may require for the purposes of paragraph (*a*) of that subsection, but nothing in paragraphs (*a*) to (*c*) of that subsection shall authorise a party to any such agreement to construct any buildings or works.

Rationalisation of holdings of property, and of functions.

8.—(1) It shall be the duty of every water authority to consider, in consultation with any other water authority concerned, the desirability, in the interest of rationalisation, of doing either or both of the following, that is to say—

(*a*) altering the boundaries of their area for the purposes of any functions of theirs ;

(*b*) transferring property of theirs to some other water authority.

(2) In discharging their duty to consider the desirability of altering the boundaries of their area for the purposes of any functions, a water authority shall first consider those boundaries which are different for the purposes of different functions, and in discharging their duty to consider the desirability of transferring any property, they shall first consider any property of theirs held for the purposes of any functions which is situated outside their area as constituted for the purposes of those functions.

(3) If a water authority decide that it is desirable to do either or both of the things mentioned in subsection (1) above, they shall make a recommendation to the appropriate Minister or Ministers accordingly, and the appropriate Minister or Ministers may—

(*a*) if the water authority recommend the alteration of the boundaries of their area, make an order under section 2 above altering those boundaries in accordance with the recommendation ; and

(*b*) if the water authority recommend the transfer of any property of theirs, make an order transferring that property and any rights or liabilities of theirs in connection therewith to a water authority specified in the recommendation.

(4) A statutory instrument containing an order under subsection (3)(*b*) above shall be subject to annulment in pursuance of a resolution of either House of Parliament.

(5) Where a water authority area adjoins any part of Scotland, and it appears to the water authority that there may be water in watercourses or underground strata in that part of Scotland, or in the water authority area, which could be transferred from that part of Scotland to the water authority area, or from the water authority area to that part of Scotland, as the case may be, the water authority shall, in so far as they consider it appropriate to do so, consult with regional water boards, river purification authorities and other authorities in that part of Scotland with a view to securing the best use of that water in the public interest.

(6) In subsection (5) above " river purification authority " has the same meaning as in section 17 of the Rivers (Prevention of Pollution) (Scotland) Act 1951.

1951 c. 66.

PART II

FUNCTIONS OF WATER AUTHORITIES

9. Subject to Part IV of Schedule 5 to this Act and to the provisions of any instrument under this Act, the functions which immediately before 1st April 1974 are exercisable by river authorities as respects their respective areas under any enactment or instrument shall be exercisable by water authorities as respects water authority areas and accordingly, but subject to any such provision, in any enactment or instrument—

Transfer to water authorities of functions of river authorities.

    (*a*) any reference to a river authority or any reference which falls to be construed as a reference to a river authority shall, except where it is a reference to a specified river authority or is to be construed as such, be construed as a reference to a water authority ; and

    (*b*) any reference to a river authority area or any reference which falls to be construed as a reference to a river authority area shall, except where it is a reference to a specified area or is to be construed as such, be construed as a reference to a water authority area.

10.—(1) It shall be the duty of each water authority to take all such action as the authority may from time to time consider necessary or expedient, or as directions under this Act or the Water Resources Act 1963 may require them to take, for the purpose of conserving, redistributing or otherwise augmenting water resources in their area, of securing the proper use of water resources in their area, or of transferring any such resources to the area of another water authority.

Water conservation.
1963 c. 38.

(2) The reference in this section to action for the purpose of augmenting water resources includes a reference to action for the purpose of treating salt water (whether taken from the sea or elsewhere) by any process for removing salt or other impurities.

11.—(1) It shall be the duty of a water authority to supply water within their area.

(2) It shall be the duty of every local authority to take such steps from time to time as may be necessary for ascertaining the sufficiency and wholesomeness of water supplies within their area and to notify the water authority of any insufficiency or unwholesomeness in those supplies.

(3) Where the following conditions are satisfied, that is to say—

(*a*) a local authority notify a water authority that the supply of water to specified premises in the local authority's area is insufficient or unwholesome to the extent of causing a danger to health ; and

(*b*) a supply of wholesome water by the water authority for domestic purposes is required for those premises and it is not practicable to provide such a supply in pipes, but is practicable to provide such a supply otherwise, at a reasonable cost ;

it shall be the duty of the water authority to provide a supply of wholesome water otherwise than in pipes for domestic purposes to, or within a reasonable distance of, those premises.

(4) Any dispute between the local authority and the water authority as to the insufficiency or unwholesomeness of any supply of water or whether it causes a danger to health shall be determined by the Secretary of State.

(5) If any question arises under subsection (3) above whether or not any description of supply of water can be provided at a reasonable cost in the area of a local authority, the Secretary of State, if requested to do so by the local authority, by a parish or community council or by ten or more local government electors in that area, shall after consulting that authority and the water authority, determine that question, and the water authority shall give effect to his determination.

(6) Subject to subsections (7) and (9) below, any functions exercisable by statutory water undertakers as such under any enactment or instrument shall be exercisable also by water authorities and shall not be exercisable by local authorities, and accordingly (but subject as aforesaid) references in any enactment or instrument to statutory water undertakers as such shall be construed as references to water authorities, statutory water companies, joint water boards and joint water committees, and to no other body.

(7) The following provisions shall have effect with respect to the supply of water: —

> (*a*) in sections 27, 36 and 37 of the Water Act 1945 (miscel- 1945 c. 42. laneous duties as to the supply of water) references to statutory water undertakers shall be construed as references only to water authorities ;
>
> (*b*) subject to any provision to the contrary contained in any instrument made under or by virtue of this Act, Parts VII and IX of Schedule 3 to that Act (supply of water for domestic purposes, and duties as to constancy of supply and pressure) shall apply throughout every water authority area, whether or not applied by or under any other enactment ; and
>
> (*c*) references in those Parts to statutory water undertakers shall be construed as references only to water authorities.

(8) Section 10 of that Act (variation of limits of supply) shall not authorise the Secretary of State to vary the boundary between two water authority areas.

(9) No functions shall be exercisable by local authorities under Part IV of the Public Health Act 1936, except under 1936 c. 49. sections 123, 124(1) and (2), 125(1) and (2), 137, 138, 140 and 141, and accordingly that Part of that Act, except those provisions and section 142, shall cease to have effect.

(10) In this section, except subsection (6), " local authority " does not include a county council or the Greater London Council.

12.—(1) Where the area of a water authority includes the Supply of whole or part of the limits of supply of a statutory water water by company, the authority shall discharge their duties with respect statutory water to the supply of water within those limits through the company. behalf of water

(2) Where it appears to a water authority that subsection (1) authorities. above will apply to their area on 1st April 1974 they shall, on or before 1st November 1973, or such later date as the Secretary of State may authorise in the case of that authority generally or in any particular case, send to the company concerned a draft of arrangements to be entered into between the authority and the company whereby the company undertake to act on behalf of the authority for the purposes of that subsection and provision is made for such incidental, supplementary and consequential matters (including matters of a financial nature) as the authority think desirable.

(3) Arrangements for the purposes of subsection (1) above may include provision for—

(a) the management or operation of sources of supply;

(b) the supply of water in bulk by or to the company;

(c) the company's charges for the supply of water.

(4) If, within a period of two months beginning with the date on which a draft of any such arrangements was sent by a water authority to the company, the water authority and the company have not entered into the arrangements, the water authority shall, within seven days of the end of that period, notify the Secretary of State of that fact and the Secretary of State shall settle the terms of the arrangements, which shall, subject to subsection (5) below, be binding on the authority and the company.

(5) The parties to any arrangements in force by virtue of the foregoing provisions of this section, as varied (if it be the case) under this subsection, may vary the arrangements or either of the parties may, in default of agreement, apply to the Secretary of State to vary the arrangements and the Secretary of State may by direction to the parties vary the arrangements in a manner specified in the direction and the arrangements as varied shall, subject to a further application of this subsection, be binding on the parties.

(6) The Secretary of State shall not so settle or vary arrangements under this section as to oblige the company to fix their charges at a level which will endanger their ability, so long as their undertaking is managed efficiently, to provide a reasonable return on their paid-up capital, having regard to their probable future expenditure and to the need to provide for any contributions which they may lawfully carry to any reserve fund or contingency fund, to make good depreciation (in so far as provision therefor is not made by any such fund as aforesaid) and to meet all other costs, charges and expenses properly chargeable to revenue.

(7) It shall be the duty of a water authority on whose behalf water is being supplied by a statutory water company to take all reasonable steps for making water available to the company to enable them to meet the foreseeable demands of consumers within their limits of supply.

(8) Subject to the provisions of any order made under section 254 of the 1972 Act as applied by section 34 below, so much of the enactments relating to the undertaking of a statutory water company as imposes on the company any duty to supply water,

except Part VIII of Schedule 3 to the Water Act 1945 (supply PART II
for public purposes) and any local statutory provision which is 1945 c. 42.
similar to any provision of that Part, shall cease to have effect.

(9) For sections 12 and 13 of the Water Act 1945 (supply of
water in bulk and default powers) there shall be substituted the
sections set out in Part I of Schedule 4 to this Act.

(10) Sections 2(1)(*b*) and (4) and 4(2) to (4) of the Water Act 1948 c. 22.
1948 (which also relate to the supply of water in bulk) shall
cease to have effect.

(11) Part II of Schedule 4 to this Act shall have effect in
relation to the making and confirmation of orders by a water
authority under sections 12 and 13 of the Water Act 1945 as
substituted by Part I of that Schedule.

13.—(1) Statutory water undertakers shall have power to Power of
make agreements with other statutory water undertakers to statutory water
supply water outside their limits of supply, subject to such undertakers
conditions as may be specified in the agreement. to supply
places
outside their
(2) An agreement under subsection (1) above may contain limits of
such incidental, consequential and supplementary provisions supply.
as the statutory water undertakers consider necessary or expedient for the purposes of the agreement.

(3) While statutory water undertakers are supplying water
outside their limits of supply in pursuance of an agreement
under subsection (1) above, the enactments relating to that part
of their limits of supply which is contiguous to the area in
which they are supplying water in pursuance of the agreement
shall have effect, subject to subsection (4) below, as if the area
within which they are thus supplying water were an area within
their limits of supply and to which those enactments extend
apart from this subsection.

(4) Where an area in which undertakers are supplying water
in pursuance of such an agreement is contiguous to areas within
the undertakers' limits of supply but to which different enactments apply, the Secretary of State may determine, upon the
application of the undertakers, which of those enactments are
to apply to the area in which the undertakers are supplying
water in pursuance of the agreement ; and the Secretary of State
may determine under this subsection that different enactments
shall apply to different parts of the area and that any enactment
is to apply to the whole of the area or to any part of it subject
to such modifications or exceptions as he may specify.

14.—(1) It shall be the duty of every water authority to provide, either inside or outside their area, such public sewers as may be necessary for effectually draining their area and to make such provision, whether inside or outside their area, by means of sewage disposal works or otherwise, as may be necessary for effectually dealing with the contents of their sewers ; 1936 c. 49.   and accordingly section 14 of the Public Health Act 1936 (general duty of local authority with respect to sewerage and sewage disposal) and section 16 of that Act (provision of sewers and sewage disposal works outside a local authority's district) shall cease to have effect.

(2) Subject to subsection (3) below, the functions conferred on local authorities by the following enactments, that is to say—

   (*a*) sections 15 to 24, 27 to 31, 33 to 36 and 42 of the Public Health Act 1936 and so much of Part XII of that Act as relates to those sections ;

1937 c. 40.   (*b*) the Public Health (Drainage of Trade Premises) Act 1937 ;

1953 c. 26.   (*c*) section 13 of the Local Government (Miscellaneous Provisions) Act 1953 ; and

   (*d*) sections 12 to 14 and Part V of and Schedule 2 to the
1961 c. 64.   Public Health Act 1961 ;

shall be exercisable by water authorities, and accordingly references in those enactments to a local authority and their district, except any such reference in section 24(4) of the said Act of 1936, shall be construed respectively as references to a water authority and their area, and any reference in Part II of the Public Health Act 1936 and, subject to any order made by virtue of this Act, in any other enactment, to a sewerage authority and their district shall be similarly construed.

(3) Notwithstanding anything in subsection (2) above, the power conferred on local authorities by section 21(1)(*a*) of the Public Health Act 1936 (use of highway authorities' drains and sewers to carry off surplus water) shall be exercisable by local authorities as well as being exercisable by water authorities.

(4) In section 34(1) of the said Act of 1936 (right to drain into public sewers) for all the words before the proviso there shall be substituted the words " Subject to the provisions of this section, the owner or occupier of any premises or the owner of any private sewer shall be entitled to have his drains or sewer made to communicate with the public sewers of any water authority and thereby to discharge foul water and surface water from those premises or that private sewer ".

(5) Before constructing, diverting or closing a public sewer in the area of a local authority a water authority shall consult the local authority and the water authority shall inform a local authority of the construction, diversion or closure of a public sewer by the water authority in the area of the local authority.

(6) Where it is proposed to erect or extend a building over a water authority's sewer of which a map is kept under section 32(1) of the said Act of 1936 and plans of the building or extension are in accordance with building regulations deposited with the council of a district or outer London borough, or notice of the building or extension is served on the proper officer of the Greater London Council under section 83 of the London Building Acts (Amendment) Act 1939, the council of the district or borough or the Greater London Council, as the case may be, shall notify the water authority of the proposal.

(7) A water authority may give directions to the council of a district or outer London borough as to the manner in which the council are to exercise their functions under section 25(1) of the said Act of 1936 (requirement for local authority's consent to erection or extension of buildings over sewers).

(8) In this section " local authority " does not include a county council and, except in subsection (2), does not include the Greater London Council.

15.—(1) Subject to subsection (6) below, it shall be the duty of a water authority and every relevant authority whose area is wholly or partly situated in the water authority's area to endeavour to make arrangements for the relevant authority to discharge as respects their area the functions of the water authority under Part II of the Public Health Act 1936, other than those excepted by subsection (3) below.

(2) Arrangements under subsection (1) above shall—

   (*a*) require the relevant authority to prepare and annually revise a programme for the discharge of the said functions as respects their area, having regard to any guidance given to them by the water authority, and to submit every such programme to the water authority for their approval ;

   (*b*) require the relevant authority to carry out any programme approved by the water authority under paragraph (*a*) above ;

   (*c*) provide for vesting in the water authority any public sewer provided by the relevant authority in pursuance of the arrangements ;

Part II

1939 c. xcvii.

Arrangements for discharge of sewerage functions.

1936 c. 49.

(*d*) require the relevant authority to provide such vehicles and equipment as may be necessary for maintaining the sewers which it is their function to maintain under the arrangements;

(*e*) provide for the water authority to reimburse the relevant authority any expenses incurred by the latter in the discharge of the said functions;

(*f*) provide for the relevant authority to conduct on behalf of the water authority any prosecutions or other legal proceedings in connection with the discharge of those functions; and

(*g*) provide for the transfer to the water authority of officers of the relevant authority in the event of the ending of the arrangements under subsection (7) below and for the compensation of any such officers who suffer loss as a result of any variation or the ending of the arrangements under that subsection.

(3) Subsection (1) above shall not apply to any functions of a water authority relating to—

(*a*) sewage disposal;

(*b*) the maintenance or operation of any sewer which immediately before 1st April 1974 was vested in a joint sewerage board or the Greater London Council.

(4) Subject to subsection (6) below, a water authority shall, not later than 1st November 1973, or such later date as the Secretary of State may authorise in the case of that authority generally or in any particular case, send to every relevant authority with whom they are under a duty to endeavour to make arrangements under subsection (1) above a draft of the arrangements with the relevant authority.

(5) Subject to subsection (6) below, if within a period of two months beginning with the date on which any such draft was sent by a water authority to a relevant authority, the two authorities have not entered into the arrangements, the water authority shall, within seven days of the end of that period, notify the Secretary of State of that fact and the Secretary of State shall settle the terms of the arrangements, which shall be binding on both authorities.

(6) If at any time before arrangements are settled under this section a water authority and a relevant authority come to the conclusion that in the interests of efficiency it would be inexpedient to enter into any arrangements under subsection

(1) above or, as the case may be, to be bound by arrangements settled by the Secretary of State under subsection (5) above—

    (*a*) the water authority shall not take the action required by subsection (4) or (5) above ; or

    (*b*) where the water authority have already notified the Secretary of State under subsection (5) above that arrangements have not been entered into, they shall further notify him of the conclusion and he shall not settle the terms of the arrangements.

(7) The parties to any arrangements in force by virtue of subsection (1) or subsection (5) above, as varied (if it is the case) under this subsection, may vary or end the arrangements, or either of the parties may, in default of agreement, apply to the Secretary of State to vary or end the arrangements and the Secretary of State may by direction to the parties vary the arrangements in a manner specified in the direction or end the arrangements, and—

    (*a*) in the case of variation, the arrangements shall (subject to a further application of this subsection), be binding on the parties ; and

    (*b*) the ending of the arrangements shall not preclude the parties from entering into further arrangements under this section.

(8) Where by virtue of this section any functions of a water authority are to be discharged by a local authority, then, subject to the terms of the arrangements, the local authority may arrange for the discharge of those functions by a committee, sub-committee or officer of theirs and—

    (*a*) where by virtue of this subsection any such functions may be discharged by a committee of a local authority, then, unless the water authority or local authority otherwise direct, the committee may arrange for the discharge of any of those functions by a sub-committee or an officer of the local authority ; and

    (*b*) where by virtue of this subsection any such functions may be discharged by a sub-committee of a local authority, then, unless the water authority, the local authority or the committee otherwise direct, the sub-committee may arrange for the discharge of any of those functions by an officer of the local authority.

(9) Any arrangements made by a local authority or committee under subsection (8) above for the discharge of any functions by a committee, sub-committee or officer shall not prevent the authority or committee by whom the arrangements are made from discharging those functions.

(10) In this section " relevant authority " means—

    (*a*) except in relation to a new town as respects which an order is in force under section 34 of the New Towns Act 1965, the council of a district or London borough or the Common Council of the City of London ; and

    (*b*) in relation to any such new town, whichever of the following bodies is selected by the water authority, that is to say, the development corporation and any such council within whose area the town is wholly or partly situated.

Requisitioning of sewers for domestic purposes.

16.—(1) It shall be the duty of a water authority to provide any public sewer to be used for domestic purposes for the drainage of premises in their area—

    (*a*) if the owners or occupiers of the premises require the authority to provide a public sewer, otherwise than for the drainage of new buildings which they propose to erect on the premises, and the conditions mentioned in subsection (2) below are satisfied ; or

    (*b*) if the owners of the premises require the authority to provide a public sewer for the drainage of new buildings which they propose to erect on the premises and the conditions mentioned in subsection (3) below are satisfied ; or

    (*c*) if the conditions specified in subsection (4) below are satisfied.

(2) In a case to which paragraph (*a*) of subsection (1) above applies, the conditions which must be satisfied are—

    (*a*) that the reckonable charges payable in respect of the premises will not be less than the qualifying amount ; and

    (*b*) that the persons making the requisition agree severally with the water authority to pay the reckonable charges in respect of the premises for three years at least from the date on which the laying of the sewer is completed.

(3) In a case to which paragraph (*b*) of subsection (1) applies, the conditions which must be satisfied are—

    (*a*) that the sewer which the owners of the premises require the water authority to provide is a sewer communicating (in such manner and in such place as the authority consider appropriate) with a private sewer provided by the owners ; and

    (*b*) that the owners undertake to meet any relevant deficit.

(4) The conditions mentioned in paragraph (*c*) of subsection (1) above are—

    (*a*) that the reckonable charges payable in respect of the premises will be less than the qualifying amount ; and

    (*b*) that the local authority in whose area the premises are situated undertake to meet any relevant deficit.

(5) Any obligation to pay an annual sum under subsection (3) or (4) above shall cease on the expiration of a period of twelve years from the date on which the laying of the sewer is completed.

(6) A water authority may require a landowner (other than a public authority) to deposit with them, as security for the payment of an annual sum under subsection (3) above, such sum, not exceeding the total expense of laying the sewer, as the water authority may require.

(7) The water authority shall pay interest at a rate prescribed by regulations made by the Secretary of State or, if no rate is for the time being prescribed, at 4 per cent. per annum, on any sum in their hands by virtue of subsection (6) above, and—

    (*a*) shall, on the request of the landowner appropriate out of that sum any amount due under his undertaking ; and

    (*b*) when the undertaking is finally discharged, repay to him any sum remaining in their hands.

(8) A water authority may agree with a local authority or any other person who is obliged by virtue of this section to meet any portion of the expense of providing a sewer that the whole or any part of the amount for which that person is liable shall be deemed to be satisfied by payment of a capital sum.

(9) If the conditions mentioned in subsection (2), (3) or (4) above are satisfied and the water authority do not lay the necessary sewer within six months or such longer period as may be agreed between the parties or be determined under subsection (10) below, they shall, unless they show that the failure was due to unavoidable accident or other unavoidable cause, be liable on summary conviction to a fine not exceeding £400.

(10) Any dispute arising under this section—

    (*a*) as to the qualifying amount in the case of any premises ;

    (*b*) as to the nature or extent of the work necessary for laying a sewer ; or

    (*c*) as to the period within which a sewer is to be laid,

shall be determined by a referee appointed by the parties or in default of agreement by the President of the Institution of Civil Engineers.

(11) In this section—

"local authority" does not include a county council or the Greater London Council;

"qualifying amount", in relation to any premises, means one eighth of the expense of providing such a sewer as is sufficient to satisfy the requirements of subsection (1) above in the case of those premises and of providing any other sewer which it is necessary or appropriate to provide in consequence;

"reckonable charges", in relation to a sewer, means charges in respect of the drainage of premises attributable to its use and includes such proportion of any charge payable under Part III of this Act for services which include sewerage as is stated by the water authority to be so attributable;

"relevant deficit" means the difference between the qualifying amount and the reckonable charges received by a water authority in respect of each year.

(12) A sewer shall be treated for the purposes of this section as used for domestic purposes if it is used for removing the contents of a lavatory or removing water used for cooking or washing other than water used for the business of a laundry or a business of preparing food or beverages for consumption otherwise than on the premises.

(13) It shall be the duty of a water authority, at the request of any person, to state the proportion of any charge under Part III of this Act which is a reckonable charge for the purposes of this section.

(14) Nothing in section 14 above or any arrangements made under section 15 above shall be taken to impose on a water authority any such obligation to provide a public sewer as may be imposed on them under this section without the requirements of this section being satisfied.

River pollution.

17.—(1) The Rivers (Prevention of Pollution) Acts 1951 to 1961 shall have effect in relation to new or altered outlets or discharges of a water authority subject to such exceptions and modifications as may be prescribed by regulations made by the Secretary of State.

(2) Any such regulations may in particular provide for securing—

(a) that consent to the bringing into use of a new or altered outlet or the making of a new discharge shall be granted (or be deemed to be granted) by the Secretary of State;

(*b*) that, in such cases and subject to such conditions as may be prescribed by the regulations, any necessary consent shall be deemed to be granted by the Secretary of State unless the Secretary of State requires an application for it to be made to him by the water authority; and

(*c*) that where a consent is deemed to be granted as mentioned in paragraph (*b*) above, the water authority shall give such notice of that fact as may be prescribed by the regulations.

(3) A statutory instrument containing regulations under this section shall be subject to annulment in pursuance of a resolution of either House of Parliament.

(4) In section 7 of the Rivers (Prevention of Pollution) Act 1951 (restrictions on new or altered outlets for the discharge of trade or sewage effluents), subsection (9) and the proviso to subsection (16) shall cease to have effect.

(5) Where an estuary is situated in the areas of two or more water authorities, the Secretary of State may direct those authorities to make arrangements under section 6 above for the discharge by a joint committee of theirs of their functions relating to the restoration and maintenance of the wholesomeness of rivers and other waters.

18.—(1) It shall be the duty of every water authority—

(*a*) to maintain, improve and develop the salmon fisheries, trout fisheries, freshwater fisheries and eel fisheries in the area for which they exercise functions under the Salmon and Freshwater Fisheries Acts 1923 to 1972;

(*b*) to establish advisory committees of persons who appear to them to be interested in any such fisheries in that area and consult them as to the manner in which the authority are to discharge their duty under paragraph (*a*) above.

(2) The duty to establish advisory committees imposed by paragraph (*b*) of subsection (1) above is a duty to establish a regional advisory committee for the whole of the area mentioned in paragraph (*a*) of that subsection and such local advisory committees as the water authority consider necessary to represent the interests referred to in paragraph (*b*) of that subsection in different parts of that area.

19.—(1) A water authority shall exercise a general supervision over all matters relating to land drainage in their area but shall arrange for the discharge by their regional land drainage committee (without prejudice to any scheme for the appointment of local land drainage committees) of all their land drainage

PART II

1951 c. 64.

Fisheries.

Land drainage.

functions except the making of drainage charges, the levying of precepts and the borrowing of money.

(2) A water authority may give their regional land drainage committee directions as to the exercise of any land drainage function other than an internal drainage function, so far as the exercise of that function appears to the authority likely to affect materially the authority's management of water for purposes other than land drainage.

(3) In subsection (2) above " internal drainage function " means the functions of a water authority under the following enactments (which relate to internal drainage boards and internal drainage districts) namely—

  (*a*) sections 4, 7, 10, 11, 21 and 24(6) and (7) of the Land Drainage Act 1930 ;
  (*b*) sections 18, 21(1), 26(3), (4) and (7), 27 and 36 of the Land Drainage Act 1961.

(4) Parts I to III of Schedule 5 to this Act shall have effect in relation to the land drainage functions of water authorities.

(5) Land drainage functions relating to the London excluded area shall continue to be exercised by the Greater London Council and other authorities by whom they are exercisable immediately before the passing of this Act, and in accordance with the enactments by virtue of which they are exercisable, but Part IV of Schedule 5 to this Act shall have effect for the purposes of their exercise.

(6) Nothing in sections 29 to 32 below shall apply in relation to a water authority's land drainage functions until a charges option order comes into force for the area of that authority.

(7) If—
  (*a*) at any time after 31st March 1978 a water authority apply to the Minister for a charges option order ; and
  (*b*) the Ministers are satisfied that—
      (i) the authority's regional land drainage committee recommended the authority to make the application ; and
      (ii) the making of an order would be in the public interest,
the Ministers may make such an order.

(8) In this section " charges option order " means an order that sections 1 and 1A of the Land Drainage Act 1961 (general drainage charges), and Part II of Schedule 5 to this Act shall cease to have effect in relation to a water authority area and shall thereupon be treated for the purposes of section 38(2)
of the Interpretation Act 1889 (effect of repeals) as if they had been repealed in relation to that area by another Act.

(9) When a charges option order comes into force for a water authority area, sections 29 to 32 below shall apply to the water authority for that area in relation to their land drainage functions, but with the substitution of references to the Ministers for references to the Secretary of State in relation to any direction—

(a) which is proposed to be given to the authority after the date when the order comes into force; and

(b) which relates to the authority's land drainage functions.

(10) A charges option order shall be subject to special parliamentary procedure.

(11) A charges option order may make such incidental, consequential, transitional or supplemental provision as the Ministers consider necessary or expedient.

20.—(1) Every water authority and all other statutory water undertakers may take steps to secure the use of water and land associated with water for the purposes of recreation and it shall be the duty of all such undertakers to take such steps as are reasonably practicable for putting their rights to the use of water and of any land associated with water to the best use for those purposes.

General provisions as to recreation.

(2) In discharging their duty under subsection (1) above statutory water undertakers other than a water authority shall consult the water authority for the area in which the water or land in question is situated and shall take account of any proposals formulated by the authority for discharging their own duty under that subsection.

(3) A water authority may, with the consent of the owner of an inland water which they have no right to use for the purposes of recreation or of land associated therewith and of any other person having a right to use the water or an estate or interest in the land, use the water or land for those purposes.

(4) In exercising their functions under subsection (1) or (3) above a water authority shall not obstruct or otherwise interfere with navigation which is subject to the control of a harbour or navigation authority without the consent of the harbour or navigation authority.

In this subsection "harbour authority" has the same meaning as in the Harbours Act 1964 and "navigation authority" has the same meaning as in the Water Resources Act 1963.

1964 c. 40.
1963 c. 38.

(5) Where the Secretary of State makes an order under section 23 of the Water Act 1945 or section 67 of the Water Resources Act 1963 authorising a water authority to carry out works for

1945 c. 42.

PART II

or in connection with the construction or operation of a reservoir in England or conferring compulsory powers for that purpose on a water authority, and it appears to him that the works to be carried out may permanently affect the area in which they are situated and are not primarily intended to benefit the inhabitants of that area, he may include in the order provision with respect to facilities for recreation or other leisure-time occupation for the benefit of those inhabitants.

Discharge of functions with respect to recreation in Wales.

21.—(1) The Welsh authority shall, after consultation with the **Severn-Trent Water Authority, prepare a plan for the use for** the purposes of recreation of the rights of both authorities to **the use of water in Wales and of any land in Wales** associated with water.

(2) Any such plan, in so far as it falls to be carried out in **the area of the Severn-Trent Water Authority, shall be carried** out by that authority in accordance with a scheme agreed between them and the Welsh authority or, in default of agreement, in accordance with any directions of the Secretary of State.

(3) Without prejudice to paragraph 2 of Schedule 3 to this Act, the Welsh authority may acquire by agreement any right to use water in Wales and any estate or interest in, or right over, land in Wales which is associated with water for the purpose of using the water or land for the purposes of recreation.

(4) Where the Welsh authority acquire any estate, interest or right under subsection (3) above which relates to water or land in the area of the Severn-Trent Water Authority, they may instead of using it themselves for the purposes of recreation grant the Severn-Trent Water Authority such derivative estate, interest or right as may be appropriate for enabling that authority to use it for those purposes.

(5) It shall be the duty of a water authority who are carrying out works for or in connection with the construction or operation of a reservoir in Wales which permanently affect one or more communities and are not primarily intended by the authority to benefit the inhabitants of that or those communities to provide, or assist others to provide, facilities for recreation or other leisure-time occupation for the benefit of those inhabitants.

(6) A water authority shall, in discharging their duty under subsection (5) above, consult the community councils of the communities affected in the case of communities having such councils, and in any case the council of any district in which any community affected is situated.

Duties with regard to nature conservation and amenity.

22.—(1) In formulating or considering any proposals relating to the discharge of any of the functions of water authorities, those authorities and the appropriate Minister or Ministers shall have regard to the desirability of preserving natural beauty, of conserving flora, fauna and geological or physiographical features of special interest, and of protecting buildings and other objects of architectural, archaeological or historic interest and shall take into account any effect which the proposals would have on the beauty of, or amenity in, any rural or urban area or on any such flora, fauna, features, buildings or objects.

(2) In formulating or considering any such proposals, water authorities and the appropriate Minister or Ministers shall have regard to the desirability of preserving public rights of access to areas of mountains, moor, heath, down, cliff or foreshore and other places of natural beauty and shall take into account any effect which the proposals would have on the preservation of any such rights of access.

(3) Where the Nature Conservancy Council are of opinion that any area of land, not being land for the time being managed as a nature reserve, is of special interest by reason of its flora, fauna or geological or physiographical features and may at any time be affected by schemes, operations or activities of a water authority, it shall be the duty of that council to notify that fact to the water authority in whose area the land is situated.

23.—(1) For the purpose of exercising the functions conferred on them by this section there shall be a body to be known as the Water Space Amenity Commission consisting of— Water Space Amenity Commission.

(a) a chairman appointed by the Secretary of State from among the members of the Council ;

(b) the chairmen of the water authorities ; and

(c) not more than ten other members appointed by the Secretary of State.

(2) Of the members of the Commission, other than the chairman, appointed by the Secretary of State—

(a) one shall be appointed after consultation with the Countryside Commission ;

(b) one shall be appointed after consultation with the English Tourist Board ;

(c) one shall be appointed after consultation with the Sports Council or some other organisation appearing to him to be concerned with the encouragement of sport and recreation and prescribed for the purposes of this paragraph by an order made by him ;

(d) the remainder shall be appointed after consultation with such associations of local authorities, and such bodies representing persons interested in the use of water and of any land associated with water for the purposes

X 2

of recreation or in the enhancement and preservation of amenity, as the Secretary of State considers desirable, and with the Greater London Council.

(3) It shall be the duty of the Commission—

(a) to advise the Secretary of State, after consultation with the Countryside Commission, the English Tourist Board and either the Sports Council or an organisation prescribed for the purposes of subsection (2)(c) above, on the formulation, promotion and execution of the national policy for water so far as relating to recreation and amenity in England ;

(b) to advise the Council and water authorities on the discharge of their respective functions so far as so relating ;

(c) to submit to water authorities any proposals which the Commission consider appropriate for the discharge of the authorities' functions so far as so relating ; and

(d) to encourage and assist the water authorities in the preparation of plans and programmes under section 24 below for the discharge of those functions so far as so relating.

(4) The Commission may collate and publish information and reports on matters relating to recreation and amenity in connection with water.

(5) The members of the Commission, other than the chairmen of the water authorities, shall hold and vacate office in accordance with the terms of their respective appointments and shall, on ceasing to hold office, be eligible for reappointment ; but any such member may at any time by notice addressed to the Secretary of State resign his office.

(6) The Council shall provide the Commission with such officers and such accommodation as the Secretary of State considers appropriate and shall defray any expenditure incurred by the Commission with the approval of the Secretary of State in the discharge of their functions.

(7) The Council may pay members of the Commission, other than the chairmen of the water authorities, such allowances as may be determined by the Secretary of State with the consent of the Minister for the Civil Service.

(8) Paragraph 40 of Schedule 3 to this Act shall have effect with respect to annual reports of the Commission.

24.—(1) It shall be the duty of each water authority, as soon as practicable after 1st April 1974, in consultation with any water authority or authorities likely to be affected by the matters mentioned below—

  (*a*) to carry out a survey of the water in their area, the existing management of that water, the purposes for which it is being used and its quality in relation to its existing and likely future uses, and to prepare a report setting out the results of the survey ;

  (*b*) to prepare an estimate of the future demand for the use of that water during the period of twenty years from the date on which the survey is completed or such longer or shorter period from that date as the appropriate Minister or Ministers may in any particular case direct ; and

  (*c*) to prepare a plan as to action to be taken during that period by the authority (whether by way of executing works or securing the execution of works by other persons or otherwise) for the purpose of securing more efficient management of water in their area, including the meeting of future demands for water and the use of water and restoring or maintaining the wholesomeness of rivers and other inland or coastal waters in their area.

(2) Where a statutory water company are supplying water in a water authority area, the water authority may require that company—

  (*a*) to carry out a survey of the existing consumption of and demand for water supplies in the part of the water authority area within their limits of supply ;

  (*b*) to prepare an estimate of the future water supply requirements of that part of the area ;

  (*c*) to formulate proposals for meeting the existing or future water supply requirements of that part of the area, including proposals for the joint use with any other statutory water undertakers of any existing or proposed new source of water supply ; and

  (*d*) to submit a report on any of the matters mentioned in paragraphs (*a*) to (*c*) above to the water authority within such time as the authority may specify.

(3) Each water authority shall keep under review the particulars contained in any report or estimate prepared by them, and any plan prepared by them, under subsection (1) above, and shall at the times required by subsection (4) below revise those particulars and that plan, either by way of amendment or by taking fresh steps under subsection (1) above, or both,

PART II
as the authority may consider appropriate having regard to changes which have occurred since the previous survey or (as the case may be) the revision last effected by them under this subsection.

(4) The times at which a water authority are to carry out a revision under subsection (3) above shall be at intervals of not more than seven years, and, subject to that requirement, such times as they consider appropriate having particular regard to the times at which like revisions are proposed to be carried out by other water authorities.

(5) Subsection (1) above shall not apply to water authorities' land drainage functions, but it shall be the duty of each water authority to carry out from time to time, and in any event at such times as the Minister may direct, a survey of their area in relation to those functions.

(6) A water authority shall from time to time prepare, in the light of the most recent surveys (if any) carried out and the most recent plan (if any) prepared by them under the foregoing provisions of this section, one or more programmes of a general nature for the discharge of their functions over a period of not more than seven years and shall submit any such programme for the approval of the appropriate Minister or Ministers, and, if the appropriate Minister or Ministers so direct, shall at such time or times as may be specified in the direction, prepare and submit for his or their approval one or more such programmes, containing particulars of any description so specified, for the carrying out by the authority during a period so specified of projects of any class so specified.

(7) Any programme of a water authority under subsection (6) above relating to the supply of water shall take account of any operations proposed under subsection (2) above to be undertaken in their area by a statutory water company, joint water board or joint water committee and involving a substantial outlay on capital account.

(8) In carrying out their duty under the foregoing provisions of this section a water authority shall—

    (*a*) consult every local authority whose area is wholly or partly included in the area of the water authority ; and

    (*b*) have regard to any of the following plans prepared for any part of that area under the Town and Country Planning Act 1971, that is to say, a structure plan, a local plan and any development plan within the meaning of Schedule 5 to that Act.

1971 c. 78.

(9) A water authority or other statutory water undertakers shall, in carrying out any project involving substantial outlay on capital account, act in accordance with any approved programme for the time being applicable to the discharge of their functions or the carrying out of their operations under subsection (6) above.

(10) Each water authority shall make arrangements for the carrying out of research and related activities (whether by the authority or by others) in respect of matters affecting the authority's functions, and in particular, but without prejudice to the generality of this subsection, may make arrangements for the carrying out of research and related activities in respect of such matters by subscribing or otherwise financially contributing to an organisation formed for that purpose.

(11) The appropriate Minister or Ministers may give directions to a water authority with respect to the making of arrangements under subsection (10) above.

(12) In the performance of their functions under this section a water authority shall consult the appropriate Minister or Ministers ; and every authority—

  (a) shall send to the appropriate Minister or Ministers, to every local authority whose area is wholly or partly included in the area of the water authority and to the Water Space Amenity Commission a copy of any report prepared by the water authority in consequence of a survey under this section and of any amendments made by them to any such report ;

  (b) shall furnish a copy of any such report or amendments to any person on payment of such reasonable sum as the authority may determine ; and

  (c) shall furnish the appropriate Minister or Ministers with such other information as he or they may reasonably require with respect to anything done by the water authority in pursuance of this section.

25.—(1) The Thames Water Authority shall, after consulting the interested bodies, submit to the Secretary of State not later than 1st April 1975 proposals for the transfer to the Greater London Council of the recreation and amenity functions of water authorities as respects the whole or part of the watercourses and land to which this section applies and, subject to subsection (3) below, the Secretary of State may by order give effect to the proposals, either as submitted to him or with modifications.

Discharge of recreation and amenity functions in and around Greater London.

X 4

(2) The Secretary of State may himself at any time after consulting the interested bodies amend or revoke an order under subsection (1) above or, where any such order has been revoked, provide for the transfer of all or any of the recreation and amenity functions of water authorities as respects the whole or part of the watercourses or land to which this section applies to the Greater London Council.

(3) If it appears to the Secretary of State that it is desirable to make an order under subsection (1) above giving effect to any proposals with modifications which appear to him to be substantial, he shall direct the Thames Water Authority, after consulting the interested bodies, to reconsider the proposals and submit revised proposals to him under that subsection within a time specified in the direction, but the foregoing provisions of this subsection shall not apply to an order under this subsection giving effect to the revised proposals.

(4) While any recreation and amenity functions are exercisable by the Greater London Council by virtue of an order under this section, section 23(3) above shall have effect as if references therein to water authorities included references to the Greater London Council.

(5) In this section " the interested bodies " means—

    (*a*) the Water Space Amenity Commission ;

    (*b*) the Greater London Council ;

    (*c*) in the case of proposals made by the Secretary of State under subsection (2) above, the Thames Water Authority and in any case any other water authority whose recreation and amenity functions will be affected by these proposals in question ;

    (*d*) the Port of London Authority ;

    (*e*) the Common Council of the City of London ;

    (*f*) the London Boroughs Association ;

    (*g*) such other bodies representing persons interested in the use of the watercourses and land to which this section applies as the Thames Water Authority consider desirable or the Secretary of State directs in the case of proposals submitted to him and as he considers desirable in the case of his own proposals.

(6) In this section " recreation and amenity functions " means, in relation to any authority, the authority's functions under section 20 above and, so far as relating to those functions, their functions under sections 22 and 24 above, not being in any case functions with respect to navigation conferred by or under any enactment.

(7) The watercourses to which this section applies are—

   (*a*) so much of the River Thames as lies within Greater London;

   (*b*) every watercourse, other than the River Thames, which is for the time being a main metropolitan watercourse within the meaning of Schedule 14 to the London Government Act 1963; 1963 c. 33.

   (*c*) so much of the River Beam, the River Ingrebourne and the River Roding as lies within Greater London; and

   (*d*) so much of any other watercourse situated wholly or partly within, or adjoining the boundary of, Greater London as lies within the flow and reflow of the tides of the River Thames;

and the land to which this section applies is any land associated with any watercourse to which this section applies.

(8) Without prejudice to any power exercisable by virtue of section 34 below, an order under this section may contain such transitional, incidental, supplementary or consequential provision as the Secretary of State considers necessary or expedient for the purposes of the order.

(9) A statutory instrument containing an order under this section shall be subject to annulment in pursuance of a resolution of either House of Parliament.

26.—(1) Each water authority and all other statutory water undertakers shall make provision for advancing the skill of persons employed by them and in doing so shall comply with any scheme for training and education in force under section 4 above. Duties of statutory water undertakers and Council to their staff.

(2) Except so far as the Council are satisfied that adequate machinery exists for the purpose it shall be the duty of the Council to seek consultation with any organisation appearing to them to be appropriate with a view to the conclusion between the Council and that organisation of such agreements as appear to the parties to be desirable with respect to the establishment and maintenance of machinery for the settlement by negotiation of terms and conditions of employment of persons employed by the Council, the water authorities and other statutory water undertakers with provision for reference to arbitration in default of such settlement in such cases as may be determined by or under the agreements.

(3) It shall be the duty of every water authority and all other statutory water undertakers to comply with any such agreement.

(4) The Council shall send copies of any such agreement, and of any instrument varying the terms of any such agreement, to the Secretary of State.

PART II
Superannua-
tion of
employees of
statutory
water
undertakers.

27.—(1) Statutory water undertakers may establish and administer pension schemes and pension funds in the interests of persons who are or have been employed by them, and may pay pensions, allowances and gratuities to or in respect of such persons or enter into and carry into effect agreements or arrangements with any other person for securing or preserving pension rights for any such persons.

(2) It shall be the duty of all statutory water companies, by participating in a scheme for or in respect of persons who are or have been employed by any such company, to secure benefits in respect of their service after their entry into the scheme not less in amount than the corresponding benefits for employees and former employees of water authorities in the standard water authority scheme and on terms (including terms as to the transferability of benefits) not less favourable to the persons entitled to the benefits than the terms of that scheme ; and in this section " standard water company scheme " means a scheme under this subsection and " standard water authority scheme " means a scheme designated by an order under subsection (3) below.

(3) The Secretary of State may by order—

(a) designate any scheme made for or in respect of employees and former employees of water authorities (including in particular a scheme contained in regulations under section 7 of the Superannuation Act 1972) as the standard water authority scheme ;

(b) designate a corporation to manage the standard water company scheme ; and

(c) prescribe a date before which any person who is in the employment of a statutory water company on 31st March 1974 and intends to remain in the employment of such a company after that date, and for whom on that date superannuation arrangements will be in operation, may opt that the standard water company scheme shall not apply to him.

(4) A person who has exercised the option conferred by subsection (3)(c) above may revoke it at any time after 31st March 1974.

(5) Every employee of a statutory water company who is eligible for membership of the standard water company scheme shall be a member of that scheme unless he has exercised the option conferred by subsection (3)(c) above and has not revoked it.

(6) Any question whether the terms of the standard water company scheme are less favourable than the terms of the standard water authority scheme shall be determined by the Secretary of State.

(7) The powers conferred on statutory water undertakers   PART II by this section are without prejudice to any of their other powers.

28. Where an emergency or disaster involving destruction of Emergencies or damage to life or property occurs or is imminent or there and disasters. is reasonable ground for apprehending such an emergency or disaster and a water authority are of opinion that it is likely to affect the whole or part of their area or all or some of its inhabitants in a way connected with the discharge of their functions, they shall assist any principal council within the meaning of section 138 of the 1972 Act in taking any action under that section which is calculated to avert, alleviate or eradicate in the water authority area or among its inhabitants the effects or potential effects of the event.

PART III

FINANCIAL PROVISIONS

29.—(1) It shall be the duty of every water authority so General duties to discharge their functions as to secure that, taking one year and powers with another, their revenue is not less than sufficient to meet relating to their total outgoings properly chargeable to revenue account. finance.

(2) The Secretary of State may with the approval of the Treasury and after consultation with the Council by order direct—

(*a*) that an authority shall discharge their functions during any period specified in the direction with a view to securing that they achieve in respect of that period a rate of return on the value of their net assets (as for the time being defined for the purposes of this section by the Secretary of State) which is not less than such rate as the Secretary of State specifies in the direction as the rate of return which he considers it is reasonable for the authority to achieve ;

(*b*) that an authority shall in the discharge of their functions be under any such other financial obligation (in addition to or instead of an obligation imposed by virtue of paragraph (*a*) above) as the Secretary of State may think fit.

(3) An order made by virtue of paragraph (*a*) of subsection (2) above shall be subject to annulment in pursuance of a resolution of either House of Parliament.

(4) An order shall not be made by virtue of paragraph (*b*) of subsection (2) above unless a draft of the order has been laid before, and approved by resolution of, each House of Parliament.

(5) It shall be the duty of every water authority to secure that their charges make a proper contribution to the discharge of their duty under this section and Part III of Schedule 3 to this Act, taking into account their present circumstances and future prospects and any directions given to them under this section.

Water
charges.
30.—(1) Subject to the provisions of this Act, a water authority shall have power to fix, and to demand, take and recover such charges for the services performed, facilities provided or rights made available by them (including separate charges for separate services, facilities or rights or combined charges for a number of services, facilities or rights) as they think fit.

(2) A water authority may fix any of their charges by means of a scheme under section 31 below or by agreement with any person.

(3) Subject to subsections (4) to (6) below, a water authority may fix their charges by reference to such criteria, and may adopt such system for the calculation of their amount, as appears to them to be appropriate.

(4) In fixing charges for services, facilities or rights a water authority shall have regard to the cost of performing those services, providing those facilities or making available those rights.

(5) A water authority may make different charges for the same service, facility or right in different cases, but it shall be the duty of every water authority to take such steps as will ensure that, as from a date not later than 1st April 1981, their charges are such as not to show undue preference to, or discriminate unduly against, any class of persons.

(6) The Secretary of State may, after consultation with the Council, give all or any of the water authorities directions as to the criteria to be applied or the system to be adopted by them under subsection (3) above and in giving a direction under this subsection the Secretary of State shall have regard to the provisions of subsections (4) and (5) above.

(7) Where a water authority introduce a new system of charges, they may make such transitional charging arrangements as they think fit applying for a period not exceeding five years.

(8) Nothing in any enactment passed before this Act shall so operate, in relation to a water authority, as to oblige them to fix separate charges for separate services, facilities or rights.

(9) No local statutory provision, other than one which expressly provides, in relation to any service, facility or right, that no charge shall be made for it, shall limit the discretion of a

water authority or of a statutory water company through whom such an authority are supplying water as to the charges to be made by them, whether it purports to limit them by specifying or providing for specifying the charges to be made, or by fixing or providing for fixing maximum charges, or otherwise.

(10) Any such limitation in a local statutory provision shall cease to have effect on 1st April 1974, but water authorities and companies through whom water authorities are supplying water shall, in fixing their charges as respects any period beginning not earlier than 1st April 1974 and ending before 1st April 1981, have regard to any special circumstances which appear to them to be relevant and, in particular, to any differences in the levels of charges which would, apart from the cesser, have been likely to be in force after the former date in different parts of the area to which the provision applied.

31.—(1) A water authority may make a scheme (in this Act referred to as a " charges scheme ") for the charges to be paid for any services performed, facilities provided or rights made available by the authority.

Charges schemes.

(2) The charges to be paid to an authority for any services, facilities or rights to which a charges scheme of that authority relates shall be those for which the scheme provides.

(3) The Secretary of State may give directions to all water authorities or any particular water authority as to the services, facilities or rights for which provision is to be made in a charges scheme.

(4) All charges schemes shall be so framed as to show the methods by which and the principles on which the charges are to be made, and shall be published in such manner as in the opinion of the authority will secure adequate publicity for them.

(5) A charges scheme may revoke or amend any previous charges scheme made by the authority.

(6) Nothing in any charges scheme shall affect any power of a water authority to make any such agreement as to charges as they are empowered to make by any enactment passed before this Act, and in particular by—

(a) section 7 of the Public Health (Drainage of Trade Premises) Act 1937 (reception and disposal of trade effluents) ; 1937 c. 40.

(b) section 27 of the Water Act 1945 (supply of water for non-domestic purposes) ; and 1945 c. 42.

(c) section 63 of the Water Resources Act 1963 (special charges in respect of spray irrigation). 1963 c. 38.

32.—(1) In any case where charges are payable to a water authority by reference to the volume of water supplied to any premises or the volume of effluent discharged therefrom (whether or not the charges are payable by reference to any other factors), the authority may install on those premises a meter for measuring that volume, and the register of the meter shall, subject to the provisions of any regulations under this section, be prima facie evidence of that volume.

(2) The Secretary of State may by regulations make provision with respect to the installation of meters, whether under this section or otherwise, their connection and disconnection and their maintenance, authentication and testing and other related matters, and a statutory instrument containing regulations under this section shall be subject to annulment in pursuance of a resolution of either House of Parliament.

(3) Any officer authorised by a water authority may at all reasonable times, on the production of some duly authenticated document showing his authority, enter any premises in the water authority's area in which there is a service pipe connected with the water authority's main, or a drain or private sewer connected with a public sewer, for the purpose of—

(a) installing meters under this section, or connecting or disconnecting them ;

(b) inspecting or examining any such meters, together with any ancillary fittings and associated works, and ascertaining from any such meter the volume of water supplied or effluent discharged ;

but admission to any premises shall not be demanded as of right unless twenty-four hours' notice of the intended entry has been given to the occupier.

(4) If it is shown to the satisfaction of a justice of the peace on sworn information in writing—

(a) that admission to any premises has been refused or that refusal is reasonably apprehended, or that the premises are unoccupied, or that the occupier is temporarily absent, or that the case is one of urgency, or that an application for admission would defeat the object of entry ; and

(b) that there is reasonable ground for entry into the premises for any purpose mentioned in subsection (3) above ;

the justice may by warrant authorise the water authority by any authorised officer to enter the premises, if need be by force, but shall not issue such a warrant unless he is satisfied that notice of the intention to apply for it has been given to the occupier, or that the premises are unoccupied, or that the occupier is temporarily absent, or that the case is one of urgency, or that the giving of such a notice would defeat the object of the entry.

(5) An authorised officer entering any premises by virtue of this section or any warrant issued thereunder may take with him such other persons as may be necessary, and on leaving any unoccupied premises which he has so entered shall leave them as effectually secured against trespassers as he found them.

(6) Every warrant under this section shall continue in force until the purpose for which the entry is necessary has been satisfied.

(7) If any person who in compliance with the provisions of this section or a warrant thereunder is admitted into a factory or workplace discloses to any person any information obtained by him in the factory or workplace with regard to any manufacturing process or trade secret, he shall, unless the disclosure was made in the performance of his duty, be liable on conviction on indictment to a fine and on summary conviction to a fine not exceeding £400.

(8) A person who wilfully obstructs another person exercising any power conferred by this section or any warrant thereunder shall be liable on summary conviction to a fine not exceeding £50.

(9) In this section—

" drain " has the same meaning as in the Public Health 1936 c. 49. Act 1936 ;

" effluent " means any liquid, with or without particles of matter in suspension therein ; and

" main " and " service pipe " have the same meanings as in Schedule 3 to the Water Act 1945.   1945 c. 42.

PART IV

MISCELLANEOUS

33. The following bodies shall cease to exist on 1st April Abolition of 1974, that is to say— existing
central and
local bodies.

(a) the Water Resources Board ;

(b) the Central Advisory Water Committee ;

(c) all river authorities ;

(d) the Conservators of the River Thames and the Lee Conservancy Catchment Board ;

(e) the Isle of Wight River and Water Authority ;

(f) all statutory water undertakers existing immediately before the passing of this Act, except statutory water companies, joint water boards, joint water committees and existing local authorities and other bodies exercising functions not affected by this Act ;

 (*g*) all joint sewerage boards and joint committees of sewerage authorities existing immediately before the passing of this Act ;

 (*h*) the Water Supply Industry Training Board ;

and section 263 of the 1972 Act (continuation of existing joint boards and committees) shall not apply to bodies which cease to exist by virtue of this section.

Consequential, transitional and supplementary provision.

34.—(1) The following provisions of the 1972 Act, that is to say—

 section 254 (consequential orders, etc.) and section 68 (transitional agreements as to property and finance) as applied by section 254 ;

 section 255 (transfer of officers) ;

 section 256 (continuity of employment) ;

 section 257 (staff commission) ;

 section 259 (compensation for loss of office) ;

 section 260 (option for early retirement) ;

shall apply for the purposes of this Act as they apply for the purposes of that Act or, as the case may be, Part IV of that Act, but subject to the exceptions and modifications contained in Part I of Schedule 6 to this Act.

(2) The provisions of Part II of that Schedule, being provisions which reproduce with modifications certain provisions of section 262 of the 1972 Act (local Acts and instruments), shall have effect with respect to local statutory provisions in force immediately before 1st April 1974.

(3) An order under section 2(5) above altering the boundaries of a water authority area and an order under section 25 above may include the like provision in relation to the order as may be made by regulations of general application under section 67 of the 1972 Act by virtue of subsection (2) of the latter section.

Isles of Scilly.

35.—(1) The Secretary of State may, on the application of the Council of the Isles of Scilly, make an order providing for the exercise as respects the Isles of Scilly of functions corresponding to any of those transferred to water authorities by this Act.

(2) Without prejudice to section 254 of the 1972 Act as applied by section 34 above, an order under this section may—

 (*a*) apply, with or without modifications, any provision of this Act to the Isles of Scilly ;

 (*b*) save the application to the Isles of Scilly of any enactment applying there immediately before 1st April 1974 and repealed as respects England in general by this Act.

(3) Except as provided by an order under this section, this Act shall not extend to the Isles of Scilly.

36.—(1) Any power to make orders or regulations conferred Orders, on the appropriate Minister or Ministers by or by virtue of this regulations Act shall be exercisable by statutory instrument. and byelaws.

(2) Any power to make an order conferred by or by virtue of any provision of this Act shall include power to make an order varying or revoking any order previously made under or by virtue of that provision.

(3) Part I of Schedule 7 to this Act shall have effect with respect to the making of byelaws by the appropriate Minister or Ministers by virtue of any enactment under which water authorities discharge their functions and Part II of that Schedule shall have effect with respect to the making of byelaws by water authorities, other statutory water undertakers and internal drainage boards under any enactment.

37. There shall be defrayed out of moneys provided by Expenses. Parliament—

   (*a*) any expenses incurred by any Minister under this Act ;

   (*b*) any increase attributable to the provisions of this Act in the sums payable out of moneys so provided under any other enactment.

38.—(1) In this Act, unless the context otherwise requires, Interpretation. the following expressions have the following meanings respectively, that is to say—

   " the appropriate Minister or Ministers " and " the Ministers " have the meanings assigned to them by section 1 above ;

   " the Council " means the National Water Council ;

   " county ", " district ", " county council ", and " district council ", mean respectively a county, district, county council and district council established by the 1972 Act ;

   " development corporation " means a development corpora- tion established under the New Towns Act 1965 or 1965 c. 59. any Act replaced by that Act ;

   " existing local authority " means a local authority within the meaning of the Local Government Act 1933 ; 1933 c. 51.

   " joint water board " and " joint water committee " mean respectively a joint board and a joint committee which has been constituted under section 9 of the Water Act 1945 c. 42. 1945 and on which a statutory water company is represented ;

" land drainage " includes defence against water (including sea water), irrigation other than spray irrigation, warping and the provision of flood warning systems, and " land drainage functions " shall be construed accordingly ;

" local authority " means a county council, the Greater London Council, a district council, a London borough council or the Common Council of the City of London ;

" local land drainage committee " and " regional land drainage committee " mean respectively the committees established by those names under Schedule 5 to this Act ;

" local land drainage district " means a local land drainage district established under that Schedule and any part of a water authority area which is to be treated as a local land drainage district for the purposes of Parts II and III of that Schedule ;

" local statutory provision " means a provision of a local Act (including an Act confirming a provisional order) or a provision of a public general Act passed with respect to some area or a provision of an instrument made under any such local or public general Act or of an instrument in the nature of a local enactment made under any other Act ;

" London excluded area " means so much of Greater London, and of any area adjoining Greater London, as—

(*a*) in relation to a time before 1st April 1974, does not at that time lie within the Thames catchment area, the Lee catchment area or the area of any river authority ;

(*b*) in relation to a time after 31st March 1974, does not at that time lie, for the purpose of the exercise of land drainage functions, within the area of any water authority ;

1972 c. 70.

" the 1972 Act " means the Local Government Act 1972 ;

" public authority " includes a statutory water company ;

1936 c. 49.

" public sewer " has the same meaning as in the Public Health Act 1936 and " private sewer " shall be construed accordingly ;

1967 c. 78.

" regional water board " and " water development board " have the same meanings respectively as in the Water (Scotland) Act 1967 ;

" river authority ", " underground strata ", " inland water ", " watercourse " and " water resources " have the same meanings respectively as in the Water Resources Act 1963;

" statutory water company " means a company authorised immediately before the passing of this Act by any local statutory provision to supply water or a company in whom the assets of any company so authorised have subsequently become vested ;

" statutory water undertakers " has the meaning assigned to it by section 11(6) above ;

" supply of water in bulk " and " water fittings " have the same meanings as in the Water Act 1945 ;

(2) Section 269 of the 1972 Act (which relates to the meaning of " England " and " Wales " in Acts passed after 1st April 1974) shall apply to this Act as if this Act had been passed after that date.

(3) Except in so far as the context otherwise requires, any reference in this Act to an enactment shall be construed as a reference to that enactment as amended, applied or extended by or under any other enactment, including this Act.

39.—(1) The following provisions of this Act shall come into operation on 1st April 1974, that is to say—

section 9, except so far as relating to sections 21 and 22 of the Land Drainage Act 1930, Part VI of the Local Government Act 1948, section 21 of the Land Drainage Act 1961 and section 82 of the Water Resources Act 1963 ;

section 10 ;

section 11, except subsection (6) so far as relating to section 12 of the Water Act 1945 ;

section 12(1) and (6) to (11), except subsections (9) and (11) so far as relating to section 12 of the Water Act 1945 ;

section 13(3) and (4) ;

section 14 ;

section 16 ;

section 17 ;

section 18 ;

section 19(6) to (11) ;

section 20 ;

section 21(3) to (6).

section 24 ;

section 25 ;

section 28 ;

section 29(1) ;

section 33 ;

1957 c. 20.

section 40(2), except so far as relating to the amendments of the House of Commons Disqualification Act 1957 made by Schedule 8 ;

section 40(3).

(2) Any provision of, or any instrument made under, another Act which is modified or amended by a provision of this Act which comes into operation before 1st April 1974 shall between the passing of this Act and that date have effect both as modified or amended by this Act and as it would have had effect without the modification or amendment.

Short title, minor amendments, repeals and extent.

40.—(1) This Act may be cited as the Water Act 1973.

(2) The enactments specified in Schedule 8 to this Act shall have effect subject to the amendments, modifications and adaptations set out in that Schedule, being amendments, modifications and adaptations which are consequential on the foregoing provisions of this Act and minor amendments.

(3) The enactments specified in Schedule 9 to this Act (which include enactments that were obsolete or unnecessary before the passing of this Act) are hereby repealed to the extent mentioned in column 3 of that Schedule.

(4) The following provisions of this Act, that is to say—

(*a*) section 4(5) to (8), so far as relating to the matters mentioned in section 4(5)(*d*) and (*e*) ;

(*b*) section 9, so far as relating to any enactment which extends to Scotland ;

(*c*) section 18 ;

(*d*) paragraphs 43, 69 and 93 of Schedule 8 ;

1967 c. 78.

(*e*) in Schedule 9, the repeals in the Water (Scotland) Act 1967 ; and

(*f*) so much of this Act as relates to the interpretation or commencement of the foregoing provisions ;

extend to Scotland, but except as aforesaid this Act does not extend to Scotland.

(5) This Act, except section 4(5) to (8), so far as relating to the matters mentioned in section 4(5)(*d*) and (*e*) and paragraph 69 of Schedule 8 and so much of this Act as relates to the interpretation of those provisions, does not extend to Northern Ireland.

1920 c. 67.

(6) For the purposes of section 6 of the Government of Ireland Act 1920 (which relates to the powers of the Parliament of Northern Ireland) this Act shall be deemed to be an Act passed before the appointed day.

SCHEDULES

SCHEDULE 1

REGIONAL WATER AUTHORITY AREAS

Name of Authority	*Area*
North West Water Authority.	The areas of the Cumberland, Lancashire and Mersey and Weaver River Authorities.
Northumbrian Water Authority.	The area of the Northumbrian River Authority.
Yorkshire Water Authority.	The area of the Yorkshire River Authority.
Anglian Water Authority.	The areas of the East Suffolk and Norfolk, Essex, Great Ouse, Lincolnshire and Welland and Nene River Authorities, except the part of the area of the Essex River Authority which is included in the area of the Thames Water Authority.
Thames Water Authority.	The Thames Catchment Area, the Lee Catchment Area and the London excluded area.
	The part of the area of the Essex River Authority the drainage of which is directed to the Thames above the point where the western boundary of the catchment area of the Mar Dyke meets the Thames.
	The part of the area of the Kent River Authority the drainage of which is directed to the Thames above Greenhithe.
Southern Water Authority.	The Isle of Wight and the areas of the Hampshire, Kent and Sussex River Authorities, except the part of the area of the Kent River Authority which is included in the area of the Thames Water Authority.
Wessex Water Authority.	The areas of the Avon and Dorset, Bristol Avon and Somerset River Authorities, except the part of the area of the Avon and Dorset River Authority which is included in the area of the South West Water Authority.
	The part of the area of the Severn River Authority the drainage of which is directed to the Severn below Sharpness.

Name of Authority	*Area*
South West Water Authority.	The areas of the Cornwall and Devon River Authorities.
	The part of the area of the Avon and Dorset River Authority the drainage of which is directed to the River Lim.
Severn-Trent Water Authority.	The areas of the Severn and Trent River Authorities, except the part of the area of the Severn River Authority which is included in the area of the Wessex Water Authority.

Section 2.

SCHEDULE 2

Boundaries of Water Authority Areas and Area and Main River Maps

Part I

Boundaries of Water Authority Areas

General

1.—(1) An order under section 2 above which establishes a water authority or alters the boundaries of a water authority area shall define the water authority area to which it relates, and any waters comprised in it which it is necessary to define for the purpose of the exercise of any of the water authority's functions, in such a way that that area and any such waters can be identified by members of the public and, without prejudice to the generality of this paragraph, any such order may define the whole or any part of a water authority area or of any such waters—

(a) by reference to areas or waters defined for the purposes of the exercise of functions relating to water in enactments in force immediately before the passing of this Act;

(b) by reference to any map;

(c) by reference to any instrument made under an enactment;

or partly by one of those means and partly by another or the others.

(2) For the purposes of this Schedule a map of any area or any waters may consist of a number of maps of parts of that area or those waters and there may be different maps in relation to different functions of a water authority.

(3) In this Part of this Schedule " low-water mark " means low-water mark of ordinary spring tides, and " the sea " includes any bay, estuary or arm of the sea.

Seaward boundaries of water authority areas for general purposes

1961 c. 48.

2.—(1) Without prejudice to section 19(1) of the Land Drainage Act 1961, the seaward boundary of a water authority area for the purposes of the functions of the authority shall, except as provided by an order under section 2 above or paragraph 3, 4 or 5 below, be low water mark on the coast of the area.

(2) Subject to any order made under section 2 above, where a river, stream or other watercourse, whether natural or artificial and whether tidal or not, or any creek in so far as it does not form part of such a watercourse, discharges into the sea, the whole of the mouth of the watercourse within a line from low-water mark at the seaward extremity of one bank to low-water mark at the seaward extremity of the other bank, or the whole of the creek within such a line, as the case may be, shall form part of a water authority area, and, if both banks are in the same water authority area, shall form part of that water authority area.

(3) Where the entrance to a dock is on the coast, the whole of the dock shall form part of a water authority area, and, if both sides of the dock are in the same water authority area, shall form part of that water authority area.

(4) Where sub-paragraph (2) or sub-paragraph (3) above applies, but the banks of the watercourse or creek or the sides of the dock, as the case may be, are in different water authority areas, an order under section 2 above may designate the water authority area in which any part of the watercourse, creek or dock is to be comprised.

3. In any such case as is mentioned in paragraph 2(4) above, an order under section 2 above may designate any tidal waters and direct that, so far as they are below low-water mark, they shall be excluded from all the water authority areas ; and an order made solely for that purpose may designate the waters to which it applies as being all tidal waters which, in so far as they are below low-water mark, lie to seaward of a line specified in the order by reference to a map.

Seaward boundaries for the purposes of fisheries functions

4.—(1) Subject to any order under section 2 above, for the purposes of the functions of a water authority relating to fisheries, the area of the authority shall include those tidal waters and parts of the sea adjoining the coast of the water authority area in which Her Majesty's subjects have the exclusive right of fishing.

(2) Any question arising under this paragraph as to the extent of the area of a water authority shall be determined by the Minister, whose decision shall be final.

Seaward boundaries for the purposes of river pollution functions

5.—(1) Subject to any order under section 2 above, for the purposes of the functions of a water authority relating to the restoration and maintenance of the wholesomeness of rivers and other waters, the area of the authority shall include those tidal waters and parts of the sea adjoining the coast of the water authority area to which any of the provisions of the Rivers (Prevention of Pollution) Act 1951 1951 c. 64. apply—

(a) by virtue of an order made, or having effect as if made, under section 6 of that Act ; or (*b*) by virtue of section 9(2) of the Rivers (Prevention of Pollution) Act 1961 (which applies certain provisions of that Act to controlled waters as defined in the Clean Rivers (Estuaries and Tidal Waters) Act 1960).

(2) Any question arising under this paragraph as to the extent of the area of a water authority shall be determined by the Secretary of State, whose decision shall be final.

PART II

MAPS

6. In this Part of this Schedule—

" area map " means a map of a water authority area ;

" main river map " means a map of a water authority area relating to a water authority's land drainage functions—

(*a*) which shows by a distinctive colour the extent to which any watercourse in that area is to be treated as the main river, or part of the main river, for the purposes of Part II of the Land Drainage Act 1930, and

(*b*) which indicates (by a distinctive colour or otherwise) which (if any) of those watercourses are watercourses designated in a scheme made under section 3 of the Land Drainage Act 1961 (designation of watercourses for drainage works in the interests of agriculture).

7. As soon as practicable after the coming into force of an order under section 2 above establishing a water authority or altering a water authority area, the Secretary of State shall send the authority one or more maps which are to be their area map in relation to their functions, except their land drainage functions, or shall notify them of one or more maps which are to be their area map as aforesaid, or partly one and partly the other.

8. The main river maps on 1st April 1974 shall consist of the following maps, in so far as not replaced by maps sent to water authorities under paragraph 9 below : —

(*a*) in the case of the areas which immediately before that date consisted of the Thames Catchment Area and the Lee Catchment Area, of maps prepared under section 5 of the Land Drainage Act 1930 and current immediately before that date,

(*b*) in the case of other areas, of main river maps kept by river authorities immediately before that date under section 11 of the Water Resources Act 1963,

and in either case, shall also consist of any maps sent to water authorities under paragraph 9 below.

9. The Minister may at any time send a water authority one or more new maps to be substituted for the whole or part of the main river map of the authority's area, and containing a statement to that effect specifying the date on which the substitution is to take effect ; and the substitution shall take effect in accordance with the statement.

10. Until a main river map of a water authority area has been prepared showing the boundaries of that area for the purposes of the water authority's land drainage functions, the boundaries of the water authority area as shown on the area map for the purposes of the authority's functions relating to water conservation shall be treated also as the boundaries of the water authority area for the purposes of their land drainage functions.

11.—(1) Where—

(a) the area of a water authority is altered so as to affect any of the particulars shown on their main river map, or

(b) the Minister confirms a scheme under section 3 of the Land Drainage Act 1961, or

(c) a water authority apply to the Minister for the variation of their main river map, so far as it shows the extent to which any watercourse is to be treated as the main river or part of the main river,

the Minister shall take such action as he considers appropriate either—

(i) by requiring the relevant water authority to send him any part of their main river map, altering it and sending it back to them, or

(ii) by preparing a new main river map and sending it to the water authority, or

(iii) by notifying the authority that he does not intend to vary their main river map.

(2) Before altering a map or preparing a new map under sub-paragraph (1) above the Minister shall give notice of his intention to do so in such manner as he thinks best adapted for informing persons affected, and shall consider any objections made to him within the time and in the manner specified in that notice, and may then alter or prepare the map, whether in accordance with the proposals contained in the notice or otherwise.

12.—(1) Every water authority shall, subject to paragraph 11(1) above, keep their area maps at their principal office and provide reasonable facilities for inspecting those maps and taking copies of and extracts from them.

(2) Any local authority whose area is wholly or partly within a water authority area shall, on application to the water authority, be entitled to be furnished with a copy of any of the authority's area maps, on payment of such sum as the local authority and the water authority may agree.

13.—(1) An area map relating to any functions shall be conclusive evidence for all purposes as to the boundaries of the water authority area in relation to those functions.

(2) A main river map shall be conclusive evidence for all purposes as to what is the main river.

(3) An area map shall be taken to be a document within the meaning of the Documentary Evidence Act 1868, as that Act applies to the Secretary of State and the Minister ; and that Act, as it so applies shall have effect—

(*a*) in relation to an area map other than a main river map, as if it had been issued by the Secretary of State and the Minister acting separately and not jointly ;

(*b*) in relation to a main river map, as if it had been issued by the Minister.

Part III

Alteration of Boundaries

14.—(1) Before making an order altering the boundaries of a water authority area the Ministers shall—

(*a*) consult with such persons or representative bodies as they consider it appropriate to consult at that stage ;

(*b*) prepare a draft order ;

(*c*) cause a notice to be published in the London Gazette and in such other manner as they think best adapted for informing persons affected—

(i) stating their intention to make the order and its general effect ;

(ii) specifying the places where copies of the draft order and of any map to which it refers may be inspected by any person free of charge at all reasonable times during the period of twenty-eight days beginning with the date on which the notice is first published otherwise than in the London Gazette ; and

(iii) stating that any person may within that period by notice in writing to the Ministers object to the making of the order.

(2) The Ministers shall also cause copies of the notice and of the draft order to be served on any public authorities who appear to them to be concerned.

15.—(1) Before making an order altering the boundaries of a water authority area, the Ministers shall consider any objections which may be duly made to the draft order, and may if they think fit cause a local inquiry to be held with respect to any such objections ; and the Ministers may make the order either in the form of the draft or in that form as altered in such manner as they may think fit, but no order shall be made so as to include in any water authority area any tidal waters which would have been outside all the water authority areas if the order had been made in the form of the draft.

(2) Subsections (2) to (5) of section 250 of the 1972 Act shall apply in relation to a local inquiry under this paragraph as they apply to a local inquiry which a Minister causes to be held under subsection (1) of that section, but with the substitution in subsection (4) for the words " such local authority or " of the words " such water authority or ".

16.—(1) Where an objection has been duly made by any body on whom notice is required to be served under paragraph 14 above and has not been withdrawn, then, if the order is made, the Ministers shall serve notice of the making of the order on every such body who has duly made an objection which has not been withdrawn.

(2) Where a notice is required to be served under sub-paragraph (1) above, the order shall not have effect before the expiry of a period of twenty-eight days from the date of service of that notice ; and if within that period any such body gives notice to either of the Ministers objecting to the order, and the objection is not withdrawn, the order shall be subject to special parliamentary procedure.

17. A statutory instrument containing an order altering the boundaries of a water authority area which is not subject to special parliamentary procedure shall be subject to annulment in pursuance of a resolution of either House of Parliament.

18. After making an order altering the boundaries of a water authority area the Ministers shall publish in the London Gazette, and in such other manner as they think best adapted for informing persons affected, a notice stating that the order has been made and naming the places where a copy of the order may be seen at all reasonable hours:

Provided that, in the case of an order to which paragraph 16(2) above applies, the notice shall not be published until the expiry of the period of twenty-eight days referred to in that sub-paragraph, and shall state whether or not the order is to be subject to special parliamentary procedure.

19.—(1) Subject to sub-paragraph (2) below, if any person desires to question the validity of an order altering the boundaries of a water authority area on the ground that it is not within the powers of this Act, or that any requirement of this Act has not been complied with, he may, within six weeks after the first publication of the notice required by paragraph 18 above, make an application for the purpose to the High Court ; and if any such application is duly made, the court, if satisfied that the order is not within the powers of this Act or that the interests of the applicant have been substantially prejudiced by any requirements of this Act not having been complied with, may quash the order either generally or in so far as it affects the applicant.

(2) Sub-paragraph (1) above shall not apply to any order which is confirmed by Act of Parliament under section 6 of the Statutory Orders (Special Procedure) Act 1945, and shall have effect in relation to any other order which is subject to special parliamentary procedure by virtue of the provisions of this Schedule as if for the reference to the first publication of the notice required by paragraph 18 above there were substituted a reference to the date on which the order becomes operative under the said Act of 1945.

(3) Except as provided by sub-paragraph (1) above, the validity of an order altering the boundaries of a water authority area shall not, either before or after the order has been made, be questioned in any legal proceedings whatsoever.

SCHEDULE 3

ADMINISTRATION, FINANCE, ETC., OF WATER AUTHORITIES AND THE NATIONAL WATER COUNCIL

PART I

WATER AUTHORITIES

General

1. A water authority shall be a body corporate.

2. A water authority shall have power to do anything (whether or not involving the expenditure, borrowing or lending of money or the acquisition or disposal of any property or rights) which in the opinion of the authority is calculated to facilitate, or is conducive or incidental to, the discharge of any of their functions.

Terms of office of members of water authorities

3. The chairman of a water authority and the other members appointed by a Minister shall hold and vacate office in accordance with the terms of their appointment.

4.—(1) This paragraph applies to members of a water authority appointed by a local authority or local authorities.

(2) The first members to whom this paragraph applies shall come into office on the day on which the water authority comes into existence, or, in the case of a member who is for any reason appointed after that day, on the day on which the appointment is made, and, subject to the following provisions of this Schedule, shall hold office until the end of May in such year as may be specified for the purposes of this paragraph in the order establishing the authority.

(3) Any other members to whom this paragraph applies shall come into office at the beginning of the June next following the day on which they are appointed, and, subject to the following provisions of this Schedule, shall hold office for a term of four years:

Provided that if for any reason any member is appointed on or after the day on which he ought to have come into office, he shall come into office on the day on which he is appointed and shall hold office for the remainder of the said term.

Vacation of office by members

5.—(1) A member of a water authority may resign his office at any time by giving notice in writing to the chairman of the authority and also, if he was appointed by a Minister, to that Minister.

(2) The chairman of a water authority may resign his office at any time by giving notice in writing to the Secretary of State.

6.—(1) The office of a member of a water authority shall become vacant upon the happening of any of the following events, namely, if he—

(*a*) is adjudged bankrupt, or makes a composition or arrangement with his creditors ; or

(*b*) is convicted in the United Kingdom, the Channel Islands or the Isle of Man of any offence and has passed on him a sentence of imprisonment (whether suspended or not) for a period of not less than three months without the option of a fine ; or

(*c*) is disqualified for being elected or for being a member of a local authority or water authority under Part III of the Representation of the People Act 1949 or under Part VIII of the 1972 Act ; or

1949 c. 68.

SCH. 3

(*d*) has, for a period of six consecutive months, been absent
from meetings of the authority, otherwise than by reason of
illness or some other cause approved during that period
by the authority.

(2) For the purposes of sub-paragraph (1)(*d*) above, the attendance
of a member of a water authority at a meeting of any committee of
the authority of which he is a member, or at any joint committee
to which he has been appointed by the authority, shall be treated
as attendance at a meeting of the authority.

Appointments to fill casual vacancies

7. Where, for any reason whatsoever, the place of a member
of a water authority becomes vacant before the end of his term of
office the vacancy—

(*a*) shall, if the unexpired portion of the term of office of the
vacating member is six months or more, be filled by the
appointment of a new member ; and

(*b*) may be so filled in any other case.

8. A person appointed by virtue of paragraph 7 above to fill a
casual vacancy shall hold office so long only as the former member
would have held office.

Disqualification for, and re-appointment to, membership of water authorities

9.—(1) Subject to the following provisions of this paragraph, a
person shall be disqualified for appointment as a member of a water
authority if he—

(*a*) is a paid officer of the authority ; or

(*b*) is a person who has been adjudged bankrupt, or made a
composition or arrangement with his creditors ; or

(*c*) has within the period of five years ending on the day on
which his qualification for appointment falls to be determined, been surcharged by a district auditor to an amount
exceeding £500 under Part X of the Local Government 1933 c. 51.
Act 1933 ; or

(*d*) has within five years before the day of his appointment
been convicted in the United Kingdom, the Channel
Islands or the Isle of Man of any offence and has had
passed on him a sentence of imprisonment (whether suspended or not) for a period of not less than three months
without the option of a fine ; or

(*e*) is disqualified for being elected or for being a member of
a local authority or water authority under Part III of the
Representation of the People Act 1949 or Part VIII of the 1949 c. 68.
1972 Act.

(2) Where a person is disqualified under sub-paragraph (1) above
by reason of having been adjudged bankrupt, then—

(*a*) if the bankruptcy is annulled on the ground that he ought not
to have been adjudged bankrupt or on the ground that
his debts have been paid in full, the disqualification shall
cease on the date of the annulment ;

(*b*) if he is discharged with a certificate that the bankruptcy was caused by misfortune without any misconduct on his part, the disqualification shall cease on the date of his discharge ; and

(*c*) if he is discharged without such a certificate his disqualification shall cease on the expiration of five years from the date of his discharge.

(3) Where a person is disqualified under sub-paragraph (1) above by reason of his having made a composition or arrangement with his creditors and he pays his debts in full, the disqualification shall cease on the date on which the payment is completed, and in any other case it shall cease on the expiration of five years from the date on which the terms of the deed of composition or arrangement are fulfilled.

(4) For the purposes of sub-paragraph (1)(*c*) and (*d*) above, the ordinary date on which the period allowed for making an appeal or application with respect to the surcharge or conviction expires or, if such an appeal or application is made, the date on which it is finally disposed of or abandoned or fails by reason of non-prosecution shall be taken to be the date of the surcharge or conviction, as the case may be.

(5) Section 92 of the 1972 Act (proceedings for disqualification) shall apply in relation to disqualification under this paragraph for appointment as a member of a water authority as it applies in relation to disqualification for acting as a member of a local authority.

10. Subject to the provisions of this Schedule, a member of a water authority shall be eligible for reappointment.

Remuneration and allowances

11.—(1) A water authority—

(*a*) shall pay their chairman and the chairmen of their regional land drainage committee and their local land drainage committees such remuneration and such allowances as may be determined by the Ministers with the consent of the Minister for the Civil Service ; and

(*b*) if the Ministers with the consent of the Minister for the Civil Service so determine in the case of any person who is or has been chairman of a water authority or any such committee, shall pay or make arrangements for the payment of a pension, allowance or gratuity to or in respect of that person in accordance with the determination.

(2) Sections 173 to 175 of the 1972 Act (allowances to members of local authorities) shall apply to water authorities, and for the purposes of those sections as applied by this paragraph a member of a committee or sub-committee of a water authority shall be deemed to be a member of that authority.

Officers

12. Sections 114 to 119 of the 1972 Act (which contain miscellaneous provisions relating to officers and former officers) shall each have effect in relation to a water authority and to officers of a

water authority subject to the necessary modifications and, in par-
ticular, but without prejudice to the generality of this paragraph,
with the substitution in section 115 of that Act for the
reference to the proper officer of the local authority of a reference
to such officer of the water authority as that authority may appoint
for the purposes of this paragraph.

13. Without prejudice to paragraph 2 above, a water authority
may—

    (*a*) provide housing accommodation for persons employed by
        them (whether by constructing, converting, enlarging or
        acquiring any buildings and whether by selling such accom-
        modation or letting it or permitting it to be occupied with
        or without requiring the payment of rent or other charges) ;

    (*b*) permit a person for whom the authority provided housing
        accommodation while employed by them to occupy such
        accommodation provided by them after ceasing to be so
        employed.

Meetings and proceedings of water authorities and committees

14.—(1) In paragraph 1 of the Schedule to the Public Bodies   1960 c. 67.
(Admission to Meetings) Act 1960 (bodies to which in England and
Wales that Act applies), for paragraph (*c*) there shall be substituted
the following paragraph : —

" (*c*) water authorities ".

(2) Without prejudice to section 2(1) of that Act (application of
section 1 of that Act to any committee of a body whose members
consist of or include all members of that body), section 1 of that Act
shall apply to every committee appointed or established by one or
more water authorities under any provision of this Act or otherwise.

(3) Where section 1 of that Act applies to a committee by virtue of
this paragraph, then, for the purposes of subsection (4)(*c*) of that
section, premises belonging to the water authority or one or more of
the water authorities which established or appointed the committee
shall be treated as belonging to the committee.

15.—(1) Subject to the following provisions of this paragraph, a
person nominated by one or more local authorities may act as
deputy for a member of a water authority appointed by that local
authority or those local authorities and may accordingly (instead of
that member) attend and vote at a meeting of the water authority or
any committees or sub-committees to which the member for whom
he is a deputy belongs.

(2) A person acting as deputy for a member of a water authority
shall be treated for the purposes for which he is nominated as a
member of that authority.

(3) A person shall not act as deputy for a member of a water
authority unless his nomination has been notified to an officer of
the authority appointed to receive such nominations.

(4) A nomination shall be in writing and may apply either to a particular meeting or to all meetings during a stated period or until the nomination is revoked.

(5) A person shall not act as deputy for more than one member of a water authority.

(6) The reference to committees and sub-committees in this paragraph does not include a reference to regional or local land drainage committees.

16. The proceedings of a water authority, or of any committee or sub-committee of such an authority, shall not be invalidated by any vacancy in their number, or by any defect in the appointment, or the qualification for appointment, of any person as a member or as chairman.

17.—(1) Subject to the following provisions of this paragraph, the provisions of sections 94 to 98 of the 1972 Act (pecuniary interests of members of local authorities) shall apply in relation to members of a water authority, or of any committee or sub-committee of a water authority, as those provisions apply in relation to members of local authorities.

(2) In their application by virtue of this paragraph the said provisions shall have effect in accordance with the following provisions—

    (*a*) for references to meetings of the local authority there shall be substituted references to meetings of a water authority or of any committee or sub-committee of such an authority ;

    (*b*) in section 94(4) for the reference to provision being made by standing orders of a local authority there shall be substituted a reference to provision being made by rules of the water authority ;

    (*c*) in section 96 for references to the proper officer of the local authority there shall be substituted a reference to an officer of the water authority appointed for the purposes of this paragraph ;

    (*d*) in the case of members of a committee or sub-committee of a water authority, the right of persons who are members of the committee or sub-committee but not members of the authority to inspect the book kept under section 96(2) shall be limited to an inspection of the entries in the book relating to the members of that committee or sub-committee ;

    (*e*) section 97 shall apply as it applies to a local authority other than a parish or community council.

(3) Without prejudice to section 97(4) of the 1972 Act, section 94 of that Act shall not by virtue of this paragraph apply—

    (*a*) to any interest which a member of a water authority or committee or sub-committee may have in the preparation or revision of a charges scheme or in the raising of any drainage rates, the levying of any general or special drainage charges or the levying of any other charges by a water authority ; or (*b*) to any interest in any other matter which such a member **Sch. 3** may have as the holder of, or as an applicant or prospec- tive applicant for, a licence under the Water Resources 1963 c. 38. Act 1963 where it is an interest which he has in common with all other holders of, or applicants or prospective applicants for, such licences, or in common with all other persons belonging to a class of such holders, applicants or prospective applicants.

18.—(1) A minute of the proceedings of a meeting of a water authority, or of any committee or sub-committee of such an authority, purporting to be signed at that or the next ensuing meeting by the chairman of the meeting to the proceedings of which the minute relates or by the chairman of the next ensuing meeting, shall be evidence of the proceedings and shall be received in evidence without further proof ; and, until the contrary is proved, every meeting in respect of the proceedings of which a minute has been so signed shall be deemed to have been duly convened and held, and all the proceedings had at the meeting to have been duly had, and, where the proceedings are the proceedings of a committee or sub-committee, that committee or sub-committee shall be deemed to have been duly constituted and have had power to deal with the matters referred to in the minute.

(2) Subject to sub-paragraph (3) below, the minutes of proceedings of meetings of a water authority shall be open to the inspection of any local government elector for any part of the water authority area, and any such local government elector may make a copy of or extract from the minutes.

(3) Sub-paragraph (2) above does not apply to any part of such minutes which contains information with respect to any manufacturing process or trade secret obtained in the exercise of powers under this Act or any enactment amended by this Act.

(4) In this paragraph " local government elector " means a person registered as a local government elector in the register of electors in accordance with the provisions of the Representation of the People Acts.

Authentication of documents

19. Any notice or other document which a water authority are required or authorised to give, make or issue by or under this Act or any other enactment may be signed on behalf of the authority by any member or officer of the authority generally or specially authorised for that purpose by a resolution of the authority ; and any document purporting to bear the signature of a person expressed to be so authorised shall be deemed, until the contrary is proved, to be duly given, made or issued by authority of the water authority.

In this paragraph " signature " includes a facsimile of a signa- ture by whatever process reproduced.

Contracts

20.—(1) A water authority shall make rules with respect to the making by or on behalf of the authority of contracts for the supply of goods or materials or for the execution of works.

Y

(2) Rules made by a water authority with respect to contracts for the supply of goods or materials or for the execution of works shall include provision for securing competition for such contracts and for regulating the manner in which tenders are invited, but may exempt from any such provision contracts for a price below that specified in the rules and may authorise the authority to exempt any contract from any such provision where the authority are satisfied that the exemption is justified by special circumstances.

(3) A person entering into a contract with a water authority shall not be bound to inquire whether the rules of the authority which apply to the contract have been complied with ; and non-compliance with such rules shall not invalidate any contract entered into by or on behalf of the authority.

Interpretation

21. In this Part of this Schedule references to a committee or sub-committee of a water authority include references to a committee or sub-committee of two or more such authorities and to a committee or sub-committee established under Schedule 5 to this Act or by a scheme thereunder.

PART II

THE NATIONAL WATER COUNCIL

22. The Council shall be a body corporate.

23. The Council shall have power to do anything (whether or not involving the expenditure, borrowing or lending of money or the acquisition or disposal of any property or rights) which in the opinion of the Council is calculated to facilitate, or is conducive or incidental to, the discharge of any of their functions.

24. The members of the Council, other than the chairmen of the water authorities, shall hold and vacate office in accordance with the terms of their respective appointments, but those terms shall not provide for any of them to hold office for more than five years at a time.

25.—(1) Any such member of the Council may by notice in writing addressed to the Minister who appointed him resign his office.

(2) A member of the Council who ceases to be a member shall be eligible for re-appointment.

26. Paragraphs 6 and 9 above, except sub-paragraph (1)(*a*) of paragraph 9, shall apply to the Council as they apply to a water authority.

27.—(1) The Council—

(*a*) shall pay to the appointed members such remuneration and such allowances as may be determined by the appointing Minister with the consent of the Minister for the Civil Service ; and

(*b*) if the appointing Minister with the consent of the Minister for the Civil Service so determines in the case of any person who is or has been an appointed member of the Council, shall pay or make arrangements for the payment of a pension, allowance or gratuity to or in respect of that person in accordance with the determination ;

and if a person ceases to be an appointed member of the Council and it appears to the appointing Minister that there are special circumstances which make it right that that person should receive compensation, that Minister may require the Council to pay to that person a sum of such amount as that Minister may with the consent of the Minister for the Civil Service determine.

(2) In sub-paragraph (1) above " appointed member " means any member of the Council other than the chairmen of the water authorities and, in relation to any such member, " appointing Minister " means the Minister by whom he was appointed.

(3) Without prejudice to the generality of paragraph 23 of this Schedule, the Council may establish and administer pension schemes and pension funds in the interest of persons who are or have been employed by them and may pay pensions, allowances and gratuities to or in respect of such persons, or enter into and carry into effect agreements or arrangements with any other person for securing or preserving pension rights for any such persons.

28.—(1) The quorum of the Council and the arrangements relating to its meetings shall, subject to any directions given by the Ministers, be such as the Council may determine.

(2) A person who is a member of the Council by virtue of his office as chairman of a water authority may authorise another person, being a member of that authority, to attend in his stead at a meeting of the Council, and any person so attending shall be treated for the purposes of that meeting as a member of the Council.

(3) Any authorisation under sub-paragraph (2) above shall be in writing and may apply either to a particular meeting or to all meetings during a stated period or until the authorisation is revoked.

29. The Council may arrange for the discharge of any of their functions, except their power to borrow money or require contributions from the water authorities to the expenses of the Council, by a committee, a sub-committee or an officer of the Council, and any such committee may, unless the Council otherwise direct, arrange for the discharge of any of their functions by a sub-committee or officer of the Council.

30. The validity of any proceedings of the Council shall not be affected by any vacancy among the members of the Council or any defect in the appointment of any of their members.

Part III

Financial and Administrative Provisions

Revenue and reserves

31.—(1) A water authority shall charge to revenue account in every year all charges which are proper to be made to revenue account, including such allocations to reserve as they consider adequate or as may be necessary to comply with any directions under paragraph 32 below and including any payments to the Council under paragraph 33 below.

(2) Revenue raised by a water authority in a local land drainage district—

    (*a*) under or by virtue of Part II of Schedule 5 to this Act ;

    (*b*) by contributions required under section 21(1) of the Land Drainage Act 1930 (contributions from internal drainage boards) ; or

    (*c*) by special drainage charges under section 3 of the Land Drainage Act 1961 ;

shall, except for any amount which they consider appropriate to set aside towards research or related activities and paying their administrative expenses and an appropriate proportion of any amount allocated to reserve under sub-paragraph (1) above and of any payment to the Council under paragraph 33 below, be spent only in the discharge of their land drainage functions in or for the benefit of that district.

(3) Any amount specified in a resolution under section 21(1) of the Land Drainage Act 1961 (resolution passed by a water authority who are the drainage board of an internal drainage district allocating a portion of their revenue in lieu of contributions which they would require from the drainage board of that district under section 21(1) of the Land Drainage Act 1930) shall be treated for the purposes of this paragraph as if it were revenue actually raised by contributions required under section 21(1) of the said Act of 1930.

32.—(1) The Ministers may with the approval of the Treasury and after consultation with the Council direct a water authority—

    (*a*) to allocate to reserve generally or to reserve for a particular purpose either a specified amount or such amount as the authority consider adequate, or

    (*b*) to re-allocate for a specified purpose the whole or part of any amount previously allocated for some other purpose, or

    (*c*) with respect to the application of amounts allocated to reserve.

(2) Directions under this paragraph requiring the allocation of any amount to reserve may provide for it to be so allocated either at a specified time or during the course of a specified period.

33. Expenditure of the Council shall, so far as not defrayed out of their own resources, be defrayed, if it is properly chargeable to revenue account, by the water authorities and any payment of a water authority towards defraying that expenditure shall be such proportion of that expenditure as the Secretary of State may direct.

Loans and grants

34.—(1) A water authority and the Council may borrow money in accordance, and only in accordance, with the provisions of this paragraph.

(2) Subject to sub-paragraph (5) below, a water authority and the Council may borrow temporarily, by way of overdraft or otherwise, such sums as they may require for meeting their obligations and discharging their functions—

    (*a*) in sterling from the Secretary of State, or

(*b*) with the consent of the Secretary of State and the approval of the Treasury, or in accordance with any general authority given by the Secretary of State with the approval of the Treasury, either in sterling or in a currency other than sterling from a person other than the Secretary of State.

(3) Subject to sub-paragraph (5) below, a water authority and the Council may borrow otherwise than by way of temporary loan such sums as they may require for capital purposes—

(*a*) in sterling from the Secretary of State, or

(*b*) with the consent of the Secretary of State and the approval of the Treasury, in a currency other than sterling from a person other than the Secretary of State.

(4) Subject to sub-paragraph (5) below, a water authority and the Council may, with the consent of the Secretary of State and the approval of the Treasury, borrow (otherwise than by way of temporary loan) from the Commission of the European Communities or the European Investment Bank sums in any currency.

(5) The aggregate amount outstanding in respect of the principal of—

(*a*) sums borrowed by water authorities and the Council; and

(*b*) sums borrowed or treated by or by virtue of any enactment as borrowed by local authorities, towards the discharge of the principal or interest of which water authorities are making contributions;

shall not exceed £3,750 million or such greater sum not exceeding £5,000 million as the Secretary of State may by order specify.

(6) The Secretary of State may also by order specify a limit for the borrowing of any water authority or of the Council.

(7) No order shall be made under sub-paragraph (5) above unless a draft of the order has been laid before the House of Commons, and has been approved by a resolution of that House.

35.—(1) The Secretary of State may with the approval of the Treasury—

(*a*) make to a water authority out of money provided by Parliament grants of such amounts as the Secretary of State thinks fit;

(*b*) give a water authority a direction providing that the whole or part of a grant made in pursuance of paragraph (*a*) above is not to be used by the authority otherwise than for the purpose of such of the authority's functions as are specified in the direction, not being land drainage functions.

(2) The Secretary of State may, with the approval of the Treasury, lend to a water authority or to the Council any sums which they have power to borrow by virtue of paragraph 34 above.

(3) Any loan which the Secretary of State makes in pursuance of sub-paragraph (2) above shall be repaid to him at such times and by such methods, and interest on the loan shall be paid to him at such rates and at such times, as the Secretary of State may with the approval of the Treasury from time to time determine.

(4) The Treasury may issue out of the National Loans Fund to the Secretary of State such sums as are necessary to enable him to make loans in pursuance of sub-paragraph (2) above, and any sums received by the Secretary of State in pursuance of sub-paragraph (3) above shall be paid into that Fund.

36.—(1) The Treasury may guarantee, in such manner and on such conditions as they think fit, the repayment of the principal of and the payment of interest on any sums which an authority or the Council borrow from a person other than the Secretary of State.

(2) Immediately after a guarantee is given under this paragraph the Treasury shall lay a statement of the guarantee before each House of Parliament ; and where any sum is issued for fulfilling a guarantee so given the Treasury shall, as soon as possible after the end of each financial year (beginning with that in which the sum is issued and ending with that in which all liability in respect of the principal of the sum and in respect of the interest thereon is finally discharged), lay before each House of Parliament a statement relating to that sum.

(3) Any sums required by the Treasury for fulfilling a guarantee under this paragraph shall be charged on and issued out of the Consolidated Fund.

(4) If any sums are issued in fulfilment of a guarantee given under this paragraph, the authority or, as the case may be, the Council shall make to the Treasury, at such times and in such manner as the Treasury from time to time direct, payments of such amounts as the Treasury so direct in or towards repayment of the sums so issued and payments of interest, at such rate as the Treasury so direct, on what is outstanding for the time being in respect of sums so issued.

(5) Any sums received by the Treasury in pursuance of sub-paragraph (4) above shall be paid into the Consolidated Fund.

37. It shall be the duty of the Secretary of State as respects each financial year—

(a) to prepare, in such form and manner as the Treasury may direct, an account of sums issued to the Secretary of State in pursuance of paragraph 35 above and of any sums required to be paid into the National Loans Fund in pursuance of that paragraph and of the disposal by the Secretary of State of those sums respectively ; and

(b) to send a copy of the account to the Comptroller and Auditor General not later than the end of the month of November next following that year ;

and the Comptroller and Auditor General shall examine, certify and report on the account and shall lay copies of it and of his report on it before each House of Parliament.

Accounts and audit of authorities and Council

38.—(1) It shall be the duty of a water authority and of the Council—

(a) to keep proper accounts and proper records in relation to the accounts ;

(*b*) to prepare in respect of each financial year a statement of accounts, in such form as the Ministers may direct with the approval of the Treasury, showing the state of the affairs of the body preparing the statement.

(2) Without prejudice to sub-paragraph (1) above, the Minister may direct a water authority to keep such accounts and records and to prepare such statements with regard to money expended in the performance of their land drainage functions as he may think fit.

(3) As soon as the accounts and statements mentioned in sub-paragraphs (1) and (2) above for any financial year have been audited under paragraph 39 below, the authority or the Council shall send to the Ministers a copy of the statement together with a copy of any report made by the auditor on it or on their accounts, and the Ministers shall lay a copy of every statement and report of which a copy is received by them in pursuance of this sub-paragraph before each House of Parliament.

(4) A copy of any document required under sub-paragraph (3) above to be sent by a water authority to the Ministers shall also be sent by the authority, as soon as the accounts kept and each statement prepared for any financial year in pursuance of sub-paragraph (1) or (2) above have been audited under paragraph 39 below, to every local authority whose area is wholly or partly included in the water authority's area.

(5) Any person, on application to an authority or to the Council, shall be entitled to be furnished with copies of the statements of their accounts prepared under this paragraph and of the auditor's report on those accounts on payment of such reasonable sum as the authority or the Council may determine, and to inspect and to take copies of, or extracts from, an abstract of the accounts of the authority or Council free of charge.

39. All accounts of a water authority and the Council shall be audited in accordance with Part VIII of the 1972 Act by a district auditor or an approved auditor appointed under that Part of that Act, and accordingly the relevant provisions of that Part of that Act, that is to say, sections 154 to 167, shall apply to all such accounts as they apply to the accounts of a county council, and in section 161(2)(*b*) and (7) (disqualification), as applied by this paragraph, the references to a local authority shall include references to a water authority and the Council.

Annual reports of authorities, Council and
Water Space Amenity Commission

40.—(1) Each water authority, the Council and the Water Space Amenity Commission shall make to the Ministers, as soon as possible after the end of each financial year, a report on the discharge by them of their functions during that year and of their policy and programme.

(2) If the Ministers so direct, a report under sub-paragraph (1) above shall be in such form and contain such information as is specified in the direction.

(3) A water authority shall send a copy of their report for any year to the Council and to every local authority whose area is wholly or partly situated in the area of the water authority.

(4) The Council shall send a copy of their report for any year to every water authority.

(5) The Water Space Amenity Commission shall send a copy of their report for any year to the Council, every water authority and every county council.

(6) The report for any year of a water authority or of the Council shall set out any direction given to them during that year under this Act.

(7) The Ministers shall lay a copy of every such report before each House of Parliament.

(8) Any person shall be entitled to be furnished with a copy of the report of a water authority, the Council or the Water Space Amenity Commission for any year on applying to the body who made the report and on payment of such reasonable sum as that body may determine.

41. It shall also be the duty of every water authority to furnish the Ministers and the Council with such information as they may from time to time require with respect to the authority's property, financial position, activities or proposed activities, and with respect to the water resources in the authority's area, and to afford to the Ministers facilities for the verification of information so furnished.

Relationship of Welsh and Severn-Trent Water Authorities

42.—(1) The Severn-Trent Water Authority shall consult the Welsh authority on any substantial development or matter of policy arising from the exercise of the former's functions, in so far as the development or matter affects so much of their area as is within Wales.

(2) It shall be the duty of the Welsh authority to keep the Secretary of State informed of their views on all matters about which they are in consultation with the Severn-Trent Water Authority.

43.—(1) Where the Severn-Trent Water Authority acquire an estate or interest in land in Wales for or in connection with the construction and operation of a reservoir, they shall convey the estate or interest in the land to the Welsh authority who shall grant the Severn-Trent Water Authority, for the purposes for which the latter originally acquired the estate or interest, a lease or sub-lease of the land or such other interest in it as may be appropriate.

(2) A conveyance or grant under sub-paragraph (1) above shall be on such terms as may be agreed between the two water authorities or as, in default of agreement, may be settled by the Secretary of State.

SCHEDULE 4

SUPPLY OF WATER IN BULK AND DEFAULT POWERS

PART I

SECTIONS TO BE SUBSTITUTED FOR SECTIONS 12 AND 13 OF THE WATER ACT 1945

12.—(1) An agreement may be made between any statutory water undertakers and any other persons, whether statutory undertakers or not, for the giving by those other persons, and the taking by the statutory water undertakers, of a supply of water in bulk for any period and on any terms and conditions, and, where the supply is to be given by persons who are themselves statutory water undertakers, either within or outside the limits of supply of those undertakers.

Supply of water in bulk by agreement or compulsorily.

(2) An agreement under this section to which a statutory water company is a party shall require the approval of the water authority on whose behalf the company are supplying water, and the water authority shall withhold their approval in any case where a supply of water is to be given by a statutory water company if it appears to the authority that the giving of the supply would be likely to interfere with the supply of water for any purpose within the company's limits of supply.

(3) Where it appears to a water authority that it is expedient—

(a) that any statutory water company through whom the authority are supplying water should give a supply of water in bulk to any other such statutory water company or to the authority and that that other company or the authority should take such a supply, or

(b) that the authority should give such a supply to such a company,

and the water authority are satisfied that the giving and taking of such a supply cannot be secured by agreement, they may by order require the giving and taking of such a supply for such period and on such terms and conditions as may be provided in the order.

(4) The power conferred by subsection (3) above may be exercised jointly by two or more water authorities in any case where the transfer of a supply of water in bulk between their areas appears to them to be expedient.

(5) Where it appears to the Secretary of State that it is expedient that one water authority should give to another a supply of water in bulk, and he is satisfied that the giving and taking of such a supply cannot be secured by agreement, he may by order require the respective authorities to give and to take such a supply for such period and on such terms and conditions as may be provided in the order.

(6) For the purpose of laying any pipes or installing any apparatus connected therewith, being pipes or apparatus required for giving

and taking a supply of water in pursuance of an agreement or order made under this section, statutory water undertakers may exercise, either within or outside their limits of supply, the like powers as are exercisable under Parts V and VI of Schedule 3 to this Act for the purpose of laying mains by undertakers to whose undertaking those Parts apply, but subject to the like conditions and obligations.

(7) Without prejudice to section 254 of the Local Government Act 1972, as applied by section 34 of the Water Act 1973, where immediately before 1st April 1974 statutory water undertakers are under an obligation to give a supply of water in bulk to any other statutory water undertakers, and the obligation arises otherwise than under an agreement or order made under this section, the obligation shall, as from that date, be deemed to be created by an agreement under this section, and—

(a) the parties may accordingly by agreement vary or terminate the obligation to supply water in bulk and the terms and conditions relating to it ; but

(b) the Secretary of State may, on the application of either of them, terminate that obligation on such terms and conditions as he thinks fit.

13.—(1) If a complaint is made to the Secretary of State that a water authority have failed—

(a) to give an adequate supply of water, either as respects quantity or quality, to any part of their area, or to give any supply which they have been lawfully required to give, or

(b) to take such steps as are reasonably practicable to obtain new powers or to extend their existing powers for the purpose of remedying any such failure, or

(c) to do anything which they are required to do by or under this Act,

or the Secretary of State is of the opinion that an investigation should be made as to whether a water authority have failed in any of the matters mentioned in paragraphs (a) to (c) above, he may cause a local inquiry to be held into the matter.

(2) Where a statutory water company are supplying water on behalf of a water authority and a complaint is made to the water authority that the company have failed—

(a) to give an adequate supply of water, either as respects quantity or quality, to any part of the water authority area which they are supplying, or to give any supply which they have been lawfully required to give, or

(b) to take such steps as are reasonably practicable to obtain new powers or to extend their existing powers for the purpose of remedying any such failure, or

(c) to do anything which they are required to do by or under this Act,

or a water authority are of opinion that an investigation should be made as to whether any statutory water company through whom

they are supplying water have failed in any of the matters mentioned   Sch. 4
in paragraphs (*a*) to (*c*) above, the authority may cause a local
inquiry to be held into the matter.

(3) Subsections (2) to (5) of section 250 of the Local Government 1972 c. 70.
Act 1972 shall apply in relation to a local inquiry under sub-
section (2) above as they apply in relation to a local inquiry which a
Minister causes to be held under subsection (1) of that section—

> (*a*) with the substitution of a reference to the water authority
> holding the inquiry for any reference to the Minister, and
>
> (*b*) with the omission from subsection (4) of the word " local ".

(4) If after a local inquiry has been held in pursuance of subsection (1) or (2) above it appears to the Secretary of State or, as
the case may be, the water authority holding the inquiry, that there
has been such a failure as is mentioned in subsection (1) or (2)
above on the part of the statutory water undertakers in question,
the Secretary of State or the water authority, as the case may be, may
make an order declaring the undertakers to be in default and
directing them for the purpose of remedying the default to discharge
such of their functions in such manner and within such time or
times as may be specified in the order or, as the case may be, to take
such steps within such time or times as may be specified in the order
to obtain new powers or to extend their existing powers.

(5) If a water authority declared to be in default by an order made
under subsection (4) above fail to comply with any requirement of
the order within the time limited by it for compliance with that
requirement, the Secretary of State, in lieu of enforcing the order by
mandamus or otherwise, may make an order transferring to himself
such of the functions of the water authority as he thinks fit.

(6) If a statutory water company declared to be in default by an
order made under subsection (4) above fail to comply with any
requirement of the order within the time limited by that requirement
for compliance with the requirement, the water authority, in lieu
of enforcing the order by mandamus or otherwise, may make an
order suspending the whole or any part of any arrangements made
with the statutory water company in question under section 12 of
the Water Act 1973, as appears to them necessary in view of the
failure, and transferring to themselves such of the functions of the
company as they think fit.

(7) Where functions transferred to the Secretary of State under this
section include the function of applying to the Secretary of State
for any new powers or for an extension of existing powers, the
Secretary of State may grant the new powers or the extension as if
an application had been made therefor, and shall give all such notices
and do all such other things as would have been required to be given
or done in connection with such an application, and any enactment
relating to the application for and grant of such new powers or
extension of existing powers shall have effect with the necessary
adaptations and modifications.

SCH. 4

(8) Where any functions have been transferred to the Secretary of State or a water authority under this section, any expenses incurred by the Secretary of State or the water authority in discharging those functions shall be paid in the first instance by the Secretary of State or the authority, but the amount of those expenses as certified by the Secretary of State or the authority shall on demand be paid to the Secretary of State or, as the case may be, the authority, by the body in default, and shall be recoverable accordingly, and the body in default shall have the like power of raising the money required as they have of raising money for defraying expenses incurred directly by them.

(9) Any order made under subsection (5) or (6) above may provide for the transfer to the Secretary of State or the water authority, as the case may be, of such of the property and liabilities of the body in default as, in the opinion of the Secretary of State or the water authority, may be necessary or expedient, and when any such order is revoked the Secretary of State or the authority may, either by the revoking order or by a subsequent order, make such provision as appears to him or them to be desirable with respect to any property or liabilities held by him or them for the purposes of the functions transferred.

Interpretation of ss. 12 and 13.

13A.—(1) Expressions used in either of the last two foregoing sections and in the Water Act 1973 have the meanings assigned to them by that Act.

(2) Any reference to a statutory water company in the last two foregoing sections includes a reference to a joint water board or joint water committee, and in relation to such a board or committee any reference to the water authority on whose behalf a statutory water company are supplying water is a reference to the water authority on whose behalf a statutory water company represented on the board or committee are supplying water.

PART II

MAKING AND CONFIRMATION OF WATER AUTHORITY ORDERS

1945 c. 42.

1. No order made by a water authority under section 12 or 13 of the Water Act 1945 shall have effect until confirmed by the Secretary of State under this Part of this Schedule.

2. A water authority shall, at least one month before they apply for the confirmation of any such order,—

   (*a*) cause a notice of their intention to make the application to be published in the London Gazette and in such other manner as they think best adapted for informing persons affected, and

   (*b*) cause copies of the notice to be served on the bodies to whom the order relates and any other public authorities who appear to them to be concerned.

3. For at least one month before an application is made for the confirmation of such an order, a copy of it shall be deposited at the offices of the water authority.

4. The water authority shall provide reasonable facilities for the inspection without charge of an order deposited under paragraph 3 above.

5. Any person on application to the water authority shall be entitled to be furnished free of charge with a printed copy of such an order.

6. The Secretary of State, with or without a local inquiry, may refuse to confirm an order submitted for confirmation under this Part of this Schedule, or may confirm the order either with or without modifications ; and the authority shall, if so directed by the Secretary of State, cause notice of any proposed modifications to be given in accordance with such directions.

7. The Secretary of State may fix the date on which an order confirmed under this Part of this Schedule is to come into operation, and if no date is so fixed the order shall come into operation at the end of the period of one month beginning with the date of confirmation.

8. An order confirmed under this Part of this Schedule shall be printed and deposited at the office of the water authority and copies of it shall, at all reasonable hours, be open to public inspection without charge.

9. Any person on application to the water authority shall be entitled to be furnished with a copy of it, on payment of such reasonable sum as the authority may determine.

10. Subsections (2) to (5) of section 250 of the Local Government 1972 c. 70. Act 1972 shall apply in relation to a local inquiry under this Part of this Schedule as they apply to a local inquiry which a Minister caused to be held under subsection (1) of that section but with the omission of the word " local " from subsection (4).

SCHEDULE 5

LAND DRAINAGE

PART I

REGIONAL AND LOCAL LAND DRAINAGE COMMITTEES

Regional Land Drainage Committees

1.—(1) Every water authority shall establish not later than 1st December 1973 or such later date as may be authorised in their case under sub-paragraph (2) below a committee, to be known as a regional land drainage committee.

(2) The Minister may, on the application of any water authority, authorise them to establish their regional land drainage committee not later than such date after 1st December 1973, but not after 31st March 1974, as he may specify.

(3) A regional land drainage committee shall consist of—

    (*a*) a chairman and a number of other members appointed by the Minister ;

    (*b*) two members appointed by the water authority ; and

    (*c*) a number of members appointed by or on behalf of constituent councils.

(4) If any part of a county is in a water authority area, the council of that county shall be a constituent council for the authority's regional land drainage committee.

(5) If any part of Greater London is in a water authority area, the council of any London borough wholly or partly within that area shall be a constituent council for the authority's regional land drainage committee.

(6) The Greater London Council shall be a constituent council for the Thames Water Authority's regional land drainage committee.

(7) Subject to the following provisions of this paragraph, the water authority shall determine the total number of members of their regional land drainage committee and may from time to time make a determination varying that number.

(8) The total number of such members shall be not less than eleven and, except where an order under sub-paragraph (11) below provides otherwise, not more than seventeen.

(9) A water authority shall submit any determination under sub-paragraph (7) above to the Minister.

(10) Any determination that a regional land drainage committee should consist of more than seventeen members shall be provisional, and shall only take effect if the Minister makes an order under sub-paragraph (11) below.

(11) If the water authority submit a provisional determination to the Minister, he may by order—

    (*a*) confirm it ; or

    (*b*) substitute for the number of members determined by the water authority some other number not less than seventeen.

(12) When the number of members of a regional land drainage committee has been fixed under this paragraph (whether on the first or any subsequent determination), the Minister shall by order specify, subject to paragraphs 3 and 15 below, the number of members to be appointed to the committee by or on behalf of constituent councils.

(13) An order under sub-paragraph (12) above shall be so framed that the total number of members appointed under sub-paragraph (3)(*a*) and (*b*) above is one less than the number of those appointed by or on behalf of constituent councils.

2.—(1) The chairman of a regional land drainage committee shall Sᴄʜ. 5 be one of the members of the water authority appointed to that authority by the Minister.

(2) The remaining members appointed to such a committee by the Minister under paragraph 1(3)(*a*) above shall be appointed from among persons who in his opinion have had experience of, and have shown capacity in, or otherwise have special knowledge of, matters relating to land drainage or agriculture and, in particular, matters so relating which affect the area of the water authority or part of that area.

3.—(1) In determining for the purposes of an order under paragraph 1 above the number of persons to be appointed to a regional land drainage committee by or on behalf of each constituent council, the Minister shall have regard to the appropriate penny rate product for each relevant area of that council for the relevant year; and where, having regard to the proportion which that product bears to the aggregate of the appropriate penny rate products for the relevant areas of all the constituent councils for that year—

(*a*) he considers it to be inappropriate that that council should appoint a member of the committee, or

(*b*) he considers that one or more members should be appointed jointly by that council and one or more other constituent councils,

he may by the order so provide.

(2) Where, in accordance with sub-paragraph (1)(*b*) above, an order provides for the joint appointment of one or more members of a regional land drainage committee, and the councils by whom that appointment is to be made are unable to agree on an appointment, the member or members in question shall be appointed by the Minister on behalf of those councils.

(3) In the appointment of members of a regional land drainage committee, that committee's constituent councils or the Minister, as the case may be, shall, so far as may be practicable, select persons appearing to them or him to have a practical knowledge of land drainage or agriculture.

(4) In this paragraph " relevant year " means, in relation to any determination, the latest financial year for which, at the time when that determination falls to be made, precepts have been issued under section 87 of the Water Resources Act 1963 (precepts by 1963 c. 38. river authorities) or paragraph 11 below.

Local Land Drainage Committees

4.—(1) It shall be the duty of every regional land drainage committee, subject to any direction given under sub-paragraph (3) below, to submit to the water authority for their area not later than 1st January 1974 or such later date as may in their case be authorised under sub-paragraph (5) below a local land drainage scheme, and any scheme submitted under this sub-paragraph is hereafter in this Part of this Schedule referred to as an initial scheme.

(2) In this Part of this Schedule " a local land drainage scheme " means a scheme—

> (a) for the creation in a water authority area of one or more districts to be called " local land drainage districts " ; and
>
> (b) for the constitution, membership, functions and procedure of a committee for each such district, to be called the " local land drainage committee " for that district.

(3) The Minister may, on the application of any water authority, direct—

> (a) that no initial scheme is required for their area ; or
>
> (b) that such a scheme is required for part of their area, but no such scheme is required for the remainder.

(4) It shall be the duty of a water authority to send any scheme submitted to them under sub-paragraph (1) above to the Minister not later than 1st February 1974 or such later date as may in their case be authorised under sub-paragraph (5) below.

(5) The Minister may, on the application of any water authority—

> (a) authorise their regional land drainage committee to submit an initial scheme to them not later than such date after 1st January 1974, but not later than 31st March 1974, as he may specify ;
>
> (b) authorise the authority to submit an initial scheme to him on such date after 1st February 1974, but not after 31st March 1974, as he may specify.

(6) A regional land drainage committee may at any time submit to a water authority a local land drainage scheme for any part of their area for which there is then no such scheme in force.

(7) Before submitting a scheme to a water authority under sub-paragraph (6) above, a regional land drainage committee shall consult—

> (a) the councils of counties and districts any part of which will fall within the area to which the scheme is proposed to relate, and
>
> (b) such organisations representative of persons interested in land drainage or agriculture as the regional land drainage committee consider to be appropriate.

(8) It shall be the duty of the water authority to send any scheme submitted to them under sub-paragraph (6) above to the Minister.

(9) A local land drainage scheme may define a local land drainage district—

> (a) by reference to areas established for the purposes of functions relating to land drainage under any enactment in force immediately before the passing of this Act ;
>
> (b) by reference to the water authority area in which that district is situated ;
>
> (c) by reference to a map ;

or partly by one of those means and partly by another or the others.

(10) A local land drainage scheme may contain incidental, consequential and supplementary provisions.

(11) The Minister may approve a local land drainage scheme with
or without modifications, and—

(*a*) an initial scheme approved by him shall come into operation
on 1st April 1974 ; and

(*b*) any other scheme so approved shall come into operation on
a date fixed by him.

5.—(1) Subject to sub-paragraphs (2) and (3) below, a local land
drainage scheme shall provide that any local land drainage committee to which it relates shall consist of not less than eleven and
not more than fifteen members.

(2) A regional land drainage committee may include in a local
land drainage scheme which they submit to the water authority a
recommendation that a committee to which the scheme relates
should consist of a number of members greater than fifteen ; and a
scheme so submitted shall be taken to provide for the number of
members of a committee if it contains a recommendation under this
sub-paragraph relating to that committee.

(3) The power conferred on the Minister by paragraph 4(11)
above shall include power to direct that a committee to which a
recommendation under sub-paragraph (2) above relates shall consist
either of the recommended number of members or of some other
number of members greater than fifteen.

(4) A local land drainage committee shall consist of—

(*a*) a chairman appointed from among their own members by
the regional land drainage committee ;

(*b*) other members appointed by that committee ; and

(*c*) members appointed, in accordance with and subject to the
terms of the local land drainage scheme, by or on behalf
of constituent councils.

(5) If any part of a county is in a local land drainage district,
the council of that county shall be a constituent council for the
local land drainage committee for that district.

(6) If any part of Greater London is in a local land drainage
district, the Greater London Council and the council of any London
borough wholly or partly within that district shall each be constituent councils for the local land drainage committee for that district.

(7) The total number of members appointed to a local land
drainage committee by the regional land drainage committee shall
be one less than the number of those appointed by or on behalf of
constituent councils.

(8) The members of a local land drainage committee appointed
to that committee by the regional land drainage committee shall
be appointed from among persons who in the opinion of the regional
land drainage committee are qualified to be appointed to the local
land drainage committee by their knowledge and experience of
land drainage or agriculture.

6.—(1) A regional land drainage committee may at any time submit to the water authority for their area a scheme varying a local land drainage scheme or revoking such a scheme and, if the committee think fit, replacing it with another such scheme.

(2) Sub-paragraphs (7) to (11) of paragraph 4 above and paragraph 5 above shall apply to a scheme under this paragraph as they apply to a local land drainage scheme which is not an initial scheme.

General

7.—(1) Members of a regional or local land drainage committee other than those appointed by or on behalf of constituent councils shall hold and vacate office in accordance with the terms of their appointment.

(2) The chairman of a regional land drainage committee may resign his office at any time by giving notice in writing to the chairman of the water authority and to the Minister.

(3) Any other member of such a committee may resign his office at any time by giving notice in writing to the chairman of the committee and also to the Minister if he was appointed by him.

(4) Section 3(12) of this Act shall apply in relation to members of a regional or local land drainage committee appointed by or on behalf of a constituent council or constituent councils as it applies in relation to members of a water authority appointed by a local authority or authorities.

(5) Any member of a regional or local land drainage committee appointed by or on behalf of a constituent council who at the time of his appointment was a member of that council shall if he ceases to be a member of that council, cease also to be a member of the committee at the expiration of the period of three months beginning with the date when he ceases to be a member of the council or on the appointment of another person in his place, whichever first occurs ; but for the purposes of this sub-paragraph a member of a council shall not be deemed to have ceased to be a member of the council by reason of retirement if he has been re-elected a member thereof not later than the date of his retirement ;

(6) The chairman of a local land drainage committee may resign his office at any time by giving notice in writing to the chairman of the regional land drainage committee.

(7) Any other member of such a committee may resign his office at any time by giving notice in writing to the chairman of the committee.

(8) Paragraph 4 of Schedule 3 above shall apply in relation to members of a regional or local land drainage committee appointed by or on behalf of a constituent council or constituent councils as it applies in relation to members of a water authority appointed by a local authority or authorities, but with the substitution in sub-paragraph (2) of a reference to the resolution or scheme establishing the committee for the reference to the order establishing the authority.

(9) A person shall, so long as he is, and for twelve months after he ceases to be, a member of a water authority's regional land drainage committee or any of their local land drainage committees,

be disqualified from being appointed to any paid office by the water authority other than the office of chairman of the authority or chairman of their regional land drainage committee or one of their local land drainage committees.

8.—(1) Paragraphs 6 to 10 and 19 of Schedule 3 above shall also apply in relation to regional and local land drainage committees and their proceedings as they apply in relation to water authorities and their proceedings, but as if paragraph 19 gave any such committee power to authorise the signature of documents on their behalf by an officer of the water authority.

(2) Subsections (1) and (2), (4) to (7) and (9) of section 6 above shall apply to every regional and local land drainage committee as they apply to a water authority, but a regional land drainage committee shall not make arrangements under those provisions, as applied by this paragraph, for the discharge in a local land drainage district of any functions which fall to be discharged there by the local land drainage committee.

(3) A water authority may not make rules with regard to the proceedings of their regional land drainage committee or any of their local land drainage committees.

9.—(1) Subject to the following provisions of this paragraph, a person nominated by one or more constituent councils may act as deputy for a member of a regional or local land drainage committee appointed by or on behalf of that council or those councils and may accordingly (instead of that member) attend and vote at a meeting of the committee.

(2) A person nominated under sub-paragraph (1) above as deputy for a member of a regional land drainage committee may by virtue of that nomination attend and vote at a meeting of a sub-committee of that committee (other than a meeting of a local land drainage committee) to which the member for whom he is a deputy belongs.

(3) A person nominated under sub-paragraph (1) above as deputy for a member of a local land drainage committee may attend and vote at a meeting of a sub-committee of that committee to which the member for whom he is a deputy belongs.

(4) A person acting as deputy for a member of a regional or local land drainage committee shall be treated for the purposes for which he is nominated as a member of that committee.

(5) A person shall not act as deputy for a member of a regional or local land drainage committee unless his nomination has been notified to an officer of the water authority appointed to receive such nominations.

(6) A nomination shall be in writing and may apply either to a particular meeting or to all meetings during a stated period or until the nomination is revoked.

(7) A person shall not act as deputy for more than one member of a regional or local land drainage committee.

PART II

FINANCIAL PROVISIONS FOR LAND DRAINAGE

Notional local land drainage districts

10. For the purposes of this Part of this Schedule and of Part III below, a water authority area in relation to which no scheme under paragraph 4 or paragraph 6 above is in force shall be treated as a single local land drainage district, and any parts of such an area in relation to which no such scheme is in force shall be treated as included in a single such district.

Precepts by water authorities

11.—(1) For the purposes of this paragraph the aggregate amount required to be raised by precepts to local authorities by a water authority in respect of a local land drainage district for any financial year shall be ascertained as follows, that is to say—

(a) subject to paragraph (b) below, that aggregate amount shall be an amount equal to so much of the relevant expenditure of the water authority for that financial year as is neither defrayed out of any reserve fund, replacement fund or sinking fund maintained by the authority nor defrayed out of sums received by the authority in respect of that year and that district otherwise than by virtue of this paragraph ;

(b) there shall also be added to (or, as the case may be, deducted from) that amount—

(i) any amount required to be provided in that financial year by way of new working capital ;

(ii) any amount required to be brought forward from a previous financial year ;

which is required to be added or deducted in accordance with this paragraph.

(2) Not later than the month of February immediately preceding each financial year, each water authority shall estimate the aggregate amount required to be raised for that year by precepts to local authorities in respect of each local land drainage district in their area ; and the amount so estimated shall be apportioned by the water authority among the local authorities any part of whose area is comprised in a local land drainage district on the basis of the appropriate penny rate product for the relevant area for the relevant year (calculated in accordance with Part III of this Schedule).

(3) A water authority may issue precepts to local authorities requiring payments of amounts apportioned to those authorities under sub-paragraph (2) above ; and each such authority shall pay, in accordance with any precept issued to them, the amount demanded by that precept.

(4) If at any time during a financial year it appears to a water authority that the aggregate amount for which they have issued precepts for that year in respect of any local land drainage district will fall short of the aggregate amount required to be raised by precept by them for that year in respect of that district, they shall

estimate the amount of the deficiency ; and sub-paragraphs (2) and (3) above shall have effect in relation to an amount estimated under this sub-paragraph as they have effect in relation to an amount estimated under sub-paragraph (2) above, except that the words from the beginning of sub-paragraph (2) to " financial year " shall be omitted.

(5) Subject to sub-paragraph (6) below, the aggregate amount for which precepts in respect of a local land drainage district may be issued under this paragraph for any one financial year to a local authority shall not, unless special consent has been obtained, exceed 1·7 times the appropriate penny rate product for the relevant area of the authority for the relevant year.

(6) Where a water authority have borrowed or propose to borrow any money under this Act, if a special resolution is passed sub-paragraph (5) above shall have effect, during the currency of the loan, as if for the reference to 1·7 times the appropriate penny rate product for any relevant area there were substituted a reference to such greater amount as may be specified in the resolution.

(7) In this paragraph " special consent " and " special resolution " mean respectively a consent given and a resolution passed—

  (*a*) in the case of a local land drainage district with a local land drainage committee, by a majority of the whole number of the local authority members of that committee ; and

  (*b*) in the case of any other local land drainage district, by a majority of the whole number of those of the local authority members of the regional land drainage committee who were appointed to that committee by or on behalf of constituent councils any part of whose area is in the district.

(8) It shall be the duty of a water authority to prepare, in such form as the Minister may direct, a statement of the purposes to which the amount demanded by any precept by the authority under this paragraph is intended to be applied, and of the basis on which it is calculated ; and a local authority shall not be liable to pay the amount demanded by any such precept until they have received such a statement.

(9) It shall also be the duty of a water authority, as soon as practicable after the end of each financial year, to calculate the amount by which the amount demanded by any precept for that year issued under this paragraph to a local authority in respect of any relevant area exceeds, or falls short of, the amount which would have fallen to be so demanded from that authority if the apportionment under sub-paragraph (2) above had been made, in relation to each of the local authorities referred to in that sub-paragraph, on the basis of the actual penny rate product for that year for the relevant area, multiplied by the appropriate factor for that year notified to the authority with the notification of the conclusive calculation of the amount (if any) of the resources element of rate support grant payable to the authority for that year ; and—

  (*a*) if in any case the calculation under this sub-paragraph shows an excess, the amount of the excess shall be recoverable by the local authority from the water authority ;

SCH. 5   (b) if in any case it shows a deficiency, the amount of the
                deficiency shall be recoverable by the water authority from
                the local authority.

(10) As soon as practicable after the end of each financial year,
each water authority shall ascertain the actual amount which was the
aggregate amount required to be raised by precept by them for that
year in respect of each local land drainage district in their area and
shall determine whether, and (if so) how far, the aggregate amount
for which precepts have been issued by them for that year exceeds
or falls short of the amount ascertained under this sub-paragraph.

(11) If the comparison under sub-paragraph (10) above shows an
excess or a deficiency, the amount of the excess or deficiency shall
be brought forward to the next financial year and (if an excess) shall
be deducted, or (if a deficiency) shall be added, in ascertaining the
aggregate amount required to be raised by precept by the water
authority for that next financial year.

(12) The duty imposed on water authorities by sub-paragraph (2)
above shall apply in relation to the financial year beginning on
1st April 1974 as it applies in relation to any subsequent financial
year; and the power of a water authority to issue precepts under
sub-paragraph (3) above shall accordingly be exercisable before that
day.

(13) In this paragraph—

" the appropriate factor " means the appropriate factor as defined
        by regulations for the time being in force under section 5
        of the Local Government Act 1966 ;

1966 c. 42.

" the conclusive calculation " means the conclusive calculation
        notified under such regulations ;

" local authority " means the council of a county or a London
        borough ;

" local authority members ", in relation to a committee, means
        the members of that committee appointed by, or on behalf
        of, constituent councils ;

" relevant expenditure ", in relation to a local land drainage
        district, means expenditure by a water authority in the
        performance of land drainage functions in or for the benefit
        of that district ;

" the relevant year " means, in relation to any precepts, the
        financial year for which they are to be issued.

General drainage charges

1961 c. 48.   12.—(1) For section 1 of the Land Drainage Act 1961 (general
drainage charges) there shall be substituted the following sections : —

" Power of   1.—(1) Subject to subsection (2) below, a water
water   authority may raise at an amount per acre of chargeable
authority   land in a local land drainage district a charge to be
to raise   known as a general drainage charge and to be levied
revenue by   on the occupiers of the land in accordance with the
means of   following provisions of this Part of this Act and sections
general   24 to 27 and 29 of the Agriculture (Miscellaneous
drainage   Provisions) Act 1968.
charges.
1968 c. 34.

(2) A water authority shall not levy a general drainage charge in respect of any local land drainage district unless the regional land drainage committee for the authority's area have recommended that such a charge should be raised.

(3) In this section and section 1A below, "local land drainage district" has the meaning assigned to it by the Water Act 1973.

Amount of general drainage charge.

1A.—(1) The general drainage charge raised by a water authority for a local land drainage district for any year shall be at a uniform amount per acre of chargeable land in that district, and that amount shall be ascertained, subject to subsection (2) below, by—

(a) dividing the aggregate amount demanded by the precepts issued by the water authority under sub-paragraphs (2) and (3) of paragraph 11 of Schedule 5 to the Water Act 1973 in respect of the year for which the charge is raised by the aggregate amount of the appropriate penny rate products on the basis of which the amount so demanded was apportioned in pursuance of the said sub-paragraph (2) ; and

(b) multiplying the quotient by one new penny and by such number as the Minister may specify by order made for the purposes of this paragraph.

(2) The number specified in an order made under subsection (1) above shall (apart from any adjustment made to it to take account of rough grazing land) be such as the Minister considers will secure, so far as reasonably practicable, that the aggregate amount produced by any charge levied by reference to a quotient ascertained in pursuance of subsection (1)(a) above will be equal to the aggregate amount which, if the chargeable land in the local land drainage district were liable to be rated, would be produced by a rate levied on that land at an amount in the pound (of rateable value) equal to that quotient multiplied by one new penny.

(3) An order under this section may be made so as to apply either to all general drainage charges or to the general drainage charges proposed to be raised in any one or more water authority areas specified in the order or in any one or more local land drainage districts situated in one or more water authority areas and there specified, and any such order applying to more than one local land drainage district may make different provision as respects the different districts to which it applies.

(4) In subsection (1) above "appropriate penny rate product" has the same meaning as it has for the purposes of Schedule 5 to the Water Act 1973 ; but the reference

to precepts in paragraph (*a*) of that subsection does not include precepts issued by virtue of the application of sub-paragraph (3) of paragraph 11 of the said Schedule to amounts estimated under sub-paragraph (4) (which authorises the issue of supplementary precepts)."

1968 c. 34.
(2) In accordance with sub-paragraph (1) above section 21(1) of the Agriculture (Miscellaneous Provisions) Act 1968 (introduction of system of drainage charges on an acreage basis) shall cease to apply to general drainage charges.

PART III

CALCULATION OF APPROPRIATE PENNY RATE PRODUCT

13.—(1) For the purposes of the application of this Schedule to any water authority area, " relevant area " means, in relation to any local authority, so much of their area as is comprised in any local land drainage district in the water authority area, and the appropriate penny rate product for each relevant area of any local authority for the relevant year shall be calculated in accordance with this paragraph.

(2) There shall be estimated, in such manner as the Ministers may direct, the amount of the product of a rate of one new penny in the pound for each relevant area of the authority for the relevant year.

1966 c. 51.
(3) The appropriate penny rate product for each relevant area of the authority for the relevant year shall be the product of a rate of one new penny in the pound for that area for that year as estimated in accordance with sub-paragraph (2) above, multiplied by the appropriate factor as defined by regulations for the time being in force under section 5(3) of the Local Government Act 1966 and as it was most recently estimated and notified by the Secretary of State to the local authority before the time when the calculation in accordance with this paragraph falls to be made.

(4) In this Part of this Schedule " local authority " has the meaning assigned to it by paragraph 11(13) above and " relevant year "—

(*a*) has the meaning assigned to it by sub-paragraph (4) of paragraph 3 above in any case where the appropriate penny rate product falls to be calculated for the purposes of that paragraph ; and

(*b*) has the meaning assigned to it by sub-paragraph (13) of paragraph 11 above in any case where the appropriate penny rate product falls to be calculated for the purposes of that paragraph.

PART IV

LONDON

General

14. Nothing in section 9 or section 19(1) above shall make any land drainage function exercisable in the London excluded area by the Thames Water Authority (in this Part of this Schedule referred to as " the water authority ") or any other water authority.

15. The Greater London Council shall be entitled to appoint one member of the water authority's regional land drainage committee.

16.—(1) No part of the London excluded area shall be treated as being in the area of the water authority for the purposes of paragraph 1(5) above.

(2) No part of the London excluded area shall be included in any local land drainage district.

Duties and powers of Greater London Council and Thames Water Authority

17.—(1) The following provisions of this Act, namely—

section 4(5)(*a*) and (*b*) ;

section 8(1) to (4) ;

section 22 ; and

section 24(5) and (6) and (8) to (12).

shall have effect in relation to the land drainage functions of the Greater London Council as if that Council were a water authority and the London excluded area were their water authority area.

(2) The Greater London Council shall send the water authority a copy of any report which sets out the results of a survey made by them under section 24(5) above, as applied by sub-paragraph (1) above, and of any programme submitted by them to the Minister under section 24(6) above as applied by that sub-paragraph.

18.—(1) If the Greater London Council intend to carry out any works for the purpose of their land drainage functions or to exercise any of those functions in a manner which is likely to affect the exercise by the water authority of any of their functions in the London excluded area, the Council shall notify the water authority in writing of their intention.

(2) The water authority may within two months of the date of a notice under sub-paragraph (1) above require the Council to consult with them about any of the matters to which the notice relates.

(3) If, within a period of two months beginning with the date on which a requirement under sub-paragraph (2) above was sent by the water authority to the Council, the authority and the Council have not reached agreement as to any of the matters to which the notice relates, the authority shall notify the Ministers of that fact and the Ministers shall give directions to the Council as to any such matter.

19.—(1) If the water authority intend—

    (*a*) to carry out works in their area for the purpose of their land drainage functions or to exercise any of those functions in a manner which is likely to affect the exercise by the Greater London Council of their land drainage functions ; or

SCH. 5

    (*b*) to carry out any works in the London excluded area for the purpose of any of their functions or to exercise any of those functions in that area in a manner which is likely to affect the exercise by the Greater London Council of their land drainage functions ;

the authority shall notify the Greater London Council in writing of their intention.

    (2) The Greater London Council may within two months of the date of a notice under sub-paragraph (1) above require the water authority to consult with them about any of the matters to which the notice relates.

    (3) If, within a period of two months beginning with the date on which a requirement under sub-paragraph (2) above was sent to the water authority by the Greater London Council, the authority and the Council have not reached agreement as to any of the matters to which the notice relates, the Council shall notify the Ministers of that fact and the Ministers shall give directions to the authority as to any such matter.

    20. The Minister may give the Greater London Council directions, either of a general or of a particular character, as to the exercise by the Council of their land drainage functions.

1963 c. 33.

    21. Paragraphs 11 to 14 of Schedule 14 to the London Government Act 1963 shall have effect in relation to the expenses incurred by the Greater London Council in the discharge of the functions conferred on them by virtue of this Part of this Schedule as they have effect in relation to the expenses incurred by them in the discharge of the functions conferred on them by virtue of that Schedule.

Amendments of enactments relating to London excluded area

    22.—(1) The amendments specified in this paragraph shall have effect in relation to the London excluded area, and in any such amendment " the metropolitan watercourses " and " the main metropolitan watercourses " have the meanings assigned to them by paragraph 15 of Schedule 14 to the London Government Act 1963.

1930 c. 44.

    (2) After section 36(3) of the Land Drainage Act 1930 (enforcement of obligations to repair) there shall be inserted the following subsection : —

    " (4) The reference in subsection (2) above to the drainage board in whose district a watercourse, bridge or drainage work is situate shall be construed—

        (*a*) in relation to the main metropolitan watercourses, as a reference to the Greater London Council ;

        (*b*) in relation to the metropolitan watercourses, as a reference to that council and the council of the London borough in which it is situate (or if it is situate in the City of London, or in the Inner Temple or the Middle Temple, to the Common Council of the City) ;

and the reference to a drainage board in subsection (3) above shall be construed accordingly."

(3) After section 44(9) of that Act (obstructions in watercourses) there shall be added the following subsection:—   Sch. 5

" (10) Any reference to a drainage board in this section shall be construed—

> (*a*) in relation to the main metropolitan watercourses, as a reference to the Greater London Council ;

> (*b*) in relation to the metropolitan watercourses, as a reference to that council and the council of the London borough in which it is situate (or if it is situate in the City of London, or in the Inner Temple or the Middle Temple, to the Common Council of the City)."

(4) In section 34 of the Land Drainage Act 1961 (power of local authorities to undertake drainage works against flooding), after sub-section (2A) (which was added to that section by paragraph 25(4) of Schedule 29 to the Local Government Act 1972) there shall be inserted the following subsections:—   1961 c. 48. 1972 c. 70.

" (2B) Neither the council of a London borough nor the Common Council of the City of London shall execute any drainage works authorised by this section in connection with any watercourse, except with the consent of the Minister and in accordance with any reasonable conditions imposed by him.

(2C) A consent required under subsection (2B) of this section shall not be unreasonably withheld and shall, if neither given nor refused within two months after application therefore is made, be deemed to have been given.

(2D) Subsection (2B) of this section shall not apply to any work executed in an emergency, but a council executing any work excepted by this subsection shall as soon as practicable inform the Minister in writing of the execution and all the circumstances in which it was executed.

(2E) It shall be the duty of a council to send a copy of any application to the Minister under subsection (2B) of this section to the Greater London Council ".

23. In Schedule 14 to the London Government Act 1963 (land drainage etc.)—   1963 c. 33.

> (*a*) in paragraph 8, for the word " lie " there shall be substituted the words " immediately before 1st April 1974 lay " ; and

> (*b*) in paragraph 15(3), for the definition of the London excluded area there shall be substituted the following definition—

>> " London excluded area " has the meaning assigned to it by section 38 of the Water Act 1973 ;

and, notwithstanding anything to the contrary in any enactment or instrument, no part of any of the metropolitan watercourses (within the meaning of that Schedule) shall be or form part of a public sewer.

SCHEDULE 6

CONSEQUENTIAL, TRANSITIONAL AND SUPPLEMENTARY PROVISION

PART I

ADAPTATIONS OF 1972 ACT

General Adaptations of 1972 Act

1. Any reference in any of the applied provisions of the 1972 Act to that Act, other than a reference to a specified provision or Part of that Act, shall be construed as including a reference to this Act.

2. Any reference in any of the applied provisions to another of the applied provisions, as the former provision applies for the purposes of this Act, shall be construed as a reference to that other provision as applied.

3. Any reference in any of the applied provisions to an authority or local authority, as that provision applies for the purposes of this Act, shall—

  (*a*) if the reference is, or is to be construed as, a reference to an existing authority, be construed as a reference to a transferor body ;

  (*b*) if the reference is, or is to be construed as, a reference to a new authority, be construed as a reference to a transferee authority ; and

  (*c*) if the reference is, or is to be construed as a reference to existing and new authorities, be construed as a reference to transferor bodies and transferee authorities.

Specific adaptations of 1972 Act

4. In section 68, as it applies for the purposes of this Act—

  (*a*) for the reference in subsection (1) to public bodies affected by the alteration, abolition or constitution of any area by an order under Part IV there shall be substituted a reference to transferor bodies and transferee authorities, and the references in subsection (4) to a public body shall be construed accordingly ;

  (*b*) for the second reference in subsection (1) to alteration, abolition or constitution there shall be substituted a reference to the provisions of this Act ; and

  (*c*) subsections (6) to (9) shall be omitted.

5.—(1) In section 254, as it applies for the purposes of this Act—

  (*a*) subsections (2)(*f*), (*g*) and (*i*), (7) and (8) ; and

  (*b*) in subsection (3), the words " outside Greater London ", in both places where they occur ;

shall be omitted, and in subsection (6) the references to Parts I and II shall include a reference to this Act.

  (2) An order under that section may include provision—

  (*a*) with respect to the supply of water in bulk where the relevant source of supply serves areas which by virtue of

this Act become comprised in more than one water authority Sᴄʜ. 6
area ;

(*b*) with respect to the making of financial adjustments or the termination of financial liabilities in connection with the transfer of functions or property by or by virtue of this Act ;

(*c*) for the calculation, collection and recovery on behalf of a water authority by a local authority during a transitional period of amounts payable in respect of services provided in the local authority's area by the water authority and for the apportionment during that period of any payment in whole or in part of any demand by a local authority which includes any such amount as between those services and the other purposes for which the demand is made ;

(*d*) conferring on a local authority whose interest in any land is on 1st April 1974 transferred to a water authority, or the successor of any such local authority, a right to reacquire the interest on terms provided for by the order if the land subsequently ceases to be used for the purpose for which it was transferred and, while the land is vested in the water authority, a right to use it in circumstances specified in the order ;

(*e*) enabling any body whose documents on that date are transferred to a water authority or the successor of any such body to inspect and take copies of those documents.

6.—(1) In section 255(2), as it applies for the purposes of this Act,—

(*a*) the reference to a local authority who are a council which ceases to exist by virtue of section 1 or 20 shall include a reference to a transferor body ;

(*b*) the second reference to sections 1 and 20 shall include a reference to the transfer of functions and abolition of bodies effected by or under this Act ; and

(*c*) the second reference to a local authority shall include a reference to a transferee authority.

(2) Section 255(4) shall not apply for the purposes of this Act.

7. In section 256(1), as it applies for the purposes of this Act, the reference to sections 1 and 20 shall include a reference to this Act.

8.—(1) In section 257, as it applies for the purposes of this Act—

(*a*) in subsection (1) the words from " after consulting " to " concerned " and " for England " shall be omitted and the reference to the Secretary of State shall include a reference to the Minister ;

(*b*) " relevant authority " means a transferor body and a transferee authority ; and

(*c*) subsection (4) shall be omitted.

(2) The staff commission established by virtue of this paragraph shall be known as the Water Services Staff Commission.

9. In section 259(4), as it applies for the purposes of this Act, for the reference to the reorganisation of local government effected by the 1972 Act there shall be substituted a reference to the provisions of this Act.

Supplemental

10.—(1) In this Part of this Schedule—

" applied " means applied by section 34 above ;

" existing " and " new " have the same meanings as in the 1972 Act ;

" transferee authority " means a water authority or the Council ; and

" transferor body " means a development corporation, the Water Supply Industry Training Board or any authority or statutory water undertakers whose functions will by virtue of this Act become exercisable by a water authority or an association of such other authorities or such undertakers.

(2) Any reference in this Part of this Schedule to any enactment without specifying the Act in which it is contained is a reference to a provision of the 1972 Act.

Part II

Local Acts and Instruments

11. Subject to paragraph 12 below, any local statutory provision to which this Part of this Schedule applies and which is not continued in force by any other provision of this Act shall—

(a) notwithstanding the transfer of functions and abolition of bodies effected by or under this Act and, in the case of an instrument made under any enactment, notwithstanding the repeal of that enactment, continue to apply on and after 1st April 1974 to, but only to, the area, things or persons to which or to whom it applies before that date ;

(b) have effect subject to any necessary modifications and to the modifications made by paragraph 13 below ;

but the continuation by this paragraph of an instrument made under any enactment shall not be construed as prejudicing any power to vary or revoke the instrument which is exercisable apart from this paragraph.

12. Paragraph 11 above shall have effect subject to the provisions of—

(a) this Act and any Act passed after this Act and before 1st April 1974 ;

(b) any order made under section 254 of the 1972 Act, as applied by section 34 above, or paragraph 14 or 15 below.

13. As from 1st April 1974 any local statutory provision to which this Part of this Schedule applies and which immediately before that date applies to an area which on that date becomes comprised in one or more water authority areas shall have effect, so far as relates to functions which on that date become exercisable by a water authority and to things done or falling to be done in the exercise of those functions, as if for any reference to the body by whom the functions were exercisable immediately before that date there were substituted a reference to that water authority, or where

the former area becomes comprised in two or more water authority areas, the water authority for the water authority area in or as respects which that thing falls to be done.

14. Paragraph 13 above shall have effect subject to any provision to the contrary made by, or by any instrument made under, this Act and, without prejudice to the foregoing, the Secretary of State may by order provide for the exercise of functions conferred by any local statutory provision to which this Part of this Schedule applies and exclude the operation of that paragraph where it would otherwise conflict with any provision of the order.

15. Where any local statutory provision is continued in force in any area by paragraph 11 above or is amended or modified in its application to any area by an order under section 254 of the 1972 Act, as applied by section 34 above, the appropriate Minister or Ministers may by that order, or in the case of a provision continued as aforesaid, by an order under this paragraph—

(a) extend the provision throughout the water authority area in which it is continued in force or extend it to a part of that area in which it was not previously in force ;

(b) provide that that provision as so continued, amended, modified or extended shall have effect in that area or part to the exclusion of any enactment for corresponding purposes, including any enactment contained in or applied by this Act ;

(c) make such modifications of any such enactment in its application to that area or part as would secure that the enactment will operate harmoniously with the said provision in that area or part ;

(d) repeal or revoke any local statutory provision to which this Part of this Schedule applies and which appears to the appropriate Minister or Ministers to have become spent, obsolete or unnecessary or to have been substantially superseded by any enactment or instrument which applies or may be applied to the area, persons or things to which or to whom that provision applies ;

(e) make such modifications of any local statutory provision to which this Part of this Schedule applies in its application to a water authority area or part of such an area as appear to the appropriate Minister or Ministers to be expedient.

16. A statutory instrument containing an order under paragraph 15 above shall be subject to annulment in pursuance of a resolution of either House of Parliament.

17. This Part of this Schedule applies to any local statutory provision in force immediately before 1st April 1974 and relating to—

(a) a body abolished by section 33 above ;

(b) functions which immediately before that date are exercisable by an existing local authority and on that date become exercisable by a water authority ; or

(c) some area constituted for the exercise of functions affected by this Act and situated wholly or partly within Greater London.

SCHEDULE 7
Procedure Relating to Byelaws
Part I
Byelaws made by the Secretary of State or the Minister

1. At least one month before a byelaw relating to the whole or part of a water authority area is made by the appropriate Minister or Ministers, by virtue of any enactment under which water authorities perform their functions, the appropriate Minister or Ministers shall cause a notice of his or their intention to make the byelaw to be published in the London Gazette and in such other manner as is in his or their opinion best adapted for informing persons affected.

2. The appropriate Minister or Ministers shall also cause copies of the notice under paragraph 1 above to be served on any public authorities who appear to him or them to be concerned.

3. For at least one month before the date on which the byelaw is to come into operation, a copy of it shall be deposited at the offices of the water authority.

4. A water authority shall provide reasonable facilities for the inspection without charge of a byelaw deposited under paragraph 3 above.

5. Any person, on application to the water authority, shall be entitled to be furnished free of charge with a printed copy of such a byelaw.

6. The appropriate Minister or Ministers may fix the date on which a byelaw is to come into operation, and if no date is so fixed it shall come into operation at the end of the period of one month beginning with the date on which it is made.

7. Any byelaw made in accordance with this Part of this Schedule shall be printed and deposited at the office of the water authority, and copies shall, at all reasonable hours, be open to public inspection without charge.

8. Any person on application to the water authority shall be entitled to be furnished with a copy of it, on payment of such reasonable sum as the authority may determine.

9. If it appears to the appropriate Minister or Ministers that the revocation of a byelaw is necessary or expedient, he or they may, after giving notice to the water authority and considering any objections raised by the authority and, if required by the authority, holding a local inquiry, revoke that byelaw.

10. The production of a printed copy of a byelaw purporting to be made in accordance with this Part of this Schedule and upon which is endorsed a certificate purporting to be signed on behalf of the water authority, stating—

    (a) that the byelaw was made in accordance with this Part of this Schedule ;
    (b) that the copy is a true copy of the byelaws ;

(c) the date, if any, fixed under paragraph 6 above for the coming into operation of the byelaw,

shall be prima facie evidence of the facts stated in the certificate, and without proof of the handwriting or official position of any person purporting to sign the certificate.

11. Subsections (2) to (5) of section 250 of the 1972 Act shall apply in relation to a local inquiry under this Part of this Schedule as they apply to a local inquiry which a Minister causes to be held under subsection (1) of that section, but with the substitution in subsection (4) for the words " such local authority or " of the words " the water authority or by such ".

PART II

BYELAWS MADE BY WATER AUTHORITIES AND OTHER STATUTORY WATER UNDERTAKERS AND INTERNAL DRAINAGE BOARDS

12.—(1) No byelaw made by an authority to whom this Part of this Schedule applies shall have effect until confirmed by the appropriate Minister or Ministers, under this Part of this Schedule.

(2) This Part of this Schedule applies to water authorities and other statutory water undertakers and to internal drainage boards within the meaning of the Land Drainage Act 1930.   1930 c. 44.

13. An authority to whom this Part of this Schedule applies shall, at least one month before they apply for the confirmation of any byelaw,—

(a) cause a notice of their intention to make the application to be published in the London Gazette and in such other manner as they think best adapted for informing persons affected, and

(b) cause copies of the notice to be served on any public authorities who appear to them to be concerned.

14. For at least one month before an application is made for the confirmation of any byelaw, a copy of it shall be deposited at the offices of the authority.

15. The authority shall provide reasonable facilities for the inspection without charge of a byelaw deposited under paragraph 14 above.

16. Any person on application to the authority shall be entitled to be furnished free of charge with a printed copy of such a byelaw.

17.—(1) Subject to sub-paragraph (2) below, the appropriate Minister or Ministers, with or without a local inquiry, may refuse to confirm any byelaw submitted for confirmation under this Part of this Schedule, or may confirm the byelaw either without or, if the authority consent, with modifications ; and the authority shall, if so directed by the appropriate Minister or Ministers, cause notice of any proposed modifications to be given in accordance with such directions.

(2) A byelaw made by a water authority under section 5 of the Rivers (Prevention of Pollution) Act 1951 shall not be confirmed without a local inquiry if any written objection to its confirmation has been received by the appropriate Minister or Ministers and has not been withdrawn, unless in the opinion of the appropriate Minister or Ministers the person making the objection has no material interest in the stream or part of a stream to which the byelaw relates ; and in relation to any such byelaw sub-paragraph (1) above shall have effect with the substitution for the words " if the authority consent, with modifications ; and the authority " of the words " after consultation with the water authority making the byelaw, with modifications ; and that authority ".

18. The appropriate Minister or Ministers may fix the date on which any byelaw confirmed under this Part of this Schedule is to come into operation, and if no date is so fixed the byelaw shall come into operation at the end of the period of one month beginning with the date of confirmation.

19. Any byelaw confirmed under this Part of this Schedule shall be printed and deposited at the office of the authority and copies of it shall, at all reasonable hours, be open to public inspection without charge.

20. Any person on application to the authority shall be entitled to be furnished with a copy of it, on payment of such reasonable sum as the authority may determine.

21. If it appears to the appropriate Minister or Ministers that the revocation of a byelaw is necessary or expedient, he or they may, after giving notice to the authority and considering any objections raised by them, and, if required by them, holding a local inquiry, revoke that byelaw.

22. The production of a printed copy of a byelaw purporting to be made by an authority to whom this Part of this Schedule applies upon which is indorsed a certificate, purporting to be signed on their behalf, stating—

(*a*) that the byelaw was made by the authority ;

(*b*) that the copy is a true copy of the byelaw ;

(*c*) that on a specified date the byelaw was confirmed under this Part of this Schedule ; and

(*d*) the date, if any, fixed under paragraph 18 above for the coming into operation of the byelaw,

shall be prima facie evidence of the facts stated in the certificate, and without proof of the handwriting or official position of any person purporting to sign the certificate.

23. Subsections (2) to (5) of section 250 of the 1972 Act shall apply in relation to a local inquiry under this Part of this Schedule as they apply to a local inquiry which a Minister causes to be held under subsection (1) of that section, but with the omission of the word " local " from subsection (4).

SCHEDULE 8

MINOR AND CONSEQUENTIAL AMENDMENTS, ETC.

Salmon and Freshwater Fisheries Act 1923

1. In section 1(2) of the Salmon and Freshwater Fisheries Act 1923 (prohibition of fishing with lights, spears, etc.) for the words " fishery board, or where there is no fishery board, of the Minister " there shall be substituted the words " water authority for the area in which the act was done ".

2. In section 5 of that Act (saving for acts done for artificial propagation or scientific purposes) for the words from " fishery board ", in the first place where those words occur, to the end of the section there shall be substituted the words " water authority for the area ".

3. In section 9(1) of that Act (prohibition of use of explosives, etc.) for paragraph (*b*) of the proviso (as substituted by section 1 of the Salmon and Freshwater Fisheries Act 1965) and the words following that paragraph there shall be substituted the following paragraph : —

> " (*b*) with the permission in writing of the water authority for the area ;

but as respects the use of any noxious substance such permission shall not be given by a water authority otherwise than with the approval of the Minister.".

4. In section 11(2) of that Act (prohibition of placing or using fixed engines for taking or obstructing salmon or migratory trout) for the words " fishery board, or, where there is no fishery board, by the Minister " there shall be substituted the words " water authority for the area ".

5. In section 14(3) of that Act (rules for fishing mill dams) for the words from " and ", in the second place where it occurs, to " district ", in the second place where it occurs, there shall be substituted the words " and the water authority for the area ".

6. In subsections (1) and (3) of section 18 of that Act (supply of water to dams and fish passes) for the words from " fishery board ", in the first place where they occur in each subsection, to " the Minister " there shall be substituted the words " water authority for the area ".

7. In section 19 of that Act (penalty for making obstructions without fish passes)—

    (*a*) in subsection (1), for the words " fishery board, or, where there is no fishery board, by the Minister " there shall be substituted the words " water authority for the area " ;

    (*b*) in subsection (3), for the words from the beginning of the subsection to " Minister " there shall be substituted the words " The water authority ".

8. In section 22(5) of that Act (penalty for injuring or obstructing fish pass or free gap) for the words " fishery board (if any) " there shall be substituted the words " water authority in whose area the dam is or was situated ".

9. In section 23(1) of that Act for the words " fishery board (if any) " there shall be substituted the words " water authority for the area ".

10. In the provisos to sections 26(2) and 31(2) of that Act (close season) for the words " fishery board (if any) ", in each place where they occur, there shall be substituted the words " water authority in whose area the act was done ".

11. In section 36(3) of that Act (prohibition on using eel baskets, etc., at certain times) for the words from " fishery board ", in the first place where those words occur, to the end of the subsection there shall be substituted the words " water authority for the area with the consent of the Minister ".

12. In section 39(1) of that Act (applications for orders) for the words from " fishery " to " Act ", in the fourth place where that word occurs, there shall be substituted the words " water authority ".

13. In section 54(1) of that Act (general powers) for the words from the beginning to " board ", in the second place where that word occurs, there shall be substituted the words " A water authority shall have ".

14. In section 59(1) of that Act (byelaws) for the words from the beginning to " Minister " there shall be substituted the words " A water authority ".

15. In section 68 of that Act (power to enter lands)—

    (a) for the words from the begining to " board ", in the second place where it occurs, there shall be substituted the words " Any water bailiff or other officer of a water authority may, under a special order in writing from the authority, " ;

    (b) after the words " this Act " there shall be inserted the words " or the Salmon and Freshwater Fisheries Act 1972 ".

16. In section 69 of that Act (order to enter suspected places)—

    (a) for the words from " any ", in the first place where it occurs, to " Act " there shall be substituted the words " a water bailiff or any other officer of a water authority it appears to any justice of the peace that the officer has good reason to suspect that any offence against this Act or the Salmon and Freshwater Fisheries Act 1972 " ;

    (b) for the words " such member or bailiff " there shall be substituted the words " that officer ".

17. In section 70 of that Act (warrant to enter suspected premises)—

    (a) after the word " Act " there shall be inserted the words " or the Salmon and Freshwater Fisheries Act 1972 " ;

(*b*) for the words " water bailiff, member of a fishery board " there shall be substituted the words " water bailiff or other officer of a water authority ".

18. For section 72 of that Act (powers of officers appointed by Minister) there shall be substituted the following section:—

" 72. The Minister may appoint persons to exercise in a water authority area—

(*a*) the powers of a water bailiff under sections 67 and 71 of this Act ; and

(*b*) the powers of an officer of a water authority under sections 68, 69 and 70 of this Act ;

and those sections shall accordingly apply to any such person, except that for the reference in section 67 to a special order from the water authority there shall be substituted a reference to an order in writing from the Minister " '.

19. For section 77(1) of that Act (certificates of conviction) there shall be substituted—

" (1) Where any person is convicted of an offence against this Act, the clerk of the court before which that person is convicted shall, within one month of the date of conviction, forward a certificate of the conviction to the water authority for the area in which the offence was committed."

Land Drainage Act 1930

20.—(1) In subsection (1) of section 1 of the Land Drainage Act 1930 (drainage districts and drainage boards) for the words from the beginning to " section " there shall be substituted the words " There shall continue to be internal drainage districts for the purpose of the drainage of land ".

(2) For subsections (2) and (3) of that section there shall be substituted the following subsections:—

" (2) An internal drainage board shall be a body corporate.

(3) An internal drainage board shall exercise a general supervision over all matters relating to the drainage of land within its district and shall have such other powers and perform such other duties as are conferred or imposed on internal drainage boards by this Act.".

(3) In subsection (5) of that section, for the words from the beginning to " districts ", in the second place where that word occurs, there shall be substituted the words " Internal drainage districts constituted ".

21.—(1) In subsection (1) of section 4 of that Act (schemes) for the words from the beginning to " authority ", in the second place where that word occurs in paragraph (*a*)(i), there shall be substituted the following words:—

" 4.—(1) A water authority may at any time and, if so directed by the Minister, shall—

(*a*) prepare and submit to the Minister for confirmation a scheme making provision—

(i) for the transfer from any drainage authority to the water authority of all rights, powers, duties,

Z 3

obligations and liabilities (including liabilities incurred in connection with works) over or in connection with the main river, and of any property held by the drainage authority."

(2) For the words from the beginning of paragraph (*b*) of that subsection to "matters" there shall be substituted the following words: —

" (*b*) submit to the Minister for confirmation a scheme making provision for any of the following matters: — ".

(3) In the said paragraph (*b*)—

(*a*) in sub-paragraph (vii) for the word "existing" there shall be substituted the word "internal";

(*b*) for the words in sub-paragraph (ix) from "drainage boards", in the first place where those words occur, to "drainage boards", in the second place where they occur, there shall be substituted the words "a water authority or internal drainage board of any property, rights, powers, duties, obligations and liabilities vested in or to be discharged by the water authority or internal drainage board".

(4) After the said subsection (1) there shall be inserted the following subsection: —

" (1A) A water authority shall not submit a scheme to the Minister under subsection (1) above by virtue of paragraph (*b*) of that subsection except one which their regional land drainage committee have submitted to them, but it shall be their duty to present any such scheme which that committee have submitted to them to the Minister without modification.".

22.—(1) In subsection (1) of section 8 of that Act (power to vary awards) for the word "Where" there shall be substituted the words "Subject to subsection (1A) below, where".

(2) After the said subsection (1) there shall be inserted the following subsection: —

" (1A) Where any such award relates to an internal drainage district, a water authority shall not submit to the Minister under subsection (1) above any scheme except one which their regional land drainage committee have submitted to them; but it shall be the duty of an authority to submit any scheme which their committee submit to them to the Minister without modification.".

23. Section 11 of that Act (transfer of functions of internal drainage boards) shall be renumbered as subsection (1) of that section, and after it there shall be added the following subsection :—

" (2) A water authority shall not present a petition under subsection (1) above except one which their regional land drainage committee have submitted to them; but it shall be their duty to present any petition which that committee have submitted to them to the Minister without modification.".

24.—(1) For subsection (1) of section 22 of that Act (precepts) there shall be substituted the following subsection:—

" (1) A water authority may issue precepts to internal drainage boards requiring payment of any amount required to be contributed by them under section 21 of this Act, and an internal drainage board shall pay, in accordance with any precept so issued to it, the amount thereby demanded."

(2) For subsection (4) of that section there shall be substituted the following subsection :—

" (4) There shall not be any obligation upon an internal drainage board to pay the amount demanded by any precept issued under this section until they have received the statement referred to in subsection (3) of this section ".

25. In section 23(1) of that Act (expenses) for the words from " under " to " Board " there shall be substituted the words " to a water authority from a county council under the Water Act 1973 ".

26.—(1) For subsection (1) of section 24 of that Act (rating powers) there shall be substituted the following subsection:—

" (1) The expenses of an internal drainage board under this or any other Act (including any contribution made by the board towards the expenses of the water authority for their area) shall, in so far as they are not met by contributions from the water authority, be raised by means of drainage rates made by the drainage board under and in accordance with this Act."

(2) Any reference to a drainage board in subsections (2), (4), (8) and (10) of that section shall be construed as a reference to an internal drainage board.

(3) In subsections (6) and (7) of that section for the words from the beginning of each of those subsections to " Catchment Board " there shall be substituted the words " An internal drainage board, after consultation with the water authority for their district,".

27. In the following provisions of that Act, namely, sections 26 to 31 (rating), section 33 and Schedule 3 (membership and proceedings of board), section 43 (power of entry), section 45 (power to buy, sell or exchange land), section 46 (borrowing by drainage boards) and section 48 (officers), any reference to a drainage board shall be construed as a reference only to an internal drainage board and not to a water authority.

28.—(1) In section 47(1) of that Act (byelaws) for the words from the beginning to " district " there shall be substituted the words " A water authority and an internal drainage board may, subject to the provisions of this Act and to Part II of Schedule 7 to the Water Act 1973 (which relates to the procedure for making byelaws) make such byelaws as they consider necessary for securing the efficient working of the drainage system in their area or, as the case may be, their district ".

(2) In paragraphs (a), (c) and (d) of that subsection for the words " the control of the board ", in each place where they occur, there shall be substituted the words " their control ".

(3) In subsection (8) of the said section 47, after the word " section " there shall be inserted the words " including a byelaw made under this section as applied by section 34 of the Land Drainage Act 1961 ".

(4) In subsection (8A) of that section, after the word " section ", in the first place where it occurs, there shall be inserted the words " including a byelaw made under this section as so applied, the water authority or ".

29. In subsections (1) and (5) of section 49 of that Act (reports and accounts of boards) any reference to a drainage board shall be construed as a reference to an internal drainage board, and for subsection (4) of that section there shall be substituted the following subsection: —

" (4) The accounts of the receipts and expenditure of an internal drainage board and of the officers of such a board shall be made up in such manner and to such date in each year, and shall be audited by such persons and in such manner as the Minister may from time to time direct."

30. In section 76(2) of that Act (accretion of land resulting from drainage works) for the words from " contained " to " with ", in the first place where that word occurs, there shall be substituted the words " of the Water Resources Act 1963 with ".

31. In section 81 of that Act (interpretation) for the definitions of " internal drainage district " and " internal drainage board " there shall be substituted the following: —

" ' internal drainage district ' and ' internal drainage board ' mean respectively a drainage district within a water authority area and the drainage board for such a district: ".

Public Health Act 1936

32. In section 15(1) of the Public Health Act 1936 (power to construct or acquire sewers and sewage disposal works) for the words before paragraph (i) there shall be substituted the words " A water authority may, either inside or outside their area,".

33. For section 20 of that Act (vesting of public sewers and sewage disposal works in a local authority) there shall be substituted the following section: —

Vesting of sewers and sewage disposal works in water authority.

" 20.—(1) In addition to the sewers and sewage disposal works vested in a water authority by virtue of section 254 or 68 of the Local Government Act 1972, as either section applies for the purposes of the Water Act 1973, there shall vest in a water authority—

(a) all sewers and sewage disposal works constructed by the water authority at their expense, or vested in the authority in pursuance of arrangements under section 15 of the Water Act 1973, or otherwise acquired by the authority ;

(b) all sewers constructed under Part IX of the Sch. 8
Highways Act 1959, except sewers belonging to 1959 c. 25.
a road maintained by a highway authority;

(c) all sewers and sewage disposal works with respect
to which a declaration of vesting under the
foregoing provisions of this Part of this Act
has taken effect.

(2) Sewers which by virtue of the said section 254
or 68 or this section become vested in a water authority
shall be known as, and are in this Act referred to as,
public sewers."

34. In section 24(4) of the Public Health Act 1936 (lengths of 1936 c. 49.
public sewers to which that section applies) references to the local
authority shall be construed, in relation to any area, as references to
the local authority who immediately before the commencement of
that Act had the function of providing for the drainage of that area,
the sewers within the meaning of the Public Health Act 1875 which 1875 c. 55.
by virtue of section 254 or 68 of the 1972 Act, as either section applies
for the purposes of this Act, are vested in the water authority in
question.

35. Section 28 of that Act (communications between sewerage
authorities' sewers) and section 35 of that Act (use of public sewers
by persons outside the district) shall cease to have effect.

36.—(1) Notwithstanding the repeal by this Act of section 37
of the London Government Act 1963 (which applied certain pro- 1963 c. 33.
visions of the Public Health Act 1936 to Greater London and the
sewerage area of the Greater London Council)—

(a) the following provisions of the Public Health Act 1936,
that is to say, section 32 (map of public sewers) and
sections 39 to 41 (miscellaneous provisions as to drainage)
shall continue to apply throughout Greater London (except
the Inner Temple and the Middle Temple); and

(b) the following provisions of the said Act of 1936, that is
to say, section 25 (need for consent to building over public
sewers, etc.) and sections 37 and 38 (drainage of new buildings) shall continue to apply to the outer London boroughs.

(2) In the said provisions in their application to a London
borough or the City of London references to a local authority shall
be construed as references to the borough council or the Common
Council of the City, as the case may be, except that references in
section 41 of the said Act of 1936 to a local authority shall, in
relation to a private sewer or a cesspool or other receptacle for
drainage, be construed as a reference to the council of the London
borough in which the sewer, cesspool or other receptacle is situated
or, if it is situated in the City of London, the Common Council of
the City.

SCH. 8

(3) At the end of section 32 of the said Act of 1936 there shall be added the following subsection:—

"(4) The council of every inner London borough and the Common Council of the City of London shall supply a copy of the said map to the Greater London Council."

37.—(1) Where a person proposes under section 34 of that Act (right of owners and occupiers to drain into public sewers) to make a communication between a drain or sewer and a main sewer in Greater London, the grounds on which the local authority may refuse under subsection (3) of that section to permit the communication shall be such grounds as they think fit, and no application to a magistrates' court may be made under the proviso to that subsection in respect of any such refusal by the water authority.

(2) In this paragraph "main sewer" means a public sewer used for the general reception of sewage from other public sewers and not substantially used for the reception of sewage from private sewers and drains.

38. In section 40(4) of that Act (soil pipes and ventilating shafts) after the words "local authority" there shall be inserted the words "or the water authority for the area".

39.—(1) In section 48(1) of that Act (examination and testing of drains, etc.) for the word "local" there shall be substituted the word "relevant".

(2) After the said subsection (1) there shall be inserted the following subsection:—

"(1A) In subsection (1) above "relevant authority" means, in relation to a drain or private sewer connecting with a public sewer, the water authority for the area, and in any other case the local authority.".

40. In section 50(1) of that Act (overflowing and leaking cesspools) after the words "the local authority" there shall be inserted the words "or the water authority for the area".

1945 c. 42.

41. In section 137(1) of that Act, as amended by section 29 of the Water Act 1945, (securing sufficient water supply to new houses) the words "the local authority or other" shall cease to have effect.

42.—(1) In section 138(1) of the said Act of 1936, as amended by section 30 of the Water Act 1945, (securing sufficient water supply for occupied houses) the words "the local authority or other" shall cease to have effect.

(2) In section 138(4) of the said Act of 1936, as amended by Schedule 4 to the Water Act 1945, for the words from "section thirty-five" to "that section" there shall be substituted the words "section 29 of Schedule 3 to the Water Act 1945 or under that section".

(3) In section 138(5) of the said Act of 1936, the words " the local authority or other " shall cease to have effect. SCH. 8

Diseases of Fish Act 1937

1937 c. 33.

43. For section 8(2) of the Diseases of Fish Act 1937 (penalties and legal proceedings) there shall be substituted the following subsections—

" (2) In England and Wales a water authority shall have power to take legal proceedings to enforce provisions of this Act as respects waters in their area.

(3) Offences against this Act committed in Scotland (including offences committed in waters with respect to which functions under this Act are exercisable by the North West Water Authority) shall be prosecuted and fines recovered in manner directed by the Salmon Fisheries (Scotland) Act 1868." 1868 c. 123.

Public Health (Drainage of Trade Premises) Act 1937

1937 c. 40.

44. Section 4(4) of the Public Health (Drainage of Trade Premises) Act 1937 (exemption of laundries from need for consent to discharges) shall cease to have effect.

Rural Water Supplies and Sewerage Act 1944

1944 c. 26.

45. In section 1(1) and (4) of the Rural Water Supplies and Sewerage Act 1944 (government contributions towards expenses of rural water supplies and sewerage) for the word " local " there shall be substituted the word " water ".

46. Section 2 of that Act (contributions by county councils towards expenses of rural water supplies and sewerage) shall cease to have effect.

Water Act 1945

1945 c. 42.

47. For subsections (1) and (2) of section 10 of the Water Act 1945 (variation of limits of supply) there shall be substituted the following subsections: —

" (1) Subject to section 11(8) of the Water Act 1973 (which relates to the boundaries of water authority areas), the Secretary of State may—

(a) on the application of any statutory water undertakers, by order vary their limits of supply, but not so as to include any area which is within the limits of supply of any other statutory water undertakers ;

(b) on the application of two or more statutory water undertakers, by order provide for the variation by agreement of any common boundary between their respective limits of supply.

(2) Subject to section 11(8) of the Water Act 1973, where it appears to the Secretary of State that it is expedient to vary the limits of supply of any statutory water undertakers and he is satisfied that such variation cannot be secured under the

last foregoing subsection, the Secretary of State may make an order providing compulsorily for such variation."

48.—(1) In the second paragraph of subsection (10) of section 14 of that Act (control of abstraction and prevention of waste) for the words from " application " to " take " there shall be substituted the words " application of the water authority within whose area the well, borehole or other work is situated, authorise them to take ".

(2) In subsection (12) of that section—

(*a*) for the words from the beginning to " concerned " there shall be substituted the words " Any officer of a water authority authorised for the purpose by the authority ", and

1963 c. 38.
(*b*) for the words " area of the river authority " (which were substituted by the Water Resources Act 1963) there shall be substituted the words " water authority area ".

49. In the proviso to section 15(1) of that Act (agreements as to drainage, etc.) for the words from " otherwise " to the end of the subsection there shall be substituted the words " into a watercourse otherwise than through public sewers, the undertakers shall before entering into the agreement—

(*a*) consult any water authority exercising functions in relation to the watercourse ; and

(*b*) if the watercourse is subject to the jurisdiction of a navigation authority, consult that authority."

50. In section 19(1) of that Act (byelaws) for the words from " the provisions " to " Act " there shall be substituted the words " Part II of Schedule 7 to the Water Act 1973 ".

51. In paragraph (*a*) of the proviso to section 22(2) of that Act (acquisition of land and execution of works) for the words from " watercourse " to the end of the paragraph there shall be substituted the words " watercourse—

(i) consult any water authority exercising functions in relation to the watercourse ; and

(ii) if the watercourse is subject to the jurisdiction of a navigation authority, consult that authority ; ".

52. In section 34 of that Act (temporary discharge of water into watercourse)—

(*a*) in paragraph (*a*) of subsection (2), for the words from " to the " to the end of the paragraph there shall be substituted the words " to any water authority exercising functions in relation to any watercourse into which the water is to be discharged ; " and

(*b*) in subsection (3), for the words from " under ", in the second place where it occurs, to the end of the subsection there shall be substituted the words " to send to a water authority under paragraph (*a*) of the last foregoing subsection ; ".

53.—(1) The following provisions of this paragraph shall have Sch. 8 effect for amending and modifying sections 36 to 38 of that Act (obligation to supply water and recovery of water rates) and for adapting references in Schedule 3 to that Act to a water rate and related expressions.

(2) Subject to the following provisions of this paragraph—

    (*a*) any reference in section 38 to a water rate shall be construed as including a reference to any charge payable under Part III of this Act ; and

    (*b*) any reference in Schedule 3 to a water rate shall be construed as including a reference to any such charge for services which include a supply of water for domestic purposes.

(3) Without prejudice to the power of a statutory water company to act as agent for a water authority apart from this sub-paragraph, a statutory water company who are supplying water on behalf of a water authority may recover on behalf of the authority any charge payable under Part III of this Act for services provided by the authority within the company's limits of supply and exercise on behalf of the authority any other powers of the authority under section 38, and references in that section to the undertakers shall be construed accordingly.

(4) Any reference in sections 36 and 37 and in sections 29 and 40 of Schedule 3 to a water rate shall be construed as including a reference to that proportion of any such charge as is stated by the water authority to be payable for a supply of water for domestic purposes, and it shall be the duty of a water authority when fixing any such charge to state the proportion of the charge which is so payable.

(5) In sections 46 and 54 to 58 of Schedule 3 any reference to a water rate shall include a reference to any such charge in the nature of a rate for a supply of water and the provision of other services, and in section 55(1) any reference to the rate poundage shall be construed accordingly.

(6) Any reference in any of the provisions mentioned in this paragraph to an instalment of a charge so mentioned shall be construed as a reference to a payment.

(7) In this paragraph " a supply of water for domestic purposes " has the same meaning as in Schedule 3 to the Water Act 1945. 1945 c. 42.

54. At the end of section 42(2) of that Act (accounts) there shall be added the words " and to any water authority on whose behalf the undertakers are supplying water in pursuance of arrangements made under section 12 of the Water Act 1973."

55. In section 55(1)(*c*) of that Act (authentication of documents) for the words " not being a local " there shall be substituted the words " other than a water ".

56. In section 59(1) of the Water Act 1945 (interpretation), in the definition of " watercourse ", for the words " joint board of local authorities " there shall be substituted the words " water authority ".

57. In paragraphs 2 and 11 of Schedule 1 to that Act (procedural provisions) for the words " the Metropolitan Water Board ", in both places where they occur, there shall be substituted the words " a water authority ".

58. In paragraph 3 of that Schedule, for sub-paragraphs (ii) and (iii) there shall be substituted the following sub-paragraphs: —

" (ii) on any water authority exercising functions in the area affected by the order ; and

(iii) where it is proposed that the order shall authorise the execution of works, on any navigation authority exercising functions in relation to a watercourse affected by the works proposed to be executed."

59. In paragraph 12 of that Schedule—

(*a*) for sub-paragraph (ii) there shall be substituted the following sub-paragraph: —

" (ii) on any water authority exercising functions in the area affected by the order ; and " ;

(*b*) in sub-paragraph (iii) after the word " undertakers " there shall be inserted the words " not being a water authority " ;

(*c*) for sub-paragraphs (iv) and (v) there shall be substituted the following sub-paragraph: —

" (iv) where it is proposed that the order shall authorise the execution of works, on any navigation authority exercising functions in relation to a watercourse affected by the works proposed to be executed."

60. In section 1(1) (interpretation) of Schedule 3 to that Act (procedural provisions), in the definition of " watercourse " for the words " joint board of local authorities " there shall be substituted the words " water authority ".

Water Act 1948

61. For section 9 of the Water Act 1948 (subscriptions to associations of water undertakers) there shall be substituted the following subsection: —

" 9. A statutory water company and a joint water board and joint water committee within the meaning of the Water Act 1973 may pay reasonable subscriptions whether annually or otherwise to the funds of any association representing any description of water undertakers and formed for the purpose of consultation as to their common interests and the discussion of matters relating to the supply of water."

62. In section 14(1) of that Act (duty of statutory water under- Sch. **8**
takers to make reports etc. to Secretary of State) for the words
from the beginning to " authorities " there shall be substituted the
words " Every statutory water company and every joint water board
and joint water committee within the meaning of the Water Act
1973 ".

Rivers (Prevention of Pollution) Act 1951   1951 c. 64.

63. In section 2(1) of the Rivers (Prevention of Pollution) Act
1951, for the words " a local authority " there shall be substituted
the words " a water authority, a harbour authority within the
meaning of the Harbours Act 1964 or a development corporation 1964 c. 40.
established under the New Towns Act 1965 or any Act replaced 1965 c. 59.
by that Act " and for the words " the local authority " there shall be
substituted the word " they ".

Town Development Act 1952   1952 c. 54.

64. In section 2(2) of the Town Development Act 1952 (Exchequer
contributions to councils of receiving districts), after paragraph (e),
there shall be inserted the following paragraph : —

" (ee) payments under section 16 of the Water Act 1973 in
respect of the provision of a public sewer needed for the
purposes or in consequence of the development."

65.—(1) In section 7 of the Town Development Act 1952 (authorities eligible to participate) for paragraph (d) there shall be
substituted the following paragraph : —

" (d) a water authority ",

and any other reference to a joint water or sewerage board in
sections 7 and 8 of that Act shall be construed as a reference to a
water authority.

(2) Section 8(4) of that Act (exercise of sewerage functions by
participating authorities) shall cease to have effect.

Local Government (Miscellaneous Provisions) Act 1953   1953 c. 26.

66. For section 12 of the Local Government (Miscellaneous
Provisions) Act 1953 (application of provisions of Schedule 3 to the
Water Act 1945 to the water undertakings of local authorities) there 1945 c. 42.
shall be substituted the following section : —

"Water   12.—(1) Subject to any provision to the contrary con-
undertakings tained in any instrument made under or by virtue of the
of water
authorities. Water Act 1973, Part XIII of Schedule 3 to the Water
Act 1945 (provisions for preventing waste of water),
except section 61 (power to test water fittings), shall apply
throughout every water authority area except in the limits
of supply of a statutory water company within the
meaning of the Water Act 1973.

(2) Section 64 of that Schedule (waste of water by non-
repair of water fittings) shall have effect, in its application
to the undertaking of a water authority, as set out with
modifications in the Schedule to this Act.

(3) Notwithstanding anything in section 41(3) of the
said Schedule 3 (recovery from owners or occupiers of

SCH. 8

1945 c. 42.

expenses incurred by the undertakers in laying communication pipes), as it applies in relation to the water undertaking of a water authority, or in any corresponding provision of a local enactment within the meaning of the Water Act 1945 relating to the supply of water by a water authority, that authority may, if they think fit, themselves bear the whole or any part of any expenses recoverable by them under that subsection or the corresponding provision."

1954 c. 30.

Protection of Birds Act 1954

1966 c. 38.

67. In section 14(1) of the Protection of Birds Act 1954 (interpretation) for the words in paragraph (c) of the definition of " authorised person " from " that is to say " to " 1945 " there shall be substituted the words " that is to say, the Nature Conservancy Council, a water authority or any other statutory water undertakers, a local fisheries committee constituted under the Sea Fisheries Regulation Act 1966, ".

1955 c. 13.

Rural Water Supplies and Sewerage Act 1955

68. In section 1(1) of the Rural Water Supplies and Sewerage Act 1955 (government contributions) for the word " local " there shall be substituted the word " water ".

1957 c. 20.

House of Commons Disqualification Act 1957

69. In Part III of Schedule 1 to the House of Commons Disqualification Act 1957 (offices the holders of which are disqualified for membership of the House of Commons) there shall be inserted at the appropriate places in alphabetical order—

" (a) Chairman, or other member appointed by a Minister, of the National Water Council ;

(b) Chairman of a regional water authority ;

(c) Chairman of the Welsh National Water Development Authority ".

1959 c. 25.

Highways Act 1959

70.—(1) In subsection (4) of section 103 of the Highways Act 1959 (drainage of highways and proposed highways) for the words " local authority " there shall be substituted the words " water authority ".

(2) In subsection (4A) of that section (notice to be given before exercise of powers under subsection (4)) after the word " district " there shall be inserted the words " and the water authority ".

71. For section 227(2) of that Act (determination of differences about vesting and use of highway drains and sewers) there shall be substituted the following subsection :—

" (2) Any difference arising under this section—

(a) between a county council and the council of a district—

(i) as to the council in whom a drain is vested, or

(ii) as to the use of a drain or sewer ; or

(*b*) between a county council and a water authority as to the   SCH. 8
    use of a sewer ;

shall, if either party to the dispute so elect, be referred to and determined by the Secretary of State ".

Land Drainage Act 1961

1961 c. 48.

72.—(1) In subsection (1) of section 3 of the Land Drainage Act 1961 (designation of watercourses and special drainage charge) for the words from the beginning to " river board ", in the second place where those words occur, there shall be substituted the words " Where it appears to a regional land drainage committee that the interests of agriculture in the water authority's area or any part of it require the carrying out of drainage works in connection with watercourses in that area, they may pass a resolution to that effect ; and if the committee pass such a resolution, the water authority ".

(2) After the said subsection (1) there shall be inserted the following subsection—

> " (1A) A water authority shall not submit a scheme under subsection (1) above except one which their regional land drainage committee has submitted to them ; but it shall be their duty to submit any scheme which that committee has submitted to the Minister without modification.".

(3) In subsection (5) of that section, for the words from " as modified " to the end of the subsection there shall be substituted the words " and, subject to subsections (7) to (10) of this section, that Act shall apply to such a scheme, except so far as subsection (1) of section 4 enables the Minister to direct a water authority to submit a scheme, as it applies to a scheme under paragraph (*b*) of that subsection ".

73.—(1) In subsection (1) of section 34 of that Act (power of local authority to undertake drainage works against flooding), after the word " shall ", in the second place where that word occurs, there shall be inserted the words " except as provided by subsections (1A) and (1B) of this section ".

(2) After that subsection there shall be inserted the following subsections :—

> " (1A) A byelaw made in pursuance of this section shall not be valid until it has been confirmed by the Minister.

> (1B) Notwithstanding subsection (1) of this section, section 236 of the Local Government Act 1972 (and not Part II of 1972 c. 70. Schedule 7 to the Water Act 1973) shall have effect in relation to byelaws made in pursuance of this section ".

74. In section 40(1) of that Act (powers of entry) for the words " any drainage board other than a river authority " (which were inserted in that subsection by the Water Resources Act 1963) there 1963 c. 38. shall be substituted the words " an internal drainage board ".

75. In section 43 of that Act (provision by drainage board of housing accommodation for employees) for the word " A " there shall be substituted the words " An internal ".

Public Health Act 1961

76. In paragraph 8 of Schedule 2 to the Public Health Act 1961 (supplementary provisions concerning sewerage contributions) for the words " the clerk of the local authority " there shall be substituted the words " a duly authorised officer of the water authority ".

Water Resources Act 1963

77.—(1) In section 16(2) of the Water Resources Act 1963 (inspection and copying of records), for the words from " records kept " to " scheme " there shall be substituted the words " any records kept by them of the rainfall, the evaporation of water and the flow, level and volume of inland water and water in underground strata in their area.".

(2) In section 16(3) of that Act for the words from " such fees " onwards there shall be substituted the words " such reasonable fees as the authority may determine ".

78. After section 24(9) of that Act (exceptions from general restrictions) there shall be added the following subsection : —

" (10) In this section, ' land drainage ' includes the protection of land against erosion or encroachment by water, whether from inland waters or from the sea, and also includes warping and irrigation other than spray irrigation."

79. At the end of section 38(2) of that Act (reference of applications for licences to Secretary of State) there shall be added the following paragraph : —

" (c) may except from the operation of the direction such classes of applications as may be specified in the direction in such circumstances as may be so specified."

80.—(1) For subsection (1) of section 60 of that Act (exemptions from and reduction of charges) there shall be substituted the following subsection : —

" (1) A water authority may, on the application of any person who is liable to pay charges to the authority for the abstraction of water under a licence under this Act, make an agreement with him either exempting him from the payment of charges or providing for charges to be levied on him at reduced rates specified in the agreement."

(2) In paragraph (a) of subsection (2) of that section for the words " river authority's new functions " there shall be substituted the words " functions conferred on the water authority by section 9 of the Water Act 1973 ".

(3) In subsection (6) of that section for the words from the beginning to " the scheme " there shall be substituted the words " No charges shall be levied ".

81.—(1) In subsection (8)(d) of section 63 of that Act (special charges in respect of spray irrigation) for the words " any charging scheme for the time being in force " there shall be substituted the words "Part III of the Water Act 1973 and any charges scheme under that Part of that Act".

(2) In subsection (9) of that section for the words from "anything contained" to the end of the subsection there shall be substituted the words "any provision of Part III of the Water Act 1973 or any charges scheme under that Part of that Act, but nothing in this section or in any agreement made thereunder shall affect the operation of any such provision or scheme in relation to a licence in so far as it authorises water abstracted in pursuance of the licence to be used on any land other than the relevant land.".

82. In paragraph (*d*) of section 79(4) of that Act (byelaws relating to reservoirs) after the word "undertakers" there shall be inserted the words "other than the water authority".

83.—(1) The following provisions of this paragraph shall have effect with respect to section 82 of that Act (transfer of functions or property of other authorities) and orders under that section.

(2) In section 82 references to a navigation authority, conservancy authority and harbour authority shall each include references to a body which no longer has any members but which, if it had members, would be such an authority.

(3) The Ministers shall not be under any duty under paragraph 1 of Schedule 10 to that Act to consult or consider representations from any body from which functions or property are proposed to be transferred by an order under section 82 if the body no longer has any members.

(4) Where an application is made to the Ministers to make an order under section 82 transferring functions or property from a body which no longer has any members, the Ministers need not cause any such notice as is mentioned in paragraph 2 of Schedule 10 to that Act to be served on that body.

84. In section 120 of that Act (service of documents), in subsections (1) and (5), after the words "this Act" there shall be inserted the words "or the Water Act 1973".

85. In section 135(1) of that Act (interpretation) for the definition of "land drainage" there shall be substituted the following definition :—

"land drainage" includes defence against water (including sea water), irrigation other than spray irrigation, warping and the provision of flood warning systems.

86. In section 135(3) of that Act (definition of "local authority sewer") for the words from "a sewerage authority" to the end of paragraph (*b*) there shall be substituted the words "any of the following, that is to say—

(*a*) a water authority ;

(*b*) a local authority ".

Harbours Act 1964

87. In section 58 of the Harbours Act 1964 (authorities not to be treated as harbour authorities), for the words from " a river board " to " Catchment Board " there shall be substituted the words " a water authority, a river purification authority, a district board nor an improvement committee ".

New Towns Act 1965

88. In section 34 of the New Towns Act 1965 (power to authorise provision of sewers and sewage disposal works by development corporation)—

    (*a*) in subsection (1), for the words " local authority " there shall be substituted the words " water authority " ; and

    (*b*) in subsection (2), after " district " there shall be inserted the words " and the water authority for every water authority area ".

89. For section 40 of that Act (power to transfer sewerage and sewage disposal undertakings of development corporations to local authorities) there shall be substituted the following section :—

" Transfer of sewerage and sewage disposal undertakings to water authorities.

40.—(1) A development corporation for a new town who have, in pursuance of an order under section 34 of this Act, been carrying on a sewerage or sewage disposal undertaking may by agreement with a water authority, and with the consent of the Secretary of State and the Treasury, transfer the whole or any part of the undertaking to that authority.

(2) The Secretary of State may by order provide for the transfer to a water authority of the whole or any part of a sewerage or sewage disposal undertaking which has, in pursuance of an order under section 34 of this Act, been carried on by the development corporation for a new town, and any such order may contain such incidental, consequential and supplementary provisions as the Secretary of State thinks necessary or expedient for the purposes of the order.

(3) The terms on which the whole or any part of an undertaking is transferred by an order under this section shall be such as the Secretary of State, with the consent of the Treasury, may specify in the order, and those terms may provide for the payment by the water authority of such sums, to be satisfied in such manner, as may be so specified :

Provided that the total of the sums so paid shall not exceed the total capital cost of the undertaking less depreciation written off.

(4) Before making an order under this section the Secretary of State shall consult with the water authority and with any other authority appearing to him to be concerned.

(5) The Secretary of State shall give notice of any order which he proposes to make under this section to the water authority and the development corporation and, if within twenty-eight days after he has given notice to them either authority give notice to him that they object to the proposal and the objection is not withdrawn, the order shall be subject to special parliamentary procedure ".

SCH. 8

National Insurance (Industrial Injuries) Act 1965

1965 c. 52.

90.—(1) In relation to accidents happening to insured persons (within the meaning of the National Insurance (Industrial Injuries) Act 1965) who attend courses or avail themselves of training facilities provided or approved by the Council, sections 7 to 9 of that Act (which make provision for treating certain accidents as arising out of and in the course of an insured person's employment) shall have effect subject to the following modifications.

(2) For the purposes of section 7, any act done by the insured person for the purposes of and in connection with his training shall, if it is not done for the purposes of and in connection with his employer's trade or business, be deemed to be so done.

(3) For the purposes of section 8, any vehicle (within the meaning of that section) which is operated by or on behalf of the Council or some other person by whom it is provided in pursuance of arrangements made with the Council shall, if not operated and provided as mentioned in subsection (1)(*b*)(i) of that section, be deemed to be so operated and provided.

(4) For the purposes of section 9, any premises at which an insured person is for the time being employed for the purposes of his training shall, if they are not premises at which he is employed for the purposes of his employer's trade or business, be deemed to be such premises.

Sea Fisheries Regulation Act 1966

1966 c. 38.

91. In section 18(3) of the Sea Fisheries Regulation Act 1966 (areas of jurisdiction), for the words from " section 119 " to " river authority) " there shall be substituted the words " section 36(3) of the Water Act 1973 (procedure relating to byelaws made by a water authority) ".

Countryside Act 1968

1968 c. 41.

92. In section 22 of the Countryside Act 1968 (recreational facilities at reservoirs, etc.), the following amendments shall be made :—

(a) in subsection (2), for the words " subsection (1) above " there shall be substituted the words " section 20(1) of the Water Act 1973 " ; and

(b) in subsections (3) to (5), for the words " subsections (1) and (2) above " there shall be substituted the words " section 20(1) of the Water Act 1973 and subsection (2) above."

Agriculture Act 1970

93. In section 98 of the Agriculture Act 1970 (duty of local authority in Scotland whose area adjoins England to consult English authorities about flood warning systems), for the words from " river " to " 1963 " there shall be substituted the words " regional water authority established for that area under section 2 of the Water Act 1973 ; ".

Town and Country Planning Act 1971

94. In section 147(4) of the Town and Country Planning Act 1971 (exclusion of compensation for refusal of planning permission, etc., where development is premature by reference to (*a*) the order of priority in the development plan or (*b*) any existing deficiency in the provision of water supplies or sewerage services), for the proviso there shall be substituted the following proviso : —

" Provided that this subsection shall not apply if the reason or one of the reasons so stated is that that development would be premature by reference to the matters mentioned in paragraph (*a*) of this subsection and the planning decision refusing the permission is made on an application made more than seven years after the date of a previous planning decision whereby permission to develop the same land was refused for the same reason, or for reasons which included the same reason."

Salmon and Freshwater Fisheries Act 1972

95. In section 3(2) of the Salmon and Freshwater Fisheries Act 1972 (byelaws about close season, etc.), for the words from " and paragraphs " to the end there shall be substituted the words " and Part I of Schedule 7 to the Water Act 1973 shall apply accordingly ".

96. In section 9(1) of that Act (production of fishing licences) for the words from the beginning to the end of paragraph (*c*) there shall be substituted the words " A water bailiff appointed by a water authority on producing evidence of his appointment, or any constable,".

97. For paragraph 18 of Schedule 1 to that Act (provisions with respect to licences) there shall be substituted the following paragraph :—

" 18. The production of a printed copy of a statement purporting to be issued by a water authority as to a licence duty fixed and, if it be the case, approved by the Minister under this Schedule or under the 1923 Act shall be prima facie evidence that the licence duty was fixed or approved as there mentioned and of the amount of the duty, and without proof of the handwriting or official position of any person purporting to sign the statement.".

Local Government Act 1972

98. In section 223(2) of the Local Government Act 1972 (appearance in legal proceedings), for the word from " river " to the end of the subsection there shall be substituted the words " water authority ".

SCHEDULE 9

REPEALS

Chapter	Short title	Extent of repeal
13 & 14 Geo. 5. c. 16.	The Salmon and Freshwater Fisheries Act 1923.	In section 6, the words " in any fishery district ". In section 17(1), the words " in any fishery district ". Section 37. In section 38(1), in paragraph (*a*) the words " of the fishery district " and paragraphs (*b*), (*c*), (*g*), (*h*) and (*i*). Section 41. Sections 43 to 53. In section 54, in subsection (1) paragraph (*a*), subsection (2), and in subsection (3) paragraph (*c*). Sections 56 to 58. Section 60. Section 66. In section 67(4), the words from " purporting " to "Act ", in the first place where it occurs. Section 81. In section 92(1), the definitions of " fishery board " and " chairman ". Schedule 3.
20 & 21 Geo. 5. c. 44.	The Land Drainage Act 1930.	In section 1, in subsection (4) the words from the beginning to " constituted, and ". Section 2. Section 3. Section 5. In section 7(1), the words from " shall " to " and " where it first occurs. In section 8(2), in paragraph (*c*) the words from " submitted " to the end of the paragraph. Section 12. Section 15. Sections 17 to 20. Section 22(2). In section 33(4), paragraph (*a*). Section 46(6). In section 47, subsections (2) to (7). Section 49(3).

Chapter	Short title	Extent of repeal
20 & 21 Geo. 5. c. 44. *cont.*	The Land Drainage Act 1930. —*cont.*	In section 50, subsection (1), in subsection (2) the words from " (whether " to " area) ", and subsections (3) and (4). Section 73. Sections 79 and 80. Schedule 1.
26 Geo. 5 & 1 Edw. 8. c. 49.	The Public Health Act 1936.	Section 14. Section 16. In section 20(2), the proviso. Section 28. Section 35. In section 41(1), the words from the beginning to "this Act". In section 90(1), the definition of sewerage authority. Sections 111 to 122. Section 124(3). Section 125(3). Sections 126 to 136. In sections 137(1) and 138(1) and (5), the words " the local authority or other ", wherever occurring. In section 142, in the definition of " statutory water undertakers ", the words from " either " to " (b) ". Section 310.
1 Edw. 8 & 1 Geo. 6. c. 40.	The Public Health (Drainage of Trade Premises) Act 1937.	Section 4(4). Section 12(2).
7 & 8 Geo. 6 c. 26.	The Rural Water Supplies and Sewerage Act 1944.	Section 1(6). Section 2. Section 4.
8 & 9 Geo. 6. c. 42.	The Water Act 1945.	Sections 1 to 5. Section 8. Section 9(4). Section 11. Section 15(3). In section 19, in subsection (1), the words from " and the " to the end of the subsection, subsection (6)(b) and the word " and " immediately preceding it and subsection (7). In section 23(1), paragraph (ii) of the proviso, and the words from " A consent required " to the end of the subsection.

Chapter	Short title	Extent of repeal
8 & 9 Geo. 6. c. 42—*cont.*	The Water Act 1945 —*cont.*	In section 24(4), the words " local authority or ". Section 28. In section 32, in subsection (1) the words " or section forty ", in subsection (2) the words " supplying water under a local enactment " and the proviso, and subsections (4) and (5). Section 33(3). In section 34, in subsection (2) the words " board or " and in subsection (4) the word " boards ". Section 35(3). In section 38, in subsection (1) the words from " whether " to " enactment ", and subsections (6) and (7). Section 40. In section 46, the words from " or ", in the third place where it occurs, to the end. In section 55(1)(*a*)(ii) the words " the water engineer or manager of the water department or ". In section 59(1), the definitions of " catchment board " and " catchment area ", " fishery board " and " fishery district " and " joint water board ", in the definition of " limits of supply " the words from " so " to the end of the definition, and the definitions of " rivers board " and " statutory water undertakers ". In Schedule 1, in paragraph 16, the words " board or ", and Parts III, IV and V. In Schedule 2, in paragraphs 3, 5, 6 and 7 the words " local authority or " wherever occurring. In Schedule 3, in section 1(1), the definitions of " catchment board " and " catchment area ", " fishery board " and " fishery district " and " rivers board ", section 46(1), sections 47 to 51, and in section 78, paragraphs (*a*) to (*c*) of subsection (1), and subsection (2).

Chapter	Short title	Extent of repeal
8 & 9 Geo. 6. c. 42—*cont.*	The Water Act 1945 —*cont.*	In Schedule 4, the whole Schedule with the exception of the provisions amending sections 275 and 279 of the Public Health Act 1936.
11 & 12 Geo. 6. c. 22.	The Water Act 1948.	Section 1. In section 2, subsections (1)(*b*) and (4). In section 4, subsections (2), (3) and (4). In section 8, in subsection (1), the words " local authority or " and in the proviso the words " authority or "; in subsection (2), the words " local authority or " and " authority or "; in subsection (4), the words " local authority or " in the first place where they occur and " that local authority or "; and in subsection (5) the words " local authority or ". Section 12. Section 13.
14 & 15 Geo. 6. c. 64.	The Rivers (Prevention of Pollution) Act 1951.	Section 1(1)(*b*). In section 7, subsection (9) and the proviso to subsection (16). Section 9. In section 11(1), the definitions of " excluded area " and " local authority ". In Schedule 2, paragraphs 5, 6, 8 and 10.
15 & 16 Geo. 6 & 1 Eliz. 2. c. 54.	The Town Development Act 1952.	In section 2, in subsection (2)(*d*), the words " main water supplies". Section 8(4). Section 9(3). Section 15.
6 & 7 Eliz. 2. c. 67.	The Water Act 1958.	Section 4(2).
7 & 8 Eliz. 2. c. 25.	The Highways Act 1959.	Section 295(6).
8 & 9 Eliz. 2. c. 54.	The Clean Rivers (Estuaries and Tidal Waters) Act 1960.	Section 1(6)(*c*).
9 & 10 Eliz. 2. c. 29.	The Rural Water Supplies and Sewerage Act 1961.	The whole Act.
9 & 10 Eliz. 2. c. 48.	The Land Drainage Act 1961.	Section 3(6). In section 34, in subsection (6), the words from " or " to the end of the subsection, and in subsection (10) the words " or, as the case may be, the Minister,".

SCH. 9

Chapter	Short title	Extent of repeal
9 & 10 Eliz. 2. c. 48—*cont.*	The Land Drainage Act 1961—*cont.*	Section 50. In Schedule 1, paragraphs 4, 20(4) and 24.
9 & 10 Eliz. 2. c. 50.	The Rivers (Prevention of Pollution) Act 1961.	In section 13(2), the words from " and in sub-paragraph (2) " onwards.
9 & 10 Eliz. 2. c. 57.	The Public Health Act 1961.	Section 15. Section 65.
1963 c. 33.	The London Government Act 1963.	Sections 35 and 36. In section 37, subsections (1), (3) and (4). Sections 38 and 39. In Schedule 9, Part I; in Part II, paragraphs 1 to 4, 7 to 10, 12 to 16 and 19; in Part III, paragraphs 4(3), 5, 7, 8 and 10 to 12. Schedule 10. In Schedule 14, paragraphs 5, 6 and 9; in paragraph 10, the words from " and the transitional " to the end of the paragraph; and in paragraph 15(3), the words from " except " in the definition of " watercourse " to the word " tides ", in the last place where it occurs.
1963 c. 38.	The Water Resources Act 1963.	Section 1(1). In section 3, subsections (1) to (4), (6) and (7). Sections 4 to 15. Section 16(1). Section 18. Section 19(2). In section 21, subsections (1) and (2); in subsection (3), the words " and the Water Resources Board "; and in subsection (4), the words from " draft " to " and to ". In section 22(3), the words from " the Water Resources Board " to " or ", and the words " the Board or " and " as the case may be ". In section 25, subsection (4) and in paragraph (*a*) of subsection (7), the words " and the Water Resources Board ". In section 32(5), the words from " or is " to " 1936 ", the words " sold or leased " and the words " and, in the case of a lease, for the period of the lease ".

Chapter	Short title	Extent of repeal
1963 c. 38 —*cont.*	The Water Resources Act 1963—*cont.*	Section 33(3). In section 48(1), the words " and of section 103 thereof ". Sections 57 to 59. Sections 61 and 62. In section 63(1), the words from " either " to " authority ", in the first place where that word occurs. In section 64, subsection (1) and in subsection (2) the words from the beginning to " subsection ". Section 69(2). Section 76(3). Section 80. In section 81(2), the words " and after prior consultation with the Water Resources Board ". In section 82(1), in paragraph (*c*) the words from " and " to the end of the paragraph and in paragraph (*d*) the words from " and ", where it secondly occurs, to the end of the paragraph. Sections 83 to 87. Section 88(2). Sections 89 and 90. Sections 92 and 93. Part IX. Sections 101 to 104. Section 107(3). In section 108, in subsection (1), the words from " either " to " otherwise " and in subsection (4) the words " to the Water Resources Board or ". Section 110. Section 119. Section 121. In section 123(1)(*a*), the words from " other " to " Board ". Section 124. Section 125. In section 126(1), paragraph (*a*) of the proviso. Section 127. Section 129. In section 131, in subsection (6) the words " notwithstanding anything in section 58 of this Act" and "under any charging scheme ", and in subsection (7) the words " under a charging scheme ".

Chapter	Short title	Extent of repeal
1963 c. 38 —*cont.*	The Water Resources Act 1963—*cont.*	In section 135, in subsection (1) the definitions of " additional members ", " charging scheme ", " constituent council ", " first appointed day ", " functions " and " statutory water undertakers ". Section 136, except subsection (4). Schedules 1 to 6. In Schedule 7, paragraph 14. Schedules 11 to 14.
1965 c. 4.	The Science and Technology Act 1965.	In Schedule 2, the entry relating to the Water Resources Act 1963.
1965 c. 56.	The Compulsory Purchase Act 1965.	In section 33(1)(*b*), the words from " that ", in the second place where it occurs, to the end of the paragraph, in subsection (2)(*b*) the words " a local authority within the meaning of the Act of 1946, or " and in subsection (4) the words " a local authority within the meaning of the Act of 1946 or ".
1967 c. 78.	The Water (Scotland) Act 1967.	In section 36(2), the words " (except paragraph 16 of Schedule 2) ". In Schedule 2, paragraph 16.
1968 c. 34.	The Agriculture (Miscellaneous Provisions) Act 1968.	Section 22. Section 27(6). Section 28. Section 50(2).
1968 c. 41.	The Countryside Act 1968.	Section 22(1). In section 49(2), the definitions of " river authority " and " statutory water undertakers ".
1968 c. 73.	The Transport Act 1968.	Section 115(4).
1969 c. 19.	The Decimal Currency Act 1969.	In Schedule 2, paragraph 30.
1970 c. 40.	The Agriculture Act 1970.	In section 88, subsections (2) and (3). In section 89, in subsection (4) the words " the Isle of Wight Authority, the Conservators, the Catchment Board ". Section 90(2).
1971 c. 34.	The Water Resources Act 1971.	In section 2(2), the words from " and ", where secondly occurring, to the end of the subsection.
1972 c. 21.	The Deposit of Poisonous Waste Act 1972.	In section 7, the words from " and any " to the end of the section.

Chapter	Short title	Extent of repeal
1972 c. 37.	The Salmon and Fresh-water Fisheries Act 1972.	Section 11(3). In section 15(3), the words from " and ", in the second place where it occurs, to the end.
1972 c. 70.	The Local Government Act 1972.	Section 177(1)(*b*). In section 181, subsections (3) to (8). In section 262(13), the word " water ", in the second place where it occurs. In Schedule 29, paragraph 24(1) and (4).

INDEX

TO THE

Public General Acts

A

ACTS OF PARLIAMENT.

Consolidation Acts. *See* COSTS IN CRIMINAL CASES ACT (c. 14); INDEPENDENT BROADCASTING AUTHORITY ACT (c. 19); MATRIMONIAL CAUSES ACT (c. 18); POWERS OF CRIMINAL COURTS ACT (c. 62).

D

E

F

FAIR TRADING ACT—*continued*

FAIR TRADING ACT—*continued*

FAIR TRADING ACT—*continued*

G

GUARDIANSHIP ACT—*continued*

H

I

J

L

LAND COMPENSATION ACT—*continued*

LOCAL GOVERNMENT (SCOTLAND) ACT—*continued*

LOCAL GOVERNMENT (SCOTLAND) ACT—*continued*

LOCAL GOVERNMENT (SCOTLAND) ACT—*continued*

LOCAL GOVERNMENT (SCOTLAND) ACT—*continued*

PART VIII.—FUNCTIONS—*continued*

LOCAL GOVERNMENT (SCOTLAND) ACT—*continued*

M

MATRIMONIAL CAUSES ACT—*continued*

PART II.—FINANCIAL RELIEF FOR PARTIES TO MARRIAGE AND CHILDREN OF FAMILY—*continued*

N

NATIONAL COAL BOARD. *See* COAL INDUSTRY ACT (c. 8).

O

P

PARLIAMENT—*continued*

Orders, regulations, etc. subject to annulment in pursuance of a resolution
of either House of Parliament under—

Administration of Justice Act (c. 15, s. 10(7))   ...   ...   I, p. 124
Badgers Act (c. 57, s. 6(2)) ...   .   III, p. 1726
Breeding of Dogs Act (c. 60, s. 1(3))   ...   .   III, p. 1792
Bangladesh Act (c. 49, s. 3(2)(*d*))   ...   .   II, p. 1374
Counter-Inflation Act (c. 9, ss. 1(4)(*a*)(5), 5(6), 8(2), 9(7), 10(5), 11(3),
13(4), sch. 2 para. 4(2), sch. 3 para. 5(4))
                                  I, pp. 39, 40, 42, 44, 45, 46, 48, 65, 68
Education Act (c. 16, ss. 3(3), 4(2))   ...   ...   I, pp. 152, 153
Employment Agencies Act (c. 35, s. 12(5))...   ...   ...   I, p. 558
Employment of Children Act (c. 24, s. 1(6))   ...   ...   I, p. 290
Employment and Training Act (c. 50, s. 13(5))   ...   ...   II, p. 1394
Fair Trading Act (c. 41, s. 134(1)) ...   .   II, p. 1208
Finance Act (c. 51, ss. 56(4), 58(2))   ...   ...   II, pp. 1484, 1485
Fire Precautions (Loans) Act (c. 11, s. 1(6))   ...   ...   I, p. 82
Fuel and Electricity (Control) Act (c. 67, s. 4(6)) ...   ...   III, p. 2243
Hallmarking Act (c. 43, s. 21(6), sch. 1 Pt. IV para. 1(2)(*b*))
                                                          II, pp. 1279, 1286
Land Compensation Act (c. 26, ss. 30(2), 51(5)) ...   I, pp. 328, 356
Land Compensation (Scotland) Act (c. 56, ss. 28(2), 47(5))
                                                          II, pp. 1663, 1687
Law Reform (Diligence) (Scotland) Act (c. 22, s. 1(3))   ...   I, p. 286
Local Government (Scotland) Act (c. 65, ss. 7(7), 17(4), 24(3), 50(2),
83(6), 98(2), 105(4), 111(2), 112(5), 116(7), 150(3), 215(8), 216(5),
219(4), 220(7), 222(5), 225(7), 229(4))
III, pp. 1925, 1930, 1932, 1947, 1964, 1972, 1979, 1982, 1983, 1988, 2012,
                            2050, 2051, 2053, 2055, 2057, 2061, 2065
Maplin Development Act (c. 64, ss. 2(9), 18(3))   ...   III, pp. 1897, 1904
Matrimonial Causes Act (c. 18, s. 50(4))   ...   .   I, p. 207
National Health Service Reorganisation Act (c. 32, s. 56(1)(*a*))
                                                                I, p. 494
Northern Ireland Assembly Act (c. 17, ss. 2(6)(*c*), 3(4)(*c*))   I, p. 161
Northern Ireland Constitution Act (c. 36, s. 27(9))   ...   I, p. 583
Pensioners' Payments and National Insurance Act (c. 61, s. 7(4))
                                                                III, p. 1804
Powers of Criminal Courts Act (c. 62, s. 54(2))   ...   ...   III, p. 1853
Protection of Aircraft (c. 47, s. 26(5), sch. para. 6)
                                                          II, pp. 1359, 1361
Protection of Wrecks Act (c. 33, s. 3(2))   ...   .   I, p. 547
Water Act (c. 37, ss. 8(4), 17(3), 25(9), 29(3), 32(2), sch. 2 para. 17,
sch. 6 para. 16)   ...   ...   I, pp. 626, 639, 649, 651, 654, 667, 703

Resolution of both Houses required for approval of orders, etc. under—
Administration of Justice Act (c. 15, ss. 2(6), 6(2))   I, pp. 118, 119
Counter-Inflation Act (c. 9, ss. 2(5), 4(4)) ...   . I, pp. 40, 42
Employment and Training Act (c. 50, s. 13(5))   ...   ...   II, p. 1394
Fair Trading Act (c. 41, ss. 22(4), 91(1))   ...   ...   II, pp. 1122, 1174
Hallmarking Act (c. 43, s. 21(5))   ...   .   II, p. 1279
Independent Broadcasting Authority (c. 19, ss. 8(9), 14(3), 23(3), 28(6))
                                                I, pp. 234, 245, 253, 261
Insurance Companies Amendment Act (c. 58, s. 53(2)) ...   III, p. 1773
Land Compensation Act (c. 26, ss. 20(9)) ...   .   I, p. 318
Land Compensation (Scotland) Act (c. 56, s. 18(8))   ...   II, p. 1654

PARLIAMENT—*continued*

PAY BOARD.   *See* COUNTER-INFLATION ACT (c. 9).

PENSIONERS' PAYMENTS AND NATIONAL INSURANCE ACT: c. 61 ...   III, p. 1797

§ 1.   Lump sum payments to pensioners, III, p. 1797.
   2.   Interpretation of provisions as to lump sum payments, III, p. 1798.
   3.   Administration of lump sum payments, III, p. 1801.
   4.   Financial provisions in connection with lump sum payments, III, p. 1802.
   5.   Increase in flat-rate contributions, III, p. 1803.
   6.   Special provisions as to pneumoconiosis, III, p. 1804.
   7, and schedule.   Consolidation of social security legislation, III, pp. 1804, 1806.
   8.   Commencement and transitory provision, III, p. 1804.
   9.   Supplementary, III, p. 1805.
   Schedule.   Enactments relating to social security, III, p. 1806.

PENSIONS.   *See* ADMINISTRATION OF JUSTICE ACT (c. 15, ss. 10–14); OVERSEAS
PENSIONS ACT (c. 21); SOCIAL SECURITY ACT (c. 38).

PIERS.   *See* LOCAL GOVERNMENT (SCOTLAND) ACT (c. 65, s. 154, sch. 19).

PLATE.   *See* HALLMARKING ACT (c. 43).

POINDING, SCOTLAND.   *See* LAW REFORM (DILIGENCE) (SCOTLAND) ACT (c. 22).

POLLUTION OF RIVERS.   *See* WATER ACT (c. 37, s. 17).

PLANNING BLIGHT.   *See* LAND COMPENSATION ACT (c. 26); LAND COMPENSA-
TION (SCOTLAND) ACT (c. 56).

POWERS OF CRIMINAL COURTS ACT: c. 62 ...   .   III, p. 1807

PART I.—POWERS OF COURTS TO DEAL WITH OFFENDERS
Preliminary
§ 1.   Deferment of sentence, III, p. 1807.

POWERS OF CRIMINAL COURTS ACT—*continued*

S

SOCIAL SECURITY ACT—*continued*

T

U

V

W

WATER ACT—*continued*

STATUTORY PUBLICATIONS OFFICE

Selected Publications

Annotations to Acts

Instructions for noting up those Acts which were affected by the year's legislation, direct or delegated. Substituted provisions are printed on adhesive slips, and the annotations can be carried out by a junior clerk on any set of statutes within a few weeks.

£9 (by post £9·21)

Chronological Table of the Statutes

A chronological list of all the Public General Acts from 1235 onwards, showing as to those totally repealed, the enactments by which they were repealed and, as to those still in operation, the effect of all subsequent legislation on them, section by section.

With the aid of this annual publication a practitioner can tell instantly the present position of any enactment to which he has been referred.

£8·50 (by post £8·79)

A free list of Statutory Publications Office titles is obtainable from Her Majesty's Stationery Office, PM1A(ZPG1), Atlantic House, Holborn Viaduct, London EC1P 1BN

Government publications can be bought from the Government Bookshops in London (Post Orders to P.O. Box 569, SE1 9NH), Edinburgh, Cardiff, Belfast, Manchester, Birmingham and Bristol, or through booksellers

 **HMSO BOOKS**

HER MAJESTY'S STATIONERY OFFICE

Government Bookshops

49 High Holborn, London WC1V 6HB
13a Castle Street, Edinburgh EH2 3AR
41 The Hayes, Cardiff CF1 1JW
Brazennose Street, Manchester M60 8AS
Southey House, Wine Street, Bristol BS1 2BQ
258 Broad Street, Birmingham B1 2HE
80 Chichester Street, Belfast BT1 4JY

Government publications are also available
through booksellers